W9-BPK-639

Bulgaria

Richard Watkins, Tom Masters

Contents

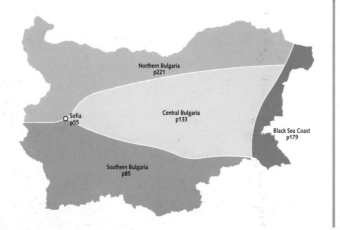

Northern Bulgaria
p221

Sofia
p55

Central Bulgaria
p133

Black Sea Coast
p179

Southern Bulgaria
p85

Destination Bulgaria

Tucked away at the southeastern extremity of Europe, Bulgaria is a land of pine-clad mountains, fairy-tale villages and, yes, long stretches of sandy Black Sea beaches. For such a small country it certainly packs a lot in, but only in recent years have foreign travellers really begun to explore the varied landscapes and unique culture of this forgotten corner of the continent.

Increasing numbers of British, and especially German visitors, jet in for cheap package-holidays at the built-up Black Sea beach resorts, but step away from the parasols and the all-inclusive deals and you'll discover a country with a rich culture and a fascinating history. Thracian and Roman ruins dot the lush countryside, alongside richly frescoed monasteries and timber-framed villages seemingly lost in time.

The capital, Sofia, is the first port of call for most visitors, and although no grand metropolis, its museums, monuments and parks are worth a few days of anyone's time. Other big cities, such as Plovdiv and Varna, are also rewarding destinations, while Koprivshtitsa, with its unrivalled national revival architecture, and the church-filled seaside town of Nesebâr are unmissable.

Bulgaria is a country made for hikers, boasting seven major mountain ranges, each with unique terrain, flora and fauna. Skiing, too, is a very popular pursuit, and you'll pay a fraction of the prices charged in more established resorts in Western Europe.

Five centuries of Ottoman rule virtually removed Bulgaria from the map as far as the rest of the world was concerned, and four decades of communism made it a little-known and difficult place to visit. Since the collapse of the Soviet bloc, Bulgaria has turned its attention westwards; already a member of NATO, it's now looking forward to joining the EU in 2007.

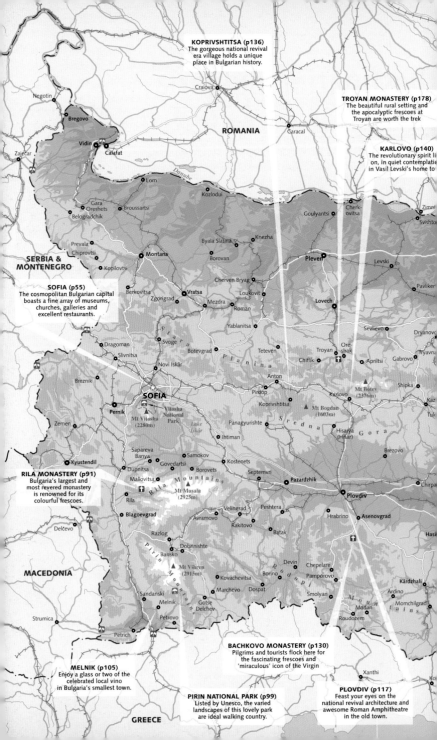

KOPRIVSHTITSA (p136)
The gorgeous national revival era village holds a unique place in Bulgarian history.

TROYAN MONASTERY (p178)
The beautiful rural setting and the apocalyptic frescoes at Troyan are worth the trek.

KARLOVO (p140)
The revolutionary spirit li
on, in quiet contemplati
in Vasil Levski's home to

ROMANIA

SERBIA & MONTENEGRO

SOFIA (p55)
The cosmopolitan Bulgarian capital boasts a fine array of museums, churches, galleries and excellent restaurants.

RILA MONASTERY (p91)
Bulgaria's largest and most revered monastery is renowned for its colourful frescoes.

MACEDONIA

MELNIK (p105)
Enjoy a glass or two of the celebrated local vino in Bulgaria's smallest town.

BACHKOVO MONASTERY (p130)
Pilgrims and tourists flock here for the fascinating frescoes and 'miraculous' icon of the Virgin

PIRIN NATIONAL PARK (p99)
Listed by Unesco, the varied landscapes of this lovely park are ideal walking country.

PLOVDIV (p117)
Feast your eyes on the national revival architecture and awesome Roman Amphitheatre in the old town.

GREECE

Negotin
Bregovo
Vidin
Calafat
Zaječar
Lom
Kozlodui
Craiova
Caracal
Zimni
Svishto
Gara Oreshets
Broussartsi
Belogradchik
Prevala
Chiprovtsi
Kopilovtsi
Byala Slatina
Knezha
Goulyantsi
Pleven
Cherk-ovitsa
Levski
Pavliker
Montana
Borovan
Berkovitsa
Vratsa
Cherven Bryag
Loukovit
Lovech
Dryanov
Zgorigrad
Mezdra
Roman
Sevlievo
Nyanva
Dragoman
Svoge
Botevgrad
Yablanitsa
Teteven
Troyan
Ore-shak
Apriltsi
Gabrovo
Slivnitsa
Novi Iskâr
Chiflik
Shipka
Breznik
SOFIA
Anton
Pirdop
Mt Botev (2376m)
Kaz
Zemen
Pernik
Mt Vitosha (2280m)
Vitosha National Park
Lake Iskâr
Koprivshtitsa
Karlovo
Mt Bogdan (1603m)
Tulc
Sredna Gora
Kyustendil
Sapareva Banya
Samokov
Kostenets
Panagyurishte
Ihtiman
Hisarya (Hisar)
Brezovo
Dupnitsa
Govedartsi
Borovets
Septemvri
Pazardzhik
Chirpa
Maliovitsa
Rila
Mt Musala (2925m)
Rila
Plovdiv
Delčevo
Blagoevgrad
Velingrad
Peshtera
Hrabrino
Asenovgrad
Razlog
Rakitovo
Batak
Hasi
Dobrinishte
Bansko
Devin
Chepelare
Kârdzhali
Mt Vihren (2915m)
Kovachevitsa
Borino
Pamporovo
Ardino
Momchilgrad
Strumica
Marchevo
Dospat
Smolyan
Madan
Sandanski
Melnik
Gotse Delchev
Roudozem
Petrovo
Petrich
Xanthi
Ko

Danube
Danube
Stara Planina
Pirin Mountains
Rila Mountains
Rodopi Mountains

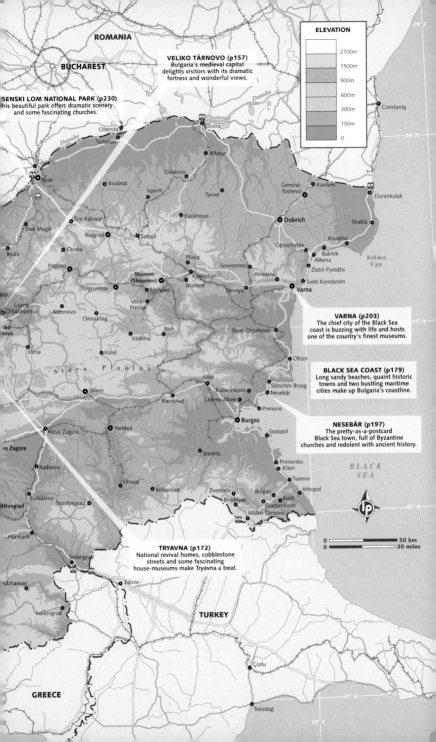

ROMANIA

BUCHAREST

VELIKO TÁRNOVO (p157)
Bulgaria's medieval capital delights visitors with its dramatic fortress and wonderful views.

SENSKI LOM NATIONAL PARK (p230)
his beautiful park offers dramatic scenery and some fascinating churches.

ELEVATION

	2100m
	1500m
	900m
	600m
	300m
	150m
	0

Danube

Constanța

Oltenița
Turtakan
Silistra

Giurgiu

Ruse

Alfatar

Dve Mogili

Doulovo

Koubrat

Byala

Tsar Kaloyan

Isperih

Tervel

Kaolinovo

General-Toshevo

Kardam

Durankulak

Razgrad

Samuil

Opaka

Pliska

Dobrich

Shabla

Kavarna

Popovo

Shumen
(Shoumen)

Kaspichan

Madara

Souvorovo

Obrochishte

Balchik
Albena

Kaliakra
Cape

up

Gorna
Oryakhovitsa

Turgovishte

Kochovo

Devnya

Aksakovo

Zlatni Pyasātsi

iko
iovo

Antonovo

Veliki
Preslav

Rish

Sveti Konstantin

Elena

Omourtag

Várbitsa

Staro Oryahovo

Varna

VARNA (p203)
The chief city of the Black Sea coast is buzzing with life and hosts one of the country's finest museums.

Stara Planina

Kótel

Obzor

Sliven

Aitos

Slánchev Bryag
Nesebár

BLACK SEA COAST (p179)
Long sandy beaches, quaint historic towns and two bustling maritime cities make up Bulgaria's coastline.

Kableshkovo

Cherno More

Pomorie

Karnobat

Nova Zagora

Yambol

Burgas

Sozopol

NESEBÁR (p197)
The pretty-as-a-postcard Black Sea town, full of Byzantine churches and redolent with ancient history.

ra Zagora

Radnevo

Sredets

Primorsko
Kiten

Tsarevo

*BLACK
SEA*

Gulubovo

Topolovgrad

Eihovo

Bolyarovo

Zvezdets

Brushlyan

Bulgari

Gramatikovo

Kosti

Ahtopol

Harmanli

Malko Tárnovo

LP

itrovgrad

Svilengrad

TRYAVNA (p172)
National revival homes, cobblestone streets and some fascinating house-museums make Tryavna a treat.

| 0 | | 50 km |
| 0 | | 30 miles |

dzharovo

Edirne

Ivailovgrad

TURKEY

Çorlu

GREECE

Tekirdağ

Bulgaria has something for everyone, from picturesque villages and monasteries to glorious, unspoilt countryside, sandy beaches and soaring mountains. For deserted beaches and an unhurried pace, go to **Sinemorets** (p196). Indulge in a glass or two of home-produced wine at the remarkable village of **Melnik** (p105) or visit remote **Kotel** (p151) for its village architecture and carpets. Check out **Balchik** (p217), a charming fishing town with a lovely palace and botanic garden. Dine out at a traditional *mehana* (tavern) anywhere in the country and sample some authentic Bulgarian food (p48) and atmosphere.

MARTIN MOOS

Enter the past at Tsarevets Fortress (p159)

Admire the national revival architecture of the house-museums in Plovdiv (p123).

TOM COCKREM

Take home some traditional Bulgarian embroidery (p37)

TOM CK

Contemplate the majestic Pirin Mountains from the village of Bansko (p99)

Vow to visit the historic
Bachkovo Monastery (p130)

Explore Rila Monastery (p91): the biggest monastery
in Bulgaria and a Unesco World Heritage Site

PAUL GR

Take in a show the old-fashioned way at the Roman Amphitheatre (p120) in Plovdiv

PHILIP GAME

Hike Mt Vihren (p101) in the Pirin Mountains

Getting Started

Although most foreign tourists come to Bulgaria on all-inclusive package deals, travelling independently is cheap, relatively hassle-free and immensely rewarding. Bulgaria is a modern and well-organised country with an efficient public transport system linking the big towns and cities, though if you're looking to explore the place in any great depth, you'll certainly require your own wheels, especially for the more remote, rural areas.

English, (and to a lesser extent) French and German are understood to varying degrees in the big cities and tourist centres, but elsewhere knowledge of foreign languages is rare. Remember that Bulgarians use the Cyrillic alphabet, and you should get acquainted with this before you travel.

If learning some Bulgarian words and phrases, and the Cyrillic alphabet, seems too difficult, you crave some comfort or your time is short, consider an organised tour (see p266 and p270). The downside is that tours are expensive and inflexible, concentrate solely on a few major attractions, and often only operate during the peak season (July and August). But if you're on a package tour based at a beach or ski resort, it's easy to visit nearby attractions by public bus, hire car or locally organised tours. Some agencies based in Sofia (see p68) run a huge range of multiday activity and special-interest tours, so if you're keen on archaeology, bird-watching, botany, caving or climbing (to name just a few), or if you fancy trying something new, such as snowshoeing, these are a good way to see the best that the country has to offer.

Doubtless, many travellers will link their visit to Bulgaria with a jaunt around Eastern Europe and/or the Balkans. If so, it's important to spend some time considering the best places to enter and leave Bulgaria so you can see everything you want without backtracking.

WHEN TO GO

Bulgaria has a temperate climate with cold, damp winters and hot, dry summers. The Rodopi Mountains form a barrier to the moderating Mediterranean influence of the Aegean, while the Danube Plain is open to the extremes of central Europe. Sofia's generally favourable climate is one of its main attributes, with average daytime highs of 28°C in July and August and 3°C from December to February. The Black Sea moderates temperatures in the east of the country. Rainfall is highest in the mountains, and in winter life throughout Bulgaria is sometimes disrupted by heavy snowfalls.

See Climate Charts (p249) for more information.

DON'T LEAVE HOME WITHOUT...

- Valid travel insurance (see p254)
- Sturdy boots and a day-pack if you intend doing any hiking
- Toilet paper
- Towel if staying at budget accommodation
- Sunscreen and a sun-hat if travelling in summer
- Adapter plug
- Water bottle for filling at public fountain
- Camera

Spring (particularly April to mid-June) is an excellent time to visit. The days are getting longer, the weather is good, the theatres and other cultural venues are in full swing, off-season rates still generally apply, and locals are not yet jaded by waves of summertime visitors. Summer (mid-June to early September) is ideal for hiking and festivals, but is the peak season for travellers from elsewhere in Europe. Temperatures can be very high during this period too. September is perhaps one of the best months to see Bulgaria. The autumn trees are glorious, fruit and vegetables are plentiful, shoulder-season tariffs are in effect, the tourist hordes have returned home, and you can still swim and sunbathe at the Black Sea.

By mid-October, almost all Black Sea resorts have closed down. As the days get shorter and the weather gets colder over the next two months, a gloom about the impending winter (December to March) permeates Bulgaria. Then, as soon as the first snows fall in around mid-December, Bulgarians start to perk up and flock to the ski resorts, which sometimes stay operating until mid-April.

The peak season along the Black Sea coast is mid-July to late August; at the ski resorts, it's Christmas/New Year and February to mid-March. If you avoid these places at these times, you may be astounded at how few tourists there are in Bulgaria.

COSTS & MONEY

LONELY PLANET INDEX

Litre of petrol 1.80 lv

1.5 litres of bottled water 0.50 lv

Large bottle of beer in a bar 1.20 lv

Souvenir T-shirt 20 lv

Street snack (banitsa) 1 lv

Despite having to pay more than Bulgarians for most hotel rooms and admission fees (see the next section), travelling around the country is relatively cheap. All food, drink and forms of transport are surprisingly inexpensive compared with Western European countries, but imported luxury goods, such as Western fashion and cosmetics, cost much the same as anywhere else.

A camp site costs about 10 lv per person and a room in a private home is about 22 lv. In a budget hotel (outside Sofia) a single room costs from 15 lv, 25 lv for a double. In a mid-range hotel a single room is 35 lv, a double 55 lv. You can get a simple meal at a cheap café from as little as 3 lv, and you're unlikely to spend more than about 12 lv for a main course, even in more upmarket restaurants.

Many museums and galleries offer free entry on one day of the week, a bonus if you're travelling with a family. These details are noted where relevant in reviews throughout the book. Also, if you fancy staying at a top-class hotel but don't fancy paying the top-class tariff, remember that most offer discounted weekend rates (which usually means Friday to Sunday night).

If you stay at budget hotels or in private rooms, eat cheap Bulgarian food and catch public buses and 2nd-class trains, allow at least 40 lv per person per day. If you want to stay in mid-range hotels, eat at higher-quality restaurants, charter occasional taxis, take 1st-class trains and buy souvenirs, allow about 70 lv per person per day. If you're staying in Sofia, you can basically double this cost.

Dual Pricing

One annoying aspect of travelling around Bulgaria is that foreign tourists are often charged considerably more for some things than Bulgarians and foreign residents (those with documents to prove they live and/or work in Bulgaria). However, this practice is not as widespread as it once was, and when Bulgaria does eventually join the EU (probably in 2007), this dual-pricing system will become illegal. Throughout this book tourist prices are given: where the dual-pricing system is not operating, this is noted.

TOP TENS

Bulgaria's most picturesque villages

The heart of Bulgaria can be found in its small, rural communities, and the country has numerous little timber-framed villages where the style and pace of life seem to belong to another time. The following villages are worth visiting for their architecture, ambience and surrounding landscapes.

- Koprivshtitsa (p136)
- Kovachevitsa (p117)
- Kotel (p151)
- Shiroka Lûka (p115)
- Melnik (p105)
- Govedartsi (p97)
- Momchilovtsi (p111)
- Arbanasi (p166)
- Yagodina (p116)
- Shipka (p145)

Bulgaria's Most Engaging Festivals

Bulgarians love to socialise and celebrate, and do so in many different ways. Celebrations of food, wine and other harvests occur throughout the year, while music and folklore festivals offer the visitor a particularly evocative introduction into the local culture. The following are among the more accessible and interesting, but for a complete list of Bulgaria's many festivals, see p252.

- Trifon Zarezan Festival, Melnik (1 or 14 February)
- Kukeri Festival, Shiroka Lûka (first Sunday in March)
- Re-enactment of the April Uprising, Koprivshtitsa (1–2 May)
- Varna Summer International Festival, Varna (May–October)
- Festival of Roses, Kazanlâk and Karlovo (June)
- International Folklore Festival, Veliko Târnovo (June–July)
- Thracia Summer Music Festival, Plovdiv (August)
- Pirin Sings Folk Festival, Bansko (August, odd-numbered years)
- Apollonia Arts Festival, Sozopol (September)
- Young Red Wine Festival, Sandanski (December)

Bulgaria's Best Religious Artworks

Bulgaria is well known for its beautiful religious icons, a rich tradition going back many centuries, into the Byzantine and Slavic past. Churches and monasteries across the country are a blaze of colour, with wonderful frescoes, murals and icons on show, while many ancient and precious examples of this art can now be seen in museums. Listed below are the best places to see Bulgaria's most important and most exquisite religious art.

- Museum of Icons (Aleksander Nevski Crypt), Sofia (p61)
- Boyana Church, Sofia (p80)
- Rila Monastery (p91)
- Bachkovo Monastery (p130)
- St Stefan Church, Nesebâr (p199)
- Nativity Church, Arbanasi (p166)
- Troyan Monastery (p178)
- Sts Peter & Paul Church, Veliko Târnovo (p161)
- Church of Sts Konstantin & Elena, Plovdiv (p125)
- Museum of Icons, Tryavna (p173)

HOW MUCH?

Coffee at street kiosk 0.40 lv

Bus/tram ticket 0.50 lv

Kebabche (grilled spicy meat sausages) and chips 3 lv

Bottle of decent Bulgarian wine 5 lv

CD of Bulgarian music 12 lv

Under the current system, accommodation can cost about two or three times more for foreigners than locals. This can be avoided to some degree by camping, staying in private rooms or looking for hotels that do not discriminate against foreigners.

Admission to tourist attractions costs between two and five times more for foreigners – which is even more galling when you consider that most museums don't label exhibits in any language but Bulgarian. While accommodation and admission fees may eat into your daily budget, this is easily offset by remarkably cheap food, drink and public transport.

Before you complain too much about dual pricing, however, it's worth noting that the average wage is Bulgaria is just €150 per month – one of the lowest in Europe.

TRAVEL LITERATURE

There are relatively few books by foreign writers devoted solely to Bulgaria; most include the country as part of a journey around Eastern Europe and/or the Balkans.

A Time of Gifts and *Between the Woods and the Water* by Patrick Leigh Fermor are among the most intriguing travel books on Eastern Europe. They detail Fermor's walk from the Netherlands to Turkey in 1933–34 on a budget of UK£1 a week.

Stealing from a Deep Place by Brian Hall details his extensive travels through Hungary, Romania, Bulgaria and parts of former Yugoslavia.

Balkan Ghosts by Robert D Kaplan offers a contemporary traveller's view of a region torn by ethnic strife and economic upheaval.

Molvania – A Land Untouched by Modern Dentistry by Santo Cilauro, Tom Gleisner and Rob Sitch is a wry guide to a fictional Balkan-like country not too far away from Bulgaria.

INTERNET RESOURCES

The World Wide Web is a rich resource for travellers. You can research your trip, hunt down bargain air fares, book hotels, find property for rent, check on weather conditions or chat with locals and other travellers about the best places to visit (or avoid!).

There's no better place to start your Web explorations than the Lonely Planet website (www.lonelyplanet.com). Here you will find succinct summaries on travelling to most places on earth, postcards from other travellers and the Thorn Tree bulletin board, where you can ask questions before you go or dispense advice when you get back. The subWWWay section links you to the most useful travel resources elsewhere on the Web.

Other useful websites (all in English) to access before you travel:

BG Globe (www.bgglobe.net) Comprehensive site with details of accommodation around the country and suggestions for visitors.

Bulgaria (www.bulgaria.com) Basic travel information, exchange rates, weather reports and so on.

Bulgarian Ministry of Foreign Affairs (www.mfa.government.bg) Good for current affairs and links to all government departments.

Bulgarian Properties (www.bulgarianproperties.com) Houses, flats and holiday-apartments for sale and rent all around Bulgaria.

Get Info Bulgaria (http://get.info.bg/visit) Excellent portal with information on a wide range of topics.

HotelsCentral.com (www.hotelsbulgaria.com) Offers attractive discounts for hotel rooms (if booked for three or more nights).

Sofia Echo (www.sofiaecho.com) Up-to-the-minute news about Bulgaria as well as restaurant and entertainment reviews for the capital.

Travel Bulgaria (www.travel-bulgaria.com) Excellent site for travel information, including links.

Itineraries
CLASSIC ROUTES

BULGARIAN HIGHLIGHTS
Two to Three Weeks

Start off in the capital, **Sofia** (p55), which has more than enough going on to keep you occupied for a few days, including some excellent museums and galleries and Bulgaria's best restaurant and nightlife scene. For a complete contrast, take the train to the beautifully restored village of **Koprivshtitsa** (p136), with its plethora of national revival–era house-museums. It's a lovely spot to stay for a day or two.

From here, take a bus to busy **Plovdiv** (p117), where you can easily pass a couple of days browsing through the art galleries, exploring the Roman remains or just taking it easy at one of the many street cafés.

From Plovdiv, head to the Black Sea coast, and the amenable city of **Burgas** (p181) for an overnight stop, before heading up to the country's biggest tourist draw, **Nesebâr** (p197), famed for its Byzantine churches. Spend a few days here, maybe taking a day trip to the beach at **Slânchev Bryag** (p202), then continue up the coast towards **Varna** (p203). The city's superb Archaeological Museum and Roman Thermae are definitely worth a visit, and the extensive Primorski Park are a pleasant place to escape the worst of the summer heat or to take a leisurely morning stroll.

Start back westwards, stopping at historic **Veliko Târnovo** (p157) on the way; its ancient fortress is unmissable and the views fantastic. Spend at least one night here before returning to Sofia.

Two weeks is not a lot of time to see all that Bulgaria has to offer, but it's enough to give you a taster, and maybe give you ideas about where you'd like to return to at a later date.

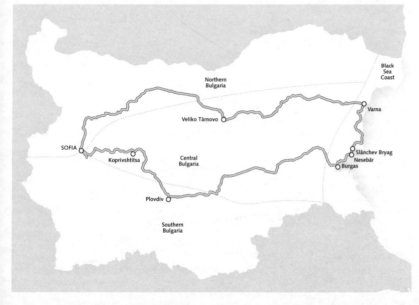

MONASTERIES & MOUNTAINS

One Week

Staying in Sofia, take a trip to **Dragalevtsi** (p82) in **Vitosha National Park** (p80), just on the outskirts of the city. Take a peek at the much-revered Dragalevtsi Monastery, and then take the chairlift up to Goli Vrâh. Depending on the season you can then go walking or skiing on **Mt Vitosha** (p82), which affords some spectacular views back over Sofia, weather permitting.

This quick trip will give you a good idea of the attractions around the capital and the conveniently close hiking and skiing areas, and take you to Bulgaria's most popular tourist attraction, Rila Monastery.

From Sofia, take the minibus for the short journey to **Samokov** (p94), which is worth a quick look over for its History Museum and mosque, then catch another minibus to Bulgaria's most popular ski resort at **Borovets** (p95). Again, depending on the time of year, you can either slip on your skis and take to the slopes or, in summer, enjoy hiking in the beautiful **Rila National Park** (p88), south of town.

Stay in Borovets for a few days, then go back to Samokov for a connecting minibus to Dupnitsa, from where you can get another bus to the village of **Rila** (p91). You could either stay overnight in the village's sole hotel, or at one of the places near **Rila Monastery** (p91), which is just a short bus ride away. The spectacular monastery is the most holy pilgrimage site in Bulgaria, and is the country's most visited attraction. Try to ignore the inevitable tour buses and crowds and just admire the stunning frescoes and beautiful architecture of the place.

From Rila village, you can catch a bus back to Sofia.

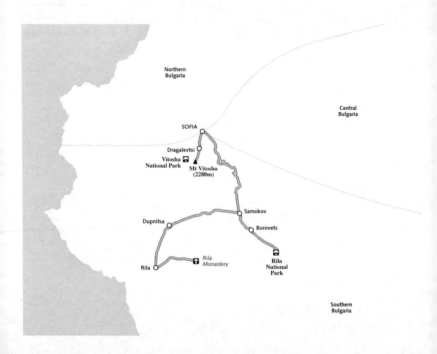

ROADS LESS TRAVELLED

THE NORTHERN LINE   Two Weeks

Starting at Sofia, head north by train to **Vidin** (p236), where you can stay overnight, see the Danube and visit the **Baba Vida Museum-Fortress** (p237). From here, travel south to gorgeous **Belogradchik** (p234), where you can explore the even more interesting fortress and see the fantastic Belogradchik rocks.

The next day, continue by train to **Vratsa** (p231) and spend a day walking in the nearby mountains before moving on to **Lovech** (p175). The old town is a great place to explore and you can make an excursion to nearby **Troyan Monastery** (p178) to see some of Bulgaria's best fresco painting.

Next, travel to **Veliko Târnovo** (p157), where, instead of staying in the town, you could enjoy a relaxing few days in nearby **Arbanasi** (p166). Take time to visit the **Ètar complex** (p171) and other local attractions, such as **Tryavna** (p172) or the **Dryanovo Monastery** (p174), before heading on to **Shumen** (p152). Here you'll find the most intricately decorated mosque in Bulgaria as well as another great fortress. You could also take interesting excursions from here to **Veliki Preslav** (p156) or **Kotel** (p151).

Carry on to **Dobrich** (p242) with its excellent open-air ethnological museum. Finally, head to the coast, and the off-the-beaten-track destination of **Balchik** (p217). This lovely place makes for a total contrast to the resorts down the coast, and while there isn't a great beach, the swimming is still good and there's the superb botanical gardens and Queen Marie's palace to visit.

This trip takes you across the often neglected northern region of Bulgaria, beginning in the far northwest at Vidin on the Danube and ending up at charming Balchik on the Black Sea.

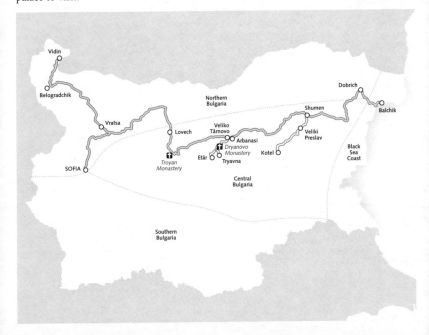

SOUTHERN SPLENDOUR

Two Weeks

Start off in Sofia, and take the bus down to **Blagoevgrad** (p88), which, though it might not be brimming over with sights, is a lively provincial town and a convenient overnight stop. From here, travel on to **Sandanski** (p103), birthplace of Spartacus and a popular and sunny spa town. The town makes an ideal base for a day trip to nearby **Melnik** (p105), famous for its wine and its bizarre sand pyramids, and you could also, perhaps, carry on to **Rozhen Monastery** (p108).

From Sandanski you catch a bus to the charming mountain town of **Bansko** (p99): outside the tourist high seasons in winter and midsummer, it's a quiet, laid-back place to rest up. The more energetic can take advantage of the excellent hiking country nearby.

Continue by bus to **Plovdiv** (p117). Bulgaria's second city is worth a few days' stopover, with one of the country's best preserved old towns and a host of art galleries to visit. The lovely **Bachkovo Monastery** (p130) is also an easy day trip from Plovdiv.

Following this route, you'll get away from the main tourist centres and see southern Bulgaria at its best.

Head south to **Smolyan** (p113), Bulgaria's highest (and longest) town. The climate here is often cool and refreshing, and the town has an excellent historical museum. Take a day trip to nearby **Shiroka Lûka** (p115), a typically charming Rodopian village famed for its *kukeri* festival and humpbacked bridges. Carry on to the spa town of **Devin** (p115), where you can indulge in some hydrotherapy or a massage. This peaceful little town makes a great base for visiting the spectacular caves at **Trigrad** (p116) and **Yagodina** (p116). You can then head back to Sofia either directly or via Plovdiv.

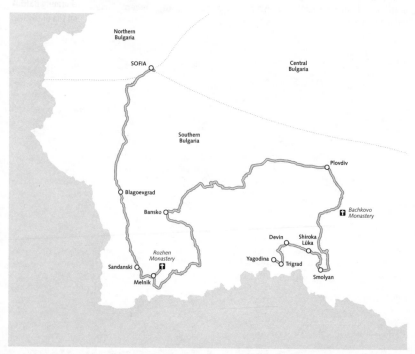

TAILORED TRIPS

THE BLACK SEA

As well as the huge beach resorts, this trip will take you to small coastal villages, ancient peninsula towns and charming Varna.

Arriving in **Burgas** (p181), spend a night in town and soak up its party atmosphere before heading south to **Sozopol** (p188) by bus. Spend a couple of days here exploring the old town and enjoying the town's two beaches. Further south, head to **Primorsko** (p193) for more nightlife, **Kiten** (p194) for family fun or **Ahtopol** (p195) for quieter, uncommercial beach-life. Nobody should miss **Sinemorets** (p196) with its access to the **Strandzha Nature Park** (p195) and its two beaches, some of the quietest on the entire Bulgarian coast.

Head back to Burgas, then on to lovely, if commercialised, **Nesebâr** (p197). Stay either in the old town itself, or in the nearby super-resort of **Slânchev Bryag** (p202), where you'll also find a great beach, albeit one totally colonised by package tourists in summer.

Head north to bustling **Varna** (p203) via swaths of deserted coastline; with a car you can discover your own beaches (although the road is often quite a way from the coast). In Varna you'll find cultural diversions, including the first-rate Archaeological Museum and the attractive Primorski Park.

North of Varna, head for one of the resorts if you haven't had enough beach.

THE UNESCO HERITAGE TOUR

This tour takes you to nearly all of Bulgaria's Unesco World Heritage Sites. Some are awkward to reach by public transport; see relevant sections for details. From Sofia, take a day trip to the suburb of Boyana, and the delightful **Boyana Church** (p80), with its important 13th-century murals. Heading south, visit the splendid **Rila Monastery** (p91) on a (long) day trip from Sofia, or from Blagoevgrad. It's the country's largest monastery, and a true highlight. The **Pirin National Park** (p101), best explored via Bansko, offers numerous walking trails and remarkable scenery.

Travelling east to Kazanlâk, you'll come upon the **Thracian Tomb of Kazanlâk** (p142). The 4th-century BC tomb is open to the public.

In the north, the impressive **Ivanovo Rock Monastery** (p230) is inside the Rusenski Lom Nature Park, near Ruse, and the **Srebârna Nature Reserve** (p242) is best reached from Silistra. Get a bus down to Shumen, from where it's possible to visit the **Madara Horseman** (p155), an 8th-century cliff-carving.

Finally, travel to Varna and then down the coast to picture-postcard **Nesebâr** (p197), the last stop on the Unesco trail.

The Authors

RICHARD WATKINS
Coordinating Author, Sofia, Southern Bulgaria

Richard studied Ancient History at Oxford University, and his first job after graduating was teaching conversational English to college students in Sofia, back in the summer of 1995. He quickly developed a real affection for this rugged little country and its welcoming people, and has since returned to Bulgaria several times, discovering something new on each visit. He is slowly amassing collections of *Troyanska kapka* pottery and Bulgarian movie posters and is already looking forward to his next bowl of *tarator*.

Richard has written about Bulgaria for other guidebooks, and has also written for several other Lonely Planet titles, including *Eastern Europe*, *Poland* and *Best of Prague*.

Richard's Favourite Trip

Although most tourists seem to bypass it as quickly as they can, I've always been fond of Sofia (p55), and can easily spend a week exploring the city, seeing what's new and just ambling between amenable cafés. The train ride between the capital and Koprivshtitsa (p136) is a particular favourite of mine, and this little town really is something special, like a timber manifestation of the national psyche.

Taking a bus across the Sredna Gora, I reach Plovdiv (p117), and despite the increasingly touristy overtones, I still enjoy the artistic ambience of the old town, its galleries and fantastic Roman remains. The restaurants aren't bad either.

It's good to get away from the city, too, and rest up in a laid-back village like Shiroka Lûka (p115).

TOM MASTERS
Central Bulgaria, Black Sea Coast, Northern Bulgaria

Tom's travel career began when he went to visit family friends in Bulgaria alone at the tender age of 14. Returning several times since then to Sofia, the Black Sea and the mountains, his love of stuffed peppers and *shopska* salad (made with chopped tomatoes, cucumbers and onions covered with feta cheese) remains undiminished. Tom lives and works in London and among other titles was also the coordinating author of Lonely Planet's *Eastern Europe* book.

Snapshot

Some 15 years after the fall of communism, Bulgaria is still a country in transition, struggling to assert its unique identity in the modern world. Resurgent capitalism has brought new opportunities for many, but has meant social deprivation and hardship for others; the average wage is one of the lowest in Europe and unemployment is high. Although things are certainly improving, the dramatic economic turnaround promised by the government in the 2001 elections has failed to materialise in the minds of an unforgiving electorate, and demonstrations organised by trades unions of up to 20,000 people brought traffic to a standstill in Sofia in 2004.

Elderly Bulgarians are still struggling to cope with the evolving market economy and the shattering of the dictatorial but structured society in which they once lived. Many now live in real poverty, and who can blame them for longing for the relatively affluent days of socialism?

On the other hand, most younger Bulgarians who grew up after the collapse of communism in 1989 have very little interest in, or, it would seem, knowledge of, the country's totalitarian past, something that has caused some concern in the wider society.

One unfortunate side effect of the free-market economy has been the growth of organised crime. In recent years, turf wars have broken out across the country between rival gangs involved in drug-trafficking and racketeering, with high-profile killings, shootings and even bomb attacks in the capital. There has been much public criticism of the ineffectiveness of the judicial system in dealing with this escalating problem, although, thankfully, visitors are highly unlikely to ever come into contact with this seamier side of Bulgaria.

Bulgaria's judiciary also came under fire in 2004 after criminal charges were made against two journalists, one British and one Romanian, under a controversial article of the penal code reminiscent of the Cold War era, which forbids 'using technical devices for secret recording'. A journalist from the BBC had secretly filmed the head of Bulgaria's Olympic Committee, Ivan Slavkov, for a documentary on high-level corruption (Slavkov was temporarily suspended), while the Romanian TV reporter had used a hidden camera to film corrupt practices at a duty-free shop on the Bulgarian–Romanian border. Both were threatened with up to three years in prison, causing a national and international outcry, with the law being denounced as 'absurd and archaic' and much debate in the media about the backwardness of a legal system that disallows investigative journalism.

Bulgaria joined NATO in 2004, and is now gearing up for accession to the EU in 2007, firmly orienting itself towards Western Europe. Some have expressed misgivings, though, about these rapid, major developments. There are also worries about the overdevelopment of the countryside for the increasing demands of tourism (see the boxed text on p39 for tips on how to minimise the impact of your visit), and controversy drags on about the pros and cons of the plans for the country's second nuclear power station at Belene (see p42).

Increasingly, though, Bulgaria is moving closer to mainstream 'Western' culture: Western pop music and fashion are abundant everywhere, while television is moving in the same way; in 2004, the first airing of the Bulgarian version of the reality game-show *Big Brother* – a phrase which once had a very different connotation here – attracted over half the population of Sofia. How times change!

FAST FACTS

Population: 7.5 million

Area: 110,910 sq km

GDP per capita: US$7600

Inflation: 2.3%

Unemployment rate: 15%

Average life expectancy: 68 (m), 75 (f)

Literacy rate: 98.6%

Highest point: Mt Mussala (2925m)

Rose oil production: Bulgaria produces 10% of the world's rose oil

Body language: Bulgarians shake their heads for 'yes' and nod for 'no'

History

Bulgaria is a country with a long, tumultuous and fascinating history. It is the land of Spartacus and Orpheus, a land invaded and conquered by Romans, Byzantines and Turks, all of whom left their indelible marks on the landscape. Bulgaria's medieval 'Golden Age', when the Bulgar Khans ruled over one of the largest empires in Europe, was bright but brief, while five hundred years of subsequent, brutal Turkish domination isolated the country from the rest of Europe. More recently, Bulgaria spent four decades as a totalitarian Soviet satellite, again leaving this small Balkan nation in the shadows as far as most foreigners were concerned. It's no wonder, then, that Bulgarians are so passionate about preserving their history and their culture, which has survived so often against the odds. In the last years of the 20th century Bulgaria began opening up, and is now looking forward to EU accession.

PREHISTORY

Excavations of caves near Pleven (in the Danubian plains in northern Bulgaria) and in the Balkan Mountains have indicated human habitation as far back as the Late Palaeolithic Period around 40,000 BC. However, archaeologists now believe that the earliest permanent settlers, arriving around 6000 BC, were Neolithic people who lived in caves, such as at Yagodina in the southern Rodopi Mountains (p109) and later, between about 5500 BC and 4500 BC, in round mud huts. The best preserved of these can be seen in Stara Zagora (see p146). Burnt grain found here indicates these people were farmers. Chalcolithic (copper-using) cultures developed during the fourth millennium BC, and a superb collection of artefacts from this period, including possibly the earliest gold jewellery ever discovered, is on show at Varna Archaeological Museum (p205).

THRACIANS

According to the Greek historian Herodotus, the population of Thrace was 'greater than that of any country in the world except India', and if the disparate tribes ever united under a single leader, then they would be the most powerful nation on earth; history, of course, tells us that they never did get their act together. Several tribes, who came to be known as the Thracians, settled around most of modern-day Bulgaria, and later expanded into Anatolia and Greece during the Middle Bronze Age about 2000 BC. In the early stages, they built settlements in and around caves and near springs. Later, they built larger permanent villages around rudimentary fortresses, established on elevated sites for defensive purposes.

Despite their disunity, the Thracian tribes shared much in common, and were respected by outsiders as great warriors: one look at the fierce Thracian weaponry displayed at archaeological museums around the country will give an idea of what Greeks, Romans and others were up against. Writing in the 2nd century BC, the Greek historian Polybius tells us of the 'insoluble state of war' that existed between the Thracians and the Byzantine Greeks. It was impossible, he says, to gain a decisive victory

DID YOU KNOW?

The Thracian Getae tribe would send 'messengers' to their god, Salmoxis, by hurling them onto a row of upturned spears.

TIMELINE	6000 BC	4000–1000 BC
	Neolithic settlements established	Thracians dominate the region

over these 'barbarians', or to end the fighting, due to the sheer number of different chieftains and their followers: 'If the Byzantines overcome one chieftain, three others still more formidable invade his territory'.

The Thracians were also accomplished artists and farmers, and grew wealthy from trading jewellery and metal products, such as copper and gold. They worshipped several gods, especially Dionysus, whom they celebrated in orgiastic rites, and many strongly believed in an afterlife, while their promiscuity and use of inhaled intoxicants were often regarded with disdain by foreign chroniclers.

The Thracians significantly influenced the religion, architecture and culture of the subsequent Roman and Greek rulers. Some geographical names used today, such as 'rila' (for Rila Monastery) and 'yantra' (the name of the river through Veliko Târnovo) probably originate from Thracian words.

Remains of Thracian settlements can be found along the Black Sea coast near Burgas and at the town of Mesembria (Nesebâr), which the Thracians settled in about 3000 BC. Other remnants can be found on Nebet Tepe in Plovdiv, where they built the fortress of Eumolpias in about 5000 BC (see p121). Because of the attractive climate and fertile land, the Thracians also built towns in and around modern-day Stara Zagora, Sandanski, Melnik, Bansko, Smolyan, Shumen and Madara.

By the first millennium BC the Thracians had spread as far north as Cherven, near the Danube, and as far west as Sofia. One tribe known as the Serdis created Sardonopolis, which was later renamed Serdica, and subsequently became Sofia, the modern-day capital.

The most famous Thracian remains are the tombs dating from about 4000 BC which are displayed in the excellent Archaeological Museum in Varna (see p205) and the tomb at Kazanlâk built in the 4th century BC (see p142). Close by, the area around Shipka has been termed the 'Bulgarian Valley of the Kings' due to its high concentration of Thracian burial mounds. In 2004 archaeologists unearthed a solid gold mask here, possibly representing the Thracian king, Teres I. It's one of the most important Thracian treasures ever found, and will hopefully soon be on display in Sofia. Other Thracian artefacts can be seen in museums in Haskovo, Smolyan, Sofia and Sliven.

ORPHEUS IN THRACE

The legend of Orpheus, the semidivine lyre-player and singer, was one of the most popular and enduring in antiquity, even spawning a 'mystery cult' in Greece and elsewhere in the Hellenistic world, but it is thought that the original Orpheus was a real person, born somewhere in the neighbourhood of Gela, north of Shiroka Lûka. His story is well known: his music soothed men, beasts and even trees; he travelled with Jason and the Argonauts in search of the Golden Fleece, when his lyre-plucking helpfully drowned out the alluring wails of the Sirens; and, of course, he descended into the underworld to rescue his dead wife, Eurydice, from the clutches of Hades. Having lost her again at the last moment, Orpheus spent the rest of his days wandering around the Rodopi Mountains, until his mournful singing drove the Bacchantes (ecstatic female devotees of Dionysus) to tear him into pieces and dump his dismembered remains in the river. Harsh critics indeed. It is said that his blood splattered, and permanently stained, the endemic Rodopian flower, the Silivriak (see p40).

AD 46

Thrace made a Roman province

681–1018

First Bulgarian Empire

Legend tells that Orpheus, the semimythical musician and day-tripper from Hell, was born in Thrace, near the modern-day village of Gela (see the boxed text, p21), while Spartacus, his famous fellow Thracian who led a slave revolt against the Romans, came from the vicinity of modern Sandanski.

GREEKS & MACEDONIANS

From the 7th century BC, seafaring Greeks made their way up the Black Sea coast of Bulgaria and founded settlements they called Apollonia (modern-day Sozopol), Odessos (Varna), Mesembria (Nesebâr), Kruni (Balchik) and Pirgos (Burgas). They established large ports for exporting wheat, fish and salt, and traded Greek pottery for Thracian metalwork and jewellery.

Despite the proximity to their homeland, the Greeks avoided most of southern and central Bulgaria because the belligerent Thracians had settled there in large numbers; estimates suggest that during the first millennium BC the Thracians outnumbered the Greeks by four to one between the Danube and the Aegean.

Only a few towns away from the Black Sea show any evidence of Greek settlement. These include Pataunia (Kyustendil), southwest of Sofia, and Silistra on the Danube in northern Bulgaria.

However, the Greeks did have a profound influence on religion, arts and culture throughout the Balkans for over 900 years. The Greek language was used extensively by non-Greeks for business, administration and education. The Bulgarian language still has many words of Greek origin, and the patriarch of the Bulgarian Orthodox Church was based in Athens for centuries.

In the middle of the 4th century BC, the Macedonians, under the leadership of Philip II, and later his son, Alexander the Great, conquered all of Thrace. Philip made his capital at Philipopolis (Plovdiv), which developed into an important military outpost, while Odessos (Varna) and modern-day Sofia were also occupied. Macedonian rule was to be brief, though, and they soon had the might of Rome to contend with.

ROMANS

Although they had defeated the Macedonian Empire in 168 BC, it wasn't until the middle of the 1st century AD that the Romans began making inroads into the territory of the Thracians, and occupying major Greek ports, such as Mesembria (Nesebâr). They set up a base at Odessos (Varna), where the largest Roman ruins in Bulgaria, the great Roman Thermae complex, can still be seen (see p206).

By AD 46 the Romans had conquered the entire Balkan Peninsula, and the territory of modern-day Bulgaria was initially divided into the provinces of Thrace, in the south, and Moesia, in the north. To shore up vital defensive lines, the Romans built numerous military strongholds and fortified major Thracian and Greek towns along the Danube at Ruse and Bononia (Vidin), and at Debeltus (Burgas) along the Black Sea coast. Although they burned and looted the major Greek settlement of Apollonia, the Romans rebuilt it to become a vital port within the Roman Empire.

The Bulgarians from Pagan Times to the Ottoman Conquest by David Marshall Lang has maps, illustrations and lucid text that make this book well worth reading and help bring medieval Bulgaria to life.

863	971
Sts Kiril and Metodii create Cyrillic alphabet	Bulgarian capital at Pliska falls to Byzantines

Ulpia Serdica (Sofia) was established as the capital of the Roman province of Inner Dacia (northwestern Bulgaria) and the most visible reminder of their presence still standing is the Sveti Georgi Rotunda (Church of St George; p64). Other towns established by the Romans, or built on existing Thracian, Greek and Macedonian settlements, include Sevtopolis (Kazanlâk), Ulpia Augusta Trayana (Stara Zagora), Nikopolis-ad-Istrum (north of Veliko Târnovo) and Trimontium (Plovdiv), where a magnificent amphitheatre was built, which is still used for performances today (see p120). By the late 3rd century AD, Serdica had become a major regional imperial capital, where Diocletian and subsequent emperors held court.

Remnants of Roman settlements can be admired in many places, even as far west as Belogradchik. In central Bulgaria, the Romans were the first to build a proper fortress on top of Tsarevets Hill in Veliko Târnovo (see p159). They built extensive walls, which partially still stand, at Hisarya (Hisar; see p141) to protect prized sources of mineral water.

Goths, Visigoths, Vandals, Huns and a distressing array of other 'barbarian' tribes began descending on the Roman provinces of Bulgaria from the 3rd century AD onwards, causing much havoc, although such raids were sporadic and short-lived.

BYZANTINES & BULGARS

In 330 the city of Constantinople (modern Istanbul) was founded by the Roman emperor Constantine the Great on the site of ancient Byzantium, and was declared the capital of the Eastern Roman Empire. The division of the empire meant that the Bulgarian provinces were now ruled from that city. By the late 4th century, the Western Roman Empire was in serious trouble and gradually fell apart, but the East continued for another thousand years, as the Byzantine Empire. The 6th-century rule of Emperor Justinian the Great was a relatively peaceful time for Bulgaria – Sofia's original Church of St Sofia (p65) was built at this time – but the following centuries saw growing numbers of Slavs, Avars and Bulgars breaching the empire's borders.

Bulgarians: Civilisers of the Slavs by Bojidar Dimitrov is a small and readable, but somewhat biased, telling of the country's religious and cultural history. It's also available in French and German.

In 632 the numerous Bulgar tribes, whose territories stretched from the Black Sea to the Caspian Sea, were united under the overlordship of Khan Kubrat, and by the middle of the 7th century they had moved into the land of modern-day Bulgaria. The Byzantines, unable to cope with the vast influx, allowed them to stay. This fierce Turkic tribe settled throughout the region, subjugating and integrating with the Slavs and the last few Thracians.

Khan (Tsar) Asparukh (r 681–700) was responsible for establishing what became known as the First Bulgarian Empire (681–1018). He created a capital at Pliska, near modern-day Shumen. The empire expanded south and west under Khan Tervel (r 701–718) and was revered for repelling an Arab advance on Constantinople.

Conflict between Byzantium and the Bulgars continued over the centuries, with Khan Krum 'The Dreadful' (r 803–814) besieging Constantinople after the Byzantines burnt down Pliska.

The 9th century was Bulgaria's apogee in many ways, with several tsars expanding the kingdom's territory: Khan Omurtag (r 814–831) captured

1014

15,000 Bulgarian soldiers are captured and blinded by Byzantine Emperor Basil II 'the Bulgar Slayer' and sent back to Tsar Samuel

1185–1396

Second Bulgarian Empire

Hungary in 829, and by the end of Khan Presian's reign (r 837–852) the Bulgarian state encompassed a huge swathe of southeastern Europe, including modern-day Romania, Moldova and Macedonia.

In 863 Tsar Boris I (r 852–889) tried to unify the fledgling Bulgar-Slav Empire by converting it to Christianity. At about this time, an independent church was established and a Slavonic alphabet devised by two monks, Kiril and Metodii, known in English as Cyril and Methodius (see the boxed text, p24).

DID YOU KNOW?

Bogomilism was a 10th-century Bulgarian heresy based on the notion of two deities, one good, one evil. It later spread to France in the form of Catharism.

Boris retired to a monastery in 889, leaving his son Vladimir in control. Vladimir's attempts to restore paganism led to his own father deposing and blinding him, and his younger brother Simeon (r 893–927) ascended the throne. The empire reached its zenith under Tsar Simeon, who moved the capital to Veliki Preslav and ushered in a cultural golden age. The Bulgarian Empire, which stretched from the Adriatic Sea to the Aegean Sea and to the Dnieper River (northeast of Bulgaria) was the largest and most powerful in Europe at that time, and the powerful Bulgarian army routed the invading Byzantines at the Battle of Acheloi (near modern Sunny Beach) in 917.

Tsar Peter's reign (r 927–968) was long and peaceful, but internal conflicts led to decline, and in 971 Preslav fell to the Byzantines and the capital moved to Ohrid (in modern-day Macedonia) under Tsar Samuel (r 978–1014). At the Battle of Belasitsa in 1014, the Byzantines defeated the Bulgars and the emperor Basil II, 'the Bulgar-Slayer', ordered 15,000 Bulgarian soldiers to be blinded and sent back to Samuel, who promptly dropped dead of a heart attack at the gruesome spectacle. In 1018 Ohrid fell, and Bulgaria officially became part of the Byzantine Empire.

In 1185 two aristocratic brothers, Asen and Petâr, led a general uprising against the Byzantines and the Second Bulgarian Empire (1185–1396) was founded, with Veliko Târnovo as the capital.

In 1204 the Byzantines fell victim to the forces of the Fourth Crusade, whose leader, Baldwin of Flanders, declared himself emperor. Invading Bulgaria the following year, though, he was captured and spent the rest of his days imprisoned in a tower (which still bears his name) at the fortress in Veliko Târnovo (see p159).

With skilful diplomacy rather than military force, Asen's son, Tsar Ivan Asen II (r 1218–1241), became the most powerful ruler in southeastern

---

STS KIRIL & METODII

The two brothers Kiril (Cyril) and Metodii (Methodius) were born in Thessaloniki in the early 9th century to a noble Byzantine family of Slavic-Bulgarian origins. Both were scholars and monks who studied and worked throughout the Balkans. They are revered in Bulgaria for developing in 863 the first Bulgarian alphabet, called Glagolic, which was later simplified by one of their disciples, Clement, and became known as the Cyrillic alphabet. But, more importantly, they helped spread Orthodox Christianity throughout the Balkans by promoting the use of Slavic as the fourth accepted language of the Church (after Latin, Greek and Hebrew).

The Cyrillic alphabet is now used in Bulgaria, Russia, Macedonia, Ukraine, Belarus, Serbia and Mongolia. Bulgarians even celebrate Cyrillic Alphabet Day (also known as the Day of Bulgarian Culture) on 24 May.

1205

Latin Byzantine emperor Baldwin of Flanders is captured after invading Bulgaria and is imprisoned in Veliko Târnovo

1762

Bulgarian national revival begins

Europe and established Veliko Târnovo as an influential literary and arts centre. His title, 'King of Bulgarians and Greeks', reflects the extent of his domain, which included newly gained parts of modern-day Serbia and Hungary. His most famous military victory was the crushing defeat of the Byzantines under Comnenus at the Battle of Klokotnitsa in 1230. After the death of Tsar Ivan Asen II, invasions by the Tartars and Arabs sapped the empire's strength, but it was internal fighting among Bulgarian leaders that fatally weakened it.

DID YOU KNOW?

Peasant revolt leader Ivailo the Swineherd was crowned Tsar in 1277. He was killed by the Tartars three years later.

OTTOMANS

The Ottoman Turks started to invade the northern Balkan Peninsula in 1362. Within the next 30 years they had conquered all of Bulgaria, which officially become part of the Ottoman Empire in 1396. Turkish rule meant the imposition of a harsh feudal system, and the isolation of Bulgaria from the rest of Christian Europe. Huge numbers of Bulgarians were either killed or carried off into slavery, the apparatus of the Bulgarian state was dismantled and many churches and monasteries were destroyed or closed. In one year alone (1657), the Turks burned down 218 churches and 33 monasteries. Numerous uprisings were put down with cruel ferocity, and many Bulgarians emigrated.

Turkish overlords settled in urban areas, forcing Bulgarians to flee into the mountains and rural regions. *Haidouks* (armed rebels) took to the hills and fought the occupiers in any way they could. Bulgarian national and cultural identity managed to survive in isolated monasteries, such as Rila, which were allowed to remain open, or were never found or controlled by the Turks. Taxes owed to the Sultan by the Christian Bulgarians were oppressive, but Pomaks (Slavs converted to Islam) were exempt, as were the wealthy citizens of Arbanasi, near Veliko Târnovo.

BULGARIAN NATIONAL REVIVAL

The era known as the Bulgarian national revival period was prompted by the work of a monk, Paisii Hilendarski, who wrote the first complete history of the Slav-Bulgarian people in 1762. He travelled across Bulgaria reading the history to illiterate people and igniting a long-forgotten national identity. By the early 19th century, the Bulgarian economy was growing fast. Merchants in towns like Plovdiv and Koprivshtitsa were supplying wool, wine, metals and woodcarvings to the ailing Ottoman Empire and Western Europe, and a new educated, prosperous, urban middle class was emerging.

These merchants built grand private homes and public buildings, often designed in a unique form (see Architecture, p37). They were decorated by woodcarvers from Tryavna and painters from Samokov, who had developed a particular Bulgarian style.

Bulgarian art, music and literature also flourished at this time, and schools with instruction in the Bulgarian language were opened. There were *chitalishtes* (reading rooms) in nearly every town and village, which provided the people with a communal forum for cultural and social activities – and for political discussions. Official Turkish recognition of an autonomous Bulgarian Orthodox Church in 1870 was a crucial step towards independence.

The Legend of Basil the Bulgar-Slayer by Paul Stephenson offers a scholarly reinterpretation of the medieval Byzantine emperor and his campaigns in Bulgaria.

1876	1877–78
April Uprising in Koprivshtitsa	Russian-Turkish War; Treaty of Berlin signed

THE END OF OTTOMAN RULE

Rebel leaders, such as Georgi Rakovski, Hristo Botev and Bulgaria's iconic hero Vasil Levski (see the boxed text, p140), had been preparing a revolution against the Turks for years before the rebellion, known as the 1876 April Uprising, prematurely started at Koprivshtitsa.

The Turks suppressed the uprising with unprecedented brutality: an estimated 30,000 Bulgarians were massacred and 58 villages were destroyed. The largest massacre occurred in the town of Batak (see the boxed text, p110). According to one story, Pazardzhik (near Plovdiv) was saved by a daring clerk who moved one comma in an official order, turning 'burn the town, not spare it' into 'burn the town not, spare it.'

The Balkans: A Short History by Mark Mazower is a thin book that covers most of what the average traveller needs to know about the turbulent region.

These atrocities caused outrage in Western Europe and led Russia to declare war on the Ottomans in 1877 after the Constantinople Conference failed to resolve anything. Decisive battles were fought at Pleven and Shipka Pass and about 200,000 Russian soldiers were killed throughout Bulgaria during the year-long Russian-Turkish War. As the Russian army, and its Bulgarian volunteers, crushed the Turks and advanced to within 50km of Istanbul, the Ottomans accepted defeat. It ceded 60% of the Balkan Peninsula to Bulgaria in the Treaty of San Stefano, signed on 3 March 1878.

However, fearing the creation of a powerful Russian ally in the Balkans, the powers of Western Europe reversed these gains at the Treaty of Berlin, signed 13 July 1878. They decided that the area between the Stara Planina ranges and the Danube, plus Sofia, would become the independent principality of Bulgaria. The Thracian Plain and Rodopi Mountains to the south would become Eastern Rumelia and, inexplicably, were placed under Ottoman control. The Aegean Thracian plain and Macedonia were returned outright to Turkey. The legacy of the Treaty of Berlin carved up the region irrespective of ethnicity and left every Balkan nation feeling cheated and angry. These redefined borders have haunted the peninsula ever since: between 1878 and WWII the Balkan countries, including Bulgaria, fought six wars over border issues.

On 16 April 1879 the first Bulgarian national assembly was convened at Veliko Târnovo in order to adopt a constitution, and on 26 June of that year Alexander Battenberg, a German prince, was elected head of state. On 6 September 1885 the principality of Bulgaria and Eastern Rumelia were reunified after a bloodless coup. This contravention of the Treaty of Berlin greatly angered the central European powers and Turkish troops advanced to the southern border of the reunified Bulgaria.

Serbia, with the backing of the Austro-Hungarian Empire, suddenly declared war on Bulgaria. Heroic Bulgarian border guards defied the odds and repelled advancing Serbian troops while the Bulgarian army hurriedly moved from the Turkish border to the western front. Eventually, the Bulgarians defeated the Serbs and advanced deep within Serbian territory. Austria intervened, calling for a ceasefire, and the Great Powers recognised the reunified Bulgaria.

THE WAR YEARS

Alexander was forced to abdicate in 1886 and was replaced by Prince (later King) Ferdinand of the Saxe-Coburg-Gotha family. Around this

1885	1912–13
Treaty of Berlin overturned; Bulgaria is reunified	The Balkan Wars

time the prime minister, Stefan Stambolov, accelerated the country's economic development and two Bulgarian political parties were founded that would wield enormous influence in the years ahead. These were the Social Democrats, forerunner to the communists, and the Agrarian Union, which represented the peasantry.

King Ferdinand I declared Bulgaria's complete independence from Ottoman control on 22 September 1908. But only four years later, the First Balkan War broke out when Bulgaria, Greece and Serbia declared war on Turkey. Although these states succeeded in largely pushing the Turks out of the Balkans, squabbling among the victors, especially over claims to Macedonia, led to the Second Balkan War (1913), from which Bulgaria emerged a loser.

Bulgaria entered WWI on the side of the Central Powers (which ironically included Turkey) in 1915. Facing widespread opposition to his pro-German policies, Ferdinand abdicated three years later in favour of his son, Boris III (father of the current Bulgarian prime minister). In the 1919 Treaty of Neuilly, Bulgaria lost Aegean Thrace to Greece, and was saddled with humiliating and crippling war reparations. The interwar period was marked by political and social unrest. The radical prime minister Alexander Stamboliyski was assassinated in a right-wing military coup in 1923, while in 1925 communist terrorists tried, unsuccessfully, to kill Boris III at Sofia's Sveta Nedelya Cathedral (p64), murdering 123 people in the process. The 1930s, meanwhile, saw the rise of the right-wing Zveno group, which staged a coup d'état in 1934, suspending the constitution. At the beginning of WWII Bulgaria declared its neutrality. However, by 1941 German troops advancing towards Greece were stationed along the Danube on Bulgaria's northern border with Romania. To avoid a war it could not win, the militarily weak Bulgarian government decided to join the Axis. Bulgaria allowed the Nazis into the country and officially declared war on Britain and France, but it refused to accede to demands that it declare war on Russia. Spurred by public opinion, the Bulgarian government also declined to hand over the country's 50,000 Jews to the Third Reich. Tsar Boris III died mysteriously on 28 August 1943, one week after meeting Hitler. According to one popular theory, the *Führer* had Boris III poisoned for his intransigence. Boris's young son succeeded him, as Simeon II.

During the winter of 1943–44, Allied air raids inflicted heavy damage on Sofia and other major towns in central Bulgaria. Antiwar activity increased, including communist guerrilla actions against the fascist Bulgarian government. A hastily formed coalition government sought a separate peace with the Allies, but to no avail. Then Russia declared war and invaded Bulgaria. On 9 September 1944 the Fatherland Front, a resistance group coalition that included communists, assumed power. Even before WWII had ended, 'people's courts' were set up around the country at which thousands of members of the wartime 'monarch-fascist' government were sent to prison or executed.

THE RISE OF COMMUNISM

The Fatherland Front swept the November 1945 elections and the communists undermined their coalition partners to gain control of the new national assembly. Under leader Georgi Dimitrov, a new constitution,

Beyond Hitler's Grasp: The Heroic Rescue of Bulgaria's Jews by Michael Bar-Zohar is a thought-provoking account of the heroism of ordinary Bulgarians in protecting their Jewish neighbours from the Nazis during WWII.

Voices from the Gulag: Life and Death in Communist Bulgaria (ed Tzvetan Todorov) is a collection of first-hand accounts from inmates, guards and bureaucrats of the horrors of the communist system.

1934	1941
Coup d'état by right-wing Zveno group	Bulgaria joins the Axis powers in WWII

BULGARIAN DEMOCRACY

Since 1990 Bulgaria has been a multiparty, democratic republic (see www.parliament.bg). Elections for the prime minister, who is also leader of the unicameral national assembly (with 240 members), are usually held every four years; the president, as the head of state, is elected every five years. The cabinet consists of 20 ministers, including three deputy prime ministers. Voting is not compulsory, but an impressive 67% of eligible voters made their choice during the 2001 parliamentary elections; marginally over 50% voted during the subsequent presidential elections.

The major political forces are the former communist party, now known as the BSP (senior party in the Coalition for Bulgaria, CFB); the National Movement Simeon II (NMSII), led by the former king, Simeon Saxe-Coburg; and the Union of Democratic Forces (UDF), a disparate coalition of right-wing groups. Other, very much smaller, parties include the NSA; a coalition headed by the Turkish Movement for Rights and Freedoms (MRF) party; the People's Union (PU); Euroleft; and the Green Party. Bulgaria is divided into 28 *oblasti* (districts) and 262 *obshtina* (municipalities).

Eastern Europe and Communist Rule by JF Brown is a readable political history of Eastern Europe's four decades of communism with special attention to the 1970s and 1980s. Also worth reading is Brown's *Surge to Freedom: The End of Communist Rule in Eastern Europe.*

created on the Soviet model, proclaimed the People's Republic of Bulgaria on 15 September 1946. The royal family, which included the current prime minister, Simeon II, was forced to flee.

From the late 1940s, industrialisation and the collectivisation of agriculture was imposed. Under Todor Zhivkov, Bulgaria's leader from 1962 to 1989, the country became one of the most prosperous in Eastern Europe. Unlike Dimitrov, Zhivkov was not a cult figure, but a shrewd politician and bureaucrat. He juggled government and party leaders among different posts, while managing to keep a balance between the young and old and conservatives and reformists.

LATE 20TH CENTURY

By 1989 *perestroika* was sending shock waves throughout Eastern Europe and veteran communists became uneasy. On 10 November 1989 an internal Communist Party coup led to the resignation of the ageing Zhivkov, ending his 27-year reign. The Communist Party agreed to relinquish its monopoly on power, and changed its name to the Bulgarian Socialist Party (BSP). In opposition, a coalition of 16 different groups formed the Union of Democratic Forces (UDF). However, the BSP comfortably won the first parliamentary elections in June 1990, so Bulgaria had the dubious honour of being the first country from the former Soviet Bloc to elect communists back into power.

DID YOU KNOW?

The body of communist leader Georgi Dimitrov, who died in 1949, lay embalmed in Sofia until 1990. His mausoleum was dynamited in 1999.

But the BSP, hamstrung by ineffective leadership and popular unrest over austerity measures, soon lost favour. Assisted by a disgusted electorate, the UDF managed to eke out a narrow victory in the October 1991 parliamentary elections, but their government collapsed within a year. After a caretaker government of technocrats was similarly unable to deal with the financial disarray, the BSP again captured, in overwhelming fashion, the December 1994 parliamentary elections. Meanwhile, Zhelyu Zhelev of the UDF became the new Bulgarian head of state after the first democratic presidential elections in January 1992.

From 1994 to 1996, the BSP squandered their mandate and led the country into economic chaos. This period was marked by hyperinflation and a sharp drop in living standards, which included the return of bread

1946	1989–90
The People's Republic of Bulgaria proclaimed	Communist regime collapses; first parliamentary elections won by the Bulgarian Socialist Party

lines and fuel shortages, while legitimised criminal networks flaunted their new-found wealth. Where hope had burgeoned just a few years before, a culture of desperation took hold.

The election of liberal lawyer Petâr Stoyanov of the UDF as president in November 1996, coupled with the resignation of the unpopular socialist prime minister Zhan Videnov, signalled that the electorate was finally fed up. Nationwide protests and highway blockades eventually forced the discredited BSP to agree to new parliamentary elections.

April 1997 ushered in the seventh change of government in as many years. Ivan Kostov of the United Democratic Forces (UtDF), a coalition which included the UDF, became prime minister and promised to combat corruption and attract foreign investment while adhering to market reforms and strict fiscal policies. But like leaders of all former communist countries, Kostov had to make harsh economic decisions, which pleased the International Monetary Fund (IMF) and EU, but not the voters.

BULGARIA TODAY

In June 2001 Bulgaria briefly made headlines across the world when the people voted the National Movement Simeon II (NMSII) party – led by the charismatic and popular former king of Bulgaria, Simeon Saxe-Coburg or Simeon II – into power during parliamentary elections. What made this result so remarkable was that the party had only formed two months before the election and that Saxe-Coburg, who did not actually run for a parliamentary seat (but could still become prime minister), had lived most of his life in Spain (see The Return of the King, below).

The NMSII won exactly half of the parliamentary seats and almost 43% of the vote, but did not have a clear majority, so it entered into a coalition with the Turkish Movement for Rights and Freedoms (MRF), the party with the smallest number of elected representatives. Simeon II persuaded some prominent Bulgarian economists to return home in order to, as he promised, turn Bulgaria's fortunes around in '800 days'. He claimed that he was not interested in restoring the monarchy, something which, in any case, had very little support among the public, and only accepted the appointment of prime minister grudgingly. Immediately after being elected, he raised the minimum wage from 85 lv to 100 lv per month.

In a major upset five months later, Petâr Stoyanov, regarded as one of Bulgaria's most popular politicians, was beaten by Georgi Parvanov in the presidential elections. Parvanov, who had lost two parliamentary elections and one presidential election in the past decade, is leader of the

A Concise History of Bulgaria by RJ Crampton gives an incisive and detailed, if somewhat dry, history of the nation.

THE RETURN OF THE KING

Simeon Borisov Saxe-Coburgotski II became king of Bulgaria at the age of six following the death of his father, Tsar Boris III, in 1943. Three years later, the Red Army rolled in, and the royal family had to flee the country. Simeon II lived in Egypt for a while, before moving to Madrid, where he married a Spanish aristocrat, Dona Margarita Gomez-Acebo y Cejuela, and became a successful businessman. They have four sons and a daughter. Although he did not return to his homeland again until 1996, he remained a popular figure. He is a distant relative of Queen Elizabeth II.

1990	2001
Zhelyu Zhelev is first democratically elected president of Bulgaria	Former king, Simeon II, is elected prime minister

BSP. He stood as the candidate for the new Coalition for Bulgaria, which did not exist three months earlier.

As far as most Bulgarians are concerned, the economy has not been turned around in quite the way promised at the 2001 general election, and low wages and high unemployment remain painful features of daily life. Other major concerns, such as the growth of organised crime and the government's support for the US-led occupation of Iraq, have led to disillusionment with the NMSII, and at the time of research, the left-leaning BSP was ahead in the opinion polls, leading up to the next general election in 2005.

Bulgaria's entry into NATO in 2004, along with a number of other former Warsaw-Pact countries, was welcomed by a Bulgarian population keen to engage with the wider world, and the country is well on course to accede to the EU in 2007.

2004

Bulgaria joins NATO

2007

Bulgaria to accede to the EU

The Culture

THE NATIONAL PSYCHE

Who are the Bulgarians? It's a question few foreigners would be able to answer with any confidence. Images of squat Olympic weightlifters, shadowy Cold War assassins and headscarfed babushkas would probably be high on the list of dated – and often negative – stereotypes, but Bulgaria and its people remain something of an enigma to most Westerners.

Warm and open to strangers, Bulgarians are a welcoming and hospitable people, with an often worldly-wise, cynical outlook on life: decades of totalitarian rule and corruption and uneven economic fortunes since have taught them not to expect much of politicians and bureaucrats. Family and friends are of paramount importance and regional loyalties (and rivalries) are often strong too, although that doesn't diminish their national sensibilities, especially when an international football match is in the offing.

Bulgarians have a fierce pride in their own, often tempestuous, history, and their centuries of struggle against foreign occupation. However, as the country has begun to integrate into the wider world and to welcome more foreign tourists, many have come to question what exactly it means to be Bulgarian, and are frustrated at the country's lack of a tangible international image. A recent campaign to create a 'brand' and a new promotional logo for Bulgaria aims to rectify this.

LIFESTYLE

Bulgarians love a party, and it seems there's something going on somewhere throughout the whole year. Religious occasions and public holidays are vigorously celebrated, as are more personal, family events, such as christenings, 'first steps' (celebrated when a child starts to walk), weddings, house-warmings and birthdays. More importantly, name days, the saint's day after which someone is named (for example, Aleksandâr celebrates his name day on 30 November, St Aleksandâr's Day), are also a much-venerated tradition.

Each year, most villages have a fair day. Locals stop work so they can eat, drink and enjoy games such as horse racing and wrestling and practise traditions such as fire-dancing on live coals (still performed at remote villages in the Strandzha Nature Park).

Bulgaria is still largely a conservative and traditional society, and rural life goes on much as it has done for the last century or so. Things are of course very different in the cities, where Western boutiques, tacky casinos and strip clubs have proliferated and racks of porn magazines openly decorate every newsstand, alongside children's comics and daily newspapers. The gay 'scene', meanwhile, is still very discreet and virtually nonexistent outside Sofia and Plovdiv.

The painful economic changes which Bulgaria has gone through in recent years have resulted in many casualties. Beggars are a common sight in Sofia and other urban centres, as many elderly and sick people have struggled to make ends meet, and disadvantaged groups such as the Roma do what they can to survive. Prostitutes walk the city streets at night and groups of glue-sniffing youths hang out in darkened corners. Despite this, most visitors are unlikely to encounter any problems.

One thing Bulgarians are proud of is their education: the literacy rate in Bulgaria is over 98%, one of the highest in the world. However, the

Holidays of the Bulgarians in Myths and Legends by Nikolay Nikov is a fascinating account of the traditions and customs associated with all the major festivals.

Lonely Planet's *Eastern Europe Phrasebook* is a convenient pocket guide which also includes languages of neighbouring countries, such as Romania.

average wage is low: just €150 per month, and of course many live on less than that, provoking discontent and demonstrations in the capital. Most Bulgarians scrape by, however, and look forward to any economic upturn which EU membership might provide.

POPULATION

Bulgaria is a small nation of just under 8 million people, some 70% of whom now live in urban centres including Sofia, the largest city by far, and (in order of population size) Plovdiv, Varna, Burgas, Ruse, Stara Zagora, Pleven and Sliven. Around 14% of Bulgarians call the capital home.

Bulgarians are of Slavic origin, and constitute roughly 85% of the population. The largest minorities are the Turks (9%) and the Roma (4.5%), while the remainder belong to tiny ethnic groups such as the Armenians, Wallachs and Circassians, as well as small numbers of Jews and ethnic Greeks and Russians. Greek populations are found in places such as Sozopol and Sandanski. Most of Bulgaria's 757,000 Turks live in the northeast and in the foothills of the eastern Rodopi Mountains, especially, of course, towards the Turkish border.

About 250,000 Pomaks live in the Rodopi Mountains. Pomaks are Slavs who converted to Islam during the Ottoman occupation in the 15th century. In the past, they have been subjected to the same assimilatory pressures as the Turks. Some villages in the Rodopis, such as Borino, are almost entirely Pomak.

At the outbreak of WWII, about 50,000 Jews lived in Bulgaria. Although forced to assemble in provincial labour camps, none were turned over to the Nazis despite the fact that the Bulgarian government had formed an alliance with Germany. After the war most Jews left for Israel and only about 5000 still remain in Bulgaria, most in Sofia.

MULTICULTURALISM

Despite the fact that it's been invaded, conquered, occupied and generally trampled upon by countless foreign powers throughout its long history, Bulgaria remains a fairly homogenous nation, with some 85% of the population declaring themselves Bulgarian.

In 1985 the communists mounted a programme to assimilate the country's Turkish inhabitants by forcing them to accept Bulgarian names. At this time mosques were also closed and even wearing Turkish dress and speaking Turkish in public were banned. Mass protests erupted and in early 1989 about 300,000 Turkish Bulgarians and Pomaks left for Turkey (though many subsequently returned to Bulgaria when the repressive policies were overturned). Many Turkish Bulgarians were experienced tobacco farmers so their departure significantly affected the economy at the time.

Relations between Bulgarians and the ethnic Turkish minority have improved since the establishment of democracy, and in the 2001 election he victorious National Movement Simeon II party (led by the former Bulgarian king Simeon II) entered into a coalition with the Turkish Movement for Rights and Freedoms party, which has a small number of MPs. Turks and Bulgarians also work well together in local government, although some low-level prejudice against the old imperial occupier still remains.

Bulgaria's Roma, on the other hand, have a tough time getting their voice heard. They suffer huge rates of unemployment, social deprivation, poverty and prejudice, and remain the convenient scapegoat for everything from street crime to national economic woes. They tend to live in ghettos in cities such as Sofia, Sliven and Pazardzhik, and can be seen begging on the streets all over the country. Their future remains uncertain.

One topic which excites massive controversy is the 'Macedonian question'. The historical region of Macedonia covered areas of modern-day northern Greece and southwestern Bulgaria, as well as the Former Yugoslav Republic of Macedonia (FYROM). In fact, many Bulgarians regard the people of the FYROM as ethnic Bulgarians (much to their fury). Their language is basically a dialect of Bulgarian, and some say that the purest form of the language is actually spoken in Ohrid, which was once the capital city of the medieval Bulgarian state, and later its spiritual heart.

During the last 130 years the region has been the primary cause of several wars between Balkan countries, some of which (including Bulgaria) have claimed some Macedonian territory as their own.

In 1945 the inhabitants of the Pirin region were named a Macedonian ethnic minority and there were plans to merge Bulgaria and Macedonia into one country, though all this came to nothing in the end and by the 1960s the ethnic minority status was rescinded. The majority of people living in the Pirin region regard themselves first and foremost as Bulgarian, and vocal movements for regional autonomy such as Internal Macedonian Revolutionary Organisation (IMRO) have only managed to attract small numbers of locals to the cause.

RELIGION

Orthodox Christianity has been the official religion since 865, though modern Bulgaria is a secular state which allows freedom of religion. The vast majority of the population – around 83% – still profess adherence to the Bulgarian Orthodox Church, although only a fraction of this number actually attends church services on a regular basis. However, major holy days do draw out the crowds, both young and old, and attending an Orthodox service is an unforgettable experience for the visitor. Worshippers light candles and kiss icons as bearded, golden-robed priests sing and swing their incense burners.

Some 12% claim to be Muslim – ethnic Turks, Pomaks and most Roma. Over the centuries, the Islam practised in Bulgaria has incorporated various Bulgarian traditions and Christian beliefs and has become known as Balkan Islam. Mosques in Sofia, Shumen, Plovdiv and Haskovo are attended by the faithful few.

There's also a small Jewish population. Judaism was introduced by refugees from Catholic Spain in the 15th century and is still practised at synagogues in Sofia and Vidin.

Roman Catholics account for just under 2% of the nation. Other Christian sects such as Armenians maintain Armenian Orthodox churches in Sofia, Varna and Plovdiv.

DID YOU KNOW?

Dunovism, founded in Bulgaria after WWI by Peter Dunov, is a religion which combines Orthodox Christianity with yoga, meditation and belief in reincarnation.

ARTS

Bulgaria has an ancient tradition of icon painting, and these religious images are still the most accessible and memorable of Bulgarian art. Five centuries of Turkish rule suppressed much of native Bulgarian culture but the national revival of the late 18th–19th centuries saw a creative blossoming, as writers and artists strove to reignite the national consciousness. During the communist era, however, most Bulgarians with artistic, literary, theatrical or musical talents were trained in the former Soviet Union and therefore heavily influenced by the Russians. These days, artistic activity in Bulgaria is at an all-time high.

Painting & Sculpture

Most of Bulgaria's earliest artists painted on the walls of homes, churches and monasteries. The most famous was unquestionably Zahari Zograf (1810–53), who painted magnificent murals, which can still be admired in the monasteries at Rila, Troyan and Bachkovo. Many of Zograf's works were inspired by medieval Bulgarian art, though they display a more human (if often gory and sadistic) spirit, with naked sinners being inventively tortured by demons a common and seemingly much-relished motif, alongside the prettier scenes of angels and saints.

www.christojeanne-claude.net
For further details on the lives and work of the avant-garde Bulgarian artist Christo and his wife, Jeanne-Claude.

Famous Bulgarian artists of the last 150 years include Vladimir Dimitrov, often referred to as 'The Master', and Dimitâr Kazakov, whose work have been shown in the Louvre. Other renowned artists are Georgi Mashev, Michail Lutov, Zlatyu Boyadjiev, Tsanko Lavrenov, Ivan Angelov and the Mitov brothers (Georgi, Anton and Boris). These, and other, artists have been immortalised in museums and galleries that are dedicated to their work and lives. You can see their work in museums and galleries in Plovdiv, Sofia, Kyustendil, Tryavna, Stara Zagora and Pleven.

Contemporary Bulgarian artists include the renowned sculptor Asen Botev and the abstract painter Kolyo Karamfilov, while Slav Bakalo has won awards for his illustrations. Without doubt, though, the most widely recognised modern Bulgarian artist is Christo Yavasheff – usually known just as Christo – famous for wrapping large buildings in sheeting for his 'installation art', including the Pont Neuf in Paris and Berlin's Reichstag.

Literature

The first recognised literary work written in Bulgarian was probably *Slav Bulgarian History* by Paisii Hilendarski. This thin, but detailed, volume was the catalyst for a resurrection of Bulgarian cultural heritage and ethnic identity from the mid-18th century. Some of Bulgaria's more respected writers, poets and playwrights were also fierce nationalists. Several of them, such as Georgi Rakovski and Hristo Botev, met violent deaths at about 30 years of age fighting the Turks (see Hristo Botev, p232).

Bulgaria's most revered author was Ivan Vazov, who wrote *Under the Yoke*, a stirring novel based on the 1876 April Uprising against the Turks. He is commemorated with two house museums, in Sopot and Sofia. Other famous literary figures who have been immortalised in museums throughout Bulgaria include Nikola Vaptsarov (in Bansko), Yordan Yovkov (Dobrich), Geo Milev (Stara Zagora), Petko Slaveikov and his son Pencho (Tryavna), Hristo Danov (Plovdiv) and Dimcho Debelyanov and Lyuben Karavelov (Koprivshtitsa).

Elias Canetti (1905–94) was probably the best internationally known Bulgarian writer of the 20th century. He was born into a Jewish family in Ruse, though lived most of his life in England, writing in German. He most famous work was *Die Blendung* (Auto-da-Fé), published in 1935, and he won the Nobel Prize for Literature in 1981.

Music

OPERA & CHORAL

Bulgaria has an impressive musical tradition, and musical academies continue to produce world-class opera stars such as a Nikolai Gyuzelev, Gena Dimitrova, Boris Hristov and Anna Tomova-Sintova. All of these stars have performed on international stages.

Emanuil Manolov (1860–1902) wrote the first opera in Bulgarian, *Siromahkinia*, based on a work by Ivan Vazov, while Pancho Vladigerov (1899–1978) is acknowledged as Bulgaria's greatest, internationally renowned, classical composer.

Bulgarian ecclesiastic music dates back to the 9th century and conveys the mysticism of chronicles, fables and legends. To hear Orthodox chants sung by a choir of up to 100 people is a moving experience.

Dobri Hristov (1875–1941) was one of Bulgaria's most celebrated composers of church and choral music, and wrote his major choral work, Liturgy No 1, for the Seven Saints ensemble, Bulgaria's best-known sacred music vocal group, based in Sofia's Sveti Sedmotchislenitsi Church.

TRADITIONAL

Alongside the scholarly Byzantine traditions maintained in Orthodox church music is the Turkish influence evident in the folk songs and dances of the villages. Following are the most common traditional folk instruments:

Daire Similar to a tambourine.

Gadulka A small pear-shaped fiddle, also known as a *rebec.*

Gayda A goatskin bagpipe.

Kaval A long, open flute.

Tambura A four-stringed, long-necked lute akin to the Greek *bouzouki,* called a *drunka* in the Pirin Mountains.

Tâppan A large, cylindrical, double-headed drum.

As in many peasant cultures, Bulgarian women are not given access to musical instruments so they usually perform the vocal parts. They often practise singing while weaving and doing household chores. Bulgarian female singing is polyphonic, ie featuring many voices and shifting melodies. Characteristic sudden upward leaps of the voice are unearthly in their beauty. Women from villages in the Pirin Mountains are renowned for their unique singing style. Some of the more famous performers include Koyna Stoyanova and Yanka Rupkina.

During the communist era, Bulgarian village music was transformed into a sophisticated art form and communicated worldwide by groups such as the Philip Kutev National Folk Ensemble and recordings such as *Le Mystère des Voix Bulgares.*

CONTEMPORARY

The most common of the contemporary Bulgarian sounds that you're likely to hear is a spirited, warbling pop-folk idiom often derided as *chalga* (or truck-driver music) by those who dislike it. Six- or seven-piece bands (often featuring a scantily clad female lead vocalist) soon get people dancing by playing traditional Balkan tunes on instruments such as the electric guitar, clarinet and synthesizer. Velentin Valdez and Gloria are particularly admired exponents of this music. Also popular is

DID YOU KNOW?

The legendary lyre-player Orpheus is said to have been born in the Rodopi Mountains.

Seven Saints www
.thesevensaints.com
Learn more about
Bulgaria's leading
sacred music vocal
ensemble.

Music in Bulgaria by
Timothy Rice and Bonnie
Wade is a thorough
academic overview of
the historical and cultural
routes of traditional
Bulgarian music, and
its development in the
modern world.

the experimental band Isihia, which incorporates traditional elements into their music. The most innovative music today comes from Teodosi Spassov, an inspired *kaval* player who is blazing new musical pathways by fusing traditional Bulgarian folk with jazz. He is also a member of the popular 'progressive rock' combo Balkan Horses Band, an international ensemble whose members come from Bulgaria and other countries in the region.

Popular Bulgarian groups that play other types of modern music include AKAGA, Wikeda, Stoian Iankulov, Elitsa and PIF. Pop music from elsewhere in Eastern Europe, and even the Middle East, is also very popular in Bulgaria.

Theatre

Every city and major town has at least one theatre, often built during the communist era, which offers Bulgarian and foreign plays, classical music, puppet shows, choral music and operas. Because the government can rarely afford to subsidise the arts these days, some theatres are closing down or playing in front of smaller audiences. Despite the revival in Bulgarian arts and culture since the demise of communism, most young people still shy away from high culture.

Musical theatre has also taken off and one of the biggest hits of recent years is *Twin Kingdoms*, which offers a contemporary take on Bulgaria's folk-cultural heritage, written by composer Georgi Andreev. It uses traditional Bulgarian instruments and a variety of musical influences, ranging from baroque to Byzantine Orthodox and Balinese styles, to tell a lavish fairy tale of abducted maidens, dragons and witches.

Sofia, Plovdiv, Varna, Veliko Târnovo, Blagoevgrad and Ruse are home to renowned opera, ballet and theatre companies and are ideal places for foreigners to enjoy a robust production. Note that most theatres close during July and August, while Sofia's National Palace of Culture (p75) offers a year-round programme of international acts.

Cinema

Bulgarian cinema is probably a closed book for most foreigners, but an increasing number of films are being produced for domestic consumption, with around three or four new features coming out each year. Recent well-received productions include *And God Came Down to See Us*, *Journey to Jerusalem*, *One Calorie of Tenderness*, *The Other Possible*

RECOMMENDED LISTENING

- **Bulgarian Folk Songs and Dances featuring Petko Radev and Petko Dachev** (2000) – a top-selling collection of traditional tunes
- **Twin Kingdoms** (2001) by Georgi Andreev – the music from the colourful stage show (see p36)
- **Orthodox & Sacred Chants** (2003) by The Seven Saints – sounds from Bulgaria's leading sacred vocal group
- **Contact** (2004) by The Balkan Horses Band – innovative folk-rock played with traditional Balkan instruments
- **Le Mystère des Voix Bulgares** (1990) – traditional Bulgarian vocals at their best
- **Bulgarian Impressions** (2000) by Pancho Vladigerov – Some of the composer's most popular works

Life of Ours and *Mila from Mars*, which won the award for the best Bulgarian feature film at the 2004 Sofia International Film Festival (www .cinema.bg/sff).

Few Bulgarian films get seen overseas; international releases include *Christmas Eve*, *Blueberry Hill*, *The Devil's Trail*, *The Prize* and *Goat's Horn*. Renowned Bulgarian directors include Peter Popzlatev, Ivanka Grabcheva and Ivan Nitchev, who directed the joint German-Bulgarian drama *After the End of the World*.

Foreign films – such as *I Am Here* and *The Cherry Orchard*, starring Alan Bates – are sometimes shot in Bulgaria because of the cheap labour, reliable weather and beautiful and varied landscapes.

Traditional Crafts

Bulgarian carpets, rugs and traditional costumes were first made as early as the 9th century but were most popular and creative during the Bulgarian national revival period. Sadly, weaving is a dying art, only practised in a few remote villages such as Chiprovtsi, Kotel and Koprivshtitsa. Weaving is still done on handmade looms and undertaken almost entirely by women. It's more of a social occasion than a business these days.

Carpets and rugs made in the southern Rodopi Mountains are thick, woollen and practical, while in western Bulgaria they're often delicate, colourful and more decorative.

Embroidery usually features extensively on traditional costumes, but tourists can also buy embroidered coasters, tablecloths and shawls. Most traditional designs are geometric but colours and symbolism vary from one region to another.

Woodcarving reached its peak during the Bulgarian national revival period. While weaving was practised mostly by women, woodcarving was almost exclusively a male domain. Men would spend hours designing and creating wooden crosses, chests, cradles, walking sticks, traditional flutes and pipes. More experienced and respected carvers could produce intricately carved ceilings (which can be seen in homes and museums in Koprivshtitsa, Kotel, Tryavna and Plovdiv) and iconostases and altars in churches and monasteries.

> 'Weaving is a dying art, only practised in a few remote villages.'

The craft is still practised in Koprivshtitsa, Teteven and Lovech but the most famous town in Bulgaria for woodcarving is undoubtedly Tryavna (see the boxed text, p172). One of the best places to admire woodcarvers at work is the Etâr Ethnographic Village Museum (p171), which you will find near Gabrovo.

Another ancient Bulgarian craft is pottery, and the most famous design is the so-called *Troyanska kapka* pattern, which literally means 'Troyan droplet', after the town of its origin and the runny pattern made by the paint. Everything from plates and bowls to *rakia* (a clear and potent kind of brandy, usually made from grapes) jugs and honey pots are made with this design, and blue, brown and green are the most common colours used, though you will also see less traditional yellow too. Bulgarians still use this Troyan ware in the home, though fancier pieces are made for the tourist trade. It's sold all across the country and makes a perfect souvenir.

Architecture

Probably the most obvious product of the prodigious and creative Bulgarian national revival period is the unique architectural style of homes seen throughout the country. These were either built side-by-side along narrow cobblestone streets, so the homes facing each other almost seem to touch, as in Plovdiv, or surrounded by pretty gardens, as in Arbanasi.

The wood-and-stone homes were often painted brown and white (though some were painted bright blue, crimson or yellow), and there would be one or two bay windows, often curved with a seat inside offering views. On top, the roof was always tiled. Inside, ceilings were often intricately carved and/or painted with bright murals and there would be several small fireplaces and low doors.

Architectural designs and styles of furniture differed from one region to another. The colour, shape and size of the typical home in Melnik contrasts significantly with those found in Arbanasi. Some of the most stunning examples of Bulgarian national revival period homes can also be appreciated in traditional villages like Koprivshtitsa, Tryavna, Shiroka Lûka, Bansko, Nesebâr and Belogradchik. There are also examples among the old towns of Plovdiv and Veliko Târnovo and at the re-created Etâr Ethnographic Village Museum (p171), near Gabrovo.

Bulgarian football www
.bulgarian-football.com
For all you want to know
about the national sport.

The most prodigious architect of the National Revival era was the self-taught Nikola Fichev (1800–81), also known as Master Kolyo Ficheto. He built bridges, churches and fountains across central Bulgaria, including the bridge at Byala, the bell tower at Preobrazhenski Monastery (p168) and the Holy Trinity Church in Svishtov. A museum is dedicated to him in his birthplace of Dryanovo.

SPORT

Football (soccer) is the main Bulgarian spectator sport, and teams are followed with partisan zeal. The Sofia-based team, CSKA, is the current Bulgarian champion, and is reasonably competitive in matches against other European sides. Football games normally take place on Saturday or Sunday, from about 4pm, and on Wednesday evening at about 7pm. The football season lasts from late August to late May, with a winter break in January and February. Tickets to matches cost from 3 to 10 lv.

The high point for the Bulgarian national side, meanwhile, was the 1994 World Cup, in which it finished in a very respectable fourth place. Since then, however, the team's performance has been disappointing; Bulgaria lost all three of its games in the Euro 2004 tournament, only managing to score a solitary goal.

Other sports followed throughout Bulgaria, and in which the country has had some international success, include volleyball, basketball, boxing, Greco-Roman wrestling and weightlifting. In the 2004 Olympics in Athens, Milen Dobrev and Maria Grozdeva brought home gold medals for weightlifting and women's pistol shooting respectively, while their team-mate Jordan Jovtchev took silver in the men's rings event.

Environment

THE LAND

Bulgaria covers just under 111,000 sq km at the heart of the Balkan Peninsula, yet encompasses an amazing variety of landscapes and landforms. Although its average elevation is not impressive, about 5% of Bulgaria is over 1600m high and about one-third of its terrain is mountainous. The country boasts seven distinct mountain ranges, each with a unique range of flora and fauna, and all covered with well-marked walking trails.

From the northern border with Romania, a windswept fertile plain gradually slopes south as far as the Stara Planina mountains, the longest mountain range in the Balkans, which, as the geographical backbone of Bulgaria, nearly splits the country into two. To the south, the Sredna Gora mountains are separated from the main range by a fault in which the Valley of Roses lies.

Southern Bulgaria is even more mountainous. Mt Musala (2925m) in the rugged and floriferous Rila Mountains, south of Sofia, is almost equalled by Mt Vihren (2914m) in the wild Pirin Mountains further south. The Rila Mountains' sharply glaciated massifs, with their bare rocky peaks, steep forested valleys and glacial lakes are the geographical core of the Balkans and a paradise for hikers (and, in parts, skiers). The Rodopi Mountains stretch along the Greek border east of the Rila and Pirin Mountains and spill over into Greece. The fascinating Yagodina and Trigrad caves are geological must-sees in the Rodopis, while Melnik's dramatic and unique sand pyramids are one of the unexpected highlights of the Pirin region.

www.bluelink.net Probably the best website for environmental news, with details of current campaigns and projects and lots of useful links.

The Thracian plain opens onto the Black Sea coast. The 378km-long coast is lined with beaches and also features coastal lakes near Burgas, spectacular cliffs near Kaliakra and several huge bays. In addition to the mighty Danube, which forms much of the border with Romania, the major rivers include the Yantra, which meanders its way through the town of Veliko Târnovo; the Iskâr, which stretches from south of Samokov to the Danube, past Sofia; and the Maritsa, which runs through Plovdiv.

RESPONSIBLE TRAVEL

Everyone travelling to Bulgaria can minimise the impact of their visit. Try to conserve water and electricity, respect traditions in villages, behave appropriately in religious buildings and leave ruins as they are. In addition, don't litter and don't destroy flora and fauna. Driving is often an ideal way to get around, but please bear in mind that traffic, and air and noise pollution, are increasing problems in Bulgaria.

One local organisation promoting sustainable alternative tourism is the **Bulgarian Association for Alternative Tourism** (BAAT; ☎ 02-989 0538; baat@spnet.net), which publishes the excellent *Bulgaria Bed & Breakfasts Guidebook*, a compendium of family-run guesthouses and off-the-beaten-track itinerary ideas. **Zig Zag Holidays** (☎ /fax 02-980 3200; www.zigzag.dir.bg) is a leading tour operator running ecologically sensitive trips and activities (see p270). They also sell BAAT's guidebook. According to its literature, the **Bulgarian Association for Rural & Ecological Tourism** (BARET; ☎ /fax 02-971 3485; baret@aster.net) hopes to 'ensure alternative sources of income for the population of rural and semi-mountainous areas, and to support sustainable development through the preservation of natural, cultural and historical heritage.'

WILDLIFE

Balkani Wildlife Society
www.balkani.org
Especially active in many
environmental campaigns,
including that to save the
Kresna Gorge.

Although not a large country, Bulgaria has a significant quantity and diversity of flora and fauna, no doubt helped by the varied climate and topography, relatively small human population, and the fact that almost a third of the country is forested. However, all environmental groups believe that the future of Bulgaria's ecology is at a critical stage and that local and international action is urgently needed before the environmental damage already caused becomes irreversible.

Animals

Bulgaria is home to some 56,000 kinds of animal, including almost 400 species of birds (about 75% of all species found in Europe), 36 types of reptiles, over 200 species of freshwater and saltwater fish (of which about half are found along the Black Sea coast of Bulgaria) and 27,000 types of insect.

Many larger animals live in the hills and mountains, and understandably far from the urban centres, so most visitors will probably see little wildlife in Bulgaria. If you are keen to see some natural fauna, join an organised tour (see p266 and p270). Alternatively, hike in the Strandjha Nature Park; the Rusenski Lom National Park, home to 67 species of mammals (about two-thirds of those found in Bulgaria); the Rila National Park; or the Pirin National Park, where 42 species of animals such as the European brown bear, deer and wild goats thrive.

Bird-lovers can admire plenty of our feathered friends at Burgas Lakes, the largest wetland complex in the country, and home to about 60% of all bird species in Bulgaria; the Ropotamo Nature Reserve, with more than 200 species of birds; the Strandzha Nature Park, with almost 70% of all bird species found in Bulgaria; and the Rusenski Lom National Park, home to 170 species of water birds. White storks, black storks, Dalmatian pelicans, sandpipers, corncrakes and pygmy cormorants are some of the species that can be seen in these areas.

ENDANGERED SPECIES

DID YOU KNOW?

After intense international pressure, the cruel practice of 'dancing' bears was banned in 1993 and confiscated bears have since been rehoused in open sanctuaries, with support from Brigitte Bardot.

Included in the official list of the endangered animals of Bulgaria are seals and dolphins, both of which were hunted ruthlessly but can still be seen in limited numbers off the northern part of the Black Sea coast.

Bulgaria has one of the largest brown bear populations in Europe (last estimate around 800 individuals). However, they are becoming rarer because of illegal poaching and legal hunting. Wolves and lynxes have begun to recover from hunting and persecution in recent years.

The Balkan chamois is an endangered wild goat, now confined to the West Rodopis although a breeding programme has been set up with individuals brought to Vitosha National Park, hopefully for eventual release.

Rare birds, including Egyptian vultures, lesser kestrels and great eagle owls, are protected in the Rusenski Lom National Park, and small cormorants, Ferruginous ducks and Dalmatian pelicans thrive in the Srebârna Nature Reserve. The Imperial eagle is one of Bulgaria's most threatened birds, now down to around 25 pairs, while Tengmalm's owl is another scarce species.

Plants

Of Bulgaria's 10,000 or so plant species, 31 are endangered. About 250 are endemic and many have indigenous names, such as Bulgarian blackberry and Rodopi tulip. The Silivriak, with its small pink flowers, grew all over

Europe before the last Ice Age, but is now found only in southern Bulgaria, particularly in the Rodopi Mountains, where it's reasonably abundant. The wonderfully named splendid tulip, with its large red flowers, is extremely rare, and was only discovered in 1976, near Yambol. It has been found nowhere else, and you'll be very lucky to spot it: only around 20 plants are known to exist.

Squeezed between the mighty Stara Planina and Sredna Gora ranges, the Valley of Roses was, until recently, the source of 70% of the world's supply of rose oil. Roses are still grown there extensively, and can be seen and enjoyed most of the year.

Forests are also protected in the national parks and reserves. The Strandzha Nature Park contains vast areas of oaks and beeches. The Unesco-protected Pirin National Park boasts about 1100 species of flora, and the Vrachanski Balkan National Park is home to 700 species of trees.

DID YOU KNOW?

Bulgaria is the third-largest exporter of herbs in Europe.

NATIONAL PARKS

The Bulgarian government has officially established three national parks – Rila, Pirin and Vrachanska Balkan (Central Balkan) – where the flora, fauna and environment are (in theory) protected. Besides the three officially protected national parks, which do not include any towns or villages, Bulgaria has many natural parks, which do, and nature reserves, which are unique managed ecosystems. The latter category receive the strictest protection, and access is often regulated or even prohibited. Confusingly, the term national park is regularly used to describe parks in any of these categories. Throughout this book we have followed the usual local usage for park names. For further information about the parks and reserves, visit www.bulgariannationalparks.org.

Environmental groups continue to lobby the Bulgarian government to expand areas already under protection and create new parks and

National Park/Reserve	Features	Activities	Best time to visit	Page
Pirin National Park	mountains, lakes; bears, deer, birds	hiking	Jun-Sep	p99
Rila National Park	alpine forests and pastures; deer, wild goats, eagles	hiking	Jun-Sep	p88
Ropotamo Nature Reserve	marshes, sand dunes; rare birds	boat trips, hiking	Apr-Jul	p193
Rusenski Lom National Park	river banks, valleys and mountains; rare birds, rock churches	bird-watching, caving	Jun-Sep	p230
Strandzha Nature Park	varied forest, beaches; birds and mammals; archaeological ruins	hiking	Jun-Aug	p195
Vitosha National Park	mountain trails	hiking, skiing	Apr-Aug & Dec-Jan	p80
Vrachanska Balkan (Central Balkan) National Park	forest; varied tree life and caves	hiking, caving	Jun-Sep	p233

reserves, especially in the unprotected Rodopi Mountains and along the Black Sea coast.

The most accessible and worthwhile parks and reserves are listed in the table on the previous page.

ENVIRONMENTAL ISSUES

Like most postcommunist countries, the lure of fast cash has outweighed ecologically sustainable development. Logging, poaching and insensitive development continue in protected areas and excessive and harmful air and water pollution is infrequently controlled and rarely illegal. Locals often rely on finite fossil fuels, such as coal for heating, and on nuclear power for electricity, and farmers continually (and illegally) clear land by burning, which causes many devastating fires each summer.

'The lure of fast cash has outweighed ecologically sustainable development'

Tourism and Transport Development

Bulgaria's increasing profile in international tourism, coupled with rampant new capitalism, has tempted developers to build new ski runs, which by definition disturb precious mountain landscapes. In 2003 a highly controversial new ski centre was completed in the heart of the (supposedly) protected Pirin National Park near Bansko. Thousands of hectares of trees were felled, and huge disruption was caused to the natural habitat. Outraged environmentalists have called this an 'environmental crime', and fear that it may set a precedent for the development of more ski runs in Pirin National Park and other protected mountain ranges. Adding insult to injury, it is thought that there may not even be enough snow here to make the runs viable, and artificial snow may be used.

The proposed construction of the Struma Motorway, linking Sofia with Kulata, has also raised environmental concerns, especially as it's projected to run through the ecologically rich 17km-long Kresna Gorge, which is home to bears, wolves, otters and over 450 plant species. Disruption and pollution will also be brought to the population of the village of Kresna, and campaigners hope to get the route diverted. For more information, see www.kresna.org.

Nuclear Energy

Bulgaria's only nuclear power plant – at Kozlodui (www.kznpp.org) near the Danube, about 200km north of Sofia – was once rated as one of the world's most dangerous nuclear facilities. Since opening in 1974, minor accidents have periodically forced partial shutdowns, leading to power cuts across the country. Massive pressure and financial aid from the EU convinced the Bulgarian authorities to close two of the facility's reactors in December 2002, and to carry out vital upgrades. Independent safety checks in 2003 praised its 'high technical standards,' and it is now regarded as one of the safest in Europe. Since the plant is such an important source of energy, the government plans to use the remaining four reactors until at least 2013.

In 2004 the government gave the go-ahead for construction of a second nuclear power plant at Belene. The project has been dogged by controversy and protests from environmentalists, who claim the building of this facility in an earthquake-prone area poses particular dangers.

Pollution

Other than pollution of the Black Sea, the main concern is the Danube, which is often heavily polluted before it even reaches Bulgaria (see the boxed text, p228). In an effort to increase production some small-scale Bulgarian farmers continue to use pesticides and fertilisers, which often find their way into various rivers and spill into the Danube or Black Sea. Some of these pesticides, such as DDT, have long been illegal, but there are hundreds of often very dilapidated and unguarded storehouses in villages across the country where these have been kept since communist times. The health risks posed not just to the farmers who use them, but also to those consuming the food produced on this land are serious, but the government seems to have no real plan for dealing with this time bomb.

The proposed construction of a national hazardous-waste treatment centre near Stara Zagora has provoked outrage from local residents, who protested on the streets of Sofia in late 2004, while environmental activists have highlighted the potential dangers of transporting such material into central Bulgaria. When building work is likely to start, though, is another matter.

DID YOU KNOW?

The Silivriak is also known as the Orpheus flower; legend says that its flowers were stained pink with the blood of the divine musician after he was hacked to pieces by the frenzied Bacchantes.

Environmental Organisations

The Bulgarian Green Party (www.greenparty.bg) was one of the first opposition parties to be formed in the wake of the collapse of the communist government in December 1989, and though initially scoring some success, it performed poorly in the 2001 elections.

Anyone with genuine interest in a specific ecological issue can contact one or more of the following organisations. Apart from Neophron, these groups do not, however, provide tourist information or offer tours. (For some companies that offer environmental tours, see p270.)

Bulgarian Association for Alternative Tourism (☎ 02-989 0538; www.alternative-tourism .org; bul Stamboiyski 20-V, Sofia) The biggest tourist non-government organisation (NGO) in Bulgaria supports small businesses and organisations involved in sustainable tourism development across the country.

Bulgarian-Swiss Biodiversity Conservation Programme (BSBCP; ☎ /fax 02-230 014; www.bsbcp.org) With support from Swiss NGOs, and the Bulgarian Ministry of the Environment and Waters, the BSBCP aims to maintain and enlarge protected areas and raise public awareness. It's involved in the Burgas Lakes, coastal Dobrudja, Strandzha Nature Park, the east Rodopis and Ropotamo Nature Reserve.

Bulgarian Society for the Protection of Birds (BSPB; www.bspb.org) The BSPB helps to protect bird life and their habitats and proudly claims to have reintroduced an extinct species, the cinerreous vulture. It's part of BirdLife International.

Ekoglasnost (☎ 02-986 2221) The local Friends of the Earth affiliate in Sofia.

Neophron (☎ 052-302 536; www.neophron.com; PO Box 492, Varna) Based in Varna, Neophron is an ecological tour agency run by the BSPB, offering bird-watching, bear-watching and botany trips around Bulgaria

The Great Outdoors

Bulgaria's mountainous, heavily forested terrain makes for great hiking, mountaineering and skiing. While on the Black Sea coast, you can indulge in an array of water sports from paragliding to scuba diving, although these tend to be confined to the big package-holiday resorts. In addition, travel agencies organise a wide range of activity and special-interest holidays, including bird-watching, wildlife-spotting, botanical and archaeological tours.

HIKING

Hiking has long been a hugely popular activity in Bulgaria, and with distinctive mountain ranges covering a third of the country, and some 37,000 km of marked trails to follow, it's easy to see why. Walkers are well supported, with numerous *hizhas* (mountain huts) along the more popular tracks, as well as in real wilderness areas. It's one of the more positive legacies of the old communist regime, which believed that hiking was a healthy and productive proletarian pastime.

'Hiking was a healthy and productive proletarian pastime.'

The standard of accommodation at these huts varies greatly, ranging from the simplest wooden shacks with only the most rudimentary of facilities for an overnight stop, to cosy hostels with kitchens, cafés and even shops attached. These huts only provide the basics and are not intended for lengthy stays. For a rundown of what you can expect at each *hizha*, log on to www.geocities.com/the_bulgarian_mountains.

If you intend doing some serious walking, you will need a detailed map of the region you're visiting. The main publisher of hiking maps is Kartografia, which produces *Pirin* (1:55,000), *Rila* (1:55,000), and separate maps for the east and west Rodopis (both 1:100,000). All are printed in English, German and Bulgarian and cost about 6 lv each. Maps of the central and west Rodopi Mountains (both 1:100,000) are issued by YEO-Rhodope and contain marked trails and details of sights and accommodation in the area. The handy *Troyan Balkan* map (1:65,000) covers the Stara Planina (10 lv).

The Rila Mountains are a rugged, rocky, heavily forested range with plunging glacial valleys and rich plant life. One of the most attractive and accessible walking routes heads into the Maliovitsa range, south of the small town of the same name and based around soaring Mt Maliovitsa (2729m). Happily, one of Bulgaria's more comfortable mountain huts, Hizha Rilski Ezera, is along this route.

Another relatively easy and very pleasant walk runs along the Rilska reka (Rilska river) towards the magnificent Rila Monastery, passing through Kiril Meadow along the way.

The Pirins offer some of the very finest walking country in Bulgaria. It's an alpine landscape of glacial valleys and lakes, and the climate is blessed with a moderating Mediterranean influence. The Pirin National Park office in Bansko (see p100) produces a CD-ROM (8 lv) with detailed information about the Unesco-listed park.

The Sredna Gora is the highest, most visited section of the Stara Planina, with hundreds of marked tracks and the highest number of *hizhas*. The Stara Planina is noted for its sudden weather changes, and some of Bulgaria's highest rainfalls and strongest winds have been recorded here, so be prepared. September is the most amenable month for walking. Camping out is discouraged at all times, due to bears and adverse weather.

Travel agencies running organised hiking trips include Odysseia-In (p271). Their Rodopi and Pirin hike (14 days, €620 per person in groups of six to nine) is a challenging trek which includes the ascent of Mt Vihren (2915m) and around seven hours of walking each day. If you have limited time, or don't want to join a large group, Zig Zag Holidays (p270) offers a three-day hiking trip including Mt Vihren, starting from Bansko (€100 per person, in groups of at least two). All are led by experienced, English-speaking guides.

Further information on hiking in Bulgaria can be found at http://bgmoun-tains.hit.bg/hiking.

MOUNTAINEERING

With seven major mountain ranges squeezed into such a small geographical area, Bulgaria is a paradise for climbers. The **Bulgarian Federation of Alpine Clubs** (☎ 02-930 0532; www.bac.netbg.com) in Sofia is the main organisation worth contacting for information, advice and details of guides. Also in Sofia, **Club Extreme** (www.clubextreme.org) offers the services of professional guides. Prices vary, and are of course dependent on where and when you want to go. Shops such as Stenata (p75) can provide gear.

The most popular areas for mountaineering are the Rila, Pirin and Stara Planina mountain ranges. The Rila Mountains (p87) are the highest range in the country boasting well over a hundred alpine peaks more than 1000m in height, including the highest peak in Bulgaria, Mt Musala (2925m), and some 180 clear, burbling streams and placid lakes. Mt Malïovitsa (2729m), reached from the town of Malïovitsa, is one of the prime climbing peaks here. Note that snow and low temperatures persist at higher levels even into summer.

The sparsely inhabited Pirin Mountains (p99) are another alpine range in the southwest, with three peaks above 2900m and almost a hundred above 2500m. It's a typical alpine landscape of cirques and ridges. The mountains were named after the Slavic god of thunder, Perun, who apparently once lived atop the highest peak here, Mt Vihren (2915m). The northern face of Vihren is the most popular climb in this region and can be reached via Bansko (p99).

For comprehensive online information on mountaineering, try http://climbingguidebg.com.

The 550km-long Balkan Range (or Stara Planina; literally 'Old Mountains') cuts right across the country from Serbia to the Black Sea, and acts as a climatic barrier between the north and south of Bulgaria, with the northern side significantly colder. It's a huge, diverse area, covering 10% of Bulgaria's territory. Due to its relatively easy access (from Vratsa) and the variety of routes offered, the most frequented section of this mighty range is the Vratsa Rocks in the far west, the largest limestone climbing area in Bulgaria. The north face of the range's highest peak, Mt Botev (2376m) is another popular climb.

Odysseia-In (p271) and Zig Zag Holidays (p270) in Sofia run guided climbing trips; contact them for current itineraries and costs.

SKIING

Though hardly in the same league as Chamonix or Aspen, Bulgaria's ski resorts have an increasing international profile and, encouraged by cheap prices, more foreign tourists than ever are choosing to spend their winter breaks here, although advanced skiers are less likely to be impressed. Borovets is the premier resort, with family-friendly Pamporovo also popular. Bansko and Chepelare see fewer foreigners, while facilities at Mt Vitosha, overlooking Sofia, are basic, but convenient for day-tripping city folk. Most foreign tourists are here on package deals, arranged at home, and this is likely to work out a lot cheaper than turning up without a reservation.

Borovets (p95), Bulgaria's oldest, biggest and most advanced resort, has four ski areas, and a variety of runs for beginners and intermediate skiers, including gentle nursery slopes and a ski kindergarten for the kids. Those looking for a challenge can try the World Cup run in the Yastrebets area, used for international competitions, or the slopes of nearby Mt Musala. There are 18km of cross-country ski tracks in the vicinity, and Borovets is also one of Europe's highest ridable areas for snowboarding. Artificial snow is always at hand should the real stuff fail to fall.

Pamporovo (p112) is another big, purpose-built ski resort at the foot of Mt Snejanka (1926m), with good snow cover from December to April. It's a great place for beginners to find their feet. The more experienced will be drawn towards the giant slalom run and, most difficult of all, the infamous 1100m-long Wall.

Skiing lessons are available at both resorts; see the relevant sections for price details.

Bansko (p99) has been largely ignored by foreign tourists. It has two ski areas: the low-altitude Chalin Valog (1100m to 1600m) and the high-altitude Shiligarnika (1700m to 2500m). There are several ski runs favourable for beginners, plus a few for more experienced skiers.

The **Bulgarian Extreme & Freestyle Skiing Association** (www.befsa.com) organises events like the annual Big Mountain competition at Bansko. They also offer freestyle skiing excursions to remote, undeveloped locations if you want to escape the crowds.

Snowshoeing excursions in the Rila Mountains are run by companies including **Discover-Bulgaria** (☎ 02-981 0971; www.discover-bulgaria.com), offering eight days from €465, and Odysseia-In (p271), eight days from €440. It's a novel way to see this fascinating corner of the country decked out in its winter finery.

> The website www.bulgariaski.com has resort details, snow reports, an online booking system and other useful information.

BIRD-WATCHING, BOTANY & BEARS

Bulgaria is a haven for all kinds of wildlife, including such elusive creatures as brown bears and wolves, plus 400 species of birds (around 75% of the European total). Bird-watching is a popular hobby and several companies run bird-watching tours. The nesting period (May to June) and migration period (September to October) are the best times to come. The Via Pontica, which passes over Bulgaria, is one of Europe's major migratory routes for birds, while Atanasovsko Lake, north of Burgas, is the country's most important reserve, frequented by 314 different species.

Neophron (☎ 052-302 536; www.neophron.com; PO Box 492, Varna) runs 10- to 14-day guided birding trips across the country, which can be combined with botany and bear-watching tours. It's run by professional ornithologists, and raises funds for the **Bulgarian Society for the Protection of Birds** (www.bspb.org).

Odysseia-In (p271) also runs bird-watching tours (14 days, from €990), and tours specialising in botany (12 days, from €740) and geology (nine days, from €830).

The **Bulgarian-Swiss Biodiversity Conservation Programme** (BSBCP; ☎ /fax 02-230 014; www.bsbcp.org) produces a multimedia CD-ROM, *Flora Bulgarica* (12 lv) in English and Bulgarian, with details of 3850 plant species for those who wish to learn more.

WATER SPORTS

The big Black Sea resorts have their fair share of organised watery fun, although elsewhere provision is patchy. The major base for waterborne activities is the resort of Albena (p214), where windsurfing and water-skiing courses are offered by outlets on the beach. Zlatni Pyasâtsi (p213) is the place to go if you want to try out some jet skiing or parasailing, while a branch of the **International Dive-Centre Deep Blue** (☎ 088 506 520) is based inside the Hotel Preslav here. Its **head office** (☎ 0888 506 520; www .diving-bg.com) is in Sofia. Deep Blue runs a good selection of PADI courses, and arranges dive trips in the Black Sea. Contact them for current prices and availability. A professional outfit like Deep Blue is preferable to some of the less organised places that spring up in the summer months along the coast.

CYCLING & MOTORBIKING

Cycling doesn't have a big following in Bulgaria, but is still an excellent way to see the countryside. Few places actually rent out bikes, but **Moto-roads** (☎ 0888 957 649; www.motoroads.com; bul Bratya Bukston 208, Sofia) has a good choice of bikes from €5 per day (plus €150 to €300 security deposit). They also have motorbikes (from €50 per day) and can organise a series of motorbike trips: a challenging nine-day off-road riding and mountain tour of the Sredna Gora and Rodopis (around 1300km) costs €1690 for two, including accommodation, or €990 for a self-guided trip.

Odysseia-In (p271) in Sofia runs eight-day mountain-biking trips through the Rodopis, covering around 50km per day (€590 per person, groups of six to nine).

'Cycling is an excellent way to see the countryside.'

Food & Drink

Bulgarian cuisine has been heavily influenced by Greek and Turkish cookery as well as home-grown Balkan traditions. Fresh vegetables and fruit form the basis of much of Bulgarian cooking, and pork, veal and chicken are popular meats. In the countryside, duck and rabbit also feature in many traditional recipes, while cheese and tripe are both common. Fish is plentiful along the Black Sea coast, but not so common elsewhere.

STAPLES & SPECIALITIES

Breakfast is rarely more than a coffee and maybe some bread for most Bulgarians, but those with more time may partake of cheese, salami and even cake and jam. Lunch again is normally a small, casual meal, while dinner is the main meal of the day, often of two or three courses, including grilled meat, salad and soup.

Popular Bulgarian dishes with a Turkish influence include the omnipresent *kebabche* (grilled spicy meat sausages) and *kyufte* (basically the same thing, but round and flat). Salads are an essential part of most Bulgarian meals, normally eaten as a starter, but some are so large that they could be a full meal in themselves. *Shopska* salad, which is made with chopped tomatoes, cucumbers and onions covered with feta cheese, is perhaps the most popular, while *snezhanka* salad is made with pickled cucumbers and plain yoghurt. Bread is a staple of Bulgarian meals and it will be brought to you, almost always at a small extra cost, whether you ask for it or not, when you order a main meal.

Offal, in various forms, is a distressingly common feature of many a restaurant menu.

Some tasty regional specialities are *patatnik* (a hearty cheese and potato omelette; from the Rodopi region), *kapama* (meat, rice and sauerkraut simmered and served in a clay pot; around Bansko), and *midi*

TRAVEL YOUR TASTEBUDS

Grilled meat and cheese feature on virtually every Bulgarian restaurant menu, and are sometimes combined, as in the *kyufte tatarsko* (seasoned pork burger filled with melted cheese). Considering that there are only two traditional kinds of Bulgarian cheese, *sirene* ('white', similar to feta) and *kashkaval* ('yellow', hard cheese), it's amazing how much Bulgarians make out of these traditional ingredients. *Pârzheni kartofi sâs sirene* (white cheese-topped fried potatoes) are a regular side dish in many cafes and restaurants. *Sarmi* (stuffed vine leaves), usually filled with rice, show evidence of Greek influence, while *Balkanska sharena sol* (Balkan mixed salt) is a common condiment found in most restaurants, which includes fenugreek and red pepper. Perhaps a less appetizing Bulgarian specialty is offal, which includes such 'delicacies' as ox tongue, ducks' hearts, lamb's brains and pig spleens.

We dare you...

Bulgarians are very keen on using up the parts of animals most Western abattoirs would throw away, but if you have the stomach for it, you might like to try, well, stomach soup for a start (*shkembe chorba*), or maybe some brain (*mozâk*) or tongue (*ezik*), which come in various forms, including in omelettes. Spleens and intestines also turn up in soups and grills. It's all a load of tripe anyway.

BULGARIAN WINE

The production (and imbibing) of wine in Bulgaria is an ancient tradition dating back to the 6th century BC, and Thracian wines are even mentioned by Homer. Today, Bulgaria is among the world's top wine-producing nations, and though once a big exporter of cheap wines, the withdrawal of state funding has slowed this output. However, private winemakers are now making strides, both in the quality and quantity of the wine they produce.

The five recognised wine-growing regions produce decent red wines, including Cabernet Sauvignon from around Sliven and Melnik, and Merlot from Haskovo and Pazardzhik; and whites, such as Chardonnay from Veliki Preslav, and Sauvignon Blanc from Varna. Other native wine varieties include Mavrud, from south of Plovdiv, and Dimiat. One of the more charming places to try a drop is Melnik, where a bottle of home-made plonk costs about 3 lv and a far better brand costs from 5 lv.

More information about wines from the Melnik region can be gathered from the websites www.melnikwine.bg and www.bulgariawines.com. In addition, winery tours are available at the Damianitza Winery, near Melnik (p107).

---

tzigane (mussels sautéed with a spicy cheese-and-mustard sauce; along the Black Sea coast).

Popular desserts of Turkish origin include *baklava*, made with honey and pistachios, and *lokum* (Turkish delight). *Mlechna banitsa* is a sweet pastry made with milk and eggs, and is one of the best Bulgarian desserts. Gooey cream and chocolate cakes rarely taste as good as they look, while ice cream features on menus everywhere.

DRINKS

Bulgarians do love their coffee, and drink it morning, noon and night at kiosks, cafés and bars across the country. While you might encounter some instant coffee, good espresso coffee is available everywhere. Smarter places also offer cappuccinos, though in cheaper outlets this might simply be instant coffee with a dollop of sprayed cream on top.

Tea is mostly the *bilkov* (herbal) and *plodov* (fruit) variety. If you want the real, black tea, ask for *cheren chai*. This will normally come with a slice of lemon; if you'd prefer milk, ask for '*mlyako*'.

Beer *(pivo* or *bira)* is very popular in Bulgaria, and is served everywhere, either in bottles or in draught form. The leading nationwide brands are Zagorka, Kamenitsa and Astika, while there are several regional beers, such as Shumensko (from Shumen) and Pirinsko (from Blagoevgrad), which are only rarely available elsewhere in the country.

Bulgaria produces huge quantities of both white and red *vino* (wine), which varies greatly in quality, from basic plonk to fine (and expensive) wines of high, international standard (see the boxed text above).

www.wines-bg.com
If you want to learn more about Bulgarian wines.

The national spirit is *rakia* (a clear and potent kind of brandy, usually made from grapes, although versions made from plums can also be found). Slivenska Perla, Lovico Suhindol, Burgas-63 and Simeon I are just a few of the many brands available. It's served with ice in restaurants and bars, which often devote a whole page on their menus to a list of the regional *rakias* on offer.

Whisky, gin and vodka made in Bulgaria are a lot cheaper than the imported brand names, but are probably best left to the Bulgarians.

CELEBRATIONS

Festivals throughout Bulgaria invariably involve eating and drinking, and there are often particular meals prepared for each holiday. One age-old custom is the baking of special loaves of bread, for example for saints' days, each marked with a distinctive design and used in some elaborate ritual; you'll see these displayed in ethnographic museums. On 28 February (Horse Easter), for example, women in rural communities traditionally bake bread in the shape of horseshoes, which are then fed to horses and new brides to ensure fertility. St George's Day (6 May), also known as Gergyovden, originated as an ancient pagan festival to do with sheep farming, and is one of the most important rural festivals, especially in eastern Bulgaria, and involves a big, ritual meal of lamb and bread.

www.travel-bulgaria
.com/content/receipts
.shtml If you're looking for
a quick and easy Bulgar-
ian recipe, this website
gives instructions for
several popular dishes.

At Easter (Velikden, or Pasha) a traditional bread is baked, containing whole eggs which have been dyed red. The bread is broken – never sliced – by the eldest member of the family, and pieces are distributed to all family members present. Other celebrations throughout the year are also marked with bread in many forms, including snakes (Jeremiah or Snake Day, May 1) and crosses (Krastovden or Holy Cross Day, 14 September) or decorated with patterns such as beehives (Prokopi Pchelar or Procopius the Beekeeper Day, 8 July) and bunches of grapes (Preobrazhenie or Transfiguration Day, 6 August). In age-old tradition, Preobrazhenie is the first day on which Bulgarians ate the new crop of grapes, while eating blackberries (once known as devil's grapes) on this day was regarded as taboo.

One rather cheerful time to be anywhere near a winery is 1 February, when the Trifon Zarezan festival takes place to honour the patron saint of vineyards, St Trifon. On this day, wine producers start pruning their vines, and pour wine on the vine roots in the hope for a bountiful harvest. The grower who has produced the largest quantity of wine is declared 'king' and is driven around in an open cart. Plenty of tasting and drinking is also undertaken (all in the name of tradition of course).

WHERE TO EAT & DRINK

Most eateries providing seating describe themselves as restaurants, while a *mehana* (tavern) is a more traditional restaurant, often decorated in a folksy village style, and offering only authentic Bulgarian cuisine. Some of these, of course, are tourist traps, luring foreign travellers with 'folk shows' – waiters in fancy dress and so on – though the real places provide a pleasant atmosphere to linger over a well-made meal. Look out for those frequented by locals and steer clear of any that employ touts to harangue passers-by.

Cafés are cheaper affairs and include basic cafeterias serving precooked Bulgarian food, soups and salads, although more often they will only serve beverages and simple snacks. In the cities, small, basic cafés or snack bars offer drinks and snacks, sometimes with a few chairs outside, or just a table to lean on. These are popular with office workers and teenagers grabbing a quick coffee and a sandwich. Look out for signs reading закуски (*zakuski*; breakfast).

In the big cities and main tourist destinations, most restaurants will offer menus in English and, occasionally, French or German. But beware: prices on any menu written *only* in a foreign language may be considerably higher than those listed on a bilingual menu. In this case, simply insist on seeing the bilingual menu. Restaurant bills will usually be 'rounded up', and a service charge of 10% is sometimes added. If it isn't, a small tip is expected.

Most restaurants are open daily from about 11am to 11pm, although outside the big towns some may close on one or two days of the week. Cafés and street kiosks usually have longer opening hours, roughly 9am to 11pm in cities, although many open earlier to offer a quick breakfast to people hurrying to work.

Quick Eats

Bulgarians are great snackers and in big towns you will see old ladies on the streets or in parks selling *semki* (sunflower seeds) wrapped in paper cones, or home-made bread rolls from sacks. Both go for around 0.40 lv. In the colder months, steamed corn-on-the-cob is proffered by street vendors, while *banitsas* (cheese pasties), *palachinki* (pancakes) and other sweet and savoury pastry products are always popular, and are widely available, most reliably at stalls outside bus and train stations. Prices are normally around 1 to 2 lv.

Western fast-food outlets can be found all over Bulgaria, while plenty of takeaway places serve tasty, and far cheaper, hamburgers and pizzas, as well as Turkish-style doner kebabs.

DID YOU KNOW?

The bacteria used to make yoghurt is called *Lactobacillus bulgaricus*, named in honour of its Bulgarian origins.

VEGETARIANS & VEGANS

Vegetarianism is an alien concept to most Bulgarians, but vegetarians will not be disappointed with the number of meatless dishes on the menus. On the down side, variety may be lacking. Most restaurants offer a dozen or more salads, which are sometimes large enough for a main course. Omelettes, vegetarian pizzas and pasta dishes are common, but note that 'vegetarian' meals may simply mean that they include vegetables (as well as meat) or fish. Sometimes this designation doesn't seem to mean anything at all. Vegans will have a much harder time: Restaurant Kibea in Sofia (p73) is probably the only place in Bulgaria serving genuine vegan dishes.

Other tasty vegetarian meals and snacks include *sirene po shopski* (cheese, eggs and tomatoes baked in a clay pot), *mish-mash* (scrambled eggs with peppers and tomatoes), *kashkaval pane* (fried breaded cheese) and the ever-popular *banitsa*.

WHINING & DINING

Most restaurants in Bulgaria welcome children, although few offer specific children's menus and fewer still will have such things as highchairs for babies. The more modern, Western-style restaurants such as the Happy Bar & Grill chain serve up dependable and recognisable food of the sausage-and-chips variety, while pizzas, in various sizes, are available almost everywhere. Similarly, you'll have no problem finding sweets, chocolates, crisps and other treats, while chocolate and jam-filled croissants are a popular local snack. Larger supermarkets will normally have a good supply of baby food and formula. See p249 for further information on travelling with children.

HABITS & CUSTOMS

Dining out in Bulgaria is normally a casual and convivial experience, and the usual Western table manners prevail. Few Bulgarian restaurants, however, have smoke-free zones, and nonsmokers will have to put up with their fellow diners puffing away before, after and even during their meals: if you can, it's best to sit outside.

Breakfast, if eaten at all, is almost invariably eaten at home. Lunch is a light meal, while dinner is often the time for family get-togethers, and is a longer, more sociable affair. Bulgarians tend to eat dinner quite late, and restaurants fill up after about 9pm; you'll have trouble getting a seat at popular places after this time. For a quiet meal, aim to eat dinner around 6.30pm to 7pm.

DOS & DON'TS

Bulgarians are by and large a laid-back lot when it comes to behaviour at the table, although the usual Western rules of 'good manners' still apply when dining out. Obviously, these standards will vary according to where you are eating: street-bar patrons won't be shocked if you use your fingers to eat, for example, but it would certainly draw attention in a smart restaurant.

■ *Molya* is the word used to attract the attention of a waiter/waitress.

■ If service is good (and not included in the bill), leave a tip of 10%.

■ If you're invited to dine at a Bulgarian home, it's traditional to bring flowers (an odd number – even numbers are for funerals), though it's not normally expected of foreigners.

EAT YOUR WORDS

If you want to know the difference between *kebabche* and *kyufte*, or are looking for a meal without meat, you'll first need to learn the Cyrillic alphabet. For language guidelines, see p277.

Bulgarian Cuisines by Dimitâr Mantov is a good recipe book (and souvenir) if you want to impress friends with a tasty Bulgarian meal when you get home.

Useful Phrases

Can you recommend ...?
mo·zhe·te li da pre·po·*râ*·cha·te   Можете ли да препоръчате ...?
   a restaurant
   re·stor·*ant*   ресторант
   a bar/pub
   bar/za·ve·*de*·ni·e   бар/заведение

Where would you go for ...?
kâ·*de* ser·*vi*·rat ...?   Къде сервират ...?
   local specialities
   me·stni spe·tsi·a·li·*te*·ti   местни специалитети
   a cheap meal
   ef·ti·na khra·*na*   евтина храна
Are you still serving food?
ser·*vi*·ra·te li *o*·shte?   Сервирате ли още?
We've booked a table.
i·ma·me za·*pa*·ze·na *ma*·sa.   Имаме запазена маса.
(I'd like) a table for (two), please.
bih *i*·skal *ma*·sa za *dva*·ma.   Бих искал маса за двама.
Excuse me, is this chair/table free?
iz·vi·*ne*·te sto·*lât*/   Извинете, столът/
ma·sa·ta svo·*bo*·den/svo·*bo*·dna li e?   масата свободен/свободна ли е?

I'd like to reserve a table for ...
bih *i*·skal da za·*pa*·zya *ma*·sa za ...   Бих искал да запазя маса за ...
   (two) people
   dva·ma (*du*·shi)   двама (души)
   (eight) o'clock
   o·sem cha·*sâ*   осем часа

Do you have ...?
i·ma·te li ...?   Имате ли ...?
   a menu in English?
   me·*nyu* na an·*gliy*·ski?   меню на английски?
   vegetarian foo
   ve·ge·ta·ri·*an*·ska khra·*na*   вегетарианска храна

I'd like a local speciality.
   mo·zhe li *me*·sten spe·tsi·a·li·*tet*?   Може ли местен специалитет?
I'd like the set menu, please.
   mo·zhe li *pâl*·no·to me·*nyu*   Може ли пълното меню?
What are the daily specials?
   kak·*vi* sa spe·tsi·a·li·*te*·ti·te za de·*nya*?   Какви са специалитетите за деня?
What would you recommend?
   kak·*vo* shte mi pre·po·*râ*·cha·te?   Какво ще ми препоръчате?
I'm a vegetarian.
   ve·ge·ta·ri·*a*·nets sâm   Вегетарианец съм.
Is it cooked in meat stock?
   v *me*·sen bu·*lyon* li e pri·*got*·ve·no?   В месен бульон ли е приготвено?
What's in that dish?
   kak·*vo i*·ma f to·*va ya*·sti·e?   Какво има в това ястие?

I'd like ... , please.
mo·lya *a*·ko o·*bi*·cha·te ...   Моля, ако обичате ...
   a cup of tea/coffee
   cha·sha chay/ka·*fe*   чаша чай/кафе
   with (milk)
   s (*mlya*·ko)   с мляко

The bill, please.
   smet·ka·ta *a*·ko o·*bi*·cha·te   Сметката, ако обичате.
Bon appétit!
   do·*bâr* a·pe·*tit*   Добър апетит!
Cheers!
   naz·*dra*·ve!   Наздраве!
That was delicious!
   be·she *mno*·go *fku*·sno   Беше много вкусно!

Traditional Bulgarian Cooking by Atanas Slavov gives more than 140 recipes you might like to try out, including all the favourites such as *kavarma*, *banitsa* and *shopska salad*.

Menu Decoder
баница (*ba*·ni·tsa) – thin, flaky pasties stuffed with white cheese.
баклава (ba·kla·*va*) – flaky pastry with walnuts or pistachios and honey.
боб (bob) – seasoned bean soup.
гювеч (gyu·*vech*) – peppers, tomatoes, aubergine, onions etc, cooked in the oven. It can also be prepared with meat.
каварма (ka·*var*·ma) – meat or vegetable stew, normally pork or chicken, in an earthenware pot.
кебапчета на скара (ke·*bap*·che·ta na *ska*·ra) – grilled, sausage-shaped pork meatballs, mixed with finely chopped onion.
кюфте (ki·*yuf*·te) – round meatballs, similar to the above.
миш-маш (*mish*·*mash*) – baked peppers, onions tomatoes and cheese.
риба-плакия (*ri*·ba pla·*ki*·ya) – one of the best-known Bulgarian fish dishes, usually with carp, baked with lemon and onion in oil, garlic, salt and pepper, with paprika, sugar and tomato paste.
сърми (sâr·*mi*) – vine leaves stuffed with rice, sometimes with sour cream or yogurt.
таратор (ta·ra·*tor*) – chilled soup made with finely chopped cucumber and yogurt.
шопска салата (*shop*·ska sa·*la*·ta) – salad of fresh tomatoes, cucumbers, sweet peppers and grated white cheese.
шкембе чорба (shk·*em*·be ch·*or*·ba) – tripe soup.

Food Glossary
BASICS
хляб	khlyap	bread
краве масло	kra·ve *mas*·lo	butter
сирене	*si*·re·ne	cheese

шоколад	sho·ko·*lat*	chocolate
яйца	yay·*tsa*	eggs
мед	met	honey
мляко	mlya·ko	milk
пипер	*pi*·per	pepper
ориз	o·*ris*	rice
сол	sol	salt
захар	*za*·khar	sugar
кисело мляко	*ki*·se·lo *mlya*·ko	yogurt

MEAT

пиле	*pi*·le	chicken
рива	riba	fish
шунка	*shun*·ka	ham
агнешко месо	*ag*·nesh·ko me·*so*	lamb
свинско	*svin*·sko	pork
скариди	ska·*ri*·di	shrimp
език	ezik	tongue
телешко	*te*·lesh·ko	veal

VEGETABLES

син домат	sin do·*mat*	aubergine
(зелен) боб	(ze·*len*) bop	(green) beans
зеле	*ze*·le	cabbage
морков	*mor*·kof	carrot
карфиол	kar·fi·*ol*	cauliflower
целина	*tse*·li·na	celery
краставица	*kras*·ta·vi·tsa	cucumber
маруля	ma·*ru*·lya	lettuce
гъби	*gâ*·bi	mushrooms
лук	luk	onions
грах	grakh	peas
пипер	pi·*per*	pepper
картоф	kar·*tof*	potato
домат	do·*mat*	tomato

FRUIT

ябълка	*ya*·bâl·ka	apple
кайсия	kay·*si*·ya	apricot
банан	ba·*nan*	banana
смокиня	smo·*ki*·nya	fig
грозде	*groz*·de	grapes
лимон	li·*mon*	lemon
портокал	por·to·*kal*	orange
праскова	*pras*·ko·va	peach
круша	*kru*·sha	pear
слива	*sli*·va	plum
ягода	*ya*·go·da	strawberry

DRINKS

бира	*bi*·ra	beer
плодов сок	*plo*·dof sok	fruit juice
минерална вода	mi·ne·*ral*·na vo·*da*	mineral water
кафе	ka·*fe*	coffee
чай	chay	tea
вино	vino	wine

DID YOU KNOW?

Wartime British PM Winston Churchill was particularly partial to a glass or two of red Melnik wine, and one brand is named after him.

Sofia СОФИЯ

HIGHLIGHTS

- **Culture**
  Take in the atmosphere of the stunning Aleksander Nevski Memorial Church (p61).

- **History**
  Explore the rich treasures of the Archaeological Museum (p61).

- **Green Haven**
  Go for a stroll around the vast, leafy Borisova Gradina park (p65), with its flowerbeds, cafés and decaying communist monument.

- **Winter Sports**
  Take to the slopes at Dragalevtsi (p82).

- **Dining**
  Treat your tastebuds to some top Bulgarian cuisine at Pri Yafata (p73).

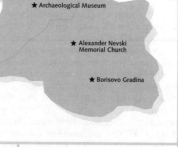

★ Archaeological Museum

★ Alexander Nevski Memorial Church

★ Borisovo Gradina

- TELEPHONE CODE: 02
- POPULATION: 1.1 MILLION

Sofia, Bulgaria's bustling, cosmopolitan capital, is where most visitors to the country will begin and end their journeys. Although it is, by far, Bulgaria's largest city, Sofia is a pleasingly compact and characterful place. First impressions, especially for those taking the grey, skyscraper-lined route from the airport into town, might seem unpromising, but modern Sofia is a young, lively and appealing city which rewards exploration and offers numerous sociable bars and cafés where you can sit back and take it all in. Soaring, onion-domed churches, treasure-filled museums, art galleries, leafy parks and evocative communist monuments jostle for your attention, and can easily keep you busy for a week or longer, while the capital also boasts some of Bulgaria's best restaurants and most happening nightlife.

As Bulgaria continues to 'Westernise' following the demise of communism, the problems and inequalities of the new market economy are more evident in Sofia than elsewhere. Pensioners sit outside trendy boutiques with battered bathroom scales, encouraging passers-by to weigh themselves in return for a few coins, while others resort to begging. As if airlifted in from a different planet, tacky casinos and sleazy strip clubs seem to have an increasing presence in the city, alongside the gleaming glass towers of luxurious hotels and numerous Western brand-name stores doing a brisk trade with Sofia's well-dressed and well-heeled teenagers. In recent years, Sofia has benefited greatly from the EU's Beautiful Bulgaria Project, which is sprucing up historic buildings and energising old neighbourhoods.

Sitting on a 545m-high plateau at the foot of Mt Vitosha, Sofia is the highest capital in Europe, and has excellent hiking and skiing spots virtually on its doorstep. The city is also the hub of much of Bulgaria's public transport network, and makes an ideal base for forays into the surrounding countryside.

HISTORY

The Thracian Serdi tribe settled the Sofia region as far back as the 7th and 8th centuries BC. The area was briefly occupied by the Macedonians in the 4th century BC, but the city as we know it today was founded by the Romans, who conquered the region in AD 29, and built the town of Ulpia Serdica. In the late 3rd century AD, Serdica became a major regional imperial capital, reaching a zenith in the early 4th century under Emperor Constantine the Great. The St George Rotunda is the most prominent reminder of the Roman era still standing.

The Bulgar king Khan Krum came through in AD 809, and made it one of the main towns of his empire. The Byzantines occupied it in the 11th century, and it was during the Second Bulgarian Empire (1185–1396) that the name of the city was changed (for the last time) to Sofia, after the Church of St Sofia, which still exists, albeit much rebuilt. Sadly, few monuments survive from this crucial period; the most important, and most precious to all Bulgarians, is the impressive Boyana Church.

The Ottomans, sweeping through the Balkans, captured the city in 1382, and held it for nearly 500 years. Sofia became the regional capital and a major market town. The Ottomans built baths and mosques, such as the Banya Bashi Mosque (which still stands), but many churches were destroyed or abandoned; the tiny Church of Sveta Petka Samardjiiska is a very rare survivor.

The city declined during the feudal unrest of the mid-19th century, and it was in Sofia that the famed anti-Turkish rebel Vasil Levski was hanged in 1873, after first being interrogated and tortured in the building that later became the Royal Palace. After the liberation of the city from the Turks in early 1878, Sofia officially became the capital of

Bulgaria on 4 April 1879. The new roads and railway lines linking Sofia with the rest of Europe and the Balkans soon boosted the city's fortunes. However, Bulgaria picked the wrong side during WWII so, tragically, a lot of the city's heritage was destroyed during bombing raids.

The Red Army 'liberated' Sofia in 1944 – the monument (p66) to their arrival still stands near Borisova Gradina – and a People's Republic was set up after the war. Socialist architects set to work in the following years, rebuilding the heavily damaged city on the Soviet model, complete with high-rise housing blocks in the suburbs and monstrous monuments in the city centre, such as the old Party House which dominates pl Nezavisimost. Some of the more distasteful reminders of the communist era, such as the mausoleum of postwar leader Georgi Dimitrov, have been wiped off the landscape, while others have been allowed to slowly decay since the fall of the communist government in 1989.

High unemployment and declining living standards were serious problems through the 1990s, and today Sofia is still a city in transition, a blend of the decrepit and the ultramodern, of affluence and poverty. The city has certainly been smartened up over recent years, and Sofians hope EU membership will bring more lasting benefits.

ORIENTATION

At the heart of Sofia is pl Sveta Nedelya, dominated by the great church of the same name. To the north, bul Maria Luisa runs past the Central Hali Shopping Centre and the Banya Bashi Mosque towards the central train and bus stations. To the south, Sofia's main shopping street, bul Vitosha, lined with boutiques and restaurants, heads towards Yuzhen Park and the massive National Palace of Culture (NDK) complex.

East of pl Sveta Nedelya you'll come upon pl Nezavisimost (also known as the Largo) and bul Tsar Osvoboditel, watched over by the former Royal Palace. Continuing down bul Tsar Osvoboditel, you'll pass pl Narodno Sabranie and the parliament building on the way to the huge park of Borisova Gradina.

See p78 for details on getting to and from the airport.

Maps

The *Sofia City Map* (1:24,500), published by Domino, and Datamap's *Sofia City Plan* (1:20,000), both printed in English, are widely available. The *Sofia City Info Guide* (see p59) also includes a good tourist map of the city centre. All bookshops listed in the next section sell maps of Sofia and other places in Bulgaria, as do stalls at pl Slaveikov. One of the best sources of maps,

---

SOFIA IN...

Two Days

Start your day with a coffee at one of the outdoor cafés in and around the **City Garden** (p65) and call into the former Royal Palace to get acquainted with Bulgarian folk art at the **Ethnographical Museum** (p61) inside. Afterwards, take in Sofia's most impressive sight, the **Aleksander Nevski Memorial Church** (p61). While you're there, visit the **Aleksander Nevski Crypt** (p61) to see the impressive Museum of Icons. In the evening, drop by **Pri Yafata** (p73) for an excellent traditional Bulgarian meal.

Four Days

Follow the above itinerary, and on the third day admire the treasures on show at the **Archaeological Museum** (p61), and take a leisurely stroll around **Borisova Gradina** (p65). On the next day, wander down to **Yuzhen Park** (p65), and maybe go to a show at the **NDK** (p75).

One Week

After the above itinerary, take a trip out to Boyana to see the **National Museum of History** (p80) and the lovely **Boyana Church** (p80). Ride the chairlift up **Mt Vitosha** (p82) and take a day trip out to **Koprivshtitsa** (p136).

especially for hiking, is **Odysseia-In** (Map pp62-3; ☎ 989 0538; www.odysseia-in.com; bul Stamboliyski 20-V); also see p60.

INFORMATION
Bookshops

Booktrading (Map pp62-3; ☎ 986 1728; pl Slaveikov 7a; ☯ 8.30am-8.30pm) Has a fair range of English-language novels as well as some nonfiction and maps.

Dom Na Knigata (Map pp62-3; ☎ 981 7897; pl Slaveikov 7b; ☯ 9am-10pm) A bookshop located in a courtyard off pl Slaveikov. This jumble of a place sells a mixture of mostly second-hand Bulgarian and foreign literature and nonfiction. However, prices are surprisingly high.

Euro-Bulgarian Cultural Centre (Map pp62-3; ☎ 988 0084; bul Stamboliyski 17) This place has an eclectic range of titles, including some classic English literature.

Fine Arts Gallery bookshop (Map pp62-3; ☎ 946 7113; ul Shipka 6) Sells books about Bulgaria in French and English, as well as guidebooks.

Open-air Book-market (Map pp62-3; pl Slaveikov) Dozens of bookstalls crowd this square daily, selling mostly Bulgarian novels and technical manuals, but plenty of books on Bulgarian history, culture and cuisine are available in foreign languages.

Second-hand bookstall (Map pp62-3; Sofia University underpass) Cheap English and French second-hand novels are on sale here.

Cultural Centres

American Cultural Center (Map pp62-3; ☎ 980 4838; ul Kârnigradska 8; ☯ 8.30am-5pm Mon-Fri)

British Council (Map pp62-3; ☎ 942 4344; www.britishcouncil.org/bulgaria; ul Krakra 7; ☯ 9am-5pm Mon-Fri)

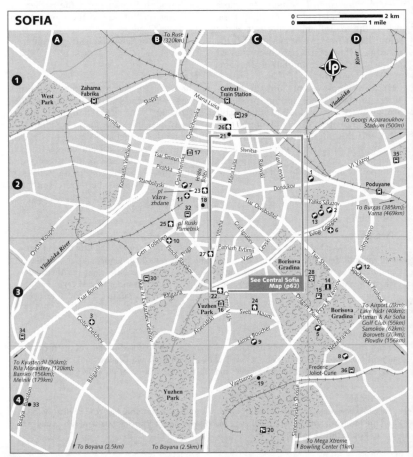

French Cultural Institute (Map pp62-3; ☎ 981 6927; www.ambafrance-bg.org; bul Vasil Levski 2; ☒ noon-6pm Mon-Fri)
Goethe Institute (Map pp62-3; ☎ 939 0100; ul Budapeshta 1; ☒ 9am-noon & 3-5pm Mon-Fri)

Emergency
Ambulance (☎ 150)
Fire (☎ 160)
Mountain Rescue (☎ 963 2000)
Police (☎ 166, English ☎ 988 5239, French ☎ 982 3028; ☒ translators available 8.30am and 6pm daily)
Traffic Police (☎ 665 060)

Internet Access
BTC Centre (Map pp62-3; ul Gurko; per hr 0.80 lv; ☒ 24hr) Offers several computers in a modern office-style environment.
Internet Centre (Map pp62-3; Euro-Bulgarian Cultural Centre, bul Stamboliyski 17; ☒ 9am-6pm Mon-Fri).
National Palace of Culture complex (Map pp62-3) Several Internet agencies are inside and also along the underpass beneath this complex, though connections are slow.
Site Internet Cafe (Map pp62-3; ☎ 986 0896; bul Vitosha 45; ☒ 24hr) One of the more central and more reliable Internet centres, with a nonsmoking room. Prices are slightly cheaper after 10pm.

Internet Resources
www.cska.bg News about Sofia's premier football club.
www.programata.bg Comprehensive eating, drinking and clubbing information.
www.sofiacityguide.com The website of the invaluable pocket guide (right) is an excellent place to start.
www.sofia.bg Official municipal website, mostly with business information.

Media
Programata (www.programata.bg) A useful, widely available free weekly listings magazine, with details of cinemas, restaurants and clubs. It's only in Bulgarian, but the website is in English.
Sofia City Info Guide (free) An excellent source of information for anyone staying in the capital for more than a few days. Printed in English and German every month, it includes reviews of hotels and restaurants, plus basic practicalities. It's available at hotel reception desks and sporadically at restaurants.
Sofia Echo (www.sofiaecho.com; 2.40 lv) An English-language newspaper published each Friday and available at some central newsstands. Mainly aimed at the expat business community, it also has restaurant and entertainment reviews useful for visitors.
Sofia Inside & Out (free) A quarterly publication carrying reviews of restaurants, bars and clubs, as well as comprehensive practical information and even a few walking routes. You can pick copies up at some hotels or at travel agencies such as Zig Zag Holidays (p60). An annual French version (5 lv) is sometimes available at central newsstands.

Medical Services
Apteka Sveta Nedelya pharmacy (Map pp62-3; ☎ 950 5026; pl Sveta Nedelya 5; ☒ 24hr)
Dento (Map pp58-9; ☎ 958 4841; ul Atanasov 11) English-, French- and Italian-speaking dentists.
International Medical Centre (Map pp58-9; ☎ 944 9326; ul Gogol 28) The IMC has English and French-speaking doctors who will make house calls at any time. They also deal with paediatrics and dental care.
Poliklinika Torax (Map pp58-9; ☎ 91 285; bul Stamboliyski 57) A competent, privately run clinic with English-speaking staff.
Pirogov Hospital (Map pp58-9; ☎ 915 4411; bul Gen Totleben 21) This reasonably acceptable hospital is the major public hospital for emergencies.

Money
The Foreign Exchange Office has numerous outlets on bul Vitosha, bul Maria Luisa and bul Stamboliyski.

Biochim Commercial Bank (Map pp62-3; ul Alabin)

Bulbank (Map pp62-3; cnr ul Lavele & ul Todor Alexandrov)

MegaTours (Map pp62-3; ☎ 980 8520; cnr ul Vasil Levski 21 & ul Graf Ignatiev) AmEx representative. It won't change AmEx travellers cheques, but otherwise provides the normal services for AmEx customers.

United Bulgarian Bank (Map pp62-3; ul Sveta Sofia)

Post

Central post office (Map pp62-3; ul General Gurko 6; ⌚ 7.30am-8.30pm)

Telephone

BTC Centre (Map pp62-3; ul General Gurko; ⌚ 24hr) State-of-the-art communications centre, run by the Bulgarian Telecommunications Company. Inside, there are booths for local and international calls, an office from where faxes can be sent, and an Internet centre. All services are neatly signposted in English.

Toilets

Central Hali Shopping Centre (Map pp62-3; bul Maria Luisa; free)

NDK Underpass (Map pp62-3; Yuzhen Park; 0.30 lv)

Public Toilets (Map pp62-3; bul Maria Luisa; 0.40 lv) Beside Banya Bashi Mosque.

Tsum Retail Centre (Map pp62-3; bul Maria Luisa; free)

Tourist Information

National Information & Advertising Centre (Map pp62-3; ☎ 987 9778; www.bulgariatravel.org; ul Sveta Sofia; ⌚ 9.30am-5.30pm Mon-Fri) The only place for independent tourist information. It's not a real tourist office (the centre is run by the Ministry of Economy), but they have a small assortment of brochures on Bulgaria as a whole, and the English-speaking staff can help with other information.

Zig Zag Holidays (Map pp62-3; ☎ 980 5102; www .zigzag.dir.bg; bul Stamboliyski 20-V, enter from ul Lavele; ⌚ 9am-6pm) Although essentially a private travel agency, Zig Zag is happy to provide tourist information, and sells a range of maps and books. It charges a reasonable 5 lv for consultation, though this fee is deducted if you book a tour (eg hiking or climbing) or accommodation with the agency.

Travel Agencies

Alma Tours (Map pp62-3; ☎ 986 5691; almatour@dir.bg; bul Stamboliyski 27) Books tours, private rooms and hotel rooms in Sofia and elsewhere in Bulgaria, and can also organise car hire. Note that the business's former name, Balkantour, is still displayed outside.

Odysseia-In Travel Agency (Map pp62-3; ☎ 989 0538; www.odysseia-in.com; 1st fl, bul Stamboliyski 20-V, enter from ul Lavele) Odysseia-In can book you on

hiking, skiing, climbing, bird-watching or numerous other trips across the country. They deal with groups; individuals should contact Zig Zag (see previous section) on the ground floor of the same building.

DANGERS & ANNOYANCES

The main danger you're likely to face in Sofia comes from the often dreadful traffic: pedestrian crossings and traffic lights don't appear to mean anything in particular to many drivers, so be extra careful when crossing roads. As elsewhere in Bulgaria, pavements on side streets are frequently blocked with parked cars, forcing pedestrians to walk on the road. This annoying practice also leaves the pavements themselves in permanently potholed condition, ideal for twisting the odd ankle or two. The toxic fumes belched out by dirty, ageing vehicles add to the unpleasantness.

Sofia is a generally safe city, but the areas around the central train station and the northern end of bul Maria Luisa are best avoided after dark, and can appear sleazy and slightly threatening once the gluesniffers and prostitutes emerge.

Beggars are a depressingly common sight in central Sofia, especially along bul Vitosha and around some churches and larger squares. Most are in genuine need and appreciative of a few coins, though be wary of gangs of grabby children. As always, be careful with bags, wallets and purses on crowded public transport and, in particular, busy areas such as the Ladies Market. Some foreign travellers have reported being robbed in the street, but thankfully this is still a very rare occurrence.

You may be approached by shady customers wanting to change money; needless to say, this is illegal and you're pretty certain to be ripped off. Drivers, meanwhile, might be faced with window-washers when they stop at traffic lights in the city centre. If you're a foreigner in a nice car, you'll naturally be asked for more for this unwanted service, though it's worth bearing in mind the high unemployment rate and very poor wages which force people into these kinds of activities.

SIGHTS

Most of Sofia's sights are handily located in the compact city centre, and you won't have to do too much walking to get round them all. Further afield, the suburb of Boyana (p79) is the location of the city's biggest museum and its most revered church.

Aleksander Nevski Memorial Church

This massive, awe-inspiring **church** (Map pp62-3; pl Aleksander Nevski) is one of *the* symbols not just of Sofia but of Bulgaria itself. It was built between 1882 and 1912 as a memorial to the 200,000 Russian soldiers who died fighting for Bulgaria's independence during the Russian–Turkish War (1877–78).

Designed by the renowned Russian architect AN Pomerantsev (also responsible for Moscow's GUM department store), the church was built in the neo-Byzantine style favoured in Russia at the time. Note the marble at the main entrance, the mosaics above the doorways and the domes laden with 8kg of gold. The cavernous, incense-scented interior is decorated with naturalistic but now darkened murals, pendulous chandeliers and elaborate onyx and alabaster thrones.

A door to the left of the main entrance leads to the **Aleksander Nevski Crypt** (Museum of Icons; ☎ 981 5775; admission 3 lv; ⏲ 10.30am-6.30pm Tue-Sun). It displays Bulgaria's biggest and best collection of religious icons from the last 1000 years, brought here from churches and monasteries all over the country. A shop inside the museum sells reproduction icons.

Archaeological Museum

The Buyuk Djami (Great Mosque), with its nine lead-covered domes, was built in 1496, and now houses Sofia's excellent **Archaeological Museum** (Map pp62-3; ☎ 988 2406; ul Saborna 2; admission 5 lv; ⏲ 10am-6pm Tue-Sun). On the ground floor there's a fascinating collection of Thracian and Roman tombstones and rich grave-goods, weaponry and jewellery. The 2nd-century AD bronze-gilt head of Apollo and the 4th-century AD stone plaque showing animal and gladiatorial fights in the circus in Roman Serdica (modern-day Sofia) are two of the highlights. Upstairs there are displays of Chalcolithic and Neolithic artefacts, such as pottery, tools and cultic objects, and more Thracian treasures. On the gallery level, a private collection features ancient weaponry and ceramics, and the walls are lined with icons and frescoes taken from churches in Nesebâr and

elsewhere in Bulgaria. The wall facing the main entrance, meanwhile, is dominated by a reproduction of the Madara Horseman figure; the original can be seen near Shumen (p155). Everything in the museum is labelled in English.

Ethnographical Museum

This **museum** (Map pp62-3; ☎ 988 4191; pl Battenberg 1; admission 3 lv, guided tour 10 lv; ⏲ 10am-5.30pm Tue-Sun) is housed in the former Royal Palace (built in 1887), which it shares with the National Art Gallery (p64). The museum contains an interesting series of displays, on two floors, of Bulgarian arts and crafts (including costumes, textiles and ceramics), and exhibits on the 19th-century Bulgarian communities in what are now Macedonia, Albania and northern Greece. Also here are traditional costumes once worn by the former king, Simeon II, and his sister, Princess Maria Luisa, as children. Everything is captioned in English.

Also worth noting are the grand – albeit rather timeworn – rooms themselves, with their marble fireplaces and ornate plasterwork; look out for the lobster, fish and dead birds on the ceiling of what was once, presumably, a royal dining room.

The exit from the museum leads directly into the Centre of Folk Arts and Crafts souvenir shop (p76).

National Gallery for Foreign Art

This huge **gallery** (Map pp62-3; ☎ 980 7262; ul 19 Fevruari 1; admission 1.50 lv, free on Sun, guided tours 7 lv; ⏲ 11am-6pm Wed-Mon) is home to a varied and intriguing collection of international art, although it does give the impression of having been assembled from random job lots rather than with any particular creative vision in

---

TOP FIVE FREE ATTRACTIONS

- Aleksander Nevski Memorial Church (left)
- Borisova Gradina (p65)
- Sundays at the National Gallery for Foreign Art (p61)
- Sofia Municipal Gallery of Art (p66)
- The changing of the guard at the Presidency (hourly; p66)

SOFIA

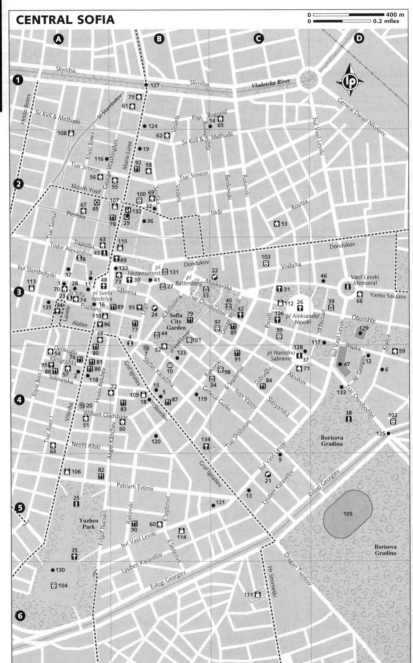

CENTRAL SOFIA

0 _____ 400 m
0 _____ 0.2 miles

SOFIA

mind. The ground floor is dominated by a vast array of 19th- and 20th-century Indian woodcarvings, including a roomful of Catholic religious sculptures from Goa. Also here is a display of West African woodcarvings and an exhibition of colourful Japanese prints. Upstairs there are several galleries of European paintings, mostly by little-known artists, plus some minor scribbles by Degas and Matisse and a few small bronze studies by Rodin. Millet's pencil sketch, *Young Woman*, and *Girl in an Oriental Dress* by the Czech Art Nouveau master Alfons Mucha are among the more eye-catching artworks. Look out too for Jean-Jacques Caffieri's marble bust of Madame du Barry. The top floor is used as a temporary exhibition space for contemporary artworks. Most captions are in English.

Church of St George

Regarded as the oldest preserved building in Sofia, the **Church of St George** (Map pp62–3), in the courtyard between the Sheraton Hotel and the Presidency, dates back to the 4th century AD. This circular Roman structure, also called the Sveti Georgi Rotunda, was converted into a church in the 6th century. It was badly damaged in bombing during WWII and only fully opened to visitors again in 1998 after much restoration. The murals inside were painted on three layers between the 10th and 14th centuries.

Inside the entrance there's a small explanation in English about the church. You're also allowed to wander around the extensive, but unexplained, Roman ruins behind the church.

Sveta Nedelya Cathedral

This magnificent domed **church** (Map pp62-3; pl Sveta Nedelya) is one of the city's major landmarks. Built between 1856 and 1863 on the foundations of several previous churches stretching back to the Middle Ages, the cathedral features a rich, mural-bedecked interior. Visitors are welcome to attend services; particularly atmospheric are those held on Thursday mornings, when worshippers are blessed against the effects of black magic. A small plaque near the southern entrance explains, in English, how the cathedral was blown up by communists on 16 April 1925, in an attempt to assassinate Tsar Boris III. Over 120 people were killed in the attack, including most of the cabinet, but Boris escaped unharmed.

National Art Gallery

Despite the promising name, the **National Art Gallery** (Map pp62-3; ☎ 980 0093; pl Battenberg 1; admission 4 lv; ☻ 10.30am-6.30pm Tue-Sun), housed in the east wing of the former Royal Palace, is disappointing, since the sizeable collection of Bulgarian paintings once displayed was removed several years ago. Today it's used for temporary exhibitions of modern art.

National Museum of Natural History

This rather dry, old-fashioned **museum** (Map pp62-3; ☎ 988 5115; ul Tsar Osvoboditel 1; admission 2 lv; ☻ 10am-6pm) contains a vast collection of animal, plant and mineral specimens (allegedly over one million), though there's very little labelling in anything but Bulgarian. The ground floor holds a display of rocks, crystals and minerals, while on the next two floors you can cast an eye over cases full of tatty-looking stuffed birds and animals, including a brown bear dangling a Nazi hunting medal from its claw and some threadbare apes that would give Edgar Allan Poe the creeps. Also presented for your delectation are jars of pickled fish, reptiles and amphibians, while the topmost floor showcases the museum's extensive collection of desiccated insects. Lining the stairs to each floor are small tanks containing live specimens, such as snakes, lizards and the delightful Madagascan hissing cockroaches.

St Nikolai Russian Church

This gorgeous **church** (Map pp62-3; ul Tsar Osvoboditel) with its glittering mosaic exterior, was built between 1912 and 1914 for the Russian diplomatic and immigrant community, and named in honour of St Nikolai, the 'miracle worker'. Like the Aleksander Nevski Church, the design is strongly influenced by Russian architecture, most notably in its five golden onion domes. The interior features colourful murals and icons painted between the 11th and 14th centuries. Bishop Serafim (1881–1950), one of Bulgaria's most revered spiritual leaders, lies entombed here, and worshippers write their prayers and wishes on pieces of paper to leave beside his monument. Sitting in a flower-filled garden, the church is one of the most photographed sites in the capital.

Church of St Sofia

Originally built in the mid-6th century, during the reign of the Byzantine emperor Justinian the Great, the **Church of St Sofia** (Map pp62-3; ul Panzh) is the oldest Orthodox church in the Bulgarian capital, to which it gave its name. However, the building was heavily damaged by fire and earthquake several times over the centuries, and the present, rather sober, red-brick structure dates largely from the 19th century. Outside stands the **Tomb of the Unknown Soldier**, with its eternal flame and stone lions.

Sveta Petka Samardjiiska Church

This tiny **church** (Map pp62-3; admission 5 lv; ☺ 7am-6pm) is incongruously located in the underpass below the Tsum Retail Centre. Named in honour of St Peter of the Saddlers, the church was built during the early years of Ottoman rule (late 14th century), which explains its sunken profile and inconspicuous exterior. Inside there are some remarkable, but faded, murals painted during the 16th century, but nothing is explained or captioned in any language, and there's little else to justify the admission fee. It is rumoured that the Bulgarian freedom fighter and national icon Vasil Levski is buried here.

Borisova Gradina

This vast park in the southeast of the city is home to the **Vasil Levski Stadium** (Map pp62-3), **CSKA Stadium** (Map pp58-9) and **Maria Luisa Pool** (Map pp58-9; ☎ 963 0054; ☺ 9am-8pm summer), as well as bike tracks and tennis courts. It's Sofia's most pleasant expanse of greenery, laid out with statues and flowerbeds, and it's a relaxing place to take a leisurely stroll on a sunny Sunday afternoon. The eastern end of the park is dominated by a gigantic **communist monument** (Map pp58-9), featuring the usual array of socialist-realist icons: lunging, dramatically gesturing soldiers clutching Kalashnikovs and stocky, stoic workers shaking hands. It has long been neglected by the authorities, and is slowly crumbling away and gaining a coat of graffiti, but small groups of pensioners come on occasion to lay flowers in remembrance of the red old days.

Yuzhen Park

Bul Vitosha leads down to the sprawling **Yuzhen Park** (Southern Park; Map pp62-3), where you'll find the massive National Palace of Culture (NDK) complex (p75). There are a few kiosks and sociable bars here, for those in search of a cheap alfresco beer, as well as carts selling popcorn, candyfloss and other snacks, and you'll also find some children's rides. It's also a favourite venue for Sofia's many skateboarders. At the northern end is the towering and shockingly decrepit **1300 Years Monument** (Map pp62-3), built in 1981 to celebrate the anniversary of the creation of the First Bulgarian Empire. At the time of research, the monument was fenced off and looked about ready to collapse, so don't get too close!

Nearby is a poignant contrast: a **memorial and chapel** (Map pp62-3) to those 'who died in the communist terror' (according to the sign in Bulgarian). Either side of the memorial is a list of 10,000 names, just some of those who died under the communists, and behind it is a register of towns and places where massacres took place.

Steps just in front of the NDK building lead down into an underpass crammed with shops and cafés. Also down here is the United New Cinema (p75).

Sofia City Garden

The **City Garden** (Map pp62-3) is a leafy oasis of calm, with cafés, swings, a stylish newsstand and a lovely fountain where old men gather to play chess. Until its sudden and unceremonious demolition in 1999, the mausoleum of Bulgaria's first communist ruler, Georgi Dimitrov, squatted at the northern end of the park, facing the Royal Palace. It has since been replaced by some shrubbery.

Sofia University Botanic Garden

The **Botanic Garden** (Map pp62-3; ul Moskovska; 1 lv; 10am-6pm Tue-Sun) is a small but well-tended plant collection, which includes a glasshouse filled with palms and cacti, a rose garden and various trees and flowers, labelled in Bulgarian and Latin. There are also some potted plants for sale.

Mineral Baths

The **Mineral Baths** (Map pp62-3; ul Triaditsa) – also known as the Turkish Baths – was built between 1911 and 1913. With its elegant striped façade and ceramic decorations, it's one of Sofia's architectural gems, but it was allowed to fall into dereliction and has been undergoing sporadic restoration for several years. When this restoration will be complete, and what the baths will eventually house, though, is anybody's guess. The hot mineral-water springs that once filled the little square between the baths and the Banya Bashi Mosque have been removed and the area has recently been smartened up with a fountain and lots of benches. A brand new **drinking-fountain complex** has been constructed just behind the baths, where locals fill up their bottles with free steaming mineral water.

Ivan Vazov House Museum

This **museum** (Map pp62-3; ☎ 881 270; ul Ivan Vazov 10; admission 1 lv; 1-6pm Tue-Wed, 1-5pm Thu, 9am-5pm Fri & Sat) is kept as a kind of shrine to Bulgaria's most revered author, whose novel *Under the Yoke* describes the 1876 April Uprising against the Turks. Vazov (1850–1921) lived here from 1895 until his death in 1921, and several rooms have been restored to their early-20th-century appearance. In the study, you can even meet Vazov's beloved pet dog, Bobby, whom Vazov had stuffed after he was run down by a tram. Downstairs, there's a small exhibition of photographs and documents, though labelling is only in Bulgarian. There's a small café attached to the house.

Visitors to the museum are infrequent, and you'll probably have to ring the doorbell to gain admittance.

Museum of Earth & Man

This **museum** (Map pp62-3; ☎ 656 639; ul Cherni Vrâh 4; admission 0.80 lv; 10am-6pm Tue-Sat) holds an extensive but poorly labelled collection of rocks, minerals, crystals and metal ores. This one's mainly for committed geology buffs.

Sofia Municipal Gallery of Art

This **gallery** (Map pp62-3; ☎ 981 2606; ul Gurko 1; admission free; 10am-6pm Tue-Sat, 11am-5pm Sun) at the southern end of the City Garden stages rotating exhibitions of modern Bulgarian art over two floors.

Monument to the Soviet Army

Near the entrance to Borisova Gradina, this giant **monument** (Map pp62–3) was built to commemorate the Russian 'liberation' of Bulgaria in 1944 and is a prime example of the bullish and intimidating socialist-realism of the period. The place of honour goes to a gang of Red Army soldiers atop a column, surrounded by bronze sculptural groups and panels depicting soldiers and workers in dramatic poses.

Banya Bashi Mosque

Sofia's only working **mosque** (Map pp62-3; bul Maria Luisa) was built in 1576 by the Turks. It's certainly an eye-catching edifice and the minaret makes a convenient landmark. At the rear of the building is a small, recently excavated section of the bathhouse that once joined onto the mosque.

Sofia Synagogue

This grand **synagogue** (Map pp62-3; ul Ekzarh Yosif 16) was consecrated in 1909. It is the largest Sephardic synagogue in Europe, and boasts a 2250kg brass chandelier. However, visitors are only welcome if invited or of the Jewish faith.

National Polytechnic Museum

This small **museum** (Map pp58-9; ☎ 931 3004; ul Opalchenska 66; admission 5 lv; 9am-5pm Mon-Fri) is a specialist collection concentrating on the history of technology, with exhibits covering such subjects as photography, TV, radio and time measurement.

Presidency

The Bulgarian president's **office** (Map pp62-3; pl Nezavisimost) occupies the eastern end of the grey, monolithic building which also houses the Sheraton Hotel. It's not open to the public, but the **changing of the guard** ceremony (on the hour) is a spectacle not to be missed, as soldiers in raffish Ruritanian uniforms stomp their way to their sentry boxes.

Sofia Monument

This 24-metre high **monument** (Map pp62-3; bul Maria Luisa) is the city's latest symbol, erected in 2001 on the site where a gigantic statue of Lenin once stood. The bronze female figure at the top of the column represents Sofia, personification of wisdom and fate.

ACTIVITIES

There isn't a great deal in the way of organised activities in Sofia itself. For details about hiking, skiing and other popular activities, see Vitosha National Park (p80).

Golf

A round of golf is possible at this **Air Sofia Golf Club** (☎ 0724-3530; bul 6 Septemvri, Ihtiman; 8am-10pm), about 55km southeast of Sofia at Ihtiman. The course may not be exceptional, but expats and wealthy Bulgarians also enjoy the club's swimming pool, horse riding, and tennis, basketball and squash courts. Contact the club for bookings and current costs.

Bowling

The **Mega Xtreme Bowling Center** (☎ 969 2601; ul Stefanov 12, Studentski Grad; per game 3-5 lv; 10am-4am) is a vast, state-of-the-art complex featuring

an 18-lane bowling alley, pool tables, a disco with live music Friday and Saturday nights and even a supermarket. To get there, catch minibus No 7 from bul Maria Luisa.

Bungee Jumping

If you feel like throwing yourself off something high, you might like to contact the **Sofian Bungi Club** (☎ 945 6229) which arranges bungee jumps in Sofia and the surrounds for 15 to 30 lv. Phone ahead for bookings.

WALKING TOUR

Fortunately, most of Sofia's attractions are in the city centre and easily accessible on foot. Allow most of the day to fully appreciate the best of what the city has to offer.

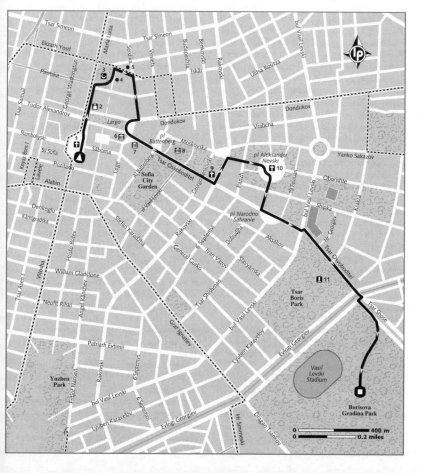

Start outside the magnificent **Sveta Nedelya Cathedral** (**1**; p64) and head north, past the **Tsum Retail Centre** (**2**; p76), to the **Banya Bashi Mosque** (**3**; p66). Walk through the pleasant little square at the back of the mosque and see how repairs are progressing on the dilapidated **Mineral Baths** (**4**; p65). Cross the road and turn right on ul Ekzarh Yosif to get to the **drinking fountains** (**5**; p66); bring a bottle to fill with mineral water.

Continue southeast on ul Serdika, emerging on the eastern end of pl Nezavisimost, facing the colossal Party House. Cross over to the **Presidency** (**6**; p66) where you can witness the changing of the guard ceremony. Just opposite, the **Archaeological Museum** (**7**; p61) holds some of Sofia's greatest treasures. Follow the yellow brick road (bul Tsar Osvoboditel), and admire the lemon-hued grandeur of the former Royal Palace which now houses the **Ethnographical Museum** (**8**; p61), perhaps stopping for a coffee, or something stronger, at Toba & Co round the back. Carry on eastwards, past the glittering glory of the **Russian Church** (**9**; p64). Cross ul Rakovski (be very careful of the traffic!) and you'll see pl Aleksander Nevski, dominated by the awesome bulk of the **Aleksander Nevski Memorial Church** (**10**; p61).

Head south onto pl Narodno Sabranie and continue in a southeasterly direction, stopping to take in the immense, socialist-realist **Monument to the Soviet Army** (**11**; p66). Just beyond this, you'll cross the dinky Eagles Bridge which spans the unassuming stream-like trickle known, rather grandly, as the River Perlovska. You'll then come upon the entrance to the vast Borisova Gradina, where you can rest your feet, sitting on one of the many benches beneath the horse-chestnut trees.

COURSES

Kibea Health Centre (Map pp62-3; ☎ 988 0193; www.kibea.net; in Kibea Restaurant, ul Valkovich 2a) Nutritional Healing courses can be followed here. Three- to five-day courses, in English, start at €150, and cover various aspects of nutritional science.

Sofia University (Map pp62-3; ☎ 710 069; www.deo.uni-sofia.bg; bul Tsar Osvoboditel) Bulgarian language courses for foreigners are offered by the university. One-to-one courses cost €100 for 20 hours tuition; group courses cost €60 per person for 20 hours. Classes in Bulgarian culture, dance and folklore are also offered; the standard three-week course costs €220.

SOFIA FOR CHILDREN

Sofia has few obvious attractions for children, but you could try the following:

Sofia Land (Map pp58-9; ☎ 962 1111; www.sofialand.bg; bul Nikola Vaptsarov; attractions 1-3 lv, all-day ticket 15 lv; ☉ 11am-7pm Mon-Fri, 10am-7pm Sat & Sun) The main attraction is undoubtedly the city's unimaginatively named new theme park, located between Yuzhen Park and Borisova Gradina. It has all the usual fairground attractions such as merry-go-rounds, rides, Ferris wheels, dodgems, a shooting gallery, maze and trampolines, as well as a cinema (tickets 2 to 5 lv).

Sofia Zoo (Map pp58-9; ☎ 962 0449; bul Simeon ovsko Shosse; admission 0.50 lv; ☉ 9am-5pm) Nearby is the zoo, which is looking a little dated these days. There's very little shade, but it does have a few play areas for children, and a couple of simple cafés. It's free for children under seven years old.

Play areas can also be found in Borisova Gradina, which has wide open green spaces that young children might enjoy. Their older siblings might prefer a game of bowls at Mega Xtreme Bowling Center (p67). There are no reliable baby-sitting agencies working with foreign tourists, although some top-end hotels may be able to provide such services.

TOURS

There's little point taking an organised tour around Sofia unless you're really pressed for time; almost everything to see in Sofia is accessible on foot, and other attractions at Boyana and Mt Vitosha, for example, are easy to reach by public transport or taxi.

The magnificent Rila Monastery (p91) is awkward to visit in one day by public transport from Sofia, so an organised tour is not a bad idea. However, renting a car, or even chartering a taxi, for the day will probably be cheaper for a group of two to four people and will certainly be more flexible. For details about renting cars and hiring taxis, see p267.

The following companies offer tours in and around Sofia for foreigners.

Alexander Tour (Map pp62-3; ☎ /fax 983 3322; www.alexandertour.com; ul Pop Bogomil 44) An upmarket outfit offering numerous tours all over Bulgaria, including bird-watching, archaeology and wine tours.

Alma Tours (Map pp62-3; ☎ 986 5691; almatour@dir.bg; bul Stamboliyski 27) Runs day trips to Rila costing

€69/54 per person for a group of two/four people; day trips to Koprivshtitsa cost €63/54 per person and three-hour guided walking tours around Sofia cost €20/15 per person. Multiday trips (including accommodation) run to destinations such as Veliko Târnovo, Plovdiv and Smolyan. Prices decrease for larger groups.

Balkantourist (Map pp62-3; ☎ 987 5192; www .balkantourist.bg; ul Sveta Sofia 2) The original monolithic government organisation, Balkantourist is now privatised, and offers all sorts of midpriced tours.

Eurotours (Map pp58-9; ☎ 931 1500; basement, central train station) Offers various day trips by car, including tours to Rila Monastery for around €60. The cost is per car, seating up to four people.

Odysseia-In Travel Agency (Map pp62-3; ☎ 989 0538; www.odysseia-in.com; 1st fl, bul Stamboliyski 20-V, enter from ul Lavele) Larger groups should contact this agency, upstairs from Zig Zag, who offer multiday activities such as snowshoeing in Rila National Park (€540 per person for eight days full-board, including equipment, in a group of six to nine people).

Tourist Service (TUI; Map pp58-9; ☎ 832 4032; ul Klokotnitsa 1) Opposite the Princess Hotel, the TUI runs three-hour tours by car around Sofia (€25 per person) and 'folkloric evenings' of music, food and dance (€55). Other day trips, which include lunch, go to Rila Monastery (€75) and Plovdiv and Bachkovo Monastery (€85).

Zig Zag Holidays (Map pp62-3; ☎ 980 5102; www .zigzag.dir.bg; bul Stamboliyski 20-V) Offers all sorts of tailor-made outdoor activities, including hiking, climbing, caving and biking trips, with an emphasis on environmentally sustainable tourism. They run day trips to Rila Monastery and Koprivshtitsa (both €90), as well as walking tours of Sofia (€36). Prices are for groups of up to three.

FESTIVALS & EVENTS

Sofia International Film Festival (www.cinema .bg/sff) Movie buffs descend on the capital each March.

Sofia International Folklore Festival Takes place in and around the capital for five days in late August.

Sofia Fest (about 14-18 Sep) Includes cultural events, concerts and exhibits held at various galleries and museums, as well as the Church of St Sofia.

St Sofia's Day (17 Sep) Widely celebrated in the capital. St Sofia is the Mother of Hope, Love and Faith.

SLEEPING

As you might expect, accommodation in Sofia tends to be more expensive than anywhere else in Bulgaria, with prices at many establishments comparable to those in Western Europe, and in recent years there has been a surge in the number of top-end hotels. Fortunately for budget travellers, Sofia now has several modern, good-quality hostels, although there is nowhere to camp in the immediate vicinity. Note that most places now quote prices in euros, though of course you can also pay in leva. The website www.sofiahotels.net lists many city hotels and offers various promotions.

Budget
HOSTELS

Over the last few years, several good-value, modern hostels have sprung up around Sofia. Most are quite small, though, and advance bookings in summer are advisable.

Hostel Mostel (Map pp62-3; ☎ 889 223 296; www .hostelmostel.com; ul Denkoglu 2; dm/d €10/30; P ☐) Highly recommended by several readers for its friendly atmosphere and helpful staff, Mostel has six- and eight-bed dorms, and the price includes breakfast, a beer and a pasta meal (though hopefully not all at the same time). Free pick ups from the bus and train stations are offered, as are day trips for guests. There's a 10% discount on stays of more than two nights, and if you're just looking for a bare bed to lay your sleeping bag, it's yours for €5.

Hostel Kervan (Map pp62-3; ☎ 983 9428; www .kervanhostel.com; ul Rositza 3; dm/d incl breakfast €10/15; ☐) Kervan is a recent addition to Sofia's hostel scene, and offers clean, simple rooms with stripped wood floors. There's an unlimited supply of free tea and coffee. Bike rental costs €10 per day and various day trips can be organised.

Hostel Turisticheska Spalnya (Map pp62-3; ☎ 983 6181; www.ts-hostel.com; ul Tsar Simeon 63; dm/d from €9/14) This bright, clean hostel is in a great central location, and offers pleasant, high-ceilinged dorms of between three and five beds, as well as a double room, and modern bathrooms.

Internet Hostel Sofia (Map pp62-3; ☎ 989 9419; interhostel@yahoo.co.uk; 2nd fl, ul Alabin 50a; dm/d incl breakfast from €8/13; ☐) One of Sofia's newest hostels, this very central place is just off bul Vitosha and offers clean, modern rooms (no bunks). There's free coffee and tea, cable TV, communal kitchen and laundry service.

Art Hostel (Map pp62-3; ☎ 987 0545; www.art -hostel.com; ul Angel Kânchev 21a; dm incl breakfast €10; ☐) This bohemian hostel stages art exhibitions, drama performances, live music and more during the summer. It has a garden at the back. Accommodation consists of a couple of small dorms (one en suite) plus summer-only 'basic accommodation' (ie a sleeping bag on the floor) for €5. There's also a communal kitchen. It's starting to look a bit scruffy compared with some of Sofia's newer hostels, but is certainly a unique place to stay. ISIC and HI cardholders get a 10% discount.

Red Star Hostel (Map pp62-3; ☎ 986 3341; ul Angel Kânchev 6; dm/tr €10/30) This small hostel, under the same management as the Internet Hostel (earlier), has just a few rooms in an apartment block off pl Slaveikov. It's clean and handily located, though staff don't speak a word of English.

Sofia Hostel (Map pp62-3; ☎ /fax 989 8582; hostel_sofia@usa.net; ul Pozitano 16; dm incl breakfast €8) This hostel offers basic accommodation, and a communal kitchen and lounge. It's a friendly, sociable place and the staff speak English and French. They also offer free Bulgarian lessons. It's above a Chinese restaurant, but is not well signposted.

PRIVATE ROOMS
Sofia has plenty of private rooms available to foreign tourists, including many in the city centre. These usually offer a much better deal than Sofia's few budget hotels. The accommodation agency at the airport is rarely staffed, but may be worth checking out if you arrive by air.

Eurotours (Map pp58-9; ☎ 931 1500) This friendly agency in the basement of the central train station offers rooms from around €10 per person.

THE AUTHOR'S CHOICE

Hotel Maya (Map pp62-3; ☎ 980 2796; 2nd fl, ul Trapezitsa 4; s/d/tr €15/20/30) This very central and friendly guesthouse, presided over by a chatty but non-English speaking landlady, has large, comfortable rooms, all with TV and minibar; one has a superb view over the Sofia Monument. The bathrooms are detached but private (you have a key), and there is one en-suite double (€25). One unexpected bonus is the rooftop terrace, with a well-stocked bar and plenty of seats, and there's an ancient, rattling lift to save your leg muscles. It's excellent value, and has lots of character.

Zig Zag Holidays (Map pp62-3; ☎ 980 5102; www.zigzag.dir.bg; bul Stamboliyski 20-V) Arranges rooms with a shared bathroom in private homes. Singles cost €15 to €18, doubles €24 to €30, including breakfast.

Markela Accommodation Agency (Map pp62-3; ☎ 980 4925; www.markela.hit.bg; 1st fl, ul Ekzarh Yosif 35; s/d with shared bathroom from 25/32 lv) This is run by helpful English-speaking staff who can show you photos of the rooms on offer.

Alma Tours (Map pp62-3; ☎ 986 5691; almatour@dir.bg; bul Stamboliyski 27) Pricier single/double central rooms for €16/20.

Olga Rooms (Map pp62-3; ☎ 980 9818; 3rd fl, bul Stamboliyski 27b; s/d €9/18) Olga's is typical of the private rooms on offer in Sofia. There's just one, cosy room in a very central apartment block, and Olga, an ebullient, retired Ukrainian engineer, will cook you up a filling breakfast at no extra charge.

The website www.sofiaapartments.com offers one-bedroom apartments around town from €40 per night.

HOTELS
Good-quality budget hotels are scarce in Sofia. The cheap hotels that cluster around the top end of bul Maria Luisa, in the vicinity of the Lions Bridge and towards the train station, are often pretty squalid and best avoided – private rooms or hostels are a much better deal.

Hotel Central (Map pp62-3; ☎ 983 7332; 3rd fl, ul Serdika 19; r 33 lv) This small guesthouse – not to be confused with the four-star hotel of the same name (opposite) – is clean, central and very good value. The large rooms have a TV and three or four beds, and are ideal for anyone travelling in a small group. However, it can get a bit noisy if there's a full house.

Hotel Enny (Map pp62-3; ☎ 983 1649; ul Pop Bogomil 46; s 40 lv, s/d with bathroom 50/80 lv) The Enny is a neat, quiet place, but a little overpriced, and some rooms, especially the singles, are small. On the other hand, the outdoor courtyard area is a great place to relax. It's well signposted from bul Mara Luisa.

Mid-Range
Hotel Niky (Map pp62-3; ☎ 952 3058; fax 951 6091; ul Neofit Rilski 16; s/d/ste from €30/40/50; P ✗) Offering excellent value and a good city-centre location, Niky is a modern, recently refurbished place with smart, comfortable

rooms and gleaming bathrooms, as well as a communal garden and restaurant. Suites all come with microwave ovens, fridges and tea- and coffee-making facilities.

Hotel Serdika (Map pp62-3; ☎ 846 5485; www .serdikahotel.com; bul Yanko Sakazov 2; s/d/ste Mon-Thu from €51/69/85, Fri-Sun from €45/64/77; P ☒ ☐) Overlooking the Vasil Levski Memorial, the Serdika is a vast edifice on a particularly busy road junction. It has perfectly decent, if unremarkable rooms, but the price is good for this class of hotel in Sofia. There are also a couple of restaurants on site.

Hotel Light (Map pp62-3; ☎ 917 9090; www.hotel light.com; ul Veslets 37; s/d/ste from €75/99/129; P ☒) One of the newest and best hotels in this somewhat scruffy part of town, Hotel Light is a bright, friendly place offering all the expected mod cons. The comfortable rooms all come with modem connections, minibars, electronic safes and smart bathrooms, and there's a gym and restaurant. The hotel runs a free shuttle service to the airport. Discounts are often available.

Hotel Lozenetz (Map pp58-9; ☎ 965 4444; www.loz enetzhotel.com; ul Sveti Naum 23; s/d €60/80; P ☒ ☐) This modern hotel south of the city centre has fresh and contemporary rooms, all with TV and minibar, and represents good value for the capital. There's a decent restaurant on site, and free Internet access for guests. Weekend discounts are available.

Art'Otel (Map pp62-3; ☎ 980 6000; www.artotel .biz; ul William Gladstone 44; d/ste from €90/145; P ☒) Tucked down a narrow, traffic-clogged side-street off bul Vitosha, this stylish modern hotel has 22 spacious rooms with bright bathrooms. In keeping with its name, there are contemporary artworks dotted around the building. There's also a good restaurant attached.

Princess Hotel (Map pp58-9; ☎ 933 8888; bul Maria Luisa 131; s/d from €90/110; P ☒ ☒ ☒) This gigantic place claims to be the biggest hotel in the Balkans and, with over 600 rooms, who's to argue? Rooms are comfy and spacious and top-notch facilities include a gym, sauna, massage parlour, tourist agency and shops. Size really does matter here, and the hotel also encompasses Bulgaria's biggest casino. It's convenient for the train and bus stations, but it's rather bland and, a little disturbingly, everyone entering the building has to pass through a metal detector.

Hotel Central (Map pp58-9; ☎ 981 2364; www .central-hotel.com; bul Hristo Botev 52; s/d/ste from €65/ 80/120; ☒) The Central is a classy, contemporary business hotel just west of the city centre. Rooms are neat, clean and comfortable, though it's a little lacking in character. Weekend discounts of between 10% and 20% are available.

Hotel Sveta Sofia (Map pp62-3; ☎ 981 2634; www .svetasofia-alexanders.com; ul Pirotska 18; s/d €62/72; P ☒) This new three-star hotel-cum-restaurant on the busy pedestrianised ul Pirotska has plain but cosy rooms, all with TVs, minibars and up-to-date bathrooms. Weekend and long-stay discounts are on offer.

Hotel Ametist (Map pp62-3; ☎ 983 5475; ul Tsar Simeon 67; s/d/tr incl breakfast from €38/50/70; P) This is a quiet, modern place in a good location, just round the corner from the Central Hali. Rooms are fairly plain, but all have TVs. It has its own restaurant.

Sun Hotel (Map pp62-3; ☎ 983 3670; sunhotel@tech no-link.com; bul Maria Luisa 89; s/d/tr/ste €45/59/74/100) This well-kept hotel in a renovated 19th-century building near the Lions Bridge is one of the smarter establishments in this area. It's handy for the central train and bus stations, but not so convenient for the sights. Rooms are small but clean and functional, and all have TVs and minibars. The hotel also has a piano bar and a pastry shop.

Hotel Baldjieva (Map pp62-3; ☎ 987 2914; baldjieva@abv.bg; ul Tsar Asen I 23; s/d/tr incl breakfast €48/58/68; ☒) This pleasant three-star hotel is in an excellent spot. The comfortable, pine-furnished rooms have fans and TVs but are small and rather plain.

Tsar Asen Hotel (Map pp58-9; ☎ 547 801; elena@ mbox.infotel.bg; ul Tsar Asen I 68; s/d €25/40; P) On a quiet suburban street, the Tsar Asen offers clean and comfortable rooms with TVs, but it only has four rooms, so book ahead. Breakfast costs an extra €2 per person.

Hotel Rodina (Map pp58-9; ☎ 917 9999; www .rodina.bg; bul Gen Totleben 8; s/d/ste Mon-Thu €80/90/110, Fri-Sun €65/80/100; ☒ P ☒ ☐) The high-rise Rodina needs to be dragged out of the 1970s and it's awkwardly placed, at a busy road junction, but it has excellent facilities, including a sauna, gym, four restaurants, bars and a nightclub.

Hotel Pop Bogomil (Map pp62-3; ☎ 983 7065; hotelpopbogomil@dir.bg; ul Pop Bogomil 5; d from €37; P) This small hotel has 10 clean and comfy rooms, all individually decorated.

It's handy enough for the central train and bus stations, though a little out of the way for anything else.

Top End

Sofia certainly has no shortage of top-end accommodation, at international prices, although most offer better-value weekend rates.

Hilton Sofia (Map pp58-9; ☎ 933 5000; www.sofia .hilton.com; bul Bâlgaria 1; d Mon-Thu from €245, Fri-Sun from €130; P ⊠ ⊠) The Hilton is a huge glassy structure rising up just behind the NDK, and offering all the international five-star facilities you would expect, including a gym, sauna, restaurants and shops.

Grand Hotel Sofia (Map pp62-3; ☎ 811 0811; www .grandhotelsofia.bg; ul General Gurko 1; d/ste Mon-Thu from €240/390, s/d Fri-Sun from €135/150; P ⊠ ⊠) Sofia's newest five-star hotel is a soaring 109-room glass and granite affair at the southern edge of the City Garden. It's a stylish place, with uniformed doormen and lots of marble, and the large rooms are fitted with the latest mod cons. Facilities include a fitness centre, a couple of restaurants, bars, boutiques and a café.

Hotel Crystal Palace (Map pp62-3; ☎ 948 9488; www.crystalpalace-sofia.com; ul Shipka 14; s/d from €120/140; P ⊠ ⊡) The Crystal Palace is another new luxury hotel, and an unusual architectural mix of 19th-century classicism and (you guessed it) 21st-century glass. It has good-sized, tastefully decorated rooms, some with balconies, and all have modem connections, TVs and minibars.

Radisson SAS Grand Hotel (Map pp62-3; ☎ 933 4334; www.radissonsas.com; pl Narodno Sabranie 4; r Mon-Fri from €207, s/d Sat & Sun from €144/162; P ⊠ ⊠) This big glass curve facing the parliament building is ideally placed and offers the high standards you would expect from this international chain. Rooms are large and tastefully decorated, and there's a gym, a couple of restaurants, an 'Irish' pub, a casino and a nightclub.

Sheraton Sofia Hotel Balkan (Map pp62-3; ☎ 981 6541; www.luxurycollection.com/sofia; pl Sveta Nedelya 5; d/ste from €300/420; P ⊠ ⊠) This imposing Sofian landmark is the epitome of luxury. Marble floors, gigantic chandeliers and large, elegantly furnished rooms provide the perfect setting for the Prada-clad jet set, and you can even have your own private butler. The official rates are startlingly high,

and the bar menu seems to be under the delusion that it's in Mayfair rather than Sofia, but sizeable discounts are frequently available.

Hotel Downtown (Map pp62-3; ☎ 930 5200; www .hotel-downtown.net; bul Vasil Levski 27; d/ste from €120/ 160; P ⊠ ⊠) Downtown is another of Sofia's new generation of gleaming, upscale business hotels (at upscale prices) offering a high standard of comfort and great facilities, including a well-equipped fitness centre. Rooms are tastefully furnished and have modem connections and satellite TVs.

EATING

Compared to the rest of Bulgaria, Sofia is gourmet heaven, with an unrivalled range of international cuisines represented and new, quality restaurants springing up all the time. It also has more than its share of snack bars, fast-food outlets and cafés dotted across town. The places listed here are among the best in terms of quality, ambience or value for money. For up-to-date information and reviews in English, check out the relevant section at www.sofiaecho.com.

Bulgarian Restaurants

Krim (Map pp62-3; ☎ 981 0666; ul Slavyanska 17; mains 7-10 lv) Krim offers Bulgarian, Russian and French cuisine in several elegant rooms of a restored early-20th-century house, or outdoors in the summer garden. It's a clubby, upmarket place, with a formal air.

Background (Map pp62-3; ☎ 986 3529; bul Vitosha 14; mains 5-20 lv) There's a wide choice of pasta, salads and traditional roast meats on offer at this little courtyard pub-restaurant, and the menu is in English. There's also a cosy cellar if you don't fancy eating outdoors.

Trops Kâshta (Map pp62-3; bul Maria Luisa; mains 2-4 lv; ⏱ 8am-9pm) There are several branches of this cheap cafeteria around town, offering traditional Bulgarian meat 'n' veg dishes. Although the menu isn't written in English, you can just point at whatever takes your fancy and trust to luck. Best to get here early, as the more popular items get snapped up and the remainders get cold.

International Restaurants

Fox & Hound (Map pp62-3; ☎ 980 7427; ul Angel Kantchev 34; mains 4-10 lv) As you might have guessed, this is an English-style pub-restaurant, replete with polished wood and

The buildings and gardens of Sofia (p55)

Sveta Nedelya Cathedral
(p64), Sofia

Overleaf:
St Nikolai Russian Church
(p64), Sofia

Vendors selling vegetables at the market in Sofia
(p74)

horsey décor. Predictably, the menu features fish and chips, jacket potatoes and English breakfasts, and there's also a big cocktail list. Try not to sit too near the toilets, though.

Kibea Health Food Restaurant (Map pp62-3; ☎ 980 3067; ul Valkovich 2a; mains 5.80-9.20 lv) Possibly the only restaurant in Bulgaria to completely ban smoking, this modish place offers a refreshingly different menu of mostly vegan dishes, such as polenta with rosemary and white beans. Some of the prices are a little high, such as 4 lv for a coffee, but it makes a welcome change for your tastebuds. There's a bookshop and 'health centre' downstairs, including a shop selling healthy organic products.

Pizza Troll (pizzas 3-10 lv; bul Vitosha (Map pp62-3; ☼ 24hr); pl Slaveikov 6a (Map pp62-3; ☎ 980 6659; ☼ 8am-midnight) This cheery pizzeria serves up a lengthy menu of good quality pizzas as well as plenty of chicken and fish dishes, such as salmon in saffron sauce, if you're not keen on melted cheese.

Taj Mahal (Map pp62-3; ☎ 987 3632; ul Rakov-ski 181; mains 5-9 lv) This cosy place serves up good-quality Indian dishes, including vegetarian options, at reasonable prices. The food is authentic and the service attentive, but it's quite small, so booking ahead is a good idea in the evenings. It's not the easiest place to find either, tucked away in a courtyard off ul Rakovski; look out for the solitary sign high above the archway.

Nine Dragons (Map pp62-3; ☎ 981 8878; bul Tsar Osvoboditel 8a; mains 5-10 lv) This upstairs restaurant directly opposite the Russian Church serves tasty Chinese food in pleasant surrounds. It might not be entirely authentic, but the portions are huge and the service is quick and friendly.

Tambuktu (☎ 988 1234; ul Aksakov 10; mains 6-20 lv; ☼ 10am-2am) This big brash place specialises in seafood, with a menu full of fish and crustaceans, cooked in a variety of ways.

Happy Bar & Grill (Map pp62-3; ☎ 980 7353; pl Sveta Nedelya 4; mains 4-8 lv) This big branch of the nationwide chain offers a reliable menu of salads and grills in a great location. You can sit outside and watch the sports channels on the numerous silent TVs, or inside among the Planet Hollywood–style mess of movie posters and musical instruments, while smiley, microskirted waitresses flit between the tables. It gets very busy in the evenings.

Restaurant Peter I (☎ 980 6577; ul Pozitano 2; mains 7-20 lv) This slightly kitschy Russian restaurant is in a cellar plastered with portraits of Tsar Peter the Great, just off bul Vitosha. The extensive menu, in English, offers palatable Russian- and Ukrainian-inspired chicken, fish and pork dishes. Service is impeccable and there's occasional live music in the evenings.

Cafés

In summer, cafés seem to occupy every piece of garden and footpath in Sofia. Some are just basic spots for a coffee and a sandwich, while others offer a more refined setting for cocktails and cakes. Most cafés are open from about 8am to midnight.

Club Lavazza (Map pp62-3; ☎ 987 3433; bul Vitosha 13; mains 6-8 lv) A chic spot to sip a cappuccino or a Manhattan, Lavazza also offers a brief food menu, including 'English' and 'Continental' breakfasts. It gets very smoky though.

Cafe Theatre (Map pp62-3; ul Vasil Levski; cakes from 2.50 lv) Facing the imposing Ivan Vazov National Theatre, this summer-only pavement café is one of the most attractive in town, abutting the City Garden. It mainly sells drinks and cakes.

Cafe de Sofi (Map pp62-3; ul Pirotska; cakes from 2.50 lv) This is another pleasant summer

---

THE AUTHOR'S CHOICE

Pri Yafata (Map pp62-3; ☎ 980 1727; cnr ul Solunska & ul Tsar Assen; mains 5-15 lv; ☼ 10am-midnight) For the best Bulgarian cuisine in the capital, Pri Yafata is hard to beat. It's a big place, done out as a traditional *mehana* (tavern), with agricultural tools, rifles, *chergas* (patterned rugs), paintings of 19th-century Bulgarian *haidouks* (outlaws) and other rustic reminders adorning the walls. Hearty dishes of duck, rabbit, pork and chicken are on the lengthy menu, which also includes plenty of vegetarian options – the monastery salad (tomatoes, spinach, peppers, stuffed vine-leaves, onions and more; 4.90 lv) is particularly excellent – and portions are huge. There are also plenty of wines to sample. It's a very popular place, and reservations are advisable for the evenings, which regularly feature live music and 'folklore' shows.

outdoor café beside the Central Hali, which makes a handy pit stop for drinks and snacks.

Toba & Co (Map pp62-3; ☎ 989 4696; ul Moskovska 6; snacks from 3 lv) Hidden away in the gardens at the back of the Royal Palace, this discreet café is a relaxing spot to indulge in one of the many inventive cocktails on offer, as well as ice cream and cakes. Occasional live music in the evenings.

Lobby Bar (Map pp62-3; inside Central Hali; pastries from 2 lv) This 'French-style' bar in the Hali (complete with white-aproned waiters) is a good place to stop for a drink. Croissants, pastries, quiche and other snacks are on offer.

Quick Eats

There are plenty of kiosks around town where you can buy tasty local fast food such as *banitsas* (cheese pasties) and *palachinki* (pancakes), as well as the inevitable hot dogs and burgers.

Goody's (Map pp62-3; ☎ 980 8847; pl Sveta Nedelya 3; mains 3-5 lv) This giant fast-food outlet next to the Happy Bar & Grill offers a range of cheap and filling meals including salads, club sandwiches and plenty of burgers. Photos of menu items are displayed behind the counter but there is no labelling in English.

Dunkin' Donuts (Map pp62-3; ☎ 933 9999; bul Vitosha 25; doughnuts around 0.30 lv) This slice of sugary Americana is the place to go if you're hankering for a Boston Creme and a coffee. There's also a takeaway counter and delivery service.

Central Hali Shopping Centre (bul Maria Luisa 25) There are several outlets in the upstairs food court in this market complex (see p75) Centres selling cheap fast food such as kebabs, pizzas and ice cream.

Self-Catering

All manner of consumables can be yours at the Central Hali (Map pp62–3), while the Ladies' Market (Map pp62–3) and the stalls (Map pp62–3) along ul Graf Ignatiev (outside the Sveti Sedmochislenitsi Church) offer an abundance of fresh fruit and veg. Branches of Bonjour Supermarket (Map pp62–3) and Oasis Supermarket (Map pp62–3), at the northern end of the Tsum shopping centre, are the places to go for everything else.

DRINKING

There's a seemingly inexhaustible supply of watering holes all over Sofia. The cheapest places to grab a beer are the kiosks in the city's parks; if you're looking for a more sophisticated ambience, the city centre has an increasing number of trendy new bars.

Buddha Bar (Map pp62-3; ☎ 989 5006; ul Lege 15a; ☯ 24hr) Very hip, very trendy and very crowded, this Buddha-bedecked drinking spot also serves food, and has a nightly disco from around 9pm.

Svejk Pub (Map pp62-3; ☎ 988 8240; bul Vitosha 1a) Although a bit dark and smoky, this is an ideal place to head for in cold weather. It offers about the widest range of beers in the city as well as meals every day and live music on weekends.

Exit (Map pp62-3; ☎ 0887 965 026; ul Lavele 16) This modern and fashionable bar-diner is one of Sofia's latest gay venues, with a DJ party every evening.

Sofia also has its share of 'Irish' pubs, frequented by expats knocking back overpriced imported beers and stouts. These include **JJ Murphy's** (Map pp62-3; ☎ 980 2870; ul Kärnigradska 6) and the **Irish Harp** (Map pp62-3; ☎ 989 8737; ul Sveta Sofia 7), which offers live music and satellite TV showing international football matches.

ENTERTAINMENT

The 'Culture Shock' supplement of *The Sofia Echo* lists current cinema offerings and concerts. If you read Bulgarian, or can find someone who does, *Programata* is a much more comprehensive source of listings; otherwise check out its excellent English-language website, www.programata.bg.

Nightclubs

Some clubs charge a nominal admission fee, mostly late at night and on weekends.

Jazzy (Map pp62-3; ☎ 0888 479 191; www.be-jazzy.com; ul San Stefano 33; ☯ 10am-4am) This trendy, relatively new nightspot hosts live bands and DJ parties, with a mix of house, rock, Latino and Bulgarian music. Check the website for current schedules.

Checkpoint Charly (Map pp62-3; ☎ 988 0370; ul Ivan Vazov 12) This cool club functions as a restaurant during the day and stages live jazz music on Friday, Saturday and Sunday nights after 10pm.

Spartacus (Map pp62-3; ☎ 955 1279; Sofia University underpass; ⏱ 6.30pm-late Mon-Thu, 11.30pm-late Fri & Sat) Sofia's recently revamped gay club attracts a mixed crowd most nights, with discos on Friday and Saturday. Go-go dancers and drag queens liven up the Balkan evenings.

Chervilo (Map pp62-3; ☎ 981 6633; bul Tsar Osvo–boditel 9) The live music, guest DJs and themed party nights at 'Lipstick' draw in Sofia's young and fashionable set nightly. It also has a pleasant terrace for sitting, sipping cocktails and being seen.

Cinemas

Sofia has around 20 cinemas screening recent English-language films (with Bulgarian subtitles), although note that cartoons and children's films are sometimes dubbed into Bulgarian. Most tickets cost 3 to 5 lv, depending on the comfort of the seats and the times of the sessions.

United New Cinema (Map pp62-3; ☎ 951 5101; tickets 5-10 lv) The most modern and comfortable cinema is the United New Cinema, also called the Multiplex, in the underpass below the NDK. It shows recent Hollywood releases on several screens. The individual theatres are quite small, though, so it's a good idea to buy your ticket in advance.

Others include the **Euro-Bulgarian Cultural Centre** (Map pp62-3; ☎ 988 0084; bul Stamboliyski 17), **Kino Yalta** (Map pp62-3; ☎ 981 6530; Sofia University underpass) and **Dom Na Kinoto** (Map pp62-3; ☎ 980 3911; ul Ekzarh Yosif 37), which mainly shows Bulgarian-language and art-house films.

Theatre & Music

National Opera House (Map pp62-3; ☎ 987 1366; ul Vrabcha 1; ticket office ⏱ 8.30am-7.30pm) The best that Bulgaria has to offer is frequently on show inside this impressive building. Performances normally begin at about 7pm, but are held only on Tuesday and Saturday at 9pm in summer (June to September).

National Palace of Culture (NDK; Map pp62-3; ☎ 916 6369; Yuzhen Park; ticket office ⏱ 9am-7pm) The NDK (as it's usually called) has 15 halls and is easily the country's largest cultural complex. It maintains a regular programme of events in summer (when most other theatres in Sofia are closed) and offers a wide range of shows throughout the year; previous featured artists have included the Buena Vista Social Club and Jerry Lee Lewis.

Other worthwhile cultural events are held at the **Bulgaria Hall** (Map pp62-3; ☎ 987 7656; ul Aksakov 1), the home of the excellent Sofia Philharmonic Orchestra; and the baroque-style, early-20th-century **Ivan Vazov National Theatre** (Map pp62-3; ☎ 987 4831; ul Vasil Levski 5), home to the National Theatre Company.

Sport

Football (soccer) is Bulgaria's main sporting passion, and Sofia alone has four teams. The main clubs are **CSKA** (☎ 963 3477), which plays at the CSKA Stadium (Map pp58–9) in Borisova Gradina and **Levski** (☎ 989 2156), based at the Georgi Asparoukhov Stadium (bul Vladimir Vazov, Poduyane). Lokomotiv and Slavia are Sofia's two smaller teams.

The **Vasil Levski Stadium** (Map pp62-3; ☎ 988 5030; Borisova Gradina) is the city's main venue for various sports.

SHOPPING

Bul Vitosha is Sofia's main shopping street, although the pricey international boutiques that dominate it are unlikely to be of huge interest to visitors. More shops cluster along ul Graf Ignatiev, while ul Pirotska is a central pedestrian mall lined with cheaper shops selling clothes, shoes, household goods and music. Street stalls and markets are the best places to seek souvenirs.

Camping & Skiing Equipment

Stenata (Map pp62-3; ☎ 980 5491; ul Tsar Samuil 63) This is the best place to buy hiking and climbing equipment, tents, mattresses and sleeping bags, but it doesn't hire gear.

Orion Ski Shop (Map pp62-3; ☎ 986 4157; inside arcade along ul Pozitano) This shop sells (but does not rent) all sorts of new and second-hand ski gear.

Markets & Shopping Centres

Central Hali Shopping Centre (Map pp62-3; ☎ 917 6106; bul Maria Luisa 25; ⏱ 7am-midnight) This covered market hall, built in 1911 but totally refurbished in 2000, has three floors of shops and cafés. Stalls on the ground floor sell a wide array of produce, including fruit, vegetables, pastries, wine, meat and cheese, as well as one selling nothing but olives. You'll also find the attractive Lobby Bar (p74) here. Upstairs there's a food court and more shops while there's a restaurant in the basement. The centre also holds a pharmacy, a bank and ATMs. Despite the posted opening times, the place is usually closed before 10pm.

Tsum Retail Centre (Map pp62-3; ☎ 953 3133; bul Maria Luisa; ☯ 10am-8pm Mon-Sat, 11am-5.30pm Sun) Sofia's main temple to Western consumerism is housed in the former all-in-one state department store. It has five floors of bright modern shops selling brand-name clothes, perfumes, porcelain and jewellery among other things, at prices beyond the reach of most Sofians. There's a coffee shop, banks and a newsstand where you can pick up international newspapers and magazines.

Ladies Market (Map pp62-3; ul Stefan Stambolov; ☯ from 7am) The 'Zhenski Pazar' stretches several blocks along a street between ul Ekzarh Yosif and bul Slivnitsa. It's Sofia's biggest fresh produce market, with all manner of fruits and vegetables on sale, including some you might not even recognise, as well as honey, bread and other food items. There are also clothes stalls and several simple cafés and kiosks. You can buy traditional *Troyanska kapka* pottery much more cheaply here than in souvenir shops. It's great fun to wander around, but it does get very crowded so watch your belongings.

Roman Wall Market (Map pp62-3; ul Hristo Smirnenski) This small collection of stalls huddles around a well-preserved but unexplained section of Roman wall. Fruit and vegetables and household goods are on sale, but unless you're already in the area it's not worth a special trip.

Music

Tapes and CDs of Bulgarian music can be bought at souvenir shops such as those listed in the next section, and sometimes more cheaply at stalls in the underpass below the NDK and in the Central Hali, where you can also find Western and Middle-Eastern pop music. You'll also see plenty of stalls around town selling pirated CDs of Western pop music.

Music Fashion (Map pp62-3; ☎ 981 3196; pl Slaveikov 1; ☯ 10am-8pm Mon-Sat, 10am-6pm Sun) This small shop has a good range of pop as well as classical CDs.

Alexandra Video (Map pp62-3; ☎ 986 7245; bul Vitosha 69; ☯ 10am-8.30pm) This bright chain store has a seemingly random selection of music, ranging from Eminem to Charles Aznavour, as well as DVDs of Hollywood films.

Souvenirs

Tradizia (Map pp62-3; ☎ 981 7765; www.traditzia.bg; bul Vasil Levski 36; ☯ 11am-7pm Tue-Sat) This browseworthy little shop has a good selection of traditional and contemporary Bulgarian handicrafts such as ceramics, glassware, carpets and textiles. Everything is made by 'socially excluded artisans' from the Roma and Turkish ethnic minorities and by people with disabilities and this project aims to help them become self-sufficient.

Centre of Folk Arts and Crafts (Map pp62-3; ☎ 988 6416; pl Battenberg; ☯ 10am-6pm) This shop inside the former Royal Palace offers a huge selection of folk art, including traditional rugs, woodcarvings, metalwork, pottery and jewellery, as well as books, and CDs and cassettes of Bulgarian music. However, prices tend to be high.

Artists sell paintings, mainly of traditional rural scenes, near the Mineral Baths and around pl Aleksander Nevski, where you'll also find stalls selling souvenirs, embroidery and 'antiques'; there are some genuine items here, but plenty of fakes too, and prices are very much aimed at foreign tourists. The underpass below pl Nezavisimost has several decent souvenir shops selling the usual array of postcards, paintings and books. The shops in the underpass below the Tsum shopping centre are generally overpriced.

GETTING THERE & AWAY
Air

For information about international flights to and from Sofia, see p263.

The only domestic flights within Bulgaria are between Sofia and the Black Sea coast. Hemus Air flies daily, except Sunday, to Varna (single/return 100/196 lv) between March and October, with extra flights most days between July and September. Dandy Airlines flies between the capital and Burgas (single/return 90/176 lv) between April and October. See p267 for domestic airline contact details.

Bus

The spanking new **central bus station** (Tsentralna Avtogara; Map pp58-9; ☎ 952 5004; bul Maria Luisa 100), right beside the train station, is a huge, well-organised place that handles services to most big towns in Bulgaria, as well as international destinations. There are dozens of counters for individual private companies, as well as an information desk and computer screens and touch-screen monitors giving details of departures. There are cafés and shops upstairs. At the time of research, some international services were still operating from a scruffy bus terminal on the opposite side of bul Maria Luisa, although these should be moving to the central bus station in due course.

Departures are less frequent between November and April. The schedules below are for the summer:

Destination	Fare	Duration	Frequency
Albena	18 lv	8hr	3-4 daily
Bansko	7.50 lv	3hr	6-8 daily
Blagoevgrad	6.80 lv	2hr	about hourly
Burgas	15 lv	7-8hr	7-10 daily
Dobrich	17 lv	7-8hr	6-8 daily
Haskovo	12 lv	6hr	10 daily
Kazanlâk	9 lv	3½ hr	6-8 daily
Lovech	9-10 lv	3hr	5-6 daily
Nesebâr	18 lv	7hr	10 daily
Pleven	8 lv	2½ hr	8-9 daily
Plovdiv	9 lv	2 ½ hr	several hourly
Ruse	12 lv	5hr	hourly
Sandanski	8 lv	3½ hr	6-8 daily
Shumen	15 lv	6hr	10-12 daily
Sliven	13 lv	5hr	hourly
Smolyan	10-12 lv	3½ hr	3-4 daily
Stara Zagora	9 lv	4hr	hourly
Varna	about 15 lv	7-8hr	every 45 mins
Veliko Târnovo	10 lv	4hr	hourly
Vidin	10 lv	5hr	every 3-4hr

From the far smaller **Ovcha Kupel bus station** (Map pp58-9; ☎ 955 5362; bul Tsar Boris III) – sometimes called the Zapad (West) station – a few buses head south, eg to Bansko, Blagoevgrad and Sandanski (although more buses to these places leave from the central bus station). From Ovcha Kupel bus station, there are also regular buses to Dupnitsa (3 lv, 1½ hours) and Kyustendil (4.60 lv, two hours). If you're heading to the Rila Monastery in summer, it's worth ringing the station to ask about any direct buses. Tickets for services departing from this station must be bought at counters inside. Ovcha Kupel bus station is linked to the city centre by bus No 60, tram No 5 and taxi (about 4 lv one way).

From tiny **Yug bus station** (Map pp58-9; ☎ 720 063; bul Dragan Tsankov 23), buses and minibuses

leave for Samokov (3 lv, one hour, every 30 minutes, 7am to 7.30pm). The station also offers an unreliable daily service (9am) direct to Malîovitsa (6 lv, two hours).

From the ramshackle **Poduyane bus station** (Map pp58-9; ☎ 847 4262; ul Todorini Kukli) – aka Iztok (East) station – buses leave infrequently for small towns in central Bulgaria (schedule below).

Destination	Fare	Duration	Departure Times
Gabrovo	8 lv	3½ hr	7.45am
Lovech	7 lv	3hr	7.45am
Teteven	6.80 lv	2½ hr	8.30am, 9am & 5pm
Troyan	7 lv	3hr	9.45am, 2pm & 5pm

INTERNATIONAL

Several agencies operate from the central bus station, offering services to Istanbul (40 lv, 18 hours), Athens (86 lv, 12 hours) and elsewhere, while numerous kiosks on the opposite side of bul Maria Luisa, such as **Group** (☎ 832 0078), sell tickets on buses to destinations all over Europe, including Paris (190 lv), Amsterdam (190 lv), Vienna (110 lv) and even Lisbon (270 lv). The bus station here is likely to be redeveloped. International services will then all leave from the central bus station.

Eurotours (Map pp58-9; ☎ 931 1500; basement, central train station) also sells tickets for international destinations, including Belgrade (36 lv, eight hours) and Budapest (102 lv, 15 hours).

Matpu (Map pp58-9; ☎ 953 2481; ul Damyan Gruev 23) probably offers the best services to Greece, including Athens and Thessaloniki.

It pays to shop around though, as different companies offer different prices.

Train

The **central train station** (Map pp58-9; ☎ 931 1111) is a massive barn-like structure which has recently undergone a facelift, though it's still far from cheerful or user friendly.

Destinations for all domestic and international services are still listed on timetables in Cyrillic, but departures (for the following two hours) and arrivals (for the previous two hours) are listed in English on a large computer screen on the ground floor. There's a small information counter in the foyer, but don't expect anyone to speak anything but Bulgarian. Other facilities include a post office, cafés, a hotel and accommodation

DOMESTIC TRAIN SERVICES TO/FROM SOFIA

Destination	1st/2nd-class fare	Duration	Number of trains (daily)
Burgas	16/11.10 lv (fast) & 19.10/15 lv (express)	6-7hr	5 fast & 2 express
Gorna Oryahovitsa (for Veliko Târnovo)	13/9 lv (fast) &14.10/10 lv (express)	3-6hr	6 fast, 4 express & 1 slow
Plovdiv	8/5.50 lv (fast) & 8/6.50 lv (express)	2½-3½ hr	8 fast, 3 express & 8 slow
Ruse	14.70/10.80 lv 7hr	4 fast	
Sandanski	9/6 lv 3½ hr	3 fast	
Varna	18/12.50 lv (fast) & 23/17 lv (express)	8hr	5 fast & 1 express
Vidin	10/6.80 lv (fast)	5-7hr	3 fast & 1 slow

agency, bookstalls and even a cinema. The rates at the foreign-exchange offices vary, so check around.

Be aware of the uniformed porters who approach confused-looking foreigners offering to provide information or carry their bags; while these men are officially sanctioned, they will expect sizeable tips for their services, so unless you're in real need, it's probably best to politely decline their assistance.

Same-day tickets for any town along the lines to Vidin, Ruse and Varna are sold at counters on the ground floor; same-day tickets to other destinations are sold downstairs. All counters are open 24 hours. Advanced tickets, seat reservations and sleepers for domestic services are available from a downstairs office (open 6am to 7.30pm Monday to Friday and 7am to 2.30pm Saturday).

The central train station is easy to reach from pl Sveta Nedelya on tram Nos 1, 2 and 7; by taxi (about 3 lv one way); or on foot (about 30 minutes).

All tickets for international trains, and advance tickets for domestic services, can be bought at one of several **Rila Bureaux** (www.bdz-rila.com; central train station Map pp58-9; ☎ 932 3346; ☺ 7am-10pm; National Palace of Culture complex Map pp62-3; ☎ 658 402; ☺ 7am-7pm Mon-Fri & 7am-2pm Sat; ul General Gurko Map pp62-3; ☎ 987 0777; ul General Gurko 5; ☺ 7am-7pm Mon-Fri & 7am-2pm Sat). Staff at these offices usually speak some English.

Major domestic services to and from Sofia are listed in the table above.

More information about the schedules and fares for other services to and from Sofia are included in the relevant Getting There & Away sections throughout this

book. For more information about international services to and from Sofia, go to p263.

GETTING AROUND
To/From the Airport

Sofia airport (☎ 937 2211; www.sofia-airport.bg) is located 12km southeast of the city centre. Minibus No 30 shuttles between the airport and pl Nezavisimost for a flat fare of 1 lv; you can pick it up from outside the Sheraton Hotel. Less convenient is bus No 84, which takes a slow and meandering route before depositing you outside Borisova Gradina.

When you emerge into the arrivals hall you will immediately be greeted by taxi drivers offering you a lift into town, at inflated rates; ignore these and instead head to the reputable **OK-Supertrans taxi** (☎ 973 2121) office counter, where you can book an official, meter-using taxi. They will give you a slip of paper with the three-digit code of your cab. A taxi (using the meter) from the airport to the city centre should cost no more than 8 lv.

Car & Motorcycle

Frequent public transport, cheap taxis and horrible traffic all provide little or no incentive to drive a private or rented car around Sofia. But there are plenty of good reasons to hire a car to places such as the Rila Monastery (and further afield) – if you can find your way out of Sofia! For details about the approximate costs and the pros and cons of renting a car from foreign and Bulgarian agencies, see p269. Rental outlets include:

Avis (Central Map pp62-3; ☎ 981 1082; ul George Washington 17; Sofia airport ☎ 945 9224)

Choice (Map pp62-3; ☎ /fax 931 0456; bul Maria Luisa 80)

Eurodollar (Map pppp62-3; ☎ 875 779; bul Vitosha 25)

Eurorent (Map pppp62-3; ☎ 980 2911; www.eurorent.com; ul Rakovski 60)

Hertz (Central Map pppp62-3; ☎ 980 1062; bul Vasil Levski 47; Sofia airport ☎ 945 9217)

Tourist Service (☎ 981 7253; www.tourist-service.com; bul Klokotnitsa)

Public Transport

The various forms of public transport – trams, buses, minibuses and trolleybuses, as well as the underground metro – run from 5.30am to 11pm every day.

A ticket on any bus, tram, trolleybus or metro within Sofia costs 0.50 lv. Most drivers on public transport sell tickets – make sure you have the right change – but it's far easier and quicker, especially during peak times, to buy tickets from kiosks and newsstands at stops along the route before boarding.

If you're going to use public transport frequently, consider buying a pass for one day (2 lv), five days (9 lv) or one month (37 lv), which are valid for all trams, buses and trolleybuses. All tickets must be validated by punching them in the small machine inside the vehicle; once punched, tickets are nontransferable. Grumpy-looking inspectors are a regular sight, and will issue on-the-spot fines (5 lv) if you don't have a ticket. Unwary foreigners are a favourite target. Don't forget to buy an extra ticket for each piece of oversized luggage too. Officially, this means anything exceeding 60cm x 40cm x 40cm.

Probably the most useful trams for visitors are Nos 1 and 7, which link the central train station with Yuzhen Park, via pl Sveta Nedelya. Public transport routes for buses, trams and trolleybuses are indicated on Domino's *Sofia City Map*, and tram routes are marked on the excellent (free) map inside the *Sofia City Info Guide*.

Buses for Boyana, Zlatni Mostove and Aleko depart from the Hladilnika bus terminal. It is near the southern terminus of tram Nos 2, 4, 9 and 12 from pl Sveta Nedelya. (From the final tram stop, walk through the tiny park to the bus stop on the main road.)

Private minibuses, known as *marshroutki,* are a popular and efficient alternative to public transport, but cost a little more (1 lv per trip). Destinations and fares are indicated (in Cyrillic) on the front of the minibus, and you pay the driver on boarding. Most services run between the city centre and the outlying suburbs. Those of perhaps most interest to travellers include No 30, which goes to the airport, No 21 which runs to Boyana, and No 41, to Simeonovo.

Sofia's modern metro system has only one line, shuttling shoppers and commuters between the western residential suburb of Lyulin and the city centre (Serdica station). It's of little value to visitors.

Taxi

Taxis are an affordable and easier alternative to public transport. By law, taxis must use meters, but those that wait around the airport, luxury hotels and within 100m of pl Sveta Nedelya will often try to negotiate an unmetered fare – which, of course, will be considerably more than the metered fare. All official taxis are yellow, have fares per kilometre displayed in the window, and have obvious taxi signs (in English or Bulgarian) on top. Never accept a lift in a private, unlicensed vehicle, because you will (at best) pay too much or (at worst) be robbed.

The rates per kilometre may range enormously from one taxi company to another (see p270).

In the very unlikely event that you can't find a taxi, you can order one by ringing **OK-Supertrans** (☎ 973 2121) or **Yes Taxi** (☎ 91919). You will need to speak Bulgarian.

AROUND SOFIA

The places mentioned here are accessible from Sofia by public transport, but it's worth staying at least one night to avoid excessive travel and to really appreciate the surroundings.

BOYANA БОЯНА
☎ 02

Boyana is a peaceful and prosperous suburb of Sofia, lying around 8km south of the city centre. Once a favourite retreat for communist leaders and apparatchiks, these days it's home to Sofia's wealthy elite and two of the capital's major attractions. However, besides these there's little else to detain you.

Sights

NATIONAL MUSEUM OF HISTORY

Housed in the former presidential palace, the **National Museum of History** (☎ 955 4280; www .historymuseum.org; ul Vitoshko Lale, Boyana; admission 10 lv; ⏱ 9.30am-6pm) is Bulgaria's most lauded, and possibly most anticlimactic, museum and is hardly in the most convenient of locations. Having said that, it does occupy a quite stunning setting, and as a bonus you get to see the overblown splendour in which the old communist leadership once lived and held court. Unless a coach party happens to turn up, it's often eerily deserted.

A grand stairway sweeps up to the first floor, where the exhibitions begin. The star of the show is undoubtedly the fabulous 4th-century BC Thracian gold treasure from Panagyurishte (on loan abroad at the time of research), with its *rhyta* (drinking cups) in the form of animal heads. There are more Thracian and Roman artefacts on display, including some intriguing mosaics, as well as Greek pottery from the Black Sea region, and lots of reproductions of treasures kept elsewhere. Also on this floor is a large 16th-century fresco from a church in Arbanasi showing demons gleefully torturing naked sinners, and uniforms, weapons and banners from the 1876 April Uprising against the Ottomans.

Upstairs, you can look over a gallery of icons and displays illustrating the social history of Bulgaria from the late 19th century up to WWII, with theatrical costumes, photographs and documents. There are also cases of traditional folk costumes, and temporary exhibitions on various topics.

Outside, there's a collection of ancient tombstones on show, alongside a few Russian MiG fighters.

Guided tours in foreign languages cost 10 lv per group, and a museum guidebook is available in a number of languages, including English, for a hefty 15 lv. There are a couple of souvenir shops and a small café on the ground floor, and a bar at the rear of the building on the first floor level, which looks out over the gardens.

While the museum certainly has some fascinating displays, the poor labelling is frustrating, especially given the high admission fee; in fact, many artefacts aren't labelled at all, in any language.

BOYANA CHURCH

The tiny, 13th-century **Boyana Church** (☎ 685 304; ul Boyansko Ezero 3; admission 10 lv; ⏱ 9am-5pm Tue-Sun) is around 2km south of the museum. It's on Unesco's World Heritage list and is perhaps Bulgaria's most cherished and revered historic monument. The 90 murals, which date from 1259, are among the very finest examples of Bulgarian medieval artwork and they influenced later murals painted in monasteries in Serbia and Russia. Some murals are in poor condition, however, and the scaffolding is evidence of seemingly perpetual restoration. Taking photos of the interior is not permitted.

The high entrance fee allows you a quick look at the small number of murals, but nothing is explained inside the church. The small booklet (3 lv), in English, provides some details.

Getting There & Away

Minibus No 21 runs to Boyana from the city centre (pick it up on ul Praga). It will drop you right outside the gates of the museum, and also connects the museum with Boyana Church. You could also take bus No 63 from pl Ruski Pametnik, or bus No 64 from the Hladilnika terminal. Signs advertising the museum line the motorway, but it's not easy to spot the building, which is set back from the road behind a screen of trees. A taxi (about 5 lv one way) from the city centre to the museum is probably the easiest option of all; for the museum, ask for the 'Residentsia Boyana'.

VITOSHA NATIONAL PARK
НАЦИОНАЛЕН ПАРК ВИТОША
☎ 02

Mt Vitosha is the rounded mountain range, 23km long and 13km wide, just south of Sofia. It's known colloquially as the 'lungs of Sofia' for the refreshing breezes it deflects onto the often-polluted capital. The mountain is part of the 22,726-hectare Vitosha National Park, the oldest of its kind in Bulgaria (created in 1934). The highest point (2290m) is Mt Cherni Vrâh (The Black Peak), the fourth-highest peak in Bulgaria and one of 11 in the immediate area over 2000m.

As well as being a popular ski resort in winter (see p82), the national park attracts legions of hikers, berry pickers and sightseers on summer weekends. There are dozens of clearly marked hiking trails, plenty of hotels, cafés and restaurants and about 80 huts and chalets that can be booked through the Bulgarian Tourist Union (see p247).

Aleko Алеко
elevation 1800m

Aleko was named after Aleko Konstantinov, a Bulgarian writer who first developed the idea of hiking in the region during the late 19th century. In summer (especially weekends), the area is crammed with picnicking families, courting couples and hikers. One popular activity is to take a mountain bike to Aleko by gondola from Simeonovo (p82), then hurtle down the ski slopes. For mountain-bike hire, contact **Motoroads** (☎ 0888 957 649; www.motoroads.com; bul Bratya Bukston 208, Sofia).

Zlatni Mostove Златни Мостове
elevation 1400m

Zlatni Mostove (Golden Bridges) takes its name from the extraordinary series of huge boulders dumped along the stone river by glaciers many centuries ago. It's another very popular spot on summer weekends but at other times you may have the place to yourself. It's accessible by bus No 261 from Ovcha Kupel bus station every 20 minutes on Saturday and Sunday, less frequently on weekdays. A taxi from the city centre will cost about 15 lv one way.

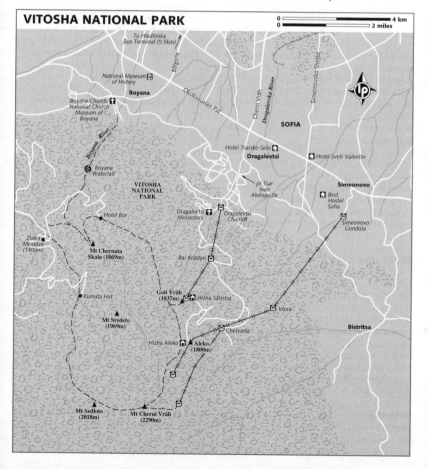

VITOSHA NATIONAL PARK

Dragalevtsi Драгалевци

A two-person **chairlift** (☎ 967 1110) starts about 5km (by road) up from the centre of Dragalevtsi village (though it's about 3km on foot if you take the obvious short cut up the hill). One chairlift (1.50 lv, 20 minutes) goes as far Bai Krâstyo, from where another (1.50 lv, 15 minutes) carries on to Goli Vrâh (1837m). Both lifts operate year-round, but most reliably on Friday to Sunday from about 8.30am to 6.30pm.

This lift is cheaper than the Simeonovo gondola so it's immensely popular, especially on sunny summer weekends. Queues of 200m are common by noon, so start early or simply take the gondola. A pleasant option is to take the chairlift to Goli Vrâh, walk (30 minutes) to Aleko and catch the gondola down to Simeonovo (or vice versa).

From the start of the chairlift, a well-marked trail (about 1km) leads to **Dragalevtsi Monastery**. Probably the oldest extant monastery in Bulgaria, it was built in about 1345, but was abandoned only 40 years later. The monastery contains particularly charming murals, and is revered as one of the many hiding places of the ubiquitous anti-Turkish rebel leader Vasil Levski.

Pl Tsar Ivan Aleksandâr in Dragalevtsi village is surrounded by charming cafés and traditional but pricey restaurants. There are also places to eat and drink along the road from the village to the chairlift.

Bus Nos 64 and 93 from the Hladilnika terminal go to the village centre; No 93 continues on to the chairlift.

Simeonovo Симеоново

Take a gondola to the mountains from Simeonovo (2.50/4 lv one way/return, 30 minutes). It operates Friday to Sunday from 9am to 6.30pm (1 October to 31 March) and 8.30am to 6pm (1 May to 30 September). It's possible to disembark at one or both of the junctions – ie Vtora and Chetvarta, from where hiking trails lead deep into the park – and then continue the trip later at no extra cost. Bus No 123 from the Hladilnika terminal goes directly to the gondola station.

Activities

HIKING

The best map is probably *Vitosha Turisti-cheska Karta* (1:50,000), printed in Cyrillic and available at bookshops around central Sofia.

Some of the shorter and more popular hikes around the park:

Aleko–Goli Vrâh A short trail (30 minutes) between the top of the gondola from Simeonovo and the chairlift from Dragalevtsi.

Aleko–Mt Cherni Vrâh A popular, but steep, 90 minutes on foot. Alternatively, take the chairlift from Aleko to within 30 minutes' walk of the summit.

Aleko–Zlatni Mostove Follow the trail to Goli Vrâh, skirt around Mt Sredets (1969m) and pass Hotel Bor; about three hours.

Boyana Church–Zlatni Mostove At the church, ask for directions to the path which hugs Boyana River and leads to the 15m-high Boyana Waterfall (best in winter). From there, obvious paths lead to Zlatni Mostove; about three hours in total.

Dragalevtsi Chairlift–Goli Vrâh Follow the chairlift from the bottom; a three-hour steep climb.

Zlatni Mostove–Mt Cherni Vrâh A tougher hike, via Kumata Hut and Mt Sedloto (2018m); about three hours.

SKIING

Mt Vitosha is one of Europe's most convenient skiing spots. The slopes here are only 22km or so from Sofia; you can easily check to see if the peak is cloudy or if the weather is lousy. Although Mt Vitosha is Bulgaria's highest ski resort, there is rarely enough snow before mid-December; nonetheless the season can often last until late April.

The 29km of alpine ski runs (the longest is about 5km) range from easy to very difficult, and start as high as Mt Cherni Vrâh (2290m), which is almost always foggy. Cross-country skiing is ideal along the 15km of trails, but snowboarding is not good because of the rocky slopes. As well as the Simeonovo gondola and Dragalevtsi chairlift there are a handful of other chairlifts and draglifts. A lift pass will set you back about 25 lv per day.

While the lift pass is cheap, there are disadvantages. Mt Vitosha is, not surprisingly, impossibly crowded on weekends. A lack of funds means the slopes are not always well maintained and the quantity and quality of ski equipment for hire is not great because so many locals use their own gear. The ski-rental shop at the start of the Simeonovo gondola and the Aleko Ski Centre at Aleko both charge about 60 lv per day for a complete set of ski gear.

The ski school at Aleko is small but enjoys a fine reputation. It does cater almost entirely to Bulgarians but instructors are multilingual.

Sleeping & Eating

In Vitosha National Park there are a several modern hotels, which are usually much cheaper than those in the city centre. Ideally, though, you'll need your own transport to stay out here. Hikers can stay at any of the numerous mountain huts.

Hizha Aleko (☎ 967 1113; dm 10 lv, s/d with shared bathroom 15/25 lv) This hut offers a number of basic rooms with two to eight beds.

Hizha Sâlzitsa (☎ 967 1054; s/d with bathroom 25/50 lv) This refurbished former rest home provides basic rooms and a restaurant. It's accessible by bus along the road to Aleko and is not far from the chairlift at Goli Vrâh.

Best Hostel Sofia (☎ 961 3046; www.bestsofiahostel .com; ul 502 No 14, Simeonovo; s/d €15/24; P ⓢ) Also known as Sportocenter Simeonovo, this place isn't actually a hostel at all, but a charming modern hotel with just eight rooms. It's a pleasant place offering superb value for money, with a gym, sauna, Jacuzzi and pools for both adults and kids, as well as its own restaurant. Various ski packages are also offered. To get here, take minibus No 41 from the city centre.

Hotel Sveti Valentin (☎ 962 2189; www.hotelsva lentin.com; bul Simeonovsko Shosse 80; s/d/tr €49/54/69; P ⓧ) Another modern, well-priced option in Simeonovo, the Sveti Valentin has a wide range of rooms available, and a pleasant garden restaurant. Breakfast is €4 extra.

Hotel Tsarsko Selo (☎ 816 0101; www.tsarskoselo .com; Oklovrasten Pat, Dragalevtsi; s/d/apt €50/60/100; P ⓧ) At the base of Mt Vitosha, this smart modern hotel complex offers large rooms at reasonable rates. There's a restaurant, gym and casino, and an airport shuttle bus. Ask about the frequent promotions.

The hiking trails branching out from Aleko are lined with cafés and bars. Most locals seem happy to bring a picnic; there are also many informal stalls around Aleko. All prices are pleasingly cheap.

Getting There & Away

To Aleko, bus No 66 (2 lv) departs from Sofia's Hladilnika terminal 10 times a day between 8am and 7.45pm on Saturday and Sunday, and four times a day on weekdays. Minibus No 41 runs from Sofia city centre to Simeonovo (1 lv).

KYUSTENDIL КЮСТЕНДИЛ

☎ 078 / pop 56,500

Kyustendil, 87km southwest of Sofia, is one of Bulgaria's most popular spa resorts and its proximity to Macedonia and Serbia has provided the town with a colourful history. The sunny climate and mineral springs, which attracted settlers during the Thracian, Greek and Roman periods, still draw tourists from across Bulgaria. For visitors, Kyustendil is a common transit point for travel to and from Macedonia, a day trip from Sofia, and a cheaper place to stay than the capital.

Bul Bulgaria is the shady stone pathway that links the train station (and adjacent bus station) with pl Velbâzhd, the central square.

Sights

The **City History Museum** (☎ 26 396; bul Bulgaria 55; admission 1 lv; ⓨ 8am-noon & 1-5pm Mon-Fri) houses an array of Thracian and Roman artefacts, and remnants of Neolithic dwellings. Not far from the museum are the ruins of the 2nd-century Roman **Asclepius Temple** and a large functioning **market**. Also worth a look is the 16th-century **Ahmed Bey Mosque** (☎ 22 381; ul Stefan Karadzha 2), about 400m northeast of pl Velbâzhd, which houses temporary archaeological displays.

On top of the forested **Hisarlâk Hill**, about 2km south of pl Velbâzhd (take a taxi), are ruins of the 2nd-century **ancient fortress** from the Roman city of Pautalia.

The **Vladimir Dimitrov Art Gallery** (☎ 22 503; ul Patriarh Evtimii 20; admission 1.50 lv; ⓨ 9.30am-11.45am & 2-5.45pm Tue-Sun) is about 200m north of pl Velbâzhd. It houses over 200 works of art, mostly by the locally born Dimitrov, also known as 'The Master'.

Sleeping & Eating

Along ul Arhimand Zinovi, directly behind Hotel Velbâzhd, several homes offer simple and clean private rooms for about 10 to 15 lv per person. Look for the signs in Bulgarian and English along the road.

Hotel Velbâzhd (☎ 26 010; fax 24 264; bul Bulgaria 1; s/d/ste 'old rooms' €8/13/16, 'renovated rooms' €25/32/44; P) This towering place is split into older and newer sections. The 'old' rooms are dreary, though still clean and reasonably comfortable, but the 'renovated' rooms are worth the extra cash. All rooms have TVs, fridges and balconies, and rates include breakfast. The hotel also offers various balneological treatments.

Hotel Bulgaria (☎ 51 200; ul Konstantinova Banja 3; s/d/apt €25/35/50; P 🖥) The Bulgaria is a modern, central option near the main square, offering a good standard of comfort for the price. There's a restaurant on site, and guests have use of a sauna.

Getting There & Away

Buses leave from the Ovcha Kupel bus station in Sofia (4.80 lv, two hours) every 60 to 80 minutes for the **Kyustendil bus station** (☎ 22 626). From Kyustendil, six daily buses go to Blagoevgrad, eight depart for Dupnitsa and one travels to Plovdiv. Buses also leave daily for Skopje in Macedonia. From the adjacent **train station** (☎ 26 041), two fast trains (7/5.50 lv in 1st/2nd class) and three slow passenger trains travel every day to Sofia.

Southern Bulgaria

CONTENTS

SOUTHERN BULGARIA

HIGHLIGHTS

■ **Pilgrimage**
Immerse yourself in Bulgarian Orthodox culture with a visit to the awesome monasteries at Rila (p91) and Bachkovo (p130).

■ **Historic charm**
Wander the cobbled streets of Plovdiv's lovingly restored old town (p117).

■ **Skiing**
Take to the slopes of Bulgaria's finest ski resorts at Borovets (p95) or Pamporovo (p112).

■ **Wining**
Drop by tiny Melnik (p105) and sample their unique red wine.

■ **Relaxing**
Treat yourself to a massage and a Jacuzzi at the laid-back spa resort of Devin (p115).

Southern Bulgaria encompasses some of the country's wildest and most spectacular landscapes, with a scattering of small towns and traditional timber-framed villages nestling among the majestic, pine-clad Rila, Pirin and Rodopi mountain ranges. The region is home to Bulgaria's foremost skiing resorts and hiking routes and its two finest monasteries: spellbinding Rila, with its fresco-covered church; and quieter Bachkovo, more popular with pilgrims than tourists. Bulgaria's second city, Plovdiv, is the main urban centre here, and its remarkably preserved old town and unique Roman remains continue to draw in the crowds.

Elsewhere, Bulgaria's smallest town, Melnik, delights travellers with its unique and plentiful wines, and the charming mountain town of Bansko makes an excellent base for walkers and is a fine place to sample traditional rustic cuisine.

SOUTHERN BULGARIA

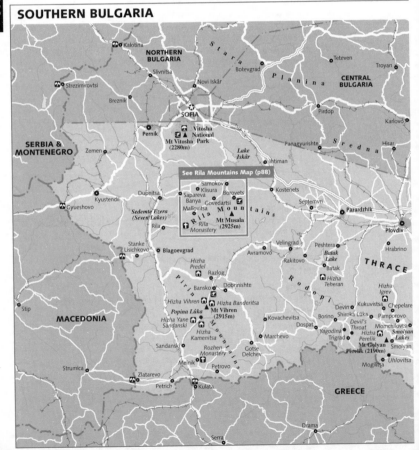

HISTORY

Historically, much of southern Bulgaria – or at least that part of it squeezed between the Sredna Gora Mountains, the Rodopi Mountains and the Black Sea coast – can be identified with the ancient region of Thrace, birthplace of the legendary figures of Spartacus, the slave leader, and Orpheus, the semimythical divine musician. This region is in fact still known as Thrace, although the Thrace of Greek and Roman antiquity was much larger, only two-thirds of which lies within Bulgaria today.

The region of southern Bulgaria can be defined as the part of the country between the Sredna Gora Mountains and the borders with Greece and Turkey. The Mar-

itsa River flows south into the Aegean Sea, which forms the border between present-day Greek and Turkish Thrace. Svilengrad is where the three nations meet. Greek, and especially Turkish, influence is apparent throughout the border areas, most notably in the minarets that tower over the Muslim villages in the Rodopis, a living reminder of the long-gone Ottomans.

RILA MOUNTAINS
РИЛА ПЛАНИНА

The majestic Rila Mountains are the most popular destination for Bulgarians who

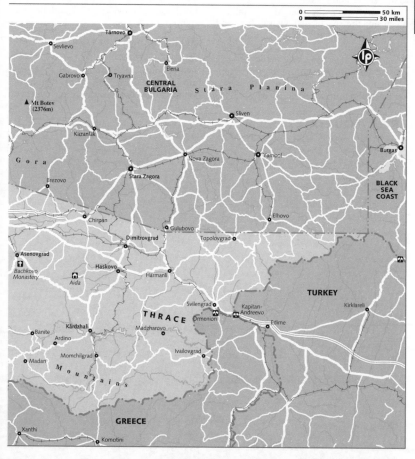

want to go hiking and skiing. While the mountain range is small (2629 sq km), the area is stunningly beautiful. It boasts a marvellous array of landscapes, including 180 perennial lakes and streams and numerous mineral springs. (In fact, *rila* comes from the Thracian word for 'mountains of water'.) Mt Musala (2925m), near Borovets, is the highest peak in the country and in the Balkans and is an excellent place to hike.

The Rila National Park, permanently open with free admission, contains 14,370 hectares of forest and 13,000 hectares of alpine pastures. It protects glorious fir trees and beechwoods (among other conifers), as well as precious wildlife, such as deer, wild goats, eagles and falcons.

As for hiking, the Rila Mountains are steep but the spectacular views, flora and fauna are definitely worth it. Snow can last until mid-June on peaks over 2000m. Mountain huts, known as a *hizha*, provide simple dormitory accommodation (from about 10 lv per person). Many serve meals but sometimes these are pretty basic, so it's advisable to bring food, or at least to inquire first.

In *The Mountains of Bulgaria*, the author, Julian Perry, details an extensive north–south trek (part of the trans-European E4 trek) across the Rila Mountains. It starts at Klisura and finishes at Hizha Predel, near Razlog, and takes from seven to 10 days. You'll need more detailed maps than those provided in this guide for the trek and for any other hiking in the Rila Mountains. Buy the *Rila* map (1:55,000), published (in Cyrillic) by Kartografia.

One of the most popular hikes starts at Maliovitsa, visits the magnificent Sedemte Ezera (Seven Lakes) and finishes at Rila Monastery (p98). For more information about exploring the mountains from the north, see Maliovitsa (p98) and Borovets (p95).

BLAGOEVGRAD БЛАГОЕВГРАД
☎ 073 / pop 77,900

Lying about 100km south of Sofia, Blagoevgrad is the capital of the Pirin region, and while it may not be brimming over with

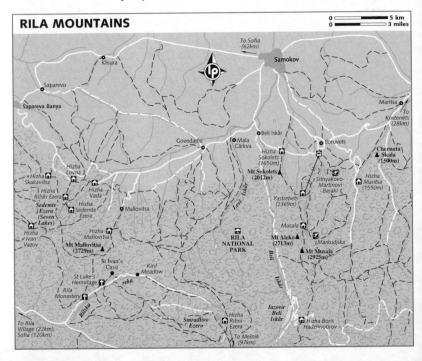

historic charm or must-see attractions, it is a lively and cosmopolitan city and home to over 16,000 students, who attend the **American University of Bulgaria** (☎ 25 241; www.aubg. bg), which dominates pl Georgi Izmirliev Makedoncheto, and the **Neofit Rilski Southwest University** (☎ 27 177), about 3km west of the town centre. Blagoevgrad is full of busy cafés, bars and clubs for those looking for a bit of nightlife, and it also makes a handy base for a trip to Rila Monastery (p91).

Formerly known as Gorna Dzhumaya, the city once had a large Turkish population, which was displaced after the Balkan Wars. It was renamed Blagoevgrad in 1950, in honour of the 19th-century Bulgarian Marxist, Dimitar Blagoev, whose statue stands on the main square, near the American University.

Information

There are foreign-exchange offices along ul Tsar Ivan Shishman, while a First East International Bank is located along a laneway southwest of pl Makedonia.

Escapenet (☎ 0899 879 042; ul Petko Petkov 2; 10.30am-10.30pm Mon-Sat; per hr 0.80 lv) A central Internet café.

Pirin Tourism Forum (☎ 881 458; www.travel-bulgaria.com/ptf/; ul Komitrov 8; 9.30am-5.30pm Mon-Fri) In the absence of an official tourist office this place can, very grudgingly, provide some basic information to travellers, but it's really a regional tourism association, working with local businesses, and its resources are limited.

Post office (ul Mitropolit Boris) Combined with the telephone centre.

Sights

The **History Museum** (☎ 823 557; bul Aleksandâr Stamboliyski; admission 3 lv; 9am-noon & 3-6pm Mon-Fri) is in a modern building just off the main road, bul Stamboliyski. The four floors house over 160,000 exhibits of religious items, archaeological artefacts from the region, information about the military history of Macedonia and plenty of traditional costumes. Try to visit the natural history section on the lowest level, which contains the best collection of stuffed animals and birds in Bulgaria. It's an interesting and well-kept museum, but unfortunately labelling is only in Bulgarian.

Between bul Aleksandâr Stamboliyski and the Forest Park is the old town of **Varosha**. Several renovated Bulgarian national revival period homes, such as the rarely opened **Georgi Izmirliev Makedoncheto House-Museum**, and art galleries (which keep erratic opening hours), such as the private **Stanislav Art Gallery**, can be found along the cobblestone streets. The area is touristy but worth strolling around.

In a small, serene garden under the Kristo Hotel is the **Church of the Annunciation of the Virgin** (ul Komitrov; 6am-8pm), built in 1844. It has an attractive, frescoed portico and faded murals inside.

A steep road (700m) from Varosha leads to the **Forest Park**, a shady and popular spot with several lookouts offering stunning city views. Towards the southern edge of the park are the small **Botanical Gardens**.

Sleeping

Alfatour Travel Agency (☎ 823 598; ul Krali Marko 4; r per person 22 lv) Alfatour can arrange rooms in private homes. Most rooms have a shared bathroom but are convenient to the town centre.

Hotel Alpha (☎ 831 122; alphablg@hotmail.com; ul Kukush 7; d/apt from 30/50 lv; P) This neat little hotel is tucked away in an unremarkable residential district near the Varosha quarter, though it's well signposted from the bus station onwards. Rooms are simple but clean and the bathrooms are very modern.

Hotel Fenix (☎ 833 400; ul Todor Alexandrov 78; s/d from 30/40 lv;) The Fenix is a small, new hotel set in the middle of a nondescript residential road just north of the train and bus stations. It's a very well-kept place and the bright, comfortable rooms all have TVs and most have balconies.

Hotel Alenmak (☎ 23 031; pl Georgi Izmirliev Makedoncheto; s/d €27/30; P) This large and rather dismal hotel faces the American University. Most of the 100 or so rooms have views of the university and square below, but they're small and dated and really don't justify the price.

Kristo Hotel (☎ 880 444; hotel_kristo@abv.bg; ul Komitrov; s/d/apt incl breakfast €30/40/80; P) The Kristo is an attractive, modern place in a serene setting just up a stone pathway from the main road and overlooking the church. The rooms are cosy, superbly furnished (many with fireplaces) and most have views. Each room is different so check out a few before deciding.

Eating

The pedestrianised streets between pl Bulgaria and pl Makedonia are awash with restaurants, cafés and bars, which seem to be forever full with the young, chain-smoking coffee-sipping crowd. The cuisine on offer at most of these places tends to be unimaginative, but those listed below offer a higher standard.

Kristo Restaurant (☎ 880 444; ul Komitrov; mains 2.50-5 lv) The restaurant of the hotel of the same name has outdoor seating overlooking the Church of the Annunciation and serves reasonably priced traditional dishes such as salads and grilled meats. They're also quite keen on offal, with brain omelette and 'lucky filled tongue' filling out the menu.

Pizza Napoli (☎ 34 649; pl Hristo Botev 4; mains 3-7 lv; ☉ 8am-midnight) This is one of Blagoevgad's better restaurants, with an attractive setting and a big menu, in English, of pizzas, pasta and grills. It's also a nice place for a drink.

Restaurant Varosha (☎ 881 370; ul Komitrov; mains 4-10 lv) The Varosha is one of several traditional, if slightly touristy, taverns in authentic Bulgarian national revival period houses around Varosha. There's an English menu and the rustic Bulgarian food is tasty and filling.

Entertainment

As expected in a university town, there are several cinemas, including a special wide-screen **Movie Max** (American University complex).

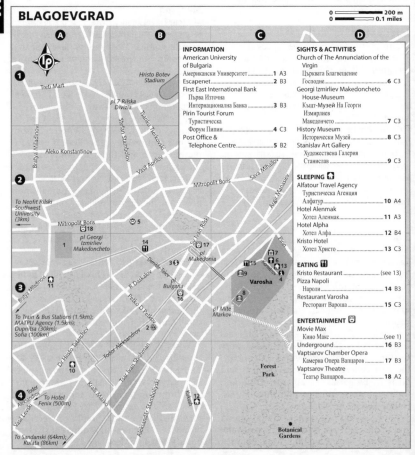

BLAGOEVGRAD

0 —————— 200 m
0 —————— 0.1 miles

INFORMATION
American University of Bulgaria
Американски Университет 1 A3
Escapenet 2 B3
First East International Bank
Първа Източна
Интернационална Банка 3 B3
Pirin Tourist Forum
Туристическа
Форум Пипин 4 C3
Post Office &
Telephone Centre 5 B2

SIGHTS & ACTIVITIES
Church of The Annunciation of the Virgin
Църквата Благовещение
Господне 6 C3
Georgi Izmirliev Makedoncheto House-Museum
Къщт-Музей На Георги
Измирлиев
Македончето 7 C3
History Museum
Исторически Музей 8 C3
Stanislav Art Gallery
Художествена Галерия
Станислав 9 C3

SLEEPING 🏠
Alfatour Travel Agency
Туристическа Агенция
Алфатур 10 A4
Hotel Alenmak
Хотел Аленмак 11 A3
Hotel Alpha
Хотел Алфа 12 B4
Kristo Hotel
Хотел Христо 13 C3

EATING 🍴
Kristo Restaurant .... (see 13)
Pizza Napoli
Нароли 14 B3
Restaurant Varosha
Ресторант Вароша 15 C3

ENTERTAINMENT 🎭
Movie Max
Кино Макс .... (see 1)
Underground 16 B3
Vaptsarov Chamber Opera
Камерна Опера Вапцаров 17 B3
Vaptsarov Theatre
Театър Вапцаров 18 A2

Later, you can join locals at one of the rowdy nightclubs, such as the **Underground** (pl Bulgaria). The respected **Vaptsarov Theatre** (☎ 823 475; pl Georgi Izmirliev Makedoncheto) and the **Vaptsarov Chamber Opera** (☎ 820 703; pl Makedonia) offer something more sedate but are closed during August.

Getting There & Away

The bus and train stations are adjacent on bul Sveti Dimitâr Solunski, about 1.5km southwest of the town centre.

Most buses leave from the well-organised **bus station** (☎ 23 750). A few buses to Sandanski, Sofia and Dupnitsa also leave from the car park in front of the train station. The bus and train stations are both accessible by bus No 2 from outside the History Museum.

Buses travel hourly (6.30am to 6pm) from Blagoevgrad to Sofia (6.80 lv, two hours) via Dupnitsa, but many more come through on their way to/from Kulata or Sandanski. Buses also go to Sandanski (4 lv, 1½ hours, 10 daily), Plovdiv (7 lv, three hours, two daily), Bansko (6 lv, two hours, six to seven daily) and Melnik (5.80 lv, two hours, one daily). Buses to Rila village (1.30 lv, 45 minutes) leave hourly between 7am and 8pm.

The **Matpu agency** (☎ 832 793; bul Sveti Dimitâr Solunski; ☯ 8.30am-10pm), opposite the bus station, runs a bus service to Bitola (24 lv) in Macedonia, leaving at 9.30pm nightly.

The **train station** (☎ 23 695) is on the main line between Sofia and Kulata, via Sandanski. There are five fast trains (1st/2nd class 8/5.80 lv, 2½ hours), and one slow passenger train, daily from Sofia, via Dupnitsa. Three of these fast trains continue to Sandanski (6/4.80 lv in 1st/2nd class, two hours) and Kulata (7.20/5.80 lv in 1st/2nd class, 2½ hours).

RILA РИЛА

Rila village is almost always ignored by the hordes of tourists who pass through on their way to the Rila Monastery, 22km to the east. However, if you're relying on public transport, you'll probably need a connection in Rila and the village does offer alternative accommodation and several foreign-exchange offices (there's nowhere to change money at Rila Monastery), but it's a very quiet place offering no real reason to linger.

Dominating the village square is **Hotel Orbita** (☎ 07054-2167; s/d 15/30 lv; P ☯). The rates are good value compared to most places near the monastery. The restaurant is popular with occasional tour buses and several cafés are nearby.

From Dupnitsa, buses go to Rila village at 10am, 11am and 4pm. From Rila village, they depart for Dupnitsa at 6.20am, 8.40am and 3pm. There are also hourly buses between Rila village and Blagoevgrad between 6.20am and 7pm (1.30 lv, 45 minutes), and buses to Sofia at 6.20am and 3.30pm.

Buses leave Rila village for the monastery at 7.40am, 12.40pm and 3.50pm and return at 9am, 3pm and 5pm (1.20 lv).

RILA MONASTERY
РИЛСКИ МАНАСТИР
☎ 07054 / elevation 1147m

Bulgaria's largest and most renowned monastery is hidden away in a narrow and forested valley of the Rila Mountains, 119km south of Sofia. It's the most revered holy place in the country, and one of the country's major attractions for Bulgarian pilgrims and foreign tourists alike. It's best to avoid weekends in summer, when the car park is full of cars and tour buses. Try to stay at least one night at a nearby hotel or camping ground (or even at the monastery itself), so you can visit during the more photogenic early mornings and late evenings. If you stay longer, you can also hike in the surrounding mountains (see p98).

Rila Monastery was founded in AD 927 by Ivan Rilski, a leader of a monastic colony of hermits. It was originally built about 3km to the northeast, but moved to the current site in 1335. By the end of the 14th century, the monastery had become a powerful feudal fiefdom. Plundered early in the 15th century, it was restored in 1469 after the relics of Ivan Rilski were returned from Veliko Târnovo. Under adverse conditions, the monastery helped to keep Bulgarian culture and religion alive during centuries of rule by the Turks, who destroyed the monastery several times.

In 1833 an accidental fire nearly engulfed all of the monastery's buildings. So many donations were received afterwards from various patrons that rebuilding commenced within a year – clearly indicating the monastery's importance and reverence to the

Bulgarian people. It was proclaimed as a national museum in 1961 by the Bulgarian government and included on Unesco's list of World Heritage Sites in 1983.

Monastery Grounds

The monastery compound is open from about 6am to 10pm, so bear this in mind if you're staying inside the monastery. Admission is free, but each of the two museums charges a 5 lv entrance fee. Photos are not permitted inside the main church but are allowed anywhere else in the grounds.

The eastern entrance is the Samokov gate but most cars and public buses park near the western Dupnitsa gate. Stalls sell souvenirs and useful English-language booklets near the Dupnitsa gate and at the base of the Hrelyu Tower, though a bit of history in English, French and German is included on notice boards nailed up at the entrances.

The monastery's forbidding exterior contrasts dramatically with the warmth and cosiness of the striped arcades inside. Four levels of colourful balconies – with monastic cells, storerooms, a refectory and kitchen – surround the large, irregular courtyard. The top balcony offers outstanding **views** of the surrounding Rila Mountains.

If you enter from the Samokov gate, you'll soon see the 23m-high stone **Hrelyu Tower**, named after a significant benefactor. Built in 1335, it is the only part of the monastery remaining from that time.

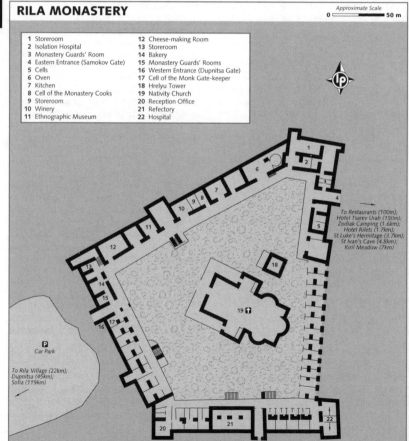

RILA MONASTERY

Approximate Scale
0 — 50 m

1 Storeroom
2 Isolation Hospital
3 Monastery Guards' Room
4 Eastern Entrance (Samokov Gate)
5 Cells
6 Oven
7 Kitchen
8 Cell of the Monastery Cooks
9 Storeroom
10 Winery
11 Ethnographic Museum
12 Cheese-making Room
13 Storeroom
14 Bakery
15 Monastery Guards' Rooms
16 Western Entrance (Dupnitsa Gate)
17 Cell of the Monk Gate-keeper
18 Hrelyu Tower
19 Nativity Church
20 Reception Office
21 Refectory
22 Hospital

To Restaurants (100m);
Hotel Tsarev Urah (150m);
Zodiak Camping (1.6km);
Hotel Rilets (1.7km);
St Luke's Hermitage (3.7km);
St Ivan's Cave (4.8km);
Kiril Meadow (7km)

P
Car Park

To Rila Village (22km);
Dupnitsa (45km);
Sofia (119km)

The **kitchen**, built in 1816, is at courtyard level in the northern wing. The 22m-high chimney, caked with centuries' worth of soot, cuts through all storeys by means of 10 rows of arches crowned by a small dome. Food, often cooked for thousands of pilgrims at a time, was prepared here in huge cauldrons, one of which was large enough to fit an entire cow!

Standing proudly in the middle of the courtyard is the magnificent **Nativity Church**, the largest monastery church in Bulgaria. The church, with its three great domes, was built between 1834 and 1837. The outside of this church is covered with colourful and dramatic frescoes, showing scenes of hell, where demons torture nude wrongdoers in various inventive ways. Other, more wholesome frescoes picture saints and angels. Several artists were involved but only the celebrated Zahari Zograf put his name to his work. The gilded and intricately carved iconostasis was created by artists from Samokov and Bansko. As with many Bulgarian churches, there is an official dress code (no shorts), although you're unlikely to be turned away for exposing your hairy legs. Photography inside the church, however, is not allowed.

The main, two-storey **museum** (admission 5 lv; ☾ 8.30am-4.30pm) is in the southeastern corner of the monastery. It houses a small and far from enthralling collection of 18th- and 19th-century ecclesiastical paraphernalia, prints and Bibles, though the star exhibit is the remarkable **Rila Cross**, a double-sided crucifix which Brother Raphael carved between 1790 and 1802. It's incised in miniature with 140 biblical scenes and inscriptions and about 650 human figures. Not surprisingly, Raphael eventually ruined his eyesight after staring through a magnifying glass for so long. Blown-up photos on the walls show just how detailed this work is. Despite the hordes of foreign tourists, nothing in the museum is labelled in any language except Bulgarian, but the booklet in English (available at the museum) will help.

Just beside the Samokov gate at the northeast of the monastery compound is the **Ethnographic Museum** (admission 5 lv; ☾ 8.30am-4.30pm) which displays the usual gathering of folk costumes, textiles and crafts from the region. Again, labelling is Bulgarian only.

Sleeping

Most places to stay are within about 100m of the eastern Samokov gate but there is also some spartan accommodation available within the monastery. Accommodation is also available at Rila village (p91) and Kiril Meadow (p94).

Zodiak Camping (☎ 2291; camp sites per person 10 lv, s/d bungalows 15/25 lv) This camping ground is not particularly private, and the bungalows are a bit shabby, but the restaurant and the riverside setting are superb. It's 1.6km past the monastery along the road to Kiril Meadow.

Rila Monastery (☎ 2208; r per person 20-30 lv) The cheaper rooms in the older western wing have three or four beds, and are sparsely furnished, but they are clean enough. The communal facilities for these rooms have toilets, but no showers. For those that would like a shower the newer rooms are far nicer, and have a private bathroom. Arrive early at the reception office (in the southern wing) because the newer rooms are often booked out by midday in summer.

Hotel Tsarev Vrah (☎ /fax 2280; s/d with bathroom €18/30) The Tsarev Vrah has been renovated but is still fairly unexciting and is overpriced for foreigners. Most balconies offer views of the forest and some have glimpses of the monastery. It's signposted about 150m from the Samokov gate.

Hotel Rilets (☎ 2106; fax 3363; s/d incl breakfast from 25/33 lv; P) The monolithic Rilets has a huge number of rooms, but it's a typically charmless leftover from the 1960s. It does have smarter 'refurbished' rooms (singles/doubles 35/45 lv), though, which are worth the extra cash. It's also a fair walk: the 500m-long access road starts 1.2km past the monastery along the road to Kiril Meadow. Guests without private vehicles will probably have to eat their evening meals at the drab dining room, or nearby Zodiak Camping, to avoid walking in the dark.

Eating

The places listed below are only a few metres from the Samokov gate. The freshest and tastiest local delicacy is trout, but beware – the price may look cheap on the menu, but the cost is per 100g.

Rila Restaurant (☎ 0488 90418; mains 2.50-12 lv; ☾ 8am-midnight) This attractive restaurant is in a 120-year-old building, again with plenty of outdoor setting. It has a similar menu to the Drushlyavitsa, though service could be friendlier.

Restaurant Drushlyavitsa (☎ 0888 278 756; mains 3-12 lv; ☺ 8am-10pm) Just outside the Samokov gate, this folksy place enjoys the best location, with outdoor tables overlooking a little brook, and it fills up quickly. The English menu offers a wide range of traditional Bulgarian cuisine.

The **bakery** (☺ daylight hr), next to the Rila Restaurant, is a popular little place offering hot, deep-fried doughnuts, as well as bread and sheep yoghurt. There are a few benches outside.

Getting There & Away

Buses to and from the monastery are frustratingly erratic. At the monastery, check the current schedules with local shopkeepers and restaurant staff (who often rely on the buses). In Sofia, it's worth ringing the **Ovcha Kupel bus station** (☎ 02-955 5362) about direct buses from the capital.

Buses leave Rila village for the monastery at 7.40am, 12.40pm and 3.50pm and return at 9am, 3pm and 5pm. (In summer, the 3pm service may continue to Sofia, but don't count on it.) From Dupnitsa, buses to Rila Monastery leave at 6.40am and 2.15pm and return from the monastery at about 9.40am and 5.15pm.

To make a really rushed day trip from Sofia to the monastery by public transport, take any bus to Dupnitsa (1½ hours) from the central bus station or Ovcha Kupel bus station before 8am. Then jump on the 10am (or 11am) bus to Rila village and catch the 12.40pm bus to the monastery. To return to Sofia, take the 5.15pm bus to Dupnitsa, and one of the hourly buses (or trains) back to the capital.

Full-day tours of Rila Monastery from Sofia cost from around €60 per person, for a group of two people, less if you're part of a larger group. For details, see p68.

AROUND RILA MONASTERY
St Luke's Hermitage & St Ivan's Cave

About 3.7km northeast of the monastery, as you drive along the road to Kiril Meadow, there's a trail on the left that leads to St Luke's Hermitage. The trail takes about 15 minutes by foot; look for the picture of St Ivan at the start of the steps. St Luke's Hermitage, built in 1798, features a large courtyard and the Church of St Luke. Continue walking along the trail for about 15 minutes to St Ivan's Cave, where Ivan Rilski lived, and is buried. According to local legend, anyone able to pass through the hole in the cave's roof has not sinned, and since it's easy to get through, the legend is very popular!

Kiril Meadow Кирилова Ливада

The road northeast of Rila Monastery continues for about 7km to Kiril Meadow, another typically gorgeous area with pine trees, picnic spots, cafés and stunning views of the craggy cliffs. Most of the road from the monastery is flat so it's a pleasant, and mostly shady, walk. There's a **guesthouse** (☎ 076-3268; r 25 lv, bungalows 50 lv) with rooms with four beds and a shared bathroom, and bungalows with five beds and a private bathroom. This is an excellent alternative for anyone who might be more interested in the quiet scenery than the busy monastery.

SAMOKOV САМОКОВ
☎ 0722 / pop 29,800

Samokov is a small and slightly scruffy-looking town about 62km southeast of Sofia, though it has a certain rustic charm and a few worthwhile sights. It's an easy day trip from the capital, and is also a handy jumping-off point for the nearby ski resort of Borovets. Samokov sprang up as an iron-mining centre in the 14th century, and was renowned during the 19th century for the Samokov School of Icon Painting and Woodcarving. Between 1910 and 1912, the local council established the famous but unsuccessful Samokov Commune. It was Bulgaria's first socialist organisation, and established to improve the safety, health and education of workers. Several foreign-exchange offices can be found near the bus station.

Sights

Easy to spot north of the bus station is the **Bairakli Mosque** (admission 1 lv; ☺ 9am-6pm Tue-Fri). It was built in the 1840s, and designed in a style epitomised by the Bulgarian national revival period. It's no longer used for worship and there's nothing to see inside other than the wonderfully ornate murals, while a little stall here sells postcards. Its minaret makes a handy landmark.

The **History Museum** (☎ 22 194; ul Liubcho Baranov 4; admission 1.50 lv; ☺ 8am-noon & 1-5pm Mon-Fri) contains archaeological and ethnographical displays, scale models of engines and furnaces, displays on the town's icon-painting heritage and a venerable printing press which produced Samokov's first Bulgarian-language magazines in 1844. Upstairs there is a gallery of photos of the old town and posed family groups from the 19th and early 20th centuries. It's a few metres west of the town square, in the middle of an unkempt garden. You may have to ring the doorbell to gain admittance.

The **Sarafska Kâshta Museum** (☎ 22 221; ul Knyaz Dondukov 11; admission 1 lv; ☺ 9am-noon & 1-5pm Mon-Fri) is about 200m north of the History Museum. This delightful 1860 national revival period home contains typical period furniture.

Sleeping & Eating

The hotel prices given below are for summer; expect to pay about 25% more in the winter season.

Hotel Koala (☎ 35 0783; ul Hristo Zagrafski 25; s/d/tr 15/22/32 lv; **P**) This small place is excellent value, with just six large, bright and well-furnished rooms with TV. It's tucked along a side street about 1km northeast of the bus station; look for the signs in English.

Hotel-Restaurant Sonata (☎ 27 534; ul Petâr Beron 4; s/d/tr €18/24/30; **P**) The Sonata is a new and fairly central hotel offering clean, cosy rooms, all with TVs and fridges. Half- and full-board options are available at an extra charge of €5 or €10. There's a children's playground and rental bikes, and the hotel also runs guided fishing and biking trips.

Plenty of cafés are dotted around the town centre. One of the better restaurants near the bus station is **Mehana Golyamata**

Cheshma (☎ 66 617; ul Tûrgovska; mains 4-10 lv; ☺ 10am-1am Mon-Sat), which serves up plenty of omelettes, grills and fish dishes. In front stands a grand 17th-century drinking fountain, which gives the restaurant its name. Alternatively, both hotels have restaurants.

Getting There & Away

Buses and minibuses to Samokov (3 lv, one hour) depart every 30 minutes between 7am and 7.30pm from the Yug bus station in Sofia. From the **Samokov bus station** (☎ 2640; ul Tûrgovska), minibuses head to Borovets (2 lv, 20 minutes), Govedartsi and Malîovitsa. Buses to Dupnitsa (3.50 lv, one hour) leave at 7.30am, 2.20pm and 5pm.

BOROVETS БОРОВЕЦ

☎ 07128 / elevation 1350m

Borovets is the most popular and established ski resort in Bulgaria, and is also an agreeable base for hiking trips in the summer. Outside these main seasons, though it's a bit of a ghost town, with some shops and restaurants closing up altogether. Although touristy and a little expensive, it's easy to escape the crowds – especially on summer weekdays, when you almost feel like you have the place to yourself. Borovets is compact and surrounded by thick pine forests, and offers plenty of things to see and do, and places to eat and drink.

Information

All places listed in this section are along, or just off, the main street (which starts from the road between Samokov and Kostenets), and are open throughout the summer. The staff at the **tourist office** (☎ 2658; Hotel Rila complex; ☺ 8.30am-11pm Nov-Feb, 9am-5.30pm Mar-Oct) can organise coach trips, walking tours and skiing lessons, among other things. The **travel agency** (☎ 306; Hotel Samokov) can provide information about hiking, and can arrange guides.

There are several foreign-exchange offices scattered around town. There is a small Internet centre in the Hotel Samokov.

Activities
SKIING

Bulgaria's oldest ski resort is built on the slopes of Mt Musala (2925m), one of the highest peaks in the Balkans. Only 70km from Sofia, Borovets is the most developed and compact resort in the country, and has twice hosted World Cup Alpine ski rounds. About 1.5m of snow is almost guaranteed between November and April. The 23 ski runs (including the longest in Bulgaria) are mostly in the main three areas of Markudjika, Yastrebets and Sitnyakovo-Martinovi Baraki. The four cross-country trails total about 19km, and start about 2km on foot from Borovets.

Borovets is reasonably good value, easy to reach from Sofia (but too far for a day trip by public transport), and there are cheap places to stay at nearby Samokov (p94), Govedartsi (p97) and Maliovitsa (p98). The downside is that Borovets, like Mt Vitosha, can get very crowded on weekends. Over a dozen places in Borovets rent ski equipment; just look for signs in English saying 'ski depot' or 'ski store'. Expect to pay 40 to 45 lv per day for a complete set of ski equipment. Plenty of well-qualified and multilingual instructors can provide training for about 300 lv (four hours per day for six days, including a lift pass and ski gear). Guests at some hotels such as the Rila (p97) and the Samokov (p97) can get cheaper training from in-house instructors.

Borovets has three chairlifts, one gondola and 10 draglifts. The gondola (open year-round) from the Borosports complex in Borovets to Yastrebets costs 8/13 lv one way/return. A one-day lift pass costs 55 lv. A free minibus between the main hotels and ski slopes is available to anyone with a lift pass.

Snowboarding at Borovets is OK, without being exceptional. A snowboard and boots can be hired for about 40 lv per day, and training can be arranged for about 120 lv (six hours). Contact the **Bulgarian Extreme and Freestyle Skiing Association** (www.befsa.com) for details of organised competitions, demonstrations and excursions in Borovets and elsewhere.

HIKING

Borovets is the best starting point for hikes along marked trails around the eastern section of the Rila Mountains. Some hikes simply follow established ski runs, which is just as well because none of the hiking trails around Borovets are included on the *Rila* map, published (in Cyrillic) by Kartografia.

Some of the shorter and more popular hikes are listed below.

Borovets–Chernata Skala Follow the road towards Kostenets, and look for the signs heading south to Hizha Maritsa; three hours (easy).

Borovets–Hizha Maritsa Use the Borovets to Chernata Skala road, and continue along the southern road; 4½ hours (medium).

Borovets–Hizha Sokolets Follow the road through Borovets – 2½ hours (easy). Another trail (1½ hours) from Hizha Sokolets heads south to Mt Sokolets (2021m).

Yastrebets–Borovets Take the gondola (see p95) to Yastrebets (2369m) and walk down; 60 to 90 minutes (easy).

OTHER ACTIVITIES

Horse riding is available in season from outside the main entrance to Hotel Rila, and costs from around 40 lv for two hours.

The mammoth **Hotel Samokov** (☎ 2581; www.samokov.com) has an indoor swimming pool (admission 4 lv), bowling alley and fitness centre, and offers saunas and massages. Each is available daily in winter, and from Friday to Sunday in summer.

The **tourist office** (☎ 2658; Hotel Rila complex) offers all-inclusive bus trips to Rila Monastery year-round (half-/full-day 37/50 lv) and Plovdiv (full day 66 lv).

Sleeping

Book well ahead (three to six months in peak times) if you want mid-range or top-end accommodation during the ski season. The rates listed here are for the summer; expect to pay about 20% more in winter. These places do not have addresses as such, because none of the streets are named. Cheaper places to stay nearby can be found in Govedartsi (p97), Samokov (p95) and Maliovitsa (p98).

Flora Hotel (☎ 2520; flora_hotel@abv.bg; s/d from 28/40 lv; **P**) The Flora is a pleasant, quiet place which offers great value for its central location. Rooms are plain but very clean and all have balconies, and there's a cosy bar and restaurant. Also on site is a small 'fishing complex' where you can catch and barbecue your own trout.

Alpin Hotel (☎ 2201; www.alpin-hotel.bg; s/d €31/38) This smart modern place just opposite the Rila has small but comfortable rooms with all the mod cons, as well as an 'English pub' and restaurant. Service is a little impersonal, though.

Hotel Sveti Ivan Rilski (☎ 2790; s/d €20/50; P) This ageing barracks-like establishment is set in secluded grounds near the centre. Rooms are small and a bit shabby, although all have TVs and the bathrooms are very new. There's a restaurant and bar, and even a small natural history museum upstairs, but it's absurdly overpriced for foreigners, and it may be worth asking about any discounts available.

Hotel Rila (☎ 2441; www.borovets-bg.com; s/d/apt 90/120/160 lv; ☻) The gigantic Rila is one of the largest and most popular hotels in town, and has superb facilities including a sports centre, tennis court, restaurants, shopping arcade and a night club. Special rates are on offer if you're staying for three nights or longer.

Hotel Samokov (☎ 2581; www.samokov.com; s/d/ste from €45/60/110; P ☐ ☻) Another giant, this colossal 11-storey place probably has the best facilities in Borovets, with three restaurants, a nightclub, shopping centre, gym, bowling alley and ski school. Rooms are comfortable, and all have balconies, but there's not a great deal of character here.

Villa Stresov (www.villastresov.com; d from €100, whole villa from €480; P ✗) This large, Swiss-style villa has four double rooms, sleeping up to eight people, a fully fitted kitchen, a garden and all the expected mod cons, and it can be rented out in its entirety. You can also just pay for the use of one, two or three bedrooms, and still have the run of the house; nobody else will be able to book into the vacant rooms. There's a two-night minimum stay. For details and reservations, check the website.

Eating

The main streets of Borovets are lined with masses of cafés, bars and restaurants serving a cosmopolitan array of cuisines, though note that many have erratic opening schedules outside the peak seasons and some close up altogether. Menus are almost always in English (and sometimes French and German), but if the menu is only in a foreign language, it's likely that the prices are two to three times higher than those on the Bulgarian menu. The cheapest eateries are at the turn-off to Borovets along the Samokov–Kostenets road.

La Bomba (☎ 483; mains 4-8 lv; ⏲ 8am-1am) Just opposite the Hotel Rila, La Bomba is typical of the many simple establishments around town serving pizzas and steak-and-chips style dishes.

White Magic (☎ 2783; mains 6-12 lv) A popular bar-restaurant opposite Hotel Samokov, run by former Olympic skier Christo Angelov, which serves up hearty international cooking.

Alpin Restaurant (mains 7-12 lv) This restaurant, at the hotel of the same name (opposite), offers a varied, if inevitable touristy, menu of pizzas, grills and barbecue meals. There's outdoor seating.

Getting There & Away

There is no direct public transport between Sofia and Borovets, so take a bus from Sofia to Samokov (3 lv, one hour) and then a minibus to Borovets (2 lv, 20 minutes). Minibuses from Samokov leave about every 30 to 45 minutes between 7am and 7pm. A taxi from Samokov costs a negotiable 5 lv.

Minibuses from Samokov usually drop off and pick up passengers outside Hotel Samokov in Borovets. Taxis congregate around the turn-off and can be chartered to Sofia for about 50 lv. It's always worth asking about sharing a taxi back to Sofia, or anywhere else in the region.

GOVEDARTSI ГОВЕДАРЦИ
☎ 07125 / elevation 1200m

Govedartsi is a pretty village 13km southwest of Samokov. It's a cheap and convenient base for visiting Borovets and/or Malîovitsa, and is a starting point for hikes along marked trails in the Rila Mountains (as detailed in the *Rila* map published by Kartografia).

There are two accommodation and eating options.

Number 53 Hotel (☎ 08857 313; kokojambazki@hotmail.com; d with shared bathroom 20 lv) has large, airy and bright rooms of outstanding value. The hotel also boasts an outdoor garden, sauna, bar and restaurant. It's a three-storey, white building along the Samokov–Malîovitsa road, about 300m east (towards Samokov) of the bus stop.

Kalina Hotel (☎ 2643; kalina-hotel@top.bg; s/d 22/44 lv) About 150m up from the town square and bus stop, the Kalina has friendly owners who can tell you everything about the local history and folklore. The rooms are smallish, but clean, comfortable and nicely furnished (with chandelier and TV). It also has a restaurant-bar and a barbecue in the garden.

From Samokov, six or seven minibuses go to Govedartsi (2 lv, 20 minutes) each day.

MALÎOVITSA МАЛЬОВИЦА
elevation 1750m

At the foot of the Rila Mountains 13km southwest of Govedartsi, Maliovitsa is far smaller, less commercial and cheaper than Borovets. It's a charmingly scenic spot with just a couple of hotels. In winter Malîovitsa is a no-frills ski resort, while in summer it's a popular place for rock climbing, mountain climbing, hiking and picnicking. Most visitors are day-trippers from Sofia with private vehicles. Those travellers without private transport will probably have to spend at least one night here if travelling from Sofia.

Activities
HIKING

Maliovitsa makes a great base for walks; the trails are well marked and easy to follow. Still, it's worth buying the *Rila* map, published by Kartografia (with the green cover), though it is only in Cyrillic.

An hour's hike from Malîovitsa is Hizha Maliovitsa at 2050m above sea level. Some rooms have four beds, but others have 20, so ask for a private room if you're in a small group. Camping is allowed for a minimal fee. Basic meals and drinks are available at the café but guests can also bring their own food and use the kitchen.

From Hizha Malîovitsa it's about seven hours to Hizha Sedemte Ezera, an older hut with simple dormitories. **Hizha Rilski Ezera** (☎ 0701-50513), at 2150m, is a little further north and is generally regarded as the nicest hut accommodation in the Rila Mountains. It offers dorm beds, as well as rooms with a shared/private bathroom from around 30/35 lv per person, including breakfast and dinner. A modest café is attached. Reservations are not normally necessary for either hut, except during the meeting of the White Brotherhood (see the boxed text, right) in August.

From the Seven Lakes, it's an easy one-hour hike down to 1985m to **Hizha Skakavitsa** (☎ 0701-50513), where there's a picturesque waterfall, or six to seven hours south to the Rila Monastery. You could bypass Hizha Malîovitsa and hike to the Sedemte Ezera (Seven Lakes) from Malîovitsa, via Hizha Vada and Hizha Lovina.

It's also possible to visit these sparkling lakes from Sapareva Banya (accessible by bus from Dupnitsa), or from Hizha Pionerska (1500m). To reach this hut from Sapareva Banya, walk 13km up the steep road, hire a taxi (more reliably from Dupnitsa), or organise a transfer (about 30/35 lv for one/two people) with Zig Zag Holidays (p69). From the hut, it's about a three-hour hike to Hizha Rilski Ezera.

SKIING

Skiing here is certainly cheaper than at Borovets, but not nearly as challenging. Ski equipment is available from the **Central Mountain School** (☎ 07125-2270) for 4 to 6 lv per person per day depending on the quality of equipment (pay extra for the better gear!). Elsewhere in Malîovitsa, equipment is about 14 lv per day. The one and only draglift costs a mere 7 lv per person per day.

OTHER ACTIVITIES

In summer, the Central Mountain School offers **rock climbing** and **mountain climbing** activities for about 30 to 50 lv per person per day, including a guide, but not transport or equipment (which is available at the School).

Between March and June, and also in September and October, **kayaking** and **rafting**

THE WHITE BROTHERHOOD

This Bulgarian-based cult is also known as Dunovism, after the priest who started it in 1918. Adherents practice a curious amalgamation of rituals such as yoga, sun-worshipping and vegetarianism, borrowed from Eastern Orthodox Christianity and Hinduism, among other religions. Followers meet at Sedemte Ezera each August; check with the Odysseia-In Travel Agency (p60) or the National Information & Advertising Center (p60) in Sofia for the exact dates. Hikers should note that the Hizha Sedemte Ezera and Hizha Rilski Ezera huts are often booked out for a week or more in August but the public are still welcome at the huts during the day to witness the pilgrimage.

is possible along local rivers; contact the Central Mountain School for current prices.

Sleeping & Eating

Hotel Malîovitsa (☎ /fax 07125-2222; d/tr/q incl breakfast from 20/30/40 lv; **P**) This huge place above the car park is atmospheric, and the rooms are nicer than the outside of the hotel, and corridors, would suggest. The hotel may change money, but it's better to do this before you come. It has a restaurant, bar, ski school and kids' playground.

Guesthouse Dzhambazki (☎ 07125-2361; info@house-djambazki.com; s/d/apt from 12/24/44 lv; **P**) This quaint and homy little place has comfortable rooms, some with balconies, as well as a sauna and mountain bikes for the use of guests – it's great value.

Central Mountain School (☎ 07125-2270; d from 25 lv; **P**) Near the car park, the school offers very basic accommodation and also has a restaurant.

Getting There & Away

In theory, a minibus travels from the Yug bus station in Sofia every day at 9am directly to Malîovitsa (6 lv, 2 hours). If this doesn't eventuate, simply catch a bus to Samokov and get a minibus to Malîovitsa (3 lv, 45 minutes) at 8.15am or 4.15pm. Minibuses return to Samokov at 9am and 5pm, and (theoretically) to Sofia at about midday.

PIRIN MOUNTAINS
ПИРИН ПЛАНИНА

Nestled in the southwest corner of Bulgaria are the compact Pirin Mountains (2585 sq km), named after Perun, the Slavic god of thunder. Over the centuries, Greeks, Turks and Slavs have been attracted to these mountains because of the mineral waters (from 230 sources) and 186 pristine lakes, often partially frozen in winter. The average height of the Pirin Mountains is comparatively low at 1033m but over 100 peaks are higher than 2000m (and 12 are more than 2700m). The highest is Mt Vihren (2915m), near Bansko.

Only 1.8km southwest of Bansko is a gate to the Pirin National Park, which is permanently open and free to enter, Bulgaria's largest at 40,447 hectares. It was placed on Unesco's list of World Heritage Sites in 1983 to protect the varied and unique landscapes, 1100 species of flora, 102 types of birds and 42 species of mammals, such as bears, deer and wild goats. The **Pirin National Park office** (☎ /fax 07443-2428; bul Bansko 4, Bansko) is not a tourist office or hiking agency, nor a place to rent equipment, but it can provide help to anyone wishing to undertake a long trek in the mountains.

BANSKO БАНСКО
☎ 07443 / pop 9740 / elevation 930m

Bansko is one of the big names in Bulgarian tourism; it's a base for top-notch skiing (see p101) and superb hiking in summer. Bansko is home to more than 150 cultural monuments, including many from the Bulgarian national revival period. These buildings were made with stone and timber and built behind fortress-style walls, with hidden escape routes, to shield inhabitants from their Ottoman occupiers. With the help of the Beautiful Bulgaria Project, many of these houses have been transformed into charming *mehanas* (taverns) and cosy pensions, and Bansko has become particularly popular with weekending Sofians. Although they may look suitably quaint, the huge, irregular cobblestones favoured along the lanes of the old quarter are hard on the feet and almost seem designed to cause accidents, so do watch your step.

Bansko was founded in the 10th century on the site of an old Thracian settlement. By the mid-18th century, it was a highly prosperous town because of its fortuitous location on the overland caravan route between the Aegean Sea and Danubian Europe. At this time, Bansko was home to traders, craftsmen and artists, as well as influential icon-painting and woodcarving schools.

Orientation

Bansko's bus and train stations stand near each other in a shabby and unpromising part of town north of the centre. The main square, pl Nikola Vaptsarov, is connected to pl Vûzhrazhdane by ul Pirin. The latter square is dominated by the mammoth Paisii Hilendarski Monument, dedicated to a locally born monk who was one of the instigators of the Bulgarian national revival in the mid-18th century. Most shops and cafés are along the pedestrian mall, ul Tsar Simeon.

Information

At the time of research, there was no official tourist office in Bansko, although this may change in the future should funds become available. In the meantime, **Oasis-A travel agency** (☎ 8076; ul Tsar Simeon 52; ◷ 9.30am-7pm Nov-Aug, 10am-1pm Sep-Oct) is happy to provide tourist information. They also run excursions and can book private rooms. The *Illustrated Map of Bansko* is printed in English and is widely available.

There are a few places to change money. Most are along ul Tsar Simeon, such as KSV

Ltd, the foreign-exchange office next to the supermarket, and the nearby DSK Bank, just over the road from the post office and telephone centre.

Internet Club Zonata (ul Bulgaria 22)

United Bulgarian Bank (ul Pirin) Next to Rodina Hotel, with ATM and foreign-exchange facilities.

Pirin National Park office (☎ /fax 2428; bul Bansko 4) For those wishing to find out about long treks in the Pirin Mountains.

Sights

House-Museum of Nikola Vaptsarov (☎ 8304; pl Nikola Vaptsarov; admission 2 lv; ◷ 9am-noon & 2-5.45pm Mon-Sat) is in the house where Vaptsarov (1909–42), respected antifascist poet and activist, was born. He was a populist writer

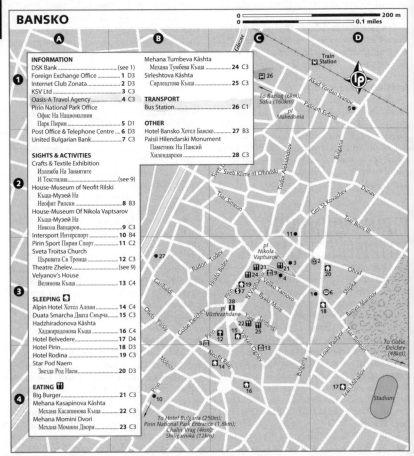

BANSKO

0 _____ 200 m
0 _____ 0.1 miles

INFORMATION
DSK Bank...(see 1)
Foreign Exchange Office 1 D3
Internet Club Zonata............................... 2 D3
KSV Ltd 3 C3
Oasis-A Travel Agency 4 C3
Pirin National Park Office
    Офис На Националния
    Парк Пирин 5 D1
Post Office & Telephone Centre 6 D3
United Bulgarian Bank.............................7 C3

SIGHTS & ACTIVITIES
Crafts & Textile Exhibition
    Изложба На Занаятите
    И Текстилна..(see 9)
House-Museum of Neofit Rilski
    Къща-Музей На
    Неофит Рилски....................................8 B3
House-Museum Of Nikola Vaptsarov
    Къща-Музей На
    Никола Вапцаров................................9 C3
Intersport Интерспорт............................ 10 B4
Pirin Sport Пирин Спорт 11 C2
Sveta Troitsa Church
    Църквата Св Троица 12 C3
Theatre Zhelev...(see 9)
Velyanov's House
    Велянова Къща 13 C4

SLEEPING 🏠
Alpin Hotel Хотел Алпин........................ 14 C4
Duata Smarcha Двата Смърча.............. 15 C3
Hadzhiradonova Kâshta
    Хаджирадонова Къща 16 C4
Hotel Belvedere..................................... 17 D4
Hotel Pirin.. 18 D3
Hotel Rodina.. 19 D3
Star Pod Naem
    Звезда Род Наем................................ 20 D3

EATING 🍴
Big Burger.. 21 C3
Mehana Kasapinova Kâshta
    Механа Касапинова Къща 22 C3
Mehana Momini Dvori
    Механа Момини Двори...................... 23 C3

Mehana Tumbeva Kâshta
    Механа Тумбева Къща 24 C3
Sirleshtova Kâshta
    Сирлещова Къща 25 C3

TRANSPORT
Bus Station 26 C1

OTHER
Hotel Bansko Хотел Банско.............. 27 B3
Paisii Hilendarski Monument
    Паметник На Паисий
    Хилендарски 28 C3

To Razlog (6km);
Sofia (160km)

To Hotel Bulgaria (250m);
Pirin National Park Entrance (1.8km);
Chalin Vrag (4km);
Shiligarnika (12km)

To Gotse
Delchev
(48km)

and labour activist influenced by communist ideology while a student at the Varna Maritime Academy. Jailed and tortured by the wartime fascist government, Vaptsarov penned his most famous poem while awaiting execution. There are a few rooms furnished in period style, plus photographs, documents and personal belongings of the man himself, though nothing is labelled in anything but Bulgarian. A short video film, followed by an audio tape in English, French or German provides some background; ask staff to run them for you. The attached **Crafts & Textile Exhibition** is basically a big souvenir shop, with a range of traditional arts, crafts and textiles from Bansko and all over the Pirin Mountains for sale. You may have to ask a member of staff to open it up. The exhibition overlooks the adjacent **Theatre Zhelev** (admission free; 9am-noon & 2-5.45pm Mon-Sat), where landscapes by the famous local painter Tenio Zhelev are on show. Again, everything is for sale, should you have the odd 700 lv or so burning a hole in your pocket.

Velyanov's House (4181; ul Velyan Ognev 5; admission 2 lv; 9am-noon & 2-5pm Mon-Fri) features the sort of elaborately painted scenes and carved woodwork that is representative of the so-called 'Bansko School' of art.

House-Museum of Neofit Rilski (2540; ul Pirin 17) is a converted school room that

was closed for renovation at the time of research. It contains some manuscripts by, and photos of, Rilski (1793–1881), who is renowned as the father of Bulgarian secular education.

The **Sveta Troitsa Church** (pl Vûzhrazhdane; 7am-7pm) was built in 1835. Surrounded by a stone wall 1m thick and 4m high, it features magnificent wooden floors and faded murals. In the church grounds is Bansko's major landmark: the 30m-high **clock tower**, built in 1850.

Activities

Nestled at the base of the imposing Mt Vihren (2915m), Bansko enjoys a climate of relatively short summers and long snowy winters. Bansko doesn't really compete with Borovets or Pamporovo, so it appeals to those who want cheaper **skiing** without the high costs and après-ski activities. Although the area's high elevation (1800m to 2500m) ensures Bulgaria's most consistent skiing, it is surprisingly ignored by foreign skiers on package tours.

On the plus side, Bansko is certainly a more atmospheric place to stay than Pamporovo or Borovets and it's not too far from Sofia. Also, the snow, which is often 2m thick between mid-December and mid-April, sometimes lasts until mid-May and the lifts and slopes are generally well

---

HIKING IN THE PIRIN MOUNTAINS

Marked hiking trails, 13 primary and 17 secondary, link 13 huts and shelters throughout the park. The primary trails are best described and mapped in the colourful and detailed map (1:55,000) in the *National Park Pirin* leaflet printed in English by the Ministry of Environment. Pick up the leaflet from the **National Park office** (/fax 07443-2428; bul Bansko 4), or from souvenir shops.

The only accurate and detailed hiking map of the whole mountain range is the *Pirin* map (1:55,000), published in Cyrillic by Kartografia, and widely available in Sofia, Sandanski and Bansko. This map indicates numerous marked trails from Bansko and contains enough detail to explore areas around Melnik and Sandanski. Also, the Domino map of *Bansko* includes a small but detailed map in English of 12 hiking trails. These include Bansko to **Hizha Banderitsa** (07443-8279), 2km southwest of Shiligarnika, and Bansko to **Hizha Vihren** (07443-8279), 2km further up. Both offer convenient bases for hikes to nearby **caves** and **lakes**, for example Hizha Vihren to Mt Vihren is about three hours one way.

From Sandanski, a popular, three-hour hike leads to the glorious **Popina Lûka** region, with lakes, waterfalls and pine forests. Hikers can stay at **Hizha Kamenitsa** (0746-30385) or **Hizha Yane Sandanski** (0746-30385). Half-board at either costs around 25 lv.

The *Mountains of Bulgaria*, by Julian Perry, describes in words (but with poor maps) a trek across the entire Pirin Mountains from Hizha Predel (at the end of the trek across the Rila Mountains) to Petrovo village near the Greek border. It's a tough trek, so allow seven to 10 days – more for delays if the weather is bad.

maintained. On the other hand, the slopes are a hassle to reach with private transport (so take a bus from Bansko), and it can get crowded on weekends.

With regard to skiing, the resort of 'Bansko' really refers to Shiligarnika, at the end of a winding, 12km road south of Bansko. Together with the far smaller Chalin Vrag, 4km southwest of Bansko, there are six ski runs (total of 14km) but only 8km of cross-country trails. There are four chairlifts and four draglifts at Shiligarnika. An all-day lift pass, which includes a free bus ride to/from the slopes, costs about 20 lv.

Equipment (from 30 lv per day) can be hired, and instructors can be arranged at **Pirin Sport** (☎ 537; ul Gen St Kovachev 8), which can also organise snowboard hire and instructors. Equipment and instructors can also be arranged at **Intersport** (☎ 4876; ul Pirin 71), **Hotel Bulgaria** (☎ 3005; ul Hristo Matov 2), **Alpin Hotel** (☎ 8075; ul Neofit Rilski 6) and **Hotel Bansko** (☎ 4275; bansko@bg400.bg; ul Glazne 37). Hotel Bansko and Intersport also hire out mountain bikes in summer, but don't expect too much in the way of quality and quantity.

Festivals & Events

St Theodor's Day (15 Mar) Celebrated with horse racing in nearby Dobrinishte.

Celebration of Bansko Traditions (17-24 May)

Pirin Sings Folk Festival (Aug) Takes place near Bansko every second (odd-numbered) year in August, bringing together thousands of folk musicians and dancers from throughout the Pirin Mountains.

International Jazz Festival (around 7-15 Aug) Attracts artists from all over Bulgaria and abroad. Most events at this festival are held on a temporary open-air stage at pl Nikola Vaptsarov and in the Theatre Zhelev.

Bansko Day (5 Oct)

Sleeping

It's worth booking ahead during any major festival and in the peak ski season. The rates listed are for summer; in winter add at least another 20% to 25%. Some hotels close for refurbishment outside the main winter and summer seasons, or operate on a much reduced level of service, so always phone ahead. Unofficial, discreet camping is possible in the nearby Pirin National Park (p99). **Star Pod Naem** (☎ 3998; bul Bulgaria 33) and **Oasis-A travel agency** (☎ 8076; ul Tsar Simeon 52; 🕑 9.30am-7pm Nov-Aug, 10am-1pm Sep-Oct) can both arrange rooms (most with a shared

bathroom) in private homes from about 22 lv per person. You'll pay slightly more in December.

Hadzhiradonova Kâshta (☎ 8276; ul Buirov 7; s/d from 13/26 lv) This charming old house offers the best value in town, with a few large, traditionally furnished rooms, complete with sheepskin bedspreads and gleaming, modern bathrooms, looking on to a picturesque courtyard. The price is unbeatable.

Alpin Hotel (☎ 8075; ul Neofit Rilski 6; s/d from 15/30 lv) The Alpin offers a range of clean and simple rooms, and is good value compared to similar places in town. Nobody seems to speak English, but climbing gear is available for hire.

Duata Smarcha (☎ 2632; ul Velyan Ognev 2; s/d incl breakfast from 16/32 lv) Set in a lovely garden, this pension is cosy and the staff speak good English. Traditional home-cooked meals are available, both to guests and the public, at the restaurant. The rooms (with TV) are excellent value, which is why it's popular and often full so book ahead.

Hotel Belvedere (☎ 8083; fax 8082; ul Ivan Mihailov 28; d €18; P) The Swiss-chalet style Belvedere is a modern hotel in a quiet residential street on the eastern edge of town. Most rooms have balconies and there's a restaurant and bar.

Hotel Rodina (☎ 8106; fax 8472; ul Pirin 7; s/d/apt €24/32/62) The Rodina is a cosy and modern hotel right in the centre of town. The public areas seem a little drab, while the rooms are plain but well cared for. There's a sauna and massage parlour to ease your aches, and a restaurant and tavern.

Hotel Pirin (☎ 8051; www.hotelpirin.bansko.bg; ul Tsar Simeon 68; s/d/apt from 50/80/95 lv; P 🖵) The Pirin is a big modern place opposite the post office offering smart, comfy rooms, a good range of facilities and an attractive garden. The price is very reasonable for a four-star establishment, though it's a little bland and impersonal.

Eating

Bansko has dozens of traditional *mehanas* offering regional delicacies – such as *kapama* (several kinds of meat, rice and sauerkraut simmered and served in a clay pot) and home-made *karvavitsa* (sausage made of pork or other meat) – all washed down with a bottle of locally made wine. Note that some places close out of season.

Big Burger (ul Tsar Simeon 4; sandwiches 2-3 lv; ☺ breakfast, lunch & dinner) One of several simple snack bars along this street offering burgers, sandwiches and drinks at a few outdoor tables.

Mehana Tubeva Kâshta (☎ 0899 888 993; ul Pirin 7; mains 3-7 lv) This amenable little bar and restaurant serves up the usual Bulgarian specialities, plus lighter meals, salads and omelettes, in a secluded, cat-filled garden. There's also a cosy interior for the colder weather.

Mehana Momini Dvori (☎ 8259; pl Vaptsarov; mains 4-5 lv) This big place, overlooking pl Nikola Vaptsarov, offers a wide range of pizzas and barbecued dishes, and has plenty of outdoor seating and a little waterfall out the front. There's a big drinks list and an English menu.

Mehana Kasapinova Kâshta (☎ 3500; ul Yane Sandanski 4; mains 4-10 lv) For excellent local food and wine in a traditional setting, the Kasapinova is probably the best place in town. Colourful local rugs bedeck the walls, wine is served up in clay beakers and on cold evenings there's a roaring fire.

Sirleshtova Kâshta (☎ 4668; ul Yane Sandanski 12; mains 5-10 lv) This *mehana* occupies a building where, in 1890, partisan Gotse Delchev organised the Macedonian Revolutionary Movement. It's a charming place to try some local Bansko cuisine and wine.

Getting There & Away

From Sofia (7.50 lv, three hours), five or six daily buses travel directly to Bansko via Blagoevgrad and several more travelling to Gotse Delchev also stop at the **Bansko bus station** (☎ 8117; ul Patriarh Evtimii). In addition, four or five buses go to Blagoevgrad only and two more depart for Plovdiv (7.50 lv, 3½ hours) at 7.10am and 8.20am. Between mid-June and mid-September, private minibuses (3 lv) run to Hizha Banderitsa (see Hiking in the Pirin Mountains on p101), leaving at 8.30am, 2.15pm and 5pm. They return to Bansko at 9.30am, 3pm and 6pm.

The **train station** (☎ 0887 038 312; Akad Yordan Ivanov) is on the narrow-gauge rail route between Septemvri (on the main Sofia–Plovdiv line) and Dobrinishte. Take this laboriously slow train (about five hours from Septemvri to Bansko) for the scenery and ambience because it's certainly not the quickest

way to/from Bansko. Ten daily trains travel along this route and stop at Avramovo, the highest station in the Balkans.

SANDANSKI САНДАНСКИ
☎ 0746 / pop 27,600

Sandanski, 65km south of Blagoevgrad, is normally only used by tourists as a connection to Melnik. However, it's a pleasant and laid-back town with a reputation as the sunniest in Bulgaria, and it's also a major spa centre. It boasts a huge, leafy park, and, with plenty of hotels and restaurants, Sandanski makes a good alternative base, both for anyone wanting a little more nightlife and excitement than Melnik (17km to the southeast) and for hiking (see Hiking in the Pirin Mountains p101). Sandanski's mineral springs, which apparently cure all sorts of ills such as bronchitis and asthma, attract tourists from all over the Balkans. Being this close to the Greek border, there's a strong Hellenic influence in town, most noticeably in the scattering of small tavernas; bar and restaurant menus translated into Greek; and promenading youths in Greek football shirts.

Sandanski was first settled in about 2000 BC by Thracians and later by the Romans and Slavs. The town is said to have been the birthplace of Spartacus, who led the legendary slave revolt in Sicily against the Romans in 74 BC. Sandanski was almost completely destroyed in the 6th century AD by barbarians but was later rebuilt and became an important town in the First Bulgarian Empire. Once known as Sveti Vrach, the town was renamed in 1949 in honour of the Macedonian freedom fighter Yane Sandanski.

Information

There was no tourist information centre in Sandanski at the time of research, but one may open in the future should funds become available. There are several banks, ATMs and foreign-exchange offices strung out along bul Makedonia. The post office and telephone centre are on pl Bulgaria.

Sights & Activities

The **Archaeological Museum** (☎ 23 188; bul Makedonia 55) was built over the remains of a Roman villa, and has a mass of poorly labelled ancient artefacts, including lots of tombstones and votive tablets, and the mosaic floor of the original villa. Of some interest is the explanation (in Bulgarian) about Sandanski's apparent link to Spartacus and items from the adjacent ruins of the 5th-century **St Joan's Basilica**. The museum was closed for renovation at the time of research, phone ahead for opening hours.

More, scrappier, **Byzantine ruins** can be seen behind, on ul Mara Buneva, possibly including a baptistry, though there's no explanation and it's not easy to make much sense out of the recumbent columns and rubble.

The **Sveti Georgi Church** (ul Sv Sv Kiril i Metodii 10; 8am-6pm) was built in 1861 and is the only church in Sandanski remaining from that period. Visitors are welcome.

The huge **Town Park** contains over 200 species of plants from the Mediterranean, as well as **mineral baths and swimming pools** (admission 1.50 lv; 9am-7pm summer), a small **lake** with paddle boats and a **Summer Theatre**. A lazy stream also runs through the park, and you can cross it on a swinging, rocking bridge.

Festivals & Events

St Vasil's Day Folk Concert (1 Jan)
Sandanski Celebrations Thursday after Orthodox Easter Sunday.
Pirin Folk National Festival (early Sep) Features plenty of dancing and music.
Young Red Wine Festival (early Dec) Merry festival of the grape.

Sleeping

Hotel Aneli (31 844; www.aneli.hit.bg, in Bulgarian; ul Gotse Delchev 1; d/apt 28/45 lv) Overlooking the main square, the Aneli offers simple, clean and cosy accommodation with smart modern bathrooms. It's excellent value and often full so do book ahead.

Hotel Balevurov (30 013; fax 24 024; ul Mara Buneva 14; tw/d 25/30 lv; P) This small modern hotel overlooks the remains of St Joan's Basilica and has neat, clean rooms with TVs and balconies. Twin rooms have separate, but large, private and lockable bathrooms. The narrow spiral staircase may prove awkward for some, though, especially if you have heavy luggage. And you're on the 4th floor.

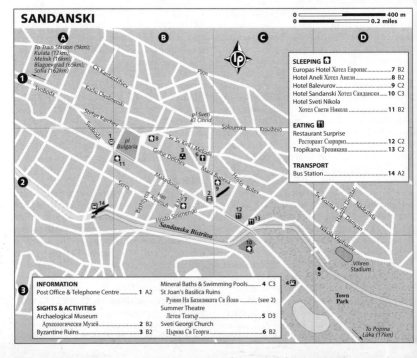

SANDANSKI

0 | 400 m
0 | 0.2 miles

To Train Station (5km);
Kulata (12km);
Melnik (16km);
Blagoevgrad (65km);
Sofia (162km)

To Popina
Lûka (17km)

Sveti Petâr and Pavel Church (p108), Melnik

Old-town architecture, Plovdiv (p117)

Rila Monastery (p91)

Plovdiv (p117)

Kiril Meadow (p94) in the Rila Mountains

A doorway off the upstairs balcony of the Rila Monastery (p91)

Wild flowers, Pirin Mountains (p99)

Europas Hotel (☎ 30 166; ul 8 Mart 11; s/d 29/40 lv;
🔀) This central place is a decent, reasonably priced option with snug, clean rooms.
All have whirring fridges and most have
balconies, if you'd like to sit out and gaze
at the local washing-lines. It can get a bit
noisy.

Hotel Sveti Nikola (☎ 33 035; www.hotel-sveti-
nikola.ltd.bg; bul Makedonia 1; s/d/ste 79/99/148 lv;
🔀 🖭 P) Outwardly resembling a nonde-
script apartment block, Sveti Nikola is right
on busy pl Bulgaria. Rooms are comfortable, if nothing special for the price, but
you're really paying for the location and
facilities, which include a sports centre and
nightclub. There's a Greek taverna attached,
with live music and nightly plate-smashing,
and lots of bars in the vicinity, so it's not the
quietest spot to stay.

Hotel Sandanski (☎ 31 165; www.interhotelsand
anski.com; bul Makedonia; s/d/apt 110/140/220 lv;
P 🗶 🔀 🖭) This minimountain of a hotel
has almost 300 restful rooms, all with balconies, and it's also a leading balneological centre, offering various hydrotherapy
treatments and weight-loss, anti-stress and
aromatherapy programmes. There's a tennis court and a pétanque pitch, and gym-
nastics classes for those fighting the flab.
The price isn't bad for four-star comfort,
and it's well-placed right beside the park.
Other features include restaurants, cafés,
bars and a nightclub.

Eating
Tropikana (☎ 0898 726 578; bul Makedonia 73; mains
3-6 lv) This place near the entrance to the
Town Park has a big menu of salads, omelettes and inexpensive traditional Bulgarian
dishes, and plenty of outdoor seating where
local cats and dogs beg for scraps.

Restaurant Surprise (☎ 31 202; bul Makedonia 63;
mains 2.50-8 lv; 🕑 lunch & diner) One of the nicer
restaurants along the main drag, Surprise
serves up fish, salads, pizza, grills and barbecue dishes. It has an English menu and
outdoor seating.

All the above hotels also have restaurants.
Dozens more cafés can be found along bul
Makedonia.

Getting There & Away
From the **bus station** (☎ 22 130; ul Hristo Smirnenski) buses to Sofia (8 lv, 3½ hours, six to eight
daily) travel via Blagoevgrad and Dupnitsa.

Buses go to Melnik, and on to Rozhen, at
7.40am, 11.40am, 3.30pm and 5.30pm (1.70 lv,
40 minutes). They return to Sandanski at
1pm, 4pm and 5pm. Check in Melnik for
times of morning buses to Sandanski.

Sandanski is conveniently on the train
line between Sofia and Athens (Greece), but
the **train station** (☎ 22 213) is about 5km west
of the town centre. From Sofia, three fast
trains (9/6.80 lv in 1st/2nd class, 3½ hours)
travel to Sandanski every day, via Blagoevgrad and Dupnitsa, and continue to Kulata
(on the Greek border). For details about
trains to Greece, see p265.

Any of the plethora of taxis around Sandanski can be chartered as far as Melnik and
Rozhen, or to Kulata.

MELNIK МЕЛНИК
☎ 07437 / pop 240
Melnik, officially the smallest town in Bulgaria, is in fact no more than a tiny, but very
striking, village, kept afloat by tourism and
its ancient wine industry. Wedged into a
narrow sandstone valley about 20km north
of the Greek border, Melnik is a unique
place. Both foreigners and Bulgarians flock
here to walk around the national revival
period homes and church ruins, and to
sample, and buy, the local Melnik wine.
Also attracting attention are the strange,
so-called 'sand pyramids' surrounding the
village, made from a yellow-white mixture
of clay and sand. Centuries of erosion by
wind, water and sun have sculpted some
amazing natural formations, such as
pyramids and also what look like giant
mushrooms, lending the area a faintly
Daliesque character.

Melnik is also a base from which to explore the southern Pirin Mountains (see the
boxed text, p101).

Most, if not all, of Melnik's attractions
can be seen in one day, though it's a peaceful and relaxing place if you'd like to stay
longer. Do note, however, that there are
no banks here. It's an easy day trip from
Sandanski.

History
The area around Melnik was first settled by
the Thracian Medi tribe, to which the legendary Spartacus belonged. It was later settled
by the Romans, then by Slavs between the
7th and 9th centuries AD. The name Melnik

probably comes from the Slavic word *mel* for 'sandy chalk', which can be seen in the surrounding cliffs.

Melnik came to prominence in the early 13th century as the regional seat of Alexei Slav (often given the title of Despot). He used the town as the capital of his personal fiefdom and built several monasteries and a large fortress (the remains of which are in evidence today). Melnik became a centre of education and culture, and local artisans produced much sought-after jewellery, woodcarving and ceramics. It also produced large quantities of red wine, which was traded as far as modern-day Croatia and Venice.

Melnik fell into decline during the Ottoman occupation, but regained prosperity through the Bulgarian national revival period in the late 18th and early 19th centuries. During this time, many traditional houses were built, often on the ruins of Roman and Slavic homes. At the turn of the 20th century, Melnik was a thriving commercial centre with some 20,000 (mostly Greek) inhabitants, but it was largely destroyed by fire during the Balkan Wars (1912–13), and it has never fully recovered its importance. Since those times, Melnik has been significantly restored and rebuilt.

Orientation & Information

Melnik's major (unnamed) thoroughfares run east–west along both sides of an often-dry tributary of the Melnishka River. Walk-

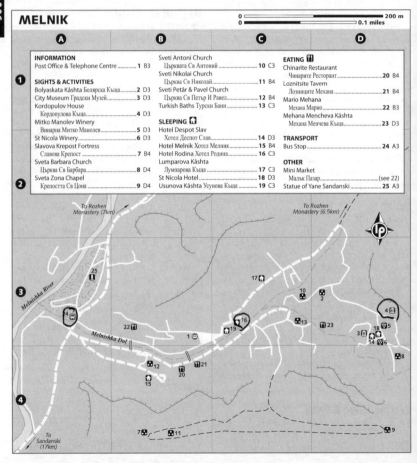

MELNIK

0   200 m
0   0.1 miles

INFORMATION
Post Office & Telephone Centre **1** B3

SIGHTS & ACTIVITIES
Bolyaskata Kâshta Болярска Къща **2** D3
City Museum Градски Музей **3** D3
Kordopulov House
   Кордопулова Къща **4** D3
Mitko Manolev Winery
   Винарна Митко Манолев **5** D3
St Nicola Winery **6** D3
Slavova Krepost Fortress
   Славова Крепост **7** B4
Sveta Barbara Church
   Църква Св Барбара **8** D4
Sveta Zona Chapel
   Крепостта Св Цона **9** D4

Sveti Antoni Church
   Църквата Св Антоний **10** C3
Sveti Nikolai Church
   Църква Св Николай **11** B4
Sveti Petâr & Pavel Church
   Църква Св Петър И Павел **12** B4
Turkish Baths Турски Бани **13** C3

SLEEPING
Hotel Despot Slav
   Хотел Деспот Слав **14** D3
Hotel Melnik Хотел Мелник **15** B4
Hotel Rodina Хотел Родина **16** C3
Lumparova Kâshta
   Лумпарова Къща **17** C3
St Nicola Hotel **18** D3
Usunova Kâshta Усунова Къща **19** C3

EATING
Chinarite Restaurant
   Чинарите Ресторант **20** B4
Loznitsite Tavern
   Лозниците Механа **21** B4
Mario Mehana
   Механа Марио **22** B3
Mehana Mencheva Kâshta
   Механа Менчева Къща **23** D3

TRANSPORT
Bus Stop **24** A3

OTHER
Mini Market
   Малък Пазар .... (see 22)
Statue of Yane Sandanski **25** A3

To Rozhen Monastery (7km)

To Rozhen Monastery (6.5km)

Melnishka River

Melnishka Dol

To Sandanski (17km)

ing paths and goat tracks run up both sides of the valley to the homes and ruins. If you're driving, please do everyone a favour and park at the western end and walk into the village. And remember, this really is a village: there's nowhere reliable to change money, the nearest banks and foreign-exchange offices are in Sandanski, and there is no Internet centre. There is, however, a **post office** (7.30am-noon & 1-4.30pm) in the centre of the village.

Sights
WINERIES

Melnik has been renowned for producing quality wines for over 600 years. The locally grown grapes produce a palatable, dark red wine, which is sold all over Bulgaria. Several wine bars and shops can be found along Melnik's cobblestone paths, and bottles of acceptable red and white can be bought for about 3 to 4 lv upwards.

The **St Nicola Winery** (286; www.bulgariawines .com) opened in 2004 and is run by the hotel of the same name (see p108). St Nicola is one of the leading brands in Bulgaria and for €3 you can taste around four of its wines. They also produce Merlot and Cabernet Sauvignon. Food can be served here by arrangement, and, of course, bottles of wine are for sale. It's in a barn-like building opposite the hotel; if it's closed, contact them to open it up for you.

The **Mitko Manolev Winery** (234) is basically a cellar dug into the rocks, and an informal hut with tables and chairs outside, where you can sample and buy both red and white wine from Melnik. It's along the short hillside trail between the Bolyaskata Kâshta ruins and the Kordopulov House. It costs 1 lv to 'look around' and you will pay for however much wine you manage to put away.

The **Damianitza Winery** (0746-30 090; www .melnikwine.bg) offers local wine tours. Contact them directly or through Hotel Despot Slav (p108) for current programmes and costs.

MUSEUMS

The houses in Melnik are typically built on the side of cliffs and on top of a basement (made of stone) in which wine is often made and/or stored. The living quarters on the upper floors usually offer glorious views. Officially, all buildings in Melnik must be built and/or renovated in the Bulgarian national revival period style, and painted brown and white.

Kordopulov House (291; admission 2 lv; 8am-8pm), built in 1754, was the home of one of Melnik's foremost wine merchants. It's now one of the country's largest and more famous revival-period structures. The lovely sitting rooms have been restored to their 19th-century appearance, with murals, stained-glass windows and exquisite carved wooden ceilings. Don't miss the huge warren of a wine cellar with 180m of labyrinthine caves hewn out of rock and its gigantic barrels, where you can taste, and buy, the house's own label wine. The house is the four-storey building on the cliff face at the end of the street, south of the creek. It's only 200m along a hillside track from the Bolyaskata Kâshta ruins.

City Museum (229; admission by donation; 9am-7pm Mon-Fri) features some traditional costumes, ceramics and jewellery from the Melnik region. Most interesting are the photos taken in the early 20th century of the bustling town. Look for the sign to the museum just before the Hotel Despot Slav, and note that it sometimes closes for lunch.

RUINS

Bolyaskata Kâshta dates back to the 10th century and is therefore one of the oldest homes in Bulgaria. However, it's now completely ruined and only some walls still stand. Nothing is explained on site in any language but it's worth the short walk for the best views of Melnik. In front of the ruins are the remains of the 19th-century **Sveti Antoni Church**, which is closed and not signposted.

Of the 70 or so churches that once graced Melnik, only 40 have survived, and most of these are now in ruins. A path (signposted in English) starts almost opposite the main entrance of the Hotel Rodina. It leads to the ruins of the **Sveti Nikolai Church**, originally built in 1756, and to the remains of the **Slavova Krepost Fortress**, built by Despot Slav. Both can be admired from the Bolyaskata Kâshta ruins, or from near the Lumparova Kâshta hotel. The trail then heads east along the ridge for about 300m to the ruins of **Sveta Zona Chapel**.

Other ruins that you can wander about include the **Turkish Baths**, which are easy to miss and difficult to recognise; they're just before the Mehana Mencheva Kâshta tavern so keep an eye out. The 1840 **Sveti Petâr & Pavel Church**, down from the car park of the Hotel Melnik, and the 15th-century **Sveta Barbara Church**, not far from the Kordopulov House, are also worth a look.

Festivals & Events

Not surprisingly, most festivities seem to centre around the local wine-making industry. **Trifon Zarezan Festival** (1 February) is celebrated wildly. Several events take place during the height of the grape-picking season in the first two weeks of October. There's also a **folkloric festival** on 1 April.

Sleeping

Many private homes in Melnik offer rooms and you may be approached by locals around the bus stop – or even while on the bus itself – with offers of accommodation. Rates vary, but hover around 15 to 20 lv per person. All rooms have a shared bathroom, but are cosy, clean, central and usually quiet (unless you happen to stay near a particularly noisy *mehana*). Look for the 'Rooms to Sleep' signs in English along the main streets.

Lumparova Kâshta (☎ 0888 804 512; r per person 20 lv; P) The cosy rooms at Lumparova contain two or three beds with thick woollen blankets and have balconies with awesome views, while the multilingual staff offer traditional food and wine tasting. It's up a steep path that starts behind Usunova Kâshta.

Hotel Rodina (☎ 249; s/d 15/20 lv) Although a bit uninspiring compared to other places, it's good value – perhaps it's a last resort if the other places are full. Enter from the lower (southern) door.

Hotel Melnik (☎ 272; d/apt 30/100 lv; P) This huge, comparatively modern hotel was built in the traditional style, albeit largely in concrete, and is situated on the hillside with great views over the village. It's a bit musty and is now looking rather dated – the décor and furnishings don't seem to have been altered in decades – although rooms are perfectly fine, and come with TV and fridge.

Usunova Kâshta (☎ 270; s/d incl breakfast 20/40 lv) This beautifully restored former Turkish prison has quiet, clean rooms which represent very good value. The rooms surround a quaint courtyard and are painted a dazzling white. It's on the flat side of the river, so no climbing is required to reach it.

Hotel Despot Slav (☎ /fax 271; s/d/tr incl breakfast 40/50/60 lv) This is one of the most traditional and authentic places in Melnik and although a short walk from most restaurants, it is quiet. The rooms are large, well furnished and feature a TV, fridge and kettle. Rates include breakfast.

St Nicola Hotel (☎ 286; stnicola@datacom.bg; d/apt Sun-Fri from €20/45, Sat & public hols from €30/75; P 🖥) Melnik's newest and most luxurious hotel, the St Nicola offers excellent value for money. Rooms are large, spotless and tastefully furnished, while the apartment comes with a sun terrace, lounge, fully equipped kitchen and big bathroom. There's also a very good restaurant and a winery.

Eating

Mehana Mencheva Kâshta (☎ 339; mains 3.50-10 lv) This tiny tavern is off the main tourist route and is popular with locals. It serves a good range of authentic Bulgarian dishes and is a nice spot to enjoy a glass of the local wine.

Mario Mehana (☎ 230; mains from 3.50 lv) Next to the Mini Market (labelled in English), Mario is one of several cosy, friendly and traditional taverns along this part of the street.

The two largest and most patronised restaurants in Melnik are opposite each other and both offer menus in English. Mains at both go from around 5 lv. Chinarite Restaurant is a bit cheerless compared to the smaller taverns, but servings are large. Loznitsite Tavern has an inviting, vine-covered outdoor setting, and an extensive menu of similar Bulgarian fare.

Getting There & Away

Bus schedules between Melnik and Sofia are erratic and often change, so check with locals in Melnik. One bus leaves Melnik for Sofia (8.80 lv, four hours) at the ungodly hour of 6am and returns to Melnik from Sofia at about 10am. Buses from Sandanski (p105) to Melnik continue to Rozhen.

ROZHEN MONASTERY
РОЖЕНСКИ МАНАСТИР

About 7km northeast of Melnik is the **Rozhen Monastery** (admission free; ☯ 7am-7pm), also known as the Birth of Virgin Mary Monastery. It was originally built in 1217, but nothing remains from that era. It was rebuilt in the late 16th century, but destroyed again by the Turks soon after. Most of what remains today was built between 1732 and the end of the 18th century. Much of the monastery has been significantly renovated in the last 30 years. Taking photos or using video cameras is not permitted. Donations of 1 to 2 lv on entry are encouraged.

The **Nativity of the Virgin Church**, originally built in 1600, contains some marvellous stained-glass windows, 200-year-old murals, woodcarvings and iconostases. Unusually, the **refectory** on the second floor also has murals. But it's the proximity to Melnik, the pleasant vine-covered courtyard, and the spectacular setting overlooking the unique sandy cliffs (particularly photogenic in the afternoon), which attract most visitors.

About 200m before the monastery car park is the (closed) **Sts Kiril & Metodii Church**, in front of which is the grave of Yane Sandanski (1872–1915), a Macedonian revolutionary leader.

For locals, the year's highlight is the **Rozhen Fair**, which is held on 8 September.

Hotel Rozhena (☎ 07437-211; s/d incl breakfast 30/40 lv; P) has comfortable rooms with TV and bathroom, and more luxurious double apartments. A sauna and gym are available to hotel guests, and there's also a restaurant.

A few *mehanas* are near the bus stop in the village. The café next to the monastery car park sells drinks and snacks.

Getting There & Away

From Melnik to the monastery by road is 7.2km, including the steep 800m uphill bit from Rozhen village. All buses from Sandanski (see previous town) to Melnik continue to Rozhen village. The popular hiking trail (6.5km) from Melnik starts from near the track up to the Bolyaskata Kâshta ruins, and continues along the dry creek bed; look for the small white, orange and green signs (in English). The trail has no shade so, in summer, walk early in the morning or late in the afternoon, and take plenty of water.

RODOPI MOUNTAINS
РОДОПИ ПЛАНИНА

The 15,000-sq-km Rodopi Mountains stretch from Velingrad to Smolyan and across into Greece (though about 85% of the mountain range is in Bulgaria). Named

after the Thracian god Rhodopa, the mountains are home to spectacular gorges and caves near Trigrad and Yagodina, the Batak and Dospat Lakes and the most extensive pine forests in Bulgaria. It's perfect for hiking in summer and skiing in winter at Pamporovo (p112) or Chepelare (p110). The average height is low (only 785m) but the highest peak – Mt Golyan Perelik, near Smolyan – is 2190m.

BATAK БАТАК

☎ 03553 / pop 4500

It's hard to imagine that this rather shabby and economically depressed town has had such a bloody history (see Massacre at Batak, p110). The major attraction for locals is nearby Batak Lake, a great spot for fishing and swimming in summer. Boats are available for rent near Hotel Panorama. For information about hiking around these ranges from Batak, see the boxed text on p111.

Sights & Activities

The Church of Sveti Nedelya, the Ethnological Museum and the History Museum are the three well-signed and adjacent attractions in town. A combined ticket costs 2 lv (admission free on Thursday). Though there are official opening times, you should visit the History Museum first to make sure the other two places are unlocked.

The **Church of Sveti Nedelya** (☼ 9am-noon & 2-6pm Tue-Sat), built in 1813, was the final refuge for 2000 locals who fought the Turks in 1876. Inside, there is obvious evidence (captions in English) of the subsequent massacre, such as bullet holes and a macabre, half-covered tomb with dozens of skulls. The nearby **Ethnological Museum** (☼ 9am-noon & 2-6pm Tue-Sat), one of the few Bulgarian national revival period houses in Batak, contains costumes and other incidental items from the late 19th century. You'll need to ask someone at the History Museum to open up.

On the main square is the **History Museum** (☎ 2339; pl Osvodozhenie; ☼ 9am-noon & 2-6pm Tue-Sat). The downstairs crypt contains names of some locals who fought against the Turks. Predictably, the upper floors contain plenty of graphic displays about the 1876 April Uprising, massacre and Russian–Turkish War. Nothing is captioned in English, but it's hard not to be moved.

Sleeping & Eating

There are no hotels in Batak itself but several are dotted along the southwestern shore of the lake. The gigantic **International Youth Tourist Centre** (☎ 3385; www.orbita.bgcatalog .com; s/d/apt incl breakfast 30/40/50 lv; P ⚡) is also known as the Orbita Hotel, and has great facilities including tennis and basketball courts. It also rents bikes and organises excursions.

These hotels, and several cafés and restaurants, are strung along the 1.2km-long access road, which starts about 7km west of Batak along the road to Rakitovo. The larger hotels stay open all year, but some cafés and restaurants only operate on weekends, especially during the winter months.

Getting There & Away

Four buses leave each day from Batak and go to Plovdiv. The three daily buses between Batak and Velingrad pass the turn-off to the lake.

CHEPELARE ЧЕПЕЛАРЕ

☎ 03051 / pop 3000 / elevation 1150m

Chepelare is a small, unremarkable village and a downmarket ski resort. It's also an alternative base to the expensive and expansive Pamporovo, which lies 6km to the south. In summer, the nearby mountains offer excellent hiking (see Hiking In the Rodopi Mountains on opposite page). The town is undergoing some impressive restoration thanks to the Beautiful Bulgaria Project, although this seems to be taking quite some time.

THE MASSACRE AT BATAK

During the 1876 April Uprising most of the population of Batak fought against the Turks under the leadership of Peter Goranov. They successfully held the Turks at bay for nine days before the aggressors eventually gained control. In brutal retaliation, the Turks burned down the village and massacred almost every citizen (between 5000 and 6000 people). The massacre was reported in the English press and (eventually) acknowledged and denounced by the British government. It was the catalyst for the Russian–Turkish War that started a year later.

Information

The combined post office and telephone centre is near the square, as is the only Internet agency.

Hebros Bank (ul Vasil Dechev) About 300m down the main street from the square.

Tourist Information Centre (☎ 2110; tic@infotel.bg; ul Murdjovska 23a; ⏰ 8.30am-12.30pm & 1.30-5.30pm Mon-Fri) It's 100m up from the town square, across the park and along the main road. It can provide a few brochures (when staff actually turn up).

Sights

Also called the Cave Museum, the **Museum of Speleology & Karst** (☎ 3051; ul Shina Andreeva 9a; admission 2 lv; ⏰ 9am-noon & 1.30-5pm Mon-Fri) is the only one of its kind in Bulgaria and, possibly, the Balkans. There are displays of minerals, bats (in bottles) and the remains of ancient cave-dwelling animals such as lions and bears, as well as exhibits about the caves near Trigrad and Yagodina. While only a few captions are in English and/or German, it doesn't matter too much because the manager can play an informative tape over the loudspeaker in either language – though trying to link the narrative with the displays is not easy! The museum is in the Hotel Pesternika building, about 200m up from the bus station on the hillside overlooking the village.

Activities

This is a quieter and cheaper **ski** resort than Pamporovo (p112), and far less established. The only ski runs, Mechi Chal I (3200m) and Mechi Chal II (5200m), are two of the best slopes in the Balkans. The chairlift (which doesn't operate in summer) is about 1.5km south of the village centre and is signposted off the road to Pamporovo. The only place to hire gear is **Orion Ski** (☎ /fax 2142) at the lift but few instructors are available. Chepelare is a good place to buy some cheap, locally made ski gear.

Sleeping & Eating

Contact the tourist office in Chepelare or Smolyan (p113) for a list of private homes in Chepelare that offer rooms for about 20 lv per person with a shared bathroom. Hotel prices increase slightly in winter.

Hotel Phoenix (☎ 3408; ul Murgavets 4; d from €21) About 200m up ul Vasil Dechev from the town square, the Phoenix is centrally located. It offers simple, spotless rooms with TV. There's also a folksy restaurant.

Hotel Savov (☎ 2036; ul Vasil Dechev 7; d/tr/apt from 25/30/40 lv; P) This homely place, opposite the Hebros Bank, offers large, comfortable and airy rooms with TV. Apartments have a sitting area, TV, fridge and an extra bed. The restaurant is popular, and worth trying even if you're staying elsewhere.

Hotel Gergana (☎ 4301; ul Hristo Botev 75; d incl breakfast from 30 lv; P) The Gergana, along the road from Plovdiv, has a handful of rooms with TV in a cosy, family-run environment. The restaurant specialises in home-cooked traditional cuisine, which heavily features potatoes (and nothing much else).

A dozen or more other hotels in Chepelare are signposted from along the Plovdiv road, but they're too far to walk to from the bus station (and there are no taxis in town).

Mehana Chepelare (mains 4-5 lv) This covered outdoor tavern, near the town square, has a limited menu (in English) and is a great place for a drink.

Getting There & Away

The bus station is across a footbridge, 200m northeast of the town square. Buses leave for Smolyan, via Pamporovo, hourly, and the regular services between Plovdiv and Madan, and Plovdiv and Smolyan, also stop in Chepelare.

MOMCHILOVTSI МОМЧИЛОВЦИ

☎ 03023 / pop 3000 / elevation 1100m

This sleepy mountainside village is about 3km up from the main (eastern) road between Chepelare and Smolyan. It's home to a number of Bulgarian painters and writers who appreciate solitude, and is full of holiday villas belonging to rich city folk from Smolyan and beyond. For travellers, Momchilovtsi is an alternative base to the ski resorts at Chepelare or Pamporovo. It's also a relaxing place to unwind or a great place for hiking in summer.

The **Historical & Ethnographical Museum** (☎ 2272; ul Byalo More), up behind the village square, is rarely open. Ring ahead for opening hours, and if you want to visit (or buy something from) one of the local artists or weavers.

The village-wide lethargy is suspended during the four-day celebrations either side of **St Konstantin & Elena Day** (21 May).

The tourist offices in Smolyan (p113) and Chepelare (p110) can provide a list of private homes in Momchilovtsi that offer rooms with a shared bathroom for about 22 lv per person. Several cosy pensions are signposted along the road from the south for about 500m before the village square. One is the **Rodopchanka Hotel** (☎ 2863; ul Byalo More 40; d incl breakfast from €20).

Shadravana Restaurant, in the park below the square, is a charming place for a meal

---

HIKING IN THE RODOPI MOUNTAINS

If you want to explore the region around Chepelare, Smolyan and Shiroka Lûka, look for the West Rhodopean Region or Western Rhodope Mountains maps (1:100,000), available at the tourist offices in Pamporovo, Chepelare and Smolyan. These maps detail (in English) various hiking trails (of three to five hours) and five routes designed for mountain bikes. The Rodopi map (1:100,000) of the whole mountain range, published by Kartografia, is detailed (in Cyrillic).

The Mountains of Bulgaria by Julian Perry describes (but with poor maps) a trek from Hizha Studenents, near Pamporovo, to Hizha Rodoposki Partizanin, near Hrabrino, about 14km southwest of Plovdiv. Hikers can stay in huts along the way. If you wish to follow the same route allow five to seven days.

The ideal base for shorter hikes is Shiroka Lûka (p115). From there, you can choose one of nine marked trails, including one to Chepelare, via Kukuvitsa (two to three hours one way) and another to Mt Golyam Perelik (five to six hours). Other excellent short hikes along marked trails:

Batak to Hizha Teheran About four hours.

Chepelare to Hizha Igrev About three hours. From there, continue to Shiroka Lûka (three hours) or Pamporovo (seven hours).

Haskovo to Hizha Aida Twenty-six kilometres west by road (four to five hours).

Pamporovo to Progled An (easy) five-hour return trip across the scenic Rozhen fields.

Smolyan to Hizha Smolyanski Ezera About three hours one way.

or drink. A handful of cafés surround the village square.

Buses between Smolyan's Ustovo bus station (2.40 lv, 45 minutes, six to seven daily) and Banite, and Plovdiv and Banite, regularly pass through Momchilovtsi.

PAMPOROVO ПАМПОРОВО
☎ 3021 / elevation 1650m

Set in the gorgeous eastern Rodopi Mountains, about 83km south of Plovdiv, Pamporovo is one of the four major ski resorts in Bulgaria. It's a pleasant and inviting area to visit in summer, offering excellent possibilities for walking, though many of the resort's facilities are closed at this time. The downside is that Pamparovo is both very expensive (in summer and winter) and expansive; there's no real centre to the place, and it lacks charm and atmosphere. The highlight of the local social calendar is the **Rozhen Folk Festival** (late August), held in the Rozhen fields between Pamporovo and Progled.

Orientation & Information
The centre of Pamporovo, such as it is, is the T-junction of the roads to Smolyan, Chepelare and Devin, via Shiroka Lûka. From this junction, the resort spreads along several roads for up to 4km. Most hotels, restaurants and shops in more remote parts of the resort are closed from May to October, but everything in and around the central Hotel Perelik is open year-round.

Activities
SKIING
The resorts of Pamporovo and Chepelare (p110) are not nearly as convenient as Vitosha, Borovets and Bansko. But being this far south, the resorts boast over 250 days of sunshine a year and with plenty of snow between mid-December and mid-April, skiing conditions are often ideal. More information about the region is available on the website www.travel-bulgaria.com/pamporovo, while www.bulgariaski.com is an excellent site, giving snow reports, advice and accommodation information for all Bulgarian ski resorts.

Pamporovo has eight major ski runs (total of 17.5km), 25km of cross-country trails and four training slopes. The advantages are that the facilities are comparatively new and the

slopes and elevators are well maintained. On the other hand, the resort at Pamporovo is very spread out and charmless, yet so popular that accommodation is hard to come by for independent skiers and travellers. Alternative places to stay are nearby Chepelare (p110), Momchilovtsi (p111), Smolyan (p114) and Shiroka Lûka (p115).

There are five chairlifts and nine draglifts. Usually, three of these chairlifts – Nos 1, 2 and 4 – open during the summer. Chairlifts cost 5/7 lv one way/return and a day pass costs about 30 lv. Minibuses from the hotels to the lifts are free to anyone with a lift pass.

Pamporovo caters well to families and provides a ski kindergarten for the kids. The slopes are ideal for beginners and training is easy to arrange. Most instructors speak English and German and charge about 150 to 200 lv per person for 12 to 24 hours' group training, spread over six to 12 days. Individual instruction costs a lot more.

Equipment can be rented from one of a dozen or more ski shops. As an example, a complete set of alpine ski gear will cost about 30 to 40 lv per day. For ski gear, try the **Sport Shop** (☎ 0888 552 354) in the Hotel Perelik complex. Pamporovo is ideal for snowboarding; visit the British-run **Snow Shack** (snowshack_uk@yahoo.co.uk) in the Hotel Markony complex if you want to hire snowboarding gear and/or join a training course.

OTHER ACTIVITIES
In summer, a number of activities are on offer. Pamporovo Sports Services, in the Pamporovo Shopping Centre sandwiched between Hotel Perelik and Hotel Murgavets, can arrange **mountain bikes** (4 lv per hour), **guides** (from 15 lv per hour) for hiking, and **tennis** courts and equipment. Around the central T-junction, a few motley **horses** can be hired (about 15 to 20 lv per hour). For **hiking**, see the boxed text (p111).

Sleeping & Eating
In winter, most foreign visitors will be on package tours (that include accommodation) from overseas, or perhaps Sofia, or be on a day trip from Plovdiv. Consequently, there's little point recommending too many hotels and most hotels in winter don't offer rates that are acceptable to individual travellers.

The following is an example of the sort of rates charged in summer by a few of the larger two- and three-star hotels. Prices in winter will be about 50% higher.

Hotel Murgavets (☎ 8317; s/d/apt from 40/50/80 lv; P ⊠ ⊑) This high-rise hotel is one of Pamporovo's giants, with large comfortable rooms and good facilities, including a gym, health and beauty centre and kids' playground. It's next to Hotel Perelik and fairly convenient.

Hotel Perelik (☎ 8405; pamporovo@bsbg.net; s/d from 40/50 lv; P ⊠ ⊑) This ex-Balkantourist monolith has undergone thorough renovations, and offers decent facilities and sensible prices. The complex also contains a bowling alley, shops, several restaurants and a disco.

Hotel Finlandia (☎ 8374; s/d from €44/58; P ⊑) One of Pamporovo's newer hotels, the four-star Finlandia has clean, classy rooms with TV and minibar, and the price includes compulsory half-board. The hotel has a nightclub, health centre and ski school with English- and German-speaking instructors, and also operates a kindergarten.

A plethora of bars, cafés and restaurants also offer all sorts of cuisines. Given the extent of the resort, you'll probably have to eat at, or near, your hotel in the evening if you don't have a car.

White Hart (Hotel Murgavets complex; mains 8-15 lv; ☺ 8am-late) This is one of several pub-cum-restaurants near Hotel Perelik that offer Western food and drinks at relatively high prices, such as 'English' breakfasts for 8.50 lv. It also features live music most nights year-round.

Getting There & Away

Every hour, buses travelling between Smolyan and Chepelare pass through Pamporovo, as do the regular services between Smolyan and Plovdiv, and Smolyan and Sofia. A couple of buses go daily to Pamporovo directly from Sofia (10 lv, four hours) and up to eight leave from Plovdiv (5.50 lv, two hours). The bus stop is at the 'Ski Lift No 1' chairlift at the central T-junction.

SMOLYAN СМОЛЯН

☎ 0301 / pop 34,300 / elevation 1000m

Very long and very narrow, Smolyan is the administrative centre of the southern Rodopi Mountains, with most of its com-ponents strung out along, or just off, the partially pedestrianised main street. It's also Bulgaria's highest town, and although fairly sedate, it does have a few decent attractions to keep you occupied for a day or two, and the location, surrounded by pine-clad peaks, is particularly attractive.

Smolyan was originally settled by a Thracian tribe in around 700 BC, but the modern town, which was created through the fusion of four separate villages, has no obvious history. For travellers, it's an alternative place to stay to Pamporovo, a transport hub for connections to villages like Shiroka Lûka (p115) and a base for exploring the seven **Smolyan Lakes** (which once numbered 20). For details about hiking, see the boxed text on p111.

Orientation

Smolyan is undoubtedly the longest (10km) town in Bulgaria and is composed of the four villages (from west to east) of Ezerovo, Smolyan, Raikovo and Ustovo. The long main street, bul Bulgaria, is pedestrianised at its western end, and lined with cafés and restaurants. The often eerily deserted civic centre complex is an outsize concrete jumble further east along this street, opposite the Hotel Smolyan, and is home to the main post office, a couple of banks, a supermarket and a sleepy café or two. There is little of interest beyond the centre of town.

Information

The main post office is in the civic centre complex, although there is another further west on bul Bulgaria, where you'll also find a number of banks and ATMs.

Regional Association of Rhodope Municipalities (☎ 62 056; bul Bulgaria 14) Just down from the tourist office. Represents the 20 local districts. It's worth contacting them if you're interested in local arts and crafts or want to organise a tour or guide.

Tourist office (☎ 62 530; www.rodopi-bg.com; ☺ 8.30am-noon & 1-5.30pm Mon-Fri, 10am-2pm Sat) Located beside the Hotel Smolyan. The helpful English-speaking staff have plenty of brochures and information.

Sights
HISTORICAL MUSEUM

Located up several flights of steps behind the civic centre, Smolyan's **Historical Museum** (☎ 27 028; pl Bulgaria 3; admission 3 lv; ☺ 9am-noon & 1-5pm Tue-Sun) has four floors of exhibits, including archaeological artefacts from as far back as the Palaeolithic era. Thracian armour and weaponry are among the highlights, and there are also fascinating displays on weaving and woodcarving, plus a huge collection of traditional musical instruments and folk costumes, most notably the fantastical Kuker outfits worn at New Year celebrations. Upstairs, photos and scale models of traditional buildings are on show.

SMOLYAN ART GALLERY

Directly opposite the museum is the **Art Gallery** (☎ 23 268; 2 lv; ⏰ 9am-noon & 1.30-5pm Tue-Sun). It houses an overwhelming 1800 paintings, sketches and sculptures by local, national and foreign artists.

PLANETARIUM

Bulgaria's biggest **planetarium** (☎ 23 074; bul Bulgaria 20; admission 3 lv) is about 200m west of the Hotel Smolyan. It offers shows (35 to 40 minutes) in English, French or German at 2pm from Monday to Saturday; and in Bulgarian at 3pm from Monday to Saturday, and Sunday at 11am and 3pm. The show with commentary in Bulgarian is still spectacular, even if you don't understand a word. The foreign-language shows are only put on for groups of five or more; otherwise, you'll have to pay 15 lv for the privilege of a solo performance.

Sleeping & Eating

The tourist office has updated lists of private homes in town offering rooms with a shared bathroom for about 22 lv per person.

Hotel Babylon (☎ /fax 63 268; ul Han Presian 22; d/tw/apt 20/24/30 lv) The Babylon is a good, central option with a range of different rooms available, including large, two-room apartments with a comfortable lounge, which are great value. It's located behind the little park, on the road above bul Bulgaria. There's a bar and restaurant downstairs, but nobody speaks any English.

Hotel Smolyan (☎ 62 053; www.hotelsmolyan.com; bul Bulgaria 3; s/d from 19/30 lv; Ⓟ) This huge, forlorn-looking former Balkantourist hotel faces the civic centre. It's a musty, dated place in need of a makeover, and although it advertises a swimming pool and sauna, both appear to be long out of commission.

Still, the price is remarkably cheap, and some rooms have balconies with fine forest views.

Three Fir Trees House (☎ 38 228; dreitannen@mbox .digsys.bg; ul Srednogorec 1; s/d 24/34 lv; 💻) This charming, well-maintained pension is around 200m east of the main bus station, down a flight of steps from bul Bulgaria; follow the signposts. The large, spotless rooms feature lots of fresh pine and most have balconies, though bathrooms are shared. The excellent breakfast (5 lv) includes home-made fruit juices, preserves, *banitsas* (cheese pasties) or whatever else is fresh, and the helpful, English- and German-speaking owner can arrange tours and rental cars and offers a cheap laundry service.

There are lots of cafés and restaurants along bul Bulgaria, including **Pizza Lucia** (☎ 6334; bul Bulgaria 57; mains 3-6 lv), which serves lots of cheap pizza and pasta dishes. Further east along this road, the **Starata Kâshta** (ul Studenska 2; mains 2-4 lv; ⏰ 4.30pm-2am), also known as the Pamporovata Kâshta, offers a small menu of the *kebabche*-and-chips variety (*kebabche* are grilled spicy meat sausages), as well as lots of beer. It's an attractive national revival–style house, built in 1840, with just a few outdoor tables and benches roughly hewn from logs. It's reached by a flight of steps up from bul Bulgaria. Menus at both are in Bulgarian only. The Hotel Smolyan's restaurant has a menu in English but the prices are double those on the Bulgarian menu. Far cheaper is the snack bar between the hotel and tourist office.

Getting There & Away

Most buses to/from Smolyan use the main **Smolyan bus station** (☎ 63 104; bul Bulgaria), at the western end of town. From there, buses leave each day for Sofia (12 lv, 3½ hours, four daily) and Plovdiv (7.50 lv, 2½ to three hours, hourly), and every hour a bus goes to Chepelare and Pamporovo. From this station, buses also go to Devin (4 lv, two hours, three to four daily) for the caves near Trigrad and Yagodina (p116). Inconveniently situated about 10km to the east is the **Ustovo bus station** (☎ 64 585; ul Trakia), which has services to/from a host of villages of little interest to travellers, as well as Momchilovtsi (2.40 lv, 45 minutes). Local bus Nos 3, 8, 9, 11, 14 and 18 travel between both bus stations, via the Hotel Smolyan. Note that the ticket offices at both close for an extended lunch break, and there's no information available in English.

SHIROKA LÛKA ШИРОКА ЛЪКА
☎ 03030 / pop 1500

Shiroka Lûka is a picturesque village famed for its three humpbacked bridges and dozens of 19th-century homes renovated in the style typical of the Bulgarian national revival period. Other attractions include the **Church of the Assumption**, which was apparently built in less than 40 days in 1834. You can't miss the wonderfully naive fresco outside picturing a funeral procession followed by dancing demons, while inside more icons and murals are on show. The iconostasis features panels explaining the story of Adam and Eve. The modest **Ethnographical Museum** in the Kalenjievi Kâshta house is very rarely open, other than for organised bus tours. The small **tourist office** (☎ 233; www.rhodope.net; 9am-5pm) near the main square has lots of information and maps, including the useful *Western Rhodope Mountains* (1:100,000). They can also book private rooms in Shiroka Lûka and surrounding villages such as tiny Gela, legendary birthplace of Orpheus, 7km to the north. For details about hiking, see the boxed text on p111.

The village is renowned for its traditional music, which is showcased during the week-long **music festival** in mid-April. The major festival is the **kukeri** (first Sunday in March), a classic folk event where locals with frightening masks, bells and elaborate costumes chase away evil spirits at the beginning of spring.

The tourist offices in Smolyan (p113) and Chepelare (p110) have updated lists of private homes in Shiroka Lûka that offer rooms.

Guesthouse Vasilka (☎ 666; sharkov@hotmail.com; r from 10 lv; P) is a simple place offering a few rooms, all with balconies. It's located at the highest point in the village, and home-cooked meals are available.

The smartest hotel in town is **Hotel Margarita** (☎ 693; d/apt incl breakfast from €20/30 lv; P). Along the main road on the western side of the creek this modern, but charming, hotel has rooms with TV. Note that prices double in winter.

The only proper restaurant is the **Restaurant Shiroka Lûka** (☎ 318; mains 4-8 lv; 11am-midnight Mon-Sat) in the centre of the village, though it's a mediocre, touristy place which only seems to come to life when a tour bus turns up.

Buses travel between Smolyan and Devin six to eight times daily, and stop anywhere along the road through Shiroka Lûka.

DEVIN ДЕВИН
☎ 03041

The little spa town of Devin is a quiet, unassuming place, and makes a handy base for visiting the caves found in the region (see p116). Although it has no particular sights or attractions in itself, it has long been one of Bulgaria's leading balneological resorts, and the source of the country's most widely distributed bottled mineral water. At the time of research, a huge new spa development was underway, alongside a new five-star hotel, so Devin's sleepy backwater character is likely to change over the coming years.

There's a tiny **tourist office** (☎ 4160; ul Osvobozhdenie 5) on the main pedestrianised street, though as staff only speak Bulgarian (and seem quite proud of the fact), and don't appear to have any leaflets or brochures, it's of somewhat limited use to foreign visitors. You can check your emails at the **Internet Club** (ul Orfei), located in the giant grey shoebox that is the House of Culture, but connections are very slow.

There are a couple of banks and ATMs along the main street and another ATM at the House of Culture.

Just opposite the Internet Club is **Devin Museum** (ul Orfei; 10.30am-12.30pm & 1.30-5.30pm Tue-Sat) which houses a display of folk arts and crafts from the Rodopis. It seems to open only on sporadic occasions.

Sleeping & Eating

Villa Ismena (☎ 0888 406 290; ul Goritsa 441; d 40 lv; P) Located at the top of a very steep road, signposted from the centre of town, the Ismena is a big, modern villa featuring lots of marble and a couple of noisy dogs. Rooms offer a high standard of décor and comfort, including TVs, minibars, balconies and sparkling bathrooms. There are superb views from the restaurant terrace, and various therapeutic programmes are available at the spa centre. The hotel can also arrange mountain guides, transport and bike rental.

Hotel Elite (☎ 2240; ul Undola 2; s/d/apt 35/45/ 70 lv; **P**) In the pedestrianised heart of Devin, Hotel Elite is a new place with large, well-kept rooms, all with TV, minibar and gleaming modern bathrooms; doubles have bathtubs rather than showers. The hotel also has its own minispa in the basement, with a sauna, Jacuzzi and massage rooms. A five-night stay, in any room, costs 115 lv and includes free use of the sauna and Jacuzzi.

Spa Hotel Devin (☎ 2513; www.spadevin.com; ul Druzhba 2; s/d/apt from 40/50/80 lv; **P** 🖳 🕭) This big, recently renovated place in the centre of Devin offers great value for money. It has its own hydrotherapy centre, with swimming pools, Jacuzzis and various therapeutic and 'anti-stress' programmes on offer, as well as beauty treatments. There's also a nightclub and casino on site and, during summer, biking, horse-riding, walking, ecology and jeep-safari tours are available to guests.

There are several basic cafés around town, though the best places to eat are at the restaurants of the three hotels listed earlier. The Spa Hotel's **Bulgarsko Selo restaurant** (mains 3-12 lv) has a big menu of pizzas and grilled meat dishes at reasonable prices, and a humorous, cartoon folk-style décor scheme going on.

Getting There & Away
From **Devin bus station** (☎ 2077) buses go to Smolyan (4.20 lv, 1½ hours, six daily), Plovdiv (6.50 lv, three hours, four daily) and Yagodina (2 lv, 40 minutes, 8am Monday to Saturday). There is one daily bus to Sofia (11 lv, four hours) leaving at the challenging hour of 6.45am. If you miss it (or would prefer to), catch a bus to Plovdiv, from where there are plenty of bus and train connections to the capital.

CAVES
Three of the largest and most fascinating of the 700 or so mapped caves in Bulgaria are in the southern Rodopi Mountains, not far from Smolyan. **Uhlovitsa Cave** (admission 4 lv; ☽ 10am-4pm Wed-Sun) is situated about 3km northeast of Mogilitsa, and boasts numerous waterfalls (most spectacular in winter) and some bizarre formations, but it's impossible to reach without private transport.

The most accessible and developed caves in this region are near Trigrad and Yagodina. Both are open daily in summer (May to September). Between mid-October and mid-April, ring first to make sure someone is there to open up. Admission to both caves includes a guided tour in Bulgarian only.

Trigrad Триград
One of the most visited **caves** (☎ 0889 163 238; admission 2 lv; ☽ 9am-5pm May-Sep, shorter hours rest of year) in Bulgaria is near Trigrad. Speleologists revel in the abundant grottoes, while visitors can admire the **Devil's Throat Cave** (Dyavolskoto Gurlo Peshtera), the name often given to the whole complex. The tour, which leaves when a few people turn up, lasts for about 20 minutes, but you are welcome to stay longer, under supervision of the caretaker. As you descend, you can hear (but unfortunately not see) a 45m-high waterfall. And don't forget to save some energy for the daunting set of steep steps at the exit and to watch out for the harmless bats.

Trigrad village is 2.3km south of the road from the cave entrance. There are a couple of small hotels in the village, including **Guesthouse Silivryak** (☎ 03040-220; s/d 20/30 lv; **P**), above the main square. With just six cosy rooms, it's an attractive little place, and the owner, Kosta Hadjiiski, is a very experienced and knowledgeable caver. Devin (p115) and Smolyan (p113) provide more accommodation options, or you could also stay in the nearby Muslim village of Borino; try the friendly **Family-Hotel Royal** (☎ 03042-2830; s/d from 10/20 lv; **P**). You will really need your own transport to stay in these places.

From Trigrad, you can hike to Yagodina (about 2½ hours).

Yagodina Ягодина
The 8km **Yagodina Cave** (☎ 03419-200; admission 4 lv; ☽ 9am-5pm May-Sep, shorter hours rest of year) is the longest known cave in the Rodopi Mountains. It has a number of abysses and labyrinthine tunnels and it is also one of the deepest caves in Bulgaria. The 45-minute tour highlights the remarkable stalagmites and stalactites, which often resemble curtains, and explains some history about the Neolithic settlers who lived in the cave dur-

ing the 6th millennium BC. Visitor numbers permitting, tours leave on the hour every hour between 9am and 4pm, except at midday. Note that from 1 October to 1 May a minimum of six visitors is required for the tour, or otherwise you can pay 15 lv. The rest of the year a minimum of 10 visitors (or 25 lv) is needed before they'll open up.

Family-Hotel Yagodina (☎ 03419-310; s/d from 12/24 lv; **P**) is a small, modern place in the centre of the village. Rooms are comfortable and spotless, and all have balconies. The cave is 6.4km south of the turn-off along the Smolyan–Dospat road, and exactly 3km south of Yagodina village.

You can hike to Trigrad (previous section) or ask directions in Yagodina village to the start of the **South Rodopi Eco-trail**; contact the tourist office in **Smolyan** (☎ 0301-62 530) or **Shiroka Lŭka** (☎ 03030-233) for details about this trail.

KOVACHEVITSA КОВАЧЕВИЦА
pop 65 / elevation 1050m

One of southern Bulgaria's most picturesque villages is also one of the most difficult to reach. Kovachevitsa has been declared an architectural and historical reservation by the Bulgarian government because of its unique building style, which is influenced by Macedonian designs and uses abundant stone rather than wood. There's little to see or do in the village, except appreciate the fresh air and stunning scenery, but this may change in the future if or when renovations of the village finish.

The only official place to stay is **Kapsazov's House** (☎ 0899 403 089; B&B per person 80 lv, full-board 110 lv), a gorgeous 19th-century home with seven rooms, set in a pretty garden. It's almost obligatory to take full-board because there's virtually nowhere else to eat. Several private homes also rent out rooms; hang around the village square for a few minutes until someone finds you and leads you to their abode.

At present, only two or three daily minibuses make it as far up the shocking road to Kovachevitsa from Gotse Delchev. If you're heading from Gotse Delchev by car, take the first (unsigned) turn-off east of the river and the right-hand (unsigned) road uphill before Marchevo village officially begins.

BULGARIAN THRACE

The territory of the ancient Thracians once covered a sizeable swathe of southeastern Europe, now within the borders of modern Bulgaria, Greece and Turkey. Bulgarian Thrace is still largely a wild, sparsely populated region of varied and dramatic landscapes and remote villages, and you'll need your own transport to explore this land in any depth. The major urban centre is Plovdiv, Bulgaria's second-biggest city and an important transport hub, while striking Bachkovo Monastery lies among wooded hills and vineyards a little further south. Further east, the ethnic Turkish influence is obvious in the small communities scattered around Bulgaria's main tobacco-growing country, although very few foreign travellers venture this far, and while hotels are beginning to appear in some otherwise out-of-the-way places, tourist facilities remain limited.

PLOVDIV ПЛОВДИВ
☎ 032 / pop 376,500

Bulgaria's second city has a long history, a rich cultural life and a host of unique attractions that will easily keep you occupied for several days. Thankfully, most of these are within the compact city centre and accessible on foot. Without doubt, the main draw is the lovely old town, which has been painstakingly restored to its mid-19th-century appearance, and is packed full with charming house-museums and art galleries. Also here is one of the best preserved Roman amphitheatres in the Balkans, which is still used for dramatic and musical performances. The modern centre of town is pleasing enough, though has perhaps less immediate visual appeal. It does have plenty of cafés, bars and clubs, though, while the lovely Tsar Simeon Garden is a pleasant, shady spot to relax, away from the hustle and bustle.

Plovdiv has always been one of Bulgaria's wealthiest and most cosmopolitan cities, and its 'bourgeois' credentials sometimes raised suspicion during the communist era. Other Bulgarians will often express negative views of the city, and the inhabitants have a reputation, not always deserved, for being rather snooty and aloof. However, it is true

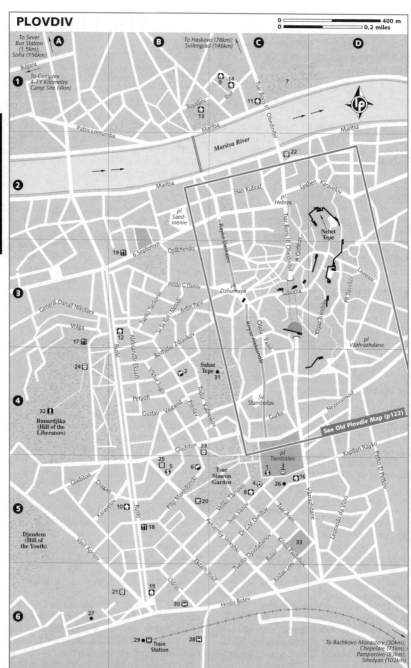

PLOVDIV

0 ——————— 400 m
0 ——————— 0.2 miles

To Sever
Bus Station
(1.5km);
Sofia (156km)

Bulgaria

To Complex
4-TY Kilometre
Camp Site (4km)

To Haskovo (78km);
Svilengrad (146km)

Patris Lomumba

Maritsa

Maritsa River

Maritsa

Maritsa

Han Kubrat

pl
Hebros

Lyaben Karavelov

Nehet
Tepe

pl
Saedinenie

Rayko Daskalov

Tsar Boris II Obedinitel

A Gladkov

Lavrenov

PR Slaveikov

Kopaz Zagorec

pl
Vazrazhdane

6 Septemvri

Opalchenska

Hristo G Danov

pl
Dzhumaya

Saborna

General Danail Nikolaev

Tsanko Tserkovski

Sv sv Kiril Metodii

Antim Parvi

Otets Paisii

Knyaz Aleksandar

Volga

Ruski

Aleksandar Ekzarh

Viktor Hugo

Bozhdar Zdravkov

Todor Kableshkov

Preslav

Sahat
Tepe

Sv
Stambolov

Gurko

Nezavisimost

Petyofi

Gustav Vaigand

See Old Plovdiv Map (p122)

Bunardjika
(Hill of the
Liberators)

Gladston

pl
Tsentralen

Kapitan Rayko

Petko D Petkov

Gladston

Dragan

Karavelov

Ruski

Filip Makedonski

Tsar Simeon
Garden

Veliko Tarnovo

Tsar Asen

Vazrazhdane

Leonardo da Vinci

Djendem
(Hill of
the Youth)

Vasil Aprilov

Avksenty Velechki

Ivan Vazov

Dr GM Dimitrov

Tsanko Dyustabanov

Bulair

Knyaz Tseretelev

Kodak Lev

Ekzarh Yosif

Odrin

Hristo Botev

Train
Station

To Bachkovo Monastery (30km);
Chepelare (71km);
Pamporovo (83km);
Smolyan (102km)

that stroppy bar staff are probably easier to find here than elsewhere in Bulgaria.

Plovdiv occupies both banks of the Maritsa River on the Upper Thracian Plain and is the second-largest road and railway hub and economic centre in Bulgaria. It's the first or last stop for many travelling between Bulgaria and Greece or Turkey.

History

Plovdiv was first settled as early as 5000 BC by the Thracians, who built a fortress at Nebet Tepe (in the old town) which they called Eumolpias. Philip II of Macedon (father of Alexander the Great) extended the settlement and named it Philipopolis in 342 BC. More walls were built around the Thracian fortress and Philipopolis became an important military centre. However, it wasn't until the Romans arrived in AD 46 that the real city began to take shape, as they built streets, towers and aqueducts for Trimontium, as it then became known. The area was plundered, and often destroyed, by the Goths in the mid-3rd century and by the Huns in AD 447, after which Trimontium fell into decline. Khan Krum seized the city in 815 and, renamed Pupulden, it became an important strategic outpost of the First Bulgarian Empire.

Pupulden was bashed about by Byzantines and Crusaders over the following centuries, and was in a sorry state by the time it fell under Ottoman control in 1365. The Turks eventually rebuilt the town, which they renamed Filibe, and over the next five centuries it thrived as an important commercial centre. The city's merchants grew wealthy and during the Bulgarian national revival period between the late 18th and early 19th centuries, erected some of Bulgaria's finest and most lavish townhouses in what is now known as the old town. It was here in 1855 that Hristo Danov founded Bulgaria's first publishing house.

The 1878 Congress of Berlin decreed that Plovdiv would remain within the Ottoman Empire, as the chief city of the province of Eastern Rumelia, while the rest of Bulgaria was granted its independence. Plovdiv had to wait until 1885 before it finally joined the new state. It is more than likely that Plovdiv would have been made Bulgaria's capital if it had been included in the original 1878 union, a fact which still rankles with many of the city's proud inhabitants.

Plovdiv's main claim to fame these days is its international trade fairs, which have been going in one form or another since the late 19th century. The fairs are the biggest in Bulgaria, and probably in the Balkans.

Orientation

Plovdiv's main points of entry, the central train station, the Rodopi bus station and the Yug bus station, are all handily located close to each other at the southern edge of town. From here, several broad streets radiate northwards, including leafy bul Ruski and ul Ivan Vazov, which runs towards the city's main square, the arid pl Tsentralen. Plovdiv's main pedestrianised thoroughfare, ul Knyaz Aleksandâr, heads north from here to pl Dzhumaya, and continues north to the river as ul Rayko Daskalov. Most of Plovdiv is south of the Maritsa River. The dreary, modern suburbs are to the north and the picturesque old town is to the east.

SOUTHERN BULGARIA

INFORMATION		
Bulbank Булбанк	**1**	C5
Greek Consulate		
Гръцка Консулство	**2**	B4
Main Post Office		
& Telephone Centre	**3**	C5
Police	**4**	C5
Raffeisen Bank Райфайзен Банка	**5**	B5
Turkish Consulate		
Турско Консулство	**6**	B5

SIGHTS & ACTIVITIES		
International Plovdiv Fairgrounds		
Интернационален		
Пловдивски Панаир	**7**	C1

SLEEPING		
Esperantsa Есперанца	**8**	C5
Hotel Avion	**9**	C1
Hotel Leipzig Хотел Лайпциг	**10**	B5
Hotel Maritsa Хотел Марица	**11**	C1
Noviz Hotel Хотел Новиз	**12**	B3

Novotel Новотел	**13**	B1
Traikov Трайков	**14**	C1
Trakiya Hotel		
Хотел Тракия	**15**	B6
Trimontium Princess Hotel		
Хотел Тримонциум Принцес	**16**	C5

EATING		
Malak Bunardzhik		
Малък Бунарджик	**17**	A3
Red Dragon	**18**	B5
Ristorante Da Lino		
Ресторант Да Лино	**19**	B3

DRINKING		
Simfoniya	**20**	B5

ENTERTAINMENT		
Cinema Geo Milev		
Кино Гео Милев	**21**	B6
Club Santo Клуб Санто	**22**	C2
Luki Cinema Кино Лъки	**23**	B4

Open-Air Theatre Летен Театър	**24**	A4
Plovdiv Opera House		
Операта На Пловдив	**25**	B5

TRANSPORT		
Avis Авис	(see 13)	
City Local Transportation Co		
Градски Транспорт Со	**26**	C5
Etap	(see 30)	
Rila Bureau Бюро Рила	**27**	A6
Rodopi Bus Station		
Автогара Родопи	**28**	B6
Tourist Service Rent-A-Car	(see 16)	
Union Ivkoni Vesna 61		
Юнион-Ивкони Весна 61	**29**	B6
Yug Bus Station Автогара Юг	**30**	B6

OTHER		
Clock Tower Часовникова Кула	**31**	C4
Monument to the Soviet Army		
Паметник На Съветската Армия	**32**	A4
University	**33**	C5

Like Rome, the city is based around seven hills, although admittedly one of these was flattened during the communist era. The closest hills to the city are Nebet Tepe, crowned with the ruins of a Thracian fort; Sahat Tepe (Clock Hill), crowned, fittingly enough, with a clock tower; Bunardjika (also known as the Hill of the Liberators) to the west; and Djendem (Hill of the Youth) in the southwest.

Bookstalls around pl Tsentralen and in the underpass beneath the train station sell maps of Plovdiv (in Cyrillic only). The best is Domino's red-covered *Plovdiv* (1:11,500). Unless you're planning a long stay, or venturing out into the suburbs, the maps in this guidebook will be sufficient.

Information

INTERNET ACCESS
There are several Internet centres along, or just off, ul Knyaz Aleksandâr. The following all claim to be open 24 hours and charge around 1.50 to 2 lv per hour.

Internet Fantasy (Map pp122-3; ul Knyaz Aleksandâr 31)
Internet Game Club (Map pp122-3; ul Knyaz Aleksadâr 10)
Internet Royal (Map pp122-3; ul Naiden Gerov 6)

MONEY
Plenty of foreign-exchange offices can be found along the pedestrian mall and ul Ivan Vazov (ideal if you're walking into town from the train or bus stations). Several exchange offices along the mall will also change travellers cheques, and some even offer cash advances with credit cards. Many exchange offices close on Sunday, except for a few along the mall, and rates vary wildly so check around.

Bulbank (Map pp118-19; ul Ivan Vazov)
Raffeisen Bank (Map pp118-19; ul Avksentiy Veleshki)
United Bulgarian Bank (Map pp122-3; pl Dzhumaya)
Has an ATM for all major credit cards.

TELEPHONE
Telephone centre (Map pp118-19; pl Tsentralen; ⏰ 6am-11pm) Inside the main post office.

TOURIST INFORMATION
Frustratingly, Bulgaria's second city still does not have a dedicated tourist office. Hotel reception staff may be able to help with some information, but don't bank on it. Otherwise, there are a few booklets and pamphlets which are widely available from street stalls,

museums and some hotels, including *Old Plovdiv* by Alexander Pizhev (4 lv), published in English, French and German and which gives some interesting background information to the sights in the city's old quarter. The free, quarterly *Plovdiv Guide,* in Bulgarian and English, lists local bars, restaurants and clubs; if you can read Bulgarian, *Programata* is another free weekly listings magazine with details of eating, drinking and entertainment options in Plovdiv, including movie listings. The website www.plovdivcityguide.com also carries some useful basic information.

Sights

RUINS
Plovdiv boasts several Roman ruins, scattered around town.

Roman Amphitheatre
This magnificent **amphitheatre** (Map pp122-3; ul Hemus; admission 3 lv; ⏰ 8am-6pm) was built during the reign of the emperor Trajan, in the early 2nd century AD. Incredibly, it was only uncovered during a freak landslide in 1972. Now lovingly restored, the amphitheatre, which at its peak could seat about 6000 spectators, is once again used for special events and concerts (often in May and June).

Visitors can admire the amphitheatre free of charge from one of several lookouts along ul Hemus or from the inevitable cafés at the top. But it's certainly worth paying the entrance fee so you can clamber around the marble seats and stage and try out the acoustics for yourself. Although accessible from ul Hemus, there's an unsigned short cut from the back of the Church of Sveta Bogoroditsa along ul T Samodomov.

Roman Stadium
Although only a very small section of the once huge **Roman stadium** (Map pp122-3) is visible today, its location, at the bottom of a kind of concrete well in the centre of Plovdiv's main thoroughfare, certainly draws attention. Just a dozen rows of the northern section have been unearthed and partially restored. It's not possible to walk around the stadium, but it can be admired from the street level. It's watched over by a modern bronze statue of the city's founder – the 4th-century BC king of Macedonia, Philip II – standing atop a column in the guise of a Roman emperor.

Roman Forum

Just down the steps at the overpass near pl Tsentralen are some visually unexciting **ruins** (Map pp118-19), where excavations continue at intervals. Although not restored, signposted or labelled, visitors can see the ruins from over the fence along the main road. On the opposite side of the post office another section of the forum has been partially excavated and restored, and can be visited, although again there are no explanations. There's a tiny, reconstructed modern amphitheatre and a few original columns.

Nebet Tepe

On this hill top are the **ruins of Eumolpias** (Map pp122-3), a Thracian settlement from about 5000 BC. The fortress and surrounding town were strategically placed on the 203m-high hill for obvious defensive purposes. The fortress was later invaded, occupied and fortified by Macedonians, Romans, Byzantines, Bulgarians and Turks. The Turks named it Nebet Tepe (Prayer Hill).

Today, it's difficult to make much sense of the overgrown rubble that remains, but the site does offer some expansive views of the city below. Nothing is fenced off, so the hill can be climbed from anywhere, but it's easier to reach from along ul Dr Chomakov through the old town. Also up here are the partially restored remains of a 13th-century reservoir – an essential facility in the desperate days of siege warfare.

MUSEUMS

Plovdiv has a dozen or so museums, but only a few are actually worth the effort of visiting, and are listed next. Opening hours can be erratic, due to lack of funds and frequent 'renovation'. If a museum looks closed during what should be opening hours, bang loudly on the front door.

Ethnographical Museum

If you only visit one museum or house in Plovdiv, make sure it's the **Ethnographical Museum** (Map pp122-3; ☎ 625 654; ul Dr Chomakov 2; admission 4 lv; ☼ 9am-5pm). It houses some 40,000 exhibits, including fascinating displays of folk art, jewellery and traditional crafts, such as weaving, metalworking, winemaking and beekeeping. Also on show are traditional tools such as grape-crushers, wine-measures and apparatus used for distilling attar of roses. Upstairs, the rooms have been restored to their elegant 19th-century appearance; the carved wooden ceilings are particularly fine. Traditional costumes and musical instruments are displayed here too.

The house, built in 1847 and owned by Agir Koyoumdjioglou, was for decades the most renowned Bulgarian national revival period style home in Plovdiv. It's famous for its niches, carved ceilings and symmetrical design. Before it became the city's preeminent museum, the building was used as a girls' boarding school and a warehouse for tobacco and flour.

Historical Museum

This is also called the **Museum of Revival & The National Liberation** (Map pp122-3; ☎ 623 378; ul Lavrenov 1; admission 2 lv; ☼ 9am-noon & 1-5.30pm Mon-Sat). It generally concentrates on the 1876 April Uprising against the Turks, and in particular, the massacre at Batak (see the boxed text, p110). The three floors also include exhibits of military uniforms and earthenware. The caretaker speaks some English but everything is labelled in Bulgarian. The museum is in a house built in 1848 by Dimitâr Georgiadi, so it's sometimes also called the Georgiadi Kâshta.

Archaeological Museum

The tiny **Archaeological Museum** (Map pp122-3; ☎ 224 339; pl Saedinenie 1) is a bit of a let down, given the city's long and turbulent history. It was closed for renovation at the time of research. There are just two rooms, one holding a selection of Thracian and Roman pottery and jewellery, the other a gathering of ecclesiastical artefacts, icons and liturgical paraphernalia. However, the museum does possess some 60,000 valuable archaeological items, and hopefully, these will be displayed here in the future or, more likely, elsewhere in Plovdiv. There are a few Roman-era tombstones on show outside the museum.

Museum of History

In the same dilapidated building as the Archaeological Museum, the **Museum of History** (Map pp122-3; ☎ 629 409; pl Saedinenie 1; admission 2 lv; ☼ 9am-noon & 1-5.30pm Mon-Sat) is dedicated to the Unification of Bulgaria in 1885, with displays of documents, photographs and personal effects of individuals connected

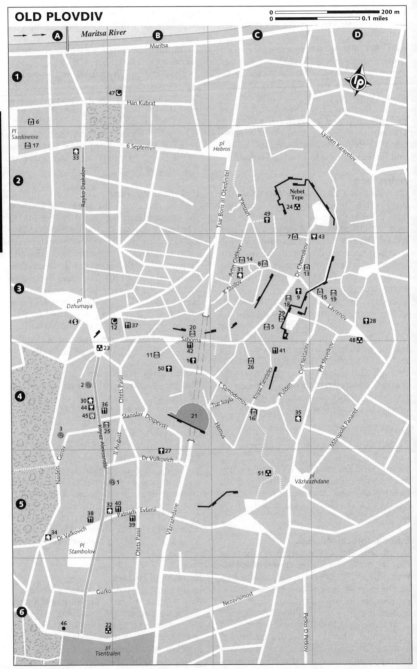

OLD PLOVDIV

0 _____ 200 m
0 _____ 0.1 miles

Maritsa River

Maritsa

Han Kubrat

Pl Saedinenie

6 Septemvri

pl Hebros

Nebet Tepe

Tsar Boris III Obedinitel

Lyuben Karavelov

Rayko Daskalov

pl Dzhumaya

Artin Gidikov

K Stoilov

Dr Chomakov

Lavrenov

Saborna

T Samodumov

Knyaz Tseretelev

Puldin

Ovil Neltchov

PR Slaveykov

Otets Paisii

Stanislav Dospevski

Tsar Ivaylo

Hemus

Mitropolit Panaret

Knyaz Aleksandar

II Avgust

Dr Vulkovich

pl Vâzhrazhdane

Naiden Gerov

Vâzrazhdane

Patriarh Evtimii

Otets Paisii

Dr Valkovich

pl Stambolov

Gurko

Nezavisimost

Petko D Petkov

pl Tsentralen

with the event. Like other museums in Plovdiv, its actual opening hours are unpredictable, and unless you can read the Bulgarian-only labelling and have an informed interest in the subject matter, it's unlikely to cause great excitement.

HOUSE-MUSEUMS

The 19th-century Plovdiv 'baroque' style house is typified by an overhanging upper storey with jutting eaves, a columned portico and a brightly painted façade. Inside, the salons, drawing rooms and bedrooms feature finely carved woodwork complemented by painted wall decorations and ornamental niches.

There are now several house-museums in Plovdiv, and unless you have a real passion for this type of architecture, you may only want to visit one or two of them. None of the displays at any of the houses have explanations in any language but Bulgarian and staff rarely speak English.

Hindlian House

Once owned by the wealthy merchant Stepan Hindlian, this **house** (Map pp122-3; ☎ 628 998; ul Artin Gidikov 4; admission 3 lv; ◷ 9am-noon & 1.30-4.30pm Mon-Fri) was built in 1835, and is one of the most opulent of Plovdiv's museum houses. The two floors of this fully restored home are full of exquisite period furniture, while the walls are painted with

real and imaginary landscapes of Venice, Alexandria and Constantinople, which took about six months to complete. The scenes were meant to illustrate the original owner's extensive overseas trading links and wealth. Look out too for the magnificent panelled ceilings and the 'Oriental style' marble bathroom on the ground floor, with its high, domed ceiling and skylight – a great luxury in the early 19th century. Visitors are welcome to enjoy the small **courtyard garden** (admission free).

In the cellar is the so-called **Wine from Bulgaria Museum & Oenology Collection** (☎ 635 376; ◷ 10am-5.30pm Tue-Sat), which is actually a venue for tutored wine tastings. The standard tasting, of three wines and bread, costs 10 lv; if you can stand the pace, a tasting of 10 wines costs 40 lv. Specialist courses are also offered, while one (full) glass of wine costs 2 lv.

Danov House

The **Danov House** (Map pp122-3; ☎ 629 405; ul Mitropolit Paisii 2; admission 2 lv; ◷ 9am-12.30pm & 2-4.30pm Mon-Sat) is dedicated to Hristo Danov (a renowned writer and publisher) and several other Bulgarian authors. The house contains a mock-up of a bookshop and a national revival–era classroom. Before you leave, have a look at the old printing press in the room next to the reception office. From the **gardens** (admission free), there are charming views of the old town and new city. The entrance is through a wall up a laneway leading to the Church of Sveta Bogoroditsa.

Balabanov House

This **house** (Map pp122-3; ☎ 627 082; ul Dr K Stoilov 57; admission 3 lv; 🕑 9am-12.30pm & 2-5pm Mon-Fri) was once owned by (and is named after) Luka Balabanov, a rich merchant from the early 19th century. The house was destroyed several decades later, but rebuilt from scratch in 1980 based on the original building plans. The ground floor is a gallery of modern, but curiously unnamed, paintings while the 1st floor contains some gorgeous antique furniture. The entrance is at the back; follow the white wall around the side.

Other Houses

Built in 1830, the **Lamartine House** (Map pp122-3; ☎ 631 776; ul Knyaz Tseretelev 19), also known as the Georgi Mavridi House, is an elegant residence now belonging to the Union of Bulgarian Writers. It's not normally open to the public, though you could call ahead to check current arrangements. The building is named in honour of its tenuous connection with the French poet, Alphonse de Lamartine, who stayed here for a mere three days in 1833, during his 'travels in the Orient'.

The **Nedkovich House** (Map pp122-3; ☎ 626 216; ul Lavrenov; admission 2 lv; 🕑 9am-noon & 1-6pm Apr-Sep, closed Sat & Sun Oct-Mar) was built in 1863. The exhibits are part of an 'Old Town Life' theme but are musty and uninteresting. It is poorly signposted but is next to the Historical Museum.

Apteka (Map pp122-3; Old Hippocrates Pharmacy; ☎ 624 594; ul Saborna 16; 🕑 9am-5pm), a small museum of pharmacy, is very rarely open despite the posted hours. You can peek through the window, though, to see what a 19th-century pharmacy looked like.

ART GALLERIES

Plovdiv has long been home to a large and thriving artistic community, and this is reflected in the number of galleries in town.

The **State Gallery of Fine Arts** (Map pp122-3; ☎ 635 322; ul Saborna 14a; admission 3 lv, free on Tue; 🕑 9am-12.30pm & 1-5.30pm Mon-Fri) occupies a grand town house built in 1846 and offers an outstanding display of art by leading Bulgarian painters from the 19th and 20th centuries. Highlights include Goshka Datsov's

symbolist work *A Samaritan*, Konstantin Velichkov's wonderful portrait *The Black Boy* and Nikolai Rainov's *A Bride of a Vampire*, showing the influence of both Art Nouveau style and 19th-century Japanese woodcuts. Look out too for Georgi Mashev's creepy mythical allegories, *A Mad Woman* and *A Nightmare*, and the works of Vladimir Dimitov. The top floor holds a collection of less immediately engaging modernist and abstract works, and there are occasional temporary exhibitions.

The **Philipopolis Art Gallery** (Map pp122-3; ☎ 622 742; ul Saborna 29; admission 2 lv; 🕑 10am-6pm) is a private collection of Bulgarian art on show in the splendidly restored Hadzhi Aleko house, dating from 1865. It's an intimate setting, the paintings displayed as they would be in a private house, and the enthusiastic (but non-English-speaking) owner actually encourages you to take photos. The mostly 19th-century works on the upper floor are the main attraction, including paintings by Michail Lutov and David Peretz. The works are only labelled in Bulgarian, but a free brochure, in English, gives basic details of the house and a few of the paintings.

Right beside the Church of Sts Konstantin and Elena, the small **Museum of Icons** (Map pp122-3; ☎ 626 086; ul Saborna 22; admission 2 lv; 🕑 9am-12.30pm & 1-5.30pm) holds a fascinating display of icons dating as far back as the 15th century. It was closed for major repairs at the time of research.

The **City Art Gallery** (Map pp122-3; ☎ 624 221; ul Knyaz Aleksandâr 15; admission 2 lv; 🕑 9am-12.30pm & 1-5.30pm Mon-Fri, 10am-5.30pm Sat) is another branch of the State Gallery of Fine Arts, in the city centre, which holds small, temporary exhibitions of modern art. Opening times can be unpredictable.

Zlatyu Boyadjiev House (Map pp122-3; ☎ 635 308; ul Saborna 18; admission 3 lv; 🕑 9am-noon & 1-6pm Apr-Sep, 8.30am-noon & 12.30-5pm Mon-Fri Oct-Mar) contains dozens of oil paintings by local artist Zlatyu Boyadjiev (1903–76), many idealising the Bulgarian peasantry. Some canvases are so huge they easily fill one side of a wall.

The **Atanas Krastev House** (Map pp122-3; ☎ 627 132; ul Dr Chomakov 5a; admission 1 lv; 🕑 10am-6pm Mar-Nov) is another attractive old house which was once the home of the famed local painter and conservationist Atanas Krastev, who died in 2003. The ground floor holds more than two dozen of his self-portraits, while upstairs you can cast an eye over Krastev's personal collection of mostly abstract 20th-century Bulgarian paintings. It still feels like a very private space, strewn with personal belongings. The terrace offers a superb view over the city, while more artworks are on show in the small garden.

RELIGIOUS BUILDINGS

Each of the following places has free admission and is open daily during daylight hours.

The huge, three-aisle **Church of Sveta Bogoroditsa** (Map pp122-3; ul Mitropolit Paisii), with its unmistakable pink and blue belltower, was built in 1844 on the site of an earlier church, from the 9th century. It contains a marvellous array of icons and murals, including one depicting a sword-wielding Turkish soldier threatening a group of chained and lamenting Bulgarian peasants.

The **Church of Sts Konstantin & Elena** (Map pp122-3; ul Saborna 24) is the oldest church in Plovdiv. Excavations reveal that a Christian sanctuary first appeared here in the late Roman period, and the church which developed was then dedicated to the Roman emperor, Constantine the Great, and his mother, St Helena. It was destroyed numerous times over the centuries and the current building was mostly rebuilt in 1832. It contains a particularly fine iconostasis, painted by Zahari Zograf between 1836 and 1840, while the covered portico is also covered in rich and colourful frescoes. Photos are not permitted inside.

Originally built in 1561, **Sveta Marina Church** (Map pp122-3; ul Dr Vulkovich 7) was burnt down 50 years later, rebuilt completely in 1783, and repaired extensively in 1856. Note the 17m-high pagoda-shaped wooden bell tower, built in 1870, and the intricate 170-year-old iconostasis inside the church.

The **Sveta Nedelya Church** (Map pp122-3; ul PR Slaveikov 40) is one of the largest in Plovdiv. Originally built in 1578 and renovated in the 1830s, it contains exquisite iconostases (carved from walnut) and faded murals from the mid-1800s. Sadly, the church is in a poor state of repair and is only sporadically open to the public, but it's worth a look from the outside.

The **Dzhumaya Mosque** (Map pp122-3; pl Dzhumaya) was built in the mid-15th century and is one of the oldest in the Balkans. It was also the largest of more than 50 mosques built in Plovdiv during the Turkish occupation, and is still used today for religious services. It's an imposing sight, despite the rather worrying looking cracks (caused by earthquakes) and crumbling masonry. Look for the 23m-high minaret and please remove your shoes before entering.

Festivals & Events

Cultural Month Festival (late May– mid-Jul)
Verdi Festival (early Jun) Two-week festival.
International Festival of Chamber Music (mid-Jun) Ten-day festival.
International Folklore Festival (early Aug)
Thracia Summer Music Festival (www.geocities.com /thracia_festival; Aug) Regional festival. Venues in Plovdiv include the Balabanov House and the Ethnographic Museum, while events also take place in Stara Zagora, Chirpan and other towns in the southern part of Bulgaria.
City Holiday (6 Sep)
International Plovdiv Fair (mid-May & late Sep) Week-long festival held in the massive **fairgrounds** (Map pp118-19; ☎ 553 146; bul Tsar Boris III Obedinitel 37), north of the river.

Sleeping

Accommodation in Plovdiv is almost as expensive as in Sofia, and there's much less of it around, so advance bookings are recommended. While the international fairs are on, in May and September, prices increase, sometimes quite substantially, and rooms are that much scarcer, so it's probably best to avoid these periods.

BUDGET

Plovdiv's budget options are limited and far from sumptuous, but they do book up very quickly. Private rooms offered through accommodation agencies can be a better deal.

Complex 4-TY Kilometre (☎ 951 360; camp sites per person 3 lv; bungalows 30-40 lv; ☼ year-round) This camping ground, also called Gorski Kat Camping, is about 4km west of central Plovdiv on the old Sofia Highway. It provides shade and privacy if you can escape the incessant traffic noise. A restaurant–bar is attached. Take bus No 4, 18 or 44 west along bul Bulgaria, or bus No 222 from the train station, as far as they go and walk another 200m down the road.

Traikov (Map pp118-19; ☎ 963 014; et_traykov@yahoo .com; 1st fl, ul Ibur 31; s/d 22/35 lv, apt 50-90 lv; ☼ 9am-5pm Mon-Sat) This reliable accommodation agency, with friendly, English-speaking staff, is a fair way from the train and bus stations, so it's well worth ringing ahead to avoid a lengthy trip in case no rooms are available; they will be happy to arrange a meeting with you outside the normal opening hours. The apartments have a kitchen, bathroom and TV.

Accommodation Agency (Map pp122-3; ☎ 272 778; ul Knyaz Aleksandâr 28; r per person 22 lv; ⏱ 9am-5pm Mon-Sat) Opening hours are occasionally irregular, but staff are helpful, friendly and speak English. The office is at the back of a small arcade; look for the black sign reading 'accommodation agency' (in English) along from the mall.

Esperantsa (Map pp118-19; ☎ 260 653; ul Ivan Vazov 14; r per person 22 lv; ⏱ 9am-5pm Mon-Sat) This accommodation agency can be a bit haphazard and the staff speak little English, but do get by in German. However, readers have commented favourably on the quality of rooms on offer. It's easy to reach from the train station, or the Yug or Rodopi bus stations, and is signposted in English.

Tourist Hotel (Turisticheski Dom; Map pp122-3; ☎ 635 115; ul PR Slaveikov 5; s/d with shared bathroom 28/48 lv) Rooms at this old and atmospheric former school are huge, with high ceilings and rather tattered furniture. The noisy nightclub at the back, musty aroma and saggy beds might not appeal to everyone, but it's cheap, convenient and very popular, so you will need to book ahead.

PBI Hostel (Map pp122-3; ☎ 638 467; hostel@pbi hostel.com; ul Naiden Gerov 13; dm €10; 🖳) Also known as the Plovdiv Bulgaria Inn, this modern hostel has a great central location, near pl Stambolov, though it's not quite up to the standards of the better hostels in Sofia, and the dorms themselves are plain and unremarkable. The owner speaks English and Japanese.

MID-RANGE

Again, Plovdiv's stock of real mid-range hotels is quite small and overpriced, and you should always book ahead. You have rather more choice if your budget can extend to the top-end options, which nearly always have room.

Trakiya Hotel (Map pp118-19; ☎ 624 101; ul Ivan Vazov 84; s/d 45.60/71.20 lv) This small, 10-room place is very convenient, about 100m from the train station. It's fairly basic, but the rooms (with fan and TV) are quiet despite the noisy location and popular bar downstairs. Breakfast costs an additional 5 lv.

Hotel Leipzig (Map pp118-19; ☎ 632 250; www .leipzig-bg.com; bul Ruski 70; s/d 44/64 lv; ℗) This ageing high-rise is one of the cheaper hotel options in town. Rooms come with TV and minibar, and some have great views of the Hill of the Liberators. However, it's in desperate need of a major overhaul, and the hard beds, antiquated plumbing and peeling paintwork reduce the appeal. Breakfast is 5 lv extra.

Hotel Elite (Map pp122-3; ☎ 624 537; ul Rayko Daskalov 53; r 100 lv; ❄) The Elite is modern and reasonably central, on the corner of the busy bul 6 Septemvri. The rooms, thankfully, are insulated from the noisy road below. It's clean and comfortable but nothing out of the ordinary, and since you pay for the room, it's poor value if you're travelling alone.

TOP END

Hotel Avion (Map pp118-19; ☎ 967 451; ul Han Presian 13-15; d/ste €50/70; ℗ ❄) Not far from the Maritsa, the Avion is a small, modern hotel offering smartly furnished doubles and suites in a quiet side street. The location's not that convenient for sightseeing, but it's a friendly, well-maintained place with its own restaurant.

Hotel Maritsa (Map pp118-19; ☎ 952 735; fax 652 899; bul Tsar Boris III Obedinitel 42; s/d/apt €56/84/142; ℗ ❄) This gleaming modern tower opposite the fairgrounds isn't in the most convenient of locations, and the dark and ostentatious foyer may be a slight put off, but rooms are attractive enough, and fair value, and facilities include a gym, a restaurant and a nightclub.

Hotel Bulgaria (Map pp122-3; ☎ 633 599; www .hotelbulgaria.net; ul Patriarh Evtimii 13; s/d incl breakfast from €35/65; ℗ ❄) Conveniently situated right in the heart of Plovdiv, the Bulgaria offers the best value in its price range. The rooms are bright and modern and all have TVs and spruce bathrooms, while the double glazing keeps out most of the noise from the busy street below. The location is hard to beat.

Noviz Hotel (Map pp118-19; ☎ 631 281; www.noviz .com; bul Ruski 55; s/d/ste 100/140/170 lv; ℗ ❄) Although not as central or convenient as you might have wished, the Noviz is good value for Plovdiv. It's a small place, but the rooms are large and well furnished, and the hotel also has a gym and sauna for guests, and a rooftop cocktail bar.

Hebros Hotel (Map pp122-3; ☎ 260 180; www .hebros-hotel.com; ul Konstantin Stoilov 51a; s/d/apt from €79/95/115; P ✗) The Hebros is undoubtedly the most characterful hotel in Plovdiv. It's a 200-year-old house filled with antique furniture, and all six rooms are individually decorated with national revival–era flair. The bathrooms, however, are sparklingly modern and there's also a Jacuzzi, sauna and well-regarded restaurant (right).

Trimontium Princess Hotel (Map pp118-19; ☎ 605 000; www.trimontium-princess.com; pl Tsentralen; s/d Mon-Thu from €80.49/101, Fri-Sun €60.49/81; P ✗) This venerable, mammoth hotel facing the arid pl Tsentralen is a grand but oddly gloomy place, which is spookily silent for much of the time. However, the rooms are smart and have a suitably elegant feel, and it's very central. The weekend prices offer better value, and there are occasional discounts. It has a restaurant, open to nonguests, and a casino.

Novotel (Map pp118-19; ☎ 934 444; www.novotel pdv.bg; ul Boyadjiev 2; s/d Mon-Fri €86/114, Sat & Sun €74/97; P ✗ ⌨) This gigantic boxy affair north of the river has all the luxuries expected of this international chain, though all with a curious '70s ambience. Rooms are large and comfortable, and there's a bar, restaurant and nightclub.

Eating

The main pedestrian thoroughfare, ul Knyaz Aleksandâr, is lined with bars and cafés, while several stalls along the northern section of ul Rayko Daskalov sell cheap and tasty doner kebabs, pizzas and other street snacks. There are a number of very good restaurants in the old town. Check out the *Plovdiv Guide* for details of some of the best places to eat in and around town.

RESTAURANTS

Restaurant Kambanata (Map pp122-3; ☎ 260 665; ul Saborna; mains 5-10 lv) Kambanata enjoys an unusual location under the grounds of the Church of Sveta Bogoroditsa, with tables set in ascending rows like a theatre, so diners can watch live music being performed most nights. If that's not your scene, there's also an outdoor terrace. The menu is in English and features the usual hearty grills and fish

dishes, as well as some less appealing items such as 'lamb's head without bone'. The service is excellent.

Hebros Hotel Restaurant (Map pp122-3; ☎ 625 929; ul K Stoilov 51; mains 6-21 lv) The excellent garden restaurant of the upmarket Hebros Hotel is the place to go for fine traditional Bulgarian cuisine, with dishes such as rabbit with plums, trout, pork with blue cheese and vegetarian options featuring on the menu.

Malâk Bunardzhik (Map pp118-19; ☎ 446 140; ul Volga 1; mains 5-10 lv) Discreetly hidden behind trees just off bul Ruski, this restaurant is an excellent place to sample some better quality Bulgarian cuisine in classy surrounds. Indoors, it's formal without being stuffy, and there's a more casual atmosphere in the garden. Live music is offered most nights.

Gusto (Map pp122-3; ☎ 623 711; ul Otets Paisii 26; mains 4-9 lv; ✪ 9am-1am) Across the road from the Bulgaria Hotel, Gusto is a bright place adorned with numerous classic black-and-white photos. It offers a varied selection of meals, including paella, kebabs, pizza and steak and chips, as well as lots of drinks.

Pulden Restaurant (Map pp122-3; ☎ 631 720; ul Knyaz Tseretelev 8; mains 8-10 lv) The Pulden has several unique dining rooms. One occupies a place where dervishes (a mystical Islamic sect) once whirled themselves into feverish exhaustion. Another is in the cellar where Byzantine-era walls and Roman artefacts make up the décor. Although predictably touristy and relatively expensive, it's worth a visit. The menu is in English and features lots of fish, meat and vegetarian dishes.

Cafe Grill Angelo (Map pp122-3; ☎ 623 973; ul Konstantin Irechek 5; mains 2-4 lv) Tucked away beneath the horse-chestnut trees behind the Dzumaya Mosque, Angelo has the usual range of cheap salads and grills, and it's also a pleasantly shady spot to grab a cold drink on a hot day.

Happy Bar & Grill (Map pp122-3; ☎ 625 193; ul Patriarh Evtimii 13; mains 4-8 lv; ✪ breakfast, lunch & dinner) Next to the Hotel Bulgaria, this is a branch of the popular country-wide chain. It offers a huge menu, in English, of salads, grills and steaks, and the food is reliable and tasty, if not exactly adventurous. 'If your waitress doesn't smile, send her away and call up another!' shouts the blurb on the menu, and service is predictably swift and friendly.

Ristorante Da Lino (Map pp118-19; ☎ 631 751; bul 6 Septemvri 135; mains 6-15 lv) Set in a converted monastery, this place offers a limited menu of Italian specialities. Prices are rather high and portions rather small, and if you turn up at a quiet time, you might find yourself dining alongside chain-smoking staff members. However, if you've had enough of *kebabche*, it might make a welcome change. In the evenings, a pianist tinkles in the corner while you munch your tortellini.

Red Dragon (Map pp118-19; ☎ 622 817; ul Filip Makedonski 27a; mains 3-6 lv) The food at this Chinese restaurant may not be the most authentic around, but the menu is extensive, the portions are large and prices are reasonable. The set lunches offer the best value, and there's also a children's lunch menu.

CAFÉS

There are plenty of pavement cafés along ul Knyaz Aleksandâr, though on a sunny day you might have trouble finding a seat. Others can be found around the old town.

Art Cafe Philippopolis (Map pp122-3; ☎ 624 851; ul Saborna 29; ☻ 10am-midnight) Located in the garden of the art gallery of the same name, this is a pleasant and stylish place to sample one of the very many intriguing cocktails available, and there's also a brief menu of snack-type food. The views of town from the terrace are breathtaking.

Dreams (Map pp122-3; ☎ 627 142; pl Stambolov; sandwiches around 2 lv; ☻ 9am-11pm) One of the busiest of central Plovdiv's numerous outdoor cafés, Dreams has a mass of seats on the edge of pl Stambolov and attracts a seemingly never-ending stream of customers with its big menu of ice creams, cakes and pastries.

Big Ben (Map pp122-3; ☎ 622 302; ul Knyaz Aleksandâr 29; mains 3-5 lv; ☻ breakfast, lunch & dinner) This Westminster clock–themed place is a pleasant spot to stop for drinks and snacks, and also offers a menu of light meals and breakfasts.

Drinking

Rahat Tepe Bar (Map pp122-3; ☎ 624 454; ul Dr Chomakov) For grand views of the old town in the company of a cold beer, head to the Rahat Tepe Bar, almost at the top of Nebet Tepe hill. They also serve simple meals such as *kebabche* and salads, and the menu also features such lip-smacking delights as 'birds' rumps on sticks' and 'pork spleen country style.' Mmmm!

Simfoniya (Map pp118-19; ☎ 630 333; Tsar Simeon Garden; ☻ 24hr) Located at the western end of the leafy city-centre park, Simfoniya is a trendy, and often full, bar-café with a big drinks and cakes menu. Right in front is the musical fountain, which is illuminated with coloured spotlights and 'dances' to trashy Euro-pop numbers in the evenings.

Sky Bar (Map pp122-3; ☎ 633 377; ul Knyaz Aleksandâr 30; ☻ 24hr) For panoramic views of the modern city, especially at night, visit the Sky Bar on the top floor of one of the tallest buildings along the mall. You can also sit outside on the terraces.

Entertainment

DISCOS & NIGHTCLUBS

Caligula (Map pp122-3; ☎ 626 867; ul Knyaz Aleksandâr 30; ☻ 10am-8am) Plovdiv's only gay club is frequented by a mixed crowd, who turn up late for the live music, DJs and 'erotic shows' which include male pole-dancers, helpfully pictured in action on the noticeboard outside. It's in the same complex as the Sky Bar (see previous section).

Club Santo (Map pp118-19; ☎ 0889 325 048; bul Maritsa 122; ☻ 11pm-6am) Overlooking the river, Club Santo is a dimly lit place with nightly DJs playing lots of Latino and dance music.

CINEMAS

Several cinemas regularly screen recent foreign films in the original language (with Bulgarian subtitles). Tickets cost from 2 to 4 lv depending on the session times and the comfort of the seats. Try the **Cinema Geo Milev** (Map pp118-19; ☎ 626 457; bul Vasil Aprilov), **Luki Cinema** (Map pp118-19; ☎ 629 070; ul Gladston 1) or **Flamingo Cinema** (☎ 644 004; bul 6 Septemvri 128).

THEATRE & OPERA

Roman Amphitheatre (Map pp122-3) This ancient theatre is the stunning venue for Plovdiv's annual Verdi Festival (June), as well as other opera, ballet and music performances during the summer months. Look for posters around town advertising upcoming events.

Open-air Theatre (Map pp118-19; Bunardjika) This theatre sometimes has performances of traditional music and dance in summer.

Nikolai Masalitinov Dramatic Theatre (Map pp122-3; ☎ 224 867; ul Knyaz Aleksandâr 38) This is one of the most respected theatres in Bulgaria. It features anything from Shakespeare to Ibsen (most performances are in Bulgarian).

Plovdiv Opera House (Map pp118-19; ☎ 632 231; opera@thracia.net; ul Avksentiy Veleshki) The Opera House features performances of classic and modern European operas, performed in Bulgarian.

Getting There & Away

AIR

Plovdiv Aiport is used only by occasional charter flights; there are no scheduled commercial flights to or from Plovdiv. The **Plovdiv Airport travel agency** (Map pp122-3; ☎ 633 081; ul Gladston 4) can book domestic and international flights for most airlines (it's the official agent for Bulgaria Air) to and from Sofia, not from Plovdiv.

BUS

Plovdiv has three well-organised bus stations. The main **Yug bus station** (Map pp118-19; ☎ 626 937) is diagonally opposite the train station and is only 10 minutes' walk from the city centre. From this station, public buses (and, where indicated, private buses) go to the destinations listed.

Destination	Fare	Duration	Frequency
Bansko	7.50 lv	3½ hr	2 daily
Blagoevgrad	7 lv	3hr	3 daily
Burgas (private)	15 lv	4hr	2 daily
Haskovo	4 lv	1hr	5 daily
Hisar	2.20 lv	1hr	12 daily
Karlovo	2.80 lv	1½ hr	half-hourly
Ruse (private)	13 lv	6hr	1 daily
Sliven	10 lv	3hr	5 daily
Sofia	9 lv	2½ hr	half-hourly
Stara Zagora	4.80 lv	1½ hr	4 daily
Varna	15 lv	7 hr	2 daily
Veliko Târnovo (private)	11 lv	4½ hr	3 daily

In summer, one or two daily buses also leave the Yug bus station for the resorts along the Black Sea coast, such as Kiten, Ahtopol, Albena and Nesebâr.

From **Rodopi bus station** (Map pp118-19; ☎ 777 607), which is accessible on foot through the underpass by the train station, there are 13 daily services to Haskovo and Karlovo and hourly buses (between 6am and 7pm) to Smolyan (7.50 lv, 2½ hours), via Bachkovo (2.70 lv, one hour), Chepelare and Pamporovo.

The **Sever bus station** (☎ 553 705), in the northern suburbs, is best accessed by taxi and is of limited use. From this bus station only one daily bus goes directly to Pleven (10 lv), Ruse (12 lv), Troyan (7 lv) and Koprivshtitsa (6 lv).

Union-Ivkoni Vesna 61 (Map pp118-19; ☎ 628 365; train station underpass; 🕒 8am-6pm) is an agency offering buses to numerous international destinations including Paris (180 lv), Rome (170 lv), Vienna (110 lv) and Amsterdam (170 lv).

Etap (Map pp118-19; ☎ 632 082; Yug bus station) is one of a number of private agencies at the Yug bus station selling tickets for coaches to Istanbul (25 lv) and Athens (95 lv), among other destinations.

City Local Transportation Co (Map pp118-19; ☎ 624 274; State Philharmonic Bldg, pl Tsentralen) offers a bus to Athens (102 lv) on Tuesday and Thursday, and between one and three daily buses to Thessaloniki (55 lv).

TRAIN

Plovdiv is along the most popular railway line in Bulgaria, between Sofia and Burgas, so trains are frequent. The major train services are listed in the table.

Destination	1st-/2nd-class fare	Duration	Number of trains (daily)
Burgas	13.60/10 lv*	4hr*	6
Hisar	4.50/3.50 lv	2hr	3
Karlovo	4.30/3.30 lv	2hr	5
Sofia	9/6.50 lv*	2½ hr*	14
Svilengrad	7.50/5.30 lv	3½ hr	3

*denotes express trains

Plovdiv's **train station** (Map pp118-19; ☎ 622 729; bul Hristo Botev) is convenient, and reasonably well organised. Recent arrivals and upcoming departures are listed in Bulgarian on a computer screen at the entrance to the station as well as in the underpass leading to the platforms. Unfortunately – and surprisingly – the platforms are not numbered and staff at the information office do not speak English.

Advance tickets for domestic services are sold upstairs. For international tickets, go to the **Rila Bureau** (Map pp118-19; ☎ 446 120; 🕒 8am-6.30pm Mon-Sat) located along a side street parallel to bul Hristo Botev. For information about international trains that pass through Plovdiv, see p265.

Getting Around

Plovdiv is pleasingly compact so it's generally quicker to get around on foot. Little of the old town (except the hotels) is accessible by vehicle, so if you have a private, rented or chartered car, park it outside the old town and walk. Happily, taxi drivers use their meters with little or no prompting.

There's no point hiring a vehicle to get around Plovdiv, but travelling around the region by car allows you to explore remote monasteries, caves and lakes. **Tourist Service Rent-a-Car** (Map pp118-19; ☎ 623 496; Trimontium Princess Hotel) and **Avis** (Map pp118-19; ☎ 934 481; Novotel) are expensive, so hire a car through one of the numerous travel agencies along the mall. Prices are more competitive, however, in Sofia, so it's probably even more economical to return to the capital and rent something from a Bulgarian company there.

AROUND PLOVDIV
Bachkovo Monastery

Бачковоски Манастир

About 30km south of Plovdiv, just past the picturesque hill-top village of Bachkovo, is the magnificent **Bachkovo Monastery** (admission free; ☾ 6am-10pm). It was founded in 1083 by two aristocrats, the Georgian brothers Gregory and Abasius Bakuriani, who were in the military service of the Byzantine Empire. The monastery was a major religious centre during the Second Bulgarian Empire (1185–1396), but was then ransacked by the Turks in the 15th and 16th centuries. It underwent major reconstruction in the mid-17th century and is now Bulgaria's second-largest monastery, after Rila.

In the centre of the courtyard stands the **Church of Sveta Bogoroditsa**, dating from 1604. Colourful frescoes in the porch include examples of Zahari Zograf's work from the early 1850s. Inside there's a 17th-century iconostasis, more 19th-century murals and a much-cherished icon of the Virgin, allegedly painted by St Luke, though in fact dating from the early 14th century. If you're here on a Sunday morning, you'll see long queues of local pilgrims waiting to pay their respects to the image, which is encased in silver.

One corner of the southern side is occupied by the former **refectory**, originally built in 1601. Covering the walls are stunning frescoes relating the monastery's history. A gate beside the refectory leads to a little courtyard (only sporadically open to visitors) where you'll find the **Church of Sveti Nikolai**, built in 1836. During the 1840s, Zograf painted the superb *Last Judgment* inside the chapel; note the condemned, nervous-looking Turks on the right and Zograf's self-portrait (no beard) in the upper-left corner.

Around 50m from the monastery entrance is the recently restored **Ossuary**, which features wonderful medieval murals. At the time of research, it was not open to the public.

An explanation board at the monastery gate provides a brief history (in English, French and German) about the monastery and a crude map of some short **hiking trails** to nearby villages. The guidebook (15 lv), available at the little shop inside the monastery compound, provides plenty of explanations and photos for keener visitors.

SLEEPING & EATING

Echo Hotel (☎ 048-981 068; d incl breakfast 50 lv) The only place to stay in the area. It's on the other side of the road, and river, from the turn-off to the monastery. It offers quiet and comfortable rooms.

The lane up to the monastery from the main road is cluttered with numerous souvenir stalls and snack bars, as well as a couple of decent restaurants. The best is **Restaurant Vodopada** (mains 3-6 lv; ☾ breakfast, lunch & dinner), at the bottom of the hill. It's a charming courtyard restaurant, centred around a little waterfall and fish-pool. The Bulgarian-only menu is full of the usual salads and sausages, and the biggest *kebabche* you'll ever see, as well as fish, and the service is cheery and attentive.

GETTING THERE & AWAY

Take any of the regular buses to Smolyan from the Rodopi bus station in Plovdiv (2.70 lv), disembark at the turn-off (obvious from the souvenir stalls and cafés) about 1.2km south of Bachkovo village and walk about 500m up the hill.

HASKOVO ХАСКОВО

☎ 038 / pop 90,600

Although few travellers bother to stop in Haskovo, it's a pleasant, café-filled little town and a convenient staging post for anyone travelling to Greece or Turkey via Svilengrad. The Turkish ambience and heritage

HASKOVO

0 ————— 200 m
0 ————— 0.1 miles

INFORMATION
Bulgarian Post Bank
Българска Пощенска Банка 1 B3
Hebros Bank 2 B2
Internet Club 3 C3
Post Office & Telephone Centre 4 A3

SIGHTS & ACTIVITIES
1000 Years Monument 5 B2
Ezhi Dzhumaya Mosque
Джамия Ежи Джумая 6 C3
Historical Museum
Исторически Музей 7 C2

SLEEPING
Hotel Aida Хотел Аида 8 B2

Hotel Central
Хотел Централ 9 B2
Hotel Oasis Хотел Оазис 10 B2

EATING
Restaurant Vesta
Ресторант Веста 11 C3

ENTERTAINMENT
Cinema Paradiso
Кино Парадизо 12 C3
Ivan Dinov Dramatic Theatre
Драматичен Театър Иван Динов ... 13 A2

TRANSPORT
Bus Station 14 D3

To Stara Zagora (61km);
Plovdiv (78km)

To Train
Station (1km);
Svilengrad (68km)

To Kârdzhali (54km)

of the town is also an ideal introduction if you're heading to Turkey. For information on hiking around these ranges from Haskovo, see the boxed text on p111.

Information

Bulgarian Post Bank (ul Otets Paisii) Come here if you need to change money.
Hebros Bank (ul Rakovski)
Internet Club (ul San Stefano)

Sights

Along the southeastern side of pl Svoboda is the **Historical Museum** (☎ 24 505; pl Svoboda; admission 1 lv). This museum houses some underwhelming displays of agricultural implements, folk costumes and archaeological finds, all in one big room. It's poorly signposted, so look out for the column fragments outside. The museum keeps erratic hours and you may have to ask staff to open up for you.

The **Ezhi Dzhumaya Mosque** (ul San Stefano) looks rather lost among the cafés in the mall. It was built in the late 14th century, and is probably the oldest mosque in Bulgaria. Visitors are welcome.

Sleeping & Eating

Haskovo has a very limited stock of hotels, but you'll nearly always be able to find a room.

Hotel Aida (☎ 665 164; pl Svoboda; d 29 lv) The Aida is a hulking old former Balkantourist hotel which doesn't look as though it's been renovated since the 1960s. Rooms are clean, though, and it's fortunately in a central and convenient location; the hideous '1000 Years' monument which stands outside is a handy landmark. A decent restaurant is attached.

Hotel Oasis (☎ /fax 663 248; ul Rakovski 10; s/d €20/22) The Oasis is a relatively new place which lies about 150m north of pl Svoboda. The rooms are clean and well appointed but it's overpriced for foreigners. Breakfast costs an additional €2.

Hotel Central (☎ 660 333; ul Varna 1; d incl breakfast 48 lv; ⚄) The Central is Haskovo's newest and most attractive hotel; it's located on a pedestrian side street right in the city centre. Its rooms are bright and cheerful, with stripped-back wooden floors and big windows.

Dozens of cafés and bars are crammed along each pedestrian mall, and huddled around the mosque. For pizzas, burgers, salads and other basic fare, try **Restaurant Vesta** (☎ 35 730; ul San Stefano 20; mains 3-6 lv; ☿ 9am-midnight).

Getting There & Away
Most bus services are operated by private companies, all of which have offices inside the chaotic **bus station** (☎ 24 218; ul Saedinenie). Every day, a dozen public and private buses depart for Sofia (12 lv, six to seven hours) and about five go to Plovdiv (4 lv, one hour). Also, several public and private buses depart daily for Varna, Burgas, Gabrovo, Kazanlâk, Stara Zagora and Svilengrad (which shares a border with Greece and Turkey). As the transport hub for southeastern Bulgaria, numerous companies at the bus station, including **ABAP** (☎ 0888 375 811), each offer at least one daily service to Istanbul (costing between 20 and 25 lv).

Central Bulgaria

CENTRAL BULGARIA

HIGHLIGHTS

- **Stunning location**
  Take in the spectacular romantic setting of Veliko Târnovo (p157).

- **Charming historic mountain village**
  Reach into Bulgaria's past at Koprivshtitsa (p136).

- **Stunning religious frescoes**
  See the powerful work of Zahari Zograf at Troyan Monastery (p178).

- **Excellent hiking**
  Take a walk in Bulgaria's 'old mountains' – Stara Planina (p148).

- **Dramatic scenery**
  Survey the Shipka Pass (p145), scene of fierce fighting in the Russian–Turkish war.

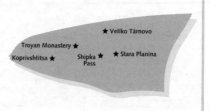

Cleaved in two by the dramatic Stara Planina mountain range, central Bulgaria appeals to anyone who enjoys good scenery, secluded mountain towns and monasteries. While its big highlights are obvious – a visit to stunning Veliko Târnovo is repeatedly mentioned by people as being the high point of their trip to Bulgaria – its less well-publicised gems are equally enjoyable and remain largely undiscovered by travellers.

As well as its considerable scenic wealth, central Bulgaria was the heartland of the Bulgarian national revival in the mid- to late 19th century. To all Bulgarians, towns

CENTRAL BULGARIA

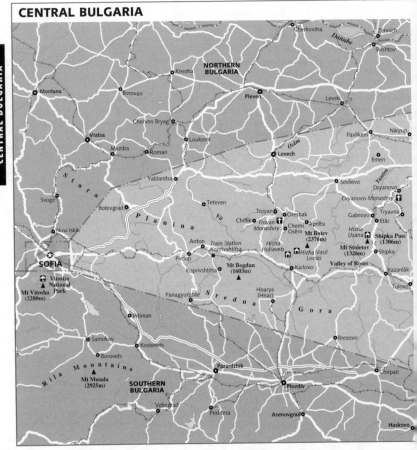

like Karlovo, Koprivshtitsa and Sliven are synonymous with the struggle against Turkish rule, breeding the generation of revolutionaries who fought for freedom against the sultan. As well as innumerable house-museums devoted to the lives of martyrs to the cause of Bulgarian independence, many of central Bulgaria's towns are fantastic showcases for revival-era architecture: remarkably well-preserved reassertions of traditional Bulgarian house design. Indeed, towns like Koprivshtitsa and Kotel are veritable open-air museums, and even in places such as Karlovo, where the modern world has encroached far more, there are delightful pockets of town where you could still be in the late 19th century.

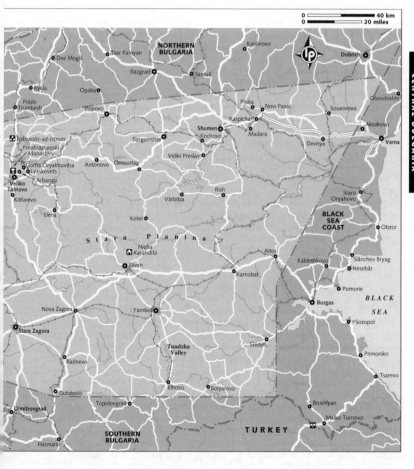

KOPRIVSHTITSA КОПРИВЩИЦА
☎ 07184 / pop 2900

Hard to pronounce, but definitely worth the effort of a little practice, Koprivshtitsa is one of Bulgaria's most lovely mountain villages, almost perfectly preserved from the Bulgarian national revival period and a fantastic place to visit between Sofia and the Black Sea. Spread across a lush pasture and pine-clad valley either side of the Topolnitsa River, Koprivshtitsa is crammed with cobblestone streets, restored churches, museums and houses with tiled red roofs, and tiny stone bridges arching across trickling rivulets. The village oozes charm and history, and nearly 400 buildings of architectural and historical impor-

tance are registered and preserved by the Bulgarian government. While it is doubtlessly a big destination for tourists, out of season you could easily be in 19th-century Bulgaria, and even at the height of summer, Koprivshtitsa is delightful.

History
Koprivshtitsa was first settled at the end of the 14th century by both ordinary folk and nobles from Veliko Târnovo fleeing Turkish conquerors. The local economy prospered from sheep, cattle and goat herding and a wealthy merchant class was soon created. Sacked by brigands in 1793, 1804 and 1809, Koprivshtitsa was rebuilt during the mid-19th century. Soon after, the popula-

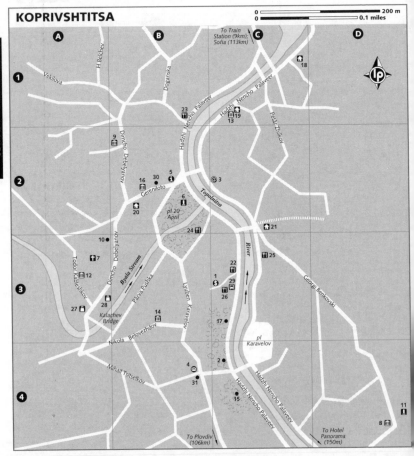

tion reached about 12,000 (almost as big as Sofia at the time).

Koprivshtitsa is famous as the place where Todor Kableshkov (or Georgi Tihanek, according to some sources) first proclaimed the national uprising against the Turks on 20 April 1876. He did this at the tiny bridge now known as the Kalachev Bridge (also called Kableshkov Bridge), built in 1813. This great day has lent its name to the main square dominated by the 1876 April Uprising Mausoleum.

After independence from the Turks in 1878, Bulgarian merchants and intellectuals left their mountain retreats for the cities, and Koprivshtitsa has survived largely unchanged to this day. The Bulgarian government declared the village a town museum in 1952, and a historical reserve in 1971.

Information

DSK Bank (next to the bus stop) is the only bank in town and has an ATM and money exchange.

Hadzhi Nencho Palaveev Cultural Centre (☎ 2034; ul Hadzhi Nencho Palaveev 78) If you are interested in festivals or cultural events, check here or with the tourist office.

Heroes Internet Club (ul Hadzhi Nencho Palaveev; per hr 1.20 lv; ☺ 9am-midnight)

Tourist Information Centre (☎ /fax 2191; koprivshtitsa@hotmail.com; pl 20 April; ☺ 9am-1pm & 2-6pm) An invaluable place in a small maroon building unmarked in English on the town's main square. Organises home stays.

Sights

The main reason to come to Koprivshtitsa is to stroll its timeless streets and absorb the charming bucolic atmosphere.

HOUSE-MUSEUMS

Touring the six house-museums is a great way to see the town, although there's none that is unmissable, so don't worry if some are closed on the day you visit. Buy a combined ticket for all six museums (adults/ students 5/3 lv) at the souvenir shop Kupchinitsa two doors up the hill from the Tourist Information Centre; most of the museums also sell them.

Karavelov House (☎ 2176; ul Hadzhi Nencho Palaveev 39; ☺ 9.30am-5.30pm, closed Tue) was occupied by the parents of Lyuben Karavelov (1834–79), a journalist and printer who worked for Bulgarian revolutionary groups based in Russia, Serbia and Romania. He was the first chairman of the Bulgarian Central Revolutionary Committee. A printing press where various seditious newspapers were produced is on show. The three separate buildings were constructed between 1810 and 1835.

The **Oslekov House** (☎ 2555; ul Gereniloto 4; ☺ 9.30am-5.30pm, closed Mon) was built by Oslekov, a rich merchant who, inevitably, took part in the 1876 April Uprising before being killed by the Turks. Oslekov House was built between 1853 and 1856 and it is possibly the best example of Bulgarian national revival period architecture in the village, evinced by the triple-arched entrance, spacious interior, stylish furniture and brightly coloured walls. Inside, there are carved ceilings, collections of 19th-century costumes, paintings and jewellery, plus several woodcarvings, some of which were bought during Oslekov's extensive travels.

Debelyanov House (☎ 2077; ul Dimcho Debelyanov 6; ☺ 9.30am-5.30pm Tue-Sun) is dedicated to Dimcho Debelyanov (1887–1916), a great poet who completed many outstanding works before he died in WWI. The property (1830) features a pretty garden and numerous displays about Debelyanov rather than period furniture usually found in other house-museums. And watch out for the *very* low ceilings!

Todor Kableshkov (1851–76), a well-travelled and astute gentleman, once resided in the glorious **Kableshkov House** (☎ 2054; ul Todor Kableshkov 8; ◷ 9.30am-5.30pm, closed Mon). Kableshkov is revered as (probably) the person who fired the first shot in anger to start the 1876 uprising against the Turks. Consequently, this house, dating back to 1845, is basically a museum about the rebellion.

Also called the Topalov House, after the original owner, the **Lyutov House** (☎ 2138; ul Nikola Belovezhdov 2; ◷ 9.30am-5.30pm, closed Tue) was built in 1854 in a style reminiscent of the baroque houses found in Plovdiv. The best-preserved house-museum in Koprivshtitsa, it features a resplendent salon with intricately carved ceilings adorned with landscapes that were hand-painted by Lyutov. The lower floor contains a permanent display (with explanations in English) of locally made felt cloths (see Shopping, opposite).

The least-visited house-museum is probably the **Benkovski House** (☎ 2811; ul Georgi Benkovski 5; ◷ 9.30am-5.30pm, closed Tue), built in 1831 on a hillside to the southeast. Georgi Benkovski (1843–76) led the insurgent cavalry on legendary exploits until he died in a Turkish ambush. Above the house, and easy to spot from the village centre, is a huge **equestrian statue** of the man astride a horse. The statue is worth the short climb for the superb views of the entire valley.

OTHER SIGHTS

The **Assumption Church** (ul Dimcho Debelyanov 26a), built in 1817, is usually closed, but visitors can peer through the window and wander around the gardens. The church grounds contain **Kableshkov's grave**, and, in the upper section, **Debelyanov's grave**. A poignant statue features Debelyanov's mother anxiously awaiting his return, and the words 'I die and am yet born again in light'.

Beside the park along ul Hadzhi Nencho Palaveev is the **Sts Kiril & Metodii School**, built in 1837.

Festivals & Events

The mammoth **International Folk Festival** (next festival summer 2010) is held every five years and folk dancers from all over the country converge here for the occasion.
Re-enactment of the 1876 April Uprising (1-2 May) The fateful historical events of the 1876 April Uprising are re-enacted in full costume by locals who prepare for weeks.
Folklore Days Festival (mid-August) Traditional Bulgarian music and dance troupes perform throughout the town.

Sleeping

The oversupply of rooms in hotels and private homes means the choice is extensive and the prices are often low. The quality of private rooms is similar to those found in most hotels, except the latter nearly always have private bathrooms. All hotels listed here, and almost all private rooms, include breakfast. The **Tourist Information Centre** (☎ /fax 2191; koprivshtitsa@hotmail.com; pl 20 April) can help you with rooms in private homes from 25 lv per person during the summer, less outside the high season. Staff can show photos of many of the rooms on offer. English is basic, but passable.

Shuleva House Hotel (☎ 2122; ul Hadzhi Nencho Palaveev 37; s/d/apt 18/24/40 lv) Although the rooms need renovation, this hotel is excellent value. The rooms are large, simple and clean, and readers have commented about the friendly staff. The apartments come with TVs.

Hotel Trayanov Kâshta (☎ 3750; ul Gereniloto 5; d/tr/apt 40/50/60 lv) This hotel/restaurant complex is excellent value. It offers huge, quiet rooms wonderfully furnished with traditional pieces, and most include TV. It's not cheap, but it's hugely atmospheric with a great garden.

Hotel Panorama (☎ 2035; ul Georgi Benkovski 40; s/d/f 34/48/60 lv) Consistently getting excellent reviews from guests, the Panorama endures as an excellent option, despite being 400m from the village centre. There are some lovely views and the rooms are comfortable and well furnished. The owners are delightful.

Hotel Kalina (☎ 2032; ul Hadzhi Nencho Palaveev 15; s/d 36/50 lv) The classiest place in town is the three-star Kalina. Rates are surprisingly good value, and it gets our 'loveliest garden in town' award.

Hotel Astra (☎ 2364; hotel_astra@hotmail.com; ul Hadzhi Nencho Palaveev 11; s/d 40/60 lv) In a gorgeous garden setting, the Astra is popular and homely, and the rooms are large and spotless. It is, however, a little pricey, and not that much better than a private room.

Eating

Koprivshtitsa is one of Bulgaria's main tourist attractions, so watch out for unscrupulous waiters and menus in English without prices. The cheapest places for a meal – at non-tourist prices, with menus in Bulgarian and prices clearly shown – are the cafés behind the market.

Pod Starata Krusha (☎ 2163; ul Hadzhi Nencho Palaveev 56; mains 3 lv) Right next to the bus station, this little tavern is charming and is a great place for a full traditional evening meal or a quick breakfast before catching your bus out of town.

Lomeva Kâshta Tavern (ul Hadzhi Nencho Palaveev 42; salads 1.50 lv, grills from 3.50 lv) Hard to miss with its striking blue exterior, this cosy place offers traditional cuisine at reasonable prices. The low ceilings and fireplace inside are reminiscent of a quaint English pub – perfect for a drink or meal on a cold evening.

Chuchura (☎ 2712; ul Hadzhi Nencho Palaveev 66; mains 3-4.50 lv) This charming place near the bus stop has a very pleasant terrace for alfresco dining. The meals are tasty and good value and there's a small hotel attached too.

Mehana Starite Borove (pl 20 April; salads 1.50 lv, mains 3.50-5 lv) Almost hidden along a laneway near the main square, Starite Borove is nearly jutting into the shady park and is the best place for a drink in summer. It's quieter than places around the main square but the food is fairly unexciting.

Na, Nazdrave Restaurant (☎ 087 624816; bul Haji Nencho Palaveev; mains 5 lv) Few places in town have the buzz of this restaurant, where tourists and locals sit side by side in a great cosy atmosphere, with a pleasant terrace for dining outside. Music policy definitely needs revision, however; when we visited it was provided by the TV on so loud the whole joint shook.

Shopping

Predictably, several souvenir shops surround the main square, but most of the stuff for sale is tacky. A fine memento of Koprivshtitsa is a carpet or bag made from felt cloth; examples are on display inside the Lyutov House (p138). Alongside the Byala Stream,

some 19th-century weaving equipment can be seen through the window of the charming Tepavitsa Valyavitsa Craft Complex, but it's often closed.

At the **Craft Shop** (☎ 2191; ul Dimcho Debelyanov; ⏰ 10am-4pm Mon-Sat), visitors can see felt cloth products being made. Some items are for sale next door.

Getting There & Away

Koprivshtitsa is normally reached by train as bus services are few and far between. Even though the train station is 9km north of the village itself, buses (0.80 lv, 15 minutes) are timetabled to meet incoming trains and to take people from the village to meet outgoing ones. The station is surprisingly busy as it's along one of the country's main west–east train lines. There are four trains a day from Sofia (3.25 lv, 2½ hours) and connections can be made there or in Kazanlâk throughout the country. There's also a direct daily train to Burgas (8.30 lv, five hours).

In Koprivshtitsa itself the little **bus stop** (☎ 2133) has a list of train times as well as connecting buses and long-distance bus routes. These were limited to one daily bus to Sofia (5 lv, two hours), one to Plovdiv (5 lv, two hours) and one to Burgas (9.50 lv, four hours) at the time of writing.

CENTRAL BULGARIA

HIKING IN THE SREDNA GORA

The Sredna Gora (Central Range) Mountains are spread over 6000 sq km from Iskâr George (near Sofia) to the Tundzha Valley (south of Yambol). The highest peak is Mt Bogdan (1603m) near Koprivshtitsa.

The Mountains of Bulgaria by Julian Perry provides a detailed description of the popular two- or three-day hike from Hisar (Hisarya) to Koprivshtitsa (or vice versa). No dedicated map of the Sredna Gora Mountains is available, but most of the mountains and hiking routes are included in the map of Stara Planina that is published by Kartografia.

The map of Koprivshtitsa, published by Domino and available in the village, includes a small, but clear, map with five enticing hiking routes around the surrounding hills. One trail (about four hours one way) leads to Mt Bogdan, and a hut where hikers can stay overnight.

KARLOVO КАРЛОВО

☎ 0335 / pop 27,700

Not as much of a one-horse town as it appears from the railway or bus station, Karlovo is an attractive place with plenty to merit a stop and even an overnight stay. Karlovo is most famous to Bulgarians as the birthplace of Vasil Levski, the revolutionary who some Bulgarians compare (rather overexcitedly) to Che Guevara. This historic connection is in evidence all over town, although the real reason to visit is to absorb the town's pleasant atmosphere, its old churches and revival-era architecture.

Orientation & Information

The town is spread out on a long hill, at the base of which are the bus and train stations. From the train station across the small park three roads go up the hill; the central one, ul Vasil Levski becomes the town's main artery (although you'd never know it from here). It stretches for 2km to the town square, pl 20 Yuli. (The bus station is about 100m up the left of the three roads from the train station, past the yellowish block of flats and to the right). There are several foreign-exchange offices and Internet centres at the top end of ul Vasil Levski.

Sights & Activities

You can see Karlovo's main sights by walking up ul Vasil Levski to pl 20 Yuli. Stop first at pl Vasil Levski, where the great man is immortalised in a bold **statue** depicting him with a lion (a common play on his surname, which means lion in Bulgarian). Turn right, and right again, to the looming pink of the marvellous **St Bogoroditsa Church** (admission free; ⏰ 7am-7pm), which contains intricate wooden iconostases (decorated partitions or screens). Opposite, the matching coloured **History Museum** (☎ 4728; ul Vûzrozhdenska 4; admission 0.50 lv; ⏰ 9am-noon & 1-5pm Tue-Sun) features a large array of ethnological displays.

Further up ul Vasil Levski is a small park with the delightful but now disused and closed **Kurshum Mosque**, built in 1485. Continue up the mall to the town square, then head left (west) for about 300m, past the **clock tower**, to the **Vasil Levski Museum** (☎ 3489; ul Gen Kartzov 57; admission 1 lv; ⏰ 8.30am-1pm & 2-5.30pm Mon-Fri). This quaint collection of rooms around a cobblestone courtyard contains several exhibits about Levski with explanations in English. Ask the caretaker to show you the modern shrine, where you can see a lock of Levski's hair while listening to taped religious chants in Bulgarian. A guided tour in English costs 2.50 lv per person.

For information about **hiking** in the region, see p139.

Sleeping & Eating

Hotel Fani (ul Levski 73; r per person 10 lv) Only signed in Cyrillic, this little family-run place adjoins a popular local lunch joint. The two rooms are basic but very clean and homely and share bathing facilities. It's definitely the best deal in town, although can sometimes be a little noisy.

Hemus Hotel (☎ 94597; ul Vasil Levski 87; s/d 20/30 lv) This small family home has four comfortable rooms and is run by kind people. It's not obviously a hotel; there's just a small sign in Bulgarian, so go by road numbers or ask.

Sherev Hotel (☎ 93380; pl 20 Yuli; renovated/unrenovated s 46/80 lv, d 60/115 lv) Definitely the best location in town, overlooking the town square amid buzzing cafés and restaurants, the Sherev is, however, totally overpriced: while the renovated rooms are just fine, the unrenovated ones are run-down.

VASIL LEVSKI

The most revered person in recent Bulgarian history may well be Vasil Levski, whose name is lent to numerous streets and squares, and who is immortalised in several statues and museums throughout the country.

Vasil Ivanov Kunchev was born on 6 July 1837 in Karlovo, and given the nom de guerre 'levski' (from the Bulgarian word for lion) by his peers. He studied and worked as a monk in Stara Zagora, but in 1862 moved to Belgrade to join the anti-Turkish rebellion led by Georgi Rakovski. Levski later moved to Romania, where he envisaged the creation of an independent and democratic Bulgaria. He then returned to Bulgaria and travelled extensively, establishing revolutionary cells, often based in remote monasteries. In early 1872 he was betrayed by a comrade, and arrested by the Turks in Lovech. Levski was hanged in Sofia in February of the next year.

You are spoilt for choice around pl 20 Yuli, which comes alive at night with restaurants and cafés; the best are either side of the Sherev Hotel, although the Voenen Klub bar-restaurant on the opposite side of the square is also good fun.

Getting There & Away

From the **bus station** (☎ 93155), about eight buses a day go to Hisar, and several depart for Stara Zagora, Troyan, Kazanlâk, Sofia and Veliko Târnovo. About every hour, a bus travelling to or from Plovdiv (2.80 lv, one hour) stops in Karlovo, not far from the Vasil Levski Museum (opposite).

The tidy **train station** (☎ 94641) is on the line between Sofia and Burgas, going via Kazanlâk and Sliven. From Sofia, one fast train and one express (7.50/5.30 lv in 1st/2nd class, 2¼ hours) stop at Karlovo. The express from Sofia continues to Burgas (9.50/6.90 lv, four hours). Six slow passenger trains a day also go to Plovdiv (4.30/3.30 lv, two hours), but the bus is far quicker and more frequent.

HISAR ХИСАР
☎ 0337 / pop 10,000

Unremarkable though its modern incarnation is, Hisar has been a popular resort since Roman times, when it was known as Diokletianopol after the Emperor Diocletian. Since ancient times Hisar's 22 mineral-water springs have been used to cure all sorts of ailments, ensuring the prosperity of the town. It's a sleepy and pleasant place today, busy with holidaying Bulgarians in the summer months and distinctly quiet in the winter. There are some remarkable Roman ruins that line the main street, although there's little to justify a specific trip to Hisar unless you want to take the waters at one of the smarter spa hotels.

Orientation & Information

From the bus station, and adjacent train station, walk (300m) down to the main road (ul Hristo Botev), with the ruins on your right, and then turn right into bul Ivan Vazov to reach the town centre and the pleasant park.

There's a DSK Bank with an ATM at the corner of Hristo Botev and bul Ivan Vazov, and an Internet café on bul General Gurko.

Sights

Originally built by the Romans and later fortified by the Byzantines, the walls protected the town and its mineral baths from raiders. The walls escaped damage from the Slavs (who did not come through this part of Bulgaria) and are probably the best preserved **Roman ruins** in Bulgaria. Still over 5m high and up to 3m thick, the walls once protected an area of 30 hectares. The most visited section (with basic explanations in French) is a short walk from the bus and train stations, while other ruins can be found along unnamed roads heading towards the town centre from the main road. Nothing is fenced, so visitors can wander around any of the ruins at any time for free. As well as the city walls, you can see the amphitheatre, baths and some dwellings.

The **Archaeological Museum** (☎ 62012; ul Stamboliyski 8; admission 2 lv; ⏱ 8am-noon & 1-5pm) features a scale model of the city walls, and some photos of early excavations. However, it's rather dull. Paradoxically, the displays about traditional regional costumes and agricultural and weaving equipment are more interesting. The museum is not well signposted; it's past the post office and accessible from the main road through a pretty courtyard.

Both hotels listed here have **balneological centres**, which offer all sorts of treatments, such as aromatherapy and hydrotherapy. Consultations with 'head physicians' cost from 30 lv for 30 minutes, depending on the type of treatment required, and the necessary (or unnecessary) extras provided, such as medications and lotions.

Sleeping & Eating

Both hotels are about 1km down bul General Gurko, which starts about 700m along the main road from the bus and train stations; look for the sign (in English) to Hotel Augusta. Both are in a rather remote part of town, but close to the mineral springs.

Augusta Spa Hotel (☎ 63821; www.augustaspa.com; bul General Gurko 3; s/d unrenovated/renovated s 75/98 lv, d 88/138 lv; Ⓟ 🖥 🏊) Hisar's other main hotel is the Augusta, a little further down the road from the Hisar and round to the right. It's divided into two buildings, one fully refurbished with air con and smart modern rooms, the other more basic. They share access to the pool and spa complex.

Hotel Hisar (☎ 62717; fax 62634; bul General Gurko; s/d 135/180 lv; P ⊠ ⊡ ⊠) Having undergone a very impressive renovation programme, the Hisar now charges similarly impressive prices to stay here. However, for this price you get very smart rooms, several restaurants, a great outdoor pool, sauna and fitness centre, as well as a modern balneological complex.

There are plenty of houses offering private rooms on bul General Gurko. Look for the signs *stay pod naem*.

Aside from the good restaurants in both hotels, there are plenty of smart *mehanas* (taverns) on bul General Gurko; try the Evropa or the National. Also, the **Tsesar** (ul Hristo Botev) serves up very good Bulgarian staples in a rustic courtyard featuring a fake windmill. Another popular traditional restaurant is Chinar near the town's church.

Getting There & Away

Conveniently, the train station and bus station are next to each other. Taking a bus is the best way to get to Hisar, with six buses a day to and from Karlovo (1.20 lv, 30 minutes) and other connections to Sofia, Troyan and Veliko Târnovo via Kazanlâk and Gabrovo. Regular buses between Karlovo and Panagyurishte also pass through and stop in Hisar. There are no direct train services to Karlovo (you have to change trains) but every day six slow passenger trains go to and from Plovdiv (2.10 lv), although only two of these are direct connections.

KAZANLÂK КАЗАНЛЪК
☎ 0431 / pop 62,750

Kazanlâk is a surprisingly interesting city and despite not being obviously attractive, it boasts plenty of history and a number of very pleasant places to stay. Tucked between the Stara Planina and Sredna Gora mountain ranges, it's at the eastern end of the Valley of Roses and is a centre for the production of rose oil. Originally settled as the Roman city of Sevtopolis, Kazanlâk still has plenty of charm, not to mention being home to a Unesco World Heritage Site. Even if you aren't tempted to come to Kazanlâk on its own merits, you may well stop off here as it's an important transport hub.

Information

Agence Pagane (☎ /fax 26900; ul Petko D Petkov) Travel agency with French- and English-speaking staff who can arrange hotel reservations and local tours.

Internet Centre (ul Otets Paisii) Big centre under a video-rental store.

Magic Exchange (ul Otets Paisii) There are surprisingly few places to change money; the most reliable is this office.

Magic Net (pl Sevtopolis, under DEPO clothes shop)

Post office (ul 23 Pehoten Shipchenski Polk) Combined with telephone centre.

Tourist Information Centre (☎ 62817; stour@kz.or bitel.bg; ul Iskra 1) Offers help with hotels, excursions and general information about the town. Good English spoken.

Sights
THRACIAN TOMB OF KAZANLÂK & MUSEUM

In the pleasant **Tyulbe Park**, just up from the Kulata Ethnological Complex, is a heavily secured **tomb** (☎ 24700; ⊙ 10am-5pm; admission 20 lv), built in the 4th century BC for a Thracian ruler. Discovered during the construction of a bomb shelter in 1944, the tomb is now a Unesco World Heritage Site, and is horrendously overpriced for foreigners, but very interesting. Along the *dromos* (vaulted entry corridor) is a double frieze with battle scenes. The burial chamber is 12m in diameter, and covered by a beehive dome that is typical of those built by Thracians between the 3rd and 5th centuries BC. The dome contains several murals that feature events such as a funeral feast and chariot race.

To satisfy those unwilling to pay 20 lv, a full-scale replica has been created in the nearby **museum** (☎ 26055; admission 2 lv; ⊙ 10am-6pm). Follow the signs along the obvious path from the tomb. The museum is tiny, however, and a little anticlimactic.

ISKRA MUSEUM & ART GALLERY

Well worth a visit is this **museum and art gallery** (☎ 23741; ul Sv Kiril i Metodii; adult/student 2/1 lv; ⊙ 9am-6pm Mon-Fri). The extensive archaeological displays include pottery, jewellery and tools from excavations of several Thracian tombs, including the one in Tyulbe Park (see above). All explanations are in Bulgarian, so the brochure (2 lv) in English, French or German is helpful.

Upstairs, a vast number of paintings are on display, including those by renowned local artists such as Ivan Milev and Vasil Barakov. Ask the caretaker for a printed catalogue (in English and French).

KAZANLÂK

0 ————————— 200 m
0 ————————— 0.1 miles

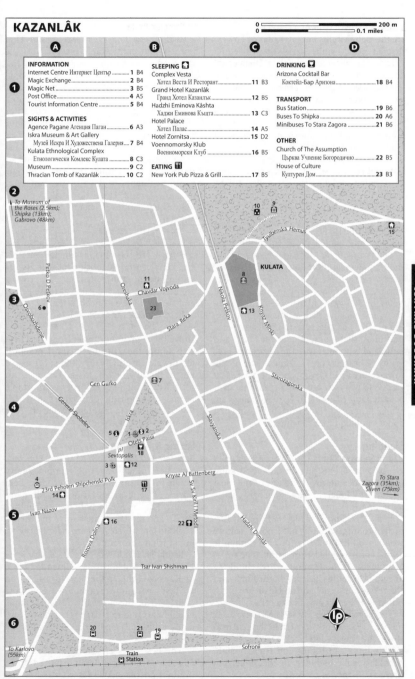

INFORMATION
Internet Centre Интернет Център	**1** B4
Magic Exchange	**2** B4
Magic Net	**3** B5
Post Office	**4** A5
Tourist Information Centre	**5** B4

SIGHTS & ACTIVITIES
Agence Pagane Агенция Паган	**6** A3
Iskra Museum & Art Gallery	
Музей Искра И Художествена Галерия	**7** B4
Kulata Ethnological Complex	
Етнологически Комлекс Кулата	**8** C3
Museum	**9** C2
Thracian Tomb of Kazanlâk	**10** C2

SLEEPING
Complex Vesta	
Хотел Веста И Ресторант	**11** B3
Grand Hotel Kazanlâk	
Гранд Хотел Казанлък	**12** B5
Hadzhi Eminova Kâshta	
Хаджи Еминова Къща	**13** C3
Hotel Palace	
Хотел Палас	**14** A5
Hotel Zornitsa	**15** D2
Voennomorsky Klub	
Военноморски Клуб	**16** B5

EATING
New York Pub Pizza & Grill	**17** B5

DRINKING
Arizona Cocktail Bar	
Коктейл-Бар Аризона	**18** B4

TRANSPORT
Bus Station	**19** B6
Buses To Shipka	**20** A6
Minibuses To Stara Zagora	**21** B6

OTHER
Church of The Assumption	
Църква Училение Богородично	**22** B5
House of Culture	
Културен Дом	**23** B3

CENTRAL BULGARIA

KULATA ETHNOLOGICAL COMPLEX

In the delightfully quaint Kulata (Tower) district near Tyulbe Park you will come across the interesting **Kulata Ethnological Complex** (☎ 21733; ul Knyaz Mirski; admission 3 lv, with rose-liquor tasting 4 lv; ⊙ 8am-noon & 1-6pm). Inside the grounds there's a replica of a one-storey peasant's home and wooden sheds with agricultural implements and carts. A courtyard leads to the two-storey House of Hadzhi Eno, built by a wealthy rose merchant in the style typical of the Bulgarian national revival period. Some explanations in German and English are nailed on the walls. The caretaker may invite you to try some rose tea, liquor or jam.

MUSEUM OF THE ROSES

The grandly named Research Institute for Roses, Aromatic & Medicinal Plants houses the tiny **Museum of the Roses** (☎ 23741; ul Osvobozhdenie; admission free; ⊙ 9am-5pm in summer). The photos and displays explain (in Bulgarian only) the 300-year-old method of cultivating the roses, picking their petals and processing the oil. The attached shop sells rose oils, perfumes, shampoos, liqueurs, tea bags and jams, and is popular with the occasional tour group. The museum is 3km north of the town centre up ul Osvobozhdenie; take a taxi (2 lv one way), or bus No 3 from the town square. Guided tours (rates negotiable) are available in English and French, but ring first about opening times in winter.

Sleeping

Hadzhi Eminova Kâshta (☎ 62595; bul Nikola Petkov 22; r/apt 20/50 lv) This picturesque guesthouse is the best deal in town and one of the most characterful hotels in the region, particularly as it doesn't implement the dual-pricing system. The handful of big, traditionally furnished rooms (with tiny bathrooms) feature woollen quilts, and overlook an authentic 19th-century walled compound. The (one) apartment is huge, and worth booking ahead. All rooms feature bathrooms and the restaurant is delightful. Unsurprisingly, booking is nearly always essential.

Voennomorsky Klub (☎ 64745; bul Rozova Dolina; s/d 41/62 lv) Excellently located in the centre of town, the Naval Club has a large number of simple but clean rooms and friendly staff. Breakfast isn't included in the price, but there are plenty of cafés nearby.

Complex Vesta (☎ 20350; complexvesta@abv.bg; ul Chavdar Vojvoda 3; s/d incl breakfast 55/68 lv) This homely and comfortable place is just off the road – so it's quiet – and behind the monolithic House of Culture. Some rooms are smaller than others, and the rooftop apartment is cramped, but all bathrooms are sparkling new. All accommodation comes with a fan, TV, fridge, bathroom and balcony.

Grand Hotel Kazanlâk (☎ 63210; hotel_kazanlak@abv.bg; pl Sevtopolis; s/d 66/88 lv; ⊠ ⌨) Despite an impressive reinvention, the legacy of Balkantourist hangs in the air here. However, the now 'Grand' Hotel Kazanlâk is on the main square and is efficiently run by pleasant staff.

Hotel Palace (☎ 62311; www.hotel-palas.com; ul Petko Stajnov 9; s/d 70/88; ⧠ ⊠ ⌨ ⌨) Bulgaria's new rich are the obvious clientele at this sparkling central establishment with its adjoining casino and restaurant. The rooms are actually very good value at these prices and the staff are extremely attentive.

Hotel Zornitsa (☎ 63939; fax 63652; www.zornica-bg.com; s/d/ste 70/98/115 lv; ⧠ ⊠ ⌨) Located above the town a short walk from the Thracian tomb, the Zornitsa is most practical for people with their own transport as it's not in the town itself. It's a great place to relax with a big pool and very comfortable rooms, although the pink chairs in reception are enough to frighten anyone off from an otherwise superb hotel.

Eating & Drinking

New York Pub Pizza & Grill (ul Knyaz Al Battenberg; mains 3-4.50 lv) During the summer pretty much the entire town seems to dine here on the large terrace overlooking the main square. Food is good – both traditional Bulgarian and modern American – and there's a 'photo-menu', so you can order by pointing at what you want.

Hadzhi Eminova Kâshta (☎ 62595; ul Nikola Petkov 22; mains 4-5 lv) The most recommended place in Kazanlâk, this is the place to eat if you are just having one meal in town. Set in the courtyard of the hotel of the same name, you'll be treated to a large selection of delicious grills and some excellent traditional cooking.

The best cafés are along ul Iskra, near Cinema Iskra. For a drink, try the trendy, outdoor **Arizona Cocktail Bar** (ul Otets Paisii).

Getting There & Away

Kazanlâk's busy **bus station** (☎ 22383; ul Sofronii) has connections to Sofia (8 lv, 2½ hours), Veliko Târnovo (6 lv, 2½ hours), Lovech (6 lv, three hours), Haskovo (6 lv, three hours) and Plovdiv (4 lv, two hours). About every hour, there's also a bus to Gabrovo (3.50 lv, 60 to 90 minutes) via Shipka.

Minibuses for Stara Zagora (2.50 lv, 45 minutes) run every 20 to 30 minutes from just outside the main station where the buses congregate. Further along the road by the roundabout, town bus No 6 (0.40 lv, hourly, 20 minutes) runs up to Shipka.

Kazanlâk is about halfway along the train line that connects Sofia and Burgas, via Karlovo and Sliven. There are regular trains to Sofia (three daily, 3½ hours), Burgas (four daily, three hours), Karlovo (six daily, one hour) and Varna (three daily, five hours).

SHIPKA ШИПКА
☎ 04324 / pop 2500

Far more attractive than Kazanlâk, Shipka is a delightful mountain village set in the foothills of the mountains below the famous Shipka Pass, which was the site of one of the most decisive battles during the liberation of Bulgaria from Turkish rule in 1877. The combination of Shipka Monastery and the wonderful Freedom Monument make this a great half-day trip from Kazanlâk, particularly if you have your own transport, although it's perfectly feasible to rely on buses as well.

Shipka has recently made the news internationally for some truly amazing archaeological finds. In 2004 a 2400-year-old burial shrine for King Seutus III, a Thracian ruler, was uncovered nearby containing vast amounts of Thracian gold and a unique golden mask. The site was still being investigated at the time of writing, although plans to promote Bulgaria's vast archaeological wealth to tourists means that it will probably soon be open to visitors.

Sights
SHIPKA MONASTERY ШИПЧЕНСКИ МАНАСТИР
Way before you arrive in Shipka you'll see the unmissable five golden, onion-shaped domes of the **Nativity Memorial Church** (admission 2 lv; photos an extra 5 lv; ☺ 8.30am-7pm) poking out from woods above the village. Part of the Shipka Monastery, and also known as the Church of St Nikolai, the magnificent structure was built in 1902 as a dedication for those who died at the Shipka Pass during the Russian–Turkish War (1877–78). The design is heavily influenced by Russian architecture of the time, and features 17 church bells that can be heard for several kilometres when rung. Inside the crypt lie the remains of many Russian soldiers who perished and there are some wonderful frescoes depicting scenes from Russian history. If it's not cloudy, the church offers marvellous views of the Valley of Roses. Follow the sign to Hram Pametnik for 1.2km through the village, or walk 300m up from the restaurant along the Kazanlâk–Gabrovo road.

SHIPKA PASS ШИПЧЕНСКИ ПРОХОД
About 13km of winding road (be careful if driving in foggy conditions) north of Shipka village is the Shipka Pass (1306m). Some 900 steps lead to the top of Mt Stoletov (1326m), which is dominated by the impressive 32m-high **Freedom Monument** (admission free; ☺ 9am-5pm). It was built in 1934 as a memorial to the 7000 Russian troops and Bulgarian volunteers who, in August 1877, died while successfully repelling numerous attacks by some 27,000 Turkish soldiers intent on relieving their besieged comrades in Pleven. To get to the pass from Kazanlâk or Shipka, take a bus to Haskovo, Gabrovo or Veliko Târnovo and ask the driver to be let off at the Shipka Pass (*Shipchensky prokhod*).

Sleeping & Eating
About 50m up from the car park at the top of the pass, **Hotel-Restaurant Shipka** (☎ 2730; Shipka Pass; s/d 10/20 lv) is excellent value because it doesn't discriminate against foreigners. Some rooms are huge and feature separate sitting areas, and all are quiet and well furnished.

Getting There & Away
Bus No 6 runs every hour between the local bus stop near the Kazanlâk bus station and Shipka village (0.40 lv, 20 minutes). Alternatively, the hourly bus between Kazanlâk and Gabrovo stops at the village and as well as at Shipka Pass, as do buses to Veliko Târnovo.

STARA ZAGORA СТАРА ЗАГОРА

☎ 042 / pop 155,600

Unremarkable Stara Zagora (literally 'old behind the mountain') is a large Bulgarian city and one that many people will pass through due to its useful train and bus connections. It's a modern place with straight, flat, tree-lined streets (signposted in English), one of the nicest central parks in Bulgaria and a smattering of sights that can fill a few hours. Stara Zagora is also famous as the home of Zagorka, Bulgaria's number one beer, and you can see the brewery as you enter the city from the west, although unfortunately it doesn't conduct tours.

History

The salubrious climate and fertile land around Stara Zagora attracted many invaders and settlers, including the Thracians (from the 4th century BC), who called it Beroe. In around AD 100, the Romans came and created a prosperous city they called Ulpia Augusta Trayana, remains of which can be seen in the city centre today. The city was later destroyed many times by the Turks and abandoned in the mid-13th century. It was the centre of fierce fighting during the Russian–Turkish War, and again completely demolished by the Turks in 1877. Most of the Thracian and Roman ruins were also wrecked at this time and the few surviving remnants of those eras are now buried under the modern city. Reconstruction of Stara Zagora commenced in 1879, and the city is now a thriving educational and cultural centre that boasts one of Bulgaria's first opera theatres.

Information

There are two large Internet cafés on ul Ruski. Plenty of foreign-exchange offices can be found along ul Tsar Simeon Veliki. and you can change travellers cheques or use a credit card to obtain cash at the United Bulgarian Bank, located in a tiny mall off ul Ruski.

Post office (ul Sv Knyaz Boris I; ⏰ 9am-noon & 2-5pm Mon-Fri)

Telephone centre (ul Sv Knyaz Boris I; ⏰ 6am-midnight) Attached to post office.

Sights

OLD CITY

Stara Zagora is built on the grid of an ancient Roman city, so some amazing discoveries have been unearthed. For example, the massive **floor mosaic**, dated to the 4th to 5th century AD, is displayed in the eastern entrance of the post office. The room relies on natural light, however, so it's a bit hard to appreciate on an overcast day.

The **Roman Theatre** (ul Mitropolit Metodii Kusev), often called the Antique Forum Augusta Trayana, was built in the 3rd century AD. It's in remarkably good repair and hosts popular alfresco concerts during the summer months. Although visitors cannot wander around, there's plenty to see from the roadside. Check out the adjacent ruins on the other side of the road too, which are accessible at all hours of the day.

NEOLITHIC DWELLINGS MUSEUM

The remains of two small one-roomed semidetached homes from the new Stone Age (about 6000 BC) are housed in a secure and airtight environment at the **Neolithic Dwellings Museum** (☎ 600 299; admission 3 lv; ⏰ 9am-noon & 2-5pm Tue-Sat). The homes were abandoned after a fire several millennia ago, so they're among the best preserved Neolithic dwellings in the Balkans.

The caretaker can provide a guided tour (which may be given whether requested or not) for 5 lv per group (minimum of five people). A tour is really the only way to determine the doors, walls, chimneys, and remains of handmade pottery, among the rubble. The Neolithic Dwellings: Stara Zagora booklet (2 lv), available at the museum, will also help explain it all.

The basement features exhibits of pottery, tools and jewellery from this and other excavations, but nothing is labelled in English, so the tour or booklet are worthwhile. Perhaps one of the strangest items on display is the 6000-year-old headless hedgehog.

The museum is not obvious at all. Enter the gates of the city's hospital, walk straight down about 100m, up the staircase and the museum is the squat building at the top.

GEO MILEV HOUSE-MUSEUM

This **house-museum** (☎ 23450; ul Geo Milev 37; admission 2.50 lv; ⏰ 9am-noon & 2-5pm Tue-Sat) is set in a lovely garden closed off from the street by a white wall. The rooms contain some manuscripts and paintings by locally born Milev (1895–1925). Milev lost an eye in WWI, but continued to write poetry dealing with

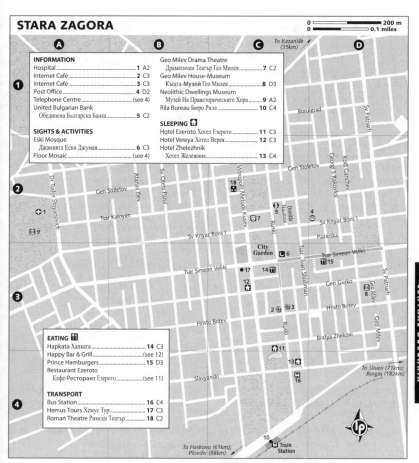

STARA ZAGORA

0 ____ 200 m
0 ____ 0.1 miles

INFORMATION
Hospital...1 A2
Internet Café....................................2 C3
Internet Café....................................3 C3
Post Office.......................................4 D2
Telephone Centre.........................(see 4)
United Bulgarian Bank
  Обединена Българска Банка.............5 C2

SIGHTS & ACTIVITIES
Eski Mosque
  Джамията Ески Джумая....................6 C3
Floor Mosaic...............................(see 4)

Geo Milev Drama Theatre
  Драматичен Театър Гео Милев.............7 C2
Geo Milev House-Museum
  Къща-Музей Гео Милев.....................8 D3
Neolithic Dwellings Museum
  Музей На Праисторическите Хора.........9 A2
Rila Bureau Бюро Рила.........................10 C4

SLEEPING
Hotel Ezeroto Хотела Езерото.................11 C3
Hotel Vereya Хотела Верея......................12 C3
Hotel Zhelezhnik
  Хотел Железник..............................13 C4

EATING
Нарката Хапката...............................14 C3
Happy Bar & Grill............................(see 12)
Prince Hamburgers.............................15 D3
Restaurant Ezeroto
  Кафе-Ресторант Езерото....................(see 11)

TRANSPORT
Bus Station.......................................16 C4
Hemus Tours Хемус Тур.........................17 C3
Roman Theatre Римски Театър..............18 C2

To Kazanlâk (35km)
To Sliven (71km); Burgas (182km)
To Haskovo (61km); Plovdiv (88km)
Train Station

CENTRAL BULGARIA

---

social themes, such as *Septemvri* about the September 1923 agrarian revolution. This work was confiscated by the authorities and Milev was arrested. After the trial, he was kidnapped by the police and murdered. Contemporary artists also sell their work in the museum. An attraction is the charming café set up in the pretty courtyard.

ESKI MOSQUE

This is one of the oldest **mosques** (ul Tsar Simeon Veliki) in Bulgaria. Built in the early 15th century, it sits incongruously among banks and department stores along the mall. The mosque has been abandoned, but remains externally attractive, despite bricked up windows and firmly locked doors.

OTHER SIGHTS

The **city garden** is one of the most attractive in Bulgaria: it's clean, and offers plenty of shade, grass, (new) seats and (functioning) fountains. At the back is the **Geo Milev Drama Theatre** (28 Mitropolit Metodii Kusev), built in 1914.

Sleeping

Nothing is cheap for foreigners in Stara Zagora, making it best to avoid spending the night unless there's a reason you need to be here.

Hotel Zhelezhnik (☎ 22158; ul Slavyanski; s/d 62/70 lv) The Zhelezhnik (Ironworker) began life as a good old Balkantourist communist hotel, but has been very nicely renovated (while maintaining its gloriously socialist name).

It's a little overpriced, but rooms are sparkling and modern and staff are very kind. Astonishingly it remains the cheapest place in town.

Hotel Vereya (☎ 26728, 618 600; fax 53174; ul Tsar Simeon Veliki 100; s/d 88/96 lv; 🔀) This vast complex with an endless array of bars and cafés surrounding it is slap-bang in the centre, but it's a relatively charmless place, and definitely overpriced. Rooms are comfortable enough though with TVs and air-con.

Hotel Ezeroto (☎ 600 103; ezeroto@mail.bg; ul Bratya Zhekovi 60; s/d/ste 100/120/150 lv; 🔀) Very nicely located and friendly, the Ezeroto is probably the best place in town: the rooms contain classy furniture, good bathrooms, fridges and TVs.

Eating

Prince Hamburgers (ul Tsar Simeon Veliki; burgers 2 lv) This immensely popular fast-food joint serves good burgers, hot dogs and other filling street food and packs in the young crowd hanging out on ul Tsar Simeon Veliki.

Restaurant Ezeroto (☎ 600 103; ul Bratya Zhekovi 60; mains 5 lv) Attached to the hotel of the same name, this place is charmingly set alongside a small lake surrounded by willow trees. The food is very good and there's an adjacent cocktail bar that is busy all day long.

Dozens of cafés are set up along ul Tsar Simeon Veliki; the most agreeable are along the eastern end, ie opposite the park and near the corner of ul Sv Patriarh. There are a couple of bakeries and places selling tasty toasted sandwiches; try Hapkata near the corner of ul Ruski and ul Tsar Simeon Veliki.

Getting There & Away

Stara Zagora's heaving **bus station** (☎ 605 349; ul Slavyanski) is opposite the Hotel Zhelezhnik and will connect you to almost anywhere in the country. Buses leave for Sofia (9 lv, four hours) and Plovdiv (4.50 lv, 1½ hours). There are also five buses each day to Varna (8 lv, five hours), hourly services to Sliven (4 lv, 1¼ hours) and seven buses a day to Veliko Târnovo (8 lv, three hours). There are also a couple of services to Burgas, Ruse and Pleven.

For Kazanlâk (2 lv, 45 minutes), catch a bus towards Veliko Târnovo (which stops at Kazanlâk), or get a direct minibus (which departs when full) from the bus station. Minibuses from Kazanlâk will drop passengers off in the centre of Stara Zagora.

From right outside its office, **Hemus Tours** (☎ 57018; ul Tsar Simeon Veliki) offers private buses to Sofia (8 lv), Pleven (11 lv) and Plovdiv (5 lv), and regular services to Athens.

HIKING IN THE STARA PLANINA

With an average height of little more than 700m, the Stara Planina (Old Mountain) range is not high, particularly compared to the Rila and Pirin Mountains. Nonetheless it is vast, covering 11,500 sq km (about 10% of Bulgaria) and, at close to 550km long, it extends almost the entire length of the country. Nearly 30 peaks are over 2000m high and the mountains feed one-third of Bulgaria's major rivers. The highest point is Mt Botev (2376m), north of Karlovo.

The Mountains of Bulgaria by Julian Perry describes the strenuous 25-day (650km to 700km) trek across the entire range. This trek – which starts at Berkovitsa, near the border with Serbia & Montenegro, and finishes at Emine Cape, about 20km northeast of Nesebâr on the Black Sea coast – is part of the trans-European E3 trek. The text in Perry's book is detailed, but the maps are poor, so buy the *Stara Planina* map, published by Kartografia and available at bookshops in Sofia. The *Troyan Balkan* map, available from the tourist office in Gabrovo (p169), is detailed, but specific to the Troyan and Apriltsi regions.

Some of the more interesting hikes along marked trails:

Cherni Osêm to Hizha Ambaritsa Four hours.
Dryanovo Eco-trail (p175)
Etâr to Sokolski Monastery One hour, Then continue to Shipka Pass (extra two to three hours – steep).
Gabrovo to Hizha Uzana Four hours.
Karlovo to Hizha Hubavets Two hours, or continue to Hizha Vasil Levski (another two to three hours) and Mt Botev (further two to three hours).
Shipka Monastery to Shipka Pass Two hours.
Sliven to Hizha Karandila Three hours

Stara Zagora train station (☎ 50145), at the southern end of ul Mitropolit Metodii Kusev, is along the commonly used train line between Sofia and Burgas, travelling via Plovdiv. For Sofia there are six trains (8 lv, four hours) every day. Heading to Burgas, there are six trains (6.50 lv, two hours) daily. Five trains a day also go to Kazanlâk, Veliko Târnovo and Ruse, changing in Tulovo. There are also three daily services to Varna.

The **Rila Bureau** (☎ 622 724), which sells advanced tickets for domestic trains and tickets for all international services, is at the train station.

SLIVEN СЛИВЕН
☎ 044 / pop 109,600

Set amid mountains that were once home to Bulgaria's anti-Turkish rebels, Sliven is certainly worth a visit to see the nearby famous 'blue rocks' although there's little to detain you in the town itself. The Thracians, Romans and Greeks all settled in this area, but little evidence of its ancient inhabitants remains. The history of Sliven is inextricably linked to the *haidouks*, the anti-Turkish rebels who lived in the rocky hills nearby from the early 18th to the mid-19th century. These insurgents eventually united under the leadership of Hadzhi Dimitâr and the revered Vasil Levski and rose up against the Turkish overlords. Sliven is a modest, yet appealing, city, under several peaks that are over 1000m high.

Orientation & Information

The city is centred around the main square, pl Hadzhi Dimitâr. To the east of the square is the town hall, to the north is the Stefan Kirov Dramatic Theatre, and to the south is the quaint Deboya Church. The post office and telephone centre are also on the square.

Several foreign-exchange offices can be found along the upper (southeastern) section of ul Hadzhi Dimitâr and the pedestrian mall, ul Tsar Osvoboditel. There's an **Internet café** (ul Tsar Osvoboitel) inside the Voenen Klub, as well as **Spider Internet** (pl Hadzhi Dimitâr) next to the Hotel Sliven in the side of the theatre building.

Sights & Activities
BLUE ROCKS СИНИТЕ СКАЛИ

These magnificent rocks are the major attraction of Sliven, beginning just a few kilo-

metres out of town. It's easy to understand how the *haidouks* were able to hide from the Turks for so long among these hills.

Take the **chairlift** (one way/return 5/10 lv; ⏱ 8.30am-5.30pm Tue-Sun, 12.30-5.30pm Mon) or walk (60 to 90 minutes) up the hill following the chairlift; however, it's not always easy going because of the occasional inexplicable sections of barbed wire you must detour around. From the top of the chairlift, take the obvious path (300m), cross the main road and walk down (another 500m) through the woods to Hizha Poveda, which serves drinks and basic meals.

To reach the chairlift from Sliven, catch minibus No 13 outside the train station or Hotel Sliven. You can also walk about 1km uphill (following the signs) from the end of the route for trolleybus Nos 18 or 20 from the city centre. Taxis are about 3 lv one way.

HADZHI DIMITÂR MUSEUM

A delightful building, which sits incompatibly among concrete apartment blocks and shops, this **museum** (☎ 22496; ul Asenova 2; admission 2 lv; ⏱ 9am-noon & 2-5pm Mon-Fri) is dedicated to the leader of the anti-Turkish rebels. It is well worth a visit, but nothing is labelled in English. It features several rooms of furniture (including antique weaving equipment) set around a cobblestone courtyard.

HISTORY MUSEUM

In a grand old building, seemingly lost among the modern shops and cafés along the mall, is the **History Museum** (☎ 22495; ul Tsar Osvoboditel 18; admission 2 lv; ⏱ 9am-noon & 2-5pm Mon-Sat). The three floors house a large array of exhibits, including archaeological and ethnological items such as coins, weapons and books. Most interesting are the displays about the anti-Turkish rebels. Nothing is captioned in English, however.

MARKET

Over the river is a surprisingly expansive (and mostly undercover) market, one of the most vibrant in Bulgaria.

HIKING

From the information centre (usually closed) along the road to the Blue Rocks chairlift, marked trails head through the hills to the (signposted) caves used by the *haidouks*. Information (in English) about the trails is

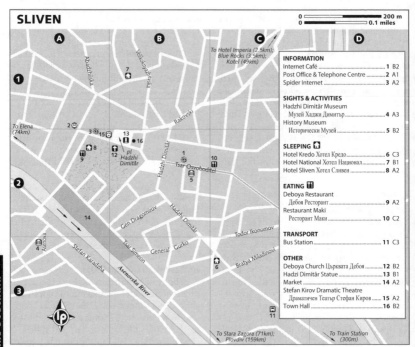

SLIVEN

```
0 ═════════ 200 m
0 ═════════ 0.1 miles
```

To Hotel Imperia (2.5km);
Blue Rocks (3.5km);
Kotel (49km)

To Elena
(74km)

To Stara Zagora (71km);
Plovdiv (159km)

To Train Station
(300m)

included in a leaflet (1.5 lv), available at the chairlift, but the leaflet has no maps.

More general information about hiking in the area is available from the local **national park authority** (☎ /fax 22926; dpp.skamani@sl .bia-bg.com). For details about hiking in the region, see p148.

Sleeping

Hotel Sliven (☎ 27065; fax 25112; pl Hadzhi Dimitâr; s/d 40/60 lv) Anyone on a budget will have little choice but to stay at this hotel. Only come here if the Kredo is booked up, as the rooms are pretty vile and the bathrooms worse. It's at least very central and the multilingual ladies on reception are surprisingly charming.

Hotel Kredo (☎ 625 080; ul Predel 1; s/d 50/60 lv) Probably the best overall value in the city, the new Kredo is a centrally located and extremely clean. English isn't spoken, though, and it often gets booked up, so try and get someone to call ahead for you.

Hotel National (☎ 662 929; www.nationalsl.bg; ul K Irecheck 14; s/d 100/120 lv; 🖳 🖳) Definitely the best place in town, the National is not cheap, but it's a lovely place, with a traditional *mehana* in the courtyard and thoroughly modern and spotless rooms. Staff are delightful and speak English.

Hotel Imperia (☎ 667 599; www.hotelimperia.net; ul Panaiot Hitov; d/ste/apt 135/180/224 lv; 🅿 🖳 🖳) This classy place offers a range of rooms, each painted a different colour, and each with a sparkling bathroom. All rooms feature air-con, balcony, fridge and TV. It's inconvenient (about 3km from the city centre and about 1km from the chairlift), as it is designed for people with cars, but boasts a swimming pool and tennis courts.

Eating

Social and culinary life thrives along Tsar Osvoboditel; it's the best place to promenade in search of some food and nightlife.

Restaurant Maki (ul Tsar Osvoboditel; mains from 3 lv) This sprawling place is one of the best in town, featuring the life-saving 'photomenu', which makes it easy for non-Bulgarian speakers to point at the meal they want. The other attraction is the huge outdoor seating area, which is abuzz on summer evenings.

Deboya Restaurant (ul General Skobolev; mains 4-5 lv) The other swinging place in town is this large eatery to one side of the Hotel Sliven. Packed for lunch and dinner alike it serves up excellent pizza and traditional Bulgarian dishes.

Hotel National Mehana (☎ 662 929; ul K Irecheck 14; mains 4-6 lv) In the courtyard of the Hotel National, this excellent *mehana* serves up traditional Bulgarian cooking and features live music. It's all alfresco, though, so only really good in the summer.

Getting There & Away

From the small **bus station** (☎ 626 629; ul Hadzhi Dimitâr), just past the massive Bila Supermarket, buses regularly go to Veliko Târnovo, Plovdiv, Stara Zagora (also minibuses) and Karlovo. Sliven is just off the main highway, so most buses travelling between Burgas and Kazanlâk, Stara Zagora and Sofia (11 lv, five hours) pass through here.

The **train station** (☎ 636 614) is a further 300m out of town but is busy with trains running between Burgas and Sofia. There are three services to Sofia (11 lv, 5½ hours) and seven to Burgas (4.90 lv, 1½ hours) as well as six trains to Kazanlâk, five to Stara Zagora and three to Plovdiv, Pleven, Ruse and Varna.

KOTEL КОТЕЛ
☎ 0453 / pop 7500

A possible substitute for the far more touristy charms of Koprivshtitsa, Kotel is a small town 49km northeast of Sliven with a proud history of anti-Turkish rebellion. While efforts are being made to attract more visitors, its out-of-the-way location means that it will be a while before its charming streets, lined with some beautiful revival-era mansions, are swamped by tourists. Kotel is also a culturally significant place in Bulgaria, being the birthplace of a remarkable number of scholars, writers and revolutionaries, including Safronii Vrachanski, Georgi Rakovski and Petâr Beron.

Locals artisans' contracts to outfit the Ottoman army in the mid-1800s spared the town from many woes of the era (including taxes), though Kotel was home for 126 'enlighteners' during the hotbed of revolutionary activity from 1877–78. As a result, Kotel is today renowned for its carpets

and rugs, which are made from wool in homes on wooden looms. The 'Kotel style' predominantly features four colours: red, black, green and blue.

Orientation & Information

From the bus station walk up a few blocks to the centre, where you'll find an ATM (and a pink city hall). Extending west, ul Izvorska (home to Monday and Thursday markets) leads to Galata old town past the **information centre** (☎ 2334; ul Izvorska 14; ☼ 9am-7pm), which has info on hikes to nearby Zherevna, plus Internet access.

Sights

Examples of the 'Kotel style' can be admired and bought at the **Exhibition Hall of Carpets & Woodcarving** (☎ 2613; ul Izvorska 17), 500m northwest of the bus station. Kotel has several museums. The best is the dramatic **History Museum** (National Revival Kotel Enlighteners; ☎ 2549; admission 3 lv; ☼ 8am-noon & 1-5pm), on the central square, showing loads of revolutionary artefacts and Georgi Rakovski's mammoth mausoleum. The enthusiastic manager knows English and likes to use it. There is also the **Ethnographic Museum** (☎ 2315; ul Altûnlû Stoyan 5; admission 3 lv; ☼ 8am-noon & 1-5pm), about 200m west of the Exhibition Hall.

You can learn to play the *gayda* and other traditional Bulgarian music and dance at the **Philip Kotev School** (☎ 2215; smu_k_l@mail.bg; ul Geori Zahariev 2, 8970), which sometimes holds recitals.

Sleeping & Eating

Your best bet is to find a private room in Kotel is by asking at the bus station or looking for the occasional *stay pod naem* signs in windows.

Kotel Hotel (☎ 2885; ul Izvorska 59; r 20 lv) Unless you are able to secure a private room, you'll be limited to this rather dreary hotel. Located towards the park about 600m west of the bus station, it's is the only hotel in town. The rooms are fine, but drab and rather old.

Starata Vodenitsa (☎ 2360; r 30 lv) Reached from the old town along ul Krum Petrov, this place has seven dark-wood, traditionally styled rooms, each with fireplace and locally made rugs. The rooms are among the best value in the country, and its restaurant is Kotel's best.

Getting There & Away

Remotely located, Kotel is best reached from either Sliven or Shumen. The best service is from Sliven, where buses leave hourly (3 lv, one hour) in both directions until around 8pm. From Shumen and Burgas there are less frequent services, and at the time of research there was no direct bus service to Sofia.

SHUMEN ШУМЕН

☎ 054 / pop 107,650

One of Bulgaria's more pleasant big cities, Shumen has a great location and several interesting sights to recommend it, although as the saying goes, it's certainly no Plovdiv. Sitting at the base of a low flat spur of the Stara Planina ranges, about halfway between the Black Sea coast and the Danube, Shumen is an industrial and military city with strong ties to the country's communist past, as evidenced by the number of statues and monuments. Shumen doesn't boast the old towns or obvious historic interest of other places in the region, but the hill-top Shumen Fortress is one of the highlights of central Bulgaria, and the city is an obvious base for day trips to Veliki Preslav (p156) and Madara (p155).

History

Both the Thracians and Romans settled in the area over several millennia. During the early Middle Ages, nearby Veliki Preslav and Pliska became the birthplaces of the medieval Bulgarian kingdom. Shumen was captured by the Turks in 1388 and for the next five centuries Chumla (as it became known) was an important market town. Later Shumen became part of the Turk's strategic quadrangle (along with Ruse, Silistra and Varna) of towns fortified as a defence against Russian advances. A comparatively large number of Jews, Armenians and Muslims live in Shumen.

Orientation

The bus station and adjacent train station are in the eastern end of the city. An extremely long pedestrian mall alongside bul Slavyanski connects the city park with the main square, pl Osvobozhdenie, and here

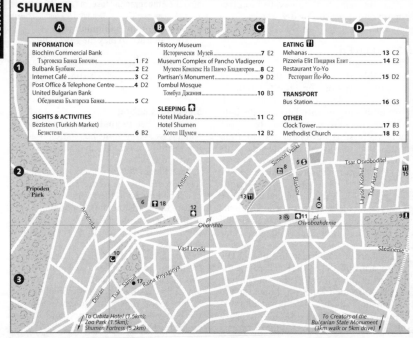

SHUMEN

INFORMATION
Biochim Commercial Bank
  Търговска Банка Биохим..........................1 F2
Bulbank Булбанк..2 E2
Internet Café...3 C2
Post Office & Telephone Centre.............4 D2
United Bulgarian Bank
  Обединена Българска Банка...................5 C2

SIGHTS & ACTIVITIES
Bezisten (Turkish Market)
  Безистена..6 B2

History Museum
  Исторически Музей....................................7 E2
Museum Complex of Pancho Vladigerov
  Музеен Комлекс На Панчо Владигеров....8 C2
Partisan's Monument..................................9 D2
Tombul Mosque
  Томбул Джамия...10 B3

SLEEPING
Hotel Madara...11 C2
Hotel Shumen
  Хотел Шумен...12 B2

EATING
Mehanas..13 C2
Pizzeria Elit Пицария Елит......................14 E2
Restaurant Yo-Yo
  Ресторант Йо-Йо......................................15 D2

TRANSPORT
Bus Station..16 G3

OTHER
Clock Tower..17 B3
Methodist Church..18 B2

you'll find pretty much everything in town, not to mention most of the local population performing the evening promenade here.

Information

Biochim Commercial Bank (bul Slavyanski)
Bulbank (bul Slavyanski)
Internet Café (bul Slavyanski)
Post office & telephone centre (pl Osvobozhdenie; ☺ 7am-10pm)
United Bulgarian Bank (ul Tsar Osvoboditel)

Sights

SHUMEN FORTRESS ШУМЕНСКА КРЕПОСТ

On the side of the hill overlooking the city is **Shumen Fortress** (☎ 58051; admission adults/students 3/1.5 lv; ☺ 8am-7pm Apr-Oct, 8.30am-5pm Nov-Mar). It's one of the oldest settlements in Bulgaria, and dates from the early Iron Age. In about the 5th century BC, the Thracians built some walls, and between the 2nd and 4th centuries, the Romans added towers and more walls.

After being ignored for several centuries, the structure was fortified by the Byzantines and became an important military base. During the Second Bulgarian Empire (1185–1396), the fortress was one of the most significant settlements in northeastern Bulgaria and was renowned as a centre for pottery and metalwork. In the late 14th century, the Ottomans invaded, burnt down part of the fortress and looted the stone.

The fortress is a fascinating place to wander through. There are some basic explanations on notice boards around the site, but the booklet (2 lv), available at the gate, is helpful (even if the photos look about as old as the fortress itself). From the Tombul Mosque, the fortress is about 5.5km uphill, so take a taxi (about 1.50 lv one way).

From the entrance to the fortress, a glorious and reasonably flat 3km path leads to the gigantic Creators of the Bulgarian State Monument, from where you can take the steps back down to the city centre.

CREATORS OF THE BULGARIAN STATE MONUMENT

This indescribably massive hill-top monument was built in 1981 to commemorate the 1300th anniversary of the establishment

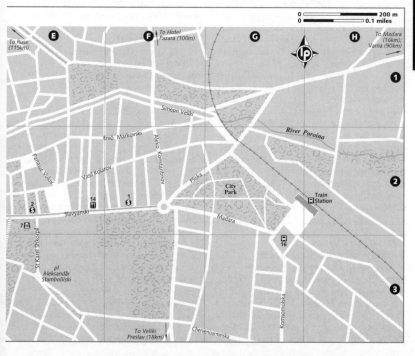

of the First Bulgarian Empire. Visible from miles away, it's a wonderful piece of communist monumentalism and it is well worth the climb from the staircase that begins in the town centre behind the History Museum (3km). The path leads from the **Partisan's Monument**, where there's definite comic value to be had in the centrepiece statue, a soldier engaged in what appears to be the 'YMCA' dance.

The 5km circuitous road to the monument starts along ul Karel Shkorpil from the History Museum. The best way up there is by taxi (about 3 lv one way), and the best way down is via the steps that lead back to the city centre and bul Slavyanski.

The **information centre** (☎ 52598; admission 3 lv; ☼ 8.30am-5pm winter, 8am-7pm summer), about 300m from the monument, features some unremarkable displays about the structure and surrounding flora. A 3km path goes past the Information Centre and car park and finishes at Shumen Fortress.

TOMBUL MOSQUE

The most beautifully decorated mosque in Bulgaria is the **Tombul Mosque** (☎ 56823; ul Doiran; admission 2 lv; ☼ 9am-6pm). Built in 1744, it is the largest mosque still in use in the country. Also known as the Sherif Halili Pasha Mosque, it was given the Turkish moniker of *tombul* (plump) because of the shape of its 25m-high dome. The 40m-high minaret has 99 steps but is not open to the public. In the courtyard there's a fountain, which some Muslims believe contains sacred water, and a couple of decent souvenir shops. Ask at the gate for an informative leaflet (in English and French) about the mosque.

Just down the main road are the ruins of the **Bezisten**, a 16th-century Turkish covered market. It was closed at the time of research (and had been for a few years), but renovations were under way so it may reopen later in some capacity.

HISTORY MUSEUM

Inside the large, ugly brick **museum** (☎ 57487; bul Slavyanski 17; admission 2 lv; ☼ 9am-5pm Mon-Fri) along the main road is a superb collection of Thracian and Roman artefacts, including many from Madara, Veliki Preslav and Pliska. There are also a number of ancient coins and icons and a scale model of the Shumen Fortress as it was in its heyday. A

rather sad little café sits largely unpatronised in the ivy-covered courtyard.

MUSEUM COMPLEX OF PANCHO VLADIGEROV

Dotted along the cobblestone western section of ul Tsar Osvoboditel are several houses built, or renovated, in the Bulgarian national revival period, or early-20th-century baroque, style. One of these, the **Museum Complex of Pancho Vladigerov** (☎ 52123; ul Tsar Osvoboditel 136; admission 1.50 lv; ☼ 9am-5pm Mon-Fri), commemorates Bulgaria's most renowned composer and pianist. The complex comprises a number of attractive buildings, including a library, arrayed around a shady courtyard garden.

PRIPODEN PARK

This large park (3930 hectares), also known as Kyoshkovete Park, is on the western edge of the city. The lower parts are spoiled a bit by the background hum from the Shumensko Pivo Brewery. Near the brewery are plenty of **hiking trails**, which lead nowhere in particular but offer plenty of shade. The **zoo park**, next to the Orbita Hotel, features some bored bison, and other caged animals.

Festivals & Events

Days of Shumen Cultural Festival (mid-May)
Folklore Festival (Aug)
Watermelon Festival (last Sun in Aug)

Sleeping

Hotel Pazara (☎ 0887 292756; ul Maritsa 15; s/d 30/35; ❄) Although not remarkable, the Pazara has the cheapest and best-value rooms in town, a 10-minute walk from pl Osvobozhdenie. It's not really marked from the street, located above the Bistro Stives (look for the Coke sign); go in through the gates and take the staircase up to the right of the café. No English is spoken, but the owners are genial and the rooms comfortable, although some share bathrooms between two rooms.

Orbita Hotel (☎ 52398; Pripoden Park; s/d 40/50 lv) Compared to the other options in Shumen, this is excellent value. The rooms are clean and comfortable, though sparsely furnished, and the apartments feature a sitting room and fridge. It's in a quiet, shady park about a 2km walk (or taxi ride) from the city centre, so it's a little inconvenient unless you are driving.

Hotel Madara (☎ 57451; fax 52591; pl Osvobozhdenie; s/d 52/80 lv) The three-star, seven-floor Madara is typically overpriced for foreigners, offering very unexciting Balkantourist-style accommodation in poky little rooms. Although central, the rooms (which have a TV and fridge) are barely two-star quality, which at these prices is a little cheeky.

Hotel Shumen (☎ 591 416; fax 58009; transmit@ psit35.net; pl Oborishte; s/d 130/180 lv, ste 200-320 lv; ☒) Twice the price of the Madara, the rooms at this four-star hotel are twice as good as those at the Madara. However, it's still overpriced for foreigners because guests are paying for amenities they may not need, including an indoor pool and sauna. Rooms contain a fridge and TV, and rates include breakfast. It's mainly used by tour groups enjoying big discounts.

Eating

Restaurant Yo-Yo (ul Tsar Osvoboditel; chicken mains about 1.50 lv; ☽ 8am-10pm) Distinctive because of the aroma of roasted chicken wafting across the road, this modest but clean eatery also offers *musaka* (about 2 lv) and all sorts of other tasty dishes.

Pizzeria Elit (bul Slavyanski; pizzas from 2 lv, other mains 2.50-3 lv) Rush here for some of the tastiest pizzas (all topped with a fried egg) in the region. A wide range of other meals is also available.

A complex of quaint 19th-century wooden buildings at the start of the western end of ul Tsar Osvoboditel contains three traditional *mehanas*. Each offers indoor tables, a courtyard garden setting and almost identical service and prices. You will pay 3 to 4 lv for grilled chicken or beef, 1.50 lv for a salad and about 1.50 lv for a small beer. Some menus are in English, but if not the largely English-speaking staff can usually help.

The best cafés are in the mall alongside bul Slavyanski, especially those opposite the History Museum.

Getting There & Away

From the **bus station** (☎ 61618), there are four buses a day to Burgas (6.50 lv, three hours), three to Ruse (6 lv, two hours), four to Dobrich (6.80 lv, two hours), three to Silistra (6.80 lv, 2½ hours), several to Veliko Târnovo (7 lv, two hours), five to Madara (1 lv, 20 minutes) and three to Veliki Preslav (1 to 1.30 lv, 30 to 60 minutes). Shumen is on

the highway between Sofia (15 lv, six hours, hourly) and Varna (4.90 lv, 1½ hours, nine per day), so numerous buses come through in both directions. Several private buses, such as those operated by Etap Adress, also stop in Shumen on the route between Sofia and Varna.

Shumen is on the main train line between Sofia and Varna. Every day, nine trains (including one express) from Varna (3.90 lv, two hours), and two fast trains from Sofia (10.70 lv, four to seven hours), stop at the grand and rather old-world **train station** (☎ 60155) in Shumen. Other daily services include one to Ruse (5.30 lv, three hours) and one to Plovdiv (9.50 lv, six hours). A couple of trains stop at Madara. There's a **left-luggage office** (☽ 24hr) inside the train station.

Call ☎ 800 184 to get a taxi, although there's usually a huge number of drivers waiting outside both the bus and train station.

AROUND SHUMEN
Madara Мадара
☎ 05313 / pop 1400

Madara was an important Thracian town around 5000 BC, and, later, during the Roman occupation. These days this village, 16km east of Shumen, probably only exists because of the famous Madara Horseman.

MADARA NATIONAL HISTORICAL & ARCHAEOLOGICAL RESERVE

This **reserve** (☎ 2095; admission 2 lv; ☽ 8am-7pm) surrounds the so-called Madara Horseman *(Madarski Konnik)*. Carved into a cliff 23m above the ground, the bas-relief features a mounted figure spearing a lion and followed by a dog. It was created in the early 8th century AD to commemorate the victorious Khan Tervel and, more profoundly, the creation and consolidation of the First Bulgarian Empire (681–1018). As the only known rock carving in Bulgaria from the Middle Ages, it's protected as a Unesco World Heritage Site.

North of the horseman, a 373-step stairway hewn out of the cliff face leads to the top of the cliffs (130m high) and the ruins of the **Madara Fortress**. The fortress was built during the Second Bulgarian Empire (1185–1396) as part of a defensive ring intended to protect the capitals of Pliska and Veliki Preslav. The sweeping views explain why the fortress was built there.

If you want to explore the area in depth, buy a copy of the *Madara* booklet (2 lv, in English or German) at the entrance gate. It also outlines some of the popular **hiking trails** to the nearby **tombs** and **caves**. Most signs around the reserve are translated into German (not English).

If you're contemplating climbing to the top of the steep steps which lead to the base of the horseman, it's worth noting that the permanent scaffolding hides more of the bas-relief the closer you get, so the whole experience can be an anticlimax up close. The **Madara Horseman Music Days Festival** is held in the reserve on four successive Thursdays from mid-June to mid-July.

SLEEPING & EATING

The two places below are a short walk from the horseman, and open all year. Watch for the signposts in English. There are plenty of cafés and souvenir shops near the car park.

Camping Madara (☎ 5313; camp site per person 7 lv, cabins 20 lv) This shady and peaceful camping spot is 500m from the horseman. It also offers a cosy little restaurant.

Hizha Madarski Konnik (☎ 2091; dm 17 lv) offers dorm rooms.

GETTING THERE & AWAY

Public transport to Madara is limited, and the horseman is 3km up a steep road from the village. Several slow passenger trains travel each day between Shumen and Varna, stopping at Madara. Buses to Madara from Shumen are infrequent, so get a bus (five times a day) to Kaspichan, then a minibus to Madara from there. A taxi from Shumen costs a negotiable 15 lv return, including waiting time. There are no taxis in Madara.

Veliki Preslav Велики Преслав
☎ 0538 / pop 10,600

Veliki Preslav (also known as just Preslav) is an unremarkable town about 18km southwest of Shumen. It's worth visiting for the ruins of the ancient capital but there's no need to stay as it's an easy day trip from Shumen. The main square is about 300m up the main road west of the bus station.

HISTORY

Veliki Preslav was founded in the early 9th century AD by the Bulgar king, Khan Omurtag, but it was Tsar Simeon who moved the capital of the First Bulgarian Empire (681–1018) from Pliska to Veliki Preslav in 893. In the new capital, Tsar Simeon decreed Orthodox Christianity as the religion of the empire, and Bulgarian as the language. Veliki Preslav soon became one of the most glorious cities in the Balkans.

The city was captured and burnt down by the Byzantines in 972. However, it was later rebuilt and flourished as a cultural and religious centre. During the Second Bulgarian Empire, the capital was moved to modern-day Veliko Târnovo, so Veliki Preslav fell into decline. In 1388 it was again sacked by the Turks, who hauled away much of the stone to construct mosques elsewhere.

RUINS

Protected by a high stone wall, the outer city spread over 5 sq km and contained churches, monasteries and residences of nobles. An inner wall encircled the 1.5-sq-km citadel with the royal palace at its centre. The most famous building was the **Round Golden Church**, built in 908 and partially restored in the last few years. It derived its name from the dome, which was gilded on the outside and covered with mosaics inside.

Visitors should first stop at the **archaeological museum** (☎ 2630; admission 3 lv; ☯ 9am-6pm Apr-Oct, 9am-5pm Nov-Mar). The artefacts from the ruins, and other items, are well displayed and labelled in English. A model of the palace helps you visualise the grandeur of the ancient city (though explanations for this are in Bulgarian only). The prize exhibits, such as seals, jewellery and the exquisite regal gold necklace, are displayed in a walkthrough safe. If you ask, staff will show a film (in English) about the ancient city.

Guided tours (in English) by an archaeologist cost 10 lv per group (maximum of five people). They are worthwhile because the ruins are spread over a large area, and nothing much is signposted. If you want to explore the site independently, ask for directions at the museum or just head down the road (away from the modern town) towards the **southern gate** and wander about.

From the bus station, walk 2km along ul Boris I, cross the road over to ul Ivanlo, turn right into ul Tsar Asen and look for the sign (in English) at the ruins of the **northern gate**. The museum is 300m down the road, with the (modern) cemetery on your left.

SLEEPING & EATING

The fairly unexciting **Hotel Preslav** (☎ 3305; s/d with bathroom 10/20 lv) is at the back of the main square. The only hotel in town, it's a bit drab, but clean enough, and the rates are low. Eat at the basic hotel restaurant, or one of cafés near the bus station.

GETTING THERE & AWAY

Every day, 11 buses travel directly between Shumen and Veliki Preslav (1.60 lv, 30 to 60 minutes), often via Kochovo. Another option is to take a bus from Shumen to Vârbitsa (six daily) – but not the ones via Rish – and jump out at Veliki Preslav.

VELIKO TÂRNOVO ВЕЛИКО ТЪРНОВО

☎ 062 / pop 75,000

There's perhaps no city in Eastern Europe with a setting more spectacular and romantic than Veliko Târnovo, city of the tsars. Here the Yantra River wends its way gracefully through a sheer tree-lined gorge atop of which sits the ancient capital of the Second Bulgarian Empire (1185–1396). Tourism here is thriving as word spreads in the evermore obscure contest to find Eastern Europe's 'new big thing'. In fact, the Bucharest–Istanbul express train which stops off here has long brought backpackers to Târnovo, but now word is well and truly out and travellers are making a beeline to Târnovo right after Prague and Budapest.

The town today incorporates its ancient quarters, including overgrown Trapezitsa Hill, one time residence of Bulgaria's kings. In the valley is Asenova, the artisans' and merchants' quarter dotted with the ruins of medieval churches, while the narrow streets of Varosha, the old town, bear imprints of the Bulgarian national revival period. A large new town has grown up to the west, but it hasn't interfered with the unreconstructed beauty of the old city. Today Veliko Târnovo is best known in Bulgaria for housing its large university, Bulgaria's most prestigious. Wherever you go in Bulgaria, don't miss this most wonderful of places, and plan to spend a few days here to do it justice.

History

The area was settled by Neolithic people between about 5500 and 4500 BC. Tsarevets Hill, on which the fortress stands today, and the nearby Trapezitsa Hill, was inhabited by Thracians in 2000 BC. The Romans built the first fortress walls, and, in the 5th century AD, a Byzantine citadel was established on Tsarevets Hill by Emperor Justinian. Next came the Slavs who captured the town in the 7th century.

Under the leadership of brothers Asen and Petâr, Târnovgrad became a centre of rebellion against the Byzantine rulers. After the foundation of the Second Bulgarian Empire (1185), Târnovgrad became the second most important town in the region (after Constantinople), and trade and culture flourished for the next 200 years.

On 17 July 1393 Târnovgrad fell again, this time to the Turks, and the fortress was destroyed. The town remained fairly stagnant until Bulgarian culture and nationalism gradually reasserted itself during the mid-19th century. In 1877 the Russian General Gurko liberated Târnovgrad from the Turks. Because of its importance during the Second Bulgarian Empire, Veliko Târnovo (as it was renamed) was chosen as the place to write the Bulgarian Constitution in 1879, and to officially proclaim the independent state of Bulgaria in 1908. The town is proud of its history, and educational, religious and linguistic heritage.

Orientation

Veliko Târnovo is based along a ridge above the Yantra River (probably from the Thracian word *yatrus* meaning 'quick flowing'). The river winds in a horseshoe bend between four hills: Tsarevets, on which the fortress is built; Momina Krepost, several kilometres to the east; Trapezitsa; and Sveta Gora (Holy Mountain). The town centre is along ul Nezavisimost and ul Stefan Stambolov between the post office and the huge underpass. The new town, which most visitors can happily avoid, spreads out to the west and southwest from ul Vasil Levski.

BOOKS & MAPS

If you're spending more than a few days here, pick up the excellent *Infoguide Veliko Turnovo* booklet (5 lv). It provides an abundance of practical and cultural information in English, and is available at the Tourist Information Centre and most bookstalls. If you're interested in the history of the various monasteries in and around the town, buy *The V Turnovo Monasteries: A Guide* (4 lv).

VELIKO TÂRNOVO

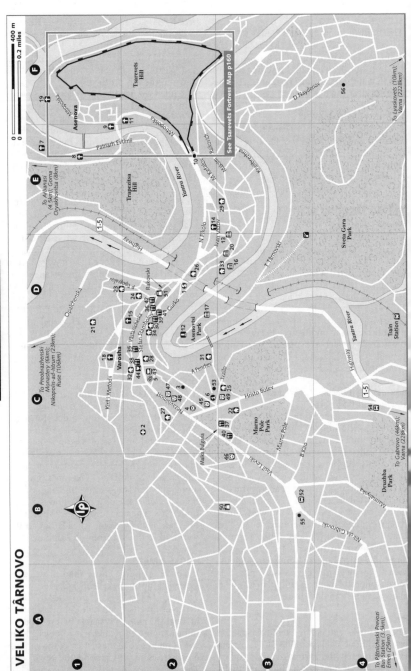

0   400 m
0   0.2 miles

See Tsarevets Fortress Map p160

The detailed and widely available *Veliko Târnovo* map, published by Domino and (mostly) translated into English, also includes helpful maps of Arbanasi and the Tsarevets Fortress.

Information

Admission fees to the museums and other attractions in Veliko Târnovo are some of the highest in Bulgaria. Students with appropriate identity cards (see p251) will appreciate discounts of up to 50% at most places.

INTERNET ACCESS

There are several Internet centres to choose from. There are two enormous ones:

I-Net Internet Centre (under Mustang Food restaurant, off ul Hristo Botev).

Navigator (ul Stefan Stambolov)

LAUNDRY

Ladybird (ul Hadji Dmitâr 25; 9am-5pm Mon-Fri & 10am-6pm Sat & Sun) Excellent same-day laundry service, around 4 lv per load.

MONEY

It seems that every third shop in the town centre is a foreign-exchange office, and most provide competitive rates with no commission. Try the following to change travellers cheques, and to obtain cash with a credit card through an ATM or over the counter:

First East International Bank (ul Stefan Stambolov 1).

United Bulgarian Bank (ul Hristo Botev 3) Near the Cinema Poltava complex.

POST

Main post office (ul Hristo Botev 1; 7am-10pm) The telephone centre is in the post office.

TOURIST INFORMATION

Tourist Information Centre (TIC; ☎ 622 148; fax 600 768; tic_vt@mobikom.com; ul Hristo Botev 5; 9am-6pm Mon-Fri, 9am-noon Sat) This is probably the best TIC in the country. The helpful fluent English-speaking staff will assist you with just about anything from excursions to private rooms and onward travel.

Sights

TSAREVETS FORTRESS

Symbol of the city and the main feature of its skyline, this place should be the first port of call for anyone visiting the city as it's *the* highlight of Veliko Târnovo and one of the major attractions in Bulgaria. The **Tsarevets Museum-Reserve** (☎ 638 841; adult/child 4/2 lv; 8am-7pm Apr-Oct, 9am-5pm Nov-Mar) is located at the end of the old town on Tsarevets Hill.

CENTRAL BULGARIA

THE SOUND & LIGHT SHOW

The sound and light show illuminates the whole of Tsarevets Hill in a stunningly colourful display, during which the road to Gorna Oryakhovitsa is closed. The show doesn't happen unless a certain number of people have bought tickets, but as a rule it happens pretty much every night during the summer, as there's always at least one tour group in town. Don't pay to see it unless you want a seat; just come along with a beer and hang out with the locals. The show is 40 minutes long and apparently relates the rise and fall of the Second Bulgarian Empire (although for most people it will just be a pretty array of flashing lights set to music).

To find out if the show is happening ring the organisers on ☎ 636 828 or ask the TIC or your hotel to check for you. Alternatively, turn up at the fortress and hope the show is on, or do what most locals and visitors do: listen for the bells, and look for the laser beams. Starting time is anywhere from 8pm to 9.30pm depending on the time of year.

Tsarevets Hill was settled by Thracians and Romans, but the Byzantines built the first significant fortress on the hill between the 5th and 7th centuries AD. The fortress was rebuilt and fortified by the Slavs and Bulgars between the 8th and 10th centuries, and again by the Byzantines in the early 12th century. The fortress reached its peak when Târnovgrad became the capital of the Second Bulgarian Empire, but was again sacked and destroyed by the Turks in 1393.

Archaeologists have so far uncovered the remains of over 400 houses, 18 churches and numerous monasteries, dwellings, shops, gates and towers. Other than the patriarch's complex and Baldwin Tower, nothing much has been restored so most of what remains, especially near the walls, is little more than rubble. This shouldn't dissuade you from visiting, however. Sadly, explanations in English are still almost nonexistent, but guided tours (rates negotiable) are possible if they are arranged in advance.

From the main entrance, pass through two more gates and veer left (northeast). You'll soon see the remains of fortress walls, some of which were once 12m high and 10m thick. You can walk along the adjoining walls – but be careful. Near the watchtower, which you can climb for views of the Asenova quarter, is a small separate gateway that was once used as a servants' entrance.

Further along the wall are the unrecognisable and poorly signposted remains of a 12th-century **monastery**, various dwellings and workshops and a couple of **churches**. At the most northerly point are the remains of a 13th-century **monastery** (with a sign in English), and **Execution Rock**, from which traitors were pushed into the Yantra River. Most famously, Patriarch Joachim III was thrown from here in 1300 for treachery.

The path hugging the eastern edge of the fortress is poorly maintained and passes nothing of interest, so head back to the middle, using the hill-top patriarch's complex as a landmark. Past one of several modern bells (used in the sound and light show; see the boxed text above) are the ruins of a **nobleman's dwelling** and two **churches** to the left (east).

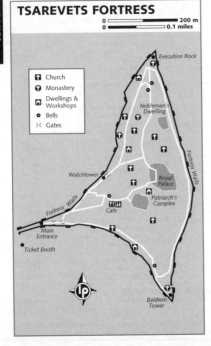

TSAREVETS FORTRESS

0 — 200 m
0 — 0.1 miles

- Church
- Monastery
- Dwellings & Workshops
- Bells
-)(Gates

Execution Rock

Nobleman's Dwelling

Fortress Walls

Watchtower

Royal Palace

Patriarch's Complex

Fortress Walls

Café

Main Entrance

Ticket Booth

Baldwin Tower

Just below the patriarch's complex are the foundations of the extensive **Royal Palace**, from where 22 successive kings ruled Bulgaria. It's hard to imagine that this palace once covered 4500 sq metres and housed a stupendous throne (about 30m by 10m) and Romans columns, probably transferred from the nearby city of Nikopolis-ad-Istrum.

From the palace, head back down (west) to the main path and walk up the steps to the **patriarch's complex**, once about 3000 sq m big. Also called the Church of the Blessed Saviour, it was probably built in about 1235, but has been extensively restored. The views of the city from the front steps are marvellous, but the modern murals inside, which outline the history of Bulgaria during in the 14th and 15th centuries, are austere.

Walk down the steps back towards the main entrance and take a sharp left along the path hugging the southern wall. At the end of the path is the restored **Baldwin Tower**, where Baldwin I of Flanders – the deposed Latin emperor of the Byzantines – was imprisoned and executed after his defeat by the Bulgars in 1205. You can climb to the top of the tower for more wonderful views.

SARAFKINA KÂSHTA

Built in 1861 by a rich Turkish merchant and moneylender, this fine five-storey Bulgarian national revival period–style house is now a **museum** (☎ 635 802; ul Gurko 88; adult/ student 4/2 lv; 🕑 9am-noon & 1-6pm Mon-Fri). The ground floor contains displays of arts and crafts, such as ceramics, metalwork, woodcarvings and jewellery, and some fascinating exhibits (with helpful explanations in English) about traditional costumes and breadmaking. The upper floor is crammed with revival-period furniture, and the walls are covered with family photos. Probably the finest museum in town, it's nevertheless best viewed from the river where you can see its full extent.

MUSEUM OF NATIONAL REVIVAL & CONSTITUENT ASSEMBLY

This **museum** (☎ 629 821; ul Ivan Vazov; adult/child under 7 4/2 lv; 🕑 8am-6pm Wed-Mon) is in a former Turkish town hall (built in 1872). It was here in 1879 that Bulgaria's first National Assembly was held to write the country's first constitution. The building is probably of more interest to some visitors than the exhibits themselves, especially because almost nothing is labelled in English.

The ground floor contains a vast number of costumes, books and photos about the history of Veliko Târnovo, while upstairs there's a lavish assembly hall with portraits of local VIPs. The basement has photos of the old town (enjoyable without any explanations in English), and some valuable icons (curiously, labelled in English).

VELIKO TÂRNOVO ARCHAEOLOGICAL MUSEUM

This very good **museum** (☎ 634 946; ul Ivan Vazov; adult/child under 7 4/2 lv; 🕑 8am-noon & 1-6pm Tue-Sun) is housed in a wonderful building with some commanding views over the valley. It contains artefacts from the Roman ruins at Nikopolis-ad-Istrum and a huge collection of Roman pottery and statues from elsewhere. There are exhibits about medieval Bulgaria (including huge murals of the tsars on the 2nd floor) and some ancient gold from regional Neolithic settlements. Frustratingly, like other museums in town, all captions here are in Bulgarian. Even if you don't go in, its colonnaded terrace and courtyard replete with Roman sculptures is definitely worth a look.

CHURCHES

In the old Asenova quarter is the **Forty Martyrs Church** (ul Mitropolska), originally built in 1230 to celebrate the victory of the Bulgars under Tsar Asen II against the Byzantines. It was used as a royal mausoleum, and then as a mosque by the Turks. At the time of research it was the site of massive renovation inside and excavations in the graveyard outside. You can't visit the church, but there are great views of the excavation site to be had from the main road.

Just across the road is the tiny **Church of the Assumption**, built in 1923 over the ruins of a 14th-century church belonging to the Nunnery of the Holy Virgin. The church is usually closed, but it's very pretty with blue-painted bas-reliefs decorating it sides.

Two blocks north is the late-13th-century **Sts Peter & Paul Church** (☎ 638 841; ul Mitropolska; adult/concession 4/2 lv), which features three layers of remarkable murals created between the 11th and 17th centuries. This is the most interesting of the churches, mainly as there are some surviving early-11th-century wall paintings, created when Bulgaria was a Catholic nation before converting to Orthodoxy in 1235. The best preserved Catholic painting is in the corner to the left of the altar, where Jesus on the cross is being comforted by the Virgin Mary.

On the other side of the river, enclosed by a high wall, is the beautifully proportioned **Church of St Dimitâr** (ul Patriarh Evtimii; admission 4 lv; ☺ by arrangement), the town's oldest church. It was built in the so-called 'Târnovo style', and named after St Dimitâr of Thessaloniki. During the church's consecration in 1185, Tsars Asen and Petâr proclaimed an uprising against Byzantine rule, which lead to the eventual creation of the Second Bulgarian Empire (1185–1396). There's little inside, so it's not usually open; you need to ask at Sts Peter and Paul Church for one of the wardens to open it up for you.

Nearby is the **Church of St Georgi** (ul Patriarh Evtimii; admission 4 lv; ☺ by arrangement), probably built in 1612 on the ruins of a medieval church. It was destroyed by the Ottomans, but restored in the early 18th century. Inside, there are some remarkable murals by unknown artists.

Just off ul Ivan Vazov is the **St Bogadaritsa Church**, the town's main cathedral, visible all over the old city with its large green neo-Byzantine domes. It's worth a look inside for its frescoes.

In the Varosha district is the **St Nikolai Church** (ul Vâstanicheska), built in 1879. Follow the steps on the left (western) side, and then turn left along ul Kiril i Metodii to the **Sts Cyril & Methodius Church**, which is distinguished by its elegant tower.

STATE ART MUSEUM
Dramatically situated in a tight bend of the Yantra River, and unmissable from most vantage points in the town centre, is the **State Art Museum** (☎ 638 941; Asenovtsi Park; adult/student 3/2 lv, free on Thu; ☺ 10am-6pm Tue-Sun). The ground floor of this uninspiring-looking building contains an array of paintings of Veliko Târnovo and the region by many different artists. The walls of the 2nd floor are full of various other works of art, mostly on permanent loan from galleries in Silistra, Dobrich and Ruse. All labels are in English, and guided tours (in English and French) are available for about 5 lv extra per person (minimum of three).

Nearby, the **Monument of the Asens** is an awe-inspiring commemoration of the establishment of the Second Bulgarian Empire in 1185. From the monument, and the adjacent café, are glorious views of the tiers of rustic houses hanging above the gorge.

Activities
At the time of research, the local tourist authorities were planning to introduce all sorts of adventure and ecotourist activities, so if you are interested in the prospect of hiking, mountain biking, horse riding and caving, contact the TIC (p159). For information about **horse riding** in Arbanasi, see p168; for **hiking** in Emen, see p169.

Trapezitsa (☎ /fax 635 823; www.trapezitsa-1902 .hit.bg; ul Stefan Stambolov 79; ☺ 9am-noon & 1-6pm Mon-Fri) can arrange rock-climbing trips and training at nearby massifs. It is based in the hotel of the same name. Serious rock climbers should pick up the *Climbing Guide* from the TIC.

Festivals & Events
Holiday of Amateur Art Activities (early May) More commonly known as the Balkan Folk Festival, it takes place over 10 days during the first half of May.
International Folklore Festival (☎ 630 223; late Jun–mid-Jul) The highlight of the cultural calendar is undoubtedly this festival held over three weeks; it features more than 300 acts from all over Bulgaria and the Balkans. More details are available from the TIC, or the organisers, from about mid-April.

Sleeping
There's now a large choice of accommodation in town, although it's wise to book ahead in summer. You'll always be able to get a private room somewhere though, so don't worry if you haven't been able to book. Wherever you stay, if possible choose a hotel in an older part of town, and a room with views of the river and gorge. Unless stated otherwise, all hotels include breakfast

BUDGET
Rooms can be booked in private homes through the **Tourist Information Centre** (☎ 622 148; fax 600 768; tic_vt@mobikom.com; ul Hristo Botev 5; ☺ 9am-6pm Mon-Fri, 9am-noon Sat) for 20 to 30 lv for a single/double. If you arrive out of hours, you'll be offered rooms by ladies on the street around the TIC. The nicest places to stay are near the Samovodska Charshiya Complex

(p165) in the Varosha district, and along the lower (southeastern) end of ul Gurko.

Hotel Trapezitsa (☎ 622 061; ul Stefan Stambolov 79; s/d/tr/q 31/46/57/76 lv) This four-storey hotel, right in the centre of town, is outstanding value and has the best possible location. Some rooms are a little small, but they're always clean and cosy. Get a room at the back to avoid the street noise, and to admire the awesome gorge views. This is probably the best choice for budget travellers (and there's a 3 lv student discount), especially if you're travelling in a group of three or four. Breakfast is not included.

Hikers Hostel (☎ 088 9691661, 088 7098279; www .hikershostel.org; ul Rezervoarska 91; dm/d 20/50 lv) Opened in 2004, this place is a clean and exceptionally friendly hostel a five-minute uphill walk from the Samovodska Charshiya Complex. It's a tiny place (two dorms and a double room) so book ahead in summer. They'll pick you up for free wherever you arrive if you call ahead (including from the Gorna Oryakhovitsa train station if they're in a good mood).

Rooms for Rent Gurko 70 (☎ 633 046; ul Gurko 70; s/d/apt 25/30/55 lv) Totally unmarked from the street, Rooms for Rent is still great value and in the heart of the old town. Ring the bell with 'to let' written on it next to the small shop. The friendly multilingual owner can arrange tours around the city for guests. Breakfast is not included in the price.

Hotel Elida (☎ 632 329; ul Rezervoarska 3; s/d/t 15/30/45 lv) On the little square above the Samovodska Charshiya Complex, the tiny Elida is an excellent budget option. The rooms are rather basic and with shared facilities, but it's excellent value in the heart of the old town. Breakfast isn't included.

MID-RANGE

Hotel Tsarevets (☎ 601 885; ul Chitalistna 23; s/d 80/ 108 lv; 🅿 😭 💻) Just a stone's throw from the fortress, this delightful and smart new hotel is well run by English-speaking staff and very good value for money. All rooms are comfortable with decent bathrooms, TVs and minibars. Discounts are available for stays of a few days or more.

Hotel-Mehana Gurko (☎ 627 838; www.hotelgurko .hit.bg; ul Gurko 33; s/d 70/100 lv; 😭 💻) The traditional town house exterior belies the huge, modern rooms (with air-con and TV) within, each individually decorated and offering great views. The Gurko is extremely popular, and so although they are planning to build a 10-room extension, it's still essential to book ahead in the summer.

Hotel Kiev (☎ 600 571; kiev@abv.bg; s/d 50/ 75 lv; 😭) A great new hotel in the middle of the old town, the Kiev's unfortunate name makes you think of a Balkantourist hotel in 1970s monolithic style, but nothing could be further than the truth: friendly owners, large and airy modern rooms and a busy café downstairs make this an excellent choice.

Kâshata Private Flats (☎ 604 129; www.the -house.hit.bg; pl Slaveikov 4; 1-/2-person studio 52 lv, 4-person apt 90 lv) An excellent alternative to a hotel or a home stay is to hire your own flat in the centre of town. Kâshata (The House) is centrally located just off the main street and boasts a selection of very decent self-contained apartments, all of which are fully equipped and will give you a huge amount of freedom. Car rental can also be organised here for 30 lv per day, and a pick-up taxi from Sofia or Varna airport is a very reasonable 80 lv. Breakfast is not included.

Hotel Comfort (☎ 628 728; fax 623 525; ul P Tipografov 5; s/d 50/60 lv) Despite some negative feedback from one reader about constant surcharges, the Hotel Comfort remains a decent option, located in a charming part of Varosha. The rooms are clean and comfortable, and feature huge bathrooms and balconies with awesome views. Breakfast is 5 lv per person.

Villa Tashkov (☎ 635 801; www.tashkoff.com; ul Gurko 19; d from 80 lv, entire villa 200 lv) This gorgeous villa can be all yours while you stay in Veliko Târnovo, or if your budget is rather more modest, a bit of the villa can be yours. Reception is at ul Stambolisky 13, and booking ahead is nearly always necessary. The fully equipped rooms with daily maid service make this place one of the smartest and most comfortable options in town.

Hotel Etâr (☎ 621 838; fax 621 890; ul Ivailo 2; s/d 40/80 lv) You can do better than stay at the somewhat overpriced Etâr, although if you need a room and other hotels are full, there's a safe bet that this aging 14-storey communist-era beauty will have something free. Views from the unexciting rooms are spectacular, though.

TOP END

Hotel Premier (☎ 615 555; hotel.premier@abv.bg; ul Sava Penev 1; s/d 120/140 lv, ste 240-480 lv; P ❄ 🖳 🖳) Târnovo's smartest and certainly its priciest hotel, the sparkling new Premier is located in the new town and has all the facilities you'd expect in this bracket of accommodation. An outdoor pool was being built when we visited, so the indoor pool, sauna and Jacuzzi will have to do until it opens.

Hotel Allegro (☎ 602 332, www.veliko-tarnovo.net /alegro; ul Todor Svetoslav 15; s/d 85/100 lv; ❄ 🖳) Opened in 2003, the Allegro is a 14-room place in the new town but with a very pleasant ambience and spotless rooms. Luxury rooms add an extra 25% to the room prices, and are larger with huge bathrooms.

Interhotel Veliko Târnovo (☎ 601 000; www .hotelvelikotarnovo.com; ul A Penchev; s/d 140/240 lv; P ❄ 🖳) The ludicrous overpricing here gets you unsmiling staff with no linguistic skills and the honour of staying in the town's most monstrous piece of Soviet architecture. The rooms are fine, with lovely views (ie you can't see it if you're in it) and many tour groups stay here at very reasonable discounts.

Eating

There's a good selection of restaurants and cafés in town, the most attractive ones being those with terraces overlooking the river and gorge.

Shtastlivetsa (mains 5 lv) This buzzing restaurant has two locations in town: most obviously the left-hand side of the Trapezitsa Hotel (ul Stefan Stambolov 79) and also at ul Marno Pole 7. In summer the terrace is hugely popular with locals and travellers alike, both for a Bulgarian meal or just some beers. Good value and excellent service.

Stratiat Restaurant (ul Rakovski 11) This excellent place is bit of a social hub, with a large outside terrace that gets busy at breakfast and remains so most of the day. Food is delicious, and the prices are reasonable considering the setting and service. They'll do a good breakfast omelette if you ask nicely (they don't have them on the menu).

Pizza Tempo (☎ 623 787; pl Slaveikov; pizzas 4 lv) A cut above the other pizzerias in town, Tempo's food is both authentic and great value, extending far beyond simple pizzas to other Italian classics such as lasagne and pasta dishes. They also deliver.

Starata Mehana (ul Stefan Stambolov; mains about 3-4 lv) Another dramatic location is on offer here, with great views over the gorge. The food is traditional and good value.

Captain Cook Fish Restaurant (ul Stefan Stambolov; mains 5 lv) Despite its rather garish chain-restaurant décor, the Captain Cook is hugely popular and serves up freshly caught Black Sea fish daily.

Restaurant Rich (ul Stefan Stambolov; salads 1.50-2 lv, mains 4-4.50 lv) The main draw here is the gorgeous balcony overlooking the gorge, lit up in the evenings by multicoloured lights. Reserve a table here, as there are only a few. The food is good, but service is often painfully slow.

Hotel-Mehana Gurko (☎ 627 838; ul Gurko 33; mains 3.50-6 lv) The traditional *mehana* in the popular Hotel Gurko is beautifully decorated and offers a wide range of Bulgarian specialities.

La Belle Époque (☎ 633 331; ul Stefan Stambolov; mains 5 lv) A rather spurious Bulgarian version of late-19th-century France is on offer here, but the food is reliable and you are usually guaranteed a seat. French and Bulgarian cuisine is served up here.

Mustang Food (pl Maika Bulgaria; grills about 3 lv) Like the Happy Bar & Grill restaurants found elsewhere in Bulgaria, Mustang offers palatable Western-style food in a modern setting at above-average prices. The menu is in English.

For a quick, cheap and filling meal, it's hard to walk past any place selling doner kebabs along ul Nezavisimost.

Drinking

Ulitsata (ul Stefan Stambolov) To one side of the Trapezitsa Hotel, this is the busiest and friendliest place in town. A young and up-for-it crowd hangs out here, enjoying great views and cheap beer on the terrace.

Pepe's Bar (pl Slaveikov) A slightly classier feel here, Pepe's attracts a well-heeled local crowd who hide out in the dark interior listening to DJs or just chill out on the terrace feeding the stray dogs.

City Pub (ul Hristo Botev) Probably the most popular bar in town is this thematic British-style pub just down from the TIC. Despite the unremarkable and pricey meals, it's always busy.

Café Aqua (ul Stefan Stambolov) A great alternative to the crowded bars is the far more laid-back Café Aqua, where people come for coffee and cake until late in the evening. It's definitely the place to be for the fashionable yet caffeine-reliant and has a great balcony overlooking the gorge.

Entertainment

A combination of local students, foreign backpackers and Bulgarians visiting the country's most charming city makes for a great atmosphere and plenty of busy drinking and dancing spots in Veliko Târnovo, particularly during the summer months.

Scream Dance Club (ul Nezavisimost 17) This is Veliko Târnovo's most popular dance place, appealing to the rather scantily clad student base.

Las Vegas Club (ul Nezavisimost 17) It may not be exciting or trendy, and the service is often slow, but the views here are almost unbeatable. If you somehow get sick of the panorama, you can play pool or order a meal.

The flashiest nightclub is the **Spyder Nightclub** (ul Hristo Botev 15; closed Sun), just near the TIC. Some of the more fashionable locals flock to the **Fashion Club** (ul Hristo Botev), which is in the Cinema Poltava complex.

For something more sedate, you could catch a movie at the **Cinema Poltava** (ul Hristo Botev), or ask the TIC about what's on at the **Konstantin Kisimov Dramatic Theatre** (☎ 623 526; ul Vasil Levski).

Shopping

From near the Hotel Trapezitsa, ul Rakovski veers upwards from the main road. It leads to an area known as the Samovodska Charshiya Complex, which is based around a cobblestone square dominated by a statue of the former prime minister, Stefan Stambolov. The area was once the home of craftsmen, including blacksmiths, potters and gunsmiths; artisans still practice their trades here. Most of the shops selling books, antiques and art, among other things, have been superbly renovated in the style typical of the Bulgarian national revival period. There are plenty of fascinating shops to grab your attention, selling traditional crafts from woodcarvings to musical instruments.

For camping, climbing, skiing and biking gear, head to the excellent **Gorgona** (☎ 601 400; www.gorgona-shop.com, in Bulgarian; ul Zelenka 2; 10am-1pm & 2-7pm Mon-Fri, 10am-2pm Sat).

Getting There & Away

BUS

There are two bus stations serving Veliko Târnovo, neither of which are in the town centre. **Pâtnicheski Prevozi bus station** (☎ 640 908; ul Nikola Gabrovski 74), about 4km from the town centre, is the main terminus for buses from other regions in Bulgaria. This station is linked to the town centre by bus Nos 10, 12, 14, 70 and 110 along ul Vasil Levski. There's a **left-luggage office** (7.30am-4.30pm). From here, there are buses to Gabrovo (3.50 lv, 40 minutes) roughly every half hour; six buses a day to Elena (2 lv, 30 minutes); five per day to Kazanlâk (5 lv, 2½ hours); eight per day to Ruse (4 lv, two hours); seven per day to Sliven (4 lv, two hours); two per day to Plovdiv (9.5 lv, 4½ hours); and one per day to Troyan (4 lv, two hours), Karlovo (7 lv, four hours) and Pleven (6 lv, two hours).

The **Yug bus station** (☎ 620 014; ul Hristo Botev) is somewhat closer to the town centre and the hub for private buses going mainly to Sofia and the Black Sea. From here there are buses throughout the day to Sofia (9 lv, four hours) as well as Varna (9.50 lv, four hours), Burgas (7 lv, 3½ hours) and Shumen (5 lv, two hours).

From outside the convenient office under the Hotel Etâr, **Etap Adress** (☎ 630 564) has air-conditioned coach departures roughly every hour to Sofia (11 lv) and Varna (11 lv), two daily buses to Dobrich (13 lv), one to Kavarna (15 lv) via Albena and Balchik and one to Shumen (8 lv).

There were no bus services at all between Bulgaria and Romania at the time of writing, because of the long delays at the border.

TRAIN

Direct services from Veliko Târnovo's tiny little station are limited and most travellers will find the major junction at Gorna Oryakhovitsa (just 8.5km away) far more useful.

From the **Veliko Târnovo train station** (☎ 620 065), there are four trains a day to Plovdiv via Stara Zagora. There are five trains to Gabrovo (change at Tsareva Livada) and regular trains to Gorna Oryakhovitsa. From the Veliko Târnovo station, bus Nos 10, 12, 14, 70 and 110 (the same ones that end up at the Pânicheski Prevozi bus station) head into town.

Gorna Oryakhovitsa train station (☎ 0618-56050) is along the main line between Sofia and

Varna. There are eight trains (three hours) every day to/from Sofia via Pleven, five trains (three hours) to Varna and 11 trains to Ruse. There are also regular connections to Stara Zagora (six trains a day) and Shumen (10 trains a day).

You can also get to the Gorna Oryakhovitsa train station from Veliko Târnovo by catching a minibus from opposite the market along ul Vasil Levski, taking bus No 14 from the Pânticheski Prevozi bus station or jumping on bus No 10 from the city centre. Alternatively, you could hire a taxi (about 6 lv).

Tickets for international trains, and advance tickets for domestic services from Veliko Târnovo and Gorna Oryakhovitsa, are available from the **Rila Bureau** (☎ 622 042; ul Tsar Kaloyan 2A; ☺ 8am-noon & 1-4.30pm Mon-Fri).

Getting Around

Taxis are not ideal for getting around the old districts because of the narrow streets; however, they are worth hiring (at fixed metered rates) to get to places like Arbanasi, or chartering (for negotiable rates) to anywhere further out. If you wish to hire a car, the TIC (p159) can put you in contact with a reliable rental company that charges a reasonable 30 lv or so per day, including insurance (but not petrol). Otherwise, getting around on foot is the best option.

AROUND VELIKO TÂRNOVO
Arbanasi Арбанаси
☎ 062 / pop 1500

Only just outside Veliko Târnovo, Arbanasi makes a wonderful contrast to the ancient capital and is a very easy trip offering a chance to see one of Bulgaria's most lovely historic monastery-villages. Today some of Bulgaria's rich and famous live here in large, traditional-style homes behind high walls, and nearly 90 churches, homes and monasteries in the village are protected as cultural monuments by the Bulgarian authorities. Originally founded by Christians from Albania in the 15th century, Arbanasi grew prosperous after Sultan Süleyman I gave the town to a son-in-law in 1538, thus exempting it from the Ottoman Empire's ruinous taxation. Residents were able to carry on trade with countrys as far away as Greece, Russia and India, and the town became a favourite summer residence for

the fabulously wealthy. All this good fortune came to an abrupt end in 1798 when the town was mostly destroyed by Turkish *kurdjali* gangs.

Arbanasi is a superb place to relax with great walking and plenty of space and tranquillity, as well as a good selection of restaurants and leisure activities such as horse riding.

SIGHTS

Despite its enormous wealth of history, there are only three open sights to visit in Arbanasi, but they are stunners. One ticket (4 lv) allows you to visit all three places; the ticket is available from each of the three attractions. Each place is officially open from 9am to 6pm every day. In practice, opening hours are erratic: places are rarely open before 9.30am. The attractions are closed between 1 October and 31 March, so check the opening times with the **Museums Department** (☎ 062-349 460) in Veliko Târnovo before visiting Arbanasi in winter.

Cameras (photographic or video) are not allowed at any of the three places. Nothing much is signposted around the village, and the streets have no names. Disappointingly, everything on site is labelled in Bulgarian, and any (brief) explanation on notice boards outside is in Bulgarian, German and Russian only. If you want any more information about the attractions, pick up one of several booklets (2 lv to 3 lv), such as *Arbanasi: A Guide,* in Veliko Târnovo.

During the 16th and 17th centuries, the comparatively benevolent Turkish rulers in Arbanasi allowed several churches to be built. The oldest remaining church in the village is known as the **Nativity Church**, and boasts arguably one of the most fascinating interiors of any church in Bulgaria. Painted between 1632 and 1649, its exquisite frescoes cover every inch of space in the five chambers, and the central iconostasis is magnificent. Over 3500 figures are depicted in some 2000 scenes throughout the church. It also contains several lavish wooden iconostases created by carvers from Tryavna.

Almost as good is the 16th-century **St Archangel Michael & Gabriel's Church**, built on the ruins of a medieval church that existed previously. The interior is also covered with marvellous murals, including one from Thessaloniki (Greece) and Bucharest (Romania), but it's rather dark inside and hard to see, so best visited when sunny, letting light filter in to a degree. The wooden iconostases were also carved by experts from Tryavna. Neither churches are used regularly in a ceremonial role any more, but the religious significance of the icon paintings makes them a popular place for Bulgarians and foreigners alike.

The ticket also includes a visit to the gorgeous **Konstantsalieva House**, built in the 17th century and rebuilt several times afterwards, most recently in a typical Bulgarian national revival style. The upper floor contains rooms of period furniture (the maternity room, or nursery, is particularly endearing), while the ground floor has a souvenir shop with an impressive range of embroidery, among other things, for sale.

There are other places that, while not open, can be admired from over the fence or through the window. Wander past the **Hadjilieva House**, the unsignposted **St Demetrius Church**, at the back of a scrappy garden, and the pretty **St Atanassius Church**, probably built in 1667, in a cemetery at the top of the lane. If you have the time, you may also want to walk by these three (closed) 17th-century buildings: **St George's Church**, the **St Bogoroditsa Monastery** and the **St Nikola Monastery**.

ACTIVITIES

One of the few places in central Bulgaria where visitors can arrange a gallop around

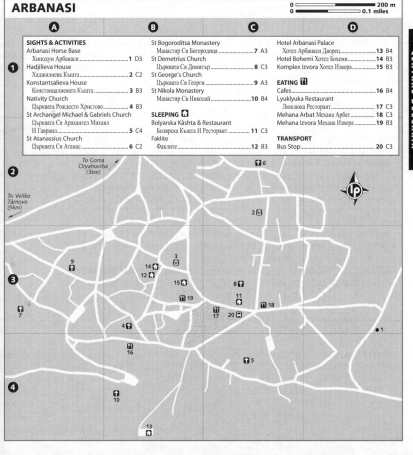

ARBANASI

0 ——— 200 m
0 ——— 0.1 miles

SIGHTS & ACTIVITIES
Arbanasi Horse Base
Хиподум Арбанаси 1 D3
Hadjilieva House
Хаджилиева Къща...................... 2 C2
Konstantsalieva House
Констанцалиевата Къща 3 B3
Nativity Church
Църквата Рождесто Христово.... 4 B3
St Archangel Michael & Gabriels Church
Църквата Св Араханел Михаил
И Гавраил............................... 5 C4
St Atanassius Church
Църквата Св Атанас................... 6 C2

St Bogoroditsa Monastery
Манастир Св Богородица 7 A3
St Demetrius Church
Църквата Св Димитър 8 C3
St George's Church
Църквата Св Георги 9 A3
St Nikola Monastery
Манастир Св Николай 10 B4

SLEEPING
Bolyarska Kâshta & Restaurant
Болярска Къща И Ресторант 11 C3
Faklite
Факлите 12 B3

Hotel Arbanasi Palace
Хотел Арбанаси Дворец............. 13 B4
Hotel Bohemi Хотел Бохеми 14 B3
Komplex Izvora Хотел Извора...... 15 B3

EATING
Cafes.. 16 B4
Lyuklyuka Restaurant
Люклюка Ресторант.................. 17 C3
Mehana Arbat Механа Арбат 18 C3
Mehana Izvora Механа Извора 19 B3

TRANSPORT
Bus Stop..................................... 20 C3

To Gorna
Oryahovitsa
(3km)

To Veliko
Târnovo
(5km)

CENTRAL BULGARIA

the countryside on horseback is the **Arbanasi Horse Base** (☎ 623 668), on the eastern edge of the village. Phone to ask about current programmes and costs. It also hosts a riding tournament each June.

SLEEPING

Arbanasi makes an equally picturesque alternative to Veliko Târnovo, offering traditional mid-range and top-end accommodation. If you are arriving in winter, ring the hotels in advance to see if they're open.

Private rooms are available; ask at the shops and kiosk at the bus stop. There's no central agency though, so it's pot luck.

Faklite (☎ 604 496; s/d 16/32 lv) Hands down the best-value place in town at the time of writing, Faklite (the torches) offers huge and beautiful en-suite rooms bursting with atmosphere, tucked away in a charming traditional villa. Ask to be in the main house to avoid the far blander and more modern rooms on the other side of the garden. The price does not include breakfast, but this can be bought in the excellent restaurant.

Hotel Bohemi (☎ 620 484; www.arbanassivt.hit.bg; s/d/apt 60/80/100 lv) This friendly and homely place has a handful of small rooms, all of which are comfortable and fair value. The large apartments feature an appealing fireplace and TV, and are worth a splurge.

Bolyarska Kâshta & Restaurant (☎ 620 484; s/d 70/80/100) Only metres from the main square and bus stop, this hotel has the same management as the Bohemi and boasts spacious rooms and a lovely garden overlooking the St Demetrius Church.

Komplex Izvora (☎ 601 205; www.izvora.hit.bg; s/d 80/120 lv, ste 160-280 lv; P ⚑ ▣) Cuteness abounds at this sprawling place that encompasses the Mehana Izvora, a large lamb barbecue that is understandably popular in its gorgeous garden setting and the hotel retreat of the same name. With a pool and farm animals aplenty, this is one of Arbanasi's most delightful hotels. The rooms are airy and comfortable.

Hotel Arbanasi Palace (☎ 630 176; www.arbanassi palace.hit.bg; s/d/ste 270/280/320 lv; P ⚑ ▣ ▣) Visible from Veliko Târnovo, the five-star Arbanasi Palace is a slice of luxury in this already well-to-do village. BMWs race up the main drive carrying wealthy Bulgarians to the hotel for the views, the Roman bath on the grounds and the superb facilities.

EATING

Mehana Izvora (grills from 3.50 lv) The Izvora is a tavern built in a 17th-century home. It's popular with tour groups, who enjoy the extensive menu of traditional food. With a swimming pool and playground, it caters well to families. In the evenings, folk music is provided (at no extra cost) if there are enough customers.

Mehana Arbat (mains 4 lv) There's a slight Russian theme to this pleasant *mehana*, although the food is mainly what Arbanasi does best: traditional Bulgarian-style grills. Located just off the main square, it's a good place to grab a bite while waiting for the bus.

Lyuklyuka Restaurant (mains from 4.50 lv) This classy place, close to the village square and bus stop, has outdoor tables that back onto the charming park.

The road around the corner from the Nativity Church is dotted with cafés. They offer the same startling views of Veliko Târnovo and the valley for which guests at the nearby Hotel Arbanasi Palace pay dearly.

GETTING THERE & AWAY

From a spot opposite the market along ul Vasil Levski in Veliko Târnovo, minibuses depart for Gorna Oryakhovitsa train station when full (about every 30 minutes). If you ask nicely, or other customers are going there too, the driver may detour through Arbanasi. If not, disembark at the turn-off to Arbanasi, along the road between Veliko Târnovo and Gorna Oryakhovitsa, and walk (about 700m) to the village. A taxi from Veliko Târnovo costs about 3 lv one way and there's always a few drivers waiting in Arbanasi to take you back.

Preobrazhenski Monastery

Приображенски Манастир

The Monastery of the Transfiguration is in a scenic forest about 6.5km north of Veliko Târnovo. Originally built in 1360, it's the largest monastery in the region, and the fourth largest in Bulgaria. It was destroyed by the Turks in the late 14th century, and rebuilt in 1825 about 500m from the original site, but later damaged by landslides. The three churches feature murals painted between 1849 and 1851 by the renowned Zahari Zograf, but the best selection of older murals is now in the archaeological museum in Veliko Târnovo.

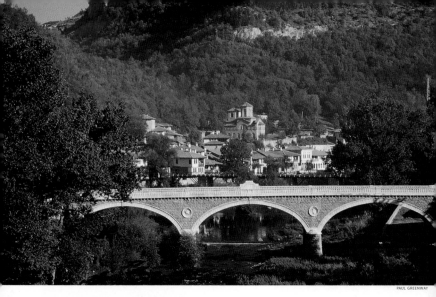

PAUL GREENWAY

Yantra River, Veliko Târnovo (p157)

MARTIN MOOS

Veliko Târnovo (p157)

St Demetrius Church (p167),
Arbanasi

PHILIP GAME

TOM COCKREM

Painted ceiling, Nativity Church (p166), Arbanasi

A hiker at the north wall of Mt Vihren (p101), Pirin Mountains

National revival architecture, Veliko Târnovo (p157)

Tsarevets Fortress (p159), Veliko Târnovo

Veliko Târnovo (p157)

Perhaps, the main reason to visit is the staggering view across the valley. The turn-off is along the road from Veliko Târnovo to Ruse and is accessible by bus No 10. From the turn-off, it's a shady, uphill (but not steep) 3km walk. A taxi from Veliko Târnovo will cost about 4 lv one way.

Emen Емен

The 3km-long **Emen Canyon**, along the Negovanka River, is the only one of its kind in Bulgaria. The surrounding area (about 25 hectares) has been declared a reserve by the locals authorities to protect species of butterflies, fish, birds and bats, as well as the 10m-high **Momin Skok Waterfall** (not so spectacular in summer).

The Bulgarian Association for Rural & Ecological Tourism (BARET) has established the **Negovanka Ecotrail** in and around the canyon. To find the start of the trail, look for signs in Emen village. Ask at the tourist office in Veliko Târnovo for current details and/or maps. Emen village and the canyon are about 25km west of Veliko Târnovo. Both are accessible by the bus to Pavlikeni, which leaves the Pâtnicheski Prevozi bus station in Veliko Târnovo at 8.30am and 6pm.

Nikopolis-ad-Istrum Никополис-ад-Иструм

Well worth a visit, especially if you have a private or chartered vehicle, are the **ruins** (admission 4 lv; ☯ 8am-6pm) of this Roman city. The city was built in AD 102 under Emperor Trayan, but destroyed by the Slavs, among others, in the late 6th century. Tragically, many of the city's treasures have been looted, but some of the greatest artefacts are housed in the archaeological museum in Veliko Târnovo. Excavations have unearthed streets, towers, gates and numerous buildings, but the highlights are the remains of the city square and town hall.

If you are driving from Veliko Târnovo, head north towards Ruse and look for the signposted turn-off to the left (west) after about 20km. But beware: some of the access road is rough. By bus, head towards Ruse, ask the driver to stop at the turn-off to Nikyup and then walk (about 4km) to the ruins following the signs. The site is not always open in the middle of summer (particularly August) because of extensive

archaeological work, so check with the tourist office in Veliko Târnovo, or ring the relevant authority (☎ 062-624 474), before heading out there at this time.

GABROVO ГАБРОВО
☎ 066 / pop 75,000

For reasons that seem lost in time, Gabrovo has been the continual butt of jokes by other Bulgarians, mostly involving their supposed miserliness (they are said to have invented the one stotinka coin). The citizens of Gabrovo – who instead of taking offence have erected a museum and organise an annual festival dedicated to this unique brand of humour – have admirably accepted this. Despite this self-deprecating streak, Gabrovo doesn't distinguish itself hugely from other provincial towns, although it's got a charming centre and is well situated for several interesting day trips to nearby villages.

The Gabrovo map, published by Domino and available in town, details 10 mountain-bike routes (from 9km to 58km), which pass local villages, monasteries and ancient ruins. These trails are also excellent for hiking (see the boxed text on p148).

Information

There are several foreign-exchange offices and an ATM on ul Radetska.

Internet Era (ul Skobelevska)

Matrix Internet Club (Hotel Balkan complex)

Tourist Office (☎ /fax 828 483; did@globcom.net; pl Vûzhrazhdane; ☯ 9am-5pm Mon-Fri) It can rent mountain bikes, advise about mountain-bike routes and hiking trails, give away brochures, arrange rooms in private homes and provide information about special events. The opening hours are erratic.

Sights

Certainly one of the more unusual museums in Bulgaria is the **House of Humour & Satire** (☎ 807 228; www.humorhouse.bg; ul Bryanska 68; adult/student & child 4/2 lv, guided tour in English, French or German 6 lv; ☯ 9am-6pm summer, Mon-Sat in winter). This huge, ugly building has four floors, but ideas relating to humour ran out by the 2nd floor; the upper floors contain unrelated art, as well as fascinating masks from all over the world. Most items are labelled in English.

There's a small number of **national revival period homes** on the eastern side of town, immediately behind the dominant (but rarely

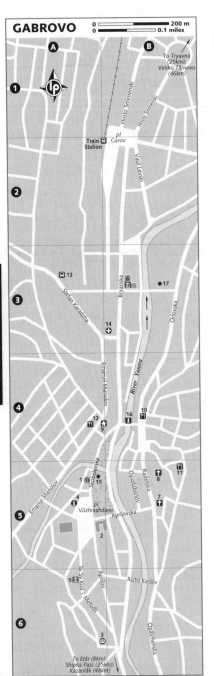

open) **St Troitsa Church**. If you want to fill in some time, the quaint **St Bogoroditsa Church** (ul Dyustabanov) is mildly interesting. The **Museum of Education** (☎ 804 071; ul Aprilovska 13) is accessible through the stunning courtyard in the Aprilov School. Also worth a peek is the **art gallery** (ul Sv Kiril i Metodii).

Festivals & Events

During odd-numbered years, Gabrovo hosts the **Biennial Festival of International Humour & Satire** (May), part of the annual **May Festivities of Culture**.

Other festivals:
Balkan Youth Festival (Aug)
Days of Chamber Music (Sep)

Sleeping & Eating

There's an alarming lack of hotels in Gabrovo, and the only option doesn't hold a candle to the two choices in nearby Etâr (p171). Ask the tourist office about rooms in private homes in Gabrovo and nearby villages, which cost about 18 lv to 22 lv per person including breakfast.

Hotel Balkan (☎ 801 911; fax 801 057; ul Emanuil Manolov 14; s/d/ste 80/90/110 lv; Ⓟ) The only hotel in town is as expensive as you'd expect given its total monopoly, although in their favour the rooms have been very well modernised and it's not the rip-off it was

CENTRAL BULGARIA

a few years ago. It's still virtually deserted, and haunted by the ghosts of its Soviet past, but if you want or need to stay in town this place is much better than many provincial hotels.

Pizza Tempo (pizzas 3 lv) This wonderful chain of pizza restaurants has brought the wood-fired oven to Bulgaria and significantly upped the national standard of pizza. The Gabrovo outlet is particularly atmospheric and busy all day long.

Tri Lovetsa (mains 4lv) Traditional-style Bulgarian specialities are served at this pleasant establishment across the road from the Hotel Balkan. There's also a nice terrace where you can dine outside when the weather allows it.

Gusto Pizza & Grill (grills about 5 lv) This place inside the Hotel Balkan is not much on Pizza Tempo, but offers fair Italian and Bulgarian food and fast service.

A number of restaurants and cafés, including Restaurant Cafe VMRO and the more touristy and expensive Strannopriemnitsa Inn, can be found in the older part of town on the eastern side of the River Yantra. In addition, plenty of cafés line ul Dyustabanov and the footbridge along ul Aprilovska.

Getting There & Away

From the **bus station** (☎ 803 277; ul Stefan Karadzha) there are up to three departures a day to Varna, Sliven, Burgas, Stara Zagora and Plovdiv. Five or six daily buses go to Pleven and one to Sofia (7 lv, 3½ hours). Buses also leave every hour for Tryavna, Veliko Târnovo (via the Dryanovo Monastery) and Kazanlâk (via Shipka and Shipka Pass).

The **train station** (☎ 827 127; pl Garov) is on a spur track off the main line between Veliko Târnovo and Kazanlâk. Services to both towns are infrequent, and of negligible use to travellers.

AROUND GABROVO
Etâr Етър
☎ 066

Prince Charles would approve of Etâr, an appealing bucolic complex of traditional artisans living as if the 20th century hadn't happened. Centred around the interesting **Etâr Ethnographic Village Museum** (☎ 801 831; www.etar .hit.bg; admission 7 lv; ☯ 8.30am-6pm), about 8km southeast of Gabrovo, this is a great trip

for anyone interested in Bulgarian crafts and the traditional Balkan way of life. First opened in 1964, this open-air museum contains nearly 50 shops and workshops. The village is designed in a style typical of the Bulgarian national revival period (19th century) and spreads over seven hectares of grass and trees. Artisans – such as bakers, cartwrights, cobblers, furriers, glass workers, hatters, jewellers, leather workers, millers, potters and weavers – practise their trades and sell their wares, some in workshops powered by water from a stream running through the complex.

There are entrances at the northern side (near the Hotel Strannopriemnitsa) and at the administration building in the middle. There is another entrance at the far southern side, near the major car park. The ticket is valid for one day (you can go in and out of the complex as often as you like on that day). Guided tours (in English, French or German) are available for 7 lv per person (minimum of five people).

A special time to visit is on **Fair Day** (14 October), which features traditional dance and music, including *kavals* (wooden flutes) made in the complex.

The *Gabrovo* map, published by Domino and available in Gabrovo, includes a detailed map of the complex.

SLEEPING & EATING

Hotel Perla (☎ 801 984; Etâr; r 44 lv) The Perla has very friendly English-speaking management and is the best deal in town, even though it doesn't have any singles (single travellers can get a double here for less than a single at the Strannopriemnitsa nevertheless). The rooms are huge and contain a TV, balcony and a very decent bathroom. Breakfast is not included and costs an extra 3 lv per person in the downstairs café.

Hotel Strannopriemnitsa (☎ 801 831; Etâr; s/d/tr incl breakfast 48/78/106 lv) At the northern (Gabrovo) end of the complex, this hotel is a little touristy, but not bad value. The doubles have balconies with views (of the less interesting part of the complex), but the singles are tiny and don't have balconies. All rooms have TV.

Restaurant Strannopriemnitsa (Etâr; mains 5 lv) Downstairs in the hotel of the same name, this *mehana* boasts interesting décor (complete with several deer antlers!) but the food is ordinary and overpriced. The service is good, however, and the outdoor tables overlook the grass and trees.

Renaissance Tavern (Etår; mains from 5.50 lv) Inside the museum complex, this tourist-oriented place charges twice as much as a normal village restaurant, but the food is tasty and the setting is charming.

The bakery inside the complex sells basic takeaway food, such as glazed *simit* buns (a local speciality), which can be enjoyed while sitting on the grass by the stream.

GETTING THERE & AWAY
Bus Nos 1, 7 and 8 go directly to the complex from along ul Aprilov in Gabrovo. Alternatively, catch one of the hourly buses between Gabrovo and Kazanlâk, get off at the turnoff (signposted in English) and walk (exactly 2km). A taxi from Gabrovo costs about 5 lv one way. You can carry on directly from here to Tryavna by taxi for about 15 lv, saving the trouble of bussing via Gabrovo.

TRYAVNA ТРЯВНА
☎ 0677 / pop 12,200
This charming town about 40km southwest of Veliko Târnovo makes for an excellent day trip. Already a big draw and working hard to attract more tourists, sleepy Tryavna has been impressively improved by the Beautiful Bulgaria Project and charms with its mixture of national revival period homes, quaint stone bridges and cobblestone streets. It is far less touristy than Arbanasi, costs nothing to wander around (unlike the complex at

Etår) and prices for everything are reasonable. Tryavna was, and to a lesser degree still is, renowned for its handicrafts, especially woodcarving.

Orientation
Helpful municipal maps are available at the Tryavna train station, at the start of ul Angel Kânchev around the corner from the train station, and opposite the Hotel Tryavna in the main square. The bus station and train station are 100m apart to the west of ul Angel Kânchev, the main road which runs through the old town and follows the curves of the train line.

Information
Bulgarian Post Bank (post office bldg, ul Angel Kânchev) The best place to change money; there's also an ATM.
Internet centre (ul Angel Kânchev 15) This reliable and cheap place is the only Internet centre.
Tourist office (☎ 2247; www.tryavna.bg; ul Angel Kânchev 22; ☼ 9am-noon & 2-5pm Mon-Fri) In the post office building and run by a friendly team of English-speakers. It can help with bus and train schedules, and will arrange private rooms.

Sights
It's easy to see everything in Tryavna on a short walking tour (allow two to three hours). From the bus station, head east (away from the train line) and then turn right along ul Angel Kânchev. The impressive **St Georgi Church** (ul Angel Kânchev 128; ☼ 7.30am-12.30pm & 2.30-5.30pm) is on the left. It was built between 1848 and 1852, and

---

WOODCARVING

During the Bulgarian national revival period, Tryavna became renowned for the quality and quantity of its woodcarvings, often intricately chiselled from local walnut, birch, poplar and oak trees. Many carvings from Tryavna were used to decorate monasteries in Gabrovo, Veliko Târnovo, Arbanasi and Rila, and carvers were sought after by builders and house owners as far away as Serbia, Turkey and modern-day Iran.

By the early 19th century, over 40 workshops in Tryavna were churning out wooden cradles, frames, icons, friezes, doors and crosses. Each design was individual, but most included the type of ornate and detailed flower motifs which became known as the 'Tryavna school' of woodcarving. Some of the most beautiful exhibits include the 'sun ceiling' inside the Daskalov House in Tryavna (see p173), which is also home to the Museum of Woodcarving & Icon Painting.

In an attempt to resurrect the tradition, courses in the Tryavna school of woodcarving are offered to tourists. Courses for one/two/three days (six hours per day) cost 35/60/80 lv, and can be arranged through the tourist office (p172) or the Staroto Shkolo school (p173). Every even-numbered year, the school also hosts the International Woodcarving Competition. Details are available from the tourist office in Tryavna.

features some worthwhile icons and carvings. Further down on the right is the **Angel Kânchev House-Museum** (☎ 2278; ul Angel Kânchev 39; admission 2 lv; ☽ 8am-6pm Apr-Oct, to 5pm Nov-Mar). Built in 1805, it contains exhibits about revolutionary hero Kânchev, and the liberation of Tryavna during the Russian–Turkish War (1877–78). Guides are available from the Shkolo.

Walk over the bridge, past the shady park and head right (still along ul Angel Kânchev) to pl Kapitan Dyado Nikola. First built in 1814 in the classic Bulgarian national revival period style, this picturesque square is dominated by a **clock tower** (1844) that chimes loudly on the hour. Facing the square is **Staroto Shkolo**, the town's old school that was built in 1836 and having been fully restored now houses the **Tryavna Museum School of Painting** (☎ 2517, 2039; adult/student 2/1 lv), which is well worth a visit. Also overlooking the square is the **St Archangel Michael's Church** (admission free; ☽ 8am-4.30pm), the oldest church in town. Burnt down by the Turks but rebuilt in 1819, it boasts some of the intricate woodcarvings for which the town is famous. It also houses a great little **Museum of Icons** (admission 1 lv; ☽ 9am-5pm) illustrating the history of Bulgarian icon painting and well worth the modest entry fee.

Continue over the stone **Arch Bridge** (1844) to ul PR Slaveikov, one of the nicest cobblestone streets in Bulgaria. On the left is **Daskalov House** (☎ 2166; ul PR Slaveikov 27a; adult/student 2/1 lv; ☽ 9am-6pm Apr-Oct, to 5pm Nov-Mar). Built between 1804 and 1808, this home, set behind a large wall and in front of a pretty garden, also contains the fascinating **Museum of Woodcarving & Icon Painting**. One of a kind in Bulgaria, the museum features some superb examples of the 'Tryavna school' of woodcarving. Ask for the informative leaflet (in English). The mounted wood portraits and figures are particularly impressive.

Housed in a former chapel, there's a second, larger **Museum of Icons** (☎ 3753; ul Breza 1; admission 2 lv; ☽ 8am-4.30pm) containing over 160 religious icons from famous local families. The museum is on the other side of the train line; follow the signs to the right from along ul PR Slaveikov.

Back on ul PR Slaveikov is the **Slaveikov House-Museum** (☎ 2166; ul PR Slaveikov 50; admission 2 lv; ☽ 8am-noon & 1-6pm Wed-Sun). Petko Slaveikov

and his son Pencho were renowned poets who lived in this house for many years. Further down on the left is the **Summer Garden Kalinchev House** (☎ 3694; ul PR Slaveikov 45; admission 1.50 lv; ☽ 9am-1pm & 2-6pm Mon-Fri). This house, built in 1830, features a charming courtyard **café** (☽ 8am-11pm) and 500 works by Bulgarian artists, including Kalinchev. More paintings, drawings and sculptures can be found next door in the **Ivan Kolev House** (☎ 3777; ul PR Slaveikov 47; admission 2 lv; ☽ 9am-1pm & 2-6pm Mon-Fri).

Sleeping

Several homes and shops along the first 200m of ul Angel Kânchev from the bus station offer rooms for rent. The tourist office can also arrange rooms in private homes (including in the old town) for about 18 lv to 22 lv per person including breakfast.

Hotel Tigara (☎ 2469; ul D Gorov 7a; s/d 25/40 lv) The Tiger Hotel is a friendly place a short walk from the Hotel Tryavna; look for the signs in English. Run by a delightful family who'll make you feel at home immediately, it's the best value in town. Rooms are clean and comfortable, but ask for the newer ones at the back. Breakfast costs 4 lv.

Komplex Brâshlyan (☎ 3019; bungalows 36 lv, d 40-60 lv) Another good option, the Brâshlyan overlooks the town from a shady spot north of the centre; its bigger rooms have huge leather sofas and balconies. There's a restaurant and outdoor deck for afternoon cocktails. Cross the tracks past the old bridge, and head up and to the right.

Hotel Tryavna (☎ 3448; fax 2598; ul Angel Kânchev 46; r 40 lv) While this is a bad deal for single travellers who have to pay the full price of a double, the newly upgraded ex-Balkantourist hotel is decent value now, being excellently located and offering comfortable standards of accommodation, if still furnished in rather Soviet browns and preglasnost oranges.

Hotel Family (☎ /fax 4691; ul Angel Kânchev 40; s/d 45/60 lv) Excellently located and with clean and smart rooms, this family-run place is still not particularly good value for foreigners compared to the Tigara. All rooms have TV and most have balconies.

Hotel Ralitsa (☎ 2262; fax 2402; hotelralica@mbox .digsys.bg; ul Kaleto; s/d incl breakfast 45/65 lv) This three-star place is set in the hills to the south of town. (Take a taxi, because it's a steep walk.) The rooms are large and have TV, and most doubles feature a balcony with great views. Book ahead on weekends in summer because it's popular with trendsetters from Gabrovo. A classy restaurant is attached.

Zograf Inn (☎ 4970/80; zograf@mbox.dgsys.bg; ul PR Slaveikov 1; s/d/apt 44/80/110 lv) Right in the heart of historic Tryavna, the Zograf is charmingly located in an old building complete with a traditional *mehana*. The rooms are not as rustic as you'd expect from the exterior: they are modern, spotless and not bad value at this price.

Hotel Seasons (☎ 2285; www.tryavna.bg/web /seasons; ul Kâncho Skorchev 11; s/d 70/100 lv; **P** 🖳 🕱) This is the local luxury option, playing host to weekending Sofians with its very smart facilities that include a large outdoor pool, sauna and Jacuzzi. The rooms are the smartest in town and walking tours in the local hills are organised for guests. Not a good option unless you have your own transport though, as there's a very steep hill to negotiate to get here.

Eating

Starata Loza (ul PR Slaveikov 44; mains 3.50 lv) The Old Vine is opposite the entrance to Daskalov House, and is probably the most enticing of the several restaurants along this cobblestone street. Although set up for the tourist crowd, prices are pleasingly reasonable. The menu is in English.

Gostilintsa (ul PR Slaveikov 35; mains 4 lv) Almost diagonally opposite the Starata Loza, this classy place is uninvitingly located behind a wooden door. The service is excellent, the meals are not too expensive and the menu is in English.

Zograf Mehana (ul PR Slaveikov 1; mains 5 lv) The traditional-style restaurant in the hotel of the same name is just off the main square and serves a reliable range of Bulgarian staples.

Getting There & Away

Pretty much all public transport to Tryavna goes via Gabrovo: all day long between every 30 minutes and an hour there's a minibus connecting the two (1.50 lv, 30 minutes). For anywhere else, get a connection in Gabrovo. Tryavna is along a rarely used spur track, and even when the nine passenger trains a day are running (2.50 lv, 50 minutes) they're infuriatingly slow.

DRYANOVO MONASTERY
ДРЯНОВСКИ МАНАСТИР
☎ 0676

Delightfully located under limestone cliffs only 5.5km from the town of Dryanovo is the charming **Dryanovo Monastery** (admission free; 🕑 7am-10pm). Originally built in the 12th century, the monastery was alternately destroyed by Turks and rebuilt by Bulgarians several times in the subsequent 500 years. The **Holy Archangel & Michael Church** was added to the monastery in 1861. The monks here are exceptionally friendly and eager to chat with tourists.

Like several other monasteries, it provided sanctuary to the revolutionary leader, Vasil Levski, and his insurgents. Later, during the Russian–Turkish War (1877–78), more than 100 locals hid in the monastery and fought against the Turks for nine days. The Turks eventually invaded the monastery and burnt down everything they could see, so most of what remains has been rebuilt since. This act of bravery is commemorated with a **mausoleum** in the monastery grounds.

Inside the Komplex Vodopadi (p175) is a **Historical Museum** (☎ 2097; admission 3 lv; 🕑 8.45am-12.30pm & 1-4.45pm Mon-Fri, 9.45am-3.45pm Sat & Sun). Not surprisingly, most displays feature the 1876 April Uprising and 1877–78 war. In particular note the large and macabre collection of skulls. Downstairs are artefacts from nearby caves, including Bacho Kiro, and some religious icons. All captions are in Bulgarian.

From the bridge near the car park, a 400m path leads through a pretty forest to the 1200m-long **Bacho Kiro cave** (admission 3 lv; 🕑 8.30am-6pm Apr-Oct, 10am-4pm Nov-Mar), inhabited during the Palaeolithic era. It's reasonably well set up, but not as exciting as other caves in Bulgaria.

BARET, with help from the Association Stara Planina tourist office in Dryanovo, has established the **Dryanovo Ecotrail**. This well-marked, circular, four-hour trail starts and finishes near the monastery, and passes through scenic forests. To find the start of the trail, ask at the Mehana Mecha Dupka (see next section) or Bacho Kiro cave. Otherwise, contact the tourist office in **Dryanovo** (☎ 2106) or the **Bacho Kiro Tourist Society** (☎ 2332), which may be able to arrange local rock-climbing and caving trips.

Sleeping & Eating

It's possible to stay in the simple **monastery rooms** (per person with shared bathroom 10 lv) for your own taste of monastic life.

Komplex Vodopadi (☎ 2314; d/apt 24/48 lv) Virtually attached to the monastery, this place offers several small but clean rooms. Many have huge balconies that overlook the monastery. The apartments are a little larger and have TV, but are not worth twice as much.

Motini Skali (☎ 2471; d incl breakfast 25 lv) Anywhere else, this place opposite the monastery gates would be heartily recommended, but the Vodopadi is better value. The apartments here contain a TV, fridge and balcony. All rates include breakfast.

About 100m from the car park along the path to the cave is the delightful riverside Mehana Mecha Dupka restaurant.

Getting There & Away

If requested, buses travelling between Veliko Târnovo and Gabrovo will stop at the turn-off to the monastery (4km south of Dryanovo). It's another 1.5km walk from there. Those with cars pay 1 lv to park.

LOVECH ЛОВЕЧ

☎ 068 / pop 49,000

Lovech is an extremely picturesque town that is popular with Bulgarian weekenders but still relatively untouched by foreign travellers. It is pleasantly located alongside the Osêm River 35km south of Pleven. Lovech has obviously benefited greatly from the Beautiful Bulgaria Project, especially in Varosha (the old town) where over 150 glorious buildings from the Bulgarian national revival period have been lovingly restored. The river has a covered bridge – the town's pride and its most enduring symbol.

During the Thracian and Roman eras, and the Second Bulgarian Empire (1185–1396), Lovech was economically and militarily important. The town reached its zenith during the Ottoman occupation, even though it was also the headquarters of the Bulgarian Central Revolutionary Committee during the mid-19th century.

Orientation & Information

The bus and train station are adjacent to each other quite a walk from the town centre. Walk along ul Tsacho Shishkov, veer to the right and follow the signs (in Eng-lish) to *centrum*. At the end of the road, turn left along ul Bulgaria to the modern town, where the banks, foreign-exchange offices and post office are huddled around the main square, pl Dimitrov. Alternatively, turn right past colourful, renovated buildings, and the Hotel Lovech, to the covered footbridge and nearby vehicle bridge leading to the old town.

Sights

Just past the Hotel Lovech is the **pokritiyat most** (covered footbridge), which is the only one of its kind in the Balkans. Built in 1872, and completely restored twice since, it now features a charming wooden exterior again. Inside there are lots of arts and crafts shops as well as a couple of cafés. If you pass through the square beyond the bridge, you'll arrive at the **Art Gallery** (☎ 23937; ul Vasil Levski 9; admission free; 9am-midday & 1-6pm Mon-Sat). It features works by local and other Bulgarian artists.

From all over the old town the fascinating, and surprisingly extensive, ruins of the **Hisar Fortress** (admission free; 8am-6pm) are visible. It was here that a treaty was signed with the Turks, which lead to the creation of the Second Bulgarian Empire. Its dramatic position affords some good views and it's a wonderful place to explore, a 10- to 15-minute walk up the hillside from the Varosha.

From near the art gallery, the cobblestone ul Hristo Ivanov Golemia, heads uphill. About 100m along is the **Ethnographical Museum** (☎ 27720; admission 3 lv, photos an extra 3 lv; 8am-noon & 2-5pm Mon-Sat). The two mid-19th-century buildings contain several fascinating exhibits and period furniture, but the highlight is probably the wine-making equipment in the dark cellar. Ask the caretaker for a (free) leaflet with explanations in English, French or German.

About 50m further up is the **Vasil Levski Museum** (☎ 27990; admission 2 lv; 9am-5pm Mon-Fri), with extensive displays about the revered revolutionary. Another 50m uphill is the renovated Byzantine **St Bogoroditsa Church**. If it's not open, you can wander around the grounds and peer through the windows.

From the church, the easy-to-see series of steps pass more renovated **national revival homes** and lead to **Stratesh Hill**, often carpeted with lilac blooms and home to a huge **Levski statue**.

Sleeping & Eating

There are a surprising number of pleasant hotels in Lovech. The best of the bunch overlook the river and are family-run places of some charm.

Hotel Tsariana (☎ 600 995; tsariana@mbox.digsys .bg; pl Todor Kirkov 10; s/d 24/30) Formerly known as the Orbita-2, the spruced up Tsariana is a decent place to stay with perfectly fine rooms, although lacking any of the atmosphere of the smaller guesthouses. It's on the main square of the Varosha, and the café life can be noisy in the evenings.

Hotel Varosha 2003 (☎ 22277; ul Ivan Drasov 23; s/ d/ste/apt 30/30/50/60 lv; P) This hugely popular place has to be the first choice for anyone staying in Lovech. Having just five spacious and well-equipped rooms means that while you need to book ahead in summer, you feel like personal guests of the owners. The friendly owners will make you feel very much at home, serving you breakfast in the garden and delicious home cooking in the evenings. Its quiet riverside location adds to its charm.

Hotel Oasis (☎ 26239; ul NV Drasov 17; s/d 25/50 lv) Overlooking the river, this quiet and homely guesthouse offers clean, comfortable rooms with TVs and heaps of furniture. Follow the signs (100m) from the vehicle bridge. A decent restaurant is attached, although some rooms can be a little noisy in the evenings from the music playing downstairs.

Hotel Lovech (☎ 604 717; ul Târgovska 12; r 65 lv) Overpriced certainly, the revamped Hotel Lovech was once the Balkantourist, but it has made good efforts to overcome this and is now a well-run and friendly place. It's in the centre of town by the footbridge.

Mehana Gallereya (ul Vasil Levski, Varosha; mains 3 lv) Located next to the eponymous Art Gallery, the Gallereya is a large courtyard restaurant with efficient service and very tasty food.

Mehana Billaya (ul Marni Poplukanov, Varosha; mains 4 lv) Up the cobbled street from the Galleraya, the Billaya is an equally charming courtyard *mehana*, although it does have ongoing loud live-music performances during the evenings which can make conversation a little strained.

There are a large number of cafés and brasseries on pl Todor Kirkov, the centre of the Varosha. This is where social life is concentrated in the evenings and it's a great place to hang out.

Getting There & Away

From the **bus station** (☎ 23204), there's an hourly connection to Troyan (2.50 lv) on the hour from 7am to 7pm. Three buses a day head further afield to Burgas, Sliven, Teteven and Veliko Târnovo, and more frequently to Kazanlâk. Buses also leave every hour for Pleven (3 lv, one hour). Six buses travel to Sofia (11 lv, three hours) every day; there are also two connections a day to Vratsa via Cherven Bryag.

Lovech is on an inconvenient spur track from the main Sofia–Varna train line, via Pleven. From the **train station** (☎ 24935), three slow passenger trains depart daily for Troyan, and another three go to Levski, where connections are possible to Sofia and Gora Oryakhovitsa (to get to Veliko Târnovo).

TROYAN ТРОЯН

☎ 0670 / pop 26,200

There's a quiet charm about Troyan, mostly known due to the proximity of the monastery of the same name, Bulgaria's third most important. If the town itself was any more laid-back, time would probably stand still here, but while it's not a very happening place, it's very pleasant to wander around. Even the deeply Soviet main square has a relaxed atmosphere fuelled by its indolent coffee drinkers taking in the afternoon sun. As well as visiting the Troyan Monastery (see next page), Oreshak, Lovech and Karlovo are easy half-day trips that can be made from here, as well as being near to some excellent hiking paths in the Stara Planina.

Troyan was strategically important in the Thracian period. It later became famous for woodcarving, metalwork and particularly pottery during the Bulgarian national revival period. Examples of these crafts can be admired at the charming museum in Troyan, or bought at Oreshak.

Orientation

The bus and train stations are on the right bank of the Bely Osâm River, whereas the town centre is on the left bank. Walk (300m) over the footbridge along ul Zahari Stoyanov. From here, turn right and walk along the mall, ul General Kartsov, to Troyan's main square, pl Vûzhrazhdane. The narrow main road, ul Vasil Levski, starts north of the square and hugs the river.

Information

Run by a friendly group of ladies, one of whom speaks good English, the Troyan **tourist office** (☎ 35064; infotroyan@yahoo.com; ul Vasil Levski 133; ☉ 8am-8pm summer, 9am-5pm Mon-Fri winter) is excellent. As well as arranging numerous activities, such as horse riding, the TIC also provides hiking maps, organises private rooms and arranges car rental from 35 lv per day.

Sights

The only real sight in town is the impressive **Museum of Folk Craft & Applied Arts** (☎ 22063; pl Vûzhrazhdane; admission 2 lv; ☉ 9am-5pm Mon-Fri). The 10 halls contain displays about textiles, woodcarving, metalwork, weaving, pottery and ceramics from the region, as well as some archaeological artefacts. Most captions are in English. There's also a **History Museum** next door (the two buildings flank the bridge); you have to ask at the Folk Craft Museum and they'll open it for you for an extra 2 lv.

Activities

A range of activities can be arranged through the tourist office. **Horse riding** (15 lv per person per hour) is possible at one of several villages near Troyan. **Mountain bikes** can be rented (1/8 lv per hour/day) and used along one of five designated mountain-bike routes, including to Troyan Monastery and Chiflik. Guides (40 lv per day), who speak French, German or English, are available for local tours and hikes.

Sleeping & Eating

The tourist office can arrange rooms in private homes in Troyan as well as in nearby villages such as Oreshak (p177). The cost is 11 to 15 lv per person, usually with breakfast. The tourist office also offers apartments in central Troyan with kitchen facilities, sitting room and bathroom for 35 lv to 45 lv per double.

All the hotels in town were undergoing renovations at the time of research, but that means that there should soon be some very good accommodation in town.

Hotel Panorama (☎ 22930; hotelpanoramatr@mail .bg; Park Kâpincho) Formerly the Hotel Kâpina, the Panorama is located in the hillside park above the town. It was due to reopen in 2005 at the time of writing. Take a taxi (1 lv) from the bus station or town centre.

Hotel Nunki (☎ 22160; ul Minko Radkovski) Also being revamped, the rooms here are large, quiet and lovingly decorated with charming national revival–style furniture, and the bathrooms sparkle. Attached is a classy restaurant with reasonable prices. The Nunki is at the start of the bridge (from where the road leads to Troyan Monastery) about 100m across from the tourist office.

For a snack, try one of the several pizza joints where ul Vasil Levski and pl Vûzhrazhdane meet.

Getting There & Away

From the **Troyan bus station** (☎ 62172), there's one daily bus to Sofia at 2pm (7 lv, three hours); every hour buses also go to Lovech (2 lv, 45 minutes), from where there are immediate connections to Pleven. There's also one direct bus a day to Pleven and three buses a day to Chiflik. For those going to Troyan Monastery, take the half-hourly to hourly bus for Cherny Osâm and ask to be dropped off at the gates (the bus goes right past). Troyan is at the end of a spur track south of Lovech, so travelling by train is futile.

AROUND TROYAN

Oreshak Орешак

About 6km southeast of Troyan is Oreshak, home of the **National Fair and Exhibition of Arts & Crafts Complex** (☎ 06952-2317; ☉ 8am-6pm Tue-Sun). This complex displays and sells embroidery, pottery, ceramics, weaving, woodcarving and metalwork. It is the best place in the Stara Planina region to pick up authentic, locally made souvenirs at reasonable prices. The week-long annual fair (usually around mid-August) is held at the complex. Another cheerful time to be in Oreshak is during the **Festival of the Plums and Plum Brandy** (late September).

Oreshak is an alternative place to stay to Troyan, and not far (4km) by bus or on foot from the Troyan Monastery. The tourist office in Troyan (see p177) can arrange rooms in private homes for about 18 lv per person including breakfast. Guests in these private homes can also order large servings of traditional meals for an extra cost.

Every hour a ramshackle bus (1 lv, 20 minutes) leaves the bus station in Troyan for Cherni Osêm, and stops at Oreshak and the Troyan Monastery.

Troyan Monastery Троянски Манастир
Only 10km southeast of Troyan is Bulgaria's third-largest **monastery** (admission free, photos 5 lv, video 15 lv; ☻ 6am-10pm) after Rila (p91) and Bachkovo (p130). Troyan stands out, however, as having some of the most powerful and disturbing frescos anywhere in the country, the work of Bulgarian master Zahari Zograf, regarded as the leading mural artist during the Bulgarian national revival period. It's a charming place and one of the highlights of central Bulgaria, even though an hour will suffice to look around the complex.

Some sections of this 16th-century monastery survived numerous attacks by the Turks between the 16th and 18th centuries, but most of what still stands today was built in 1835. The colourful murals inside the **Church of the Holy Virgin** were painted in the 1840s by Zahari Zograf. The church is very poorly lit, so it's hard to see the detail of the frescos inside. Luckily, however, the very best of Zograf's frescoes are outside on the back wall. They depict Judgment Day, the apocalypse and hell and are truly remarkable. Some of the images, including the seven-headed fire-breathing dragon and the torture of sinners in hell by demons will affect even the most devoutly atheist.

The monastery is also renowned for its remarkable woodcarvings, including the altar, created in the mid-19th century by experts from Tryavna. The highlight for most, though, is the legendary Three-Handed Holy Virgin, only seen in public during the annual monastery celebrations on **Virgin Mary's Day** (15 August).

The ubiquitous revolutionary Vasil Levski formed and trained insurgents at the monastery and even cajoled the monks here to join the fight against the Turks in 1876. This rather irreverent history is highlighted in the small, separate **museum** (adults/children 4/2 lv) on the 3rd floor. The museum door is usually locked, but you can ask someone at the reception office inside the gate to open it.

Although Troyan Monastery is not nearly as touristy as famous Rila Monastery (p91), several businesses have sprung up in and around the Troyan Monastery, including several cafés, souvenir shops and art galleries.

Visit the reception office if you want to stay in one of the basic rooms. These cost 10/20/30 lv for singles/doubles/triples with a shared bathroom.

There's a very good *mehana* next to the monastery serving up delicious food (mains 3 lv) in a wonderful location overlooking the river.

Every hour the ramshackle bus between Troyan and Cherni Osêm stops at the monastery gates. A taxi from central Troyan to the monastery costs about 5 lv for a one-way trip. Most taxi drivers will happily come back in an hour or two to take you back to Troyan.

Black Sea Coast

HIGHLIGHTS

- **History**
  Peer into the past at magnificent
  Nesebâr (p197).

- **Dining**
  Eat up the atmosphere in Varna's
  superb Paraklisa restaurant (p209).

- **Swimming**
  Take to the waters at Sinemorets and
  its two gorgeous beaches (p196).

- **Bird-watching**
  Spy on the winged inhabitants of
  Burgas Lakes (p187).

- **Green Haven**
  Explore the sublime botanical gardens
  at Balchik (p217).

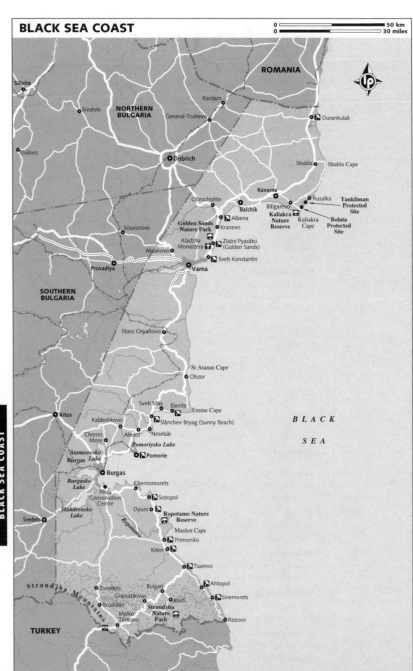

BLACK SEA COAST

It's no surprise that when you mention Bulgaria to most people, they automatically think of its coastline; after all, it attracts vast numbers of holiday-makers from all over Europe and is a serious rival to Greece and Spain for tourist numbers. Far from being black (the sea's name comes from the dangers associated with crossing it in ancient times), clean azure waters lap vast swaths of superb sandy beaches – most of which swarm with package tourists from across Europe during summer.

Over the past decade the Black Sea coast has been transforming itself from a Soviet workers' summer paradise to an exceptionally good value, Western-standard alternative to the expensive resorts of the Mediterranean. The region is used to package tourists who often fly in and out without seeing anything beyond one of the big resorts, although there's great scope for independent travellers here too – including the empty beaches to the south and north, the Strandzha Nature Park, the Burgas Lakes, several marvellous historic towns and one of Bulgaria's most pleasant cities, the unofficial regional capital of Varna. Don't allow preconceptions of cheap family package tours to put you off this, one of Bulgaria's most enchanting regions.

Climate

In summer, the climate is warm and mild, so it's obviously the best – and the busiest – time to visit. The average temperature is a warm 23°C, but sea breezes keep it cool. During winter the temperature rarely drops below freezing, but at least once a season a storm (or three) howls in from the Black Sea and buries the coast in snow.

LIFE'S A BEACH

Every day during summer, lifeguards work between 8am and 6pm at the resorts and popular beaches; they usually rescue a few tourists who ignore the warnings and don't swim between the flags. It is extremely important to pay attention to the warnings on the Black Sea – there are often very strong currents at play and there are several fatalities every year.

Topless bathing is acceptable at the major resorts, but less so elsewhere.

Top Five Beaches For...

- Pristine coast: Sinemorets (p196)
- Urban swimming: Varna (p203)
- Good water sports: Pomorie (p196)
- Endless fun: Slânchev Bryag (p202)
- Up-for-it crowds: Albena (p214)

SOUTHERN COAST

BURGAS БУРГАС

☎ 056 / pop 210,000

Most people arrive on the Bulgarian Black Sea at this busy economic centre, whether it be flying in to its busy airport on one of hundreds of summer charter flights or at the tail end of a long train journey from the Stara Planina. While the Black Sea's cultural capital (and most pleasant city) is doubtlessly Varna (p203), Burgas has plenty to merit a visit and staying for a few days allows you to visit lots of the Black Sea's best attractions.

Though less of a ghost town out of season than many of the coastal towns and resorts, Burgas is never better than during summer when its main pedestrian precinct and beachside promenade positively ache with scantily clad young holiday-makers out for as much fun as possible.

A slightly less carnally orientated crowd comes to Burgas for the four lakes around it that are havens for abundant bird life (see p187).

History

The area was inhabited for centuries by the Thracians before the Greeks came in the 2nd century AD and built the city of Pirgos

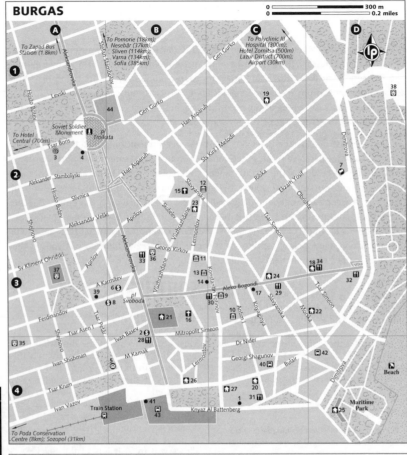

BURGAS

(Greek for 'tower'), from which the name Burgas originated. Later, the Romans invaded, fortified existing walls and expanded the city, which they renamed Debeltus. Most of what remains in present-day Burgas dates from the 17th century, when fisher folk from Pomorie and Sozopol settled in the area and called the city Burgas. The city grew quickly after the completion of the railway from Plovdiv (1890) and the development of the port (1903).

Orientation
Burgas is pleasingly compact, so almost everything, save a few hotels, is within walking distance. The train station and the main Yug bus station are both located centrally, about 250m from the main pedestrian mall, ul Aleksandrovska, which links the Burgas University in the north to centre of the city. About halfway along ul Aleksandrovska, another mall, ul Aleko Bogoridi, heads eastwards towards Maritime Park.

MAPS
The *Burgas* map (1:10,500), published by Domino, is detailed but is in Cyrillic only. Less thorough, but still adequate for most visitors, is the *Bourgas City Guide*, published by Makros in English and German and distinguishable by its blue-and-yellow cover. Both maps are available at any bookstall in the city.

Information
BOOKSHOPS
Bel Canto Bookshop (ul Knyaz Al Battenberg) Small shop by the train station offering an excellent variety of books, as well as postcards and souvenirs.
Helikon Bookshop (ul Aleksandrovska) Near the university, this bookshop is one of the best in Bulgaria, selling a wide range of books and local, regional and international maps.

INTERNET ACCESS
There are Internet cafés all over town; two of the best established are as follows:
ENet Internet Agency (ul Tsar Boris) This air-conditioned place can be found near the university.
Internet Club (ul Georgi Kirkov) This dark and dingy centre is in the Cinema Septembri building.

MONEY
Numerous foreign exchange offices can be found along ul Aleksandrovska and ul Aleko

Bogoridi. **Bulbank** (ul Aleksandrovska) has an ATM that accepts all major credit cards. Banks that change cash and travellers cheques, and have ATMs, are **United Bulgarian Bank** (cnr ul Ferdinandov & ul Aleksandrovska) and **Raffeisen Bank** (ul Ferdinandov).

POST
Long-distance telephone calls can be made from any number of booths and telephone centres along the two malls.
Post office (ul Tsar Petâr)

TRAVEL AGENCIES
Most travel agencies in Burgas cater to Bulgarian tourists, but there's no reason why foreigners can't join an organised tour. Many agencies offer all-inclusive two-day trips to Istanbul for €60 per person (but only in summer).
Tourist Services Bulgaria (☎ 840 601; Hotel Bulgaria, ul Aleksandrovska 21) Knowledgeable and helpful English-speaking staff. It can arrange tours, car rental and long-distance (but not international) bus tickets.

Sights
STS CYRIL & METHODIUS CHURCH
The city's main **church** (ul Vûzhrazhdane; admission free; ☾ 8am-5pm) is a delightful and impressive place, with its frescoes almost totally renovated (there's just one corner still waiting to be done and currently home to several families of birds). Don't be dressed for the beach if you visit, as it's still the city's main place of worship, although tourists are quite welcome.

ARCHAEOLOGICAL MUSEUM
Located incongruously along the modern mall is the **Archaeological Museum** (☎ 843 541; ul Aleko Bogoridi 21; adult/student 2/1 lv; ☾ 9am-5pm, closed Sun in winter). It houses a small collection of antiquities, such as Neolithic and Thracian artefacts from the 6th century BC, and various bits and pieces from the Roman period (1st to 3rd century AD). The staircase is lined with glass tanks of live reptiles, no doubt to boost sagging interest in antiquities. The highlight of the museum is probably the wooden tomb of a Thracian king, the only one found in the region. A leaflet provided by staff, and printed in English, French or German, makes the collection more interesting and is ideal for a self-guided tour.

ETHNOGRAPHICAL MUSEUM

This **museum** (☎ 842 586; ul Slavyanska 69; adult/student 2/1 lv; ☺ 9am-5pm Mon-Sat, closed Sat in winter) is pretty much the same as other ethnographical and ethnological museums throughout Bulgaria. Housed in the Brakalov House (which is an alternative name for the museum), the collection includes period furniture, regional costumes and exquisite jewellery, as well as displays about weaving, fishing, boating and traditional fire dancing. Everything is labelled in Bulgarian.

NATURAL SCIENCE MUSEUM

Of specific interest to anyone planning to visit the Strandzha Nature Park (p195), the **Natural Science Museum** (☎ 843 239; ul Konstantin Fotinov 20; adult/student 2/1 lv; ☺ 9am-5pm Mon-Sat, closed Sat in winter) offers informative displays about regional flora and fauna.

CITY HISTORY MUSEUM

The **museum** (☎ 841 815; ul Lermontov 31; adult/student 2/1 lv; ☺ 9am-6pm Mon-Fri) explains the history of Burgas. It contains 100-year-old photos of the city and beach, but is fairly uninteresting: cans of tuna even fill up the display cabinets on the top floor.

ART GALLERY

The small **gallery** (☎ 842 169; ul Mitropolit Simeon 24; adult/student 2/1 lv; ☺ 9am-noon & 2-6pm Mon-Fri) is within a synagogue that was built in 1909. It contains an eclectic collection of contemporary Bulgarian art and sculpture, as well as religious icons.

ST HACH ARMENIAN CHURCH

This quaint **church** (ul Lermontov; admission free; ☺ 6am-10pm), built in 1855, appears to almost touch the ugly Hotel Bulgaria. The interior of the church is charming.

MARITIME PARK

Burgas' showpiece is this swath of greenery running alongside the Black Sea coast. Within walking distance of the city centre, the park features manicured flowerbeds, spouting fountains, Soviet-era war memorials, modern sculptures and plenty of cafés. The park is full of bench-warming pensioners, boisterous kiddies in playgrounds, cuddling young lovers and rollerblading teenagers, and is particularly enjoyable and photogenic on a summer evening.

BEACH

Burgas' beach is a disappointment, so do your swimming and sunbathing at nearby Sozopol or Pomorie, or wait until you visit a resort such as Slânchev Bryag. Next to the port and overlooked by several rusting oil tankers, the beach has greyish sand (which contains iron, so it retains heat longer in summer) and scrappy facilities. **Paddle boats** (per hr 3 lv) are available for hire, but are really hard work if the waves are high, which is often. There's also a **water slide** (1 lv).

Activities

The **Safari Hunting & Fishing Shop** (☎ 841 432; ul Konstantin Fotinov) rents and sells fishing and snorkelling equipment, and **Triton Diving** (☎ 956 984; baracuda@abv.bg; ul Knyaginya) rents and sells scuba-diving gear. Triton is not interested in arranging diving tours for foreigners, and its staff speak no English. No fishing or diving trips along the Black Sea coast are available from Burgas, so you'll have to find a boat and then negotiate a price with the owner; your best chance is at one of the smaller villages along the southern Black Sea coast.

Festivals & Events

Iora Flower Exhibition (April & September) The Black Sea's semi-annual flower show.
Sladkopoyna Chouchouliga Festival (May) With children's choirs.
Emil Chakarov Music Festival (early July) Internationally attended classical music festival.
Burgas Sea Song Festival (July & August)
International Folklore Festival (late August) Burgas' main festival. The programme is well advertised and shows take place during the evening at the Summer Theatre in Maritime Park, at places along ul Aleksandrovska and ul Aleko Bogoridi, inside the Ethnographical Museum and around pl Troikata.
Saint's Day (6 December) The patron saint of Burgas is St Nikolai, whose saint's day is celebrated with gusto.

Sleeping

The lack of accommodation in Burgas has slowly been overcome by the steady opening of new mid-range and top-end hotels. It remains an expensive place to stay and one where it's pretty essential to book ahead in summer. Most people find private rooms the way to go here, although if you're travelling in a little more style there are plenty of decent options. Unless stated otherwise, all hotels offer private bathroom and TV.

HOTEL PRICES

All accommodation prices listed in this chapter (unless stated otherwise) are what you should expect to pay during the high season (July and August). During the shoulder season (May, June, September and October), room prices drop by up to 50% so, along with the continually good weather and greatly reduced crowds, this is the best time to visit.

BUDGET

Burgas has a few accommodation agencies that can arrange rooms with local families. However, these are often in the dreary Lazur residential district, which is not too far from the northern section of the Maritime Park and beach, but is a fair walk from the malls and cafés. If you arrive in Burgas during working hours, try one of the following three agencies, listed in order of reliability. Otherwise, book a room in advance.

Dimant (☎ 840 779; fax 843 748; ul Tsar Simeon 15; s/d 8.70/17.40 lv; ☺ 8am-10pm) A fair way from the bus and train stations, but it's the only agency open on weekends. Not all staff speak English, but they are extremely keen to help and most of their options are excellently located in the city centre.

TS Travel (☎ /fax 845 060; tstravel@ns.comnet.bg; cnr ul Konstantin Fotinov & ul Bulair; per person 10 lv; ☺ 9am-6pm Mon-Fri) Convenient to the train station, this agency offers a few private rooms and the staff speak English. The standards and amenities of the rooms, however, are nothing to get excited about.

Primorets Travel (☎ 842 727; ul Ivan Vazov; per person 12 lv; ☺ 9.30am-5.30pm Mon-Fri) In a bright blue-green building opposite the train station. Staff speak no English.

Hotel Mirazh (☎ 381 77; ul Lermontov 48; d with shared bathroom 44-49 lv) Central and clean, with large rooms (only the dearer ones have a TV). Most rooms have a balcony, plenty of seats and even a sofa, but those facing the street are noisy during the day.

Hotel Central (☎ 815 467; ul Ivailo 60; s/d/apt 44/50/60 lv) Its name is a misnomer, for the Central is in a pleasant suburb about 800m west of the university. These are some of the cheapest hotel rooms in town and are large and well furnished, with huge bathrooms. To get here, take a taxi.

Zornitsa Hotel (☎ 816 266; block 45, Zornitsa; per person 10 lv) Sleep with socialism in this out-of-the-way 1960s high-rise in the Zornitsa neighbourhood, 2km north of Burgas train station. Each room has three beds, with a shared bathroom for every two rooms. Take bus 12A from the centre. It's east of the giant grey hospital, past the football stadium.

MID-RANGE

Hotel Elite (☎ 845 779; ul Morska 35; s/d 50/56 lv; ✵) Well located and with new and comfy rooms, the Elite might be the best deal in town. Some rooms have balconies, all have phones. Avoid the cramped attic room.

Hotel Astoria (☎ 820 670; ul Sts Kiril I Metodii 38; s/d/apt 80/90/100 lv) In a quiet side street conveniently located between the promenade and the town centre, the Astoria is friendly and well run. Most rooms have balconies and all are well maintained and cosy.

Hotel Bulgaria (☎ 842 820; ul Aleksandrovska 21; renovated s/d 78/100 lv, unrenovated s/d 195/205 lv) This huge place dominates Burgas' central square and is very convenient. However, it's hard to get too excited about it; the rooms are fairly crummy and you pay so much for the renovated ones you're better off pretty much anywhere else.

TOP END

Hotel Plaza (☎ 846 294; www.plazahotel-bg.com; ul Aleko Bogoridi 42; s/d 99/146 lv; ✵) The hippest place in town and with one of the best locations, the Plaza opened in 2003 and is a popular spot with wealthy Sofia fashionistas. While the rooms don't quite live up to the promise of the lobby (which looks more like an expensive furniture shop), they are still smart and comfortable. Good weekend discounts of around 20% make Friday and Saturday good days to arrive.

Hotel Bulair (☎ 844 389; www.bulair.bulhoasting.com/bulair/bulair-eng.htm; ul Bulair 7; r 140 lv; ✵) Right in the centre of town, this converted mansion is now a very pleasant hotel with great rooms that enjoy peace and quiet despite the busy road outside. Single travellers will be financially better off at the Plaza.

Hotel Primorets (☎ 842 045; fax 842 934; ul Knyaz Al Battenberg 2; s/d 90/108 lv) Despite the good location fronting Maritime Park, the Primorets is a little overpriced. All rooms have balconies (some, at 120 lv, have good sea views) and most have new bathrooms.

Eating & Drinking

The best cafés are in Maritime Park, particularly those overlooking the Black Sea. Other inviting places for a drink and/or snack are along ul Aleko Bogoridi, particularly along the upper (eastern) end, and along ul Aleksandrovska, especially near the corner of ul Georgi Kirkov.

RESTAURANTS

National Restaurant & Tavern (ul Filip Kutev 6; soups 1.50 lv, meals 3-6 lv; 24hr) The chefs inside this authentically decorated Bulgarian national revival period building offer a huge array of national dishes and cuisine from all around Europe. Very few restaurants in Burgas have such a traditional or cosy feel – this one is a winner.

Marakas (ul Aleko Bogoridi 19; meals from 2.50 lv; 7am-midnight) Always busy, this excellent place on the main pedestrian strip serves up superb battered calamari as well as the usual Bulgarian favourites. Its staff are extremely friendly and this is a great place to come any time of day and watch the world go by.

Panorama Restaurant (ul Aleksandrovska 21; salads 2.50 lv, meals 8-12 lv) On the 17th floor of Hotel Bulgaria, this aptly named restaurant offers the best views along the Black Sea coast, especially at sunset. The menu features both Bulgarian and international cuisine and service is excellent, although it's definitely on the pricey side.

Nov Shanhai (☎ 843 105; ul Aleko Bogoridi 61; mains 2.50-6 lv; 11am-midnight) One of several popular choices at the eastern end of ul Aleko Bogoridi, this authentic Chinese restaurant serves heaping platters, including many veg options.

Pub Bar & Grill (ul Georgi Kirkov; grills 3.50-5 lv) This is obviously a clone of the popular nationwide chain Happy Bar & Grill, but the meals here are not quite as delicious. It offers a handy 'photo menu', featuring pictures of all available meals, which makes ordering considerably easier.

Restaurant Porto Rico (ul Aleko Bogoridi; meals about 3.50 lv) In a nicer section of the extensive mall, the Porto Rico has a pleasant setting, cheap and tasty food and a menu also in German.

QUICK EATS

A couple of stalls near the western end of ul Aleko Bogoridi sell tasty takeaway doner

kebabs and pizzas, ideal for munching on while enjoying the sea breezes in Maritime Park.

BMS (ul Aleksandrovska; meals about 2.50 lv) Popular BMS offers cafeteria-style service and huge dollops of Bulgarian food. It's one of those cheap and cheerful places where you can simply point at what you want, pay, eat and enjoy.

Fast Food Beit (ul Aleko Bogoridi; meals from 2 lv) The signs (in English) on the notice board and window list a decent range of Continental and Asian food at reasonable prices. This casual outdoor eatery is ideal for vegetarians who don't want to resort to yet another salad.

Entertainment

In summer, nightclubs and bars materialise among the trees of Maritime Park. The centre of activity is often the **Summer Theatre** (☎ 842 814). The Hotel Bulgaria (p185) has a casino that offers 'free food and drinks' to patrons – but probably only to those losing money. The Art Gallery (p184) sometimes features piano recitals.

Cinema Septembri (ul Georgi Kirkov; tickets about 3 lv) shows recent films every evening. For something a bit more sophisticated, find out what's on offer at the **Adriana Boudevska Drama Theatre** (☎ 841 524; ul Tsar Asen I 35) or the **Opera & Ballet Theatre** (☎ 843 057; ul Sv Kliment Ohridski 4).

Getting There & Away

AIR

The quaintly named Dandy Airlines links Burgas with Sofia (90/176 lv one way/return, four times a week) but only between 15 April and 30 October. The **Burgas Airport Travel Agency** (☎ 842 631; cnr ul Hristo Botev & ul Ferdinandov) is the agency for Air Bulgaria and Dandy Airlines, and its staff can book and confirm (for a small fee) other international flights.

BUS

The excellent and visitor-friendly **Yug bus station** (☎ 840 841), at the southern end of ul Aleksandrovska, is where most travellers will arrive or leave when travelling up and down the coast. It's just outside the train station and all destination signs are in English, making it one of Bulgaria's best.

Buses and minibuses leave every 30 to 40 minutes throughout the day to popular places along the Black Sea coast, including Sozopol (2 lv, 40 minutes), Nesebâr (2.50 lv, 40 minutes) and Slânchev Bryag (2.70 lv, 45 minutes). Buses also go to Primorsko (3.50 lv, one hour, every 30 minutes between 6am and 7pm) and Kiten (3.50 lv, one hour, every one to 1½ hours between 6am and 8pm), but only four times a day as far as Ahtopol (5 lv, 1½ hours). Minibuses travelling directly to 'Pomorie Central' (1.80 lv, 25 minutes) leave every one to 1½ hours.

Each day, buses travel to Plovdiv (13 lv, four hours, depart 7.30am and 9.15am), Varna (7 lv, two hours, every 30 to 40 minutes), Sofia (17 lv, seven to eight hours, about 10 daily), Stara Zagora (5.50 lv, 2½ hours, departs 10.30am) and Sliven (5 lv, two hours, about every two hours).

Coaches to Istanbul are frequent and cheap. **Nışkılı Turızm** (☎ 841 261) and **Özlem** (☎ 844 697) both have several daily departures (30 lv, seven hours). Both offices are on ul Bulair and the air-conditioned coaches depart from outside.

Enturtrans (☎ 844 708; ul Bulair) is one of several private bus companies with services to various destinations in Europe via Sofia. It also has bus services to Sliven, Pleven, Veliko Târnovo, Haskovo, Kazanlâk and Varna for slightly more than the fares on public buses.

From the **Zapad bus station** (☎ 821 094), about 2km northwest of pl Troikata, buses leave for Malko Târnovo (6.70 lv, three hours, four or five daily), in the Strandzha Nature Park. Take city bus No 4 from the train station/Yug bus station to get there.

TRAIN

The historic **train station** (☎ 845 022; ul Ivan Vazov), built in 1902, has been overhauled and is now the most attractive and cleanest in Bulgaria. Through the **ticket windows** (🕑 8am-6pm) on the right you can buy advance tickets for domestic and international services, while same-day tickets can be bought at the **windows** (🕑 24hr) on the left. At the time of research, timetables were badly signposted but this may improve. The **left-luggage office** (🕑 6am-10.45pm) is outside the station.

Seven trains travel daily between Burgas and Sofia (11.10 lv, seven to eight hours). Of these, five travel via Plovdiv (7.90 lv, four to five hours), and two travel via Karlovo (7.60 lv, 4½ hours).

Express trains run from Burgas to Kazanlâk (6.50 lv, three hours), Stara Zagora (6.90 lv, two hours) and Sliven (4.10 lv, 1½ hours).

International tickets are also available at the **Rila Bureau** (☎ 845 242) inside the station. A train to Bucharest runs in summer only.

Getting Around

Many travel agencies offer car rentals, but most seem to be representatives for TS Travel (p185). It's better to approach TS Travel directly. The cheapest car it can offer costs 86 lv per day (one to two days), including unlimited kilometres and insurance, plus petrol. A deposit of €100 to €200 is required, and the vehicle can be dropped off at Sofia, Plovdiv or Varna for a supplementary charge of 0.40 lv per kilometre from Burgas.

Any of the taxis around Burgas can be chartered for negotiable rates to nearby beach resorts and villages.

BURGAS LAKES
БУРГАСКИ ЕЗЕРА

The four lakes surrounding Burgas are Pomoriysko (or Pomorie), Atanasovsko, Mandrensko (Mandra) and Burgasko (Burgas). These are collectively known as the Burgas Lakes. Comprising over 9500 hectares, it's the largest wetland system in Bulgaria, and is home to about 60% of the country's bird species.

The **Poda Conservation Centre** (☎ 056-850 540; admission 1 lv; 🕑 8am-6pm) was opened in 1998 under the auspices of the Bulgarian Society for the Protection of Birds (BSPB). The centre ostensibly provides education about conservation issues to local people, but is also open to foreign visitors. It's worth a visit, especially if you're interested in this genuine and admirable effort at conservation and bird protection at a place so close to the urban sprawl of Burgas.

In the **Poda Protected Area**, which surrounds the centre, bird lovers will delight in spotting pelicans, black-winged stilts, ibises and spoonbills. Most birds can be seen yearround and hundreds of cormorants are always nesting on the disused electricity poles. The 15 mammal species – unlikely to be seen in the tall grass and reeds, however – include pygmy white-toothed shrews.

From the roof of the conservation centre, it is possible to observe some birds with binoculars (free of charge) and telescopes (if you ask nicely).

To really admire the bird life up close, go on a walk along the signposted 2.5km **nature trail** (entry for up to 6 people 10 lv). It takes about three hours to complete and there's an explanatory leaflet in English available from the centre. It's recommended that you get a guide (English- or German-speaking), which will cost an extra 15 lv per group.

East of Burgas, the 28-sq-km **Burgasko Lake** (or Lake Vaya) is the largest sea lake in Bulgaria. It is home to pelicans throughout the year but the best time to see them is between April and October. A 1½-hour **boat trip** around this lake costs about 5 lv per person, but a minimum of six passengers is required. A guide is recommended and costs extra. For details, contact the **conservation office** (☎ 056-849 255) in Burgas, or the Poda Conservation Centre.

The centre also offers other day trips and overnight excursions around the other lakes, and elsewhere in the region, with an emphasis on flora, fauna and bird life. The cost of these tours depends on your requirements and the numbers in the group. Tours of the lakes are also offered by **Neophron** (☎ /fax 052-634 584; www.neophron.com; ul Rakovski 57, Varna).

The *Bourgas Lakes* map (4 lv), available from the Helikon Bookshop (p183) in Burgas, is excellent. It provides maps (in Bulgarian and English) of each lake, as well as the locations of lookouts, walking trails, access roads and bird nesting areas.

The **Poda Conservation Centre** (per person 5 lv) offers a few basic bunk beds. Bring your own food to cook in the kitchen and book all accommodation in advance.

The centre is poorly signposted on the left, about 8km south of Burgas on the road to Sozopol. It's accessible by taxi (about 5 lv one way), or catch bus No 5, 17 or 18 from opposite the Polyclinic III hospital along bul Demokratsiya.

SOZOPOL СОЗОПОЛ
☎ 0550 / pop 5000

One of the Black Sea's gems, Sozopol stands out by being a historic and beautiful town rather than simply a resort. With its charming peninsula old town, two superb beaches and genial atmosphere, Sozopol makes a far better base for exploring the area than Burgas, with plentiful accommodation and good transport links. While Sozopol was a real find in the 1990s compared with tourist-saturated Nesebâr, it has caught up considerably in terms of commercialisation in the past few years. It's now a huge destination in summer, and while it's still delightful, you won't feel as if you've fallen upon an undiscovered gem. With prices still much lower than in Nesebâr, though, it's definitely worth a night or two.

History
Until about 2000 years ago, Sozopol was an island. The original inhabitants were Thracians who lived here from about 4000 BC. In 611 BC, Greek colonists from Miletus settled in the area and lived (more or less) peacefully with the Thracians. The Greeks called their home Apollonia, after the Greek god of healing, Apollo.

Despite a short-lived invasion by the Persians in 532 BC, Apollonia flourished by trading meat, salt, leather and weapons, among other things, with neighbouring states. The Romans realised the potential of the region and, under Marcus Lucullus, attacked Apollonia in 72 BC. Most of the town was destroyed and the famous 13m-high bronze statue of Apollo was taken to Rome as booty, but Apollonia later regained some importance as an economic centre in the far-flung Roman Empire.

In AD 330, the town was renamed Sozopol (Town of Salvation) and was later settled by the Slavs. It became part of the First Bulgarian Empire (681–1018) in 969. For centuries, Sozopol remained a tiny fishing village occupied by Genoan and Turkish invaders. Early in the 19th century a revival of fortunes saw about 200 houses built in the traditional Black Sea style, with stone foundations, roofs of Turkish-style tiles and walls of wood and stone.

At the end of the Russian–Turkish War (1877–78), most citizens of Sozopol fled to Russia to avoid potential retaliation by the Turks. The town remained empty for several decades before being resettled by Turks, Bulgars and Greeks. During the communist era, the town was promoted as a holiday resort, although not until the 1990s did it really take off, now attracting scores of Germans, Russians and holiday-makers from Eastern Europe.

Orientation

Sozopol is 31km southeast of Burgas and is divided into two areas. The old town to the north is a collection of narrow cobblestone streets lined with sturdy wooden dwellings built on lower floors made of stone; 180 of these buildings are listed by the Ministry of Culture for their historical and cultural significance. South of the bus station is the new town, often called Harmanite. On the western side of the peninsula is a Bulgarian naval base.

Information

Many foreign exchange offices can be found along the old town's main streets, and around the new town's main square.

Biochim Commercial Bank (ul Apolonia 17)
Internet Club (ul Republikanska; 🕒 9am-11pm)
Post office (ul Apolonia; 🕒 7am-8.30pm) Has a telephone centre.
United Bulgarian Bank (ul Apolonia 4) Has an ATM. Cash and travellers cheques can be changed here.

Sights

ART GALLERY OF SOZOPOL

This **art gallery** (☎ 2202; ul Kiril & Metodii 70; admission 1.50 lv; 🕒 10am-7pm Mon-Sat) is perched on a bluff with marvellous views of the sea. It offers a collection of sea-motif paintings and sculptures, some donated by art galleries in Sofia. The opening hours are fairly erratic: staff seem to enjoy a long lunch.

CHURCHES

The 15th-century **Church of Sveta Bogoroditsa** (ul Anaksimandâr 13; admission free; 🕒 6am-10pm) is on the ruins of another church dating from the Middle Ages and, as required by the Ottoman rulers, it was built below street level. The church contains exquisite wooden iconostases inspired by carvers from Macedonia. The gates are mostly closed, so get the keys from the Archaeological Museum. Otherwise, just peek over the fence.

Sveti Zossim Chapel (admission free; 🕒 6am-10pm) is a small working church in the shady gardens opposite the bus station. It was built in the 13th century, on the foundations of another church from the Middle Ages, to honour the patron saint of sailors.

Also worth a quick look are the **Church of St George** (ul Apolonia; admission free; 🕒 6am-10pm), the **St Nedelya Chapel** (ul Anaksimandâr; admission free; 🕒 6am-10pm) and the **Sts Cyril & Methodius**

Church (ul Han Krum), which is relatively new (built in 1899) and not open to the public.

ST JOHN'S ISLAND

The 660-hectare **St John's Island** (St Ivan's Island) is the largest along the Bulgarian coast. Although it's now uninhabited, the ruins of a 13th-century monastery and temple, and the lighthouse built in 1884, clearly indicate previous habitation. The island is now a nature reserve and protects about 70 species of birds. It can be visited by boat, or admired from the window of any restaurant along the northwestern side of the old town.

The fishing boats, docked along ul Kraybrezhna, can be rented for a negotiable fee (about 7 lv to 8 lv per person per hour, with a boatman) for trips to the island. For other boat options see below.

BEACHES

The town's two beaches are pleasant, but on most days the waves can be reasonably high. The 1km-long **Harmanite Beach** is wide and clean and offers a water slide and paddle boats. The **Town Beach** (or Northern Beach) is also long, but not as wide, and doesn't offer the same number of beachside cafés, restaurants and bars.

Along the beaches, there are the camping grounds of Zlatna Ribka, about 2km northwest of Sozopol, and Kavatsi, 2km to the south (see p191). These two beaches are open to the public and offer a couple of cafés and bars.

ARCHAEOLOGICAL MUSEUM

This unimpressive **museum** (☎ 2226; ul Han Krum 2; admission 1.50 lv; 🕒 10am-5pm, closed Sat & Sun in winter) is along an unnamed laneway leading to the port. It contains a limited array of artefacts, such as coins, pottery and ceramics from settlements along the Black Sea coast which have since been submerged. All of the better items are, however, in national museums in France and Germany. The few exhibits in the foyer, such as the anchors dated to the 4th century BC, have explanations in English, but everything else in the museum is labelled only in Bulgarian.

Activities

Sailing boats moored near the fish restaurants in the port area take passengers on trips along the coast and to St John's Island for

BLACK SEA COAST

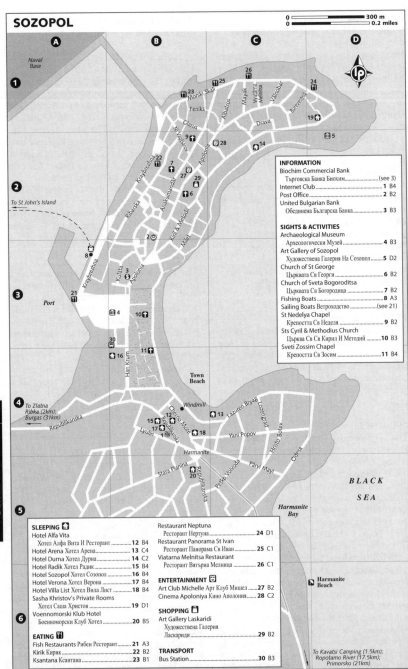

SOZOPOL

0 — 300 m
0 — 0.2 miles

To Kavatsi Camping (1.5km);
Ropotamo River (17.5km);
Primorsko (21km)

about 15 lv per person per hour (depending on the distance and number of passengers). Sunset is a particularly grand time to be on board.

Zlatna Ribka (☎ 2427) is the only spot offering water sports. Windsurfing (per hr 10 lv) is available here for experts, and lessons (for a negotiable fee) are possible for beginners. Other water sports such as jet skiing can also usually be arranged.

Monisub Scuba Dive Center (☎ 08 870 7027; www .monisub.city.bg) is not set up particularly well and it's not advisable for divers to just turn up at the office and expect to immediately join a diving tour or sign up for any training without organising it beforehand. The best time for scuba diving is between June and October; at other times, the sea is too cold and the waves too rough.

Festivals & Events

The **Apollonia Arts Festival**, held in the first half of September, is *the* highlight of Sozopol's social calendar, and is one of the most popular events along the Black Sea coast. Something akin to Bulgaria's equivalent of the Edinburgh Festival, it features all sorts of jazz, pop and alternative music at various venues in the old and new town, although names will mean nothing to most visitors.

Sleeping

Sozopol has an enormous amount of places offering rooms. Look for signs along Republikanska in the new town and pretty much anywhere in the old town.

Hotel rooms overlooking the main roads are noisy, but most of the others offer great views. Staying in the old town is possible, although unless you stay at the Hotel Durna, this will usually be in private rooms, which are advertised all over the peninsula.

BUDGET

Sasha Khristov's Private Rooms (☎ 23434; ul Venets 17; s/d/tr/apt 10/20/30/50 lv) This lovely old family homestead in the old town faces the art gallery at the very end of the Sozopol peninsula. It's run by the kind Khristov family and comprises rooms (all with bathrooms and terraces) and a family-sized apartment. Book ahead in summer.

Hotel Verona (☎ 22592; www.hotel-verona.com; ul Republikanska 8; s/d 22/44 lv; 🖳) The lovely, family-run Hotel Verona enjoys a great location with superb views over the sea from its higher floors. The rooms are great value and the restaurant downstairs packs in the crowds in the evenings. Rooms are very clean, most with balconies.

Hotel Alfa Vita (☎ 23614; ul Republikanska 9; d 40 lv; ☥ 1 Jun-25 Sep) Offers similar amenities (eg TV, fridge and balcony) to Hotel Radik, but is not great value for single travellers. The views from some rooms are superb, and the bathrooms are large. The downstairs restaurant serves up a mean selection of doner kebabs.

Voennomorski Klub Hotel (☎ 22283; vmk@infotel .bg; ul Republikanska 17; s/d 40/46 lv; 🖭 🖳) This large complex overlooks the main square in the new town. The quiet rooms are smallish but reasonably comfortable, and nicely furnished with pine wood. It's not signposted or particularly obvious, so look for the word Хотел (hotel).

Hotel Sozopol (☎ 22362, 23142; ul Han Krum; s/d 10/20 lv) During the high season, this Soviet-era relic has the best-value rooms in town. It's located next to the bus station, between the old and new towns. The rooms are unremarkable, but they all have balconies. Breakfast costs 2 lv, while full board is 9 lv.

Zlatna Ribka (☎ 2427; camping per person 7 lv, bungalows with bathroom 23 lv) About 2km northwest of Sozopol, along the road to Burgas, this huge complex offers all sorts of accommodation. It's one of the few camping grounds in the region away from the main road, so there's not much noise from passing traffic. On the downside, the bungalows are minuscule and built too close together, so peace and privacy are not guaranteed in the high season. Water sports (see p189) are available. Any bus coming from Burgas to Sozopol passes Zlatna Ribka, just state your destination and the driver will let you out at the gates.

Kavatsi Camping (☎ 2261; camping per person 9.50 lv, bungalows with toilet & shared bathroom 42 lv, d with bathroom 60 lv, cottages 100 lv) The best-equipped complex in the area, but the bungalows are tiny and crammed together. The cottages (with four beds, TV, kitchen and terrace) and hotel rooms (with TV) are overpriced. It's about 2km south of the new town's main square, along the coastal road to Primorsko. Any bus going south from Sozopol to Primorsko or beyond will pass the camping ground. Just state your destination and the driver will let you out on the main road.

MID-RANGE

Hotel Durna (☎ 0888 705023; ul Kiril & Metodii; r 70 lv) This is the only hotel proper in Sozopol's old town. It's a smart and well-appointed place, with gorgeous sea views, overlooking the southern side of the peninsula.

Hotel Radik (☎ 23706; ul Republikanska 4; s/d Jun-Aug 26/52 lv, Sep-May 22/44 lv, apt year-round 55 lv) Another good-value place, the Radik is well located and run by a friendly family. The singles are tiny, but still decent value and most rooms have balconies with sea views.

Hotel Villa List (☎/fax 22235; ul Cherno More 5; s 28-57 lv, d 40-94 lv; ☒ ☒) Has 80 excellent rooms overlooking the town beach, but gets lots of summer tour groups. The hotel is still worth trying (especially in the off season) because it's close to the beaches, has competent and friendly staff, the rooms have air-con, TV and balcony, and the rates include breakfast. The hotel also boasts a swimming pool with sea views.

Hotel Arena (☎ 22406; arena_gab@abv.bg; Tsentralen Plyazh; r 60 lv; ☒) Right on the beachfront, this pricier option is a winner for sun worshippers. Nearly all the rooms have sea views with great balconies, and although its Soviet past is still detectable, the Arena is a fun place to stay.

Eating

Local fish dishes are tasty and fresh, but usually expensive. The cheapest fish restaurants are strung along the port area. The best restaurants in town are on ul Morksi Skali, and are large and traditional affairs with some spectacular views.

Some of the best cafés are in the shady park opposite the bus station. The cafés along ul Apolonia offer no views, but the ones along the middle stretch of the street are trendy and ideal for people-watching.

Ksantana (☎ 22454; ul Morski Skali 7; mains 8 lv) The split-level terraces of this traditional establishment afford a bird's-eye view of St John's Island from the courtyard balcony. The restaurant can be entered at both the top and bottom of the steps and can be easy to miss, with a sign only in Cyrillic.

Restaurant Panorama St Ivan (☎ 08 8826 0820; ul Morski Skali 21; mains 6 lv) Similar to the Ksantana, this small and homely restaurant features a small courtyard with glorious views and breezes. Meals are reasonably priced, and the menu is in English.

Viatarna Melnitsa Restaurant (☎ 22844; ul Morski Skali 27; mains 4-6 lv) Immediately obvious from the small windmill at the entrance, and the larger one in the grounds, the Viatarna Melnitsa ('old windmill') is so popular that even the Bulgarian president dines here when he's in town. It's not as quaint or homely as other taverns, nor does it offer the same sea breezes, but the food is excellent and the prices are low.

Restaurant Neptuna (☎ 22735; ul Morski Skali 33; meals from 5 lv) The last of the big restaurants along Morski Skali, just before the peninsula ends, the Neptuna offers delicious fish meals, superb views and welcome breezes in a family-run tavern. The management also lets smart rooms for tourists who want to stay in the old town.

Kirik (ul Ribarska 77; meals from 3.50 lv) For fresh fish, it's tough to beat Kirik. The *midi tzigane*, locally raised mussels sautéed with a spicy cheese and mustard sauce, will make your tongue curl with delight.

The mall on ul Ropotamo, alongside Harmanite Beach, is absolutely packed with cafés, restaurants and bars. All of them are pretty much the same, but three places do stand out. Restaurant Paradise has a quiet, raised, off-street eating area and reasonable prices. Most of the **Fisherman Restaurant & Bar** (meals about 3.50 lv) is on the beach. The menu is extensive, but surprisingly it doesn't offer a great number of fish meals. Havana Club distinguishes itself from the others with a small swimming pool for guests (more suitable for the kiddies).

Drinking

After a hard day of swimming, eating and shopping, most visitors relax with a drink at one of the numerous bars or cafés. Any fish restaurants, or any café or bar along the northwestern coast, is ideal for a late-afternoon or evening drink. For views of the northern beach and old town, it's hard to beat the **Complex La Perla** (ul Lazuren Bryag).

Entertainment

Art Club Michelle (ul Apolonia 39) has live music most evenings, and Viatarna Melnitsa Restaurant (above) features folkloric music and dancing. The marvellous **Cinema Apoloniya** (ul Apolonia; tickets about 5 lv; ☒ Apr-Oct only) shows modern English-language films on an outdoor screen.

Shopping

Naturally, the streets in the old town are lined with souvenir stalls. **Art Gallery Laskaridi** (ul Kiril & Metodii) sells contemporary art, as well as books about Sozopol.

Getting There & Away

The small public **bus station** (ul Han Krum) is between the old and new town. Buses leave for Burgas (2.10 lv, 40 minutes) about every 30 minutes between 6am and 9pm in summer, and about once an hour in the off-season. Quicker and more comfortable minibuses also service this route for about the same price.

Only a couple of buses a day go directly to Ahtopol (2.50 lv, one hour), via Primorsko (1.40 lv, 20 minutes) and Kiten (1.80 lv, 30 minutes). Public buses leave up to three times a day for Shumen, Stara Zagora, Sofia and Haskovo.

Larger and more comfortable private buses arrive and depart from spots around the new town's main square. Daily, three or four private buses go to Sofia, one or two depart for Plovdiv, and another one or two travel up and down the southern coast as part of the overnight Haskovo–Ahtopol service.

Almost all private and public buses going from Burgas, Sofia, Sliven, Plovdiv and Stara Zagora to anywhere along the southern coast normally stop in Sozopol and pick up passengers.

Getting Around

Sozopol is easy to get around on foot and there's no need to hire one of the vampiric cabs from around the bus stop. If you do need a cab, get one on the main road in the new town. While it's perfectly possible to see the coast to the south of Sozopol by public transport, it's a lot easier by car. There are several travel agencies around the new town's main square, which can arrange car rental from about €40 per day, including unlimited kilometres and insurance, plus petrol. One agency to look out for is **Tabanov** (☎ /fax 388 725; tabanov@abv.bg).

ROPOTAMO NATURE RESERVE
НАЦОНАЛЕН РЕЗЕРВАТ РОПОТАМО

This reserve was established in 1940 to protect fragile landscapes of extensive marshes and the largest sand dunes in Bulgaria, as well as rare flora such as the endemic sand lily. The reserve also protects more than 200 species of birds (seven of which are endangered), reptiles such as snakes and turtles, and mullet and carp, which must not be caught here as fishing is illegal. This pristine reserve, which has always been surprisingly unpopulated, is now run by the Bulgarian-Swiss Biodiversity Conservation Programme (BSBCP).

At several well-signposted places along the road between Burgas and Primorsko, visitors can stop and admire some of the reserve, and wander along short **walking trails**. Explanations (in English) about the local flora, fauna and natural landscapes are provided along the trails.

Where the main road between Sozopol and Primorsko crosses the Ropotamo River is the major entrance to a **parkland** (admission free, parking 3 lv), favoured by day-trippers and bus groups. There are a couple of cafés and picnic spots, and some short **hiking trails**, but most visitors come for a **boat ride** (40/70min trip per person 7/8 lv) along the murky green-and-brown river. Boats hold up to 25 people. To get to the parkland entrance by public transport, take any bus or minibus south of Sozopol, and get off at the prominent, well-signposted bridge.

PRIMORSKO ПРИМОРСКО
☎ 0550 / pop 2500

Primorsko (meaning 'by the sea') is a busy resort 52km south of Burgas and popular mainly with Bulgarians. It is far less developed than resorts to the north, although a walk through its crowded town centre, crammed with takeaway stands, loud bars and tack-trading souvenir stalls, makes it clear that while smaller, it's just as crowded. That said, the beach is long, attractive and sheltered, so it's ideal for swimming and boating, although the water is often shallow at low tide.

From the town square, along bul Treti Mart (the main road into town), it's a short walk south to the beach. The best shops are along ul Cherno More, which heads southeast from the square.

Sleeping

The **Demin Agency** (bus station; per person 8-20 lv) organises rooms at rates that vary according to their proximity to the town centre and beach, and whether the room has a private bathroom. However, the agency is frequently unmanned, so call **Denka Mincheva** (☎ 0888 318835) if there's nobody around to help. For one of the best deals in town, you could just head straight for the private rooms at **44A ul Cherno More** (per person 8 lv), where you'll be given spotless rooms with all mod-cons, including TV. The drawback is the loud bar across the road that will really annoy anyone wanting to sleep before 1am.

Hotel Stop (☎ 0888 850820; ul Treti Mart 75; d 20 lv) Despite its odd name and even odder is-it-finished exterior, the Stop is a good deal with surprisingly smart rooms and a central location.

Hotel Prima Vera (☎ 33488; ul Cherno More 46; d 30 lv) A very decent place, with modern, clean rooms and a good pizzeria downstairs. It's right in the thick of the action so some rooms may be quite noisy in summer.

Spektar Palace (☎ 335 29; spectar-palace@infotour .org; ul Treti Mart 82; s/d 40/50 lv; 🖳 🖳) While it's among the more expensive options in town and not particularly near the beach, the Spektar Palace is nonetheless a good hotel, with very decent facilities. Being a little out of the town centre means it's a lot quieter than most hotels.

Eating

Most locals and visitors seem to be more than happy to buy a doner kebab, pizza or toasted sandwich from one of many stalls along the main road. A dozen hotels in the town centre and near the beach have eateries of some sort. Plenty of other cafés, bars and restaurants can be found around the town square and along the main road. The **Chinese Zodiak Restaurant** (ul Treti Mart) is surprisingly excellent with a Chinese chef.

Getting There & Away

Primorsko's bus station, 1km from the town centre, is where all public transport arrives and leaves. From here, there are buses to Kiten (1.20 lv, 10 minutes, roughly every hour). There's one bus to Akhtopol (2.20 lv, 45 minutes, departs 8.05am) and two buses a day to Tsarevo (2 lv, 8.10am and 3.50pm) Also, buses regularly stop at Primorsko on the way between Burgas, Sofia or Haskovo and Ahtopol or Kiten, but many of these services pass through, in either direction, late in the evening. In addition, buses travel

daily to Burgas (3.20 lv, one hour, every 30 minutes between 6am and 7pm). About six private buses a day also go to Sofia, and one or two travel to Stara Zagora, Plovdiv and Sliven via Sozopol and Burgas.

KITEN КИТЕН
☎ 0550 / pop 550

Enjoying a far more relaxed feel than Primorsko, the little resort of Kiten, 5km to the south, was first permanently settled as recently as the 1930s, but nearby excavations indicate evidence of settlement in the 6th century BC. Kiten is pleasantly situated around pockets of forest, but there's no town centre as such, so all shops, restaurants and hotels are dotted along the roads between the two beaches – the biggest concentration is on ul Atliman, which is lined with lively restaurants and bars.

The northern **Atliman Beach** is along a horseshoe-shaped bay, one of the cleanest and prettiest along the Black Sea coast, and the hills in the background thankfully hinder all possible future development. **Morski Beach** to the south is sheltered and ideal for swimming, and has plenty of beachside cafés.

Hotel Atliman (below) offers **day trips** by bus to Nesebâr (22 lv), Sozopol (10 lv) and Varna (45 lv), and all-inclusive **boat trips** (13 lv) in the Ropotamo Nature Reserve.

Sleeping & Eating

Eos Hotel Complex (☎ 36865; eoskiten@abv.bg; Petrova nive ul 1; s&d/tr/apt 60/78/110 lv; 🖳) Nicely located a short walk from the bus stop and both beaches, the Eos is a smart place that offers its guests use of the small pool, sauna and gym. The rooms are simple, bright and clean.

Hotel Assarel Medet (☎ 2445; ul Strandzha; d/tr/ apt incl breakfast 60/82/105 lv) Considerably better than the exterior suggests, this hotel is not just another boring Balkantourist-style throwback to the 1960s. The rooms are clean and bright, and have TV, bathroom and a balcony with lovely views. It's about 200m north of Morski Beach.

Hotel Atliman (☎ 2349; fax 2823; s/d 45/55 lv) This is the only place within walking distance of Atliman Beach. It offers large, clean rooms with a balcony and views, but check a few of the rooms first because some are better than others. At the time of research, all bathrooms appeared to have been recently renovated.

Yug Camping (camping per person 5 lv, s/d bungalows with shared bathroom 5/9 lv, apt 45 lv) As this place doesn't suffer from the must-overcharge-foreigners syndrome, it's remarkably cheap, but then the quality of accommodation is very ordinary indeed. The well-signed (500m) access road is about 1.5km south of the turn-off to Kiten from Burgas.

Try **Restorant Smokinya** (ul Urdoviza 20), about halfway between the two beaches, for tasty fish meals.

Getting There & Away

The smart air-conditioned bus station is at the top end of ul Strandzha, at the junction of the roads to Primorsko and Ahtopol. Daily buses to Burgas (3.50 lv, one hour, hourly) travel via Primorsko and Sozopol. There are direct buses to Plovdiv and Sofia (via Stara Zagora) throughout the day. All buses and minibuses travelling to or from Ahtopol will also stop in Kiten to pick up passengers.

AHTOPOL АХТОПОЛ
☎ 0550 / pop 1350

A little run-down compared to its smarter neighbours, Ahtopol is nevertheless very pleasant in a quiet, village-like way. The focus here is on resorts run by companies (often rather dilapidated ones from the communist days) and there are relatively few hotels, although private rooms are plentiful. The beach is about 800m from the town centre but it's very pleasant and easy to find some space to yourself. Unlike to the north, the beach is below some hills, so few cafés (and no hotels) blot the landscape.

If there is a town centre, it's based around the park where the bus stops, though the post office and administration buildings are about 500m east of this. To find the beach, walk southwest from the park and bus stop along ul Sveti Nikola towards the main coastal road for about 300m, and then head northwest along any laneway. The rocky coastline east of the town's park is also begging to be explored.

The cheapest and easiest accommodation is through **Credo Prim** (☎ 62224; per person 8-15 lv), a tiny office next to the bus 'station' letting out private rooms. Its owner is a delightful lady who only speaks Bulgarian and Russian.

Pleasingly, the **Hotel Neptun** (☎ 2164; cnr ul Sveti Nikola & ul Georgi Kondolov; s/d 10/20 lv) doesn't overcharge foreigners, but it has seen better

days. Most rooms are adequately comfortable and, as it's only metres from the sea, some have balconies with great views.

Of the several pleasant *mehanas* along the main streets, the best is probably Cafe Varna, which has a shady courtyard. It's at the northeastern end of the town park.

Public transport to Ahtopol is pretty poor. Five buses a day depart from the tiny **bus station** (☎ 08 8999 8847) for Burgas (5.40 lv, 1½ hours) via Primorsko and Sozopol, while four buses go south to Sinemorets (0.50 lv, 10 minutes), one of which continues to Rezevo (1 lv, 30 minutes), the tiny village on the closed Turkish border. To cross into Turkey, you need to travel inland to Malko Târnovo.

STRANDZHA NATURE PARK
НАЦОНАЛЕН ПАРК СТРАНДЖА
☎ 05952

In the southeastern corner of Bulgaria is the infrequently visited Strandzha Nature Park, which was established in 1995. The 1161 sq km of rolling hills protect the country's most diverse vegetation, including vast forests of oak and beech, as well as 40 species of fish, 261 types of birds (almost 70% of those found in Bulgaria), 65 species of mammals (six of which are endangered) and various unexcavated Byzantine fortresses.

The park's ecotourism potential is slowly being developed with the aid of the BSBCP and the US Peace Corps in Sofia. But the park is not – and probably never will be – set up for major tourism, if only because it's so remote and visiting is not easy without private transport. And don't stray too close to the Turkish border: this is an area of smugglers and trigger-happy border-patrol guards.

The park is ideal for **hiking** because it's sparsely populated and relatively flat. Several short hikes between 1km and 8km long, and longer treks of about 20km between the coast and the centre of the park, are detailed in the colourful *Nature Park Strandzha* map (1:70,000), available at the Helikon Bookshop (p183) in Burgas (4 lv). The park also contains what are probably the most undeveloped stretches of sandy **beach** along the Bulgarian Black Sea coast. If you visit in early June, make sure you witness the **fire-dancing festival** in Bulgari.

The administrative centre is Malko Târnovo, an economically depressed town in the park's southwest. The **History Museum** (☎ 2998) and the **Ethnographical Museum** (☎ 2126) contain some displays about the park, and staff at both museums are good sources of information. For more details, contact the **park office** (☎ /fax 2963; strandjapark@yahoo.com; ul Janko Maslinov 1, Malko Târnovo).

There are a couple of guesthouses and homes that offer cheap rooms in Malko Târnovo and Brûshlian. **Malko Târnovo Hotel** (☎ 2182; s/d 18/30 lv) has basic rooms with private bathroom. Free camping is permitted inside the nature park.

From the Zapad bus station in Burgas, buses leave for Malko Târnovo (6.70 lv, three hours, four or five a day) via Bulgari, but transport to other villages in the park is infrequent. If you have a private vehicle, Ahtopol and Kiten are convenient bases for day trips to the park.

SINEMORETS СИНЕМОРЕЦ
☎ 0550 / pop 500

Sinemorets is the Black Sea's last largely undiscovered gem, although it seems that the relentless pace of development along the coastline has set it firmly in the developers' sights. Despite the recent opening of an enormous hotel by the village's best beach, the atmosphere of remote village life and a generally slow-paced existence remains here and it's also a superb base for visiting the nearby Strandzha Nature Park and for hiking and birding in the lovely countryside.

The two beaches are excellent and this is one of the Black Sea's best places to escape the crowds and enjoy pristine white sand and clean water.

Sleeping & Eating

Villa Philadelphia (☎ 66106; www.villaphiladelphia.com; ul Butamya; s & d 50-70 lv) An excellent American-run venture, the Villa Philadelphia offers simple but clean rooms, good views towards the sea and very kind staff. The management specialises in bird-watching tours of the nearby countryside. Price depends on length of stay. There's also a very good little restaurant attached. Highly recommended.

Atlas Hotel (☎ 66200; atlas@dir.bg; ul Butamya; s/d 40/50 lv) This modern and clean place is unremarkable but the cheapest hotel in town. If you're on a real budget, a private room will serve you better, but this is a fine alternative, an easy walk to the beaches and has friendly staff.

Bella Vista Beach Club (☎ 66138; www.bellavista beachclub.com; s/d including full board 64/77 lv; ❇ P ☎) This hulking eyesore overlooking Sinemorets' charming south beach is a brand new place, catering squarely to package tourists, although walk-in guests are welcome. Facilities are excellent and all-encompassing, but it's hard to be too keen on such an out-of-place venture. There are several pricey places to eat on campus.

Getting There & Away

Transport to/from Sinemorets is very poor. From further up the coast you'll need to travel to Ahtopol and change there for one of the four daily minibuses to Sinemorets (0.50 lv, 15 minutes). It's a pleasant walk if there's not a bus coming soon. A 'taxi' to/from Ahtopol will cost about 5 lv if you can find someone willing to take you (there aren't any taxis in Sinemorets).

CENTRAL COAST

POMORIE ПОМОРИЕ
☎ 0596 / pop 14,500

Understandably overlooked by most people travelling up or down the coast, Pomorie, 18km northeast of Burgas, is probably the least attractive seaside town along the Black Sea coast. The beach is badly littered and marred by breakwaters every 100m to 200m, and the water is full of seaweed. The town centre is pleasant enough, but is far from the beach, which seems to be full of people who wished they could afford to stay somewhere nicer such as Slânchev Bryag. It's not all bad news, however: Pomorie is a comparatively cheap base from which to visit Burgas and Nesebâr, and some water sports are available.

Pomorie once rivalled Nesebâr in beauty and antiquity, but was mostly destroyed by fire in 1906.

Sights & Activities

There are still a few things to see in town, including the quaint **Sveti Bogoroditsa Church**, in the shady park in the town centre, and the ruins of **St George Monastery** (ul Knyaz Boris 1), about 700m from the main bus station towards the beach. In the older, nicer part of town, with its occasional cobblestone streets and wooden houses, is the **Preobrazhenie Hris-**

tovo Church (ul Han Kubrat 1). Many Bulgarian tourists ignore the beach and wallow in a **mud bath** (per hr 20 lv), or enjoy a **therapeutic massage** (per hr 25-30 lv), both at Hotel Pomorie.

It's often windy at the beach, making it ideal for **windsurfing** (per hr 8 lv) and **paragliding** (20/30min 30/50 lv). Pomorie is one of the few places along the coast where you can hire **motorbikes** (30min/1hr 5/9 lv). They are available from stalls at the southeastern end of the beach.

Sleeping & Eating

Hotel Horizon (☎ 6172; ul General Skobelev; d 30 lv) Looking rather abandoned at the end of the road from the central bus station, the Horizon boasts a good position and sea views, but the rooms probably haven't been updated or even maintained for about 30 years.

Hotel Byal Dom (White House; ☎ 7651; ul Raina Kniaginia 15; s/d 28/34 lv) This is a far better option than Horizon. Although the hotel doesn't overlook the beach, it's modern, clean and friendly, and some rooms have ocean views. The popular restaurant is recommended.

Hotel Pomorie (☎ 2440; fax 2280; ul Yavorov 3; d incl breakfast 65 lv) On a rocky outcrop equidistant from the town centre and beach, this place is not great value. While some rooms have views, and all have a TV and fridge, most bathrooms haven't been renovated since the '50s. The distance from the beach is offset by the indoor swimming pool with sea views.

The best restaurants and cafés overlook the nicer part of the beach to the southeast.

Getting There & Away

There are two bus stations in Pomorie – the main bus station is about 3km before the town centre (and accessible by local bus No 1 or taxi), and the central station is outside the town hall. From the latter station, it's about 200m northeast to the beach and 100m south to the town centre.

The regular buses and minibuses between Burgas and Nesebâr and/or Slânchev Bryag invariably stop at the main bus station. From this station, seven or eight daily buses go to Sofia, and several travel to Plovdiv, Sliven, Varna and Stara Zagora.

Every one to 1½ hours, daily minibuses marked 'Pomorie Central' (in Bulgarian) leave from Burgas (2 lv, 25 minutes) and Slânchev Bryag (1.50 lv, 30 minutes) and stop at Pomorie's small central bus station.

NESEBÂR НЕСЕБЪР

☎ 0554 / pop 9500

This little stunner is the pride of the Bulgarian Black Sea Coast, but unfortunately suffers from this, being virtually under siege from tour groups and souvenir sellers during the high season. Designated by Unesco as a World Heritage Site, Nesebâr is an incredibly scenic town with several Byzantine church ruins along cobblestone streets and a couple of worthwhile museums. Unlike Sozopol, Nesebâr offers plenty of great hotels in the old town, and while Sozopol has better beaches, Nesebâr is right next to the mother of Bulgarian beach resorts: Slânchev Bryag.

Arriving in Nesebâr from virtually anywhere in Bulgaria will amaze you – suddenly it's clear where all the tourists are, and prices are at least double or triple what you'd pay elsewhere. On a small rocky island 37km northeast of Burgas, connected to the mainland by a narrow artificial isthmus, it's nevertheless a delight and you should definitely afford it a day or two if you possibly can.

History

The first inhabitants were the Thracians who settled in what became known as Mesembria in about 3000 BC. In 512 BC, the Greeks came to live with the Thracians and built and/or fortified fortresses, temples, gates and towers – most of which are now submerged after the level of the Black Sea rose around 2000 years ago.

To avoid the sort of looting and fires that destroyed Apollonia (Sozopol), the populace of Mesembria accepted the Roman invaders in 72 BC. But the city fell into decline as the Romans concentrated on other ports and ignored this part of the coast.

Under Byzantine rule from AD 395, Mesembria regained its former glory as a centre of commercial and strategic importance. During the 5th and 6th centuries, a number of walls, towers and imposing churches were erected, including the basilica (p199). After the Bulgar invasion in 812, the town was renamed Nesebâr for reasons unknown. Over the next centuries, Nesebâr passed back and forth between Byzantine rulers and the First Bulgarian Empire (681–1018), but the town remained unscathed.

Even the Turks left Nesebâr alone, and decided to strengthen existing fortifications to defend it against Cossack pirates. The town

NESEBÂR

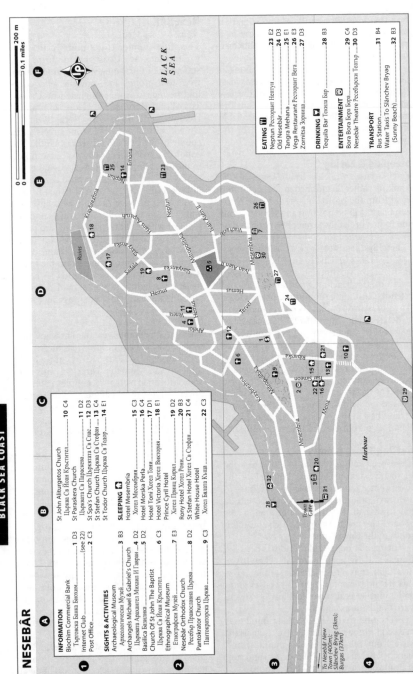

INFORMATION
Biochim Commercial Bank
Търговска Банка Биохим......................**1** D3
Internet Club..(see 22)
Post Office..**2** C3

SIGHTS & ACTIVITIES
Archaeological Museum
Археологически Музей.....................**3** B3
Archangels Michael & Gabriel's Church
Църквата Архангел Михаил И Гаврил...**4** D2
Basilica Базилика.................................**5** D2
Church Of St John The Baptist
Църква Св Йоан Кръстител................**6** C3
Ethnographical Museum
Етнографски Музей...........................**7** E3
Nesebâr Orthodox Church
Несебър Православна Църква............**8** D2
Pantokrator Church
Пантократорска Църква....................**9** C3
St John Aliturgetos Church
Църква Св Йоан Кръстител...............**10** C4
St Paraskeva Church
Църква Св Параскева........................**11** D2
St Spa's Church Църквата Св Спас.....**12** D3
St Stefan Church Църква Са Стефан....**13** C4
St Todor Church Църква Св Тодор......**14** E1

SLEEPING
Hotel Mesembria..................................**15** C3
Hotel Morska Perla..............................**16** C4
Hotel Toni Хотел Тони........................**17** D1
Hotel Victoria Хотел Виктория...........**18** E1
Prince Cyril Hotel
Хотел Принц Кирил...........................**19** D2
Rony Hotel Хотел Рони.......................**20** B3
St Stefan Hotel Хотел Са Стефан........**21** C4
White House Hotel
Хотел Бялата Къща............................**22** C3

EATING
Neptun Ресторант Нептун...................**23** E2
Old Nesebâr..**24** D3
Tangra Mehana....................................**25** E1
Vega Restaurant Ресторант Вега........**26** E3
Zornitsa Зорница................................**27** D3

DRINKING
Tequila Bar Текила бар.......................**28** B3

ENTERTAINMENT
Bora Bora Бора Бора..........................**29** C4
Nesebâr Theatre Несебърски Театр....**30** D3

TRANSPORT
Bus Station..**31** B4
Water Taxis To Slânchev Bryag
(Sunny Beach).....................................**32** B3

reached some heights between the 13th and 15th centuries, but again fell to the Byzantines and then the Ottomans in 1453. During the Bulgarian national revival of the 18th and 19th centuries, Nesebâr prospered and many merchants constructed numerous typical buildings, some of which remain today. Overshadowed by Varna and later by Burgas, Nesebâr ceased to be an active trading town from the early 20th century, and these days survives almost entirely on tourism.

Orientation

The old town is on a rocky outcrop, 850m long and 300m wide. It's connected to the new town on the 'mainland' by a narrow causeway that goes through the 3000-year-old fortress walls, built by the Thracians and later fortified by the Greeks and Byzantines. There's no reason to visit the new town: all hotels, restaurants, shops and other attractions listed here are in the old town.

The best map is the *Sunny Beach & Nessebur City Guide*, published by Makros and distinguishable by its yellow-and-blue cover. For a detailed history of Nesebâr, look for *The Ancient City of Nessebur* (9 lv), which contains plenty of photos and makes a decent souvenir. Also worthwhile is *Nessebur: A Town with History* (10 lv), a booklet with gorgeous photos and some historical details. Maps and books are available at any of the town's plethora of bookstalls.

Information

Every second or third shop seems to be a foreign exchange office. Many of these change travellers cheques but charge different commissions, so shop around.

Biochim Commercial Bank (ul Mesembria; 8.30am-7.45pm Mon-Fri, plus 11am-7.45pm Sat & Sun Apr-Oct) The only bank in town that changes travellers cheques. Also has an ATM that accepts major credit cards.

Internet Club (White House Hotel, ul Tsar Simeon 2)

Post office (ul Mesembria; 8am-8pm Tue-Sat) Has a telephone centre.

Sights

CHURCHES

Nesebâr was once home to about 80 churches and chapels, but most are now in ruins. Characteristic of the Nesebâr style of church design are the horizontal strips of white stone and red brick, which are offset by striped blind arches resting on the vertical pilasters, the façades highlighted by ceramic discs and rosettes. Except where indicated, each church is open daily during daylight hours and admission is free.

No visitor can help but be impressed by the dominant ruins of the **basilica**, also known as the Metropolitan Church and Old Bishopric. Originally built in the early 6th century and then rebuilt in the late 9th century, it served as the bishopric until about 1257, when the churched was ransacked by Venetians. It contained three naves and boasted a spacious interior with high walls and wide windows. The unmissable ruins are accessible from along the main street, ul Mitropolitska.

Typical of the characteristic Nesebâr construction is the well-preserved **Pantokrator Church** (ul Mesembria). Built in the mid-14th century, it's renowned among religious historians for its bell tower and unusually deliberate and conspicuous urban location. It now contains a classy art gallery.

Probably the most beautiful church in old Nesebâr was the **St John Aliturgetos Church**, accessible down some steps from the end of of ul Ribarska. Built in about the mid-14th century and dedicated to St John the Unbeliever, the church was mostly destroyed by an earthquake in 1913. Concerts are sometimes held here in summer.

The **Church of St John the Baptist** (ul Mitropolitska) was built in the 10th century, and features some of the best-preserved murals from the 14th and 17th centuries. It's also now occupied by an art gallery. **St Spa's Church** (ul Aheloi; admission 1.70 lv; 10am-1pm & 2-5.30pm Mon-Fri, 10am-1.30pm Sat & Sun) was built in 1609. Like all churches established during Ottoman rule, it had to be built below street level. It features some comparatively well-preserved murals, but nothing much else.

St Stefan Church (ul Ribarska; adult/child 2.10/1 lv, photos 4 lv; 9am-noon & 2-6pm) was built in three stages between the 10th and 12th centuries. It became the new bishopric (which is an alternative name for the church) after the basilica was looted. The interior of St Stefan's is almost completely covered with murals dating from the 15th and 16th centuries, and was one of the first churches in Bulgaria to be decorated with ceramics.

The **Archangels Michael & Gabriel's Church** (ul Hemus) was built over a few decades during the 13th and 14th centuries. It remains in relatively good condition, but entry is usually forbidden. Very little is known about the origins of **St Todor Church** (ul Neptun), which has been partially restored but is also usually closed. A fine example of 13th-century architecture is **St Paraskera Church** (ul Hemus), which had only one nave. The building is now occupied by a restaurant. **Nesebâr Orthodox Church** (ul Slavyanska) is the only functioning church in town and visitors are welcome.

ARCHAEOLOGICAL MUSEUM

Although the number of exhibits is limited, it's still worth visiting the **Archaeological Museum** (☎ 26 018; ul Mesembria 2; adult/child 2.50/1.20 lv, photos 4 lv; ☉ 9am-1pm & 1.30-7pm Mon-Fri, plus 9am-1pm & 2-6pm Sat & Sun Apr). The ground floor houses earthenware pots from between the 5th and 2nd centuries BC, as well as other artefacts such as anchors detailing the naval history of previous civilisations. Other highlights include Thracian tombs, Roman tablets and gold jewellery. The basement has a token collection of unremarkable religious icons recovered from Nesebâr's numerous churches.

All items are labelled in English, except, disappointingly, those detailing any history and explaining the model of the ancient city. The museum can get very busy at times, with tour-group leaders shouting at their flocks, so ideally come before 10am or after 5pm.

ETHNOGRAPHICAL MUSEUM

Ignored by the shopaholics and forgotten by the tour groups is this small **museum** (ul Mesembria 32; adult/child 1.50/0.85 lv; ☉ 10am-2pm & 3-6pm Mon-Sat). Inside a typical wooden Bulgarian national revival building (constructed in about 1840), it features regional costumes and displays about weaving. All labels are in Bulgarian and German.

BEACHES

The beaches are popular with some locals and visitors, but they're small and rocky and the water is often choked with seaweed. The best place for a dip is either side of the two jetties to the northeast. Alternatively, head to the far superior beach at Slânchev Bryag, only a few kilometres away.

Sleeping

If you come in the off-season (October to May) and/or stay for more than two or three nights, it's worth asking for a discount; the town has so many hotels that bargaining is common. Private rooms are the best options – ladies offering a room or two meet tourists off the bus.

MID-RANGE

Rony Hotel (☎ 44002; fax 44001; ul Chayka 1; s/d/apt incl breakfast 49/65/90 lv; ✷) Superbly located and staffed with extremely helpful people, Rony is highly recommended. Rooms are cosy, comfortable and clean and the ground-floor restaurant is very good. Independent travellers will probably be able to walk off the bus and straight into a room during the high season. It offers attractive discounts for longer stays.

St Stefan Hotel (☎ 43603; ul Ribarska 11; s/d/apt incl breakfast 65/70/90 lv; ✷) Opposite the picturesque St Stefan Church, this modern hotel is far better value than others in this price range. The 16 modern rooms contain a TV and fridge, and those on the upper floors have balconies with views. The hotel also has a gym, sauna and spa. It's used by tour operators to accommodate groups, so reserve in advance.

Hotel Toni (☎ 42403; ul Kraybrezhna 20; r 58 lv) Hotel Toni caters to independent travellers, but features the same sort of setting and views as adjacent hotels costing far more. Breakfast costs an extra 5 lv. It's open year-round and you'll get very generous discounts out of season.

Hotel Victoria (☎ 46000; seamex@spnet.net; ul Kraybrezhna 22; d/apt incl breakfast 80/90 lv; ✷) Another recommended three-star hotel with some wonderful views, all rooms at the Victoria have a TV and fridge. The hotel is usually full in the high season, but the off-season brings some great deals.

Prince Cyril Hotel (☎ 42215; princecyril_hotel@abv .bg; ul Slavyanska 9; r incl breakfast 80 lv; ✷) Another very good hotel. The rooms are well appointed, even if some are slightly cramped. All have modern bathrooms. It's certainly worth inquiring about off-season discounts considering the excellent location and amenities, including TV.

Hotel Mesembria (☎ 43255; ul Ribarska 6; s/d 40/50 lv) The staff here are rather unhelpful and don't speak English. While some of the rooms have decent balconies, the rooms themselves are drab and Soviet. Location is great, but this is still rather a second-rate joint.

Cathedral of the Assumption of the Virgin
(p205), Varna

Tombul Mosque (154),
Shumen

Sozopol (p188)

Sozopol (p188)

The ancient Stambul Kapiya gate, pl
Bdnitsi, Vidin (p237)

PAUL GREENWAY

ROBERTO GE

Folk music players, Vidin (p236)

Svoboda (Freedom) square, with the Monument to Freedom, Ruse (p225)

PAUL (

TOP END

Hotel Morska Perla (☎ 45606; ul Tsar Simeon 4; s/d/ apt 60/100/120 lv; 🆒) Very friendly and professionally run, the 'Sea Pearl' is extremely comfortable and agreeable, although overpriced in July and August. Outside these months, prices are 50% lower.

White House Hotel (☎ 42488; www.white-house -13.8k.com; ul Tsar Simeon 2; s/d/apt incl breakfast 60/100/ 150 lv; 🆒 🖥 P) OK, so the US president probably wouldn't stay here, but the White House is definitely one of the better hotels in town. Nesebâr's one and only Internet café functions from here and staff speak good English. Rooms all feature TV, fridge and usually a balcony.

Eating

Git your teeth and bear it – all restaurants in Nesebâr are tourist-oriented. Food prices are roughly twice what you'll pay elsewhere in the country, and the food usually not that much better. If you've been to Slânchev Bryag, you won't be shocked by the restaurant prices in Nesebâr, but you will be horrified if you've arrived from anywhere else in Bulgaria.

Freshly caught fish abounds on the menus of Nesebâr's numerous restaurants and *mehanas*. If possible, escape the crowds and find a quiet place with views and breezes in the eastern part of town. The cheapest places are the harbour-side eateries near the bus station, where locals and fishermen eat. This is also the place to eat later at night – most tourist restaurants are shut by 11pm.

Zornitsa (☎ 45231; mains 6-8 lv) Great sea views and tasty fish can be had at this place, off ul Mesembria on the southern side of the town. The absence of live music makes this a good choice for a quiet evening meal, although it fills up later on.

Old Nesebâr (☎ 44532; ul Ivan Alexander 11; mains 6-9 lv) This popular barbecue place also offers great sea views and good food. Its menu is more meat-focused that most, so it offers some respite from the fish.

Vega Restaurant (mains 4-12 lv; 🕙 9am-midnight) Off ul Mesembria and run by a friendly family that often ends nights pouring the *rakia* at a nearby table, Vega Restaurant has four terraces overlooking the water and big-portion Bulgarian meals.

Tangra Mehana (ul Neptun; mains 4.50-16 lv; 🕙 11am-10pm) One of several upscale fish res-

taurants at the end of the main drag. Seats in the vine-covered courtyard fill quickly. Go for the grilled blue fish snagged offshore (16 lv) or an English breakfast (5 lv).

Neptun (ul Neptun 1; meals from 5.50 lv) For truly fresh seafood such as *lefer* (bluefish), the Neptun is recommended. It's one of several decent restaurants at the end of the main drag, blissfully distant from the noise and crowds.

Drinking

Most locals and visitors do nothing more in the evening than sit at a café and sip on a beer or coffee. For something a little different, try Tequila Bar, set up on a pontoon. Prices are high, but it's an ideal place to watch the sun set and to throw scraps to the seagulls on the nearby rocks.

Entertainment

The only nightspot in town is Bora Bora, on the 2nd floor of the defunct maritime passenger terminal. Livelier nightlife can be had in nearby Slânchev Bryag. Bulgarian drama is performed at the small **Nesebâr Theatre** (ul Mesembria).

Shopping

Nesebâr has more tourist tat per square metre than anywhere else in Bulgaria. You can pick up all kinds of souvenirs here, although embroidery and woollen goods predominate. Price wise, it's far better to shop almost anywhere else.

Getting There & Away

Nesebâr is excellently connected to destinations both up and down the coast by public transport. If you're driving, *please* do everyone a favour and park in the new town and walk over the causeway.

The town's bus station is on the small square at the end of the causeway, just outside the city walls. Be aware that the stop before this on the mainland is for the new town, which nobody will probably want to get out for. From the bus station, there are big municipal buses to Slânchev Bryag (0.50 lv, 10 minutes, every 15 minutes), Burgas (2.10 lv, 40 minutes, every 30 minutes) Varna (6 lv, two hours, seven a day) and Sofia (18 lv, seven hours) about 10 times a day, mostly early in the morning and late at night.

To get to nearby Slânchev Bryag you can also catch a taxi (about 4 lv), but make sure the driver uses the meter; or jump into an expensive but fun water taxi (8.50 lv), which leaves from an obvious spot north of the bus station about every 30 minutes between 9am and 9pm.

SLÂNCHEV BRYAG (SUNNY BEACH)
СЛЪНЧЕВ БРЯГ
☎ 0554

Despite the cringeworthy name, Sunny Beach is one of Bulgaria's best beaches – a huge bay lined by several kilometres of sandy beach that attracts more sun worshippers than any other resort in the country. Big brother to Golden Sands up the coast, this is where to head if you want a carefree, cloistered couple of days on the coast with nothing but the warm sea and miles of browning flesh to distract you.

Almost everyone here is on a cheap package tour and few people go beyond nearby Nesebâr. The resort is home to more than 120 hotels (with nearly 30,000 beds) and about 600 cafés, restaurants, bars and shops. As the hotels are spread out among shady parks, Slânchev Bryag doesn't feel nearly as overcrowded or hectic as other resorts along the coast, so it's popular with families. Prices for everything are high, naturally.

Orientation & Information

Slânchev Bryag lines the coast, and its main drag is the coastal road that runs between Varna and Burgas. Along this road, there are plentiful ATMs, and there are also market stalls, a post office, a telephone centre with an Internet agency, and a laundry. Dozens of foreign exchange offices are set up here and elsewhere around the resort. Day-old copies of English and German newspapers can be bought at hotel reception desks and bookstalls.

Activities

Slânchev Bryag caters mainly to families, so there's plenty of activities for the kids, but surprisingly few places to organise any water sports. Unfortunately, you can't just walk onto the beach and expect to go windsurfing, paragliding or jet skiing. The most exciting thing to do on the water is splash about on a two-person **paddle boat** (per hr about 8 lv).

Sleeping

Almost everyone who stays in Slânchev Bryag is on a package tour that includes accommodation (and, often, meals and all sorts of activities), so there's little point recommending any particular hotel. Also, most independent travellers will almost certainly choose to do a day trip by bus from Burgas or Nesebâr; the latter offers the best range of budget and mid-range accommodation in the region and is linked very frequently to Slânchev Bryag by public transport. No agencies in the town offer rooms in private homes because nobody really lives here.

There are more than 120 hotels to chose from, but try to avoid any place too close to the main road. For the best deal, contact a travel agent who will have access to the weekly discounts given for tour groups, which can make time here incredibly cheap. Check out websites such as www.bulgarian coast.com for an introduction to the truly vast number of places to stay here.

Eating

The cost of a meal at a major hotel is two or three times more than at a café. In major hotels and restaurants, expect to pay 10 to 12 lv for a decent meal, 4 lv for a toasted sandwich and even 2 lv for a cup of tea.

Among the various pizzerias, fake English pubs, Indian takeaways and hamburger stalls, it is still possible to find a restaurant serving authentic Bulgarian cuisine. One of the best is Chuchura (just behind Hotel Trakia), which has folkloric music most evenings and food at reasonable prices.

Getting There & Away

There is a big central bus station just off the main road in the middle of the main strip. It's excellently laid out and easy to use (all timetables are in English as well as Bulgarian). However, if you want to go up or down the coast, you can get on at any bus stop along the main road.

City buses to Burgas (2.10 lv, 45 minutes) all go via Nesebâr; you can also get frequent buses to Varna (5 lv, two hours) and Pomorie (1.50 lv, 30 minutes).

Most buses and minibuses use the station just off the main road, about 100m up from the Hotel Svejest. Minibuses from Burgas stop anywhere along the main road (and within walking distance of your hotel) as far north as Hotel Cuban. From the bus station, several daily buses go to Sliven, Plovdiv and Stara Zagora, and eight or nine depart for Sofia.

For information about travelling between Slânchev Bryag and Nesebâr, see p201.

Getting Around

Trolleybuses (1.50 lv) shuttle along three numbered routes every 15 to 20 minutes between 9am and 11pm. The streets around the resort are uncrowded and flat, so bicycles are an ideal way of getting around. These can be rented from outside Hotel Svejest for about 3/8 lv for one/three hours, or 15 lv for the whole day. Cars can be hired through several travel agencies and at hotel reception desks; rental starts at €40 per day, including insurance and unlimited kilometres, plus petrol.

NORTHERN COAST

VARNA BAPHA
☎ 052 / pop 350,000

Varna is by far the most interesting and cosmopolitan town on the Black Sea coast, and a definite highlight of the region. A strange combination of port, city and resort, it's a changeable place – one minute large-scale grandeur and the Black Sea, the next, forgotten side streets and ancient Roman remains. Indeed, there's an air of a capital that never quite was here, but its long and interesting history is attested to by plenty of sights and activities, including the largest and most impressive museum in Bulgaria and the superb Cathedral of the Assumption of the Virgin at the city's heart.

You'll eat well here, as well as have plenty of activities to keep you going, from enjoying the great marine park and clean sea to visiting some of the city's great museums and shopping on its busy pedestrianised streets.

Varna is also an ideal base for day trips to nearby beach resorts such as Sveti Konstantin (p211) and Zlatni Pyasâtsi (Golden Sands; p213), and the charming towns of Balchik (p217) and Dobrich (p242).

History

Remnants of an ancient Thracian civilisation dated to about 4000 BC have been found at Varna Necropolis, an area of about 100 tombs near Varna. In 585 BC, the Greeks from Miletus settled in the area and created the city of Odessos. The Greeks only lived here for about 150 years before it again came under the control of the Thracians. Odessos withstood initial attacks from the Macedonians in 342 BC, but was eventually annexed by Alexander the Great. The city didn't really regain any regional importance until the Romans conquered the area and set up a base in Odessos during the 2nd century AD.

During the First Bulgarian Empire (681–1018), the city was renamed Varna but its fortunes declined. It alternated between Byzantine and Bulgarian rule during the Middle Ages, and eventually re-emerged as a prosperous settlement. Next came the Turks, who captured Varna in 1393 and turned it into a northern bastion of their empire. After the Crimean War (1853–56), Turkey allowed its allies, Britain and France, to sell their products throughout the Ottoman Empire, so Varna became a great trading centre once more.

In 1866, a railway between Ruse and Varna was built. This provided a direct route from the Danube to the Black Sea coast and proved a catalyst for an economic resurgence. Varna became a major shipbuilding centre and port, and resorts based on mineral springs and beaches were later established nearby.

Orientation

Despite its size, the centre of Varna is pleasingly compact. Ul Tsar Simeon leads from the train station into pl Nezavisimost, which acts as the city centre. From the square, a short thoroughfare heads northwest, passing the domineering cathedral towering over the market and several theatres, and turns into bul Vladislav Varenchik, which leads to the main bus station and airport. From pl Nezavisimost, another broad pedestrian mall, ul Knyaz Boris I, runs east and then northeast towards Primorski Park and the sea.

MAPS

The city is excellently mapped in the detailed *Varna City Map*, published in English by Slavena (with a blue cover). Maps are readily available from any of the plethora of bookstalls around the city and at the bus and train stations.

Information
BOOKSHOPS
Penguin Bookshop (ul 27 Juli) Two-storey bookshop just behind St Nikolai Church. Sells English-language novels.

INTERNET ACCESS
There are Web cafés all over the city; the following two are big and central:
Frag (pl Nezavisimost) Oddly named subterranean Internet café in the same building as the Varna Opera House.
Internet Cafe (Festival Hall, ul Slivnitsa) Can be quite difficult to find, downstairs in the warren of this vast complex, but has about 30 terminals.

LAUNDRY
The two places listed here offer a drop-and-collect service at very reasonable rates.

Laundrette (ul Opalchenska 23; ⏰ 8.30am-8.30pm)
Peralnya (ul Voden; ⏰ 9am-7pm Mon-Fri, 9am-6pm Sat)

MONEY
There is certainly no shortage of foreign exchange offices and ATMs around the city centre.
Biochim Commercial Bank (bul Vladislav Varenchik) Near the main post office. Changes travellers cheques, provides cash advances and has an ATM.
Bulbank (ul Slivnitsa) Changes travellers cheques, provides cash advances over the counter and has an ATM that accepts major credit cards.
United Bulgarian Bank (ul Knyaz Boris I)

POST
Main post office (ul Sâborni 36)

VARNA

BLACK SEA COAST

TELEPHONE
Telephone centre (ul Sâborni 36; ☺ 7am-11pm) Inside the main post office.

TOURIST INFORMATION
Tourist information centre (☎ 602 907; www.tourexpo .bg; ul Tsar Osvoboditel 36; ☺ 9am-7pm Mon-Fri, 9am-1pm Sun) Excellent and super-friendly, with English-speaking staff who can book hotels and give information on the entire region. It's a little out of the centre, but easily walkable. City tours can be arranged but they are rather overpriced at 70 lv per person in a small group.

TRAVEL AGENCIES
Balkan Tourism (☎ 618 051; www.balkantourism.bg; ul A Malinov 4) Can organise private accommodation, rent cars and make bookings elsewhere on the coast.

Global Tours (☎ 601 085; globaltours_varna@hotmail .com; ul Knyaz Boris I 67) Offers a full range of services, including car rental, international and internal flights and excursions.

Tourist Service (☎ 225 313; Hotel Odessos, ul Slivnitsa 1; ☺ 9am-6pm Mon-Fri) Rents cars and organises excursions and private rooms.

Dangers & Annoyances
Varna is a pricey place and taxi drivers are keener to rip you off here than anywhere else in the region. Check the tariffs before getting in and make sure the meter is running. At the bus and train stations, moneychangers offer outrageously high exchange rates, trying to set you up for a rip-off or robbery. Do *not* change money on the street. Also, watch out for large buses and silent trolleybuses speeding along pedestrian malls.

Sights
CATHEDRAL OF THE ASSUMPTION OF THE VIRGIN
This big **cathedral** (☎ 225 435; pl Mitropolitska Simeon; ☺ 6am-10pm) was built between 1880 and 1886 and is the main symbol of the city, standing right at its heart, north of pl Nezavisimost. Its golden domes are impressive and the whole structure is second in size only to the Aleksander Nevski Cathedral in Sofia. It features three altars – one dedicated to St Nicholas of Myra, one to the Russian martyr, Aleksander Nevski, and one to the Assumption of the Virgin. Note the murals (from the late 1940s), the stained glass windows and the icons and thrones carved from wood. The museum commemorates the sacrifices made by the Russian Army in liberating Bulgaria from the Turks.

ARCHAEOLOGICAL MUSEUM
For those who glaze over at the mere mention of archaeological museums, this may just well be the antidote. Varna's amazing **Archaeological Museum** (☎ 237 057; ul Maria Luisa 41; adult/student 4/2 lv; ☺ 10am-5pm Tue-Sun Apr-Oct, 10am-5pm Tue-Sat Nov-Mar). The 100,000 objects

BLACK SEA COAST

are housed in 39 rooms along two massive floors, so allow plenty of time to take it all in. All exhibits originate from the Varna area, and are placed in chronological order, from the old Stone Age to the late medieval period.

The highlights are perhaps the 6000-year-old gold and copper objects. Unearthed by chance in 1972 in the Varna Necropolis (closed to the public), about 4km west of central Varna, these items are reputedly the oldest of their kind in the world. Other rooms contain religious icons from the 16th to 18th centuries, Bulgaria's largest collection of ceramics, sculptures and bas-reliefs, and fine examples of woodcarving from Tryavna. Two other rooms contain temporary exhibits, and a huge library caters to students of archaeology.

All exhibits have detailed captions in English, and it's easy to work through the displays chronologically by following the arrows. It is not permitted to take photographs in the museum. The entrance to this massive building (a former girls' high school) faces the southeast, and is accessible through the park.

ROMAN THERMAE

One definite highlight of Varna is the well-preserved ruins of the **Roman Thermae** (☎ 456 476; ul Khan Krum; adult/child 3/2 lv; ☾ 10am-5pm Tue-Sun Apr-Oct, 10am-5pm Mon-Fri Nov-Mar). The ruins are the largest in Bulgaria and the third biggest in Europe. Only a small part of the original complex (estimated to be 7000 sq metres) still stands. The baths were built in the late 2nd century AD as part of the reconstruction of the city of Odessos by the Romans. Probably abandoned only 100 years later when the Roman Empire started to collapse, the complex was only occupied again once more – by artisans – in the 14th century.

Some boards around the complex contain basic explanations (in English) about the use of the rooms, such as the frigidarium (where guests bathed in freezing cold water) and the tepidarium, where they luxuriated in tepid water before jumping into the caldarium (with scaldingly hot water).

The ruins can be admired for free from the grounds of St Anastasios Orthodox Church (see right). However, it's far better to pay the entrance fee and explore the ruins from within – but allow enough time to enjoy it all. The booklet (2 lv) available at the entrance gate on the southwestern corner is a bit ancient itself but provides a useful summary about the baths' history and purpose.

ROMAN BATHS

The ruins described previously are called Roman *thermae* (Latin for 'baths') to differentiate them from the **Roman Baths** (bul Primorski). The baths were built in around the 4th century AD, so they're not as old as the Roman Thermae, nor are they as impressive. There's nothing much to see, and a lamentable lack of explanations on site doesn't help. The grounds are closed, but it's worth peering over the fence if you're walking past.

CHURCHES

The churches are worth exploring; admission is free, and they're open from about 6am to 10pm. The beautiful **St Anastasios Orthodox Church** (ul Graf Ignatiev) overlooks the Roman Thermae. Built in 1602, it's one of the oldest churches in the city and features an intricately carved throne. The quaint **St Nikolai Church** (ul Knyaz Boris I; cameras/video cameras 5/15 lv), which looks out of place along the modern mall, is worth a visit for its murals.

The elegant **St Sarkis Armenian Apostolic Church** (ul Han Asparuh 15) was built in 1842. It's not normally open but its exterior can be admired from over the fence or from within the church grounds.

Once the National Bulgarian Renaissance Museum under the communists, the **St Michael the Archangel Church** was founded in 1865 under the Turkish Yoke and is historically significant as it was the first place during the beginning of the Bulgarian national revival where religious services were given in Bulgarian. The building also contained Varna's first school. You are welcome to have a look around – the church is small and badly lit but there are some fine wooden icons. The lovely **garden courtyard** is worth a visit in itself.

ETHNOGRAPHIC MUSEUM

Housed in a delightful old revival-era mansion, Varna's **Ethnographic Museum** (☎ 630 588; ul Panagyurishte 22; adult/student 4/2 lv; ☾ 10am-5pm Tue-Sun Apr-Oct, 10am-5pm Tue-Sat Nov-Mar) is one of the country's best, although admittedly that's no awesome achievement. The ground floor contains a large and varied collection of agricultural implements and displays about weaving, wine-making, iron smelting and fishing from the late 19th and early 20th centuries. The 1st floor has an impressive range of costumes and jewellery, and the four rooms on the 2nd floor feature the sort of furniture that would have filled this Bulgarian national revival house (1860).

Some of the museum's captions are in English and a few are also in French and German. The booklet (2 lv), written in French, English or German, and available at the museum, provides further explanations.

NATIONAL NAVAL MUSEUM

Unmissable from the city beach is the **National Naval Museum** (☎ 633 015; bul Primorski 2; adult/child 2/1 lv; ◷ 10am-6pm Mon-Fri). Here, a superb display of boats (including the warship *Druzki*, which torpedoed a Turkish boat and turned around the Balkan Wars of 1912–13), submarines and other naval equipment greets you in the outdoors around the museum. It's well worth a look even if you don't go in. Inside, it houses various exhibits outlining the history of the Bulgarian Navy from the Russian–Turkish War (1877–78) to the present day and features anchors, artillery, uniforms and models of ships. The museum is certainly more interesting than the typical archaeological and ethnological museums found all over Bulgaria, and the only one of its kind in the country. To the north, a 1km promenade leads to the **Liberators Monument**.

PRIMORSKI PARK

This large and attractive green space overlooking the sea stretches for about 8km, and is said to be the largest of its kind in Europe. Easily accessible from the city centre, it's bursting with people and festivals in summer, and is a wonderful place for an evening promenade. It features the **Copernicus Planetarium** (☎ 684 444/1; adult/under 18 5/2 lv; ◷ showings 5pm & 7pm Mon-Sat) which does a decent show that is well worth a visit for those interested in astronomy. If you have a group of 10 or more (or, presumably, purchase 10 tickets) the staff will put on a show in English or German.

Further into the park is the **Aquarium** (☎ 222 586; ◷ 9am-7pm). Disappointingly, it's little more than a motley and outdated collection of live and bottled marine life. The entrance is on the northwestern side, near all the cafés.

In the northern section, the **Zoopark** (☎ 302 528; admission 1 lv; ◷ 8am-8pm) features a ragged collection of deer, jaguars, emus and lions. About 200m further north, the **Terrarium Varna** (admission 1.20 lv; ◷ 9am-6pm) offers a collection of creepy crawlies such as spiders and scorpions.

Another 500m further north is the **Dolphinarium** (☎ 302 199; admission 16 lv; ◷ Tue-Sun). Although the only one of its kind in the Balkans, it offers little more than what you would expect, ie dolphins jumping in and out of water. Forty-minute shows are held at 11am and 3pm (January to May), 11am, 2pm and 3.30pm (June to August) and 11am and 3pm (September to December). You can also watch the dolphins at play before or after the show for the price of a drink at the café.

ART GALLERIES

Varna has a thriving artist community and there are around 20 public and private art galleries. Devotees should pick up the *Varna Art Galleries* (2 lv) brochure from the Boris Georgiev Art Gallery. The brochure describes the exhibits at each gallery, details the opening hours and contains a useful map with locations of each gallery.

There are three galleries worth visiting here. The **Boris Georgiev Art Gallery** (☎ 243 123; ul Lyuben Karavelov 1; admission 2 lv; ◷ 10am-5pm Tue-Sun), also known as the Varna Art Gallery, features two floors of mostly Bulgarian contemporary art. The **Varna Centre for Contemporary Art** (☎ 603 238; ul Knyaz Boris I 65; admission free; ◷ 10am-6pm Tue-Sun) is another gallery with a collection of rather bizarre modern art. An equally interesting private gallery is the nearby **Artin** (☎ 614 833; ul Knyaz Boris I 57), which features the latest work of some of the best-known local artists in a charming old mansion.

Festivals & Events

Between May and October, Varna hosts the renowned **Varna Summer International Festival**. First established in 1926, the festival features outstanding events, including opera, the biennial International Ballet Competition (held in even-numbered years) and choral, jazz and folkloric music. Events are held at the **Open-Air Theatre** (☎ 228 385; Primorski Park) and in some of the nine halls in the massive **Festival Hall** (☎ 621 331; ul Slivnitsa). Programmes and information about buying tickets are well advertised beforehand in Varna and Sofia. The Festival Hall also hosts the **Annual International Film Festival** for one week or so in late August and early September.

Other special events around the city include the **Songs about Varna Competition** and the **Days of Greek Culture** festival, both held in March.

Sleeping

There has been a huge expansion in Varna's hotel market over the past few years, and although most places remain a little overpriced you shouldn't have trouble finding a room at any time of the year.

BUDGET

Victorina (☎ 603 541, 08 8772 1538; www.victorina.borsa bg.com; ul Tsar Simeon I 36; per person 22 lv) Right by the train station and highly recommended for renting rooms in private houses around the centre. Out of season, rates drop to 15 lv. You are also able to rent self-contained apartments both in the centre and on the coast. English is spoken.

Tourist Service (☎ 225 313; Hotel Odessos; high/off season per person 30/40 lv; ☽ 9am-6pm Mon-Fri) The price of rooms offered by this agency is comparatively high, but the quality of accommodation is better than most.

Tourist Information Centre (☎ 602 907; ul Tsar Osvoboditel 36; per person 15-20 lv) **Global Tours** (☎ 601 085; globaltours_varna@hotmail.com; ul Knyaz Boris I 67; 15-20 lv) Private rooms can also be organised by these two.

Flag Hostel (☎ 648 877; www.flaghostels.com; 1st fl, ul Opalchenska 25; dm €10) Opened in 2004, the Flag became the Black Sea's first hostel and is a great place to stay. Run by an Australian, the spotless place has a nice, relaxed sense of fun. As well as its 18 beds in three dorms, there's free laundry, shared kitchens and plenty of free beer available.

Voennomorski Club (☎ 238 312; ul Vladislav Varenchik 2; s/d 30/44 lv) This bright-blue building opposite the cathedral offers small but comfortable and clean rooms in an unbeatable location. It's a musty old place in general, although many rooms have now been renovated. Most rooms can be noisy. Despite this, it's excellent value.

MID-RANGE

Three Dolphins Hotel (☎ 600 911; ul Gabrovo 27; s/d 50/60 lv) In a quiet area near the train station, this small, homely guesthouse is OK value. All rooms have a TV, and recently renovated rooms that incorporate air-conditioning, minibars and Internet access are worth the price hike (s/d 70/80 lv). It's a good idea to book ahead in high season.

Hotel Santa Marina (☎ 603 826; fax 603 825; ul Baba Rada 28; s/d incl breakfast 72/92 lv; ☒) This tiny, cosy place is centrally located and good value. Rooms have a TV and fridge. It's often full, especially on summer weekends, so book ahead.

Hotel Odessos (☎ 640 300; www.odessos-bg.com; ul Slivnitsa 1; s/d incl breakfast 80/90 lv; ☒ ☐ Ⓟ) This three-star, four-storey hotel overlooking Primorski Park has modern, clean and comfortable rooms. Not all rooms have balconies with views, and those that do overlook the crowded square. It's overpriced thanks to the wonderful location, but it's always popular, so book ahead in summer.

TOP END

City Mark (☎ 603 721; www.citymark.hit.bg; pl Nezavisimost; s/d/tr 120/150/175; ☒) Right in the heart of town, the City Mark is smart and popular with a young clientele. Its rooms are sometimes on the garish side, but always very comfortable and there's a genuine air of cool about the place. Downstairs, you'll find a lively bar and restaurant that attracts the crowds from nearby pl Nezavisimost.

Grand Hotel Musala Palace (☎ 664 100; www .musalapalace.bg; ul Musala 2; s/d/ste 234/263/370 lv; ☒ ☐ Ⓟ) Varna's grandest hotel is this superb (if rather chichi) conversion of the Hotel London, which originally opened in 1912. The exceptionally opulent and large rooms are furnished in baroque-style darkwood furniture, and the overall service is top notch.

Panorama Hotel (☎ 687 300; bul Primorski 31; s/d/ste 100/140/200 lv; ☒ ☐ Ⓟ) The look and feel of the Panorama is thoroughly chic and minimalist, the latter also being true of the guest numbers when we visited. However, this is certainly one of the best deals for top-end accommodation.

Art Hotel Capitol (☎ 688 000; www.capitol.bg; ul Petko Karavelov 40; s/d 150/170 lv; ☒ ☐ Ⓟ) One of the more stylish new establishments in town, the so-called 'art' hotel does have some lovely touches, although some of the choices are on a knife edge between stylish and garish. Still, it's a superb place to stay with great rooms and demonstrates a flare for the hotel business that remains sadly rare elsewhere in the country.

Cherno More Hotel (☎ 612 235; fax 612 220; ul Slivnitsa 33; s/d 85/133 lv) Shaking off its communist legacy, this huge eyesore in the centre of town is wildly overpriced, but it's never full as it's so big. There's actually a whole range of prices available, depending on how unmodernised you are willing to go – the crappiest double will set you back 57 lv, but it's still overpriced and the plumbing is horrendous.

Orbita Hotel (☎ 612 350; orbita@abv.com; ul Tsar Osvoboditel 25; s/d 90/106 lv; 🕲) This rather characterless hotel is at the edge of the city centre and its rooms are perfectly adequate and clean, including TVs, fridges and modern bathrooms.

Eating

Varna has some superb dining and is a great place to escape from the tourist-oriented atmosphere of many other eateries along the coast.

Paraklisa (☎ 223 495; bul Primorski 47; mains 6-12 lv; 🕒 11am-11pm Mon-Sat) Set back from the road in the courtyard of a tiny church, the traditional look at this, the Black Sea's most enduring and innovative Bulgarian kitchen, is balanced by the graffiti that has accumulated on the walls over the years. Try the veal with aubergines (9 lv) or the various lamb dishes, all of which are cooked to perfection. The church outside remains open all night if you want to pop out to give thanks (and you probably will). Reservations are essential and the staff speak good English.

Morska Sirena (☎ 692 095; mains 6-12 lv; 🕒 11am-11pm Mon-Sat) If you can't get a reservation at Paraklisa, try this newer venture by the same cook – on the city's pier.

Nikova Kâshta (☎ 304 739; 8 Primorski Polk; mains 10 lv) Not in Varna proper, 'Nick's House' is on the road to Vinitsa, a short cab ride (3 lv) from the town centre. In a gorgeous pink revival-period house, this place serves up top-notch traditional dishes, although it's pricier than almost anywhere else in town.

Orient Turkish Arabic Restaurant (☎ 602 380; ul Tsaribrod 1; mains 3-4 lv) Another of Varna's best,

this Halal place serves up delicious Turkish and Middle Eastern dishes in a charming space dominated by the sound of running water and a lovely outside terrace. Highly recommended.

Chuchura (☎ 608 648; ul Dragoman; mains 3 lv) Another highlight, here you'll find classic Bulgarian cooking served by traditionally clad staff. It has a menu in English, and the service is impeccable. The daily specials often include delicious Bulgarian *musaka*.

Gabi Gostilnitsa (ul Sveti Klement 8) A very popular tavern on a small side street that serves up simple, tasty, home-cooked Bulgarian standards at bargain prices. It's always busy with locals.

Komplex Hâshove (☎ 616 877; 8 Primorski Polk; mains 3-5 lv) This charming complex features a café, bar, *mehana* and restaurant, and a fountain in the courtyard. It is always busy, especially at lunch time when the city's power brokers dine here. Excellent pizza.

Bulgaverna Nashentsy (☎ 630 186; ul Tsar Simeon I 27; mains 6-8 lv; 🕒 10am-last customer) This large and not untacky take on the traditional Bulgarian restaurant serves up high-quality dishes from its vast pictorial menu. Often filled by tour groups, it's nevertheless popular with Bulgarians too. There's live music and dancing from 8pm.

Happy Bar & Grill (pl Nezavisimost; grills about 5 lv) The Varna-based but countrywide Happy Bar & Grill chain has several restaurants in town, including at this central location. It's a cheerful place that serves tasty salads and grilled meat dishes at comparatively high prices.

Mustang Food (salads 2-3 lv, breakfast 3 lv, grills from 3.50 lv) Mustang Cinema (bul Vladislav Varenchik); Cherno More Hotel (ul Slivnitsa 33) Similar in style and popularity to Happy's, Mustang offers large servings of Western-style meals, but at more competitive prices. There are several branches around the city.

Trops Kâshta (ul Knyaz Boris I; mains 2-3 lv) This chain of nationwide cafeterias is just as busy during the working week as those in Sofia and Plovdiv. It's an ideal place to enjoy a cheap, simple meal without needing to speak Bulgarian or plough through a menu in Cyrillic. Just point and pay.

BMS (mains 2-3 lv) train station (ul Devnya); St Nikolai Church (ul Knyaz Boris I) Offers similar choices, prices and service to Trops Kâshta. It has two convenient locations.

Drinking

Some of the best cafés are in Primorski Park, near the entrance to the Aquarium and around the Summer Theatre. In the city centre, try the cafés along the northeastern end of ul Knyaz Boris I and the southeastern section of ul Slivnitsa. Along the esplanade, just down from the park, competition is fierce among cafés and bars, so prices for drinks and fish meals are excellent value.

Entertainment

Varna Opera House (☎ 602 086; pl Nezavisimost) Bulgaria's second most important opera house (after Sofia) hosts performances by the Varna Opera and Philharmonic Orchestra all year, except July and August, as does the **Storya Bachvarov Dramatic Theatre** (☎ 600 779; pl Mitropolitska Simeon) next door.

Open-Air Theatre (☎ 228 385; Primorski Park) Complete with mock, ivy-covered Roman arches, this theatre hosts anything from ballet to rock concerts. Details are available at the adjoining ticket office. Live music is also played most summer evenings at the temporary **Summer Theatre** (Primorski Park).

Mustang Cinema (bul Vladislav Varenchik; tickets about 4 lv) Next to Mustang Food, this is probably the most comfortable and most expensive cinema in town. Recent European and American films are also shown all year at **Festival Hall** (☎ 621 331; ul Slivnitsa).

Shopping

Varna has good shopping on the pedestrian mall of ul Knyaz Boris I, where there are some great fashion and music stores. If folk craft, pottery and embroidery are your things, the stalls set up around the Cathedral of the Assumption of the Virgin offer some excellent bargains. Quality paintings are sold outside St Nikolai Church. One of the best handicraft shops in town is the **Unique Gallery** (ul 27 Juli 21; ☺ 9am-6pm).

Getting There & Away

AIR

Varna's international **airport** (☎ 650 835) is an extremely busy place from late spring until autumn, with charter flights from all over Europe landing here to unload sun seekers onto the Black Sea beaches. Out of season, it's virtually deserted, but year-round flights include one a day to and from Sofia. From the centre, bus No 409 goes to the airport.

The local agency for bookings is the **Varna International Airport Travel Agency** (☎ 612 588; ul Knyaz Boris I 15). **Hemus Air** (☎ 501 039) flies between Varna and Sofia (one way/return 100/196 lv) every day except Sunday between mid-March and late October, and once or twice a day between July and mid-September. **Dandy Airlines** (☎ 501 338) flies between Varna and Sofia several times a day for roughly the same price. Bookings for Hemus and Dandy flights can be made at the relevant offices at the airport, or at the Varna International Airport Travel Agency.

BUS

Varna has two main bus stations – the old **bus station** (☎ 448 349; bul Vladislav Varenchik) is about 2km northwest of the city centre. From this depressing old place, services go to Athens (95 lv, 26 hours, one daily), Balchik (2.50 lv, one hour, 16 daily), Burgas (7 lv, two hours, three daily), Dobrich (3 lv, one hour, every 30 minutes), Istanbul (40 lv, 10 hours, two daily), Plovdiv (15 lv, six hours, two daily), Shumen (5 lv, 1½ hours, three daily), Sofia (19 lv, seven hours, 20 daily) and Veliko Târnovo (8 lv, four hours, 20 daily).

All buses to Sofia go via Shumen and Veliko Târnovo, the buses to Plovdiv go via Stara Zagora and buses south to Burgas pass through all the coastal resorts, including Slânchev Bryag and Nesebâr.

Most long-distance services are operated by private buses. Tickets for these can be bought at agencies in town (as well as at the bus station), but all departures are from the old bus station.

The second bus station in Varna is the **Chatsna Mladost Station** (☎ 500 039), about 200m along a road that starts almost opposite the public bus station; look for the sign in English opposite the bus station. From here, minibuses go to smaller places along the Black Sea coast, including Dobrich (2.50 lv, every 30 minutes), Balchik (2.50 lv, one hour, hourly), Kavarna (3.50 lv, depart 7am, 10am and 5pm), Burgas (6 lv, every 40 minutes to one hour) and Nesebâr (4.50 lv, 1½ hours, six daily), via Slânchev Bryag (4.50 lv, 1¼ hours).

Buses from the south (eg those from Burgas) usually drop off passengers at a convenient spot opposite the main post office on bul Vladislav Varenchik, so as to avoid dumping you in the far-flung bus station.

For details about buses and minibuses between Varna and the beach resorts along the northern coast, see below.

TRAIN

The **train station** (☎ 630 444; bul Primorski) was undergoing restoration at the time of research, but is very similar to that at Burgas. A computer screen in the foyer lists departures and arrivals in Bulgarian. There's a **left-luggage office** (☺ 6am-10pm).

Varna is an important destination on the rail network and there's even a connection to Moscow via Bucharest three times a week in summer. Other destinations include Ruse (6.90 lv, four hours, two daily), Sofia (12.50 lv, eight hours, five daily), Plovdiv (9.90 lv, six hours, three daily) and Shumen (3.90 lv, 1½ hours, eight daily).

The **Rila Bureau** (☎ 226 273; ul Preslav 13; ☺ 8am-7.30pm Mon-Fri, 8am-3.30pm Sun) sells tickets for international services and advance tickets for domestic trains.

Getting Around

The bus and train stations are on opposite sides of the city, and linked by bus Nos 1, 22 and 41. The most useful bus for visitors is No 409, which connects the airport with Zlatni Pyasâtsi (Golden Sands) every 15 minutes between 6am and 11pm. This bus passes the public bus station in Varna and Primorski Park (including the Dolphinarium) and stops near Sveti Konstantin. It can be caught at designated spots near the main post office on bul Vladislav Varenchik, and along ul Slivnitsa.

To tee up a rental car, **Hertz** (☎ 500 210) and **Avis** (☎ 500 832) have offices at the international section of the airport. **Vendor** (☎ 605 111; Cherno More Hotel, ul Slivnitsa 33) is cheaper: it charges US$60/50/45 per day for one/two/three days, including insurance and unlimited kilometres (but not petrol). Cheaper still is the Tourist Service Kapka 94 carrental agency at Sveti Konstantin (right).

The taxi drivers around the cathedral are notorious for ripping people off, so if they refuse to use their meter, simply get out and try another taxi. Varna is also one of the few places in the country where you should carefully check the taxi rates listed on the windows before climbing in. Newer-model taxis and those with air-con charge about three times more than others.

SVETI KONSTANTIN
СВЕТИ КОНСТАНТИН
☎ 052

Sveti Konstantin is a small beach resort about 9km northeast of Varna. Established in 1946 and called Druzhba (Friendship), it was later renamed Sveti Konstantin and Sveti Elena, but is now simply known as Sveti Konstantin. The hotels at the resort are attractively spaced out among oak, beech and pine trees. Sveti Konstantin is less commercial than other resorts, and quieter because of the lack of roads and, therefore, vehicles. The downside is that the beaches are not as spectacular, but many visitors prefer to soak in the mineral baths anyway.

Orientation & Information

The centre of Sveti Konstantin is the road between the bus stop and beach that passes the post office; and the unnamed laneway (which we've called Post Office Lane) between the post office and the Grand Hotel Varna. Hotels are astoundingly badly signposted, and many signposts (in English) are ambiguous, so you may need to invest in a map (2 to 3 lv), available at any bookstall at the resort.

There are dozens of foreign exchange offices, as well as the **Biochim Commercial Bank** (Post Office Lane). An Internet centre is on the ground floor of the International Home for Scientists F Jolet Curie (see p212).

Sights & Activities

SV KONSTANTIN & SV ELENA MONASTERY

This tiny **church** (admission free; ☺ daylight, closed Sun morning) is just off Post Office Lane. It was built below street level in the style demanded by the Ottoman rulers during the early 18th century. The church was destroyed not long after but was rebuilt in 1912. More information about the church and the general development of Sveti Konstantin is featured in a small but fascinating display (with explanations in English) on the ground floor of the International Home for Scientists.

MINERAL BATHS

Sveti Konstantin is popular with Bulgarians (but less so among foreigners) for the mineral springs, which apparently offer relief from various ailments and stress. Several 'health' complexes are signposted around the resort. The admission fee to a swimming

BLACK SEA COAST

pool is 2 lv, a sauna costs from 4 lv for 30 minutes, and a 30-minute massage will set you back about 12 lv. The most developed but expensive place for these activities, and other medical treatments, is the **Balneocentre** (Grand Hotel Varna).

BEACH

The beach is serviceable without being attractive; it's more like a series of small stretches of sand bordered by jetties, break-waters and rocky outcrops. Because of this, and the fact that the resort often attracts guests who are retired and on package tours, no water sports are available. If you want to windsurf or jet ski, head for Albena further up the coast.

Sleeping

The only option for anyone on a budget is a room in a private home – look for an 'accom-modation office' sign (in English) around the resort. **Tourist Service Kapka 94** (☎ 361 003), near the post office, charges 18 lv per person for private rooms, and 26 lv per person for a room in a two-star hotel (most probably a fair way from the beach).

If you normally stay at mid-range hotels, it's better to do a day trip from Varna. To stay here in a top-end hotel, it's cheaper to inquire about a package tour from your home country, or at a travel agency in Sofia. Examples of hotels on offer at the resort are listed here. There are no roads, so none of the hotels have addresses.

International Home for Scientists F Jolet Curie (s/d 85/112 lv) With a name like this we had to mention it, and the complex certainly domi-nates the centre of the resort. It is, however, a typical leftover from the 1960s, complete with barely functioning TVs, fridges and wall-mounted clocks. The prices charged for foreigners are far too high.

Estreya Hotel (☎ 361 135; fax 361 316; s/d incl break-fast 86/150 lv; ☒) A sparkling new place, featur-ing an immaculate garden in a central but secluded location, only metres up from the monastery. The comfortable rooms have a TV and fridge.

Hotel Dolphin (☎ 361 171; s/d 170/190 lv; ☷ ☒) Rates include all meals, drinks and some sports and activities. The Dolphin is a mas-sive new place on the waterfront, catering al-most exclusively to people on package tours. The pool is attractive.

Grand Hotel Varna (☎ 361 491; ghv_res@mail.techno-link.com; s/d 220/289 lv; ☒) The Grand Hotel is so big it has a bowling alley, casino and three swimming pools, and seems to have thousands of rooms and a couple of hundred bars. You name it and it's probably here.

Eating

The cheapest eateries are the small cafés such as Texaco at the bus stop, which offers a grilled half-chicken for less than 3 lv.

Amforia (Post Office Lane; meals 4.50 lv) This place is worth trying for a plate of tasty fish and vegetables.

Restaurant Zaliva (fish meals 5-7 lv) Despite the rather unfortunate name, the grilled fish is delicious and reasonably priced. The views and breezes are also an attraction. It's at the end of the road that passes Grand Hotel Varna towards the beach.

Bulgarska Svatba (meals about 5 lv) One of the few places that actually offers Bulgarian cui-sine. Housed in a traditional building just over the road from Hotel Plaza.

There are masses of restaurants featuring all sorts of cuisines, from the **Delhi Restaurant** (set-price 4-course meals 7 lv), near Grand Hotel Varna, to the **Ukrainian Restaurant** (Hotel Bor). Menus at all restaurants are in English and German, and restaurant staff are likely to speak both languages.

Getting There & Away

Bus No 409 travels from Varna airport to Zlatni Pyasâtsi every 15 minutes between 6am and 11pm. It stops outside the Hotel Panorama at Sveti Konstantin, from where it's a short walk down to the hotels and beach. From along the laneway down from the Panorama, turn right at the first road towards the bus stop and then left down to the beach. Every 15 to 20 minutes between 6am and 11pm, bus No 8 goes directly from Varna to Sveti Konstantin, via ul Maria Luisa, ul Slivnitsa and the northeastern end of ul Knyaz Boris I in Varna.

Getting Around

Budget (☎ 361 491) car rental has a counter in the foyer of Grand Hotel Varna. **Tourist Service Kapka 94** (☎ 361 003) offers cars for an all-inclusive fee of €35 per day (plus petrol), which is cheaper than anywhere in or near Varna.

ZLATNI PYASÂTSI (GOLDEN SANDS)
ЗЛАТНИ ПЯСЪЦИ
☎ 052

Zlatni Pyasâtsi (Golden Sands) may well sound as equally cringe-inducing as Sunny Beach, but in fact it was not a name invented by travel agents (although they can hardly have objected to its PR-friendly sound) – this is actually a centuries-old name for this superb stretch of beach 18km up the coast from Varna. Despite this, Zlatni Pyasâtsi was only developed for mass tourism in the 1960s and has since grown to become Bulgaria's second-largest coastal resort. Around 60 hotels and villas, with nearly 15,000 beds, are clustered along the 4km stretch of sandy beach, or hidden among the trees. Most hotels don't offer genuine sea frontage, unlike those in Slânchev Bryag, but the resort is so narrow that most hotels are less than 300m from the beach anyway. Out of season, the entire resort is something of a ghost town and culturally, like Slânchev Bryag, the place is a zero, but come here for relaxation and seaside fun and you won't be disappointed.

Orientation & Information

Driving a private car into the resort costs 3 lv per vehicle, but visitors arriving by private/public bus or taxi do not have to pay any entrance fees. The resort is long, thin and easy to get around, but there are plenty of helpful signs in English. Several maps are available at bookstalls; the best is *Nessebur & Sunny Beach City Guide*, published by Makros and printed in English and German (with a distinctive yellow-and-blue cover). The post office and telephone centre are near Hotel Yavor, about halfway along the resort, and there is an Internet centre a few metres up from the post office.

Sights
ALADZHA MONASTERY

Understandably, a major local attraction is the **Aladzha Monastery** (☎ 355 460; admission 3 lv, video camera 15 lv; 9am-6pm Tue-Sun Apr-Oct, 9am-4pm Tue-Sat Nov-Mar). Very little is known about this bizarre rock monastery, and reports about its history vary considerably. The cave was probably inhabited during the 5th century BC, but what remains today was probably created during the height of the Ottoman occupation (13th and 14th centuries), when normal churches and monasteries could not be built. The monastery was used by monks from the Hesychast order until the 18th century, but was not discovered again until 1928.

Several sets of stairs and walkways lead to and around these astonishing caves, which were carved up to 40m above ground. Erosion has undoubtedly caused a lot of damage to the caves, including to the extensive murals inside the monastery, but it's still quite a remarkable place. A signposted path (600m) leads to the **Catacombs**, a set of tri-level caves that were probably created in the 13th century. The second level was probably used for burials, but the exact purpose of the other two caves is unknown.

Everything at the monastery is signposted and labelled in English, but the small booklet, written in English and French and available inside the grounds, contains more explanations and makes a nice souvenir. The **museum** also provides some detailed explanations (in English, French and German) about the use and excavations of the monastery. Apparently to fill up space, some unrelated art is displayed on the 2nd floor of the museum.

To walk to the monastery from the resort, head up the road past the post office, cross the main Varna–Albena road outside the Economic & Investment Bank, and follow the signs to 'Kloster Aladja' and the markings along the obvious trail. The walk takes 50 minutes to an hour one way and wends its way through a wonderful, shady forest, part of the 1320-hectare **Golden Sands Nature Park**, which hinders any expansion of the resort into the hills.

The road (3km) is steepish in parts and starts about 500m south along the Varna–Albena road from the start of the walking trail. A good idea is to take a taxi to the monastery (about 4 lv) and walk back down to the resort through the forest. Bus No 33 from the public bus station in Varna to Kranevo drops passengers outside the front entrance of the monastery, but only runs in both directions four or five times a day.

Activities

Most of the agencies in Zlatni Pyasâtsi that once offered water sports have moved to Albena, the self-titled 'sports centre of Bulgaria'. If any outfit decides to set up a water-sports enterprise in Zlatni Pyasâtsi in the future, it will almost certainly do so along

BLACK SEA COAST

the beach near the unmissable International Grand Hotel. This part of the beach is the location of the Water Sports Centre, which offers **jet skiing** and **parasailing**.

The Equestrian Picnic Riding School offers all sorts of equine activities, such as 'advanced' **horse riding** and shorter rides (in distance) for beginners. The school is signposted about 1km up the Varna–Albena road from the southern entrance to the resort.

Water from the mineral springs in the area apparently cures stress, rheumatism, arthritis and various respiratory ailments. Most major hotels offer all sorts of **massages** (20/40min from 12/20 lv), as well as **mineral baths** (30min 25 lv) and a confusing array of 'health treatments'. The main centre of activity is the **Balneocentre** (Ambassador Hotel).

Kiddies will delight in the children's **entertainment centre**, with paddle pools, toy trains and water slides, which is just near Hotel Sirena.

Tours
Dozens of agencies and stalls along the esplanade sell tours such as three-hour yacht cruises (30 lv per person including lunch), and bus trips to Nesebâr (25 lv), Balchik (12 lv) and Kaliakra Cape (20 lv), including a stop in Balchik.

Sleeping
Almost every visitor to Zlatni Pyasâtsi will be on a package tour (with prebooked accommodation) or on a day trip from Varna or elsewhere along the Black Sea coast. Consequently, there's little point recommending any particular hotel, and most places simply don't offer rates that are acceptable to individual travellers anyway.

If you want to stay here, but haven't booked any accommodation, visit the **accommodation office** (☎ 355 683; Varna–Albena road; per person high/low season incl breakfast 33/26 lv; ☼ 9am-6pm), next to the Economic & Investment Bank. It offers rooms in two-star hotels (no doubt a reasonable walk from the beach).

Eating
Food and drink in Zlatni Pyasâtsi cost about twice as much as in Varna, but prices are not quite as outrageous as in Albena. Naturally, the plethora of restaurants, cafés, bars and fast-food joints offer the usual array of Western food as well as Chinese and Indian cuisine. For something different, try the Georgian Restaurant opposite Hotel Rodina.

Vodenitsata (starters 2.50-3.50 lv, main meals from 5.50 lv) This charming place serves traditional Bulgarian meals in a shady courtyard setting, and features live folkloric music most evenings. It's between the post office and the accommodation office.

Tsiganski Tabor (meals 5.20-6.50 lv) Although catering more to the tourists hurtling along the Varna–Albena road, this inviting place, with classic Bulgarian fare, is nevertheless worth the short walk up from Hotel Trapezitsa.

Getting There & Away
There are many entrances to the resort, but the most frequently used ones are in the far south, near the Riviera Hotel complex, at the start of the road to Aladzha Monastery, at the accommodation office and Economic & Investment Bank 500m further north and outside the Hotel Zora in the far north.

Bus Nos 109, 209, 309 and 409 leave Varna every 10 or 15 minutes between 6am and 11pm. The buses stop along the main Varna–Albena road at each main entrance to Zlatni Pyasâtsi, from where it's no more than a 10-minute walk to any major hotel or the beach. Bus No 9 from Varna stops at the southern entrance only, while No 409 goes all the way to the Varna airport. These buses can be caught along ul Maria Luisa, ul Slivnitsa and the northeastern end of ul Knyaz Boris I in Varna; one convenient bus stop is near Mustang Food (p209) along bul Vladislav Varenchik.

Getting Around
If you're not keen on walking, there are several options: hire a bicycle from outside Hotel Rodina for 5/9 lv (one/two hours) or 25 lv (all day); take a trolleybus (1.50 lv) along the esplanade; or jump into one of the (few) cute 'solar taxis', which charge about 5 lv for a trip anywhere within the resort. **Avis** (☎ 500 832; Hotel Rodina) charges from US$70 per day for car rental, including insurance and 200 free kilometres, plus petrol.

ALBENA АЛБЕНА
☎ 0579
While Zlatni Pyasâtsi probably has a livelier nightlife, Albena's more casual feel makes it appealing to a younger, fun-loving crowd.

The beach is about 4km long, up to 100m wide, and stunning. The water is shallow up to 150m offshore, and ideal for the abundance of water sports on offer. The downside is the horrendous prices charged for just about everything – this is certainly the most expensive place in Bulgaria. Opened in 1969, Albena is named after the beautiful heroine from the play of the same name written by Bulgarian playwright and author, Yordan Yovkov.

Orientation & Information

Albena is the most organised resort in Bulgaria, so there are plenty of maps along the streets and multilingual staff at tourist booths. The accommodation office (see p216) is not a tourist office, but the helpful multilingual staff can answer basic questions. Dozens of foreign exchange offices all over Albena will be able to change money, and most offer competitive rates. Along the main road, both the Biochim Commercial Bank and the SC Express Bank, at the administration building opposite the post office, change travellers cheques and offer cash advances on major credit cards. The post office has an Internet centre and plenty of telephones for long-distance calls. Most of the better shops are lined along the unnamed laneway between the Dobrudja and Dorostol Hotels.

Entry to the resort by private car costs 2 lv; admission is free for anyone travelling by taxi or private/public bus or minibus.

Sights

CULTURAL CENTRE

The **Cultural Centre** in the middle of the resort is a token effort at offering something that isn't so hedonistic. The centre hosts regular concerts (tickets about 15 lv) of Bulgarian music and dance. Posters on the centre's front door, and elsewhere around the resort, advertise upcoming programmes. The centre also houses an **Archaeological Museum** (admission 3 lv; ☺ 9am-8pm) that is, frankly, pathetic, and set up entirely for oblivious tourists. Don't forget that the best archaeological museum in the country is a short trip down the road in Varna.

Activities

Albena promotes itself as a 'sports resort' and the 'sports capital of Bulgaria'. It certainly does offer the best range of activities in the country, and adventurous and sporty types will find enough to satisfy their needs – and empty their wallets. Prices are probably lower than most places in Europe, but *very* expensive compared to the cost of almost everything else in Bulgaria.

The Borian Yacht Club in the northern part of the resort offers **windsurfing** (150 lv) and **water-skiing** (180 lv) courses over six days. Also available at the club are **jet skiing** (per 15min 35 lv), **yacht cruises** (1/4 hr 30/50 lv) and **fishing trips** (3/5 hr 30/50 lv).

Tennis (court hire day/evening 15/18 lv) is popular and is offered at a dozen or so courts all over the resort. Coaching costs from 20 lv per hour. Equipment costs extra, and the tennis complexes can even find you a partner to play with (for a supplementary fee).

The more adventurous can enjoy **microlight rides** (8-10min 45 lv) at a runway just past the Arabela restaurant in the far north. **Parasailing** is available at several places along the beach (look for the parachutes in the air) for about the same price. The best place for all types of water sports is along the beach opposite the signposted (in English) 'bazar' in front of Hotel Kardam. Several stalls here offer **jet skiing** (15min 40 lv), **parasailing** (10min 40 lv), **surfing** (board hire per hr/day 15/50 lv), **water-skiing** (10min 20 lv) and **windsurfing** (1hr 12 lv).

Konna Baza Riding Club (☎ 048-776 056), along the main road, offers equestrian activities, including 50-minute walks (costing 18 lv per person), advanced rides (one/two/three hours 40/50/70 lv), training (12 hours, 150 lv) and basic rides (two/three/four/five hours, 30/45/60/75 lv).

Albena boasts the largest number of mineral springs in Bulgaria. The **medical centre** (☎ 62305; mcalbena@mbox.digsys.bg; Hotel Dobrudja) is the country's largest therapy centre. It offers all sorts of massages (45 lv for the 'works') and therapies (eg aromatherapy and hydrotherapy) for about 50 lv per hour.

Tours

Most hotels and travel agencies around Albena can organise all sort of tacky tours, such as seeing a 'Bulgarian wedding' (not a real one!) for 120 lv per person, including food and drinks. Perhaps more enlightening are the bus trips to Varna (29 lv, or 35 lv including the Dolphinarium), and both Balchik and Kaliakra Cape (40 lv).

Sleeping

The **accommodation office** (☎ 62920; bus station; s 54-135 lv, d 70-210 lv; ☉ 8am-noon) is an agency that can organise only hotel rooms (ie not rooms in private homes). The cheaper rooms are likely to be far closer to the main road than the beach. All rates include breakfast. If you want a private room, look for the relevant signs in English, German and Bulgarian outside homes along the main Varna–Balchik road.

Practically everyone visiting Albena will be on an organised tour (with accommodation included) or on a day trip from Varna or elsewhere. Consequently, there's little need to recommend any particular hotel, and most decent places do not offer rates that are acceptable to individual travellers anyway. Rates for the two hotels mentioned here will give you some idea of what to expect.

Gorska Fey (☎ 62961; camp sites 8 lv, bungalows 80 lv, A-frame bungalows 220 lv) Also known as Albena Camping, this camping ground is spread out through the forest just behind the bus station. It's a lovely, shady place; a little remote, perhaps, but it is regularly connected to the beach and restaurants by trolleybus. The A-frame bungalows are large, luxurious and all feature four beds as well as a TV, fridge and veranda. The other bungalows (also with four beds) are not cheap compared to those in the rest of Bulgaria, but they're real bargains for Albena.

Hotel Dobrudja (☎ 62501; dobrudja@al.bia-bg.com; s/d incl breakfast 130/190 lv) This four-star hotel offers all the usual amenities in a central location. It's the only place in Albena likely to stay open in winter.

Hotel Kardam (☎ 62368; s/d Jul & Aug 80/120 lv, May, Jun, Sep & Oct 65/100 lv) One of several three-star places close to the beach and shops, the Kardam is cheaper and cosier than most others. Rates include breakfast.

Eating

At last count, Albena had over 120 places to eat. Food and drink in the resort costs about two or three times more than in Varna. If money does matter, check the menu (always with English and German translations) before sitting down. Typically, an omelette will cost 4 to 5 lv; small/large pizzas, 7/10 lv; grills with garnishes, 10 to

12 lv; a small bottle of local/imported beer, 2/4 lv; and a cup of tea, 2 lv.

Slavyanski Kut (mains 10 lv) This large complex in the southern section of the resort is one of the few places that offers Bulgarian cuisine, as well as folkloric performances most evenings.

Starobulgarski Stan (mains 8 lv) Along the road between the bus station and the Cultural Centre, this classy place also offers tasty traditional dishes.

Arabela (mains from 8 lv) For something different, try this unmissable restaurant, inside an old sailing ship along the far northern beach.

Kafe Kiz (Cultural Centre; snacks from 3 lv) This is one of the few places we can recommend for snacks (eg pizzas and sandwiches) and drinks at acceptable prices.

Getting There & Away

The well-organised **bus station** (☎ 62860) is about 800m from the beach, and is connected to the hotels and beach by trolleybus. Minibuses from Varna (2.50 lv, 45 minutes) via Zlatni Pyasâtsi (2 lv, 20 minutes) depart every 30 minutes between 8am and 7.30pm from a spot known as Makedonia Dom. Every 15 minutes between about 8am and 7.30pm, minibuses leave from Albena for Balchik (1.20 lv, 20 minutes), and to Dobrich (3 lv, 45 minutes) every 30 minutes to hourly. Three or four buses a day travel between Sofia (16 to 18 lv, eight hours) and Albena.

Getting Around

Trolleybuses (1.50 lv) putter along two set routes every 20 minutes between 9am and midnight. Other ways to get around include horse and cart at *very* negotiable rates; bicycles, which are available for rent outside the bazar and Slavyanska Hotel (one hour/two hours/all day 5/9/20 lv); motor scooters (one hour/two hours/all day 15/25/50 lv); and even rollerblades (one/two hours 5/9 lv).

Albena Rent a Car (☎ /fax 62010; Hotel Dobrudja) charges 65 lv per day (one to three days), or 45 lv per day for more than one week, including unlimited kilometres and insurance, but excluding petrol.

Plenty of predatory taxi drivers line the main roads, and need persuasion to use their meters.

BLACK SEA COAST

BALCHIK БАЛЧИК

☎ 0579 / pop 13,760

At last, you gasp on reaching this delightful place, a *real* town! After the endless resorts north of Varna, it is indeed a pleasure to visit gorgeously located Balchik, certainly one of the Black Sea's highlights, mainly due to its setting and atmosphere. Huddled below white chalk cliffs, this least embellished of the coast's old towns retains a village feel even during summer when tourists inevitably dominate the scene. The town is great, but the main attraction here is the palace, with its stunning botanical gardens, a couple of kilometres down the coast. While there's no natural beach at Balchik there are plenty of places to swim, so you can easily combine sunbathing with sightseeing.

Although it's an easy day trip from Varna, Balchik is ideally suited as a cheap base from which to explore attractions in the countryside, such as Dobrich (p242) and Kaliakra Cape (p220), as well as the beach resorts to the south.

History

Greek traders who settled here in the 6th century BC initially called the place Kruni (which sort of means 'town of 100 springs'), but later changed the name to Dionissopolis in honour of the god of wine. Centuries later, the Romans used the town to defend their northern empire. The poet Ovid, exiled to the area by Augustus Caesar, wrote of Balchik: 'Hail, whitestone city and thy unique beauty'. The town was rebuilt on higher ground in the 6th century AD after being destroyed by a tidal wave. In medieval times, Balchik (from the name of a local ruler, Balik) thrived on the export of grain from the hinterlands. In 1913, Balchik (and the rest of the region) was annexed by Romania, before it was literally sold back to Bulgaria in 1940 for 7000 'golden leva'.

Information

The hilariously bizarre *Sea Telegraph* newsletter, available at Balchik Hotel (p219), provides a potted history of the town in English, French and German. You can change money and send/receive cash via Western Union, behind the port building, as well change money at **DSK Bank** (ul Cherno More).

The post office and telephone centre are at the main square, pl Nezavisimost, while the main Internet café is just off the square in a backstreet between ul Cherno More and ul Dionisopolis. There's a semi-useful **tourist information centre** (☎ 76951; ul Primorska; ☺ 8am-8pm Apr-Oct, 9am-5pm Mon-Fri Nov-Mar) near the seafront.

Sights

SUMMER PALACE OF QUEEN MARIE & BOTANICAL GARDENS

You can't come to Balchik without seeing its magnificent **palace** (☎ 72559; adult/under 16 5/1 lv; ☺ 8am-6pm). It was built in 1924–26 by King Ferdinand of Romania because his wife, the UK-born Queen Marie, requested a place of solitude (Balchik was then part of Romania). She understandably called it 'The Quiet Nest' and it remains surprisingly tranquil despite the steady stream of daytrippers who visit in summer. In fact, to call this place a palace is absurd; it's a charming seaside retreat – don't come expecting a vast mansion.

The 35-hectare complex is a glorious collection of laneways, many lined with water mills. One laneway leads over the Venetian-styled **Bridge of Sighs** and down to the elegant palace, often called the **Quiet Nest Villa**. The palace, which overlooks the sea, is deliberately designed in styles reminiscent of Islamic architecture (note the minaret) and the Bulgarian national revival period.

The surrounding **botanical gardens** took more than five years to complete during the 1950s and, in summer, they are a riot of colour from rose beds and Mediterranean plants. In all, about 600 different species of flora are featured, including the second-largest collection of cactuses in Europe, at Allah's Garden. An **arts festival** takes place in the gardens each year in early June.

Within the complex, next to the cactuses, the **Tropical House** (adult/under 18 1.20/0.80 lv; ☺ 9am-6pm) stands out as a real highlight. Privately run by a group of zoology students, this is no quick-scam-the-tourists venture like so many, but a place where you can meet and greet a huge range of snakes, iguanas, spiders and other creepy crawlies. The knowledgeable students speak good English and make fascinating guides.

The palace and gardens can get crowded at times, but if you visit before 10am or after 4.30pm you may have much of the complex to yourself. At the main entrance,

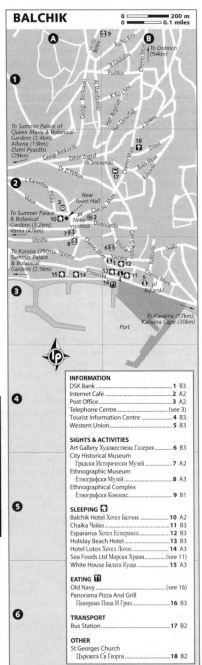

BALCHIK

0 ____ 200 m
0 ____ 0.1 miles

To Summer Palace of
Queen Marie & Botanical
Gardens (3.4km);
Albena (13km);
Zlatni Pyasatsi
(29km)

To Summer Palace
& Botanical
Gardens (3.2km);
Varna (47km)

To Korona (750m);
Summer Palace
& Botanical
Gardens (2.5km)

New
Town Hall

pl
Neza-
visimost

Port

To Dobrich
(54km)

To Kavarna (17km);
Kaliakra Cape (30km)

it's worth buying a booklet (3 lv, in French, German and English), which provides a more helpful map and list of explanations than any of the captions and signs inside the complex.

If you're travelling here by bus from the southern coast, get off at the bus stop opposite the palace – either look for the hotels and tour buses, or ask the driver to drop you off at the *dvorets* (palace). Then walk down the access road, enter the palace at the main entrance, visit the complex, exit at the beach (where there's another entrance) and stroll 3km into town along the waterfront.

OTHER SIGHTS

The **Art Gallery** (☎ 74130; admission 2 lv; ☽ 10am-noon & 1-5.30pm Mon-Fri) is in the white building on the right off ul Cherno More if you're heading uphill from the port. There are two floors of modern local and international art, but the primary attraction is the statue of Dionis, after whom the town was once named.

Further up ul Cherno More is the **City Historical Museum** (☎ 72177; pl Nezavisimost; admission 2 lv; ☽ 9.30am-noon & 12.30pm-5.30pm Mon-Fri). It contains a small but diverse collection, ranging from fossilised mammoth bones to WWII memorabilia. Check the Thracian carriage and the model of the Roman tomb discovered nearby in 1907.

Opposite the Historical Museum is the **Ethnographic Museum** (☎ 72177; ul Vitosha 3; admission 2 lv; ☽ 9.30am-noon & 12.30pm-5.30pm Mon-Fri). In a beautiful old stone house built in 1860, it features a limited but varied number of authentic costumes, as well as displays about traditional trades and crafts such as fishing and woodcarving.

The **Ethnographical Complex** (☎ 72177; ul Hristo Botev 4; admission 2 lv; ☽ 9.30am-noon & 12.30pm-5.30pm Mon-Fri), also known as the Bulgarian National Revival Complex, houses a few unremarkable displays about local folklore and education. From the bus station, walk north on ul Cherno More for 20 minutes and look out for the clock tower in the grounds. If you're near the port, take a taxi (about 1.50 lv) because it's a steepish walk.

Sleeping

The most economic option is renting a private room – some people meet arriving buses, offering rooms for as little as 10 lv, and there are accommodation agencies that can help. Down towards the seafront you'll find **Chaika** (☎ 72059; chaika@mail.bg; pl Ribarski 2) and **Sea Foods Ltd** (☎ 72531; sea_foods@hotmail.com). The tourist information centre (see p217) can also arrange rooms. All agencies charge around 10 to 16 lv per person.

Balchik Hotel (☎ 72809; www.hotel-balchik.com; pl Nezavisimost; s/d/apt 20/28/80 lv) The town's Balkantourist leftover from the 1960s is nevertheless great value for money. Its rooms may be a bit dated (Soviet deluxe class, still rather drab by modern standards) but they are big and clean with balconies. The staff are also extremely friendly and promise that a pool is soon to be built.

Holiday Beach Hotel (☎ 77071; holiday_beach@balchik.net; ul Primorska 23; r 60 lv; 🔀 P) An upscale venture that opened in 2004, the Holiday Beach has 55 smart rooms that are a bargain. All rooms are brand new and have walk-out balconies, most with great sea views.

Esparansa (☎ 75148; ul Cherno More 16; r with shared bathroom 30-40 lv) About 150m up from the port, Esparansa is a four-room hotel, open seasonally. It's a step into another (past) world, with lace tablecloths and overflowing bookcases dressing up the very eclectic rooms.

White House (☎ 73951; ul Geo Milev 18; s/d 60/90 lv; 🔀 P) Situated on the port, this great new place is well located with 10 double rooms and six apartments – all very comfortably set out with wooden floorboards.

Hotel Lotos (☎ 72195; r incl breakfast 30 lv; 🔀) One of several decent three-star hotels along the esplanade. Its rooms are unremarkable but have decent views and the restaurant downstairs is very popular. Prices double in July and August.

Eating

The western waterfront between the port and the palace is where to head for tasty food (at a fraction of the price of that elsewhere on the coast). Some popular places include the Old Navy and the upstairs Panorama Pizza and Grill, by the harbour, the albeit rather touristy Lotus Restaurant and, down towards the palace, the atmospheric Korona. All average about 4 lv per main course.

Getting There & Away

Bus is the only public transport available to and from Balchik, and the surprisingly large **bus station** (☎ 74069) is at the top of ul Cherno More, a steep 1km walk from the port. Minibuses travel from Balchik to Albena (1.40 lv, 20 minutes, about every 15 minutes), Varna (2.50 lv, one hour, hourly) and Dobrich (2.50 lv, 45 minutes, every 30 minutes). There are also six buses a day to Kavarna (1.80 lv, 30 minutes) and three to Sofia (20 lv, 10 hours).

KAVARNA КАВАРНА
☎ 0570 / pop 15,000

Kavarna, 17km east of Balchik, is an unappealing administrative town with a small nearby port It's not worth a visit in itself, but it may be useful for anyone wishing to explore the Kaliakra Cape (p220).

The town has several places to visit, including the small **History Museum** (☎ 82150; ul Chirakman 1), which is in an old mosque and includes several Thracian artefacts from the region; the rarely open **Ethnographical Revival Complex** (☎ 85017; ul Sava Ganchev 18); and the **Art Gallery** (☎ 84235; ul Aheloi 1), where most works have been inspired by the Black Sea coast.

Camping is possible at **Morska Zvezda** (bungalows per person 15 lv; s/d incl breakfast 40/45 lv), where there are tiny bungalows and overpriced singles and doubles. The best of a poor choice of hotels is **Hotel Dobrotitsa** (ul Chernomorska 22; s/d 63/85 lv).

There are four daily buses to Balchik (2 lv, 30 minutes), one bus every 30 minutes to hourly to Dobrich (4 lv, one hour) and a dozen buses to Varna (4 lv, 1¼ hours). Minibuses travel less regularly to Bâlgarevo, Rusalka and Shabla. Public transport to anywhere else further north is infrequent. The border with Romania is closed here.

THE LEGEND OF KALIAKRA

According to a local myth, a group of 40 beautiful young women tied their long hair together and, holding hands, threw themselves off a cliff along the Kaliakra Cape in the 14th century. They did this to avoid a life of slavery, dishonour or worse under the Turks who were advancing to Kavarna. Some displays about this legend are in Kavarna's History Museum, and a monument along the Kaliakra Cape is dedicated to the women.

KALIAKRA CAPE НОС КАЛИАКРА

Kaliakra (Beautiful) Cape is a pronounced 2km-long headland (the longest along the Bulgarian coastline), about 13km southeast of Kavarna. Together with Balchik, it's a popular day trip by boat and/or bus for folks staying at the southern beach resorts.

Kartografia's *Northern Black Sea Coast* map provides essential details about the reserve and its attractions.

Most of the cape is part of the 687-hectare **Kaliakra Nature Reserve** (admission 3 lv; ☉ 24hr), the only reserve in Bulgaria that partially protects the Black Sea (up to 500m offshore). The reserve also protects fragile wetlands at **Bolata** and **Taukliman** (Bay of Birds), about 100 remote **caves** and over 300 species of birds. Most of the year, the official lookouts along the cape and near Rusalka are ideal spots to watch numbers of increasingly rare dolphins and seals.

Also in the reserve are the ruins of an 8th-century **citadel**, with remnants of baths, churches and various tombs. The history of the area is explained in some detail at the **Archaeological Museum** (admission free; ☉ 10am-6pm), wonderfully located inside a cave (look for signs to the museum).

Anyone visiting the reserve must firstly go to the **Nature Information Centre** (☎ 057 44424) in Bâlgarevo village, about halfway between Kavarna and Kaliakra Cape. Set up with the aid of the BSBCP, the centre features a modest but well-intentioned display (in English) about the flora, fauna and marine life of the Black Sea.

Unfortunately, public transport from Kavarna does not reliably go any further than Bâlgarevo, so the best way to visit is with a private car, a rented vehicle (from Varna or one of the beach resorts), or in a taxi from Kavarna.

Northern Bulgaria

CONTENTS

HIGHLIGHTS

- **Stunning prehistoric natural phenomenon**
  Clamber around the Belogradchik rocks and Kaleto fortress (p235).

- **Monasteries and ancient ruins**
  Spot rare birds, rock churches and ruins in the Rusenski Lom National Park (p230).

- **Historic**
  Wander through Vidin's Baba Vida Museum-Fortress (p237).

- **Cosmopolitan**
  Enjoy Ruse's Austro-Hungarian architecture and vibrant café society (p223).

- **Charming**
  Watch artisans at work in the Stariyat Dobrich Ethnological Museum Complex (p243).

★ Vidin
★ Belogradchik
★ Ruse
Rusenski Lom ★
Dobrich ★

NORTHERN BULGARIA

It's safe to say that northern Bulgaria is not the most obvious region in the country to visit, but if you take the time you'll be rewarded with a part of Bulgaria that is still virtually untouched by tourism, and with considerable charm for that. The major highlights here are the amazing rock formations in Belogradchik, which date from millions of years ago, a slew of impressive monasteries (some of which are hewn from rock) and the magnificent Baba Vida Museum-Fortress overlooking the Danube at Vidin.

This is Bulgaria's window seat on the mighty Danube River, which, having taken in Vienna, Bratislava, Budapest and Belgrade, flows between Bulgaria and Romania before emptying into the Black Sea. Unfortunately, few Bulgarian town planners have appeared to care much about this great European river, and there are few places apart from Vidin where you can enjoy good views.

Even though many people cross into northern Bulgaria from neighbouring Romania, only few make the effort to see anything beyond the charming border boom town of Ruse. If time is short, it makes sense to head straight for Veliko Târnovo in central Bulgaria, but if you have time to explore, northern Bulgaria is well worth the time and effort.

NORTHERN BULGARIA

RUSE РУСЕ

☎ 082 / pop 182,500

Cosmopolitan Ruse (roo-*seh*) is a boom town on the Danube, a major gateway for people travelling to/from Romania, and is on one of the most important Balkan trade routes. Its prosperity is evident if you come from elsewhere in the region, and even more striking if you come from Romania. The city centre, with its grand Austro-Hungarian–influenced architecture, has been given an extensive face-lift thanks to the Beautiful Bulgaria Project. Disappointingly, however, the original town planners thought so little of the Danube that most of the riverside is dominated by ugly ports and railway lines. Riverside cafés have been slow to develop, although there are now one or two places where you can enjoy a cold beer overlooking the mighty European river.

There's relatively little to keep you in the town itself for too long (although there's plenty to merit an overnight stop); Ruse is best used as a base to explore other parts of the region, not least the fantastic Rusenski Lom National Park (p230).

History

A Roman fortress, Sexaginta Prista (Port of 60 Ships), was established here in AD 69–70 as part of the empire's northern defensive line. Although strengthened by Emperor Justinian in the 6th century, the fort was obliterated during invasions by Slavic tribes soon afterwards. Fed up with these constant raids, most of the populace of Ruse moved to Cherven, 35km south and now part of the Rusenski Lom National Park.

During the First (681–1018) and Second (1185–1396) Bulgarian Empires, Ruse remained an insignificant backwater before being destroyed by the Turks in the 14th century. Under the reforming Turkish district governor, Midhat Pasha, Roustchouk (as it became known) was rebuilt and modernised. It became an important economic and cultural centre, especially after the railway from Ruse to Varna (the first in Bulgaria and in the entire Ottoman Empire at the time) was built in 1866 to link the Danube with the Black Sea.

Being so close to Bucharest, headquarters of the Bulgarian Central Revolutionary

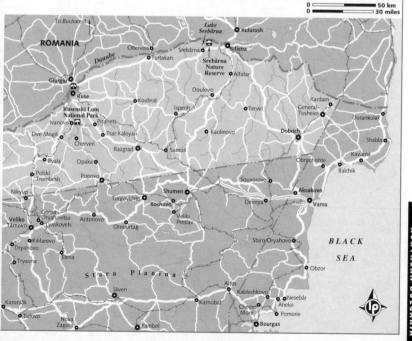

RUSE

0 ————————— 200 m
0 ————————— 0.1 miles

A **B** **C** **D**

ROMANIA

1

River

Danube

2

Brakya Obretenov

Omurtak

Polyclinic

Youth
Park

To Danube
Bridge (6km);
Silistra (112km)

19

26

3

30

Tsar Ferdinand

15

20

Lyuben Karavelov

Baba Tonka

Duhovno Vuzrazhdane

Nezavisimost

Dandolov

Rakovski

25

35

37

Tsar Osvoboditel

Aleksandrovska

Satelinerte

Revivalists'
Park

Nish

13

36
10

29

5

16

4

River
Terminal
(Disused)

21

17

Knyazheska

Borisov

Pirotska

Aleksandrovska

Olec Palai

Slavyanska

8

6

42

28

4

31

41

3

39

35

12

11

33

Konstantin Irichek

Olimpi Panov

pl
Svoboda

43

23

Petko D Petkov

pl Sveta
Troitsa

Municipal
Building

Simeon Veliki

7

1

40

14

Mukuvova

Tsatcov

Stadium

Lipnik

To Iztok Bus
Station (4km)

32

38

5

pl Knyaz Al
Battenberg

9 Fevruari

Nikolaevska

Ivan Vazov

24

9

Gen Skobelev

Rila

Bunov

Borisova

Petar Beron

Han

22

Asparukh

Rakovski

Gen Skobelev

Tsar Osvoboditel

Tsar Asen

6

27

Maria Luiza

Stefan Nikolaevska

Stambolov

34

2

P Hitov

To Ivanovo (20km);
Cherven (35km);
Sofia (320km)

To Yug Bus Station
& Train Station (2km);
Hizha Prista (4km);
Varna (203km)

To Shumen
(115km)

Committee, Ruse was a stronghold of anti-Turkish rebellion. By the end of the Russian-Turkish War (1877–78), Ruse was the largest, most prosperous city in Bulgaria, epitomised by the grand and eclectic architectural style of the city centre.

Ruse was eclipsed by Sofia in the early 20th century and never really recovered its *fin-de-siècle* status. Ruse became a major industrial centre and a focus of dissent against the government in the 1980s when its citizens formed one of the first campaign groups in Bulgaria, demanding a Romanian chlorine plant nearby clean up or close down. The plant was correctly believed to have been responsible for a huge rise in childhood illness and malformed babies in Ruse.

Orientation

The centre of Ruse is pl Svoboda, one of the biggest city squares in Bulgaria. Dominated by the huge Monument to Freedom (1908), it is always crowded with locals enjoying the shady trees, fountains and benches. Among the 18 streets that join the square is Ruse's main pedestrian mall, ul Aleksandrovska. It heads northeast to the Soviet Army Monument and southwest towards pl Knyaz Al Battenberg. The major landmark in the south is the 206m-high TV tower, apparently the highest in the Balkans.

Information

BOOKSHOPS

Pingvinite Bookshop (ul Aleksandrovska) Sells a few books in English about Bulgaria and offers one of the best ranges of maps in the country.

INTERNET ACCESS

i.netcafé (ul Aleksandrovska 37) Far and away the best Internet café in town.

MONEY

Dozens of banks, ATMs and foreign-exchange offices are along ul Aleksandrovska and around pl Svoboda.

Biochim Commercial Bank (ul Knyazheska) Near the Rila Bureau.

Bulbank (pl Sveta Troitsa) Just north of the opera house; changes cash and travellers cheques. The bank's ATM accepts major credit cards, as does the ATM in front of the post office.

United Bulgarian Bank (ul Burov)

POST

Post office (pl Svoboda; ⏰ 7am-9.45pm)

TELEPHONE

Telephone centre (pl Svoboda; ⏰ 7am-9.45pm) Inside the post office.

TOURIST INFORMATION

Rusenski Lom National Park office (☎ 872 397; n-park@acvilon.com; ul Gen Skobelev 7; ⏰ 9am-5pm Mon-Fri) Helpful staff can point out camp sites and where to hike along the river, and arrange visits of the Ivanovo Rock Monastery. They have excellent maps, but keep running out.

Tourist Information Centre (☎ 824 704; tic@tic.rousse .bg; ul Aleksandrovska 61; ⏰ 9.30am-6pm Mon-Fri) One of the best in the country, giving advice and information about how best to enjoy your stay. English spoken.

TRAVEL AGENCIES

Byala Zvezda (☎ 279 770; biala_zvezda@abv.bg; ul Vidin 10, entrance B, 2nd fl, apt 25) Local NGO organising hiking, caving, canoeing, trekking and cycling trips in Rusenski Lom National Park.

Dunav Tours (☎ 824 836; dtbktu@dunavtours.bg; ul Olimpi Panov; 9am-noon & 1-5.30pm Mon-Fri) Arranges private rooms and regional tours, and sells tickets for long-distance buses.

Retro Tours (☎ 276 108; retroturs@abv.bg; ul Angel Kânchev 14) Able to book onward plane and bus tickets, reserve hotels and organise local excursions.

Rila Bureau central (☎ 223 920; ul Knyazheska 33; 9am-noon & 12.30-5pm Mon-Fri); train station (☎ 828 016; 9am-5.30pm & 9.30pm-5.30am) The central branch sells international train and bus tickets, but not to Bucharest; these can only be bought on the day of travel at the Rila Bureau in the train station.

Sights

RELIGIOUS BUILDINGS

Behind the opera house is the Russian-style **Church of Sveta Troitsa** (pl Sveta Troitsa; admission free but donations welcome; 7am-6pm). Built in 1632, it is the oldest remaining building in Ruse and features an interesting subterranean design, brought about by the Turks, who would only allow the building of churches that were lower than mosques. The church features several large and well-preserved murals and 16th-century crosses and icons. As you walk down the stairs, look up and admire the stained-glass windows in the tower. The bell tower in the grounds was added only in the late 19th century, after the end of Turkish rule.

The **Catholic Church of St Paul the Crucified** (admission free; 7am-6pm), just off ul Pridunavski, was built between 1890 and 1892. It still retains its original, and clearly visible, murals and stained-glass windows, chandeliers and icons. It was the first church in Bulgaria to boast an organ and the massive 700-pipe instrument is still played during Sunday services.

MUSEUMS

There are many museums in Ruse, although most are connected with Bulgaria's struggle against the Turks and, as such, may not be of particular interest to foreigners.

One definite highlight is the **Transportation Museum** (☎ 803 516; ul Bratya Obretenovi 5; admission outside/indoor displays 4/2 lv; 10am-6pm Mon-Fri), which explores the history of the railways in Bulgaria (where Ruse was the first station). The outdoor display includes some great locomotives from the late 19th and early 20th centuries, while inside there's an opulent collection of private carriages, including those of Tsar Boris III, Tsar Ferdinand and even the Turkish Sultan Abdul Aziz. There are also photos documenting the development of communications and mass transport.

The **Museum of the Urban Lifestyle in Ruse** (☎ 820 997; ul Tsar Ferdinand 39; admission 3 lv; 9am-noon & 2-5pm Mon-Fri) is in the 1866 Kaliopa House (as it's sometimes known), which, according to legend, was given by the Turkish governor, Midhat Pasha, to his reputed mistress – the beautiful wife of the Prussian Ambassador. The museum features sumptuous furniture from the early 20th century and crockery, cutlery, porcelain and costumes.

The **Zahari Stoyanov House-Museum** (☎ 222 727; ul Pridunavski; adult/student 3/0.50 lv; 9am-noon & 2-5pm Mon-Fri) details the life and times of revolutionary Zahari Stoyanov, including his various guns and swords as well as some interesting early photographs.

ROMAN FORTRESS OF SEXAGINTA PRISTA

The **fortress** (☎ 825 004; ul Tsar Kaloyan 2; adult/concession 2/1 lv; 9am-noon & 1-5pm Mon-Fri) was built here as a Danube naval station between AD 69 and 79. At the height of the power of the Roman Empire, it would have been home to around 600 soldiers who guarded the edge of the empire and ensured the essential artery of the Danube remained open and safe for traders. The complex is well maintained with plenty of labelling in English. You can see the old defensive walls, including a tower, barracks and storage area. There are also a number of stone inscriptions, decorative sculptures and tombstones on display.

CANETTI TRADE HOUSE

This fine **building** (ul Slavyanska 9) was built by the grandfather of Nobel Prize–winning literature laureate Elias Canetti (1905–94). Canetti himself was born and brought up in Ruse. Of Sephardic parents, and brought up to speak Ladino, Bulgarian, German and English, Canetti was an archetypal cosmopolitan and better than anyone else represents the spirit of *fin-de-siècle* Ruse, a city where nationalities and cultures blended seamlessly. Leaving Ruse aged just 18, Canetti nevertheless recalls the city with great warmth in his memoir *Tongue Set Free*. Today, the house is a private residence so literary pilgrims will have to make do with staring in from outside.

PARKS & MONUMENTS

Around the **Revivalists' Park** are the graves of some local revolutionary heroes. The park is dominated by the gold-domed **Pantheon of the National Revival** (☎ 228 913; admission free; 9am-noon & 1-5pm Mon-Fri). Built to commemorate the 100th anniversary of the death of 453 locals who fought the Ottomans in 1878, it is of minimal interest to visitors.

North of the Pantheon, and at the end of ul Saedinenie, is the **Soviet Army Monument**, built in 1949. Behind it is the **Youth Park**, a massive area with playgrounds, swimming pools and tennis courts, and one of the few places in Ruse with river views.

Festivals & Events

March Music Days Festival (last two weeks of March) Features international musicians.

Golden Rebeck Folklore Festival (early June)

Ruse Jazz Bluezz Festival (September)

Days of Ruse festival (early October) Music, dance and theatre.

Christmas Festival (15-24 December)

Sleeping

There are no cheap hotels in central Ruse. All prices include breakfast unless otherwise stated.

BUDGET

Although not as common as elsewhere in Bulgaria, private rooms are still available in Ruse, but they are rather steeply priced. **Dunav Tours** (☎ 824 836; dtbktu@dunavtours.bg; ul Olimpi Panov 5; s/d 22/35 lv; 9am-noon & 1-5.30pm Mon-Fri) is a friendly and reliable agency that can arrange rooms at private homes in central Ruse. The **Tourist Information Centre** (☎ 824 704; tic@tic.rousse.bg; ul Aleksandrovska 61; r per person about 10 lv; 9.30am-6pm Mon-Fri) can organise cheaper rooms, but it has far fewer on its books.

National Hotel (☎ 824 120; fax 834 915; ul Nikolaevska 51; s & d 40 lv) A little way from the centre, but still well located just 15 minutes' walk from pl Svoboda, the National is one of the better deals in town. The rooms are clean and basic but absolutely fine.

Hizha Prista (☎ 820 272/6; Park Prista; beds 10 lv) This is Ruse's only true budget option, but it's a real trek: take bus 6 or 16 from anywhere along Tsar Osvoboditel, and get off at the first stop following the Metro shop. Tell the conductor you want Hizha Prista and you'll be fine. The basic accommodation is in rooms as well as dorms; all share clean facilities.

MID-RANGE

Danube Plaza Hotel (☎ 822 929; www.danubeplaza .com; pl Svoboda; s/d 60/80 lv;) Nowhere near the Danube admittedly, the Plaza is nevertheless a great place, overlooking the main square with spacious and cosy rooms, many with views. You get a better standard of rooms than elsewhere for the price, and location is unbeatable. All rooms have satellite TV, Internet connection and big bathrooms.

Splendid Hotel (☎ 235 951; www.splendid.rousse .bg; ul Aleksandrovska 51; s/d 66/82 lv;) Set back in a side street but still just metres from the main square, the Splendid is an excellent place to stay. Rooms are very comfortable, if a little unfortunately attired. Be aware that paying by credit card pushes up the prices.

Hotel Yuvelir (☎ 823 536; ul Hadzhi Dimitâr 26; s/d 46/68 lv) A little disorganised and run-down, this small hotel is in an old jewellery shop (yuvelir means 'jeweller') converted into basic but clean rooms.

Hotel Kristal (☎ 824 333; ul Nikolaevska 1; s/d 50/70 lv;) Renovated from its rather drab

---

THE DANUBE BRIDGE

This double-decker highway and railway bridge, 6km downstream from Ruse, links the city with Giurgiu on the Romanian side of the Danube. Built between 1949 and 1954, this massive structure – 2.8km long and 30m above the water – is the largest steel bridge in Europe.

Until recently the bridge was named the Friendship Bridge – fairly ironic, as relations between Bulgaria and Romania have been rather unfriendly. This was especially so during the 1980s when a chlorine-and-sodium plant in Romania caused massive air pollution and health problems in Ruse and, more recently, following another catastrophic spill in Romania (see the boxed text on p228). In a concession to reality, the bridge was recently renamed the Danube Bridge.

former self, the Kristal is not exactly central, but is just a short walk from the action. Aimed at business travellers and tour groups, it's nevertheless a good, comfortable hotel with exceptionally helpful staff. Rooms are fine, but with rather small bathrooms. Breakfast is an extra 2 lv.

Hotel Liliya (☎ 822 900; ul Zlaten Rog 1; s/d 60/80 lv; Ⓟ 🅧) Central with airy, clean and modern rooms, many of which have massive balconies, the Liliya is a good choice, but still a bit pricey. There's a cosy bar and restaurant downstairs.

TOP END

Anna Palace (☎ 825 005; www.annapalace.com; ul Knyazheska 4; s/d 105/130 lv; Ⓟ 🅧 🖳) Ruse's smart new image has been enormously enhanced by this excellent conversion of an old mansion by the river terminal. It's luxurious, if a little garish in places, but its rooms are comfortable and staff effortlessly polite. The rooms on the 4th floor are attic rooms with sloping ceilings and go for about 20% less than the rest.

Bistra & Galina Hotel (☎ 823 344; www.bghotel .bg; ul Han Asparukh 8; s/d 85/115 lv; 🅧) The rooms

THE DANUBE

The Danube is the second-longest (472km) river in Europe. Called the Dunav by Bulgarians, it rises in the Black Forest of southwestern Germany and empties into the Black Sea. It travels through four capital cities (Vienna, Budapest, Bratislava and Belgrade) and nine countries (Germany, Austria, Slovakia, Hungary, Serbia and Montenegro, Bulgaria, Romania, Moldova and Ukraine). No other river in the world is shared by so many countries. The average depth of the Danube is about 5m and the water rarely flows more than 3km/h.

In January 2000 a tailings dam burst at a gold mine in Baia Mare (Romania). About 100,000 cu metres of cyanide-contaminated water spilt into the Tisa and Danube Rivers, killing thousands of fish and birds. This spill, described as the worst environmental disaster in Europe since Chornobyl, has so far poisoned river systems in Romania, Hungary, Bulgaria, Ukraine and Serbia and Montenegro. Experts believe that wildlife habitats will not return to normal before about 2010.

at the smart Bistra & Galina are excellent, each with TV and minibar, although it's one of the city's pricier options. Great if you can afford it, although avoid the tiny singles.

Eating

Ali Baba (ul Aleksandrovska; mains 1.50) A great place to grab something quick and easy on the run. Kebabs, falafel and meat wraps are all served here for takeaway customers.

Mehana Chiflika (ul Otets Paisii; salads 1.50-2 lv, mains 2-3 lv; 🕑 11am-2am) Far bigger than the outside suggests, the Chiflika has an off-beat décor, quick service and large servings (salad and bread may be enough for a main course). It features live music in the evenings, which is great fun but precludes any conversation. A menu in English is available.

Restaurant Rila (ul Maria Luiza; mains from 3 lv; 🕑 6.30-11pm) A popular traditional *mehana* (tavern) with cheap, tasty food set in a great little space just off ul Borisova. It's always busy with a buzzing atmosphere but service is good.

Mehana Strandzhata (☎ 821 185; ul Konstantin Irichek 5; mains 3-4 lv; 🕑 noon-11pm) This lovely place serves up delicious and reliable food from all over the Balkans in its cosy premises on a great little enclosed terrace.

Happy Bar & Grill (pl Svoboda; salads about 2.50 lv, grills from 4.50 lv) This nationwide chain spills out onto the square and is ideal for a quick Western meal. It offers a menu in English.

Balkan Princess (☎ 088 827 0297; pontoon 6, Danube waterfront; mains 4-8 lv, surcharge per person for the trip 5 lv) Look no further if you want to dine while cruising the Danube. The *Balkan Princess* leaves its dock on the riverfront and cruises up and down the river while diners enjoy its large selection of fish and meat dishes or one of the cocktails from its onboard bar. Be aware that the boat only sails when there are enough paying punters – so if it's a quiet night you may just be dining on a stationary boat, although you don't pay the surcharge in this case.

Anyone wishing to self-cater should first head to the supermarket, **SVA** (ul Aleksandrovska; 🕑 24hr).

Entertainment

Ruse's nightlife is concentrated in the countless cafés and bars that line ul Aleksandrovska and pl Svoboda. Almost all of them are packed with young people drinking from the late afternoon.

Fresh (cnr ul Aleksandrovska & ul Tsar Osvoboditel) Special recommendation for its cocktails and funky crowd.

NoDo (ul Konstantin Irichek 20; ☒ 7am-midnight) Easily the coolest café in town with its gorgeous décor and fantastic cocktails.

Soundgarden (ul Knyazheska 16) The best place for live music: local bands keep the cellar club rocking most nights until 4am.

More cultural options include the **Ruse Opera House** (pl Sveta Troitsa), first opened in about 1890 and one of the finest buildings in the city, and the **Sava Ognyanov Drama Theatre** (pl Svoboda), which has a strong reputation throughout the country for its productions. You can buy tickets for both at their respective box offices. The Tourist Information Centre also sells tickets for any festivals that are going on.

Several cinemas, including **Cinema Intim** (ul Daskalov) and **Royal Cinema** (ul Olimpi Panov), show recent English-language films.

Getting There & Away
BOAT
At the time of research there were no ferries across the Danube, although you can check at the **river terminal** (☎ 846 559) in case there's a change in the situation.

BUS
The cramped **Yug bus station** (☎ 222 974; ul Pristanishtna), about 2.5km south of the city centre, is extremely busy. From here, there are regular buses to Sofia (10 lv, five hours), Veliko Târnovo (5 lv, two hours), Burgas (11 lv, 4½ hours), Shumen (5.40 lv, two hours), Varna (11 lv, four hours) and Plovdiv (12 lv, six hours). Also, one or two daily public buses go to Gabrovo and Pleven and four or five to Dobrich. Buses and minibuses leave for Silistra (5 lv, about two hours) every hour or so. To get to the station, take trolleybus No 25 or bus No 11 or 12 from ul Borisova.

From the smaller **Iztok bus station** (☎ 443 836; ul Ivan Vedur 10), about 4km east of the city centre (city bus Nos 2 and 13 go there from ul Gen Skobelev, near the roundabout four blocks east of ul Borisova), buses go to regional villages such as Ivanovo and Cherven in the Rusenski Lom National Park (p230).

TRAIN
The **train station** (☎ 820 222; ul Pristanishtna) is Bulgaria's oldest and is adjacent to the Yug bus station, about 2.5km from the town centre.

There are four daily trains to Sofia (14.70 lv, seven hours), four to Veliko Târnovo (6 lv, two to three hours), two to Varna (9.75 lv, four hours) and three to Bucharest (15 lv, 3½ hours). If heading for Bucharest, turn up at least 30 minutes before the train leaves as customs and passport checks are done in the station and last-minute arrivals will be scolded by the guards.

In the station, the **Rila Bureau** (☎ 828 016; ☒ 9am-5.30pm & 9pm-5.30am) sells international train tickets. Beware that the Rila Bureau in town does not sell tickets to Bucharest; they can only be bought at the station on the day of travel. There's a **left-luggage office** (☒ 6am-1.30pm & 2-8.30pm) at the train station; walk past the main buildings and up the small hill to the ramshackle hut at the top. To get to the train station, take trolleybus No 25 or bus No 11 or 12 from ul Borisova.

Getting Around
Naturally, there are plenty of available taxis around town and most drivers appear to be very honest, automatically using their meters. You can rent bicycles from **Byala Zvezda** (☎ 279 770; apt 25, 2nd fl, entrance B, ul Vidin 10; per day 25 lv).

Contact a travel agency such as Dunav Tours or your hotel about the options for

---

BUCHAREST BOUND

Nearly everyone visiting Ruse is coming from or heading to the Romanian capital, just a few hours away by train. There are no buses between anywhere in Romania and Bulgaria, the Ruse–Giurgiu ferry no longer runs and crossing the Danube Bridge on foot or by bicycle is not allowed, meaning that the only public transport across the border is by train. Alternatively, you can cross by taxi (Dunav Tours – p225 – can organise one from Ruse to Bucharest for €100, which isn't so bad when divided between four people). Until both countries gain EU membership, the border situation is likely to remain tedious, with customs and passport control for the train taking about an hour each side.

renting a car, which is useful for side trips such as visiting the Rusenski Lom National Park.

RUSENSKI LOM NATIONAL PARK
НАЦОНАЛЕН ПАРК РУСЕНСКИ ЛОМ
This 3260-hectare national park, established in 1970, hugs the Rusenski Lom, Beli Lom and Malki Lom Rivers near Ruse. The park is one of the best places in Bulgaria for bird-watching. It protects about 170 species of water birds, as well as endangered Egyptian vultures, lesser kestrels and great eagle owls. It's also home to 67 species of mammals (16 of which are endangered) and 23 types of bats. The park comprises endless valleys and mountains (rare among the Danubian plains), caused by unique geological shifts during the Pleistocene period.

Most visitors come to marvel at the 40-or-so rock churches built in and around the 300 caves. The rock monastery at Ivanovo is accessible, but only a few other caves are open to tourists. You can visit the second-longest cave in Bulgaria, the Orlova Chuka Peshtera (Eagle Peak Cave), between the villages of Tabachka and Pepelina. Also around the park are limited ruins of cities built by Thracians and Romans.

Information
Information centre (☎ 08116-2203; Ivanovo town hall)
Rusenski Lom National Park office (☎ 082-872 397; n-park@acvilon.com; ul Gen Skobelev 7, Ruse; 9am-5pm Mon-Fri) All visitors should pick up the *Naturpark Russenski Lom* map, published by the Green Danube Program. The map is available here and at bookstalls in Ruse.

Sights
IVANOVO ROCK MONASTERY
СКАЛЕН МАНАСТИР ИВАНОВО
Several caves near Ivanovo were used for religious purposes. The most famous was the St Bogoroditsa (Holy Virgin's) rock church, the only remaining section of the original St Archangel Mikhail Monastery complex also known as the **Ivanovo Rock Monastery** (☎ 082-231 023; admission 3 lv; 8am-noon & 1-5pm Wed-Mon). The monastery is built inside a cave that is 16m long, 4m wide and 38m above ground. It is now on Unesco's World Heritage list.

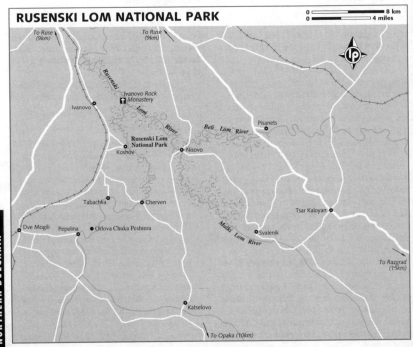

RUSENSKI LOM NATIONAL PARK

Built during the 13th century, under the sponsorship of Tsars Ivan Asen II and Ivan Aleksandâr, the monastery was linked to the Royal Court and became a regional centre of art, culture and religion. The 14th-century murals inside – which are regarded as some of the finest in Bulgaria, if not Europe – show portraits of various saints and impassioned scenes from the Last Supper. The artists are unknown.

The monastery is signposted along a good road, about 4km east of Ivanovo and 20km south of Ruse.

CHERVEN ЧЕРВЕН

Cherven was first established in the 6th century by people from Ruse who wanted to escape the constant Slavic invasions. The town became an important religious, economic and military centre during the Second Bulgarian Empire (1185–1396). Remains of the 6th-century **citadel** (☎ 082-230 123; admission 3 lv; ☯ 8am-noon & 1-5pm Wed-Mon) are remarkably intact. Recent excavations have unearthed several streets, towers and churches, now all part of a protected archaeological reserve. The ruins are a short walk north of Cherven village, about 15km south of Ivanovo.

Sleeping

The park is not particularly well set up for tourism, so it's a good idea to check with the national park office in Ruse (p225), or the information centre in Ivanovo (p230), about current accommodation options. There are rooms at private homes in Cherven, Pisanets, Nisovo and Koshov for about 18 lv per person; these can be arranged through the information centre or national park office.

Getting There & Away

From the Iztok bus station in Ruse, four buses leave daily for Cherven, via Ivanovo and Koshov, between Monday and Friday. For Pisanets, take one of the frequent buses towards Razgrad from the Yug bus station in Ruse; and for Nisovo, look for a bus leaving the Iztok station for Opaka.

CHEREPISH MONASTERY ЧЕРЕПИШКИ МАНАСТИР

The **Cherepish Monastery** (admission free; ☯ 24hr) was originally built in the 14th century. It has been razed and rebuilt several times

since and is considerably smaller than it used to be. Like many other monasteries in the area, it was used by rebels as a hiding place before and during the Russian-Turkish War (1877–78).

The attached **museum** offers little more than a few religious icons and books (in Bulgarian) for sale. At the time of research, a block of basic guest rooms (with shared bathroom) was being built. According to the monks, accommodation will cost as little as 3 lv per person.

The poorly signposted monastery is about 600m from the roadside restaurant of the same name along the road from Mezdra to Zverino. If driving from Sofia, consider taking the scenic, but slower, road through the stunning Iskâr Gorge, via Novi Iskâr. By bus from Sofia, catch anything heading towards Mezdra, Vratsa, Montana or Vidin. Disembark at the turn-off to Zverino and wait for a connecting minibus or head west for about 6km.

VRATSA ВРАЦА
☎ 092 / pop 78,900

Despite having very little in the town itself, Vratsa is well worth visiting for its spectacular location under the looming peaks of the Vrachanska Mountains, which are part of the Vrachanska Balkan National Park (p233). Vratsa is also a more pleasant and useful base than Montana for visiting nearby villages and monasteries. There's enough in the town to divert you for a few hours, but unless you plan to go walking, there's no reason to stay the night here.

Orientation & Information

The town centre is typical: the large, and mostly empty, pl Hristo Botev is dominated by a grotesque statue of Botev (see the boxed text, p232) and surrounded by ugly concrete buildings. Most locals prefer to congregate around the cafés and shops lining the main pedestrian mall called (you guessed it) ul Hristo Botev. This thoroughfare heads east from the square and finishes at the market near the train station. The banks along ul Hristo Botev change money and offer ATM services. There are two Internet cafés on pl Hristo Botev. You can get information, maps and other advice about visiting the Vrachanska Balkan National park from both the **Vrachanska Balkan**

National Park information centre (☎ 621 473; Hotel Tourist; ☺ 9am-noon & 2-5pm Mon-Fri) and the **Vrachanska Balkan National Park headquarters** (☎ 633 149; infocenter@vratsa.net; ul Ivanka Boteva 1).

Sights & Activities

HISTORICAL MUSEUM

The local **museum** (☎ 620 220; pl Hristo Botev; adult/student 5/0.5 lv; ☺ 8am-noon & 2-6pm Tue-Sun) is sometimes known as the 'Archaeological Museum'. It houses impressive displays of coins and jewellery from the Thracian period, artefacts from nearby Neolithic dwellings and historical items relating to Macedonia. Like most Bulgarian museums, however, the complete lack of captions in any language other than Bulgarian is frustrating, especially given the high admission fee for foreigners. The antiquated guidebook (2 lv), written in French, may help explain some of the displays. The museum is behind the 16th-century tower to the left (west) of Hotel Valdi Palace (right) as you face it.

ETHNOGRAPHIC COMPLEX

Confusingly, this place is also called the **Regional Historical Museum with Art Gallery** (☎ 620 209; ul Gen Leonov; adult/student 5/0.50 lv; ☺ 8am-noon & 2-6pm Mon-Sat). Several structures are built in the styles reminiscent of the Bulgarian national revival and British Tudor periods. They contain the usual array of traditional costumes, as well as displays, among other things, about the author and musician Diko Iliev. Pop into the **Museum of Carriages** at the back of the complex, where several fascinating buggies and carts lie idle. Your ticket is valid for entrance here as well.

HRISTO BOTEV

The most revered person in Vratsa is unquestionably Hristo Botev (1848–76), a rebellious teacher, poet and newspaper publisher. He later became a leader of an insurgent gang that fought against Ottoman occupation while hiding in the Vrachanska Mountains, near Vratsa. At the age of 28, Botev and several of his men were captured and killed by the Turks. Botev's deeds are commemorated on 2 June each year with a ceremony in the Vrachanska Mountains and in the Vratsa town square that bears his name.

It costs nothing to wander around the museum **gardens** and the adjacent **St Sofronni Vrachanski Church** (ul Gen Leonov; ☺ 8am-7pm). From pl Hristo Botev, head down the mall to ul Hristo Botev and turn right along the cobblestone lane of ul Gen Leonov.

HIKING

The charming hills to the southwest of the main square are ideal for short hikes; the obvious tiny **church** perched on the hill top is easily accessible along stone steps through the forest. Only about 1km from the Hotel Tourist, along the road to the Ledenika Cave, is a scenic area where locals enjoy picnicking, hiking (trails marked in Cyrillic) and watching suicidal amateur rock climbers.

Sleeping & Eating

There is no official camping ground in the vicinity but discreet, unofficial camping is possible anywhere in the hills and picnic areas and in the Vrachanska Balkan National Park (opposite).

Hotel Tourist (☎ 661 528; www.hotel.vratza.com, in Bulgarian; bul Krayrechen 1; s/d/tr 25/50/60 lv) Not nearly as bad as it looks, the Tourist has the town's best-value rooms: clean, comfortable and mostly with balconies with some great views towards the mountains. The hotel is along the road to Ledenika Cave, about 300m past the Historical Museum.

Hotel Valdi Palace (☎ 624 150; www.valdi.vratza .com, in Bulgarian; pl Hristo Botev; s/d 30/42 lv, apt 50-90 lv) The most central hotel in town and, despite its charmless exterior, has perfectly OK rooms. The staff are friendly, but the hotel hasn't evolved much beyond the Soviet era. The restaurant is a popular spot for dinner.

Restaurant Atlantik (pl Hristo Botev; mains 3 lv) This undercover and off-street complex includes a café, bar and restaurant that offers tasty food, excellent service and live music most nights.

The best places for a drink (and a meal) are the innumerable cafés along the mall. Look for the umbrellas.

Getting There & Around

The **bus station** (☎ 622 558) is slightly hidden from the main road, about 300m east of the train station. Buses travel to/from Sofia (6 lv, two hours) at least every hour daily (more frequently between 6am and 9am). There are also one or two buses daily to Gabrovo, Pleven and Lovech, and four to Vidin.

Inside the **train station** (☎ 624 415), the **Rila Bureau** (☎ 620 562) sells tickets for international trains and advanced tickets for domestic services. Each day, there are five trains to Sofia, six to Montana and four to Vidin (stopping in Gara Oreshets, from where you can get to Belogradchik easily).

Taxis are plentiful and cheap, and can be chartered to Ledenika Cave (see the next section) and Cherepish Monastery (p234).

VRACHANSKA BALKAN NATIONAL PARK
НАЦОНАЛЕН ПАРК ВРАЧАНСКИ БАЛКАН

An area of 28,845 hectares to the southwest of Vratsa was declared a national park in 1989 to protect more than nine species of birds, 700 types of trees and about 500 caves. Other fragile landscapes, such as rocky outcrops, are also protected but they are still enjoyed by rock climbers and hanggliders. Many of the park's more accessible areas are a sad reflection of its heyday. Most hotels are abandoned and the disused chairlift dangles menacingly above the road.

The **Ledenika Cave** (guided tours per person 5 lv; ⏰ 8am-6pm summer) is 15km (about three hours on foot) from the start of the road past the Hotel Tourist in Vratsa; follow the ambiguous dark-blue signs (in Bulgarian). The cave is mostly covered in ice during winter (*led* means 'ice'), but it's a popular excursion in summer. Entry is only possible on a guided tour, for which a minimum of about eight people is needed. The best time to visit is on a sunny weekend. Also, ask your hotel about concerts that are, incredibly, sometimes held inside the cave.

The hourly bus to Zgorigrad from Vratsa should stop near the cave. Locals like to take the bus, drive, hitch a ride or charter a taxi to the cafés about 12km up the road from the Hotel Tourist, and then hike down the shady road to Vratsa. Alternatively, ask at the cafés for directions to the start of the new **Vrachanska Eco-trail**.

Contact the **park headquarters** (☎ 092-633 149; infocenter@vratsa.net; ul Ivanka Boteva 1, Vratsa) for more information if you're undertaking a major hiking or caving expedition in the park.

MONTANA МОНТАНА
☎ 096 / pop 54,600

Montana is an unappealing town just off the highway between Vratsa and Vidin. It's a major transport hub so anyone visiting Chiprovtsi or the Lopushanski Monastery by bus will need to get a connection in Montana. If you get stuck here overnight, stay in the reasonable rooms at the **Montana Hotel** (☎ 626 803; pl Slaveikov; s/d with TV 30/40 lv).

The road to Lopushanski Monastery passes the picturesque **Montana Reservoir**. It's popular with locals for swimming and fishing (bring your own gear) but pack sunscreen because there's no shade. Visitors can walk along the dam wall.

From the **Montana bus station** (☎ 623 454) there are services almost hourly to Sofia, Vratsa and Vidin and about four or five daily to Chiprovtsi, Kopilovtsi, Pleven and Belogradchik. The **train station** (☎ 623 846) is on a spur track from the major line between Sofia and Vidin and is very inconvenient.

LOPUSHANSKI MONASTERY
ЛОПУШАНСКИ МАНАСТИР

Built between 1850 and 1853, this small **monastery** (admission free; ⏰ 8am-6pm) is in a serene setting about 21km west of Montana. It's dedicated to St John the Precursor and contains precious icons created by the renowned brothers Stanislav and Nikolai Dospevski. Like many other monasteries, it was also a hiding place for anti-Turkish rebels.

If the monastery is closed, ask staff at the guesthouse for permission to see inside. The **guesthouse** (☎ 09551-350; r per person about 20 lv) is only metres from the monastery and has about 20 rooms. The older rooms downstairs share a bathroom, but the newer rooms upstairs include a bathroom, a fridge and plenty of furniture. The chairs along the veranda outside the rooms are a great place to relax.

The attached café has outdoor and indoor tables. The service can be poor and the meals are nothing to get write home about, but the location is delightful. According to the official brochure published by the guesthouse, mountain bikes are available for hire, but staff knew nothing about this when we asked. Nevertheless, the surrounding countryside is ideal for cycling.

CHIPROVTSI ЧИПРОВЦИ
☎ 09554 / pop 3000

This fairly old, but charmless and quiet, village about 30km west of Montana, is famous for its carpets, though precious few are for sale. While Chiprovtsi is worth a visit, especially if you have a private car, avoid coming in winter when the climate can be appalling. Like Belogradchik, Chiprovtsi is a grateful (and needy) beneficiary of the Beautiful Bulgaria Project, which has renovated many crumbling buildings.

Sights

CHIPROVTSI MONASTERY
ЧИПРОВСКИ МАНАСТИР

Also known as the **St Ivan Rilski Monastery** (admission free; ☼ daylight hr), this modest structure was probably built in the 15th century as a Catholic church. It was burned down at least five times, mostly by Turks, because it provided sanctuary to rebels in the 17th century. What remains today was rebuilt in the 1830s as an Eastern Orthodox monastery. Despite indications to the contrary in some tourist literature, accommodation at the monastery is not available. The turn-off to the monastery is 5.8km northeast of Chiprovtsi village and is accessible on any bus between Montana and Chiprovtsi. From the turn-off, it's 400m to the monastery.

HISTORY MUSEUM

This **museum** (☎ 2194; ul Vitosha 2; admission 3 lv, free Thu; ☼ 8am-5pm Mon-Fri, 10am-4pm Sat & Sun) offers displays about regional mineral exploration, exhibits about the Turkish occupation of the area and copies of murals from Chiprovtsi Monastery (the originals are in the Aleksander Nevski Memorial Church in Sofia). One room is dedicated to traditional costumes from the region and to the type of carpets for which the village is renowned (see right).

The caretaker, who speaks good English, can provide an entertaining **guided tour** (per person 3 lv, no minimum number required). The museum is at the top of the concrete steps to the right as you face the Chiprovtsi village square from the main road.

Sleeping & Eating

The **museum** (s/d 10/20 lv) has two glorious rooms, which it rents to the public. The rooms, which share a bathroom, contain lovely antique furniture and are worth booking ahead.

There are a few cafés around the main square; the best are situated along the steps up to the museum.

Shopping

For centuries, Chiprovtsi has been famous for its handmade woollen carpets, but the industry is a small-scale affair these days. There are no workshops where the public can watch artisans ply their trade and no shops in which to buy any carpets. The museum does sell a few small items, however, such as tiny bags (about 5 lv) and small rugs (15 lv). Larger items can be ordered through the museum but allow at least one month. If you are seriously keen (rather than just curious) about locally made carpets, ask the museum caretaker to introduce you to a local who can show you some samples and take you to a home where carpets are still made.

Getting There & Away

Four or five daily buses travel in both directions between Montana and Chiprovtsi. The road to Chiprovtsi from the Vratsa–Vidin highway (E79) starts about 3km northwest of Montana. From the south, the turn-off is signposted 'Чипровски Манастир'; from the north, it's signposted 'Lopushanski' in English.

BELOGRADCHIK БЕЛОГРАДЧИК
☎ 0936 / pop 6700

The undoubted highlight of the region is gorgeous, dramatic   with its wonderful mountain location and fascinatingly weird rock formations. Despite some inevitable industrial additions courtesy of the communists, Belogradchik retains its essentially aloof and insular atmosphere – very much a mountain town barely touched by mass tourism, although visitor numbers are continually rising.

Orientation & Information

From the main square at the junction of the three major roads, ul Treti Mart leads to the fortress, which is well signposted (look for 'за крепостта' signs). One street below the village square is the bus station. The First East National Bank, near the abandoned Hotel Belogradchik Skali, will change major currencies in cash only.

7 30 am   5 30 pm
2 00 pm   12 n   1 30 pm

There's an **Internet café** (ul Knyaz Boris I) between the pink art gallery and the white history museum (look for the 'JAR Computers' sign). The useful **Tourist Information Centre** (☎ 4294; milena-tourist_centre@abv.bg; ul Poruchik Dvoryanov 5; ☺ 1-6pm) can help with hotel bookings and also gives out free maps of the town.

Sights

BELOGRADCHIK ROCKS & KALETO FORTRESS

Quite where the majestic **Kaleto Fortress** (☎ 4855; admission 2.50 lv, guided tour 5 lv, photo/video 2/5 lv; ☺ 8am-6.30pm) ends and the rocks begin is an open question. Originally built by the ingenious Romans in the 1st century BC, the design has incorporated the massive Belogradchik rocks into the fabric of the fortress, making it defensively brilliant. Several towers, walls and gates were later added and/or fortified by the Byzantines, among others. Most of what remains today was built by the Turks between about 1805 and 1837. There's no need to take a tour; just clamber around the ramparts, explore the defensive bunkers and living quarters (bring a torch if you have one) and climb up to the highest rocks (tracks are obvious and some ladders have been installed to help you on your way). These remarkable rock formations are over 200 million years old and are spread over 200 hectares. There are some other impressive examples about 100m down the road from the main square (follow the track to the Nature Department of the History Museum). It's a wonderful place to explore, and various tracks lead elsewhere around the rocks and into the forest.

The fortress is a steepish 2km hike from the main square; follow the signs. As you would expect from this height, the views from the top are outstanding. Peter Jackson missed a trick by not using this as a location for *The Lord of the Rings* – it's pure fantasy film.

MUSEUMS

The **History Museum** (☎ 3469; pl 1850 Leto; admission 1 lv; ☺ 9am-noon & 2-5pm Mon-Fri) is in Panova's House (an alternative name for the museum). As well as numerous coins, jewellery and costumes – and 6000 or so artefacts from the fortress – the museum contains displays about local anti-Turkish rebellions during the mid-19th century.

The **Nature Department** (admission 3.50 lv) is an offshoot of the History Museum. It contains various exhibits about local flora and fauna, but opening hours are irregular so ring the museum beforehand if you really want to see inside. From the abandoned Hotel Belogradchiski Skali, walk up ul Vasil Levski, turn right, walking in front of the Soviet-era youth club behind the hotel, and follow the path down about 600m. There are some amazing views over the Belogradchik rocks from here, so it's well worth the walk even if the museum isn't open.

Sleeping & Eating

The two big state-run hotels – the Hotel Belogradchiski Skali, at the main square, and the Hotel Belogradchik, one street below – have been abandoned to fate and there are no indications of any future renovations. Private rooms had not caught on at the time of research, strange perhaps for a town with such tourist draws. However, hotels are reasonably priced, so it's no problem.

Hotel St Valentine (☎ 4002; pl Benkovski 1; s/d 20/40 lv) Not as romantic as it may sound but, nevertheless, the Valentine is by far the best deal in town. Opened in 2004, it's located to one side of the condemned Hotel Belogradchik. All eight rooms are superclean, have TV and bathroom, and there's a great little restaurant and bar downstairs. Book ahead in summer.

Hotel Rai (☎ 3735; s/d 25/30 lv, r with shared bathroom 20 lv) Facing the bus station, the Hotel Rai has recently renovated rooms, one with a balcony. While it's modern and perfectly pleasant, the staff are nonexistent and it feels more like staying in a private home (you get your own key to the front door, for example). However, it's good value.

Hotel Madona (☎ 5546; www.hotelmadona.hit.bg, in Bulgarian; ul Hristo Botev 26; s/d 30/40 lv, with shared bathroom 25/35 lv) This B&B has very small, but nice, traditional rooms in a home that feels gingerbread housey. It's 600m up from the main square (follow signs to 'hotel'). There's also a decent restaurant attached.

Restaurant Elite (☎ 4558; ul Yuri Gagarin 2; mains 4-5 lv) The best place in town. Walk five minutes up steep ul Vasil Levski and turn left. It's often quiet, but the traditional Bulgarian meals are excellent.

Getting There & Away

From the decrepit **bus station** (☎ 3427), there are three or four daily services to Vidin (4.50 lv, 1½ hours) and a 7am bus to Sofia (6 lv, four hours), via Montana but not Vratsa. There are also three buses per day to the nearest train station at Gara Oreshets (1 lv, 20 minutes), timed to meet the train to Sofia. If you plan to travel by train to Belogradchik, get off at Gara Oreshets and get the bus from there.

VIDIN ВИДИН

☎ 094 / pop 69,400

Vidin suffered a great deal from the economic decline during the UN sanctions against neighbouring Serbia, which saw

international trade routes diverted to Ruse and mass unemployment hit the area. While Serbia is now a thriving new democracy, Vidin is yet to recover from its slump and the place still has a depressed feel to it several years after the end of Slobodan Milosevič's regime.

Despite this, Vidin is worth passing through if you are in the region, and while much of the city's glory is in the past, it's also one of the few places to see the Danube in Bulgaria. Vidin boasts several attractions (including a marvellous fortress) and is a worthy alternative to Ruse for travelling to and from Romania, although its remoteness is understandably a disincentive for some travellers.

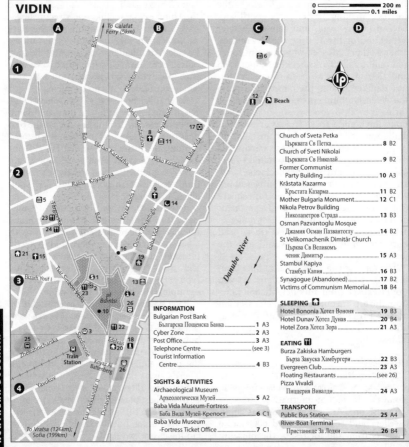

VIDIN

0 ———— 200 m
0 ———— 0.1 miles

INFORMATION
Bulgarian Post Bank
Българска Пощенска Банка **1** A3
Cyber Zone **2** A3
Post Office **3** A3
Telephone Centre .... (see 3)
Tourist Information
Centre **4** B3

SIGHTS & ACTIVITIES
Archaeological Museum
Археологически Музей **5** A2
Baba Vida Museum-Fortress
Баба Вида Музей-Крепост **6** C1
Baba Vidu Museum
-Fortress Ticket Office **7** C1

Church of Sveta Petka
Църквата Св Петка **8** B2
Church of Sveti Nikolai
Църквата Св Николай **9** B2
Former Communist
Party Building **10** A3
Krâstata Kazarma
Кръстата Казарма **11** B2
Mother Bulgaria Monument **12** C1
Nikola Petrov Building
Николапетров Страда **13** B3
Osman Pazvantoglu Mosque
Джамия Осман Пазвантоглу **14** B2
St Velikomachenik Dimitâr Church
Църква Св Великомъ
ченик Димитър **15** A3
Stambul Kapiya
Стамбул Капия **16** B3
Synagogue (Abandoned) **17** B2
Victims of Communism Memorial **18** B4

SLEEPING
Hotel Bononia Хотел Вононя **19** B3
Hotel Dunav Хотел Дунав **20** B4
Hotel Zora Хотел Зора **21** A3

EATING
Burza Zakiska Hamburgers
Бърза Закуска Хамбургери **22** B3
Evergreen Club **23** A3
Floating Restaurants .... (see 26)
Pizza Vivaldi
Пищерия Вивалди **24** A3

TRANSPORT
Public Bus Station **25** A4
River-Boat Terminal
Пристанище За Лодки **26** B4

History

Some historians believe that the Thracians were the first to settle along this part of the Danube, though this is hotly contested. On the site of the 3rd-century BC Celtic settlement of Dunonia, the Romans built a fortress they called Bononia to control the Danube crossing. During the Second Bulgarian Empire (1185–1396), Bdin (as it was known) became an important northwestern bastion and trading centre.

The fall of Bdin in 1396 marked the completion of the conquest of Bulgaria by the Ottomans, who renamed the town Vidin (which they believed was easier to say). The Turks built an extensive city wall around Vidin and strengthened the Baba Vida fortress, which remains today. By the 16th century, Vidin was the largest town in Bulgaria and one of the biggest ports along the Danube. In the late 18th century, as Turkish rule weakened, a local pasha (high official), Osman Pazvantoglu, declared the district independent of the sultan. In 1878 Vidin was returned to Bulgaria by the Romanian army. Seven years later, an attempt by Serbia to take the area was resisted.

Orientation

The town square, pl Bdintsi, is an eclectic mix of the old and new. The former Communist Party building in the south towers over the ancient Stambul Kapiya Turkish gate to the north. The train station, bus station and river-boat terminal are only one block or so apart.

Information

There are foreign-exchange offices, banks and several ATMs along ul Tsar Simeon Veliki and around pl Bdintsi, including the Bulgarian Post Bank.

Cyber Zone (ul Târgovska 3) Reliable and cheap.

Post office (🕐 7am-6.30pm Mon-Fri, 8am-1.30pm Sat) Between the square and train station.

Telephone centre (🕐 7am-6.30pm Mon-Fri, 8am-1.30pm Sat) In the post office.

Tourist Information Centre (☎ 601 421; tsviat@abv.bg; pl Bdintsi 6; 🕐 9am-6pm Mon-Fri)

Sights

BABA VIDA MUSEUM-FORTRESS

At the northern end of the riverside park, overlooking the Danube, is the magnificent **Baba Vida Museum-Fortress** (☎ 601 705; admission 2 lv, guided tour, in Bulgarian or Russian only, 5 lv; 🕐 8.30am-5pm summer, 10am-5pm winter). The Bulgars built the fortress between the 10th and 14th centuries on the ruined walls of the 3rd-century Roman citadel of Bononia. Most of what remains today was rebuilt in the 17th century by the Turks, who used it to stockpile weapons. Because it was spared destruction during the Russian-Turkish War (1877–78), Baba Vida is regarded as the best-preserved medieval stone fortress in Bulgaria.

It's interesting to wander through, although without any set itinerary or much signage, it really is just a wander. Unfortunately, there's not much inside, save a rather uninspiring collection of weaponry and a singularly terrifying waxwork prisoner sitting in the dungeon. Each wall of the fortress is about 70m long, though a few remaining outer walls continue several hundred metres further down the river towards the town centre. The main structure is surrounded by a deep moat. Notice boards in French explain some of the history and uses of each section. Coming from the town, walk around the moat to the back of the fortress to the ticket office and entry.

Many locals use the upper section for sunbathing, and alongside the wall there's a tiny beach of pebbles. Swimming here is strictly for desperadoes; a quick glance upriver to the factories and tankers, and downriver to the fishermen, will probably deter most people from taking a dip.

OTHER ATTRACTIONS

The main building of interest in the town centre is the **St Velikomachenik Dimitâr Church** (ul Tsar Simeon Veliki; 🕐 8am-6pm). The city's main cathedral, it's been partly Beautiful Bulgaria-ised. Its domes and interior are still in some need of work, but it's got some interesting frescoes and icons, as well as the usual over-supply of comically unfriendly octogenarian church cleaners.

Northwest of the main square is the **Archaeological Museum** (☎ 624 421; ul Tsar Simeon Veliki 12; 🕐 9am-noon & 2-6pm Tue-Sun). On show are Thracian and Roman artefacts, including jewellery and statues, as well as exhibits from the Bulgarian national revival period. It's housed in a pagoda-shaped wooden building, which was used in the 19th century as a *konak* (police station) by the Turks. However, it's sometimes closed for no reason.

On the riverfront, just by the Hotel Dunav, is the **Victims of Communism Memorial** – interesting mainly as it's one of the few public acknowledgements of the postwar political repression in Bulgaria. The building looks like a rather modern church and is locked. A more typically Soviet piece of civic architecture is the **Mother Bulgaria Monument** further up the riverfront in the park before the fortress. It's now covered in graffiti and red paint but has a certain sad appeal.

In the suburbs, between the main square and the fortress, are several interesting buildings such as the 18th-century **Osman Pazvantoglu Mosque** (ul Osman Pazvantoglu) and the modern Orthodox **Church of Sveti Nikolai** opposite. Also of note is the **Krâstata Kazarma** (☎ 23855; ul Knyaz Boris I), which is meant to house the local history museum but seems to be permanently closed, and the 17th-century **Church of Svetka Petka** opposite. The abandoned **synagogue** (ul Baba Vida) is worth a look.

Near the entrance to the Hotel Bononia, the lovely white **Nikola Petrov Building** houses temporary exhibitions by local artists.

Sleeping

Hotel Dunav (☎ /fax 600 177; www.dunav-vidin.dir.bg, in Bulgarian; ul Edelvais 3; s/d 23/46 lv, with shared bathroom 18/36 lv) The cheapest place in town, but it comes at a price: the rooms are largely un-renovated and don't feel very clean, although the quality of room varies enormously – some have nice new furniture, while the bathrooms in others are dire. However, the location is convenient and quiet.

Hotel Bononia (☎ 606 031; moira_bg200@yahoo.com; ul Bdin 2; s/d 35/60 lv; ❄) Convenient to the town centre, river and park, and probably the best overall value in town. Most rooms have sparkling new bathroom and TV, but those on the top floors are a little hot in summer. Breakfast is an extra 5 lv.

Hotel Zora (☎ 606 330; www.hotelzora.hit.bg, in Bulgarian; ul Naycho Tsanov 3A; s/d/apt 55/72/90 lv; ❄) This delightful place overlooks the St Velikomachenik Dimitâr Church and has great staff, some of whom speak English. All rooms have balcony, minibar, TV and even a bath rather than the ubiquitous shoddy Bulgarian hotel shower.

Eating & Drinking

Burza Zakiska Hamburgers (pl Bdintsi; burgers about 1.50 lv, soups 1.30 lv) Alongside the lower eastern side of the main square, this informal joint is one of the best of its kind in Bulgaria. The burgers are tasty and fresh and it's always packed with locals.

Pizza Vivaldi (☎ 609 334; ul Naicho Tsanov 2; mains 5 lv) This friendly place is one of the very few good restaurants in town and probably the best place to find a crowd in the evening. The pizzas are good and there's also a great range of Bulgarian dishes.

Evergreen Club (☎ 608 390; off pl Bdintsi; mains 4-6 lv) Despite a modern interior, the food here is what you would expect from a traditional Bulgarian *mehana* (albeit with a strange English name). It's cosy and the staff are attentive. Loud music sometimes predominates at the weekend, though.

The best places for a drink are any of the innumerable cafés that line the main square and malls. Especially enticing are those near the Archaeological Museum and in the riverside park. Sadly, none of these cafés offer any views of the Danube, so try one of the sporadically available floating restaurants near the river-boat terminal if you're interested in the view.

Getting There & Away

The **bus station** (☎ 23179; ul Zhelezhnicharska) is a short walk from the town centre. It's a quiet place and confusingly without a central timetable. From this station, there are 14 daily buses to Sofia (10 lv, four hours) via Vratsa, six a day to Belogradchik (2.5 lv, one hour) and one connection to Pleven (6 lv, 3½ hours). There is a sporadic service to Nagoutin in Serbia from here as well. Enquire locally about its latest timing, though, as it wasn't running at the time of research.

From the small **train station** (☎ 623 184; ul Saedinenie), three fast trains (9.65/6.80 lv in 1st/2nd class, five hours) and one slow train (7.30 lv, five hours) travel daily to Sofia via Vratsa.

TO/FROM ROMANIA

Talk about a bridge to Romania is still talk. You can cross by ferry to Calafat, Romania (8 lv), twice a day from the river-boat terminal near the centre. A more expensive car ferry is north of town. The car ferry operates 24 hours a day and is accessible on bus No 1 from the train station in Vidin.

PLEVEN ПЛЕВЕН

☎ 064 / pop 138,500

Historic Pleven, despite its strategic position, is a town that has little to offer visitors. It's the kind of place where if you are changing buses or trains you may want to look around a bit, but it's certainly not a place for which to make a diversion.

Pleven is most known for its history. In September 1877, 100,000 Russian and Romanian soldiers under General Totleben attempted (for the third time) to liberate Pleven from the Turks. The Turks eventually tried, but failed, to break the siege in December of that year. This momentous battle, which was the beginning of the end of the Russian-Turkish War, is commemorated by a number of war memorials, museums and mausoleums around the city.

Information

Along, or just off, the main thoroughfare of ul Vasil Levski is where you'll find most foreign-exchange offices.

Java Internet Cafe (ul Daniel Popov)
Post office Just off pl Vŭzrazhdane.
Telephone centre Inside the post office.
United Bulgarian Bank (ul Vasil Levski 1)

Sights

The delightful **Church of Sveti Nikolai** (☎ 837 208; pl Sveti Nikolai; admission free; ☼ 24hr) possibly dates back to the 14th century. It was built below street level in the style dictated by the Ottoman rulers at the time. There are famous icons inside and a huge bell tower. A priest may request an obligatory 'donation' of about 2 lv.

In a small, shady park is the **Museum of Liberation of Pleven 1877** (☎ 820 033; ul Vasil Levski 157; admission 2 lv; ☼ 9am-noon & 1-6pm Tue-Sat). It honours the battle against the Turks in Pleven.

The **Svetlin Rusev Art Gallery** (☎ 838 342; ul Doiran 75; admission free; ☼ 10.30am-6.30pm Tue-Sat) is housed in a red-and-white former spa. It has four floors of modern art, including Picasso and Goya on the top floor. Pavel Koichev's *The Table* is an unfinished sculpture of misshapen world figures.

The unmistakable **mausoleum** (☎ 830 033) dominates pl Vŭzrazhdane. It was built in 1907 as a memorial to the thousands of Russian and Romanian soldiers who died in Pleven in 1877. The building is not open to the public but visitors can see the cannons ominously pointed towards the main square and the eternal flame in front of the mausoleum.

The **Historical Museum** (☎ 822 691; ul Stoyan Zaimov 3; admission 2 lv; ☼ 9am-noon & 1-5pm Tue-Sat) is enormous. The 24 halls house more than 5000 exhibits about local history, flora and fauna and contain archaeological remains from Nikopolis-ad-Istrum (p169) and a nearby Neolithic settlement.

The **Military-Historical Museum** (☎ 822 919; Skobelev Park; admission 2 lv; ☼ 9am-5pm Tue-Sat) was built to commemorate the 100th anniversary of the 1877 battle. Known as the 'Panorama' or 'Epopee (Epic) of Pleven', it's on top of a hill in Skobelev Park. The four halls feature huge, haunting paintings but most locals come for the views and surrounding parklands.

Sleeping

It's hard to imagine why anyone would want to spend a night in Pleven, unless simply to break up a journey. If so, a short detour south to Lovech (p175) would be a far better plan as Pleven's hotels are overpriced and mediocre.

Hotel Pleven (☎ 836 321; pl Republika; s & d 50 lv) This place is pretty awful but it's the cheapest in town and if you just want a bed it's totally passable. The rooms are clean but extremely old and in a museum-like state of decay. Reductions are offered when hot water isn't available (which is often).

Hotel Rostov (☎ 805 005; www.rostov.dir.bg; ul Tsar Boris 2; s/d 80/115 lv) This three-star hotel is far better value than Hotel Pleven and more convenient than the Balkan. The rooms are small but have a fan, fridge and TV.

Hotel Balkan (☎ 822 215; ul Ruse 85; s/d incl breakfast 90/135 lv) Although popular, the rooms are charmless and it's inconvenient and overpriced for foreigners. The rooms have TV.

Eating

Pizza Tempo (ul Konstantinov; mains 3-4 lv) Bulgaria's best pizza chain has a great outlet in Pleven, where meals are prepared in wood-fired ovens.

Speedy Bar & Grill (ul Vasil Levski; mains 4-5 lv) Similar to the Happy Bar & Grill restaurants

PLEVEN

0 — 300 m
0 — 0.2 miles

INFORMATION

Java Internet Cafe	**1** B2
Post Office	**2** C5
Telephone Centre	(see 2)
United Bulgarian Bank	
Обединена Българска Банка	**3** B4

SIGHTS & ACTIVITIES

Church of Sveti Nikolai	
Църква Св Никола	**4** B3
Historical Museum	
Исторически Музей	**5** B6
Mausoleum Мавзолея	**6** B5
Museum of Liberation of Pleven 1877	
Музей На Освобождението	
На Плевен 1877	**7** B3
Svetlin Rusev Art Gallery	
Художествена Галерия	
Светлин Русев	**8** B4

SLEEPING

Hotel Balkan	**9** D4
Hotel Pleven Хотел Плевен	**10** B1
Hotel Rostov Хотел Ростов	**11** B4

EATING

Mehana Bulgarski Koren	
Механа Български Корен	**12** A3
Pizza Tempo Пица Темпо	**13** C5
Speedy Bar & Grill	**14** B4

TRANSPORT

Bus Station	**15** B1
Private Bus Ticket Office	**16** A1
Private Bus Ticket Office	(see 9)
Rila Bureau Бюро Рила	(see 16)

Train Station

Market

pl Republika

Lenko Milev

Oteis Paisi

Grenaderska

A Konstantinov

Daniel Popov

To Sofia (174km)

Naicho Tsanov

Dolan

Vasil Levski

Zanenhof

pl Sveti Nikolai

Dramatic Theatre

Ozvobodenie

Market

Ruse

To Varna (304km)

Ivan Vazov

Tsar Simeon

Konstantinov

Kiril & Metodii

pl Svoboda

To Skobelev Park (1km); Military-Historical Museum (1.5km)

Stamboliyski

pl Vazrazhdane

Hadzhi Dimitar

pl Slivnitsa

Stoyan Zaimov

Gen Skobelev

Hemus

San Stefano

Turguiyat

To Skobelev Park (150m); Military-Historical Museum (650m)

To Lovech (35km)

NORTHERN BULGARIA

found elsewhere, this place offers snappy service, outdoor tables and hearty servings of Western-style food.

Mehana Bulgarski Koren (ul Naicho Tsanov 4; mains 5-8 lv) This place can be a bit tricky to find down the back streets, but is a gem. If you're only having one meal in Pleven, make it here. With its gorgeous courtyard replete with water features and live music most nights, it is often packed with locals (always a good sign). Service can be slow when it's busy, but the food is excellent.

Getting There & Away

From the **bus station** (☎ 827 232; pl Republika), next to the train station, there are buses to Lovech (3 lv, 45 minutes, hourly), Sofia (8 lv, 2½ hours, 17 daily), Gabrovo (6 lv, two hours, six daily), Ruse (4 lv, 2½ hours) and Troyan (5 lv, 1½ hours, one or two daily). There's also a daily connection to Vratsa, Montana, Veliko Târnovo and Burgas.

Private buses depart hourly for Sofia (9 lv, 2½ hours) and less frequently to Burgas, Ruse and Varna from ticket offices in front of Hotel Pleven and the train station.

Pleven's **train station** (☎ 831 133) is along the main northern train line. Trains travel to Varna (11.40 lv, 4½ hours, five daily) and Sofia (7.50 lv, 3½ hours, 10 daily). Fifteen trains also stop daily at Pleven on the way from Sofia to Gorna Oryahovitsa, from where there are four connections to Ruse. The **Rila Bureau** (☎ 822 390; train station) sells tickets for international services and advance tickets for domestic trains.

SILISTRA СИЛИСТРА

☎ 086 / pop 49,900

Silistra is a likable town and one of very few along the mighty Danube to offer views and boat trips. Most of the port is a few kilometres away, which makes Silistra more agreeable than Ruse if you're looking for a Danube experience. However, it has none of Ruse's other attractions and is decidedly remote and backwards.

The bus station is 1.5km from the main square, pl Svoboda, around which there are banks and foreign-exchange offices, as well as the post office and telephone centre.

Sights & Activities

Over the centuries, Silistra has been invaded and occupied by Thracians, Romans, Greeks, Russians, Romanians and Turks, all of whom built citadels and fortresses in or near the town. Along the street between the mall and river are obvious **ruins** of the ancient Roman city of Durostorum.

The Turkish **Medzhitabiya Fortress** (built in 1848) is closed but the lovely forested **park** surrounding the fortress is great fun for **hiking**. The fortress is about 5km from town (2 lv by taxi) on the Silistra–Dobrich road, or a 3km walk up the hill. The TV tower is an adjacent landmark.

The **Art Gallery** (☎ 26838; bul Simeon Veliki 120; adult/student 2/1 lv; ☼ 9am-5pm Mon-Fri) is in a renovated yellow building along the mall, opposite the drama theatre. The gallery contains hundreds of works by contemporary Bulgarian artists, as well as Japanese engravings.

The **Archaeological Museum** (☎ 23894; adult/student 2/1 lv; ☼ 9am-noon & 2-6pm Mon-Fri) was in the same building as the Art Gallery at the time of research. It houses artefacts from the Turkish fortress and other ruins in the region, as well as costumes, jewellery and a 3rd-century Thracian chariot. The museum may move in the future, so check the current location at the Art Gallery.

The MV *Bravo* offers one-hour **boat tours** (per person 5-6 lv) along the Danube several days a week. Inquire at the travel agency in the Zlatna Dobroudja Hotel.

Sleeping & Eating

Zlatna Dobroudja Hotel (☎ 26674; fax 22661; ul Dobroudja 2; s 40-55 lv, d 66-99 lv; ✖) This was the only functioning hotel in town at the time of research. It has a central location and reasonable rates given the standard of accommodation. All rooms have a TV and the price includes breakfast.

Several cafés and restaurants are found in and around the hotel complex, including Pizzeria Zlatna Dobroudja, which offers tasty pizzas and pasta dishes for 3 to 4 lv from an English menu.

Getting There & Away

Roughly every hour, buses and minibuses leave the Silistra **bus station** (☎ 23062) for the Yug bus station in Ruse (5.50 lv, about two hours). From Silistra, there are also two or three daily buses to Varna, eight to Dobrich, four to Sofia, three to Shumen and one to Veliko Târnovo. There is one daily train to Ruse and three to Samuil.

From Silistra port to Călăraşi (in Romania), a ferry operates every few hours (25/7 lv per car/passenger). Fares are payable in euros or leva. Public transport on the Romanian side is not reliable, however, so the border at Ruse is probably easier.

LAKE SREBÂRNA ЕЗЕРО СРЕБЪРНА

Lake Srebârna is shallow (1.5m to 5m deep) and connected to the Danube by a narrow, natural canal, so it's full of unique types of vegetation and floating islands made of reeds. The lake is home to over 160 species of water birds, including colonies of endangered small cormorants, Ferruginous ducks and Dalmatian pelicans. Surrounding the lake is the 8000-hectare **Srebârna Nature Reserve**, established as a World Heritage Site by Unesco in 1983.

The **Museum of Natural History** (☎ 086-23894; admission 2.50 lv; ⏲ 9am-noon & 2-4pm Mon-Fri) is in Srebârna village. It contains a few exhibits about local bird life and flora and is the perfect place for serious bird-lovers to arrange **bird-watching trips**.

The southern part of the lake extends to within a few hundred metres of the Silistra–Ruse road. Bus Nos 22 and 222 travel several times a day between Silistra and Srebârna village. Otherwise, take the more regular Silistra–Ruse bus or minibus, disembark at the signposted turn-off and walk 1.5km into the village.

DOBRICH ДОБРИЧ

☎ 058 / pop 113,800

Dobrich is a popular trip for people staying on the Black Sea. It's a standard Bulgarian town, but compared to the resorts of the coast it's an interesting place with plenty to see on a day trip. Settled in the 15th century, Dobrich has always been renowned for its arts and crafts and, recently, for the quality of agricultural products grown in the surrounding fertile plains. Otherwise there's not much reason to come here: it's a pleasant town, but unremarkable save for the interesting ethnological complex.

Information

Around the massive pl Svoboda are the United Bulgarian Bank and the post office and telephone centre. There are Internet cafés on ul Nezavisimost and inside the Hotel Bulgaria (p243).

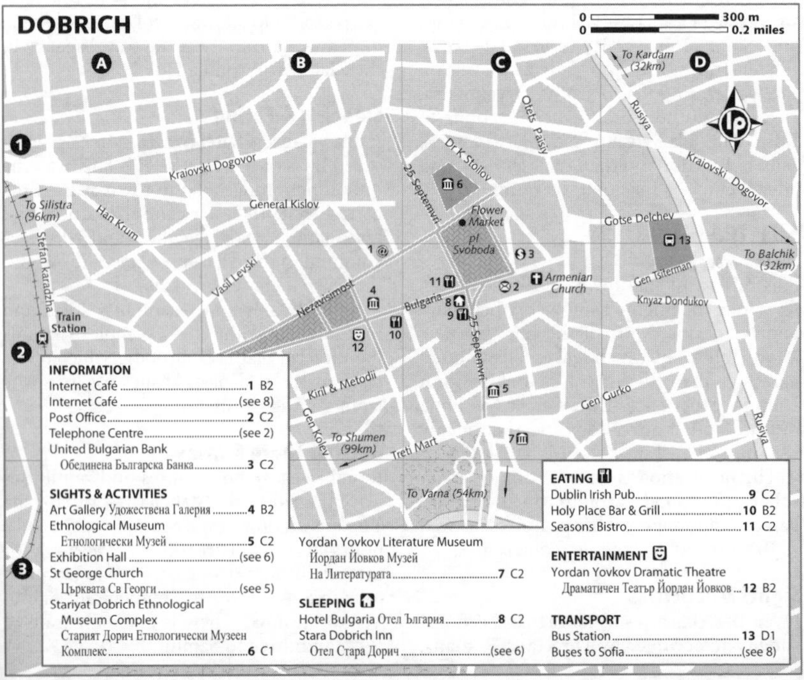

Sights

STARIYAT DOBRICH ETHNOLOGICAL MUSEUM COMPLEX

Some 37 shops, cafés, bars, restaurants and souvenir stalls form part of this charming **complex** (☎ 29068; ul Dr K Stoilov; admission free; ☽ 8am-6pm summer, 8am-5pm winter). The cobblestone streets are marvellous to wander around and it's possible to poke your head into a shop and watch blacksmiths, potters, weavers and other artisans ply their trades. The shady courtyard is lined with cafés and there's a charming hotel (see p243).

The complex is hidden behind an ugly modern building; look for the sign at the southern entrance. The map (in English) along the main street inside the complex is helpful. The **exhibition hall** (admission 1 lv) at the courtyard contains antique jewellery but is of minimal interest. The clock tower at the end is more attractive. This is a good place to wander and shop for local handicrafts.

ART GALLERY

The **Art Gallery** (☎ 602 215; www.dobrichgallery.org; ul Bulgaria 14; admission 0.50 lv, guided tour in English or German 1 lv; ☽ 9am-12.30pm & 1.30-6pm Mon-Sat) houses more than 1700 works of art collected over a period of 100 years, including many by 'The Master', Vladimir Dimitrov. The permanent displays have captions in English but the temporary exhibits do not.

YORDAN YOVKOV LITERATURE MUSEUM

This **museum** (☎ 24308; ul Gen Gurko 4; admission 1 lv; ☽ 9am-6pm Mon-Fri, 9am-4pm Sat & Sun) features a range of furniture, costumes, knick-knacks, books and photos relating to Bulgarian novelist Yordan Yovkov. All captions are in Bulgarian but the manager can provide a free information leaflet in English.

ETHNOLOGICAL MUSEUM

Inside the lovely courtyard of a Bulgarian national revival period home, this **museum** (ul 25 Septemvri; admission 2 lv; ☽ 8.30am-noon & 2-4.30pm Mon-Fri) offers the usual array of traditional costumes and jewellery. It's adjacent to a park with a statue of the ubiquitous Vasil Levski in front of the **St George Church** (admission free; ☽ 8am-6pm).

Sleeping

Stara Dobrich Inn (☎ 601 5904; Stariyat Dobrich Ethnological Museum Complex; s/d 50/60 lv) This charming guesthouse offers clean, modern and large rooms with traditional Bulgarian furniture. Rooms don't have TVs or air-con, but it's certainly a welcome break from the soulless high-rise hotels found in most other cities. The guesthouse is not signposted: coming from pl Svoboda, turn right off the square by the Rosexim sign before turning left and going through the archway by the Western Union building. Walk through the museum complex and turn left at the end. Call ahead in summer.

Hotel Bulgaria (☎ /fax 625 444; pl Svoboda; s/d 70/100 lv; P ☐ ☒) This massive central hotel has a range of large and comfortable rooms (if still with very Soviet furnishings) each with a fan, TV and fridge. It's decent value (less so for singles) and the hotel has a casino and fitness centre. However, the Stara Dobrich Inn is far better value.

Eating

Numerous charming cafés can be found along ul 25 Septemvri, in the shady park to the south. There are also a couple of excellent and traditional *mehanas* at the ethnological museum complex.

Seasons Bistro (ul Bulgaria; mains 3 lv) Just a short distance from the Hotel Bulgaria, this is an airy, smart and popular spot for food and drink at any time of day. The menu includes Bulgarian and European dishes, and the food is good.

Dublin Irish Pub (pl Svoboda; mains 3-4 lv) Irish run and owned, the Dublin is no expat joint (it would be very empty if it was!). It's a popular place for locals to dine, serving up a delicious grill selection, traditional Bulgarian and Serbian dishes and a host of good beers.

Holy Place Bar & Grill (ul Bulgaria; mains 3-4 lv) This former Happy Grill outlet has changed its name to the odd Holy Place. It offers a fairly Identikit menu and style to the Happy Grill chain, however.

Getting There & Away

From the **bus station** (☎ 622 240), on the eastern edge of town, buses and minibuses leave for Albena (3.50 lv, 45 minutes, every 30 minutes), Varna (3.50 lv, 40 minutes, every 15 minutes), Balchik (2.80 lv, 45 minutes, every 30 minutes) and Kavarna (4 lv, one hour). Two daily buses go to both Ruse (12 lv, three hours) and Silistra (5 lv, 1½ hours). All buses to Sofia (17 to 18 lv, seven to eight hours) leave from the car park of the Hotel Bulgaria in the town centre, not the bus station.

Dobrich is shabbily served by trains. From the **train station** (☎ 609 078) on the western edge of town, you can't get anywhere interesting, except Varna (change in Povelanovo). You can get a train to Kardam on the Romanian border, but you can't cross here. There's a Rila Bureau at the station, so you can book international tickets.

Directory

ACCOMMODATION

Bulgaria offers a wide range of accommodation options, from spartan mountain huts to luxurious five-star hotels. Accommodation is most expensive in Sofia and other big cities, though elsewhere prices are still cheap by Western European standards, even though foreigners usually pay considerably more for all types of accommodation than Bulgarians (see p10). If you're travelling independently around the country, one indispensable publication is the annual *Bulgaria Bed & Breakfasts Guidebook* (about 8 lv) published by the **Bulgarian Association for Al-**ternative Tourism** (☎ 02-989 0538; www.alternative tourism.org), which lists ecological, family-run guesthouses all over Bulgaria. You can buy it at Zig Zag Holidays in Sofia (p60).

Accommodation in this book has been divided into three price categories: budget, mid-range and top end. In the budget category, double rooms cost up to €25, or 50 lv; in mid-range they cost up to €50, or 100 lv;

PRACTICALITIES

- The metric system is used for weights and measures.

- Bulgaria runs on 220V, 50Hz AC and plugs are the standard round two-pin variety, sometimes called the 'europlug'.

- Videos work on the PAL system.

- If you're visiting Sofia, pick up the English-language *Sofia Echo*, published on Friday. If you can read Bulgarian, two respected daily newspapers are *Trud* (Work) and *24 Chasa* (24 Hours).

- If you get very bored, tune into the government-run TV channel (Kanal 1) or one of three private ones (BTV, Novi Televizyia and Sedemte Dni). Televisions in most – but certainly not all – hotel rooms can pick up a plethora of stations from around the region, so you can enjoy Israeli talent quests, Cypriot game shows and Russian soap operas, as well as CNN, BBC, Eurosport and MTV.

- In Sofia, tune into BG Radio (91.9FM), Radio Contact (106FM), Jazz FM (104FM) and Classic FM (89.1FM). Darrik Radio, a nationwide network of stations that usually play contemporary pop music, can be heard in Sofia (98.3FM), Varna (90.7FM), Plovdiv (94.6FM), Ruse (104FM) and Veliko Târnovo (88.9FM). Several international services can be found on the FM band in Sofia. These include Voice of America (103.9FM), BBC (91FM), Deutsche Welle (95.7FM) and Radio France Internationale (103.6FM). If you understand Bulgarian, try the national station, Horizont (102.4FM).

and anything above that is regarded as top end. However, as accommodation in Sofia is priced so much higher than anywhere else, double rooms costing up to €100, or 200 lv, are placed in the mid-range bracket for the capital, and anything over that is top end.

Budget accommodation is usually very simple, and includes private rooms, hostels and cheaper guesthouses, normally with shared bathroom facilities. Mid-range options offer a much higher standard and will almost always include en-suite bathrooms and extras such as minibars and TVs. Top-end accommodation is, naturally, the best available, or at least the most luxurious and dependable. This includes international chains as well as home-grown establishments, and most of these are very modern, with top-notch facilities. Sofia, in particular, has numerous top-end options for you to try out. Top-end hotels commonly offer discounted weekend prices (Friday to Sunday inclusive) and it may be worth asking for discounts for longer stays too. Some hostels in Sofia may also be willing to offer discounted rates for long stays.

Note that hotels in seasonal spots, such as the Black Sea or skiing resorts, frequently close down outside the holiday seasons, or may operate on a much reduced basis: closing up part of the hotel and the restaurant, for example, or cutting back staff to a minimum, so if you're thinking of staying in, for example, Bansko in October or Nesebâr in February, you really need to phone ahead to see what the current situation is.

Useful websites offering hotel booking facilities and discounts include www.bg globe.net, www.hotelbg.com, www.hotels bulgaria.com and, for the capital, www.sofia hotels.net.

Camping

These days, camping is not an ideal way to see Bulgaria. Camping grounds have struggled since losing government support, and the industry, which once included over 100 locales nationwide (with half that number along the Black Sea coast), is in serious decline. Even privatised camping grounds tend to be run-down, so don't have high expectations.

Camping grounds in Bulgaria are rarely open between November and April, and some along the Black Sea coast only operate from June to early September. These tend to be very crowded in July and August, and while camp sites will normally be available at this time, security, privacy and tranquillity are rarely guaranteed. In addition, camping grounds have a tendency to

---

BUYING PROPERTY IN BULGARIA

Recent years have seen a surge in the number of foreigners – especially British people – looking to buy holiday homes in Bulgaria, lured by low prices and the promise of long hot summers by the sea or rustic country idylls. By Western standards, house prices are often amazingly cheap; it's still possible, for example, to pick up a run-down village house (with, ahem, lots of potential) for under €10,000, although prices are rising (by an average of 25% from 2003–4) and are sure to rise even faster once Bulgaria joins the EU, most likely in 2007.

The favourite spot for property investment is, naturally enough, the Black Sea region, and this international interest has fuelled a building boom, with new developments appearing all along the coast. For a new Black Sea holiday apartment, you can expect to pay from around €35,000. Other hot spots are Sofia and the ski resorts of Bansko and Borovets.

At the present time, foreigners are allowed to buy buildings but not the land on which they stand, but to get around this anomaly you need to register a limited Bulgarian-based company and buy your property through that. This is a relatively simple process, and estate agents and developers will be able to help and advise with this. This law may well change in the future to allow more foreign investment.

For more information, visit www.bulgarianproperties.com, which has a huge number of houses, flats and studios for sale, and up-to-date news on the property scene in Bulgaria. Also try www .blackseavillas.net and www.skipropertybg.com for more localised offerings, and www.bulgarian dreams.com, a UK-based company providing news and advice on buying property in the country. The **Bulgaria Real Estate Group** (www.breg.bg) offers legal assistance to foreigners.

be placed closer to noisy main roads (to attract passing customers) than to anywhere peaceful or picturesque such as a beach or lake.

The cost of setting up a tent at a camping ground is about 8 to 10 lv per person per night, but tents are rarely available for hire, so bring your own. Most camping grounds also rent out tiny bungalows for slightly more than the cost of camp sites, but these, too, are often far from inviting.

Camping in the wild (ie outside a camping ground) is technically prohibited but normally accepted if you're discreet and, most importantly, do not build wood fires (which attract attention and damage the environment).

Hostels

Backpacker hostels are a very new phenomenon in Bulgaria, and while Sofia now boasts several excellent private establishments, you'll find very few anywhere else in the country.

There are no hostels in Bulgaria affiliated to the Youth Hostels Association (YHA) or Hostelling International (HI), and only one or two hostels in Sofia will offer small discounts for holders of HI or International Student Identity Card (ISIC) cards. Other hostels around the country are run by the Bulgarian youth agency Orbita and are more basic affairs, aimed at school groups, hikers and the like.

Hotels

Like anywhere else, the hotel scene in Bulgaria is varied and basically you get what you pay for. While many of the older, formerly state-run hotels have now been privatised and renovated, those in less-visited locations are often shabby and run-down. Some are abandoned and look as if they're going to fall down at any moment, while others which continue to operate *still* look like they're going to crumble to the ground!

Modern private hotels have sprung up everywhere and usually offer good value. Some hotels offer more expensive 'apartments'. These are usually double rooms, but more luxurious and feature more amenities. 'Suites' are often family rooms with two double bedrooms.

Hotels (but not private homes, mountains huts or hostels) are rated from one to five stars, but one- and two-star places are rarely proud of the fact so they often don't advertise their rating. Some hotels do not offer single rooms or single rates in a double room. If this is the case, only the rates for doubles are listed in this book.

International chain hotels such as the Hilton and Radisson now have a presence in Bulgaria and offer the usual high standards at the usual international rates. Although nearly all hotels are overpriced for foreigners, some are blazing new trails by adopting a more equitable pricing policy.

Most smaller and more remote ski-resort hotels are closed in summer (from about mid-April to November), while almost all places along the Black Sea coast do not open between late October and early April.

Whether breakfast is included depends on local competition. In some towns every hotel includes breakfast; in other places it's never part of the tariff. Sometimes breakfast costs an extra 3 or 4 lv per person (considerably more in a five-star hotel). This is worth considering for the convenience, but breakfast in a local café will probably be tastier and cheaper.

Unless stated otherwise in this book, reserving a room in advance is not normally necessary, except if you're determined to stay at a particular place or visiting at peak times (eg Nesebâr in August or Bansko at Christmas) or during a major festival.

Monasteries

About a dozen of the 160 monasteries around Bulgaria offer accommodation to anyone, of either sex, from pilgrims to foreign tourists. Some rooms are actually inside the monastery, such as at the Rila and Cherepish Monasteries, or at guesthouses within metres of the monastery gates, eg the Troyan, Dryanovo and Lopushanski Monasteries. Some only offer rooms on a sporadic basis, or will frequently close for 'renovation'; contact the monasteries directly to see if they have room.

Mountain Huts

Anyone, especially those enjoying long-distance treks or shorter hikes, can stay at any *hizha* (mountain hut). Normally a *hizha* only offers basic, but clean and comfortable, dormitory beds, with a shared bathroom, which cost from 10 to 35 lv per person per night. Most are only open from May to October, but those situated at or near major ski slopes are often also open in winter. In or around a town or village along a popular hiking/trekking route, you can also often find a *turisticheski dom* (tourist home; a fairly comfortable hotel with double rooms) or a *turisticheska spalnya* (tourist bedroom; a more basic, dorm-style hostel).

It's often not necessary to book these in advance, but beds at most of the 200 or more mountain huts, hotels and hostels can be reserved at the **Bulgarian Tourist Union** (BTC; Map pp62-3; ☎ 02-980 1285; bts@nat .bg; bul Vasil Levski 75, Sofia). The office is tucked inside a photo shop in the underpass at the junction of bul Vasil Levski and ul General Gurko. The BTC office also sells some hiking maps and the *Hizhite v Bâlgariya* book (written in Cyrillic) detailing the locations of, and amenities at, most places in the mountains. **Zig Zag Holidays** (Map pp62-3; ☎ 02-980 5102; www.zigzag.dir.bg; bul Stamboliyski 20-V, Sofia) can also arrange accommodation in the mountains and villages. For general information on *hizhas*, visit www.geocities .com/the_bulgarian_mountains.

Private Rooms

As well as being a cheap accommodation option for foreign visitors, private rooms also offer a glimpse into real Bulgarian life. Standards vary, but usually these will be in nondescript apartment blocks with communal bathroom facilities. The hosts always seem be elderly ladies, who are unlikely to speak English. Most are friendly and effusive and will provide breakfast and lengthy monologues in Bulgarian, whether you understand it or not, while others, of course, are in it purely for the extra cash. If you don't mind sleeping in a room surrounded by kitschy knick-knacks and B&W photos of long-dead husbands in military uniform, it's a homely and evocative choice.

Rooms cost anything between 10 and 20 lv per person, but they're normally priced per number of beds so people travelling alone sometimes have to pay for double rooms. Rooms in Sofia or Plovdiv will naturally be more expensive than those in small provincial towns and villages.

Stays in private rooms can often be arranged through an accommodation agency in a town centre, or at a bus or train station. Alternatively, you can wait to be approached in the street or keep an eye out for relevant signs in Bulgarian, English or German in shop windows or hanging outside the actual home. It's always important to find out where the rooms are before making a decision: in a village such as Melnik, all homes are central, but in a city such as Burgas the home may be in an outlying and dreary suburb.

ACTIVITIES

Bulgaria is gaining a reputation as an inexpensive and increasingly sophisticated winter-sports destination. The country's unspoilt, mountainous terrain also makes it ideal for walking and hiking, with numerous well-marked trails and a system of mountain huts, or *hizhas*, for hikers to sleep in. Mountaineering and caving are also popular activities.

Water sports are popular on the Black Sea coast, although these tend to be confined to the big package-holiday resorts. Windsurfing, paragliding, scuba diving and a host of other watery activities can be arranged during summer.

For more on outdoor activities, see p44.

BUSINESS HOURS

Normally, government offices are open on weekdays (Monday to Friday) between 9am and 5pm, but they often close for 45 minutes to one hour any time between noon and 2pm. Private businesses more or less keep the same hours, but rarely have time for a leisurely lunch break. Most shops are open from about 9am to 7pm on weekdays, and from 9am to 1pm on weekends. Some operate shorter hours on Sunday (or close altogether) but shops in big cities such as Sofia and Plovdiv are often open later on weekends. Post offices are open weekdays from 8am to 6pm, and banks operate from 9am to 4pm weekdays. Some of the foreign-exchange offices are open 24 hours but most operate between about 9am and 6pm Monday to Saturday.

Restaurants generally open from 11am to 11pm. Frustratingly, many museums and tourist attractions, even those in major cities, close for one or two days a week, usually between Sunday and Tuesday. (They often also close for lunch.) Opening times do change regularly, so don't be surprised if a museum or art gallery is closed even though it should be open.

CHILDREN

Successful travel with young children requires planning and effort. Don't try to overdo things; even for adults, packing too much into the time available can cause problems. Make sure planned activities include the kids as well – balance the morning at a stuffy museum with an afternoon swim at the beach or a walk in the hills. And include children in the trip planning; if they have helped to work out where you'll be going, they'll be much more interested when they get there. For further general information and suggestions, see Lonely Planet's *Travel with Children*.

Practicalities

Bulgaria is a safe and healthy country and medical facilities are generally pretty good. Most of the necessities for travelling with toddlers, such as nappies (diapers), baby food and fresh or powdered milk are readily available, and there are well-known international fast-food outlets all over the country.

The major international car-rental firms can provide children's safety seats for a nominal extra cost, but it's essential to book these in advance. It's also worth noting that highchairs are almost unheard of in restaurants, public nappy-changing facilities are rare and childcare (baby-sitting) agencies are only common among the expatriate community in Sofia. Breast-feeding in public is not usual and may attract stares. Cots are only available in the top-end, international chain hotels, though it's always worth asking at other modern hotels. Look out for other travellers with children and see if you can pick up some useful tips!

Sights & Activities

The most obvious attractions for young children are, of course, the long sandy beaches of the Black Sea, and the playgrounds, waterslides, toy trains and the rest offered by the big resorts such as Slânchev Bryag (p202), Zlatni Pyasâtsi (p213) and Albena (p214). Other activities, such as parasailing and horse riding, are often available. The kids may also like to visit some of the

zoo parks (though the animals are forlorn and the facilities uninspiring), while Sofia boasts the country's sole amusement park, Sofia Land (p68), which has plenty of rides and funfair-style attractions to keep children happy for an afternoon. Also, there are plenty of hills, rocks and fortresses to clamber around, and all cities and towns have parks with playground equipment.

CLIMATE CHARTS

Bulgaria enjoys a temperate climate with hot, dry summers and cold, wet winters, often with heavy snow. Southern Bulgaria and the Black Sea coast record the highest temperatures, with Sandanski (p103) often named the sunniest and hottest town in the country. Smolyan (p113), the highest town in the country, is one of the coolest, as you'd expect. The Danube plain, meanwhile, is open to the extremes of central Europe. Sofia's climate is generally favourable,

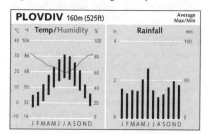

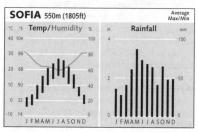

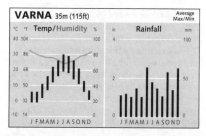

with average daytime highs of around 28°C in July and August and 3°C from December to February. Rainfall is highest in the mountains and rural life is often disrupted in winter by huge snowfalls. See p9 for further details.

COURSES

There are a few language courses that are offered to foreigners, but make sure you book them before you arrive in Bulgaria.

Sofia University (Map pp62-3; ☎ 02-710 069; www .deo.uni-sofia.bg; bul Tsar Osvoboditel) offers Bulgarian language courses for foreigners, with one-to-one courses costing €100 for 20 hours' tuition. The university also runs classes in Bulgarian culture, dance and folklore; a three-week course costs €220.

The **Sts Cyril & Methodius University of Veliko Târnovo** (☎ 062-20 070; www.uni-vt.bg) usually offers a one-month 'International Summer Seminar for Students in Bulgarian Language and Slavic Culture' every August. Contact it for current programmes and costs.

CUSTOMS

Whether you're inspected by customs officers depends on how you enter the country but, generally, bona fide tourists are left alone. You're allowed to take in and out 'gifts up to a reasonable amount', souvenirs and articles for personal use. Foreigners (over 16 years old) are also permitted to bring in the following duty-free items: 200 cigarettes or 250g of tobacco, 2L of wine or 1L of another alcoholic drink, 500g of coffee and 50ml of perfume. If you enter or leave the country with more than 8000 lv on you, you must declare it.

For information about exporting by plane unusual items such as valuable archaeological artefacts, contact the customs authorities at **Sofia airport** (☎ 02-980 4500) or **Varna airport** (☎ 052-225 532).

DANGERS & ANNOYANCES

Although some foreigners may still baulk at the thought of visiting the Balkans, with its 'troubled' international image, Bulgaria is a modern, peaceful and well-ordered country, which has thankfully avoided the kind of unrest seen in past years in neighbouring Serbia and Macedonia. If you can handle yourself in the big cities of Western Europe, North America or Australia, you'll certainly have little or no trouble dealing with the seamier sides of Bulgaria. You'll be fine if you look purposeful, keep alert and take the usual safety precautions.

Theft is not as much of a problem as it is in some countries but, obviously, look after your belongings and watch out for pickpockets in busy markets and on crowded buses. Prime targets for thieves are parked cars, especially those with foreign licence plates and/or rental-agency stickers. Never leave things inside the car; always lock everything in the boot, or take it with you.

Bulgarian drivers can be extremely reckless at times, and pedestrians should be very careful when crossing roads, especially in Sofia. There are a lot of very old and very dirty vehicles thundering around on Bulgaria's roads, many emitting dense, choking fumes. It's unpleasant, and hard to avoid, but you might want to cover your mouth and nose as these wrecks rattle past you in the cities. Cars appear to be able to park pretty much anywhere, and drivers do like parking on pavements, blocking them for pedestrians. Inevitably, footpaths in towns throughout Bulgaria are often crumbling and under sporadic repair. Also, watch out for trams and trolleybuses shuttling stealthily along what ostensibly look like vehicle-free shopping malls.

Beggars ply their trade around some churches and larger squares, but most are in real need and are very rarely aggressive or demanding. Be wary, however, of gangs of children who work the streets of big cities such as Sofia and Varna.

Bulgaria has harsh drug laws. The country is a common route for drugs (and arms) smuggled across the Black Sea from Russia and Armenia, and from Turkey, so always treat the transport, trade and use of drugs with a *great* deal of caution.

Foreigners are sometimes set up for minor monetary rip-offs, but these are fairly obvious and easy to avoid: taxi drivers at airports and beach resorts normally overcharge outrageously, and moneychangers on the street sometimes offer ridiculously high exchange rates. (Changing money on the street is illegal and unnecessary.) One source of irritation is the policy of dual pricing (see p10).

Bulgaria is a major producer of tobacco, and smoking seems to be the national pastime. Cafés, bars and restaurants are often poorly ventilated, but this is less of a problem in summer when most patrons sit outside.

Security

To keep money, passports etc safe from pickpockets, the best place is out of sight under your clothes. It's easy to make a cloth pouch that hangs around your neck or waist, or is pinned under clothing. Alternatively, buy a moneybelt. Other methods include belts with concealed compartments, and pouches worn around the leg. Try not to keep everything in one place; keep small change and a few banknotes in a shirt pocket to pay for bus tickets and small expenses without having to extract wads of cash from a secret hiding place. It may also help if you distribute valuables about your person and baggage, especially if you must carry all your belongings at once.

All important documents (eg passport data page and visa page, credit cards, travel-insurance policy, air/bus/train tickets, driving licence) should be photocopied before you leave home. Leave one copy with someone at home and keep another with you, separate from the originals.

DISABLED TRAVELLERS

Disabled travellers will often have a rough time in Bulgaria because few facilities have been established for people with special needs. Uneven and broken footpaths make wheelchair mobility problematic, and ramps and special toilets for those in a wheelchair are few and far between, except possibly in a handful of five-star hotels in Sofia. In accordance with the guidelines that have been established by European authorities, the Bulgarian government plans to upgrade wheelchair access in some existing buildings, and make it compulsory for many new edifices, but this is still a long way from fruition. One Bulgarian organisation involved with disabled locals, and possibly worth contacting, is the **Center for Independent Living in Sofia** (☎ 02-989 8857).

DISCOUNT CARDS

The ISIC is available to full-time students of any age, and the International Youth Travel Card (IYTC) is available to anyone under 26 years of age. In Bulgaria, holders of either card can obtain discounts of 10% to 20% at museums, some major attractions, hotels and hostels, some medical and dental clinics, as well as at a few restaurants. Selected travel agencies also offer card-holders discounts of up to 50% off domestic flights and 10% off train and bus tickets (depending on the agency and time of year). A brochure (in Cyrillic) listing places that offer these discounts is available from Orbita (see the boxed text, below). More general information about these cards is available on the website www.isic.org.

Also, an International Teacher Identity Card (ITIC), identifying the holder as a teacher or professor, offers similar discounts. More general information about this card is available on the website www.istc.org.

Many places in Bulgaria that should accept these cards don't advertise the fact, so it's always worth asking at the entrance (as long as you have the right card).

EMBASSIES & CONSULATES
Bulgarian Embassies & Consulates
Australia Sydney (☎ 02-9327 8067; 4 Carlotta Rd, Double Bay, NSW 2028)
Canada Ottawa (☎ 0613-789 3215; mailmn@storm.ca; 325 Stewart St, Ottawa, K1N 6K5)
France Paris (☎ 01-45 51 85 90; www.amb-bulgarie.fr; 1 Ave Rapp, 75007 Paris)

ORBITA

Student, youth and teacher discount cards can be issued to anyone with the correct documentation. International Student Identity Card (ISIC) and International Youth Travel Card (IYTC) cost 12 lv, and an International Teacher Identity Card (ITIC) costs 18 lv. All are available at the Bulgarian youth agency **Orbita** (Map pp58-9; ☎ 02-986 2216; www.orbita .bgcatalog.com; bul Hristo Botev 48, Sofia). Check the website for further details, including a comprehensive list of hotels, restaurants, clubs, museums, Internet cafes and other establishments across Bulgaria offering discounts to card-holders. Orbita also has offices, and hostels and hotels available to anyone, at Batak (☎ 03-542-3385), Burgas (☎ 056-841 254), Lovech (☎ 068-21 143), Pleven (☎ 064-33 288), Primorsko (☎ 05561-2009), Ruse (☎ 082-234 203) and Veliko Târnovo (☎ 062-621 502).

Germany Berlin (☎ 030-201 0922; fax 208 6838; Mauerstrasse 11, 10117 Berlin)

Greece Athens (☎ 01-647 8106; Str Kallari 33, Psyhiko); Thessaloniki (☎ 031-829 210; Edmundo Abot 1)

Ireland Dublin (☎ 01-660 3293; 22 Burlington Rd, Dublin)

Japan Tokyo (☎ 03-465 1021; 36-3 Yogogi 5-Chome, Shibuya-Ku, Tokyo)

Macedonia Skopje (☎ 003 8991 229 444; ul Zlatko Shnaider 3, Skopje)

Netherlands The Hague (☎ 070-350 3051; fax 358 4688; Duinroosweg 9, 2597 KJ The Hague)

Romania Bucharest (☎ 01-230 2150; Str Rabat 5)

Turkey Ankara (☎ 0312-426 7456; fax 427 3178; Atatürk Bulvari 124, Kavaklidere); Istanbul (☎ 0212-281 0115; Ahmet Adnan Saygun caddesi 44, Ulus-Levent)

UK London (☎ 020-7584 9400; www.bulgarianembassy .org.uk; 186-88 Queen's Gate, London SW7 5HL)

USA Washington DC (☎ 0202-387 0174; www.bulgaria -embassy.org; 1621 22nd St NW, Washington DC 20008)

Embassies & Consulates in Bulgaria

There is no New Zealand embassy in Bulgaria; in emergencies, New Zealanders should contact their **consulate general in Athens** (☎ 210-6874 700; 268 Kifissias Ave).

Australia Sofia (Map pp58-9; ☎ 02-950 5060; ul Trakia 37)

Canada Sofia (hMap pp58-9; ☎ 02-943 3704; ul Assen Zlatarov 11)

France Sofia (Map pp58-9; ☎ 02-965 1100; www .ambafrance.bg; ul Oborishte 27-29)

Germany Sofia (Map pp58-9; ☎ 02-918 380; gemb@vilmat.com; ul Frederic Joliot-Curie 25)

Greece Plovdiv (Map pp118-9; ☎ 032-632 003; ul Preslav 10); Sofia (Map pp58-9; ☎ 02-946 1027; ul San Stefano 33; ◷ 9am-noon Mon-Fri)

Ireland Sofia (Map pp58-9; ☎ 02-980 0642; bul Stamboliyski 55)

Macedonia Sofia (Map pp58-9; ☎ 02-701 560; ul Frederic Joliot-Curie 17; ◷ 10am-1pm Mon-Fri)

Netherlands Sofia (Map pp58-9; ☎ 02-816 0300; ul Oborishte 15)

Romania Sofia (Map pp58-9; ☎ 02-971 2858; bul Eminesku 4; ◷ 3-5pm Tue, 10am-noon Wed & Thu)

Serbia Sofia (Map pp58-9; ☎ 02-946 1633; ul Veliko Târnovo 3)

Turkey Burgas (Map p182; ☎ 056-844 2718; bul Demokratsiya 38); Plovdiv (Map pp118-9; ☎ 032-239 010; Filip Makedonski 10); Sofia (Map pp62-3; ☎ 02-935 5500; bul Vasil Levski 80)

UK Sofia (Map pp62-3; ☎ 02-933 9222; www.british -embassy.bg; ul Moskovska 9)

USA Sofia (Map pp58-9; ☎ 02-937 5100; www .usembassy.bg; ul Saborna 1)

FESTIVALS & EVENTS

Bulgaria hosts a bewildering number of religious, folkloric, music and wine festivals. Most have traditions dating back hundreds of years; others are set up mainly to attract tourists, and there's at least one major festival every summer weekend somewhere in the country. The largest event is the mammoth **International Folk Festival** held every fifth August in Koprivshtitsa (next in 2005).

More information about the festivals listed here can be found in the relevant sections throughout this guidebook, and current details about some programmes and dates can be obtained from the websites www.bulgariatravel.org and www.bulgarian space.com/bmg.

January
St Vasil's Day Folk Concert (1 Jan) Sandanski.

February
Trifon Zarezan Festival (1 Feb) Melnik; watch the wine flow.

March
Kukeri (1st Sun in Mar) Shiroka Lûka; locals parade in elaborate bell-covered costumes and startling masks in this ancient fertility rite.
Songs about Varna Competition Varna.
Days of Greek Culture Varna.
March Music Days Festival (last 2 weeks of Mar) Ruse.
Sofia International Film Festival (early Mar) Sofia.
Sandanski Celebrations (Thu after Orthodox Easter Sun) Sandanski.

April
Folkloric Festival (1 Apr) Melnik.
Music Festival (1 week in mid-Apr) Shiroka Lûka.

May
Flora Flower Exhibition (all month) Burgas.
Re-enactment of the April Uprising (1 & 2 May) Koprivshtitsa.
Holiday of Amateur Art Activities or Balkan Folk Festival (10 days in first half of May) Veliko Târnovo.
Sladkopoyna Chouchouliga Festival Burgas.
May Festivities of Culture (biennial) Gabrovo.
Varna Summer International Festival (May-Oct) Varna.
International Plovdiv Fair (1 week in mid-May) Plovdiv.
Days of Shumen Cultural Festival (mid-May) Shumen.

Celebration of Bansko Traditions (17-24 May) Bansko.
Cultural Month Festival (late May–mid-Jul) Plovdiv.

June
Fire Dancing Festival Bulgari (early Jun) Strandzha Nature Park.
Arts Festival (early Jun) Balchik.
Festival of Roses (1st weekend in Jun) Kazanlâk and Karlovo.
Verdi Festival (2 weeks in early Jun) Plovdiv.
International Festival of Chamber Music (10 days in mid-Jun) Plovdiv.
Madara Horseman Music Days Festival (mid-Jun–mid-Jul) Madara.
International Folklore Festival (3 weeks in late Jun–mid-July) Veliko Târnovo.

July
Burgas Sea Song Festival (Jul & Aug) Burgas.

August
International Folklore Festival (early Aug) Plovdiv.
International Jazz Festival (7-15 Aug) Bansko.
Folklore Days Festival (mid-Aug) Koprivshtitsa.
Annual Fair (mid-Aug) Oreshak.
Folklore Festival Shumen.
Sofia International Folklore Festival (5 days in late Aug) Sofia.
Balkan Youth Festival (early Aug) Gabrovo.
Thracia Summer Music Festival (early–mid-Aug) Plovdiv and other towns in Bulgarian Thrace.
Pirin Sings Folk Festival (mid-Aug in odd-numbered years) Bansko.
Milk Festival (last weekend in Aug) Smilyan, near Smolyan; local bovines compete for the title of 'Miss Cow'.
Annual International Film Festival (1 week, late Aug-early Sep) Varna.
Watermelon Festival (last Sun in Aug) Shumen.
International Folklore Festival (late Aug) Burgas.
Rozhen Folk Festival (late Aug) Near Pamporovo.

September
Flora Flower Exhibition (all month) Burgas.
City Holiday (6 Sep) Plovdiv.
Apollonia Arts Festival (1st half of Sep) Sozopol.
Pirin Folk National Festival (early Sep) Sandanski.
Rozhen Fair (8 Sep) Rozhen.
St Sofia's Day (17 Sep) Sofia.
Sofia Fest (14-18 Sep) Sofia.
Days of Chamber Music Gabrovo.
International Plovdiv Fair (1 week in late Sep) Plovdiv.

October
Days of Ruse (1st half of Oct) Ruse.
Grape Picking Celebrations (1st 2 weeks of Oct) Melnik.

Bansko Day (5 Oct) Bansko.
Fair Day (14 Oct) Etâr.

December
Young Red Wine Festival (early Dec) Sandanski.
Christmas Festival (15-24 December) Ruse.

FOOD
Eating out in Bulgaria is remarkably cheap, at least for Western travellers, and even if you're on a tight budget you'll have no problem eating well. In this book, we've simply divided eating options into restaurants, where prices range from around 4 to 12 lv, cafés, where you're unlikely to spend more than 3 to 4 lv, and quick eats, which are the cheapest of all, at around 2 to 3 lv. For more information on local cuisine and drink, see p48.

GAY & LESBIAN TRAVELLERS
Although homosexuality is legal in Bulgaria from the age of 18, this has more to do with the government's 'modernising' programme in preparation for EU accession in 2007 than any social liberalism. In fact, Bulgaria remains a very conservative country, and same-sex couples should refrain from overt displays of affection and be discreet when booking into hotel rooms. A few gay clubs and bars can be found in Sofia and a couple of other major cities, although most attract a mixed crowd, and there are no venues specifically aimed at lesbians.

The website www.bulgayria.com is an excellent and comprehensive source of information, in English, on all aspects of gay (male) life in Bulgaria, including details of gay-friendly bars and nightclubs. Gay women can find some information at www.bg-lesbian.com. The major gay association is the **Bulgarian Gay Organization Gemini** (☎ 02-987 6872; www.bgogemini.org). Contact the group about current gay and gay-friendly bars and nightclubs in Sofia.

The *Spartacus International Gay Guide* by Bruno Gmünder is the best male-only international directory of gay entertainment venues in Europe. Lesbians should look out for *Damron's Women's Traveller* by Bob Damron.

HOLIDAYS
During official public holidays all government offices, banks, post offices and

major businesses will be closed. All hotels, restaurants, bars, national parks/reserves and museums (unless it coincides with a normal day off) stay open, as do most shops and petrol stations; border crossings and public transport continue to operate normally.

The official public holidays are:

New Year's Day (1 Jan) Banks and other offices often also close on New Year's Eve.

Liberation Day (3 Mar) Celebrates Bulgaria's independence after the Russian-Turkish War (1877–78); also known as National Day.

Easter (Mar/Apr) Orthodox Easter falls one week after Catholic/Protestant Easter.

St George's Day (6 May) Celebrates the start of the livestock breeding cycle.

Cyrillic Alphabet Day (24 May) Also known as Day of Bulgarian Culture.

Unification Day (6 Sep) Celebrates the final reunification of Bulgaria in 1885.

Bulgarian Independence Day (22 Sep) Celebrates official independence from Turkey in 1908.

National Revival Day (1 Nov) Celebrates the Bulgarian national revival of the 19th century.

Christmas (25 & 26 Dec) During the communist era, Christmas Day was outlawed, so it was often celebrated on 26 December instead.

INSURANCE

A travel-insurance policy to cover theft, loss and medical problems is a sensible idea. Some policies offer lower and higher medical-expense options. The higher ones are chiefly for countries such as the USA, which have extremely high medical costs. There is a wide variety of policies available, so check the small print.

Some policies specifically exclude 'dangerous activities', which can include scuba diving, motorcycling and even trekking. A locally acquired motorcycle licence is not valid under some policies.

You may prefer a policy that pays doctors or hospitals directly rather than you having to pay on the spot and claim later. If you have to claim later, make sure you keep all documentation. Some policies ask you to call back (reverse charges) to a centre in your home country where an immediate assessment of your problem is made.

Check that the policy covers ambulances and an emergency flight home.

For car insurance, see p269.

INTERNET ACCESS

Bulgaria is now well and truly 'connected', and even the smallest town has at least one Internet centre. With about 150 Internet service providers throughout the country, competition is fierce and access is remarkably cheap, from as little as 0.80 lv per hour, although 1 to 1.50 lv per hour is more common. Internet centres are usually open daily between about 10am and 9pm, sometimes later. Look for places with the word 'café' or 'centre' (often in English) rather than anywhere with the word 'games', because these places are usually dingy, smoky bunkers where teenage boys endlessly play violent and deafening computer games. Bulgarian Telecommunications Company (BTC) centres offer the most reliable and speedy connections, while the more modern, privately run Internet cafés are usually pretty good. However, in older places, especially away from the big cities, connections tend to be painfully slow.

Only top-end hotels in cities such as Sofia and Plovdiv will provide modem connections for laptops in the room; elsewhere you may be able to plug into the regular phone socket, but this is by no means certain. Some Internet centres may allow you to hook up your laptop, but don't count on it.

For internet resources, see p12.

LANGUAGE

Bulgarian is a South Slavonic language that uses the Cyrillic alphabet. It became the official language of Bulgaria in 1879, when the dialect spoken in the ancient capital, Veliko Târnovo, was chosen as the national language. Dialects do exist, as in most other Eastern European countries, but they are more or less mutually comprehensible. Not surprisingly, Bulgarian incorporates words from Greek, Russian and Turkish. More recently, some words from English (eg *ofis* for office and *garadj* for garage), Italian (*ciao* for goodbye) and French (*merci* for thank you) have been incorporated into the vernacular.

Students in Bulgaria must learn at least one foreign language – either English, French, German or Russian – from an early age and many now opt for English. Older Bulgarians may speak Russian, because it was a required school subject during the communist era, and a few others may also speak French or German. These days, young people, tourism workers and business people are more likely to speak English as a second language, although German is usually preferred in the Black Sea resorts.

It's essential to learn the Cyrillic alphabet, both the standard print and written versions, because some letters are completely different and occasionally used interchangeably. You will come across what might be called 'handwritten style' Cyrillic in printed form too, which can often cause confusion. In this popular style, the 'd' sound is represented by what looks like a small Latin 'g', the 't' sound is represented by what looks like a small 'm' and 'l' looks like an inverted 'v'.

Bilingual dictionaries (in Bulgarian, and English, German or French) are available from most bookshops throughout the country. Also, Lonely Planet's *Eastern Europe Phrasebook* contains an extensive list of words and phrases in Bulgarian and languages from nearby countries, such as Romanian.

LEGAL MATTERS

Once Bulgaria gains membership of the EU, it will more or less follow the same legal system as most of the rest of Europe. The days of blatant ripping off of foreign travellers are long gone: traffic police have to abide by a certain code of ethics, but residents do complain bitterly about corruption within some government departments, especially customs. If you do get into serious trouble with the police, it's best to contact your embassy (see p252).

MAPS

Good maps are easy to find in Bulgaria, but you might want to buy one or two before you come. For a useful overview of the region, buy Geocenter's *Eastern Europe* (1:2,000,000) map. The *Baedeker Bulgaria* (1:750,000) map and Bartholomew's *Bulgaria* (1:750,000) map will probably be available in your home country.

Proper road maps are essential if you're driving around Bulgaria. One of the best is the *Bulgaria Road Map* (1:500,000), published in English by Kartografia (with a red cover). Slightly better is *Bulgaria* (1:530,000), published in English by Data-

map (with a blue cover). It's colourful, detailed and has several city maps on the other side. A smaller version (1:760,000), published in Cyrillic, has a red cover. These maps are readily available all over Bulgaria.

The maps in this guidebook will probably be more than sufficient for most visitors, but detailed maps (often in Cyrillic) are available in Bulgaria for most cities, towns and major attractions. Undoubtedly the best publisher is Domino. It offers maps (usually with a red cover) of Bansko, Burgas, Blagoevgrad, Gabrovo, Haskovo, Kazanlâk, Koprivshtitsa, Melnik, Veliko Târnovo, Pleven, Plovdiv, Ruse, Sandanski, Smolyan, Sofia, Stara Zagora, Varna and Vidin. Most maps list street names in Cyrillic (which can be handy for linking maps with street signs), provide keys in Bulgarian and English, and include other towns and places in the region. Another respected map publisher is Datamap, which produces an excellent country map as well as some city maps in English.

Also available in Bulgaria are a range of other maps for places along the Black Sea coast and for hiking (p44). If you are going to do some serious hiking, you will definitely need a detailed map. In Sofia, the best place to find these is Zig Zag Holidays (p60), while elsewhere, local travel agencies or tourist information centres are your best bet. Other detailed and useful maps, which are not always easy to find, include *The Monasteries in Bulgaria*, published by Kartografia in Cyrillic, and *Wine Map Bulgaria*, published in English by Bars Agency.

MONEY

The local currency is called leva (singular lev), which comprises 100 stotinka and is almost always abbreviated to lv. The lev is a stable currency that has been rising in value recently; see inside the front cover for the conversion rates of several major currencies at the time of research. For major purchases such as organised tours, airfares, car rental, mid-range and top-end hotels, prices are almost always quoted by staff in euros, although payment is possible in leva too. While budget hotels and some private rooms may quote their rates in euros, payments should be made in leva. The rates given in this book are in the currency stated by individual establishments; normally the leva price will simply be twice the given euro price (eg €10 = 20 lv), though some places may work out the precise exchange rate. All other transactions in Bulgaria are in leva (and listed as such in this book).

In July 1997 a Bulgarian currency board was established to officially peg the lev to the Deutschmark, ending a nightmarish skid of frequent devaluation and hyperinflation. Two years later, the lev was revalued to bring it into parity with the Deutschmark (ie DM1 = 1 lv), and old 1000 lv notes, for example, were replaced with new 1 lv notes. This caused temporary confusion, and some unscrupulous characters took advantage of confused foreigners, but happily this is all in the past.

When the euro was introduced in January 2002, the lev was automatically tied to the new currency at the rate of exchange at that time. This was roughly 2 lv to €1.

See p10 for more information.

ATMs

ATMs that accept major credit cards (ie Cirrus, Maestro, JCB, Visa, MasterCard and American Express) are an increasingly common sight and can now be found in all sizable towns and cities. It's best to use credit cards as a backup for cash in case an ATM swallows your card (more likely if the card is issued outside Europe). Otherwise, bring two or three different cards. Also, before you leave home make absolutely sure your card is hooked up to an ATM network in Bulgaria and check with your bank about exchange rates (which, of course, favour them) and commissions (which can be about 2%). The total amount you can withdraw depends on how much your bank will allow, and on how much is in your account; the maximum allowed per day by most Bulgarian banks is usually 200 lv.

Black Market

With the currency stabilisation, no black market exists in Bulgaria. Foreigners may still be approached (especially in Varna, Sofia and Plovdiv) to change money, but this is illegal and there's a high chance you'll be given counterfeit leva, short-changed or robbed.

Cash

Bulgarian banknotes come in denominations of 1, 2, 5, 10, 20 and 50 leva. Coins come in 1, 2, 5, 10, 20 and 50 stotinki and 1 lev, which is gradually replacing the 1 lev banknote. Prices for smaller items are always quoted in leva, or a fraction of a lev, ie on a bus ticket the fare will be listed as '0.50 lv' rather than '50 stotinki'.

When changing money, make sure that the foreign banknotes you have are not torn, marked or grubby, otherwise they may be refused, or you may even be given a lower rate without being told so in advance – always make absolutely sure of the precise sum in leva you will receive before handing over any of your cash. Similarly, make sure that any leva given to you are not torn or marked. Foreigners may export and import up to 5000 lv without restrictions.

Credit Cards

While credit cards are still not as common or reliable in Bulgaria as in Western or northern Europe, they are gaining ground, especially American Express, Visa and MasterCard. These three cards can usually be used at up-market restaurants, souvenir shops, top-end hotels, car-rental firms, travel agencies and some petrol stations, but rarely anywhere else – despite signs indicating acceptance of credit cards. You cannot rely on using a credit card exclusively in Bulgaria; use it to get cash from banks and for major purchases only. Some places, particularly the more expensive hotels, will add a 5% surcharge to your bill if you use a credit card.

If no ATM is available, or you're worried about using one (in case it swallows your card), some larger branches of major banks will provide cash advances in leva over the counter; this service is also sometimes offered by foreign-exchange offices. The fee is usually about 4% and you'll probably also be charged fees and commissions by your bank. The maximum withdrawal allowed for cash advances depends on what is determined by your bank.

International Transfers

Telegraphic transfers are not that expensive but they can be quite slow through a bank. Having money wired through American

Express, MoneyGram or Western Union is fairly straightforward and faster than a bank (funds are sometimes available in less than one day). You should know the sender's full name, the exact amount and the reference number when you're picking up the cash. With a passport or other ID, you can pick up the amount in euros or leva. The sender pays the fee, which can range from 5% to 15%, depending on all sorts of things.

Moneychangers

The currencies listed inside the front cover can be changed at any of the plethora of foreign-exchange offices in every city, town and at major attractions. Most don't charge commission or fees, but some do – despite signs to the contrary on notice boards outside – so always check the final amount that you will be offered before handing over your cash.

The best currencies to take are euros, pound sterling and US dollars. You may have trouble changing lesser-known currencies, such as Australian or Canadian dollars, but you should be able to find somewhere in a city such as Sofia, Plovdiv or Varna that will accept most major international currencies.

Foreign-exchange offices can generally be recognised by the huge 'exchange' signs, almost always written in English. Current rates are always displayed prominently, often on notice boards on the footpath. These offices are normally open from Monday to Saturday between about 9am and 6pm, but offices in the centre of cities and larger towns are often open every day. Foreign-exchange offices (and banks) will give you a receipt, but there's no need to keep it.

It's also easy to change cash at most of the larger banks found in cities and major towns; these include the United Bulgarian Bank, Bulbank, Bulgarian Post Bank, Raffeisen Bank and Biochim Commercial Bank. The exchange rates listed on the electronic boards in bank windows may offer slightly higher rates than foreign-exchange offices, but many banks charge commission. The other disadvantages with banks are that they're only open between 9am and 4pm from Monday to Friday, and queues can be long.

The lev is freely convertible, so there should be no problems changing excess leva back into sterling, dollars or other major foreign currencies. However, some readers have reported difficulties trying to change leva for local currency in other Eastern European countries.

Taxes

The value-added tax (VAT) of 20% is included in all prices quoted in Bulgaria, and is included in all prices listed in this guidebook. Some restaurants add service charges of 10%, and some top-end hotels list pre-VAT prices.

Tipping & Bargaining

Waiters normally round restaurant bills up to the nearest convenient figure and pocket the difference; the same applies to taxi drivers. In some restaurants an 8% to 10% service charge is already added, although this doesn't always stop the waiters rounding up the bill again, or hovering expectantly for an extra tip. If it's not added, and the service is good, add about 10%. Always leave the tip on the table (but make sure no beggars or street kids are within sight if you're sitting outside); it's socially unacceptable to give a tip to the waiter by hand.

Haggling is not customary in Bulgaria. An exception is at the seaside resorts where taxi drivers and landlords of private rooms habitually inflate prices for foreigners.

Travellers Cheques

Travellers cheques are not as easily convertible as cash, nor as convenient as credit cards, but they are a safe way of carrying money. The downside is that not all foreign-exchange offices and banks will change travellers cheques, and those that do sometimes only accept American Express and Thomas Cook, with commission rates of 3% to 5%. So if you need to change travellers cheques, always look around for the best exchange rates. Some larger banks, such as the Bulbank in Sofia, will change travellers cheques in US dollars into cash for a fee of about 2% to 3%.

Guaranteed personal cheques are another way of carrying money or obtaining cash. Eurocheques, available to European bank-account holders, are guaranteed up to a certain limit. When cashing them, you'll be asked to show your Eurocheque card bearing your signature and registration number, and perhaps a passport or ID card. Many hotels and merchants in Bulgaria refuse to accept Eurocheques, however, because of the relatively large commissions involved.

PHOTOGRAPHY & VIDEO
Film & Equipment

The people and landscapes of Bulgaria are extremely photogenic so bring (or buy along the way) plenty of film. Photographic and video film and equipment are available everywhere but, obviously, shops in the larger cities and towns have a wider selection, and everything for sale near tourist sites is overpriced. As an example of standard prices, a role of 24/36 print film from a photographic shop in Sofia or Plovdiv costs about 4.50/7.50 lv. Developing costs are about 0.30 lv per print; more for larger prints or faster service. A roll of 24-exposure slide film (without processing) costs about 10 lv but is not easy to find, so bring your own. Developing slides is also a difficult, lengthy and expensive process, so wait until you get home.

Anyone serious about taking great snaps should pick up *Travel Photography* published by Lonely Planet.

Anyone using a digital camera should check that it has enough memory to store your snaps; two 128 MB cards will probably be enough. If you do run out of memory space your best bet is to burn your photos onto a CD. Increasing numbers of processing labs now offer this service.

To download your pics at an Internet café you'll need a USB cable and a card-reader. Some places provide a USB on request but be warned that many of the bigger chain cafés don't let you plug your gear into their computers, meaning that it's back to plan A – the CD.

Restrictions

Taking pictures of anything in Bulgaria that might be considered of strategic importance – from bridges and tunnels to train stations and border crossings – is not advisable. These days officials are much less paranoid about photography than they used to be, but use common sense when it comes to this issue. And please ask permission before taking close-up photos of people.

POST

The normal cost of sending a postcard anywhere is 0.35 lv, but the 'express service' (which is usually quicker) costs 0.45 lv to all countries in Europe and 0.60 lv to the rest of the world. Letters weighing up to 20g normally cost 0.65 lv; the express service is 0.80 lv to Europe and 1 lv to anywhere else.

To send a parcel from Bulgaria, you usually have to take it unwrapped to a main post office. Anything heavier than 2kg must often be taken to a special customs post office.

SHOPPING

It's easy to spend lots of money on souvenirs but, not surprisingly, most of the stuff at popular tourist spots, such as resorts along the Black Sea coast, is tacky and overpriced. For more information about Bulgarian handicrafts such as woodcarving and weaving, see p37.

Some of the more attractive, and usable, mementos of your trip to Bulgaria may include pieces of *Troyanska kapka* pottery, decorated with the traditional *kapka* (droplet) design. Plates, bowls, cups, wine goblets and sugar bowls, among other things, are widely available. Most of these items are still made for everyday use, not just as tourist trinkets, so try looking in markets rather than pricier souvenir shops. Other worthwhile keepsakes include embroideries from Nesebâr, Varna and Sofia; paintings of traditional village life, or landscapes, from Varna, Nesebâr, Sofia and Plovdiv; woodcarvings from Tryavna; or carpets, rugs and bags from Koprivshtitsa, Chiprovtsi and Kotel. The National Fair and Exhibition of Arts & Crafts Complex (p177) in Oreshak is a marvellous place to spend up big on embroidery, pottery, ceramics, weaving, woodcarving and metalwork. The Etâr Ethnographic Village Museum (p171) near Gabrovo is a fantastic place to find traditional handmade crafts such as pottery, woodwork, metalwork and textiles. As the regional centre for the Valley of Roses, Kazanlâk is the place to buy rose oil, perfume, shampoo, liqueur, tea bags and jam, though you can pick these things up in Sofia and elsewhere. For antiques, head to the old towns in Veliko Târnovo and Plovdiv. The best range of other souvenirs, such as books, traditional costumes and jewellery, is in Sofia.

Compact discs of foreign music are usually made outside Bulgaria and tend to be expensive, but CDs of Bulgarian music often cost about 13 lv. Cassettes and CDs are available throughout the country, but the range is particularly extensive in Sofia and Plovdiv.

Note that counterfeit goods are big business in Bulgaria, ranging from pirated CDs and copy watches sold at street stalls to fake designer clothes on sale in markets and even in city-centre boutiques. Most of this is pretty obvious and priced accordingly, while some items can be quite expensive and may be designed to deceive. Be careful, too, when dealing with 'antiques', especially at street stalls in such places as Sofia. As always, use your common sense and make sure you know what you're buying.

SOLO TRAVELLERS

Solo travellers should face no specific problems in Bulgaria, other than the perennial annoyance of often having to pay for a double room in hotels, and facing the obvious disappointment of waiters in swankier restaurants when you ask for a 'table for one'. Private rooms and budget hotels are more likely to offer single prices, although it's always worth asking for discounts elsewhere, especially at weekends. Macho culture prevails in Bulgaria, and women travelling alone may attract unwelcome attention, especially outside the big cities and resorts, where foreigners are more of a novelty, and in bars and clubs anywhere.

TELEPHONE

From Bulgaria, it's easy to telephone anywhere in the world from public telephone booths, telephone centres, private homes and hotels.

The two operators are Bulfon, with its orange booths, and the slightly more up-to-date Mobika, which has blue booths. Some accept coins, although most now only take phonecards, and some Mobika booths also accept Visa and MasterCard for long-distance calls (and have instructions in English). Cards for each system, ranging in price from 5 to 25 lv, can be bought at kiosks and in some shops. You will also come across antiquated, and often battered-looking, public telephones operated by the Bulgarian Telecommunications Company (BTC), which accept 0.50 lv tokens, available at kiosks. Finding one in working order can be a challenge.

Every big town throughout the country has a BTC centre, normally inside or very near to the main post office. BTC centres are normally open from at least 8am to 6pm daily, and often 24 hours a day in larger towns. Making a local or long-distance call at a BTC centre is simple: choose a booth (or take a token indicating which booth to use), call the number and pay the amount displayed on the counter above the telephone. BTC centres will normally have fax and Internet facilities as well.

To ring Bulgaria from abroad, dial the international access code (which varies from country to country), add 359 (the country

---

UNUSUAL SOUVENIRS

If you're looking for a souvenir of your time among the Bulgars, and garish trinket boxes and amateur daubs of twee, timber-framed houses just won't do, there are plenty of more tasteful mementos for you to pick up. Hand-painted icons make a particularly evocative reminder of your stay, and though often expensive, they do involve a huge amount of skill and time. How about a patterned *cherga*? These traditional, hand-woven rugs make a colourful addition to any room and, again, involve a great deal of work. Troyanska Kapka pottery is common, but one of the more unusual products is a jug and set of shallow cups specifically made for serving and drinking the potent national spirit, *rakia*; it's sure to make a decorative conversation piece!

If you're here in March, see if you can find a *martenitza*; these little red-and-white woollen tassels, often in the form of a man and woman, are worn by women and children and later tied to fruit trees to make a wish.

Folding, horn-handled knives, traditionally used by shepherds, are also good buys – get them straight from the blacksmith at Etâr (p171), while hand-knitted woollen socks from Bansko make useful and cosy mementos.

Foodstuffs worth bringing back include the widely used local seasoning Balkanska Sharena Sol (Balkan Mixed Salt), rose-petal jam, herbal tea bags and, of course, a good bottle of *rakia*.

code for Bulgaria), the area code (minus the first zero) and then the number.

As the telecommunications systems in rural areas are being upgraded, some numbers will change, often with the addition of digits to the beginning of the number. If any numbers listed in this guidebook do not work, check the telephone directory (mostly written in Bulgarian and English) or ring one of the inquiry numbers listed here. These numbers can be dialled toll-free anywhere within Bulgaria and there's a good chance one of the operators will speak English.

International directory inquiries (☎ 124)
International operator (☎ 0123)
National directory inquiries for businesses (☎ 144)
National directory inquiries for homes (☎ 145)
National operator (☎ 121)

Mobile Phones
Mobile (cell) phones have taken off in Bulgaria and are common pretty much everywhere in the country. Mobile telephone numbers have different codes (eg 087 and 088) and are indicated by the abbreviations 'GSM' or 'mob'. Both operators, Globul and M-Tel, cover most of the country, but contact your own mobile-phone company about the usability of your phone in Bulgaria.

TIME
Bulgaria is on Eastern European Time, ie GMT/UTC plus two hours, except during daylight saving, when clocks are put forward by one hour between the last Sunday in March and the last Sunday in October. There are no time zones within the country.

Bulgaria is one hour behind Serbia & Montenegro and Macedonia, and the same time as Romania, Greece and Turkey. Therefore, if it's noon in Sofia, it's 2am in Los Angeles, 5am in New York, 10am in London, 11am in Paris and 8pm in Sydney, not taking into account daylight saving (where applicable) in these countries. The 24-hour clock is commonly used throughout Bulgaria, and always indicated on bus and train timetables.

TOILETS
With the exception of a few Middle Eastern–style squat toilets near the Turkish border, almost all toilets in Bulgaria are the sit-down European variety. All hotels provide toilet paper and soap, but these are rarely offered anywhere else. In the more basic hotels and private homes you may still come across old-fashioned toilets that have small bins beside them for used toilet paper (throwing paper down the toilet may block the pipes), but fortunately these are now becoming rare.

The standard of public toilets, especially at train and bus stations, is generally abominable and staff have the gall to charge at least 0.20 lv per visit (more for a few squares of see-through toilet paper). So if you can't get back to your hotel, visit a museum, classy bar or restaurant. Western fast-food franchises such as McDonald's always have clean toilets with toilet paper and often a queue to use these facilities. More acceptable privately run toilets are available for about 0.30 lv in central Sofia and the Black Sea resorts.

TOURIST INFORMATION
Despite large amounts of vital foreign capital obtained through tourism, and constant pleas from travel agencies and tourist operators, Bulgaria still doesn't have a dedicated Ministry of Tourism. Tourism is the responsibility of the Ministry of Economy and gets a lower profile than it deserves.

The National Information & Advertising Center (p60) in Sofia is the closest thing to a tourist office in the capital. In an effort to boost regional tourism, the government has opened a number of autonomous, local Tourist Information Centres (TICs) around the country. These TICs, however, are often little more than associations of travel agencies, rather than independent tourist offices dispensing free advice and useful maps. TICs of use to visitors are mentioned throughout this guidebook.

The former government-run tourism monopoly, Balkantourist, has been split up and privatised. The subsequent private agencies now operate under myriad different, though slightly ambiguous, names, such as Balkan Tours, Balkan Airtours and Balkan Holidays. These are essentially travel agencies and *not* tourist offices.

One of the more useful of the new private travel agencies is Zig Zag Holidays (p60) in Sofia, which can offer plenty of information to foreign travellers.

The **Bulgarian Association for Alternative Tourism** (☎ 02-989 0538; www.alternative-tourism.org; bul Stambolyiski 20-V, Sofia), in the same building as Zig Zag, promotes sustainable alternative tourism across the country.

VISAS

Citizens of Australia, Canada, Israel, Japan, New Zealand, the UK and the US can stay in Bulgaria visa-free for up to 30 days, while citizens of all EU countries, apart from the UK, can stay for up to 90 days. However, the visa situation is highly changeable, so do check the current requirements with your nearest Bulgarian embassy or consulate (see p252) before your departure.

Visa Extensions

At the time of research, 30-day tourist stamps could only be extended in exceptional circumstances within Bulgaria. If you want to stay longer, apply for the 90-day visa at the Bulgarian embassy or consulate in your own country before you leave. Better still, just leave Bulgaria for Turkey, Greece or Romania and return with a fresh 30-day stamp. At the time of writing, it was still possible to simply cross the border checkpoint and come straight back again, but this may change in future, meaning you will have to stay outside the country for a certain period before being allowed back in. Check with your embassy in Sofia for the latest travel requirements.

Extending your 30-day tourist stamp to a 90-day tourist visa is a complicated and laborious affair and, if granted, costs 200 lv. In Sofia, apply at the **Passport Office** (Map pp62-3; ☎ 02-982 3316; bul Maria Luisa 48; ❤ 8.45am-12.15pm & 1.30-5.15pm Mon-Fri).

WOMEN TRAVELLERS

In general, travelling around Bulgaria poses no particular difficulties for women travellers. For the most part, sober men are polite and respectful, especially if you're clearly not interested in their advances, and women can usually meet and communicate with local men without their intentions necessarily being misconstrued. That doesn't mean, however, that women can go into a bar or nightclub unaccompanied and expect to be left alone. If you attract unwanted attention, 'Omâzhena sâm' means 'I am married' and is a pretty firm message.

Like most desinations in Eastern Europe, common sense is the best guide to dealing with possibly dangerous situations,

such as hitchhiking, sharing hostel rooms and walking alone at night. Wear slightly conservative outfits; use dark sunglasses to avoid unwanted eye contact in particularly uncomfortable situations; or wear a wedding ring. For overnight train journeys, choose a sleeper rather than a couchette.

WORK

With so much domestic unemployment, Bulgaria isn't enthusiastic about handing out jobs to foreigners instead of locals, though the government is keen for foreigners to establish businesses as long as most of the staff are Bulgarian. Most foreigners working in Bulgaria are specialists under contracts. These contracts are most often arranged before arriving in the country.

If you intend seeking employment in Bulgaria, you will need a working visa which currently costs around 500 lv; contact your local Bulgarian embassy for details. If you do find a temporary job, the pay is likely to be very low. Do it for the experience, rather than the money, and you won't be disappointed. Teaching English is one way to make some extra cash, but the market is often saturated. A helpful website is run by the **Sofia Echo** (www.sofiaecho.com), Bulgaria's only English-language newspaper.

If you arrange a job before you arrive, your employer should plough through the frightening mass of paperwork from relevant government departments and pay the various fees. If you land a job *after* you arrive, or you're considering setting up a business in Bulgaria, urgently contact some expats for current advice about the plethora of required forms and fees. Then apply for the so-called 'blue passport' which entitles you to the same rates for museums, hotels, ski lifts etc as Bulgarians. This is a substantial saving and a great idea if you are planning to do some sightseeing.

Work Your Way Around the World by Susan Griffith provides practical advice on a wide range of issues. Its publisher, Vacation Work, has many other useful titles, including *The Directory of Summer Jobs Abroad* edited by David Woodworth. *Working Holidays* by Ben Jupp, published by the Central Bureau for Educational Visits and Exchanges in London, is another good source, as is *Now Hiring! Jobs in Eastern Europe* by Clarke Canfield.

Transport

CONTENTS

GETTING THERE & AWAY

ENTERING THE COUNTRY

One bureaucratic leftover from the communist era, which still prevails for reasons the relevant authorities cannot properly explain, is the requirement that foreigners register with the police. At hotels, hostels, camping grounds and, often, private homes, staff normally take details from your passport, fill out the registration form (in Cyrillic) and give you a copy. In theory, you must then show all of these forms to immigration officials when you leave. This requirement is almost never enforced, but it pays to keep a few copies of the registration forms with you in case you're asked for them when you leave. If you don't have any forms, or don't have enough, tell the immigration official that you lost the others, weren't given any, went camping, or whatever reasonable excuse comes to mind.

If you're staying with friends and relatives, or, sometimes, in a private home, you're supposed to personally register with the police within 48 hours. Ask someone where you're staying about the current requirements and, if you need to register, ask them to accompany you to the nearest police station (where no-one is likely to speak anything but Bulgarian and Russian). If you're camping or staying in mountain huts, registration is obviously impossible – a fact which immigration officials grudgingly accept. In theory, failure to register may result in a fine for your host of between 200 and 2000 lv.

Delays are common at border crossings, and customs officials are generally an unfriendly and suspicious lot; expect to be questioned on what business you have coming to Bulgaria and where you intend staying.

At present, to obtain a new 30-day tourist stamp you need only to cross the border into, say, Greece, and then come straight back through Bulgarian customs again. However, this can provoke questions from customs officials, and the law may be changed in the future, meaning you will have to spend at least one night outside the country before being let back in again with a new stamp.

Passport

There are no restrictions on any foreign passport-holders entering Bulgaria, other than the length of time they are allowed to stay. See p261 for details of stamps and visas.

AIR
Airports & Airlines

The Bulgarian national carrier is **Bulgaria Air** (☎ 02-865 9517; www.air.bg; code FB), operating out of Sofia airport with just eight planes. It has

---

THINGS CHANGE...

The information in this chapter is particularly vulnerable to change. Check directly with the airline or a travel agent to make sure you understand how a fare (and ticket you may buy) works and be aware of the security requirements for international travel. Shop carefully. The details given in this chapter should be regarded as pointers and are not a substitute for your own careful, up-to-date research.

only been in existence since the end of 2002 and has an unblemished safety record.

The main international airport is **Sofia airport** (☎ 02-937 2211; www.sofia-airport.bg), though in summer a few charter flights also travel to/from **Varna** (www.varna-airport.bg). Plovdiv airport is only used by occasional charter flights, for example bringing some package holiday-makers to the ski resorts.

Major airlines flying to/from Bulgaria include the following. All offices are in Sofia.

Aeroflot (☎ 943 4529; www.aeroflot.ru) Code SU; hub Moscow Airport.

Air France (☎ 980 6150; www.airfrance.com) Code AF; hub Paris Airport.

Alitalia (☎ 981 6702; www.alitalia.it) Code AZ; hub Rome Fiumicino Airport.

Austrian Airlines (☎ 981 2424; www.aua.com) Code OS; hub Vienna Airport.

British Airways (☎ 954 7000; www.britishairways.com) Code BA; hub London Heathrow Airport.

Czech Airlines (☎ 988 5568; www.csa.cz) Code OK; hub Prague Airport.

Hemus Air (☎ 945 9147; www.hemusair.bg) Hub Sofia Airport.

LOT Polish Airlines (☎ 987 4562; www.lot.com) Code LO; hub Warsaw Frederic Chopin Airport.

Lufthansa Airlines (☎ 980 4141; www.lufthansa.com) Code LH; hub Frankfurt Airport.

Malev-Hungarian Airlines (☎ 981 5091; www.malev .hu) Code MA; hub Budapest Airport.

Olympic Airways (☎ 980 1040; www.olympicairlines.com) Code OA; hub Athens Airport.

Swiss (☎ 980 4459; www.swiss.com) Code LX; hub Zurich Airport.

Turkish Airlines (☎ 980 3957; www.turkishairlines.com) Code TK; hub Ankara Airport.

Tickets

It pays to shop around for your air tickets, and though they're no substitute for the personal attention and advice you'll get from a high-street travel agent, you're likely to find some of the better deals online, either through the websites of the airlines themselves, or through one of the growing number of dedicated Internet flight shops. The following websites are worth a look:

Bargain Bucket (www.bargain-bucket.com) Useful links to many other online travel agencies.

Bulgaria Flights (www.bulgariaflights.com) Comprehensive dedicated site with cheap flights from many European cities to/from Sofia and Varna.

Cheap Flights (www.cheapflights.co.uk)

ebookers (www.ebookers.com)

Flights.com (www.tiss.com)

Sta Travel (www.statravel.com)

Travelocity (www.travelocity.com)

Full-time students and people under 26 years (under 30 in some countries) have access to better deals than other travellers. You have to show a document proving your date of birth, or a valid International Student Identity Card (ISIC), when buying your ticket and boarding the plane.

INTERCONTINENTAL (RTW) TICKETS

If you're flying to Bulgaria from the other side of the world, then round-the-world tickets may be very good value. The best places to look for these are **Star Alliance** (www .staralliance.com) and **One World** (www.oneworldalliance.com). These airline alliances will offer a limited period, usually one year, to travel around the world, stopping off at destinations of your choosing.

Tailor-made round-the-world tickets can also be assembled by travel agents, and there are numerous online agencies which offer good deals; see the following sections for some ideas.

Australia

There are no direct flights to Bulgaria from Australia, so you'll have to travel via one or more stopovers in Asia and/or Europe, such as Singapore, London, Moscow or Frankfurt. Prices do vary considerably, depending on the time of year you're travelling and the airline you choose to fly with, but a return ticket will cost from at least A$1750.

STA Travel (☎ 9231 1910; www.statravel.com.au) offers cheap tickets, and has offices in all major cities and on many university campuses. **Flight Centre** (☎ 13 31 33; www.flightcentre .com.au) also has dozens of offices throughout Australia. **Student Flights** (☎ 1800 046 462; www .studentflights.com.au) is an excellent source for discounted flights, including round-the-world options, while **M & G Travel** (☎ 1800 677 512; www.mgtravel.com.au) is another worth checking out.

Canada

Again, there are no direct flights between any Canadian airports and Bulgaria; instead you will need to fly to London, Frankfurt, Rome, Warsaw or another big European city, and pick up a connection there. Fares offered by Canadian discount air-ticket sellers are about 10% higher than those sold in the USA. **Travel CUTS** (☎ toll-free 1-866 246 9762; www.travelcuts.com) is Canada's national student travel agency and has offices in all major cities. For online flights, try **Travelocity** (www.travelocity.ca; ☎ toll-free 877-282 2925).

Continental Europe
BALKANS
Hemus Air has four flights a week to Bucharest (€169), and Tarom does the route daily at around the same price. Olympic Airways departs regularly from Athens and Hemus Air flies four times a week from the Greek capital between October and March (€140). Also, Turkish Airlines has regular flights to Sofia from Ankara and Istanbul, with prices from around €200 one way.

FRANCE
Bulgaria Air and Air France both fly between Sofia and Paris about three times a week. **OTU Voyages** (☎ 01-40 29 12 12; www.otu .fr) has branches across France but caters mostly to students and young travellers. For online flight deals, try the website www .opodo.fr.

GERMANY
There are more flights to Bulgaria from Germany than from any other European country. Bulgaria Air flies three times a week from Sofia to both Berlin and Frankfurt. Hemus Air also flies twice weekly to Cologne between December and March (€245), and to Leipzig (€205). Lufthansa Airlines flies daily from Frankfurt and Munich. Air Via and Condor Airlines fly from several German cities most days, and prices fluctuate.

STA Travel (www.statravel.de; ☎ 1805 456 422) has branches in major cities across the country. For online offers, visit www.opodo.de.

ELSEWHERE IN EUROPE
All sorts of flights to Sofia are also available from elsewhere in Europe. Prices vary quite widely, so shop around for the best deal. From Rome, Bulgaria Air flies four times a week and twice a week from Milan. Alitalia also flies regularly from Milan and Rome. Both Austrian Airlines and Lauda Air depart from Vienna three times a week.

Bulgaria Air also connects Sofia with Amsterdam, with four weekly flights. It flies twice a week to Prague, three times a week to Zurich and four times a week to Madrid.

Czech Airlines flies from Prague to Sofia five days a week and LOT Polish Airlines departs daily from Warsaw. In addition, there are regular flights from Geneva on Swiss, and from Budapest on Malev-Hungarian Airlines, which has a code-sharing agreement with KLM flying out of Amsterdam. From Moscow, Aeroflot travels regularly to Sofia and Varna all year.

Further afield, Hemus Air also flies weekly to Larnaca (in Cyprus), Beirut, Cairo (between December and March), Tripoli and Dubai, and Bulgaria Air flies twice weekly to Tel Aviv.

New Zealand
As with Australia, you will need to fly via another European country to get to Bulgaria from New Zealand. The **Flight Centre** (www.flightcentre.co.nz; ☎ toll-free 0800 243 544) has branches throughout the country, and **STA Travel** (www.statravel.co.nz; ☎ 1805 456 422) also has offices in the major cities.

UK
Both British Airways and Bulgaria Air fly daily between London and Sofia for about UK£180/240 one way/return. Bulgaria Air is usually the cheaper of the two.

STA Travel (☎ 0870 1600 599; www.statravel.co.uk) has offices across the UK. It sells tickets to all travellers, but caters especially to students and travellers under 26 years. **Student Flights** (☎ 0870 499 4004; www.studentflights.co.uk) and **Global Village Travel** (☎ 0870 442 4848; www .globalvillage-travel.com) are also worth a look over. Online ticket agencies such as www .opodo.co.uk and www.expedia.co.uk often have competitive prices.

USA
There are no direct flights between Bulgaria and anywhere in the USA. Bulgaria Air has a code-sharing agreement with Virgin Atlantic, so Virgin can fly you from one of eight cities in the USA to London, from where Bulgaria Air connects to Sofia on the same day. Alternatively, you can take a British Airways flight to London, and another on to Sofia, or fly to any major European

city, such as Rome, Frankfurt or Paris, and catch a regular flight to Sofia, or (in summer) a charter flight to Varna. The cheapest connection to Sofia is probably on LOT Polish Airlines from Chicago or New York via Warsaw. Prices are subject to change, so check around for the best deals available at the time you wish to travel.

Discount travel agents in the USA and Canada are known as consolidators. San Francisco is the ticket-consolidator capital of America, though some good deals can also be found in most major cities. **Cheap Tickets Inc** (www.cheaptickets.com) is an air consolidator offering discounts of up to 25%. Also worth checking out is the **International Association of Air Travel Couriers** (IAATC; ☎ 308-632 3273; www.courier.org).

STA Travel (☎ toll-free 800-781 4040; www.statravel.com) has offices in most major cities; ring for office locations. For online quotes, try **Airbrokers** (www.airbrokers.com).

LAND
Border Crossings
There are several crossings into Romania, but if you're driving, use the toll bridge at Ruse or a land border further east. For public transport, the quickest crossing is again at Ruse, but the crossing at Vidin is a more scenic place to enter Romania. You can also cross at Kardam–Negru Voda (accessible from Dobrich) and at Durankulak–Vama Veche (accessible from Varna), but there's no public transport to these points.

The only crossings into Greece are at Kulata–Promahonas and at Svilengrad–Ormenion.

The main border crossing into Turkey is Malko Târnovo–Derekoy. From Kapitan-Andreevo, near Svilengrad, travellers can cross the Turkish border to Edirne.

For Macedonia, the main crossings are between Gyueshevo (near Kyustendil) and Deve Bair; Zlatarevo (west of Kulata) and Delc; and Stanke Lisichkovo (near Blagoevgrad) and Novo Selo.

Travelling into Serbia, the main crossings link Kalotina (near Dragoman) and Dimitrovgrad; Vrâshka Chuka (near Vidin) and Zajc; and Strezimirovtsi (near Pernik) and Klisura. Be careful when travelling overland by train because crime is not uncommon on services within Serbia.

See p261 for details of stamps and visas.

Bus
Buses from destinations all over Europe travel to Bulgaria. From Sofia, buses run as far as Berlin (160 lv), Paris (190 lv), Rome (180 lv) and even Lisbon (270 lv). International buses also leave from Plovdiv, Varna, Burgas and Haskovo. You will have to get off the bus at the border and walk through customs to present your passport. Long delays can be expected. When travelling out of Bulgaria by bus, the cost of entry visas for the countries concerned are not included in the prices of the bus tickets.

Car & Motorcycle
Although driving is a great way to get around, bringing your own vehicle into Bulgaria is expensive, and the paperwork can be daunting. It's probably better to hire a car inside the country (see p267).

Train
Bulgarian State Railways (BDZh; www.bdz-rila.com) operates all international train services.

Greece
BUS
The main departure/arrival points for buses to/from Greece are Sofia and Plovdiv. From Sofia, buses go to Athens (12 to 14 hours, around 90 lv) and Thessaloniki (eight to nine hours, around 50 to 60 lv). Buses from Plovdiv also head to these cities; expect journey times of roughly 22 and 14 hours respectively, and prices of around 95 lv and 55 lv.

TRAIN
The *Trans-Balkan Express* (train Nos 460/461) runs between Bucharest in Romania and Thessaloniki in Greece, passing through Ruse, Pleven, Sofia, Blagoevgrad and Sandanski. From Sofia, the journey time is roughly 15 hours.

The Sofia–Thessaloniki service links the two cities every day during summer (15 June to 30 September). It takes around nine to 10 hours. A seat will cost you around 50 lv. Trains also travel between Svilengrad and Thessaloniki (nine to 10 hours).

Macedonia
Buses to Macedonia leave from Sofia, Blagoevgrad and Kyustendil. Buses from Sofia go to Skopje (six hours, 15 lv) and Ohrid (nine hours, 25 lv); buses from Kyustendil

also go to Skopje (five hours, 15 lv), while from Blagoevgrad, a daily service runs to Bitola (around eight hours, 24 lv).

No trains travel directly between Bulgaria and Macedonia. The only way to Skopje by rail from Sofia is to get a connection in Niš.

Romania
BUS
Buses don't travel directly between Romania and Bulgaria because of the long delays at the border in Ruse.

CAR & MOTORCYCLE
A toll of 210/160 lv is levied on all cars/motorbikes crossing the bridge from Giurgia in Romania into Ruse.

TRAIN
Most visitors travel to/from Romania by train and either start from, or go through, Ruse.

The *Bulgaria Express* runs between Sofia and Moscow, via Bucharest and Kiev, daily. The journey from Sofia to Bucharest takes around 12 hours. Between Sofia and Bucharest this train is called the *Grivitza*.

Every day in summer, a train from Burgas and another from Varna connect with a train leaving Ruse for Bucharest (15 hours), which carries on towards Prague.

Also, every day in summer the *Sofia-Saratov* service travels to Bucharest. It departs from Sofia at 3.20pm and travels via Pleven, Gorna Oryahovitsa and Ruse, before arriving at Bucharest about 13 hours later. It departs from Bucharest at 1.40pm.

Fares from Sofia to Bucharest are around 40 lv one way.

The *Trans-Balkan Express* (see Greece, p265) travels daily between Thessaloniki and Bucharest, with onward connections to Budapest, via Sandanaski, Sofia, Pleven and Ruse.

The *Bosfor* (train Nos 498 and 499) links Istanbul with the Romanian capital, passing through Stara Zagora, Veliko Târnovo and Ruse. The train leaves Istanbul at 10pm, Stara Zagora at 7.50am and Ruse at 1pm, reaching Bucharest at 4pm.

Serbia
Buses to Serbia leave from Sofia. There are frequent services to/from Belgrade, which cost about 40 lv and take eight hours.

The *Balkan Express* (see Turkey, below) leaves Sofia and travels through Niš to Belgrade. It takes about nine hours from Sofia and a one-way ticket costs about 47 lv.

Turkey
BUS
Several companies operate bus services to/from Turkey, departing from Sofia (Istanbul 40 lv, 18 hours), Burgas (Istanbul 30 lv, seven hours) and Varna (Istanbul 40 lv, 10 hours). From Plovdiv and Haskovo, expect to pay around 25 lv for a bus to Istanbul, with journey times of around eight to 10 hours. See the relevant sections in the regional chapters for more details.

TRAIN
The daily *Bosfor* (train Nos 498 and 499) between Istanbul and Bucharest also crosses through Bulgaria year-round. It leaves Ruse for Istanbul passing through Gorna Oryahovitsa and Stara Zagora (see www.bdz-rila.com for current times), and takes around 16 hours.

The *Balkan Express* (train Nos 490 and 491) travels daily between Istanbul and Belgrade, with onward connections to Zagreb and Venice, via Bulgaria. It passes through Plovdiv and Sofia. The journey from Sofia to Istanbul takes about 15 to 17 hours and costs roughly 40 lv.

RIVER & SEA
There are no international travel routes to/from Bulgaria either by river or sea, despite the long, inviting and accessible coastline of the Black Sea, and the mighty Danube in the north.

TOURS
Most tourists visit Bulgaria on package tours, invariably either for skiing or beach holidays, while others come on tours specialising in bird-watching or hiking. For details about tour operators based in Bulgaria, and for a discussion about the pros and cons of organised tours, see p270.

Surprisingly few foreign companies offer organised activity or sightseeing holidays to and around Bulgaria, but one reliable company that does is the London-based **Exodus** (☎ 0870 240 5550; www.exodus.co.uk). Their 15-day 'Discover Bulgaria' tour in June costs £729 per person, including flights from London.

Balkan Tours (www.balkan.co.uk) is an established firm that offers package skiing and beach holidays to Bulgaria. For example, two weeks in Slânchev Bryag (p202) costs £469 per person in July, including flights from the UK.

Balkan Holidays (www.balkanholidays.co.uk) is a leading specialist company selling similar breaks. A week in Borovets (p95) in January costs around £395 per person.

Other companies worth considering:

Crystal (☎ 01235-824 324; www.crystalholidays.co.uk)
Inghams (☎ 020-8780 4433; www.inghams.co.uk)
Sunquest (☎ 020-7499 9991; www.sunquestholidays.co.uk)

GETTING AROUND

Bulgaria is relatively easy to get around and a wide range of trains, buses and minibuses are available. To explore the country more fully, you might want to hire a car inside the country.

AIR

Bulgaria is reasonably compact, and bus and train services are reliable and cheap, so there's little point flying within Bulgaria unless you're in a real hurry.

There are two small airlines flying domestically; **Hemus Air** (www.hemusair.bg; ☎ 02-945 9147), which flies from Sofia to Varna, and **Dandy Airlines** (☎ 02-943 3674), which operates flights between Sofia, and Varna and Burgas. See the relevant regional chapters for details.

BICYCLE

Generally, cycling is not popular in Bulgaria, and isn't the most practical way of getting about in urban or built-up areas. Many roads are winding, steep and in poor condition; some major roads are always choked with traffic; and bikes aren't allowed on highways. On the other hand, traffic is light along routes between villages and long-distance buses and trains will carry your bike for an extra 5 lv or so. Spare parts are available in cities and major towns, but it's better to bring your own. Mountain bikes are a more attractive option in the countryside, and are sporadically available for rent. There are several specific mountain-bike routes (see p47).

BUS

Buses link all cities and major towns and connect villages with the nearest transport hub. In some places, buses are run by the government. These buses are old, uncomfortable (when compared with city buses) and slow. Newer, quicker and more commodious private buses often operate in larger towns and cities, and normally cost little more than the fare on a ramshackle public bus.

There are also numerous private companies running services all across the country, the biggest of which is **Etap-Grup** (☎ 02-945 3999; www.etapgroup.com), which operates from Sofia and links up with most major towns and cities.

All timetables are listed (in Cyrillic) inside the bus stations and all buses have destination signs (in Cyrillic) in the front window.

For a public bus, you normally buy a ticket from the counter marked *kasa* (каса) inside the station. This way you're guaranteed a seat and you know the correct departure time and platform number. However, in some cases the cashier will tell you to buy a ticket on the bus.

Costs

Bus travel in Bulgaria is very cheap by Western standards, with a cross-country ticket from Sofia to Varna or Burgas costing around 15 lv, and a ticket from the capital to Sandanski in the far south just 8 lv.

Reservations

Tickets for public buses can rarely be booked the day before (or earlier) but seats on private buses can be reserved one or more days in advance. However, except for long-distance services at peak times, eg between Sofia and Varna in August, there's no need to book any bus more than a few hours ahead. In fact, if you arrive at the bus stop or station about 30 minutes before departure, you'll normally get a ticket for the bus you want.

CAR & MOTORCYCLE

Probably the best way to travel around Bulgaria – especially when visiting remote villages, monasteries and national parks – is to hire a car (or motorbike). However, there's no point hiring a car and then parking it for three days while you explore Plovdiv or Varna on foot, and it can be difficult driving around any city, particularly Sofia.

Automobile Associations

The **Union of Bulgarian Motorists** (Map pp62-3; ☎ 02-980 3308; www.uab.org; pl Positano, Sofia) offers a 24-hour 'alarm centre for road assistance service' and has some helpful basic information on its website. Also possibly of some use is the related **Autotourism Travel Agency** (☎ 02-986 4942), which operates a telephone information helpline.

Bring Your Own Vehicle

It is not advisable to drive your own car into Bulgaria, especially if it's a relatively new vehicle; car theft is very common and foreign cars are an immediate target. You will need all the original registration and ownership documents, or your vehicle may be impounded by the police. It can also be an expensive business: from January 2005 tolls have been payable on motorways. For a car, the fee is €5 per week or €12 per month, though this is likely to change;

contact the Union of Bulgarian Motorists for updates. Drivers must also pay a 'disinfection fee' of around €2.50 when they enter the country. The fees can be paid in US dollars, euros, leva and most other major European currencies. Foreign drivers from must state which border crossing they plan to use when leaving.

Driving Licence

Drivers of private and rented cars (and motorcycles) must carry registration papers. Your driving licence from home is valid in Bulgaria, so an international driving licence isn't necessary (but it may be useful if you're driving elsewhere in Eastern Europe).

Fuel

Petrol is available in unleaded super 95 and unleaded super 98, as well as diesel and LPG. Major brands like Shell and OMV are often preferred by local drivers because water has been known to make its way into other brands.

Petrol stations are found roughly every 15km to 20km along the highways, and are

Road Distances (km)

	Blagoevgrad	Burgas	Dobrich	Gabrovo	Haskovo	Kulata	Kyustendil	Lovech	Pleven	Plovdiv	Ruse	Shumen	Silistra	Sliven	Smolyan	Sofia	Stara Zagora	Varna	Veliko Tărnovo	Vidin	Vratsa
Blagoevgrad	---																				
Burgas	464	---																			
Dobrich	613	185	---																		
Gabrovo	321	234	317	---																	
Haskovo	272	213	388	141	---																
Kulata	82	520	695	403	346	---															
Kyustendil	72	462	602	310	278	154	---														
Lovech	268	299	356	65	206	350	257	---													
Pleven	275	334	347	100	241	357	264	35	---												
Plovdiv	194	270	455	146	78	260	200	159	194	---											
Ruse	421	263	212	152	293	503	410	150	146	298	---										
Shumen	482	148	133	186	302	564	471	225	219	283	115	---									
Silistra	543	262	92	274	374	619	525	272	268	396	122	113	---								
Sliven	353	114	299	130	132	419	359	193	228	159	216	135	248	---							
Smolyan	244	357	541	241	141	207	302	261	296	102	393	356	474	232	---						
Sofia	101	385	512	220	234	183	90	167	174	156	320	381	443	279	258	---					
Stara Zagora	282	182	367	80	61	348	288	145	180	88	232	218	355	71	161	231	---				
Varna	571	134	51	274	371	652	559	313	304	398	203	90	143	248	477	469	316	---			
Veliko Tărnovo	342	224	271	46	187	424	331	85	120	192	106	140	228	110	287	241	126	228	---		
Vidin	300	538	558	308	433	382	289	243	208	355	356	429	478	429	457	199	388	515	328	---	
Vratsa	217	406	451	172	316	299	206	119	108	237	254	329	376	300	329	116	251	421	193	126	---

mostly open 5am-10pm. Some near Sofia and other big cities are open 24 hours.

Hire

To rent a car in Bulgaria you must be at least 21 years of age and have had a licence for at least one year. Rental outlets can be found all over Bulgaria, but the biggest choice is in Sofia. Prices start at around €25 per day, though international companies such as Avis and Hertz charge about twice that. All major credit cards are normally accepted.

Some of the more reliable agencies which have offices in the capital and elsewhere:

Avis (☎ 02-981 1082; www.avis.bg)
Autojet (☎ 02-979 0505; www.rentacar.bg)
Eurorent (☎ 02-980 2911)
Hertz (☎ 02-980 1062; office@hertz.autotechnica.bg)
Tany Rent (☎ 02-963 0797; www.tany.bg)
Tourist Service (☎ 02-981 7253; www.tourist-service .com)

There are very few places where you can rent a motorbike; one of the better places is **Motoroads** (Map pp58-9; ☎ 0888 957 649; www .motoroads.com; bul Bratya Bukston 208) in Sofia. They offer a range of motorbikes, costing from €50 per day.

Insurance

Third-party 'liability insurance' is compulsory, and can be purchased at any Bulgarian border. Buying comprehensive insurance in your home country is a better idea (but make sure it's valid in Bulgaria). The Green (or Blue) Card – a routine extension of domestic motor insurance to cover most European countries – is valid in Bulgaria.

Road Conditions

Travelling around Bulgaria by private car or motorcycle is not as relaxing as it may be in Western and northern Europe. Other than a few impressive highways, road conditions are generally taxing. Drivers must cope with potholes, roads under reconstruction, slow-moving vehicles, horses and carts and often erratic driving by other motorists.

You should never rely completely on road signs. They're often frustratingly ambiguous, or nonexistent, and most are written in Cyrillic (except around major cities, along the Black Sea coast and at the borders). It is imperative that you buy an accurate map (see p255) and be able to read Cyrillic.

Road Hazards

Vehicle security is a concern so take the usual precautions against car theft. If possible, use a guarded parking lot or hotel car park, or park under a street light. Never leave any valuables in the car.

And please take care as road accidents are common. The worst time is the holiday season (July to September) and most accidents are caused by drink-driving.

Road Rules

Although road signs are rare, the official speed limits for cars are 50km/h in built-up areas, 80km/h on main roads and 120km/h on highways. Speed limits for motorcycles, trucks and buses are 50km/h in built-up areas, and 50/80/100km/h on highways. Traffic police, who used to routinely flag down passing cars at whim for spot checks and fines, are now officially prohibited from doing so without just cause. Drivers and passengers in the front must wear seat belts, and motorcyclists must wear helmets. The blood-alcohol limit is 0.05% and these days traffic police are very unforgiving about drink-driving. Fines for the first offence range from 100 to 300 lv.

If you have an accident, you *must* wait with your vehicle and have someone call the local traffic police (see inside front cover).

HITCHING

Hitching is never entirely safe in any country in the world and we don't recommend it. Travellers who decide to hitch should understand that they are taking a small but potentially serious risk. People who do choose to hitch will be safer if they travel in pairs and let someone know where they're planning to go.

Hitchhiking is officially illegal in Bulgaria, but people still do it, and hitching in rural Bulgaria may be preferable to being restricted by infrequent public transport (but travel will tend to be in fits and starts because many cars often only travel to the next village). The upsurge in crime over the last few years has dissuaded some Bulgarians from offering lifts to hitchhikers. Bulgaria's borders are not particularly 'user friendly', so hitching across them is not recommended.

Oh, and the pretty ladies standing along the major highways near Sofia waving down male drivers are *not* looking for a lift.

LOCAL TRANSPORT
Minibus

Private and public minibuses ply routes between smaller villages, eg along the Black Sea coast and between urban centres and ski resorts in winter. Tickets for minibuses cost roughly the same as public buses but are usually bought from the driver (though it's still worth checking this first at the counter inside the bus station). If you can choose between a public bus and minibus, take the latter because it's quicker, normally more comfortable and standing is rarely allowed. Destinations (in Cyrillic) and, often, departure times are indicated on the front window. Most minibuses leave from inside, or very close to, the major public bus station. In Sofia, minibuses called *marshroutki* run between the city centre and the suburbs, acting like shared taxis (see p79).

Public Transport

All cities and major towns have buses, but they're generally not in great condition and they tend to be overcrowded and uncomfortably hot in summer. New privately run minibuses operate in some cities, such as Sofia. The few places with useful bus and minibus routes are detailed in the relevant Getting Around sections throughout this book, but you're almost always better off using a taxi (see the next section). Bus tickets are regularly checked by conductors, especially in Sofia. Don't forget to buy an extra ticket for each piece of large luggage (ie suitcase or backpack). Major cities also have trams and trolleybuses (a cross between a tram and bus) and Sofia has a modern metro system.

Taxi

Taxis, which must be painted yellow and equipped with working meters, can be flagged down on most streets in every city and town throughout Bulgaria. They can be very cheap, but rates do vary enormously, so it pays to shop around before jumping in. Taxis can be chartered for longer trips at negotiable rates, which you can approximate by working out the distance and taxi rate per kilometre, plus waiting time.

All drivers must clearly display their rates on the taxi's windows. These rates are divided into three or four lines:

- The first line lists the rate per kilometre from 6am to 10pm (about 0.35 lv per kilometre is acceptable), and the night-time rate (sometimes the same, but often about 10% more)
- The second lists, if applicable, the call-out fee of about 0.50 lv if you preorder a taxi (almost never necessary)
- The third (or second-last) lists the starting fee (0.30 lv to 0.50 lv)
- The fourth (last) lists the cost for waiting per minute (0.15 lv to 0.25 lv)

Taxi drivers in Bulgaria are probably as (un)scrupulous as their counterparts in many other countries. Some drivers do try to overcharge ignorant and unwary foreigners by rigging the meter (difficult to do), claiming the meter 'doesn't work' (it must work by law) or offering a flat fare (which will always be at least twice the proper metered fare), especially if you're negotiating a long trip, such as an intercity journey. Dishonest drivers seem to almost exclusively congregate around central Sofia, Plovdiv, Varna and the resorts along the Black Sea coast.

TOURS

As more and more independent foreign tourists 'discover' Bulgaria, new travel agencies have emerged to offer activity and special-interest tours. Some will just bus you off on the well-trod paths to Rila Monastery and the like, and large groups are normally required, while others offer a more personal service. For some overseas-based companies that offer tours, see p266.

If you are pressed for time, crave a bit of comfort or find that getting around is a little difficult, an organised tour is worth considering. Even a one-day tour can be worthwhile, especially to remote monasteries and villages. Travel agencies and tourist offices that offer local tours are listed in the regional chapters of this book. Naturally, plenty of agencies at the Black Sea resorts of Albena, Slånchev Bryag and Zlatni Pyasâtsi offer (expensive) tours.

Enterprising Bulgarian travel agencies that offer interesting tours around Bulgaria are surprisingly few and far between but you could try the following companies:

Zig Zag Holidays (Map pp62-3; ☎ 02-980 5102; www .zigzag.dir.bg; bul Stamboliyski 20-V, Sofia) Offers environmentally sensitive tours and tailor-made outdoor activities, including hiking, climbing, caving and nature trips. Contact them for prices.

Odysseia-In Travel Agency (Map pp62-3; ☎ 02-989 0538; www.odysseia-in.com; 1st fl, bul Stamboliyski 20-V, Sofia) Odysseia-In can book you on hiking, snowshoeing, caving, bird-watching, botany or numerous other trips across the country. It can also book rooms in over 100 mountain huts, monasteries and village homes.

Neophron (☎ 052-302 536, www.neophron.com; PO Box 492, Varna) runs guided bird-watching trips on the coast and in the mountains, as well as other trips for those interested in botany or wild animals. It's run by professional ornithologists.

TRAIN

Bâlgarski Dârzhavni Zheleznitsi (БДЖ) – the **Bulgarian State Railways** (BDZh; ☎ 02-931 1111; www.bdz.bg) – boasts an impressive 4278km of tracks across the country, linking most sizable towns and cities, although some are on a spur track and only connected to a major railway line by infrequent services. Most trains tend to be quite old and shabby, and journey times are slow. Buses are normally quicker, more comfortable and more frequent, especially between cities and major

towns, although on the plus side, you'll have more room in a train compartment, and the scenery is likely to be more rewarding.

Trains are classified as *ekspresen* (express), *bârz* (fast) or *pâtnicheski* (slow passenger). Unless you absolutely thrive on train travel, you want to visit a smaller village or you're travelling on a tight budget, use a fast or express train.

Two of the most spectacular train trips are along Iskâr Gorge, from Sofia to Mezdra, and on the narrow-gauge track between Septemvri and Bansko. Railway buffs often go on these trips for no other reason than the journey itself.

Classes

First-class compartments seat six people, eight are crammed into 2nd class, and the intercity express has individual seats in an open carriage. Sleepers and couchettes are available between Sofia, and Burgas and Varna but must be booked in advance. Fares for 1st class are around 30% higher than for 2nd class, but it's always worth paying the extra just to have a bit more space.

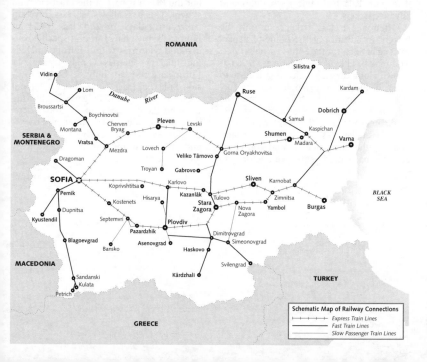

Schematic Map of Railway Connections
⊢+⊢+⊢+⊢ *Express Train Lines*
———— *Fast Train Lines*
———— *Slow Passenger Train Lines*

Costs

Train travel within Bulgaria is exceptionally cheap by Western standards, with a cross-country trip between Sofia and Varna costing approximately 12 lv (2nd class). A 1st-class ticket on this route would cost roughly 18 lv, probably the most you'd ever pay for a seat on a domestic train service in Bulgaria.

Reservations

For frequent train services, for example between Sofia and Plovdiv, there is rarely a problem if you simply turn up at the station and purchase a ticket for the next train (but be careful to allow approximately 30 minutes to queue up). Advance tickets are sometimes advisable on train services such as the intercity express to the Black Sea during a summer weekend. Advance tickets can be bought at specific counters within larger train stations and at Rila Bureaux in cities and major towns. Staff at Rila are normally far more helpful, knowledgeable and likely to speak English than anyone at a train station, so it's best to deal with Rila for advice, schedules and advance tickets.

Often a 1st-class ticket can only be bought in advance at the point of departure, eg in Sofia for the Sofia–Varna service. You may be able to buy a 1st-class ticket at a town along the way which is still close to Sofia, in Pleven for example, but any further away becomes less likely, because the station doesn't know how many 1st-class seats are available. If this is the case, buy a 2nd-class ticket, get on a 1st-class carriage, and pay the difference. Should you come across a particularly surly conductor who

---

TICKETS

All tickets are printed in Cyrillic. Other than the place of departure and destination, tickets also contain other important details:

- Клас – *klas* – '1' (1st class) or '2' (2nd class)
- Категор ия – *kategoriya* – type of train, ie T (express), 255 (fast) or G (slow passenger)
- Влак – *vlak* – train number
- Час – *chas* – departure time
- Дата – *data* – date of departure
- Вагон – *vagon* – carriage number
- Място – *myasto* – seat number

---

won't allow this, then simply return to 2nd class and try again later.

Train Passes

Most major European rail passes can be used anywhere in Bulgaria. No special individual pass is available within Bulgaria, but the BDZh is part of the Euro-Domino system. This pass allows 1st-class travel on consecutive days, or 2nd-class travel on nonconsecutive days, around specified *individual* countries within Europe, including Bulgaria. The pass is only available to Europeans and can only be bought outside Bulgaria. Inter-rail and City Star rail passes are also valid in Bulgaria, but bearing in mind the cheapness of rail travel here, they're poor value unless you intend travelling for several hours every day. For details and prices, visit the musical website www .bdz-rila.com.

Health

CONTENTS

Travel health depends on your predeparture preparations, your daily health care while travelling and how you handle any medical problem that does develop. Bulgaria will not provide any major challenges to visitors' health.

BEFORE YOU GO

Prevention is the key to staying healthy while abroad. A little planning before departure, particularly for pre-existing illnesses, will save trouble later. Carry a spare pair of contact lenses and glasses, and take your optical prescription with you. Bring extra medications in their original, clearly labelled, containers. A signed and dated letter from your physician describing your medical conditions and medications, including generic names, is also a good idea. If carrying syringes or needles, be sure to have a physician's letter documenting their medical necessity.

INSURANCE

Find out if there is a reciprocal arrangement for free medical care between your country and the country visited. If you do need health insurance, strongly consider a policy that covers you for the worst possible scenario, such as an accident requiring an emergency flight home.

INTERNET RESOURCES

The World Health Organisation's publication *International Travel and Health* is revised annually and is available online at www.who.int/ith/. Other useful websites include www.mdtravelhealth.com (travel health recommendations for every country; updated daily), www.fitfortravel.scot.nhs.uk (general travel advice for the layperson), www.ageconcern.org.uk (advice on travel for the elderly) and www.mariestopes.org.uk (providing information on women's health and contraception).

IN BULGARIA

AVAILABILITY OF HEALTH CARE

Every city and major town has a government hospital of an acceptable – albeit not excellent – standard, as well as more up-to-date private clinics. Smaller towns and villages may have a clinic, but for serious complaints you should travel to a larger town or ask your embassy/consulate to recommend a hospital, clinic, doctor or dentist. Dental clinics are easy to find in big cities and *apteka* (pharmacies) are common. Doctors at *bolnitsa* (government hospitals) are well trained and most speak English and/or German. However, equipment can be lacking and outdated. Staff at the more expensive *poliklinika* (private clinics), such as in Sofia, are more likely to be fluent in English and German, and equipment is normally of a higher standard.

INFECTIOUS DISEASES
Tickborne Encephalitis

This is spread by tick bites. It is a serious infection of the brain and vaccination is advised for those in risk areas who are unable to avoid tick bites (such as campers,

---

HEALTH ADVISORIES

It's usually a good idea to consult your government's travel-health website before departure, if one is available:
Australia: www.smartraveller.gov.au
Canada: www.travelhealth.gc.ca
UK: www.doh.gov.uk/traveladvice/
USA: www.cdc.gov/travel/

forestry workers and walkers). Two doses of vaccine will give a year's protection, three doses up to three years'.

Typhoid & Hepatitis A

These diseases are spread through contaminated food (particularly shellfish) and water. Typhoid can cause septicaemia; Hepatitis A causes liver inflammation and jaundice. Neither is usually fatal but recovery can be prolonged. Hepatitis A and typhoid vaccines can be given as a single-dose vaccine, Hepatyrix or Viatim.

Rabies

This is a potential concern considering the number of stray dogs running around Bulgaria. If bitten, seek medical attention immediately (most main hospitals will have a rabies clinic), but don't panic; while rabies is transmitted via the animal's saliva, the rabies virus is present in saliva only during the final stages of the disease in the animal, often only in the last week of the dog's life. It is therefore a relatively rarely transmitted disease. Still, do not take any chances and seek medical attention. Any bite, scratch or even lick from an unknown animal should be cleaned immediately and thoroughly. Scrub with soap and running water, and then apply alcohol or iodine solution.

TRAVELLER'S DIARRHOEA

If you develop diarrhoea, be sure to drink plenty of fluids, preferably an oral rehydration solution (eg Dioralyte). A few loose stools don't require treatment, but if you start having more than four or five stools a day, you should start taking an antibiotic (usually a quinolone drug) and an antidiarrhoeal agent (such as loperamide). If diarrhoea is bloody, persists for more than 72 hours or is accompanied by fever, shaking, chills or severe abdominal pain, you should seek medical attention.

ENVIRONMENTAL HAZARDS
Air Pollution

Due to the large number of old, poorly maintained vehicles rattling around the roads in Bulgaria, the build up of traffic fumes can be unpleasant in Sofia and other big cities, and may affect those with severe respiratory problems. Thankfully, it's easy enough to escape the urban sprawl and get some fresh air in the country. Cigarette smoke, however, is harder to avoid. Bulgarians are notorious chain-smokers, and restaurants and bars can get particularly fuggy.

Hypothermia & Frostbite

Proper preparation will reduce the risks of getting hypothermia. Even on a hot day in the mountains, the weather can change rapidly, so carry waterproof garments and warm layers, and inform others of your route.

Acute hypothermia follows a sudden drop of temperature over a short time. Chronic hypothermia is caused by a gradual loss of temperature over hours.

Hypothermia starts with shivering, loss of judgment and clumsiness. Unless rewarming occurs, the sufferer deteriorates into apathy, confusion and coma. Prevent further heat loss by seeking shelter, warm dry clothing, hot sweet drinks and shared body warmth.

Frostbite is caused by freezing and subsequent damage to bodily extremities. It is dependent on wind-chill, temperature and length of exposure. Frostbite starts as frostnip (white, numb areas of skin) from which complete recovery is expected with rewarming. As frostbite develops, the skin blisters and then becomes black. Adequate clothing, staying dry, keeping well hydrated and ensuring adequate calorie intake best prevent frostbite. Treatment involves rapid rewarming.

Water

Tap water is generally considered safe to drink in all major towns and cities, although it might not taste particularly pleasant. However, caution should be taken in smaller villages, and if staying at older or more remote hotels where the water pipes may be as old as the buildings themselves. The fountains in town parks and outside monasteries and churches provide an ideal source of drinkable water. *Cheshma* (water spouts), often found alongside main roads, also offer constant supplies of fresh, delicious and safe water.

If in doubt, purify water (with filters, iodine or chlorine) or boil it. At high altitude water boils at a lower temperature, so germs are less likely to be killed. Boil it for longer in these environments.

Easiest, and safest, of all, simply buy bottled water, which is inexpensive and sold everywhere. Fill the empty bottles up at public fountains to avoid unnecessary waste.

WOMEN'S HEALTH

Emotional stress, exhaustion and travelling through different time zones can all contribute to an upset in the menstrual pattern. If using oral contraceptives, remember some antibiotics, diarrhoea and vomiting can stop the pill from working and lead to the risk of pregnancy – remember to take condoms with you just in case. Time zones, gastrointestinal upsets and antibiotics do not affect injectable contraception. Travelling during pregnancy is usually possible, but always consult your doctor before planning your trip. The most risky times for travel are during the first 12 weeks of pregnancy and after 30 weeks.

HEALTH

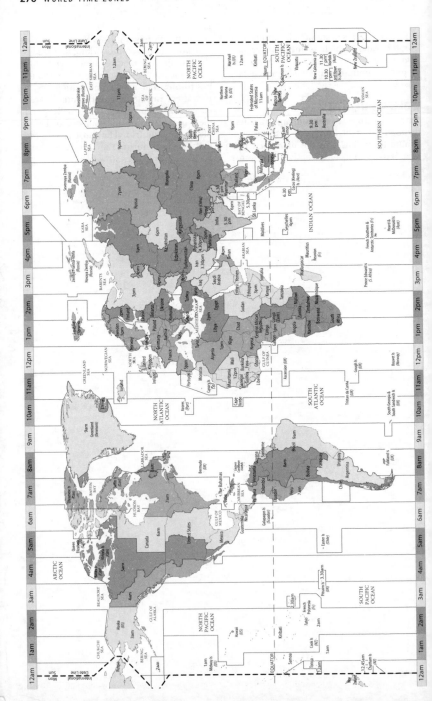

1. Община Белоградчик
2. Крепост "Калето"
3. Исторически музей
4. Природо-научен музей
5. Картинна галерия
6. Астрономическа обсерватория
7. Църква "Св. Георги Победоносец"
8. Туристически информационен център
9. Ресторант "Мислен камък"
10. Ресторант "Елит"
11. Хотел и кафе "Рай"
12. Хотел-механа "Мадона"
13. Туристически дом
14. Кафе "Маракана"

1. Municipality of Belogradchik
2. Fortress "Kaleto"
3. Museum of History
4. Museum of Nature and Science
5. Art gallery
6. Astronomical observatory
7. Church St. Georgi Pobedonosets
8. Travel information center
9. Restaurant Mislen kamuk
10. Restaurant Elit
11. Hotel and cafe Rai
12. Hotel - tavern Madona
13. Tourist house
14. Cafe Maracana

Пещера Магура
Гара Орешец
Видин
Vidin
The Magura cave
Гара Орешец Oreshets station

e-mail: belogradchik@bulmail.net
www.belogradchik.hit.bg
www.ecotracks.hit.bg
www.maguracave.hit.bg

Община Белоградчик - (0936) 31 61
факс (0936) 32 48

Туристически информационен
център (0936) 42 94

Dobre doshli v Belogradchik!

По шосе от **София** до Белоградчик се пътува по три маршрута:

1. София - магистрала Хемус - проход Витиня - Враца - Монтана - Белоградчик (215 км).

2. София - проход Петрохан - Монтана - Белоградчик (185 км).

3. София - проход Петрохан - с. Долни Лом - Белоградчик (167 км).

С лек автомобил пътуването е около 3 часа, с автобус (две линии всеки ден) - около 4 часа.

С влак се пътува до гара Орешец (на 11 км от Белоградчик). Редовна автобусна връзка с града за всеки влак.

Разстоянието до **Видин** - Белоградчик е 47 км. Редовни автобусни линии. Ж.п. връзка през гара Орешец.

You can use the following three motor transport routes from **Sofia** to Belogradchik:

1. Sofia - Hemus high road - Vitinya pass - Vratsa - Montana - Belogradchik (215 km).

2. Sofia - Petrohan pass - Montana - Belogradchik (185 km).

3. Sofia - Petrohan pass - the village of Dolni Lom - Belogradchik (167 km).

It takes about 3 hours by car and about 4 hours by bus (two lines every day) to reach the town. From Sofia can be used train to the railway station of Oreshets (at 11 km from Belogradchik). There is a regular bus connection with the town for every train. The distance from **Vidin** to Belogradchik is 47 km. There are regular bus lines. The railway connection with the town is through the railway station of Oreshets.

Welcome to Belogradchik!

Language

CONTENTS

THE BULGARIAN CYRILLIC ALPHABET

Cyrillic	Roman	Pronunciation
А а	a	as in 'father' (but shorter)
Б б	b	as in 'boy'
В в	v	as in 'vice'
Г г	g	as in 'go'
Д д	d	as in 'door'
Е е	e	as in 'bet'
Ж ж	zh	as the 's' in 'pleasure'
З з	z	as in 'zoo'
И и	i	as in 'bit'
Й й	y	as in 'yes'
К к	k	as in 'king'
Л л	l	as in 'let'
М м	m	as in 'met'
Н н	n	as in 'net'
О о	o	as in 'pot'
П п	p	as in 'pen'
Р р	r	like the trilled Scottish 'r'
С с	s	as in 'see'
Т т	t	as in 'tip'
У у	u	as in 'put'
Ф ф	f	as in 'foot'
Х х	kh	as the 'ch' in Scottish *loch*
Ц ц	ts	as in 'lets'
Ч ч	ch	as in 'chip'
Ш ш	sh	as in 'ship'
Щ щ	sht	as the '-shed' in 'pushed'
Ъ ъ	â	a neutral vowel sound, roughly resembles the 'a' in 'ago'
Ю ю	yu	as the word 'you' but shorter
Я я	ya	as in 'yard' but shorter

Modern Bulgarian belongs to the group of South Slavonic languages. It's the descendant of the oldest Slavonic literary language, Old Bulgarian (also called Old Slavic or Old Church Slavonic). Originally formulated in connection with the missionary work of the Salonica brothers, Cyril (after whom the Cyrillic script he created is named) and Methodius, during the 9th century AD, Old Bulgarian flourished in the Bulgarian lands for several centuries, giving rise to an original literary and cultural tradition that continues to thrive.

Today Bulgarian is the native language of more than nine million speakers who make up the Slavonic ethnic majority of the Republic of Bulgaria. It is the second language of several linguistic minorities in the country, including speakers of Turkish, Romany, Armenian, Greek and Romanian. While Contemporary Standard Bulgarian is the official language of the Republic of Bulgaria, historical and social factors have given rise to regional varieties in neighbouring areas. In Bulgaria itself, a number of regional dialects are common, and Bulgarian is spoken by sizable groups in the former USSR, Canada, Argentina and in some other countries.

Bulgarian has affinities with all the other Slavonic languages, and is closely related to Russian. Unlike these languages, however, Modern Bulgarian has lost its grammatical case endings, making it a lot easier for English speakers to put together gramatically correct phrases.

Bulgarians are generally friendly and very approachable. If you don't have the time to learn the intricacies of local etiquette and body language, rest assured that the use of the polite forms, accompanied by a friendly smile, will take you a long way in Bulgaria. Have a great time!

PRONUNCIATION

To a great extent Bulgarian spelling (unlike English) has an almost one-to-one representation between letter and sound. Most

Bulgarian sounds occur in English as well –
with a little practice you'll have no problem
making yourself understood.

ACCOMMODATION

I'm looking for a ...

Târ·sya ...   търся ...

  campground
  kâm·pink   къмпинг
  guesthouse
  pan·si·*on*   пансион
  hotel
  kho·*tel*   хотел
  youth hostel
  mla·*de*·shko   младежко общежитие
  ob·shte·*zhi*·ti·e

Where's a cheap/good hotel?
  kâ·*de i*·ma ef·tin/*khu*·baf kho·*tel*?
  Къде има евтин/хубав хотел?
What's the address?
  ka·*kâf* e ad·*re*·sât?
  Какъв е адресът?
Could you write the address, please?
  bikh·te li mog·*li* da mi na·*pi*·she·te ad·*re*·sa?
  Бихте ли могли да ми напишете адреса?
Do you have any rooms available?
  i·ma·te li svo·*bo*·dni *sta*·i?
  Имате ли свободни стаи?

I'd like (a) ...
bikh zhe·*lal* ...
бих желал ...

  a single room
  sta·ya s ed·*no* le·*glo*
  стая с едно легло
  a room with a double bed
  sta·ya z *dvoi*·no le·*glo*
  стая с двойно легло
  twin room with two beds
  pre·kho·den khol i *sta*·ya s po ed·*no* le·*glo*
  преходен хол и стая с по едно легло
  a room with a bathroom
  sta·ya z *ba*·nya
  стая с баня
  to share a dorm
  le·*glo* v *ob*·shta *spal*·nya
  легло в обща спалня

How much is it per night/person?
  kol·ko e na *ve*·cher na   Колко е на вечер на човек?
  cho·*vek*?
May I see it?
  mo·ga li da *vi*·dya?   Мога ли да видя?

Where is the bathroom?
  kâ·*de* e *ba*·nya·ta?   Къде е банята?
Where is the toilet?
  kâ·*de* e to·a·*le*·tna·ta?   Къде е тоалетната?
I'm leaving today.
  dnes si za·mi·*na*·vam   Днес си заминавам.
We're leaving today.
  dnes si za·mi·*na*·va·me   Днес си заминаваме.

CONVERSATION & ESSENTIALS

Hello.
  zdra·*vey*·te   Здравейте. (polite)
  zdras·ti   Здрасти. (informal)
Goodbye.
  do·*vizh*·da·ne   Довиждане. (polite)
Goodbye.
  cha·o   Чао. (informal)
Yes.
  da   Да.
No.
  ne   Не.
Please.
  mo·lya   Моля.
Thank you.
  bla·go·dar·*ya*   Благодаря. (polite)
  mer·*si*   Мерси. (informal)
That's fine/You're welcome.
  iz·vi·*ne*·te me/   Извинете ме/
  mo·lya *nya*·ma zash·*to*   Моля, няма защо.
I'm sorry.
  sâ·zha·*lya*·vam   Съжалявам.
Excuse me.
  iz·vi·*ne*·te me   Извинете ме.
What's your name?
  kak se *kaz*·va·te?   Как се казвате?
My name's ...
  kaz·vam se ...   Казвам се ...
Where are you from?
  ot·kâ·*de* ste?   Откъде сте?
I'm from ...
  as sâm ot ...   Аз съм от ...
I like ...
  kha·*res*·vam ...   Харесвам ...
I don't like ...
  ne kha·*res*·vam ...   Не харесвам ...
Just a minute.
  mo·*ment* mo·*lya*   Момент, моля.

DIRECTIONS

Where is ...?
  kâ·*de* se na·*mi*·ra ...?   Къде се намира ...?
Go straight ahead.
  vâr·*ve*·te na·*pra*·vo   Вървете направо.
Turn left.
  za·*viy*·te na·*lya*·vo   Завийте наляво.

Turn right.
za-*viy*-te na-*dyas*-no — Завийте надясно.
at the corner
na *â*-gâ-la — на ъгъла
at the traffic lights
na sfe-to-*fa*-ra — на светофара

SIGNS	
Вход	Entrance
Изход	Exit
Информация	Information
Отворено	Open
Затворено	Closed
Забранено	Prohibited
Полицейско Управление	Police Station
Тоалетни	Toilets/WC
Мъже (М)	Men
Жени (Ж)	Women

behind	zat	зад
in front of	pret	пред
far (from)	dâ-*le*-che ot	далече от
near (to)	*bli*-zo do	близо до
opposite	*sresh*-tu	срещу

beach	bryak/plash	бряг/плаж
bridge	mos	мост
castle	za-*mâk*	замък
cathedral	ka-te-*dra*-la	катедрала
island	*o*-strof	остров
lake	*e*-ze-ro	езеро
main square	tsen-*tra*-len	централен
	plosh-*tat*	площад
market	pa-*zar*	пазар
monastery	ma-na-*stir*	манастир
old city	*sta*-ri-yat grat	старият град
palace	dvo-*rets*/pa-*lat*	дворец/палат
quay	key	кей
riverbank	bre-*ga* na re-*ka*-ta	брега на реката
ruins	raz-va-li-*ni*	развалини
square	plosh-*tat*	площад
tower	*ku*-la	кула

HEALTH

I'm sick.
bo-len/*bol*-na sâm — болен/болна съм. (m/f)
It hurts here.
tuk me bo-*li* — Тук ме боли.

I'm ...
as sâm ... — Аз съм ...
asthmatic
as-ma-*tik* — астматик
diabetic
di-a-be-*tik* — диабетик
epileptic
e-pi-lep-*tik* — епилептик

EMERGENCIES

Help!
Po-mosh! — Помощ!
There's been an accident!
sta-na-la e ka-ta-*stro*-fa! — Станала е катастрофа!
I'm lost.
za-*gu*-bikh se — Загубих се.
Go away!
ma-hay-te se! — Махайте се!
Call a doctor!
po-*vi*-kay-te le-kar! — Повикайте лекар!
Call the police!
po-*vi*-kay-te po-*li*-tsi-ya! — Повикайте полиция!

I'm allergic to ...
a-ler-*gi*-chen sâm kâm ... — Алергичен съм към ...
 penicillin
 pe-ni-tsi-*lin* — пеницилин
 bees
 pche-*li* — пчели
 nuts
 o-re-hi — орехи
 peanuts
 fâs-*tâ*-tsi — фъстъци

antibiotics
an-ti-bi-*o*-ti-tsi — антибиотици
antiseptic
an-ti-sep-*tich*-no — антисептично
 sred-stvo — средство
aspirin
a-spi-*rin* — аспирин
condoms
pre-zer-va-*ti*-vi — презервативи
contraceptive
pro-ti-vo-za-*cha*-tâch-ni — противозачатъчни
diarrhoea
di-*a*-ri-ya — диария
medicine
le-*kar*-stvo — лекарство
nausea
ga-de-ne — гадене
sunblock cream
krem pro-*tif* — крем против
 slân-che-vo iz-*ga*-rya-ne — слънчево изгаряне
tampons
tam-*po*-ni — тампони

LANGUAGE DIFFICULTIES

Do you speak English/French/German?
go-*vo*-ri-te li an-*gliy*-ski/*fren*-ski/*nem*-ski? — Говорите ли английски/френски/немски?

Does anyone here speak English?
nya·koy go·*vo*·ri li an·*gliy*·ski?
Някой говори ли английски?
How do you say ... in Bulgarian?
kak e na *bâl*·gar·ski ...?
Как е на български ...?
What does ... mean?
kak·*vo* oz·na·*cha*·va ...?
Какво означава ...?
I understand.
raz·*bi*·ram
Разбирам.
I don't understand.
Ne raz·*bi*·ram
Не разбирам.
Could you write it down, please?
mo·lya *bikh*·te li go na·*pi*·sa·li?
Моля, бихте ли го написали?
Please show me (on the map).
mo·lya po·ka·*zhe*·te mi (na *kar*·ta·ta)
Моля, покажете (ми на картата).

NUMBERS

0	*nu*·la	нула
1	e·*dno*	едно
2	dve	две
3	tri	три
4	*che*·ti·ri	четири
5	pet	пет
6	shest	шест
7	se·dem	седем
8	o·sem	осем
9	de·vet	девет
10	de·set	десет
11	e·di·na·de·set	единадесет
12	dva·na·de·set	дванадесет
13	tri·na·de·set	тринадесет
14	che·ti·ri·na·de·set	четиринадесет
15	pet·na·de·set	петнадесет
16	shest·na·de·set	шестнадесет
17	se·dem·na·de·set	седемнадесет
18	o·sem·na·de·set	осемнадесет
19	de·ve·tna·de·set	деветнадесет
20	dva·de·set	двадесет
21	dva·de·set i e·dno	двадесет и едно
30	tri·de·set	тридесет
40	che·ti·ri·de·set	четиридесет
50	ped·de·set	петдесет
60	shez·de·set	шестдесет
70	se·dem·de·set	седемдесет
80	o·sem·de·set	осемдесет
90	de·ved·de·set	деветдесет
100	sto	сто
1000	hi·lya·da	хиляда

PAPERWORK

name
i·me име
nationality
na·*ro*·dnos народност
date of birth
da·ta na *razh*·da·ne дата на раждане
place of birth
mya·sto na *razh*·da·ne място на раждане
sex/gender
pol пол
passport
pas·*port* паспорт
visa
vi·za виза

QUESTION WORDS

Who?	koy?	Кой?
What?	kak·*vo*?	Какво?
What is it?	kak·*vo* e to·*va*?	Какво е това?
When?	ko·*ga*?	Кога?
Where?	kâ·*de*?	Къде?
Which?	ko·*e*?	Кое?
Why?	zash·*to*?	Защо?

SHOPPING & SERVICES

I'd like to buy ...
bikh *i*·skal da *ku*·pya ... Бих искал да купя ...
How much is it?
kol·ko *stru*·va? Колко струва?
I don't like it.
ne mi kha·*res*·va Не ми харесва.
May I look at it?
mo·zhe li da (go/ya/go) Може ли да (го/я/го)
vi·dya? видя? (m/f/n)
I'm just looking.
pro·sto *gle*·dam Просто гледам.
It's cheap.
ef·tin/*ef*·ti·na/*ef*·ti·no e Евтин/Евтина/Евтино е. (m/f/n)
It's too expensive.
mno·go e skâp/*skâ*·pa/ Много е скъп/скъпа/
skâ·po скъпо. (m/f/n)
I'll take it.
shte (go/ya/go) *vze*·ma Ще г(о/я/го) взема. (m/f/n)

Do you accept ...?
pri·*e*·ma·te li ...? Приемате ли ...?
  credit cards
  kre·di·tni *kar*·ti кредитни карти
  travellers cheques
  pâ·tni·che·ski *che*·kove пътнически чекове

more
po·ve·che/*osh*·te
повече/още

less
  *po-mal-*ko
  по-малко
smaller
  *po-ma-*lâk/*po-mal-*ka/*po-mal-*ko
  по-малък/по-малка/по-малко (m/f/n)
bigger
  *po-*gol-*yam/po-*gol-*ya-*ma/*po-*gol-*ya-*mo
  по-голям/по-голяма/по-голямо (m/f/n)

I'm looking for ...
*târ-*sya ...   Търся ...
  bank
  *ban-*ka   банка
  church
  *tsâr-*kva-ta   църквата
  city centre
  *tsen-*tâ-ra na gra-*da*   центъра на града
  ... embassy
  *po-*sol-*stvo-to na ...   посолството на ...
  the hospital
  *bol-*ni-tsa-ta   болницата
  exchange office
  ob-*men-*no-to byu-*ro*   обменното бюро
  market
  pa-*za-*ra   пазара
  museum
  mu-*ze-*ya   музея
  police
  po-*li-*tsi-ya-ta   полицията
  post office
  *po-*shta-ta   пощата
  public toilet
  *grad-*ska to-a-*le-*tna   градска тоалетна
  telephone centre
  te-le-*fon-*na-ta tsen-*tra-*la   телефонната централа
  tourist office
  byu-*ro-*to za tu-*ri-*zâm   бюрото за туризъм

TIME & DATES
What time is it?
  *kol-*ko e cha-*sât?*
  Колко е часът?
It's ... am/pm.
  cha-*sât* e ... pre-*di* o-bet/slet *o-*bed
  Часът е ... преди обед/след обед.

When?	ko-*ga?*	Кога?
today	dnes	днес
tonight	do-*ve-*che-ra	довечера
tomorrow	*u-*tre	утре
yesterday	*vche-*ra	вчера
morning	*su-*trin	сутрин
evening	*ve-*cher	вечер

Monday	po-ne-*del-*nik	понеделник
Tuesday	*vtor-*nik	вторник
Wednesday	*srya-*da	сряда
Thursday	chet-*vâr-*tâk	четвъртък
Friday	*pe-*tâk	петък
Saturday	*sâ-*bo-ta	събота
Sunday	ne-*de-*lya	неделя

January	ya-nu-*a-*ri	януари
February	fev-ru-*a-*ri	февруари
March	*mârt*	март
April	a-*pril*	април
May	may	май
June	*yu-*ni	юни
July	*yu-*li	юли
August	*av-*gust	август
September	sep-*tem-*vri	септември
October	ok-*tom-*vri	октомври
November	no-*em-*vri	ноември
December	de-*kem-*vri	декември

TRANSPORT
Public Transport
What time does the ... leave/arrive?
v *kol-*ko cha-*sa* za-mi-*na-*va/pri-*sti-*ga ...?
В колко часа заминава/пристига ...?
  boat
  *ko-*ra-bât   корабът
  bus (city)
  *grat-*ski-yat af-to-*bus*   градският автобус
  bus (intercity)
  mezh-du-*grat-*ski-yat   междуградският
    af-to-*bus*   автобус
  plane
  sa-mo-*leh-*tât   самолетът
  train
  *vla-*kât   влакът
  tram
  tram-*va-*yat   трамваят

I'd like ...
*mo-*lya *day-*te-mi ...   Моля, дайте ми ...
  a one-way ticket
  bi-*let* f e-*dna* po-*so-*ka   билет в една посока
  a return ticket
  bi-*let* za o-*ti-*va-ne   билет за отиване
    i *vrâ-*shta-ne   и връщане

I want to go to ...
*is-*kam da o-*ti-*da do ...
Искам да отида до ...
The train has been delayed.
*vla-*kât za-kâ-*snya-*va
Влакът закъснява.

The train has been cancelled.
vla·kât e o·tme·*nen*
Влакът е отменен.
the first
pâr·vi·yat/*pâr*·va·ta/*pâr*·vo·to
първият/първата/първото (m/f/n)
the last
po·*sle*·dni·yat/pos·*led*·na·ta/po·*sle*·dno·to
последният/последната/последното (m/f/n)

first class	*pâr*·va *kla*·sa	първа класа
second class	*fto*·ra *kla*·sa	втора класа
arrival	pri·*sti*·ga·ne	пристигане
departure	za·mi·*na*·va·ne	заминаване
carriage	va·*gon*	вагон
category (of train)	ka·te·*go*·ri·ya	категория
platform	pe·*ron*	перон
timetable	ras·pi·*sa*·ni·e	разписание
ticket office	gi·*she*·to za	гишето за
	bi·*le*·ti	билети
train	vlak	влак

Private Transport
I'd like to hire a ...
zhe·*la*·ya da na·*e*·ma   Желая да наема ...
car
ko·*la*   кола
4WD
ko·*la* s chet·*vor*·no   кола с четворно
pre·*da*·va·ne   предаване
motorbike
mo·*tor*   мотор
bicycle
ko·le·*lo*   колело

Is this the road to ...?
to·*va* li e *pâ*·tyat za ...?   Това ли е пътят за ...?
Where's a service station?
kâ·de i·ma ser·*vis*?   Къде има сервиз?
Please fill it up.
mo·lya na·pâl·*ne*·te go   Моля, напълнете
do·*go*·re   го догоре.
I'd like ... litres.
is·kam ... *li*·tra   Искам ... литра.

diesel
di·zel   дизел
leaded petrol
o·*lo*·ven ben·*zin*   оловен бензин
unleaded petrol
be·zo·*lo*·ven ben·*zin*   безоловен бензин

How long can I park here?
za *kol*·ko *vre*·me *mo*·ga da par·*ki*·ram tuk?
За колко време мога да паркирам тук ?

ROAD SIGNS	
Дай Път	Give Way
Опасност	Danger
Паркирането Забранено	No Parking
Отклонение	Detour
Вход	Entry
Забранено Задминаването	No Overtaking
Пътна Такса	Toll
Намали Скоростта	Slow Down
Влизането Забранено	No Entry
Еднопосочно Движение	One Way
Изход	Exit
Освободи Пътя/Платното	Keep Clear

Where do I pay?
kâ·de da pla·*tya*?
Къде да платя ?
I need a mechanic.
tryab·va mi mon·*tyor*
Трябва ми монтьор.
The car/motorbike has broken down at ...
ko·*la*·ta/mo·*to*·rât se po·vre·*di* na/do/pri ...
Колата/Моторът се повреди на/ад/при ...
The car/motorbike won't start.
ko·*la*·ta/mo·*to*·rât ne *mo*·zhe da za·*pa*·li
Колата/Моторът не може да запали.
I have a flat tyre.
spu·kakh *gu*·ma
Спуках гума.
I've run out of petrol.
svâr·shi mi ben·*zi*·nât
Свърши ми бензинът.
I had an accident.
ka·ta·stro·*fi*·rakh
Катастрофирах.

TRAVEL WITH CHILDREN
Is there a/an ...?
i·ma li ...?
Има ли ...?
I need a ...
tryab·va mi ...
Трябвя ми ...
baby change room
mya·sto/*sta*·ya za po·*vi*·va·ne na be·*be*·ta
място/стая за повиване на бебета
car baby seat
va·*gon* za *may*·ki z de·*tsa*
вагон за майки с деца
child-minding service
sluzh·ba za *gle*·da·ne na de·*tsa*
служба за гледане на деца

children's menu

det·sko me·*nyu*

детско меню

disposable nappies/diapers

pe·le·*ni* za ed·no·*kra*·tna u·po·*tre*·ba

пелени за еднократна употреба

infant milk formula

re·*tsep*·ta za pri·*got*·vya·ne na khra·*na* za *be*·be·ta

рецепта за приготвяне на храна за бебета

(English-speaking) babysitter

ba·*vach*·ka ko·*ya*·to go·vo·ri an·*gliy*·ski

бавачка, която говори английски

highchair

det·sko *stol*·che

детско столче

potty

nosht·no gâr·*ne*

нощно гърне

stroller

pro·*hot*·ka

проходка

Do you mind if I breastfeed here?

i·ma·te li *ne*·shto pro·*tiv* da *kâr*·mya tuk?

Имате ли нещо против да кърмя тук?

Are children allowed?

poz·vo·*le*·no li e za de·*tsa*?

Позволено ли е за деца?

Glossary

For food and drink terms see the Food & Drink chapter (p48). For general terms see the Language chapter (p277).

apteka – chemist or pharmacy
avtogara – bus station

Balkantourist – the former government-run tourism organisation
balneology – therapeutic bath of mineral waters, often enjoyed in a balneocentre
banya – bath; often signifies mineral baths in general
BDZh – abbreviation for the Bulgarian State Railways
bul – abbreviation of bulevard: main street or boulevard

cherga – a traditional, colourful, hand-woven rug

dvorets – palace
dzhumaya – mosque

ezero (m), **ezera** (f) – lake

gradina – garden; often referring to a public park

haidouks – Bulgarian rebels who fought against the Turks in the 18th and 19th centuries
hali – indoor market
hizha – hut; often refers to a mountain hut
house-museum – a home built in a style typical of the Bulgarian national revival period and turned into a museum

iconostasis (s), **iconostases** (pl) – a screen, partition or door in an Eastern Orthodox church that separates the sanctuary from the nave; often richly decorated
iztok – east

kâshta – house
khan – king within a Bulgar tribe, or the subsequent Bulgarian empires; also known as a *tsar*

konak – police station built during Turkish rule
knyaz – prince
krepost – fortress
kurdjali – Turkish gangs that raided several Bulgarian towns during the 18th and 19th centuries

lev (s), **leva** (pl) – monetary unit of Bulgaria; shortened to lv; equals 100 *stotinki*

manastir – monastery
mehana – tavern
most – bridge

obshtina – municipality; also another word for town hall

pasha – high official during Turkish rule
peshtera – cave
pl – abbreviation of ploshtad: town or city square
Pomaks – literally 'helpers'; Slavs who converted to Islam during the era of Turkish rule

reka – river

sever – north
stotinka (s), **stotinki** (pl) – one-hundredth of a *lev*
sveti (m), **sveta** (f) – saint

Troyanska kapka – traditional glazed pottery with a distinctive 'drip' design
tsar – see *khan*

ul – abbreviation of ulitsa: street

varosha – centre of an old town
vrâh – mountain peak

yug – south

zapad – west

Behind the Scenes

THIS BOOK

This 2nd edition of *Bulgaria* was written by Richard Watkins (coordinating author) and Tom Masters. The 1st edition was researched and written by Paul Greenway. The Health chapter was adapted from material written by Dr Caroline Evans.

THANKS from the Authors

Richard Watkins First and foremost, many thanks go to Lubomir, Rositsa, Milena, Krasi, Kiril and all the staff at Odysseia-In and Zig Zag Holidays in Sofia for their friendly and professional assistance. I could not have done it without you. Thanks also go to Stefan Tchernokolev for the wine-tasting in Melnik, Ginka Andreeva in Sofia for the movie posters, and Margarita Dinkova and staff at Eurotours. A thank you also goes to my fellow teachers and to students, who made my first visit to Bulgaria, as a TEFL teacher back in 1995, so memorable, encouraging me to return again and again to the land of Vasil Levski, Zagorka and humorous menu misprints. Merci!

Tom Masters Thanks to Caroline Bright and Andrei Pospielovsky for their hospitality in Sofia, the Kirov family for introducing me to Bulgaria when I was so young, especially Nick. Also thanks to Svilen Ivanov in Veliko Târnovo, Borislav Sorokin in Ruse, Plamina in Karlovo, Vanessa in Balchik and all the other kind people throughout Bulgaria who helped me with my research.

CREDITS

This title was commissioned and developed in Lonely Planet's London office by Fiona Christie with assistance from Judith Bamber, Heather Dickson and Imogen Franks. Cartography for this title was developed by Mark Griffiths. Project managers Ray Thomson and Eoin Dunlevy oversaw production of this title.

Dan Caleo and Barbara Delissen (coordinating editors) were assisted by Andrew Bain, Charlotte Orr, Simon Williamson and Lucy Monie. Thanks to Martin Heng and Darren O'Connell.

Coordinating cartographer Jovan Djukanovic was assisted by Malisa Plesa, Jacqueline Nguyen and Herman So. Wayne Murphy created the back cover map. Thanks to Mark Griffiths, Anthony Phelan and Valentina Kremenchutskaya.

John Shippick and Indra Kilfoyle laid out this book, assisted by Laura Jane and Wibowo Rusli. John also created the cover artwork and the colour pages. Thanks to Adriana Mammarella, Kate McDonald and Sally Darmody. Gerilyn Attebery designed the cover.

Thanks to Mark Germanchis and Lachlan Ross for technical support, and to Quentin Frayne and Jodie Martire for the language sections. Special thanks go to Bulgarian language expert Dr Angel Pachev.

THANKS from Lonely Planet

Many thanks to the travellers who used the last edition and wrote to us with helpful hints, useful advice and interesting anecdotes:

A E Adams, Dominique Adey Balinova, Pere Alzina i Bilbeny, Christoph Andert, Alexander Andruska, Luitgard Anthony, Shabnam Anvar, Hilmir Ásgeirsson **B** Bruce Bachman, Jordan Bannister, Catherine Barber, Joseph L Benatov, Jim Berry, Paul Berry, David Bertolotti, Alan & Lesley Brown, Malcolm & Joan Brown, Irena Bushandrova **C** Fergy Campbell, Ana Ceh, Mitko Chatalbashev **D** Luca Dall'Olio,

---

THE LONELY PLANET STORY

The story begins with a classic travel adventure: Tony and Maureen Wheeler's 1972 journey across Europe and Asia to Australia. There was no useful information about the overland trail then, so Tony and Maureen published the first Lonely Planet guidebook to meet a growing need.

From a kitchen table, Lonely Planet has grown to become the largest independent travel publisher in the world, with offices in Melbourne (Australia), Oakland (USA) and London (UK). Today Lonely Planet guidebooks cover the globe. There is an ever-growing list of books and information in a variety of media. Some things haven't changed. The main aim is still to make it possible for adventurous travellers to get out there – to explore and better understand the world.

At Lonely Planet we believe travellers can make a positive contribution to the countries they visit – if they respect their host communities and spend their money wisely. Every year 5% of company profit is donated to charities around the world.

Huw Davies, Matthias Dekan, Sylvia Dennerstein, Francesco Diodato, Noel Duffin **E** Boris Ederov, Emil Entchev **F** George Fescos, Med Lars Floter, John P Forgach **G** Jay Geller, Riley Graebner, Christina Guise **H** Alex Hall, Edward Hillier, Brendan Hoffman, Kevin Honan, David Hook, Steve Horlock **I** Claudia Immisch **J** Steve James, Frederik Jansen, Vicky Janssens, Jentz Jensen, Matic Jesensek, Nick Johnstone **K** Kapka Kassabova, Borislav Kiprin, Heidi Knudsen **L** Zev La Mont, GWA Lamsvelt, Christine Landry, Jesper Larsen, Anthony Leach, Brian Lema, Peter Lowthian **M** Delyan Manchev, Robert Philip Henry Mann, Brian Manson, Catherine McGurn, Debbra Mikaelsen, Melanie Miller, Gioconda Millotti, Poli Miteva, Raina Moneva **N** Raluca Nemtanu **O** Stuart Oates **P** Craig Pardey, Rossen Petrov, Rosi Petrova, Avril Phillips, Peikko Pitkanen, Mads Pockel, Valter Pratas **R** Jason Revill, Barry Ridgway, Francoise Rohaut **S** Antoinette Schapper, Larry Schwarz, Rob South **T** Anna Travali, Eric Trenson, Tonio Treschi, Adonis Tsilialis **V** Teun van der Wildt, Jan van Eijk, Elitsa Videnova **W** Terry Walker, Michael Wegner, Peter Weller, Jane Whitby, Janne Wikman, Ginette Williams, Richard Wood

ACKNOWLEDGMENTS

Globe on back cover © Mountain High Maps 1993 Digital Wisdom, Inc.

Index

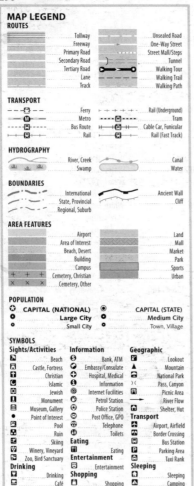

MAP LEGEND

ROUTES

Tollway	Unsealed Road
Freeway	One-Way Street
Primary Road	Street Mall/Steps
Secondary Road	Tunnel
Tertiary Road	Walking Tour
Lane	Walking Trail
Track	Walking Path

TRANSPORT

Ferry	Rail (Underground)
Metro	Tram
Bus Route	Cable Car, Funicular
Rail	Rail (Fast Track)

HYDROGRAPHY

River, Creek	Canal
Swamp	Water

BOUNDARIES

International	Ancient Wall
State, Provincial	Cliff
Regional, Suburb	

AREA FEATURES

Airport	Land
Area of Interest	Mall
Beach, Desert	Market
Building	Park
Campus	Sports
Cemetery, Christian	Urban
Cemetery, Other	

POPULATION

○ CAPITAL (NATIONAL)	◉ CAPITAL (STATE)
● Large City	● Medium City
○ Small City	○ Town, Village

SYMBOLS

Sights/Activities
- Beach
- Castle, Fortress
- Christian
- Islamic
- Jewish
- Monument
- Museum, Gallery
- Point of Interest
- Pool
- Ruin
- Skiing
- Winery, Vineyard
- Zoo, Bird Sanctuary

Drinking
- Drinking
- Café

Information
- Bank, ATM
- Embassy/Consulate
- Hospital, Medical
- Information
- Internet Facilities
- Petrol Station
- Police Station
- Post Office, GPO
- Telephone
- Toilets

Eating
- Eating

Entertainment
- Entertainment

Shopping
- Shopping

Geographic
- Lookout
- Mountain
- National Park
- Pass, Canyon
- Picnic Area
- River Flow
- Shelter, Hut

Transport
- Airport, Airfield
- Border Crossing
- Bus Station
- Parking Area
- Taxi Rank

Sleeping
- Sleeping
- Camping

LONELY PLANET OFFICES

Australia
Head Office
Locked Bag 1, Footscray, Victoria 3011
☎ 03 8379 8000, fax 03 8379 8111
talk2us@lonelyplanet.com.au

USA
150 Linden St, Oakland, CA 94607
☎ 510 893 8555, toll free 800 275 8555
fax 510 893 8572, info@lonelyplanet.com

UK
72-82 Rosebery Ave,
Clerkenwell, London EC1R 4RW
☎ 020 7841 9000, fax 020 7841 9001
go@lonelyplanet.co.uk

Published by Lonely Planet Publications Pty Ltd
ABN 36 005 607 983

© Lonely Planet 2005

© photographers as indicated 2005

Cover photographs: Traditional Bulgarian outfit, Jean Dominique Dallet/Photolibrary.com (front); Horse and cart carrying corn in northwest Bulgaria, Roberto Gerometta/Lonely Planet Images (back). Many of the images in this guide are available for licensing from Lonely Planet Images: www.lonelyplanetimages.com

Printed through Colorcraft Ltd, Hong Kong
Printed in China